Proceedings of the Mardi Gras '94 Conference

TOWARD TERAFLOP COMPUTING AND NEW GRAND CHALLENGE APPLICATIONS

February 10 - 12, 1994 Louisiana State University

Editors

RAJIV K. KALIA AND PRIYA VASHISHTA
Louisiana State University

NOVA SCIENCE PUBLISHERS, INC.

TOWARD TERAFLOP COMPUTING AND NEW GRAND CHALLENGE APPLICATIONS

Art Director: Christopher Concannon
Graphics: Elenor Kallberg and Maria Ester Hawrys
Manuscript Coordinator: Roseann Pena
Book Production: Tammy Sauter, Benjamin Fung
and Michelle Lalo
Circulation: Irene Kwartiroff and Annette Hellinger

Library of Congress Cataloging–in–Publication Data
available upon request

ISBN 1-56072-247-9

6080 Jericho Turnpike, Suite 207
Commack, New York 11725
Tele. 516-499-3103 Fax 516-499-3146
E Mail Novasci1@aol.com

Printed in the United States of America

CONTENTS

I. LARGE-SCALE APPLICATIONS

II. PARALLEL ALGORITHMS, TOOLS, AND LANGUAGES

PREFACE

High performance computing and communications (HPCC) is becoming increasingly pervasive in all areas of science, technology, and education. In order to keep abreast of the latest developments in HPCC, we have started a series of HPCC conferences at Louisiana State University, Baton Rouge. Held annually during the Mardi Gras festival, these conferences aim to foster cross-disciplinary interactions among researchers who are developing or using HPCC to address large-scale applications in the physical sciences and engineering disciplines. The first such conference called "Concurrent Computing in the Physical Sciences" was held on February 18-20, 1993.

This book contains the proceedings of the second Mardi Gras conference, called "Toward Teraflop Computing and New Grand Challenge Applications", which was held in Baton Rouge on February 10-12, 1994. The conference was mainly supported by the National Science Foundation's Divisions of Advanced Scientific Computing, Chemistry, and Materials Research. The conference was organized by LSU faculty in the physical sciences and computer science, with the help of an advisory board consisting of:

- Gary Grest, Exxon Research Corporation
- Mark Gordon, Iowa State
- Michael Klein, University of Pennsylvania
- Vincent McKoy, Caltech
- Paul Messina, Caltech Concurrent Supercomputing Facilities
- Michele Parrinello, IBM - Zürich
- Rick Stevens, Argonne National Laboratory

The conference featured an impressive group of speakers which included computational scientists in the physical sciences and engineering disciplines, as well as experts in parallel computing, high-speed networking, and scientific visualization. Eighty participants from universities, government and industrial laboratories, and federal funding agencies attended the conference.

Presentations at the conference addressed issues related to large-scale scientific computations on parallel machines across high-speed networks; strategies for modeling grand challenge applications in geophysics and climate modeling; attempts to integrate multimedia into large-scale parallel computations; and recent advances in parallel programming languages, programming environments, and compiler optimization. There were a number of talks on large-scale materials simulations that dealt with various approaches to constructing interatomic interactions for Monte Carlo and molecular-dynamics simulations of real materials; first-principles electronic structure calculations for semiconductor surfaces, and for water and metal-ammonia solutions; electronic structure methods based on finite-difference schemes and wavelet transforms; multimillion particle molecular-dynamics calculations for fracture of materials; and tight-binding calculations for solid C_{60} and graphitic tubules. The presentations in the area of chemistry dealt with parallel computations of electron-molecule collisions; quantum-dynamics simulations; Green's function Monte Carlo calculations of molecular systems; and quantum chemistry computations on parallel computers. In physics and astronomy, there were presentations on large-scale computations in condensed matter, atomic, and biophysics; simulations for galaxy formation and object-oriented schemes for parallel astrophysics simulations; and the effort to build a teraflop computer for lattice quantum chromodynamics calculations.

We are very grateful to a number of people who helped us with the conference. They include: Jerry Draayer, Sitharama Iyengar, Simon de Leeuw, Joel Tohline, Jin Yu, Aiichiro Nakano, Jim Fernandez, Cathy Mixon, Beverly Rodriguez, Arnell Jackson, John Cazes, Alok Chatterjee, Howard Cohl, Aljosa Vrancic, John Zachry, and the staff of Short Courses and Conferences at LSU, especially Doug Bourgeois. Finally, we would also like to thank Drs. Richard Hilderbrandt, Merrell Patrick, Bruce Taggart, and Robert Voigt at NSF for supporting this conference. We would also like to acknowledge the support of the Department of Physics and Astronomy and Department of Computer Science at LSU. The conference also received support from Mobil Research Corporation through the efforts of Dr. Bradley Feuston.

I. LARGE-SCALE APPLICATIONS

Toward Teraflop Computing
and New Grand
Challenge Applications

ISBN-1-56072-247-9

THE DEVILISH WORLD OF SURFACES

K. Cho and J. D. Joannopoulos

Department of Physics
Massachusetts Institute of Technology
Cambridge, MA 02139

An introduction is presented of the state-of-the-art of modern experimental and computational tools for the study of materials surfaces. Examples include predictions, from first-principles calculations, of the scanning tunneling microscopy associated with one of the classic surfaces of crystalline silicon.

The title of this work was inspired by Wolfgang Pauli, who was fond of remarking that although it is certainly God who created the beauty and simplicity of perfect crystals, the surface must have been invented by the Devil [1].

Physical phenomena explicitly associated with surfaces of materials have been studied in various guises for millenia. But it is only in the last fifty years or so that the *understanding* of surfaces and interfaces has emerged as a major scientific and technological issue. Even so, it has only been in the last decade or so that it has become possible for experiment and theory to accurately, reproducibly, and *directly* probe into the nature of the surface.

Let us begin then with a brief review of two important and exciting developments that have led to this possibility. We will draw one example from experiment and one from theory, and these two will be interwoven throughout the rest of paper.

The first important development is the invention of the Scanning Tunneling Microscope (STM) by Binnig and Rohrer [2]. In this experiment, one brings a very thin metallic tip (typically W) in proximity to the surface of interest and measures the electron tunneling current between the tip and surface. Since this current is an exponential function of the distance of the tip to the surface, by keeping the current constant and scanning the tip across the surface one can accurately map out the topography of the surface. Conventional theories of STM [3-5] are based on an approximation that does not include any significant interactions between the tip and the surface. STM images are then interpreted simply as a convolution of the tip wave function with the surface wave function. Although this is a very useful approximation for many applications, there may exist systems for which the tip-surface interaction and the surface dynamics play a crucial role in the STM measurement process. It is precisely this effect that we wish to investigate using the next development.

This is the ability to perform *ab initio* theoretical investigations of materials properties and behavior [6]. *Ab initio* formalisms are important because they can stand alone. They can complement experimental investigations but need not be guided by them. In an *ab initio* formalism one strives to calculate the total energy of an interacting many-body system of electrons and nuclei using the atomic numbers as essentially the only experimental input. There are four important ingredients that make *ab initio* calculations of real materials systems tractable. Vert briefly, these are the use of density functional theory to deal with the electron-electron interactions, pseudopotential theory to deal with the strong electron-nuclei potential, supercells to deal with aperiodic atomic configurations, and modern minimization techniques to relax the electronic and nuclear degrees of freedom [6].

Let us now use this *ab initio* formalism to investigate one of the classic problems in surface science - the scanning tunneling microscopy of the (100) (2x1) reconstructed surface of crystalline silicon.

A typical room temperature STM image of the Si(100) surface [7-9] reveals the surface reconstruction as a geometry consisting of rows of dimers which appear to be symmetric as shown schematically at the top of Fig. 1. *Ab initio* calculations, however, obtain a ground state surface geometry that involves a c(4x2) reconstruction and *asymmetric* dimers as shown at the bottom of Fig. 1. These *ab initio* results are consistent with earlier predictions of asymmetric dimers using empirical tight-binding

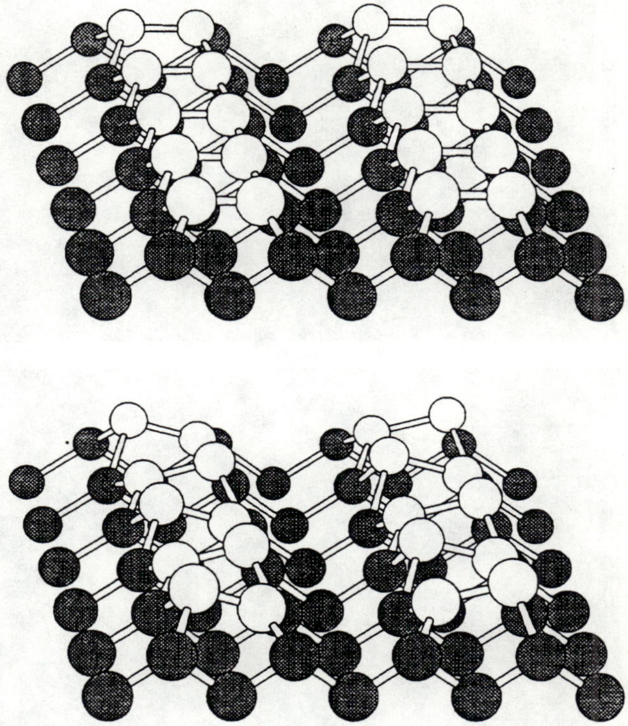

Figure 1. Ball-and-stick model of symmetric dimers (top) and asymmetric dimers (bottom) on the Si(100) surface.

techniques [10].

How then can we understand this discrepancy between theory and experiment? One might expect that this discrepancy could be reasonably resolved by arguing that thermal fluctuations in the asymmetric dimer configurations will create an averaged or "symmetric" image. Such thermal fluctuations have been predicted to be present on the surface *in the absence of a tip* [11-13]. In the presence of a tip, however, a different mechanism may be operational. To investigate this interesting possibility we have performed *ab initio* total energy calculations to determine the atomic rearrangements that may occur when a tungsten tip is brought in proximity to the Si(100) surface. The details of our calculations are presented elsewhere [14].

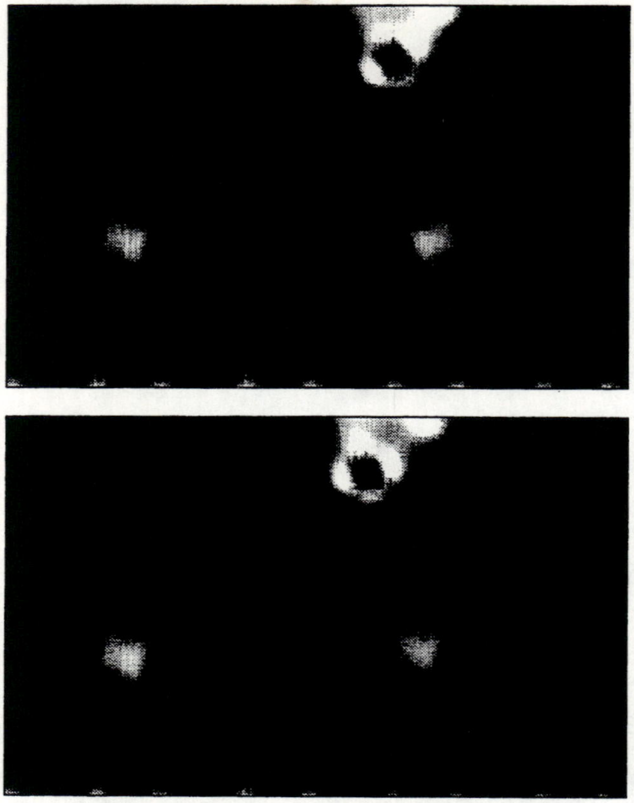

Figure 2. Charge density cross section of the tip and dimer in the metastable state (top) and in the stable state (bottom).

In Fig. 2 we show the results of our calculations for a tip restricted to lie directly above a surface atom. The top and bottom panels represent configurations that would be, respectively, metastable and stable at zero temperature. We find that the barrier, E_b, for metastable -> stable is about 0.1 eV while for stable -> metastable it is 0.3 eV. This implies a significant interaction between the tip and surface atoms which does not appear explicitly in the total charge density distributions. However, one can easily see the effects of this interaction by examining the electronic states near the top of the fermi energy. This is shown in Fig. 3. The top panel corresponds to the Si dangling bonds states in the *absence* of the tip, while the two lower panels show how one of these dangling bonds gets pushed down in energy by

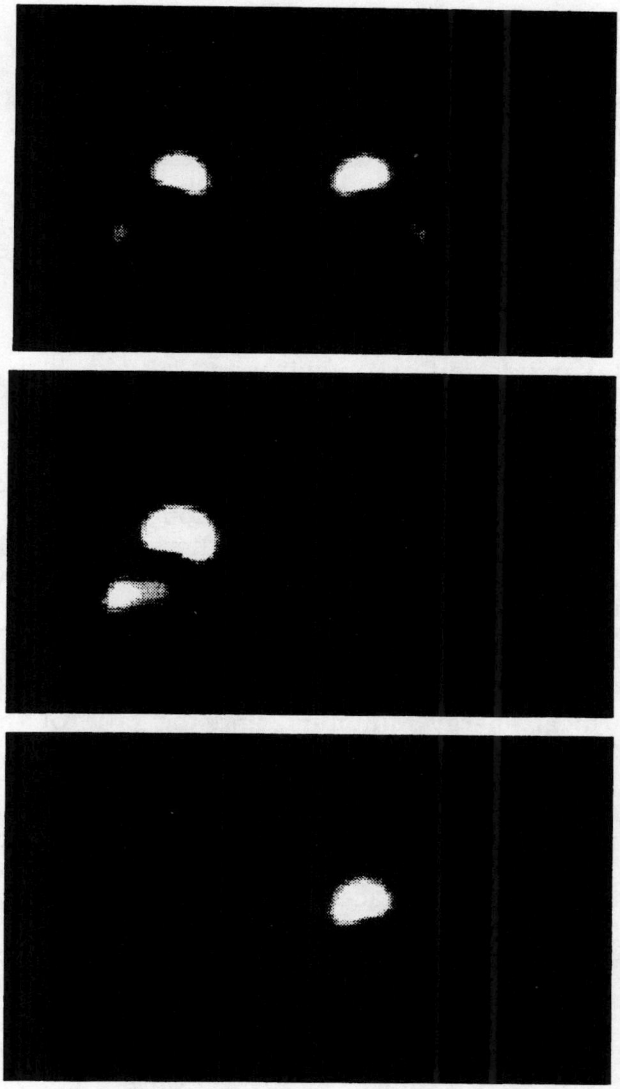

0.01 eV

-0.12 eV

Figure 3. Dangling bond states of surface dimers in the absence of the tip (top) and in the presence of the tip (middle and bottom).

the presence of the W tip.

For a given value of energy barrier, E_b, the average time that a dimer spends in one asymmetric configuration before flipping to the other is simply

$$\tau_b = 10^{-13} \exp(E_b / k_B T),$$

where the phonon frequency is estimated to be 10^{13} sec^{-1}. During an STM measurement, an STM tip typically stays $3x10^{-3}$ sec = t_{STM} above a surface atom and therefore the relative values of τ_b and t_{STM} will determine the nature of the STM image. In the *absence of interactions* between the STM tip and surface, a buckled dimer is in a symmetric potential well, and the energy barrier for flipping (0.08 - 0.09 eV) is small enough that at room temperature the dimer can flip up and down very frequently ($\tau_b = 2x10^{-12}$ sec). This would lead to a symmetric STM image that is the *average* of up-flip and down-flip configurations.

In the *presence of interactions* between the STM tip and surface, a buckled dimer is in an *asymmetric* potential well, and τ_b is different for the down-flip and the up-flip configurations. At room temperature, τ_b's are short enough ($\tau_{down} = 5x10^{-12}$ sec and $\tau_{up} = 1.3x10^{-8}$ sec) that, in principle, the dimer can flip up and down freely, and thermal equilibrium between two local energy minima of the asymmetric potential is reached during the STM imaging time.

Therefore, the dimer spends different amounts of time in each local energy minimum, and the ratio of the times is given by the Boltzmann factor of the difference of two local minimum energies ($4x10^{-4}$). Consequently, the dimer stays *in the up-flip configuration* except for intermittent rapid *round-trips* to the down-flip configuration. For all practical purposes, therefore, one is always measuring a dimer in the up-flip position as the tip moves along the surface. The resulting image is then deceptively that of a "symmetric" dimer.

As one decreases the temperature, τ_{down} and τ_{up} increase and eventually both become larger than t_{STM}. This occurs at and below a temperature T_{freeze} = 48 K for which the surface dynamics is so slow that a dimer cannot flip during the STM imaging time. Therefore, at this temperature range one can observe frozen buckled dimers in up-flip and down-flip positions from an STM image of the surface.

Let us now consider if it is possible for an STM tip to flip a dimer at very low temperatures which will remain flipped after the tip is removed. The results of this exercise are shown in Fig. 4. As we proceed from top to bottom, the tip is brought closer and closer to the surface until there is a discontinuous change in the

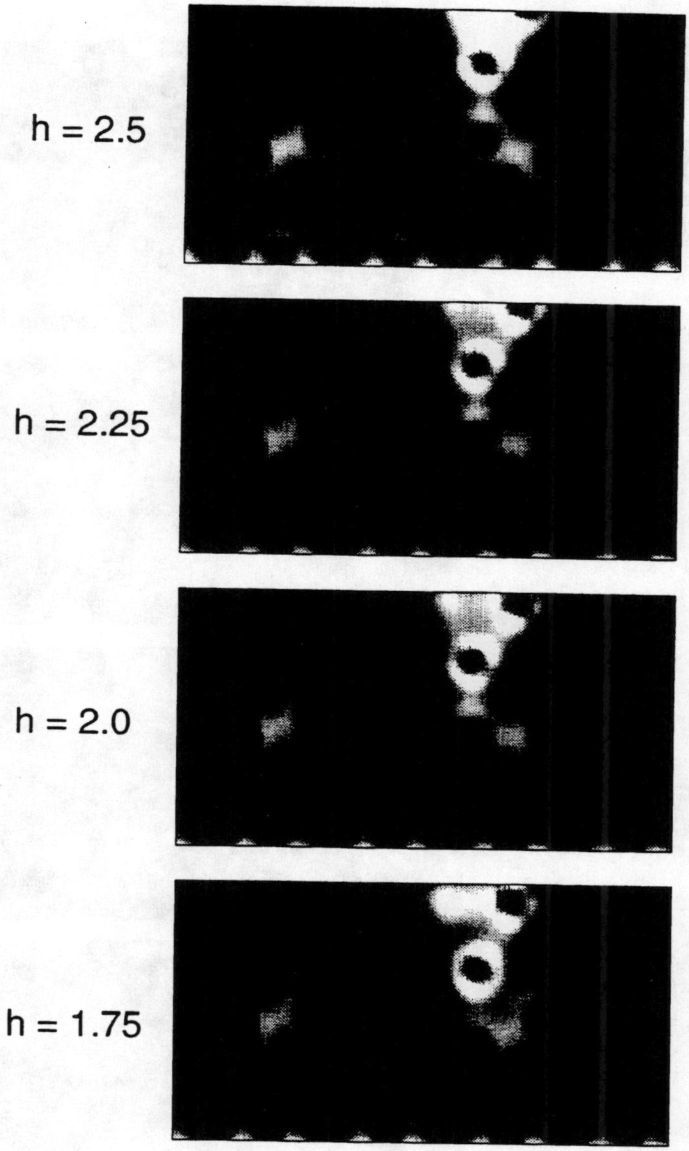

Figure 4. The sequence of charge density cross sections (from top to bottom) as the tip pushes down and flip the dimer.

equilibrium value of the dimer asymmetry angle. If we now attempt to pull the tip back up, we find that the tip eventually flips the "down"-dimer back to its original "up" position. A dimer

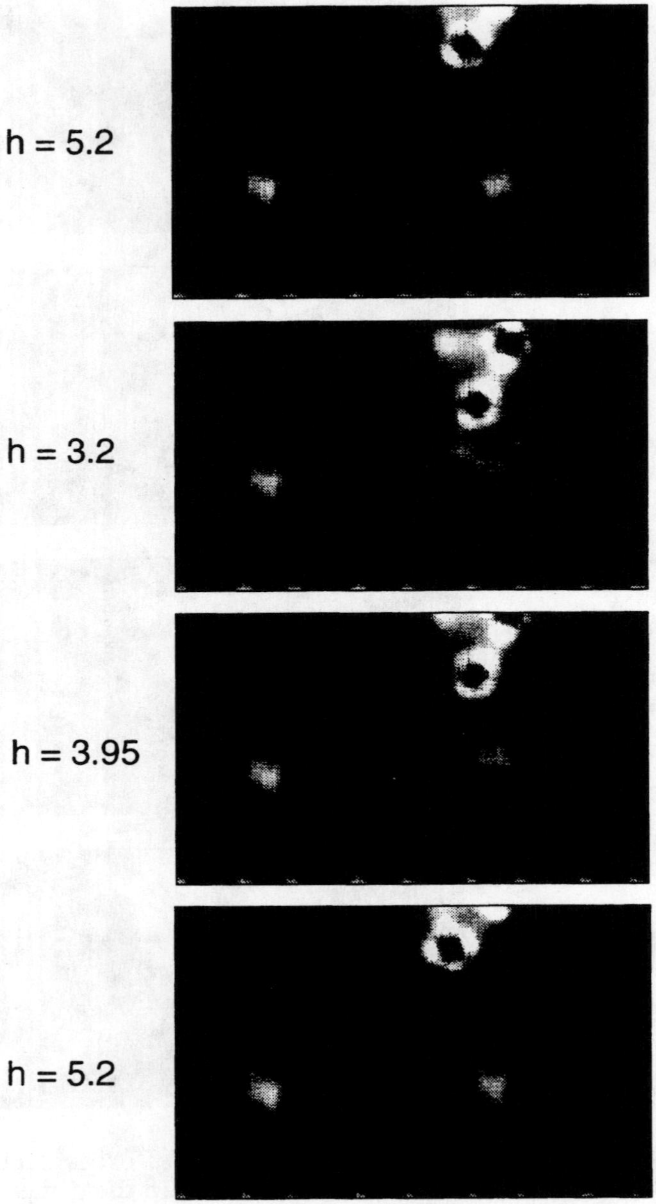

Figure 5. The sequence of charge density cross section of the tip and dimers as the tip pulls up a dimer.

on the surface *can* be "permanently" flipped, however, using the approach shown in Fig. 5. Here the process of flipping is performed by having the tip *pull* on a dimer atom rather than *push* on it. Proceeding from top to bottom, the first two panels represent a tip being brought down to a surface dimer, while the next two panels correspond to the tip being pulled back up. The net effect of this procedure is for the tip to flip a dimer on the surface that remains flipped after the tip is removed.

An idealized Si(100) surface at low temperature will have dimers as shown schematically in Fig. 6. Since each dimer can be made to flip into one of two possible positions, each dimer can conceivably store one bit of information. One could envision therefore, the intrinsic Si(100) surface as a potential ultra high density reading and writing memory device. Writing would be accomplished by simply using the technique illustrated in Fig. 5, and reading would be accomplished by simply scanning the tip horizontally at higher distance from the surface. Since the time scale for STM scans is slow compared to modern memory devices, perhaps the most useful application for this could be archival memory storage. And the gain in density compared to conventional devices would approach *six* orders of magnitude!

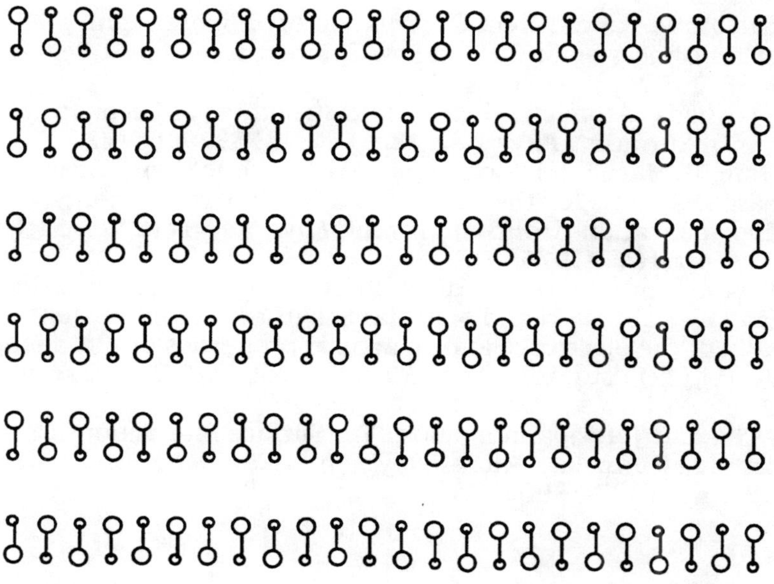

Figure 6. Schematic top view of the idealized Si(100) surface.

REFERENCES

1. V. Weisskopf, private communication.
2. G. Binnig and H. Rohrer, 'Surface Studies by Scanning Tunneling Microscopy', *Phys. Rev. Lett.* Vol. 49, 1982, pp. 57-61.
3. J. Tersoff and D. R. Hamman, 'Theory and Application for the Scanning Tunneling Microscope', *Phys. Rev. Lett.* Vol. 50, 1983, pp. 1998-2001.
4. C. Julian Chen, 'Origin of Atomic Resolution on Metal Surfaces in Scanning Tunneling Microscopy', *Phys. Rev. Lett.* Vol. 65, 1990, pp. 448-451.
5. H. Kageshima and M. Tsukada, 'Theory of scanning tunneling microscopy and spectroscopy on Si(100) reconstructed surfaces', *Phys. Rev. B* Vol. 46, 1992, pp. 6928-6937.
6. For a review see *e.g.* M. C. Payne, M. P. Teter, D. C. Allan, T. A. Arias, and J. D. Joannopoulos, 'Iterative minimization techniques for *ab initio* total-energy calculations: molecular dynamics and conjugate gradients' *Rev. Mod. Phys.* Vol. 64, 1992, pp. 1045-1097.
7. R. M. Tromp, R. J. Hamers, and J. E. Demuth, 'Si(001) Dimer Structure Observed with Scanning Tunneling Microscopy', *Phys. Rev. Lett.* Vol. 55, 1985, pp. 1303-1306.
8. R. J. Hamers, R. M. Tromp, and J. E. Demuth, 'Scanning tunneling microscopy of Si(001)', *Phys. Rev. B* Vol. 34, pp. 5343-5357.
9. Robert A. Wolkow, 'Direct Observation of an Increase in Buckled Dimers on Si(001) at Low Temperature', *Phys. Rev. Lett.* Vol. 68, 1992, pp. 2636-2639.
10. D. J. Chadi, 'Atomic and Electronic Structures of Reconstructed Si(100) Surfaces', *Phys. Rev. Lett.* Vol. 43, 1979, pp. 43-47.
11. J. Ihm, D. H. Lee, J. D. Joannopoulos, and J. J. Xiong, 'Structural Phase Diagrams for the Surface of a Solid: A Total-Energy, Renormalization-Group Approach', *Phys. Rev. Lett.* Vol. 51, 1983, pp. 1872-1975.
12. At room temperature for dimers not pinned directly to defects.
13. Jaroslaw Dabrowski and Matthias Scheffler, 'Self-consistent study of the electronic and structural properties of the clean Si(001) (2x1) surface', *Appl. Surf. Sci.* Vol. 56-58, 1992, pp. 15-19.
14. K. Cho and J. D. Joannopoulos, 'Tip-Surface Interactions in Scanning Tunneling Microscopy', *Phys. Rev. Lett.* Vol. 71, 1993, pp. 1387-1390.

Toward Teraflop Computing
and New Grand
Challenge Applications

ISBN-1-56072-247-9

ALGORITHMS FOR PREDICTING PROPERTIES OF REAL MATERIALS ON HIGH PERFORMANCE COMPUTERS

James R. Chelikowsky[1], N. Troullier[1,2], K. Wu[2], and Y. Saad[2]

[1]Department of Chemical Engineering and Materials Science, [2]Department of Computer Science, Minnesota Supercomputer Institute, University of Minnesota, Minneapolis, Minnesota 55455

1. INTRODUCTION

Perhaps *the* most exciting development in materials science has been the realization of a *practical* method for predicting properties of *real* materials. It is now possible to predict from *ab initio* methods many structural properties such as bond lengths, and vibrational modes to within ~1%. The chief obstacle for applying such methods is that these methods are computationally intensive, and, at present, cannot be applied routinely to systems containing more than a few dozen atoms.

One of the most successful methods for describing real materials is based on several simplifying assumptions. These assumptions include: (a) The *Born Oppeheimer approximation* which allows one to separate the electronic degrees of freedom from the nuclear degrees of freedom; (b) The *one electron approximation* which allows up to map the many body problem to a single body problem; (c) The *local density approximation* which approximates the effect of exchange and correlation by a functional which depends only on the charge density; (d) The *pseudopotential approximation* which allows one to consider only the valence electrons, or chemically active electron states. *None of the assumptions listed rely on experimental input.* The pseudopotentials can be determined from first principles atom calculations, and are often considered to be *ab initio* pseudopotentials. The weakest approximation of the ones listed is the local density approximation. This approximation relies on the cancellation of errors in the exchange/correlation energies between the configurations of interest. This cancellation is quite good for structural energies such as the energy difference between two closely related crystal structures. The cancellation is weakest for the cohesive energy which involves the energy difference between an isolated atom and the energy per atom of a solid.

Using the above approximations, one must choose a technique to solve the resulting one-electron Schrödinger equation for the spatial and energy distributions of the electrons. With a solution to this equation, the total electronic energy of the system of interest can be calculated, and structural energies computed. For example, one can calculate the total electronic energy of two different crystal structures, and ascertain which structure is more stable. A common procedure to solve Schrödinger's equation is to use a plane wave basis, *i.e.*, a pseudospectral approach. A plane wave basis has several desirable features: the basis is not biased, it is complete and orthonormal, and computational techniques such as three dimensional (3D) Fast Fourier Transforms (FFT) can be employed with a plane wave basis. Moreover, plane waves can be very appropriate with a pseudopotential formalism. Since the pseudopotentials are weak compared to an all electron potential, the resulting pseudo-wave functions often converge quickly in terms of a Fourier expansion. However, this need not be the case, especially for localized systems such as a small cluster, or molecule. For such systems, the the direct application of a plane wave basis is non-trivial. The lack of periodicity in these materials invalidates Bloch's theorem, and the use of Fourier transforms. One procedure to "rescue" the plane wave basis is the *supercell method*[1]. In the supercell method, the localized configuration of interest is artificially repeated to impose periodicity on the system. For example, if one wanted to examine a molecule, the molecule would be isolated in a large cell, and this cell would be artificially repeated to construct a "crystal" of isolated molecules. This "forced" periodicity of supercells allows standard "band structure" codes to be used for non-periodic systems[2-5].

The implementation of the "pseudopotential-plane wave-supercell" approach can be difficult on high performance computers. The plane wave basis is required to replicate not only the electronic states of the localized system of interest, but also "vacuum" regions imposed by the supercell geometry. Replicating the vacuum in the supercell for a localized system can be almost as costly as replicating the "real" part of the wavefunction. In a recent calculation for a complex surface, the 7x7 reconstruction of the (111) silicon surface, 700 atoms were effectively treated: approximately 400 "real" atoms in the supercell and a vacuum contribution effectively corresponding to another 300 atoms[6,7].

Another issue which complicates supercell calculations concerns interactions from one cell into another. For example, one can examine a vacancy in a crystal by considering a large supercell of the ideal crystalline solid and removing an atom from the supercell. If one wishes to examine charged systems, the problem becomes more acute. Consider a charged defect within a supercell configuration, for this situation each individual cell is charged. The total electronic energy summed over all the cells diverges. A simple "fix" to this problem is to insert a uniform compensating charge in each supercell, but determining the effect of this uniform background in terms of a total energy, or binding energy, is quite complex[8,9].

An additional complication that arises with the use of plane waves concerns the use of 3D FFT's for handling the convolutions. While 3D FFT's are a great advantage in expediting the calculation, these transforms present computational communication obstacles when one attempts to implement such codes on parallel computer architectures. A typical gain for the implementation of this procedure on a parallel machine can be an order of magnitude. While this gain is a clear improvement, it is unlikely that algorithms based on this approach will achieve teraflop performance in the near future.

In this paper, we raise the following issue: *Is there an alternative to plane waves which might be better suited for high performance machines?*

2. HIGHER ORDER FINITE DIFFERENCE METHODS

We present a new approach which eliminates many of these problems. Our approach is much simpler to implement than the plane wave basis without any loss of accuracy. The approach is based on utilizing the *finite difference method* [10,11]. The "basis" in this approach is a real space grid. It might be suspected that a grid approach would not be competitive with plane waves. The real space grid must be fine enough to replicate accurately the wave functions. A grid this fine may result in so many grid points as to result in an unworkable scheme. However, this need not be the case, especially when coupled with pseudopotentials. As we shall demonstrate, it will not be the case for most electronic structure problems involving localized systems such as clusters or molecular systems. Consider that the two approaches, i.e., plane waves expansions and finite difference descriptions are intimately related. If the wave function is slowly varying, then it should be easy to expand the function in a plane wave basis. Concurrently, for a slowly varying function, the wave function can be expanded in a Taylor series, and a finite difference method will work well. One clear limitation of the finite difference approach *and* the plane wave basis is that neither will be very effect in describing an all electron potential. The strong Coulomb part of the all electron potential results in wave functions which are difficult to expand in plane waves, and are difficult to describe in a simple expansion.

A key aspect of our work is the availability of *higher order* expansions for the kinetic energy operator, *i.e.*, approximations of the Laplacian. If we impose a simple, uniform grid on our system where the points are described in a finite domain by (x_i, y_j, z_k), we may write

$$\left(\frac{\partial^2 \psi}{\partial x^2}\right)_{x_i,y_j,z_k} = \sum_{n=-N}^{N} C_n \psi(x_i + nh, y_j, z_k) + O(h^{2N+2}) \qquad (1)$$

where h is the grid spacing. The series is converged to $O(h^{2N+2})$ if we assume that ψ is sufficiently differentiable, specifically if it has $2N + 2$ derivatives. Algorithms are available to compute the coefficients C_n for arbitrary order in h [12]. As $N \rightarrow \infty$, the finite difference expansion becomes commensurate with an FFT for a periodic system.

If the kinetic energy operator can be expanded as in Eq. (1), then we can set up a one-electron Schrödinger equation over the grid. We will employ the local density approximation. We assume a uniform grid over the three dimensions, but this is not a necessary assumption. Over these grid points we must solve:

$$
\begin{aligned}
&-\frac{\hbar^2}{2m}\Big[\sum_{n_1=-N}^{N} C_{n_1}\psi(x_i+n_1h,y_j,z_k)+\sum_{n_2=-N}^{N} C_{n_2}\psi(x_i,y_j+n_2h,z_k)\\
&+\sum_{n_3=-N}^{N} C_{n_3}\psi(x_i,y_j,z_k+n_3h)\Big] \quad + \quad [V_{ion}(x_i,y_j,z_k) \qquad (2)\\
&+\ V_H(x_i,y_j,z_k)\ +\ V_{xc}(x_i,y_j,z_k)\ ]\ \psi(x_i,y_j,z_k)=E\ \psi(x_i,y_j,z_k)
\end{aligned}
$$

If there are M grid points, the size of the resulting matrix is $M \times M$. The size of this matrix is the limiting factor is solving this finite difference equation. V_{ion} is the nonlocal ionic pseudopotential, V_H is the Hartree potential and V_{xc} is the local density expression for the exchange and correlation potential.

There are several issues which must be addressed to solve Eq. (2). The first concerns the procedure by which the self-consistent field is constructed. The exchange-correlation potential, V_{xc}, is trivial once the charge density has been constructed over the grid. The charge is trivially known once the matrix has been diagonalized. This part of the calculation requires no FFT's.

The Hartree potential can be determined by a matrix equation, which for large systems may be quite efficient. For localized systems, this procedure can involve fairly complex boundary conditions, but in terms of computational cost it is the equivalent of obtaining one additional eigenstate. Instead, we solve for V_H by direct numerical integration of the Poisson integral. The time for this integration constitutes a small computational contribution. For example, for a small cluster the solution of Poisson's equation is less than 1% of the total computational time for the systems of interest here. We use a Broyden mixing scheme to expedite the construction of the self-consistent field [13].

Another issue concerns the nonlocality of the ionic pseudopotential, *i.e.*, the angular momentum dependence of this potential. These pseudopotentials are constructed as for any electronic structure calculation. Details of their construction can be found elsewhere [14]. We employ the Kleinman-Bylander form [15] in *real space* [16]:

$$
\begin{aligned}
V_{ion}(x,y,z)\ \psi(x,y,z) &= V_{loc}(x,y,z)\ \psi(x,y,z)+\sum_{lm} G_{lm}\ u_{lm}(x,y,z)\Delta V_l(x,y,z)\\
G_{lm} &= \frac{\int u_{lm}(x,y,z)\ \Delta V_l(x,y,z)\ \psi(x,y,z)\ dxdydz}{\int u_{lm}(x,y,z)\ \Delta V_l(x,y,z)\ u_{lm}(x,y,z)\ dxdydz} \qquad (3)
\end{aligned}
$$

V_{loc} is the local ionic pseudopotential, $\Delta V_l = V_l - V_{loc}$ is the difference between other l-components of the ionic and the local ionic potential. u_{lm} are solutions to the atomic pseudopotential for the valence states of interest. Usually, one component is taken as the local component, *e.g.* $V_l = V_s$ where V_s is the s-component to the local component. The range of ΔV_l is usually much less than a bond length. The nonlocality in V_{ion} is reflected by the occurrence of $\psi(x, y, z)$ in G_{lm}. The integral involving $\psi(x, y, z)$ is performed over the relatively few grid points where ΔV_l is non-zero:

$$
\begin{aligned}
& \int u_{lm}(x,y,z)\ \Delta V_l(x,y,z)\ \psi(x,y,z)dxdydz \\
= & \sum_{ijk} u_{lm}(x_i, y_j, z_k)\Delta V_l(x_i, y_j, z_k)\psi(x_i, y_j, z_k)h^3 \qquad (4)
\end{aligned}
$$

The matrix resulting from Eq. (2) is real, symmetric and sparse. This greatly facilitates the diagonalization calculation. The sparsity of the matrix is a function of the order to which the kinetic energy is expanded. We have illustrated the structure of the matrix below (Figure 1).

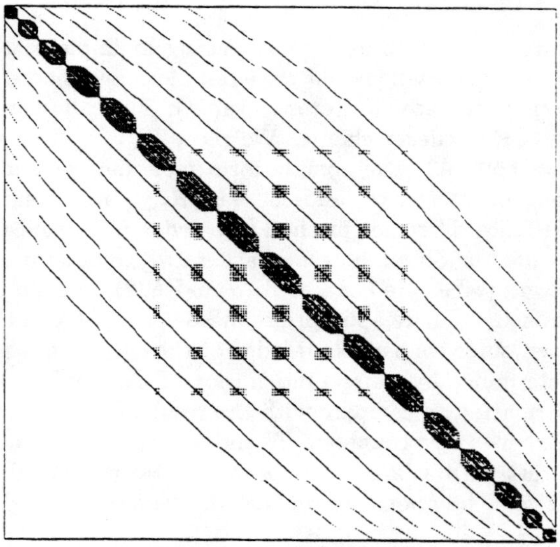

Figure 1. The structure of the Hamiltonian matrix for a diatomic molecule. Non-zero matrix elements are indicated by black dots.

Our application in this case corresponds to solving for the electronic structure of a diatomic molecule; however, the general form of the matrix for other systems would be similar. There are three distinct elements of the matrix: (1) Coefficients for the higher order expansion of the kinetic energy. These elements appear on the diagonal and as off-diagonal bands. (2) The local electronic potential evaluated over the grid points. These elements resides only on the diagonal. (3) Rank one update elements corresponding to the nonlocal contributions. These nonlocal matrix elements are properties solely of the ionic part of the pseudopotential and are not updated during the generation of the self-consistent field. Only the local parts of the potential (on the diagonal) are updated during the self-consistency cycle.

The sparsity of the matrix is a function of the order N to which the kinetic energy is expanded. We have employed an iterative diagonalization procedure which can take advantage of sparsity to compute the eigenvalues and eigenvectors. An alternate approach to exploiting sparsity is to perform the matrix-vector products required by the diagonalization routine in operator format. Using this procedure, there is no need to store the matrix in any sparse form since the coefficients $C_{n_i}, i = 1,2,3; n = -N, N$ in Eq. (2) are constant and as a result, the matrix-by-vector kinetic operations required by the diagonalization routine can be performed in "stencil" form. The non-local operations are accomplished by performing them as vector-by-vector operations. This strategy not only saves storage, it also leads to an efficient implementation on most high-performance vector and parallel computers.

3. APPLICATION TO DIATOMIC MOLECULES

We will illustrate this procedure by considering a simple diatomic molecule: the CO molecule. Given the pseudoatom wave functions, we choose a radius, R_{max} beyond which we expect the atomic states to vanish. Typically this radius encompasses at least 99% of the valence charge. We chose R_{max} to be 5.6 a.u. for both C, and O. (1 a.u. = 0.529 Å). The domain for a molecular system is constructed by requiring all atoms of interest to reside at least R_{max} from a surface.

In the standard finite difference method, the order N is fixed (at $N = 1$) and the mesh-size h is varied to obtain a desired accuracy. To determine the accuracy, the results of the two meshes are compared (h and $h/2$), and an estimate of the error is then determined. A more appropriate mesh-spacing h can then be derived, if necessary. However, since we have knowledge of the eigenvalues and the pseudowavefunctions as determined by a direct integration of the atomic pseudopotentials, we can use this information to compare with the results obtained by the finite difference method. We have two parameters, N and h, to obtain the desired accuracy. To find these, we start with a large grid spacing and continuously reduce h until the eigenvalues and wave functions are replicated. We have verified this procedure for several orders of N.

Let us illustrate this procedure for the oxygen atom. Given the localized nature of the oxygen wave functions, this atom should be a severe test. In Figure 2, we illustrate the convergence of the eigenvalues as a function of N for several values of h. For the "standard" finite difference method, $N = 1$, the eigenvalues have not converged to the known values even for $h = 0.35$ *a.u.* At this value of h, the eigenvalues differ by more than $0.1 Ry$ from those determined by direct integration. However, for $N \geq 4$, the eigenvalues are converged to within $0.01 Ry$ for $h \leq 0.4$. We have experimented higher values of N, *i.e.* with $N = 6$ and 9. We find that for most applications, orders higher than $N = 6$ do not provide significant improvement. For example, if N is increased from 6 to 9, the total electronic energy of the oxygen atom changes by less than ~0.005 Ry for $h = 0.4$ a.u.

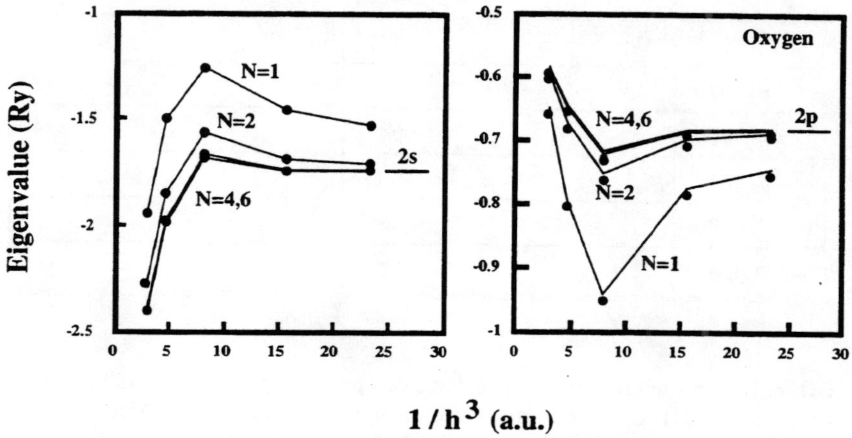

Figure 2. Convergence of atomic oxygen eigenvalues for different orders, N, and different grid spacings, h.

All the following calculations are done with $N = 6$. The grid spacing was taken to be $h = 0.4$ for carbon and oxygen. The matrix size obtained from this procedure is comparable with that obtained using plane waves, but no 3D FFT's or packing/unpacking of vectors needs to be performed. By eliminating this costly communications overhead, very efficient use of parallel algorithms/computers can be obtained. The matrix size for the CO molecule is approximately 14000 × 14000.

In Table I, we list the pseudopotential eigenvalues from the direct integration of the atomic Schrödinger for C, and O, and as calculated using the finite difference method. The largest error in the eigenvalues is on the order of ~0.02Ry. This is the type of error which one would introduce using a plane wave basis. The chief source of error from the higher-order finite difference method arises from the finite size of R_{max}. Even though the valence charge is strongly localized, the exchange-correlation potential does not decay vary rapidly. For example, if we consider an exchange potential which scales as $\sim \rho(r)^{1/3}$, if the charge falls off by three orders of magnitude at R_{max} the exchange potential decays by only one order of magnitude. By requiring the charge to vanish outside R_{max}, we also require the exchange-correlation potential to vanish at this radius. This error manifests itself in a small error in resulting self-consistent potential and in the total energy of the atom. For example, in the case of atomic oxygen the "finite difference" self-consistent potential differs by an rms error of ~ 0.01 Ry from the potential found by "direct integration."

We note that similar problems can occur for supercell approaches, *i.e.*, the exchange-correlation may not be correctly replicated unless the cell size if quite large.

	Carbon	Oxygen
E_s (FD)	-0.99	-1.74
E_s (DI)	-1.00	-1.74
E_p (FD)	-0.38	-0.68
E_p (DI)	-0.40	-0.68
$^3P \rightarrow {}^1D$ (FD)	1.31	1.87
$^3P \rightarrow {}^1D$ (Expt)	1.26	1.84

Table I. Atomic energy levels in Ry from pseudopotentials by direct integration (DI) and from finite difference calculations (FD). Also, the lowest excitation in eV as calculated from finite difference pseudopotentials and as measured from atomic spectra [17].

As a test of the atomic wavefunctions from our finite difference method, we have calculated the lowest excitations for the atomic species of interest. Using local density spin polarization formalism, we compare to measured atomic spectra [18]. In Figure 3, we illustrate the wave function from finite difference calculations, and compare the wave functions for C and O from direct integration. It is perhaps somewhat surprising that these wave functions are so accurate given that only ~10-15 points are considered along a given axis.

The diatomic molecules were computed following the same prescription as for the atomic species. By determining the electronic energy change as function of bond length, we can find the cohesive energy, the equilibrium bond length and the vibrational modes. In Figure 4, we illustrate the binding energy for CO as a function of bond length. The cohesive energy from local density calculations is not very reliable without including gradient corrections [19]. Our motivation here is not to improve on this formalism, but to test the accuracy of the finite difference method. We have determined the cohesive energy by subtracting the energy of the constituent atoms from the molecular energy without gradient corrections. We summarize our calculated binding energies in Table II. Typically, we find an overbinding by ~1-2 eV compared to experiment. Our CO molecule is slightly underbound. It may be that our grid spacing of $h = 0.4 a.u.$ is slightly too large for a highly converged solution. However, our binding energy exceeds that of previous work [21].

The bond length for the CO molecule is accurately reproduced by our calculations. Our vibrational mode is slightly lower than experiment. The vibrational mode was determined by fitting a cubic polynomial to the energy versus bond length. The vibrational modes are accurate to within a few percent on the basis of this fitting.

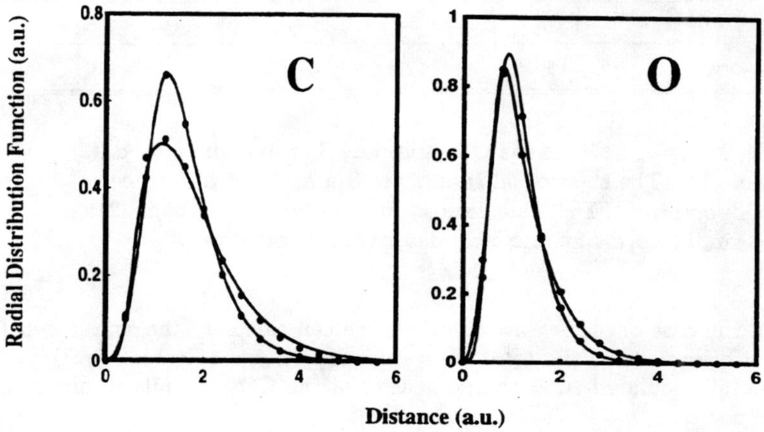

Figure 3. Pseudopotential radial distribution functions for carbon and oxygen for the *s*-state and *p*-state. The solid points correspond to a finite difference description.

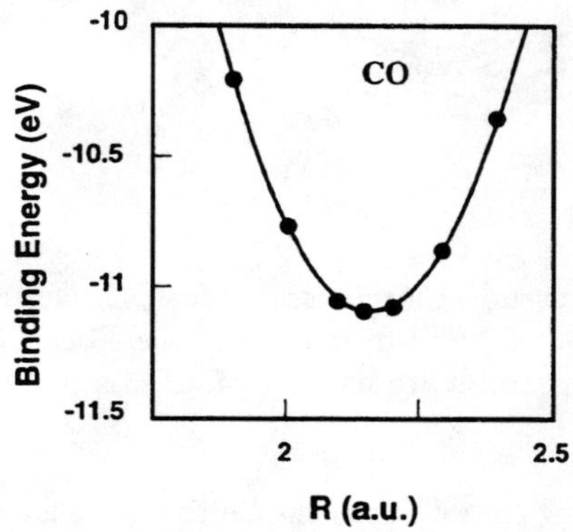

Figure 4. Binding energy of the CO molecule as function of the bond length, R, in a.u. (1 a.u. = 0.529 Å). The calculated points to a (solid circles) are fit to a cubic polynomial.

	Cohesive Energy (eV)	Bond Length (Å)	Vibrational Mode (cm^{-1})
Experiment	11.24	1.13	2170
FDP	11.1	1.13	2000
Other theory	9.6	1.17	2100

Table II. Properties of the CO molecule. The experimental data is from [20]. The theoretical results are from a finite difference pseudopotential (FDP) calculation, and from other methods [21]. using similar forms for the local density approximation.

As in the case of plane wave solutions, we can calculate the charge densities of individual orbitals, and the total charge density of the molecule. In Figure 5, we compare our calculated total charge density of the CO molecule to one computed via plane waves.

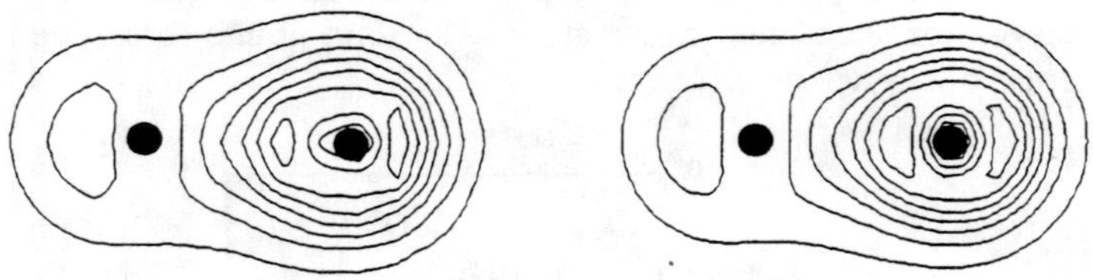

Figure 5. Total pseudo-charge density for CO. Results from a finite-difference "basis" (left) and from a plane wave basis (right) are illustrated. The contours are in units of 0.125 a.u.

It is very gratifying to note that the finite difference wave functions reproduce the dipole moment of the CO molecule. The dipole in CO is extraordinarily sensitive to the bond length and even changes in sign with changing bond length [21]. At large distances the dipole corresponds to charge configuration of C^+O^-. At smaller distance the sign reverses, and at equilibrium, the dipole corresponds to charge state of C^-O^+. The dipole we calculate is -0.10D compared to the experimental value of -0.1227D [22]. A previous local density calculation has given a value of -0.01D[21]. In Figure 6, we illustrate the dipole of the CO molecule versus the interatomic separation. We compare to the experimental results, and to two other theoretical calculations: a Hartree-Fock calculation, and an all-electron local density calculation.

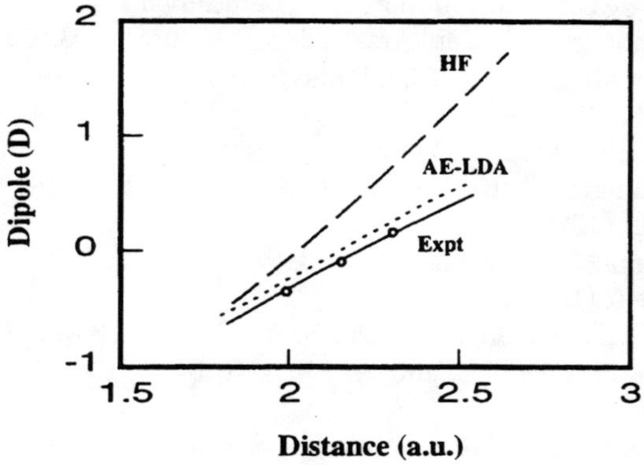

Figure 6. Dipole of the CO molecule as a function of bond length. A positive dipole corresponds to C^+O^-. Results from two theoretical calculations and experiment are illustrated. The open circles correspond to a finite difference pseudopotential calculation.

4. CONCLUSIONS

In summary, we have suggested an algorithm for performing electronic structure calculations on high performance computers. We have combined a higher order finite difference approach with *ab initio* pseudopotentials. In contrast to methods which use a plane wave basis, our calculations are performed completely in "real space." No artifacts such as supercell geometries need be introduced for localized systems. Our method is much easier to implement than methods based on a plane wave basis, and is amenable to parallel machine architectures.

ACKNOWLEDGMENTS

Support from the National Science Foundation and the Minnesota Supercomputer Institute is acknowledged.

REFERENCES

1. J. R. Chelikowsky and M. L. Cohen, "*Ab Initio* Pseudopotentials and Structural Properties of Semiconductors," *Handbook on Semiconductors*, Editor P.T. Landsberg, (Elsevier, Amsterdam), Volume 1, p. 59 (1992).
2. M. L. Cohen, M. Schlüter, J. R. Chelikowsky, and S. G. Louie, Phys. Rev. B **12**, 5575 (1975).
3. K. M. Ho, M. L. Cohen, and M. Schlüter, Chem. Phys. Lett. **46**, (1977); M. Schlüter, A. Zunger, G. Kerker, K. M. Ho, and M. L. Cohen, Phys. Rev. Lett. **42**, 540 (1979).
4. I. Stich, R. Car, and M. Parrinello, Phys. Rev. B **44**, 4262 (1991); Phys. Rev. Lett. **63**, 2240 (1989).
5. J. R. Chelikowsky and N. Binggeli, Solid State Comm. **88**, 381 (1993); J. R. Chelikowsky, N. Troullier, and N. Binggeli, Phys. Rev. B**49** 114, (1994).
6. I. Stich, M. C. Payne, R. D. King-Smith, J. -S. Lin, L. J. Clarke, Phys. Rev. Lett. **68**, 1351 (1992).
7. K. D. Brommer, M. Needels, B. E. Larson, and J. D. Joannopoulos, Phys. Rev. Lett. **68**, 1355 (1992).
8. N. Binggeli, J. L. Martins and J. R. Chelikowsky, Phys. Rev. Lett. **68**, 2956 (1992).
9. This approach has been used to study charged impurities see, e.g., C. G. Van de Walle, P. J. H. Denteneer, Y. Bar-Yam, and S. T. Pantelides, Phys. Rev. B **39**, 10791 (1989); S. Froyen and A. Zunger, Phys. Rev. B **34**, 7451 (1986).
10. G. D. Smith, *Numerical Solutions of Partial Differential Equations: Finite Difference Methods*, 2nd edition, Oxford, 1978.
11. A brief description of this method applied to diatomic molecules can be found in J.R. Chelikowsky, N. Troullier, and Y. Saad, Phys. Rev. Lett. **72**, 1240 (1994).
12. B. Fornberg and D. M. Sloan, *Acta Numerica 94*, Editor A. Iserles, Cambridge University Press, 1994 (in press).
13. C. G. Broyden, Math. Comp. **19**, 577 (1965).
14. N. Troullier and J. L. Martins, Phys. Rev. B **43**, 1993 (1991).
15. L. Kleinman and D. M. Bylander, Phys. Rev. Lett. **48**, 1425 (1982).
16. N. Troullier and J. L. Martins, Phys. Rev. B**43**, 8861 (1991).
17. C. E. Moore, *Atomic Energy Levels*, National Standard Reference Data Series (NBS, Washington, DC), 1949, Volume I.
18. J. E. Northrup, M. T. Yin, and M. L. Cohen, Phys. Rev. A **28**, 1945 (1983).
19. F. W. Kutzler and G. S. Painter, Phys. Rev. B **45**, 3236 (1992).
20. K. P. Huber and G. Herzberg, *Constants of Diatomic Molecules*, (Van Nostrand, New York), 1979.
21. O. Gunnarsson, J. Harris and R. O. Jones, J. Chem. Phys. **67**, 3970 (1977).
22. C. Charkerian Jr., J. Chem. Phys. **65**, 4228 (1976).

Toward Teraflop Computing
and New Grand
Challenge Applications

ISBN-1-56072-247-9

Wavelet–Transform Representation of the Electronic Structure of Materials

T.A. Arias[(1)], K.J. Cho[(1)], J.D. Joannopoulos[(1)], Pui Lam[(2)] and M.P. Teter[(3,4)]

[(1)] Department of Physics, Massachusetts Institute of Technology
[(2)] Department of Physics, University of Hawaii
[(3)] Corning Glass Works
[(4)] Cornell University

Abstract

We develop a three dimensional (3D) wavelet analysis to support a new formalism for electronic structure calculations which is more suited to parallel computation. The central concept from wavelet theory, multiresolution analysis [MRA], provides a uniformly improvable and tractable description of electronic wave functions and overcomes limitations of conventional basis expansions. The potential power of the wavelet formalism for *ab initio* electronic structure calculations is demonstrated by a calculation of 1s states for all the naturally occurring nuclei on the periodic table, a calculation the interaction energies of the hydrogen molecule ion, as well as an illustrative self-consistent all-electron calculation of the Kohn-Sham orbitals of the carbon atom.

1. INTRODUCTION

Spectral analysis using the Fourier transform is a powerful method for solving many problems in science and engineering. This method, however, is not appropriate for problems that require a localized description in real space for the efficient implementation of algorithms in parallel computing environments. Although several techniques, such as the windowed Fourier transform, have been invented to provide complete local bases, by far the most promising new technique is the wavelet transform[1]. Unlike the plane wave basis functions of the Fourier transform, the wavelet basis functions are localized both in real space *and* in Fourier space[1,2]. Furthermore, multiresolution analysis (MRA) of the wavelet transform provides a systematic successive approximation scheme for practical applications in many varied fields[1,3].

Applications of the wavelet transform have focused primarily on digital signal processing (1D), compact image coding (2D), and related fast mathematical algorithms[4]. More recently, the wavelet transform has been applied to the analysis of chaotic behavior and turbulence in 2D, the coherent states of quantum optics and quantum field theory, and to real space renormalization group theory[2].

In this paper, we develop yet another application of the wavelet transform, in 3D, to electronic structure investigations of material properties. Traditional *ab initio* total energy density functional methods for electronic structure calculations use either specialized basis sets which are dependent *explicitly* on the locations and types of the atoms in the system (*e.g.* atomic, Gaussian or Slater basis sets and augmented plane wave [APW] basis sets) or plane wave basis sets[5]. Specialized basis sets typically are capable of describing electronic structure with a small number of basis functions, but lack an explicit and well-defined procedure for *uniform* improvement, and thus generally complicate the calculation of forces and atomistic molecular dynamics simulations because of the presence of large Pulay terms[6] which must be compensated through explicit calculation.

On the other hand, plane wave basis sets do provide a uniform expansion of electronic wave functions, introduce no Pulay terms for supercells of fixed size and are well suited to *ab initio* atomistic molecular dynamics simulations. But, they suffer from the same limitations as the Fourier transform method. Specifically, the description of the rapid variations of electronic wave functions close to atomic nuclei (in atomic cores) requires a large number of plane wave functions even though the volume of the atomic core is only a small part of the total volume of the system. Further, the extended nature of plane waves and the ensuing communications overhead make the formulation of the electronic-structure problem unnecessarily awkward on parallel platforms for both the (plane wave based) pseudopotential approach and the APW approach.

The "best of all worlds" then would be to have a basis set that, unlike a plane wave basis, can zoom into the atomic core regions with localized functions, *and*, unlike specialized bases, does not introduce Pulay terms into the computations of atomic forces, does not complicate atomistic molecular dynamics simulations, but does provide an explicit prescription for complete expansion of electronic wave functions. The wavelet basis has all these desired properties: multiscale decomposition of wave functions, localized description of rapid variations, and a uniformly complete expansion similar to the plane wave expansion. Therefore, as we shall discuss in this paper, the wavelet basis overcomes the limitations of both specialized bases and the general plane wave expansion while retaining only the advantages of both approaches.

2. MULTIRESOLUTION ANALYSIS

2.1 General Theory

We review here briefly the central concept which we need from wavelet theory, multiresolution analysis [MRA]. (See [1,3] for more in depth discussions.) MRA begins by defining a basis of localized functions, ϕ, on a uniform grid at unit spacing. The subspace of functions formed by arbitrary linear combinations of functions in this basis,

$$f(x) = \sum_n a_n \phi(x-n), \tag{1}$$

we identify as V_0. Scaling this basis uniformly in space by factors of 2 then generates a series of subspaces

$$V_j \equiv span\{\phi(2^j x - n)\} \tag{2}$$

of greater (increasing j) and lesser (decreasing j) resolution. These spaces impose a nested hierarchy in the Hilbert space of all functions, $\hat{\mathbf{H}}$,

$$\cdots V_{-2} \subset V_{-1} \quad \subset V_0 \quad \subset V_1 \subset V_2 \cdots = \hat{\mathbf{H}} \tag{3}$$

Here we have made formal the intuitive notion that functions described by a coarse basis, V_j, also be describable within a finer basis, V_k, by insisting that $V_j \subset V_k$ for $j < k$. $V_0 \subset V_1$ implies that $\phi(x)$ is a *scaling function*, that it may be written as a linear combination of functions in the next finer space,

$$\phi(x) = \sum_n a_n \phi(2x-n). \tag{4}$$

This condition is *equivalent* to Eq. (3).

The set of suitable functions obeying the two-scale relation is characterized most easily in Fourier space. The Fourier transform of Eq. (4) becomes

$$\hat{\phi}(k) \quad = \quad \left[\sum_n \frac{1}{2} a_n e^{-i\frac{k}{2}n}\right] \hat{\phi}(\frac{k}{2}) \equiv m_0(\frac{k}{2})\hat{\phi}(\frac{k}{2}), \tag{5}$$

where $m_0(q)$ is then any arbitrary 2π-periodic function of q obeying the one condition that $m_0(0) = 1$ so that the area under $\phi(x)$ is conserved. Applying this relation recursively yields the general form for the Fourier transform of a valid scaling function,

$$\hat{\phi}(k) = \prod_{n=1}^{\infty} m_0(\frac{k}{2^n}). \tag{6}$$

With scaling functions characterized, MRA then goes on to describe the space, W_0, of the detail which is lost in going from the coarser, *approximation space* V_0 to the finer space V_1. It describes the *detail space* as spanned by another set of functions, wavelets ψ, placed on those points present in the finer lattice of V_1 but not present in the coarser lattice of V_0. For $V_1 = V_0 \dot{+} W_0$ to obtain, any function $f \in V_1$, must be expressible as the sum of a function $g \in V_0$ and a function $h \in W_0$,

$$f(x) = \sum_n f_n \phi(2x - n) \equiv \sum_n g_n \phi(x - n) + \sum_{n\, odd} h_n \psi(x - \frac{n}{2}) \tag{7}$$

The Fourier transform of this condition yields, after applying Eq. (5) and defining m_1 so that $\hat{\psi}(k) \equiv m_1(k/2)\hat{\phi}(k/2)$,

$$m_f(\frac{k}{2})\hat{\phi}(\frac{k}{2}) = m_p(k) m_0(\frac{k}{2})\hat{\phi}(\frac{k}{2}) + m_a(k) m_1(\frac{k}{2})\hat{\phi}(\frac{k}{2}), \tag{8}$$

where $m_f(q) \equiv \sum_n (f_n/2) \exp(-iqn)$ and $m_p(q) \equiv \sum_n g_n \exp(-iqn)$ are 2π-periodic functions and $m_a(q) \equiv \sum_{n\, odd} h_n \exp(-iqn/2)$ is a 2π-*anti*periodic function. Taking $k \to k + 4\pi$ in Eq. (8) yields the result that $m_1(q)$ must be a 2π periodic function, so that ψ also must have the form of a linear combination of scaling functions from V_1. (See Eq. (5).)

With the form of m_1 determined, $k \to k + 2\pi$ then gives a second equation for m_a and m_p, which when combined with Eq. (8) yields a solution for m_p and m_a for general m_f so long as

$$\det \begin{pmatrix} m_0(q) & m_1(q) \\ m_0(q+\pi) & -m_1(q+\pi) \end{pmatrix} \neq 0, \; for\ all\ q. \tag{9}$$

Given any valid scaling function, then, a W_0 satisfying $V_1 = V_0 \dot{+} W_0$ may be made up of ψ taken as any linear combination of ϕ's from V_1 which does not violate (9). This result is recursive in the sense that the condition that

$$W_j \equiv span_{\{n\, odd\}}\{\psi(2^j x - \frac{n}{2})\} \tag{10}$$

satisfy $V_{j+1} = V_j \dot{+} W_j$ becomes just Eq. (9) with $q \to 2^j q$, which clearly holds as well because Eq. (9) is valid for *all* q.

With the sequence of detail spaces, $\{W_j\}$, thus defined, the entire Hilbert space can be expressed as either the sum of the detail spaces of *all* resolutions or the sum of one approximation space and the wavelet spaces of that and *higher* resolutions:

$$\dot{\sum_j} W_j \;=\; V_{j_0} \dot{+} \dot{\sum_{j \geq j_0}} W_j = \hat{\mathbf{H}} \tag{11}$$

Any function in $\hat{\mathbf{H}}$ thus can be expanded either as a sum of the wavelet functions of *all* resolutions or as a sum of the scaling functions at resolution $j = 0$ and the wavelet functions of all *finer* resolutions $j \geq 0$.

2.2 Choice of Basis for Physical Systems

Although wavelet– scaling– function pairs are far from unique, one form that is convenient for the expansion of the continuous functions found in physical applications in general and electronic structure calculations in particular is to take the following as the 2π-periodic generating functions,

$$m_0(q) = \sum_n \exp\left(-\frac{3}{2}\sigma^2(q-2\pi n)^2\right) \tag{12}$$

$$m_1(q) = -D^2(q)\, m_0(q) \tag{13}$$

where,

$$D^2(q) \equiv \left(q - 2\pi[\frac{q+\pi}{2\pi}]\right)^2, \tag{14}$$

with $[x]$ being the greatest integer function. The condition (9) is easily seen to be satisfied as $-m_0(q)m_1(q+\pi)-m_1(q)m_0(q+\pi) = m_0(q)m_0(q+\pi)(D^2(q)+D^2(q+\pi)) > 0$ for all q because $m_0(q)$ is strictly positive and the two D^2 terms are each non-negative and are never both zero *simultaneously.* The utility of this choice comes from the fact that, for $\sigma = 1.35$, m_0 and m_1 generate a $\phi(x)$ and a $\psi(x)$ which may be approximated, respectively, as a normalized Gaussian of width σ and its second derivative, known as the Mexican hat function, to an absolute error of better than 10^{-10}. This has the advantage that in simple one-electron test calculations, all of the relevant matrix elements are known analytically between the Gaussian and Mexican hat.

As a practical verification of the representation afforded by this basis, we demonstrate how well the basis reconstructs the plane wave functions $G(x) \equiv \exp(ikx)$ as k varies from zero through the Niquist frequency corresponding to the spacing of the finest grid. For this particular test, we construct a basis consisting of Gaussians of r.m.s. width $\sigma = 1.35$, centered on the integers, and a bifrucating set of 63 Mexican-hat wavelets between each pair of successive integers. We then project the function $G(x)$ onto this basis and compute the integral overlap of $G(x)$ with this projection. A value of unity indicates a perfect representation of $G(x)$ in our basis. Table 1 summarizes the results of these calculations. The recovery is nearly perfect up to the Niquist frequency ($G(x) = e^{2\pi i \cdot 32 \cdot x}$), which is about the best one can expect for *any* set of basis functions and which we *do* expect from the fact that the Gaussian-Mexican hat basis forms a nearly exact multiresolution analysis.

2.3 Implementation

Truncation of Eq. (3) at some finest resolution j_{max} leads to the wavelet expansion of a function $f(x)$ as

$$f(x) = \sum_{\mathbf{n}} a_{j_0,\mathbf{n}}\phi_{j_0,\mathbf{n}}(\mathbf{r}) + \sum_{j=j_0}^{j_{max}}\sum_{\mathbf{n}} d_{j,\mathbf{n}}\psi_{j,\mathbf{n}}(\mathbf{r}). \tag{15}$$

This expansion generalizes directly to three dimensions, and begins with V_{j_0} containing all scaling functions at scale j_0 centered on the points in the V_{j_0} lattice,

n	$<G\|U\|G>$	n	$<G\|U\|G>$	n	$<G\|U\|G>$	n	$<G\|U\|G>$
0	1.0000	9	1.0000	18	1.0000	27	1.0000
1	1.0000	10	1.0000	19	1.0000	28	0.9997
2	1.0000	11	1.0000	20	1.0000	29	0.9975
3	1.0000	12	1.0000	21	1.0000	30	0.9819
4	1.0000	13	1.0000	22	1.0000	31	0.8806
5	1.0000	14	1.0000	23	1.0000	32*	0.5000
6	1.0000	15	1.0000	24	1.0000	33†	0.1194
7	1.0000	16	1.0000	25	1.0000	34†	0.0181
8	1.0000	17	1.0000	26	1.0000	35†	0.0025
*Niquist frequency				†Supra-Niquist Frequencies			

Table 1: Reconstruction of $G = e^{2\pi i \cdot n \cdot x}$ with 6 resolution levels ($\leftrightarrow$ 64 basis functions) per unit.

$\phi(2^{j_0}x - l)\phi(2^{j_0}y - m)\phi(2^{j_0}z - n)$. It further places wavelets at scales from $j = j_0$ up to $j = j_{max} - 1$, centering the wavelets at scale j on all those points present in the V_{j+1} lattice which are not also present in the V_j lattice. In this manner, each point of the finest scale lattice of $V_{j_{max}}$ is associated with one and only one function.

Because the wavelet functions are *localized in space*, one may retain only the basis functions that have significant coefficients in Eq. (15) for the problem at hand. This locality allows one to use different resolutions for different spatially localized regions. To describe of the rapid oscillations of the electronic wave function in an atomic core region, one need add higher resolution scales *only* to the core region. In practise, we collect the most important basis functions by introducing spheres of finite support radii at each nuclear center as Fig. 1 illustrates. Correspondingly smaller support radii are chosen for correspondingly higher resolutions so that the deep core regions have more resolution scales.

Within this basis, the Schrödinger equation, $\hat{H}|\Psi> = \epsilon|\Psi>$, becomes a generalized eigenvalue problem. Expansion of the wave function in terms of the basis functions ($|\Psi> = \sum_i c_i|b_i>$) leads to the secular equation,

$$\sum_i < b_j|\hat{H}|b_i > c_i \quad = \quad \epsilon \sum_i < b_j|b_i > c_i. \tag{16}$$

3. RESULTS

3.1 Elementary Chemistry: the Hydrogen Atom

In order to gain a sense of the optimal values of the various parameters of the formalism, we began with the hydrogen atom as a simple test case. After performing

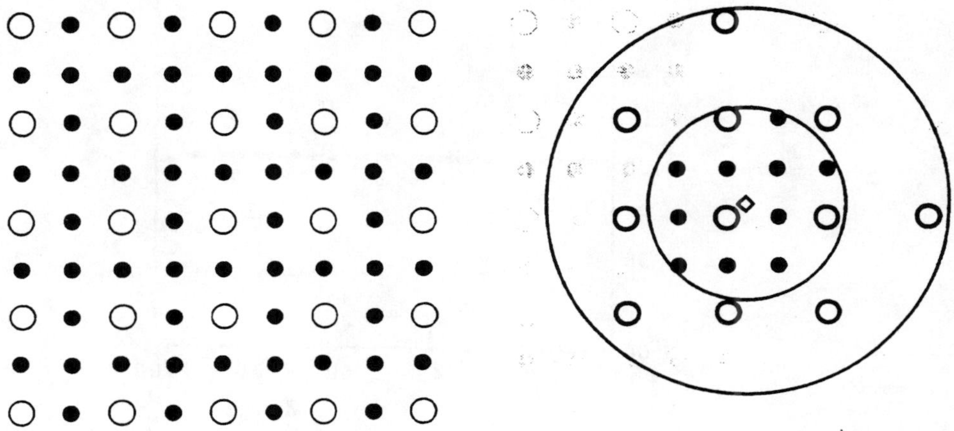

Figure 1: Left panel shows a two dimensional arrangement of the centers of basis functions on a simple square lattice. Open circles are the centers of the basis functions at resolution $j = 0$, and filled circles are the centers of the basis functions at resolution $j = 1$. Right panel shows the basis functions that lie within each support radius that is centered on an atomic position (diamond-symbol). The larger (smaller) radius corresponds to $j = 0$ ($j = 1$) resolution.

calculations using many different resolution scales and different support radii, we found that a satisfactory minimal basis set for the Hydrogen atom contains 25 basis functions with four resolution scales: (7 scaling functions from V_0 on a 1 *Bohr* grid, plus 6 wavelets from W_0, plus 6 wavelets from W_1, plus 6 wavelets from W_2) which we designate simply as (7 + three 6's). These correspond respectively to support radii of 1 *Bohr*, 0.5 *Bohr*, 0.25 *Bohr*, and 0.125 *Bohr*. The resulting 1s eigenenergy is within 2% of the exact value. This error in easily controlled by increasing the size of the basis set. Changing to 85 functions with three resolution scales (33 + two 26's), we obtain the $1s$ eigenenergy to within 0.5% of the exact value.

3.2 Across the Periodic Table: from Hydrogen to Uranium

Adding further resolution scales, one can calculate the wave functions of heavier nuclei to the same accuracy. As the atomic number increases, the Coulomb potential becomes stronger, and consequently, higher resolution scales are needed in the core region. However, only *one* additional resolution scale needs to be added each time the atomic number doubles, and the size of the basis thus grows only as $log_2 Z$, where Z is the atomic number, as opposed to the Z^3 behavior which pure plane wave approaches would exhibit. To describe the $1s$ wave functions for $Z = 1 \ldots 92$ (Hydrogen through Uranium) using a *fixed* basis set, for instance, the wavelet basis uses only eleven

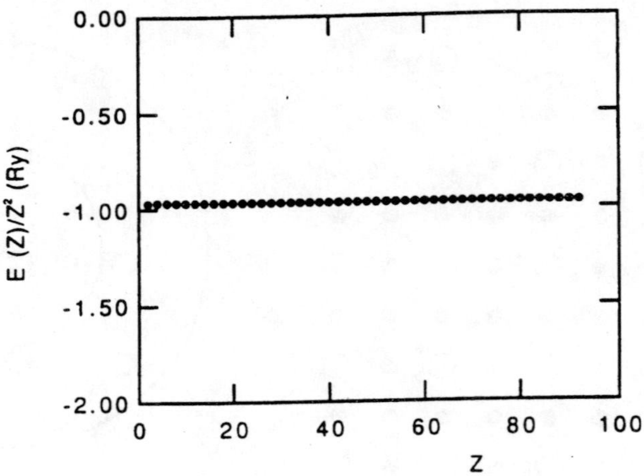

Figure 2: The filled circles are the 1s eigen energies of all the nuclei with even atomic numbers on the periodic table ($Z = 2, 4, ..., 92$) calculated with the fixed 67 basis function set.

resolution scales (7+ ten 6's), as opposed to the requirement of about 10^8 plane waves. (An augmented plane wave, or other specialized basis, calculation of just U would require a much more reasonably sized basis; however, specialized bases require the use of a *different* basis set for each atom in the periodic table.) Using this *fixed* wavelet basis set of *only* 67 basis functions, we then calculate (to within 3%) the $1s$ eigenvalues of all the naturally occurring nuclei on the periodic table! The results are shown in Fig. 2 and include, for simplicity, only the even nuclei. Note that the eigenvalue for each nucleus is larger than the exact value by very nearly a constant percentage so that the results appear to lie on a straight line.

3.3 Bonding: the Ionized Hydrogen Molecule

As a simple example of chemical bonding, we consider the energy of an H_2^+ molecule as a function of the separation R between the two protons. The total energy (electronic eigenenergy plus the Coulomb potential energy) is plotted as a function of R in Fig. 3. The basis set for the calculation is selected using the same support radii as our more accurate hydrogen atom basis set (33 + two 26's) from Sec. (3.1). As the constituent atoms of the molecule and their associated support radii move, the total number of basis functions varies in the molecular calculation between 141 and 167. The calculated values in Fig. 3 are very close to the exact values [7] but are larger by a nearly constant fraction of 1%, implying that the wavelet basis gives an efficient representation of the chemical bond with excellent representation of inter-ionic forces, even when the basis is not brought to full completion.

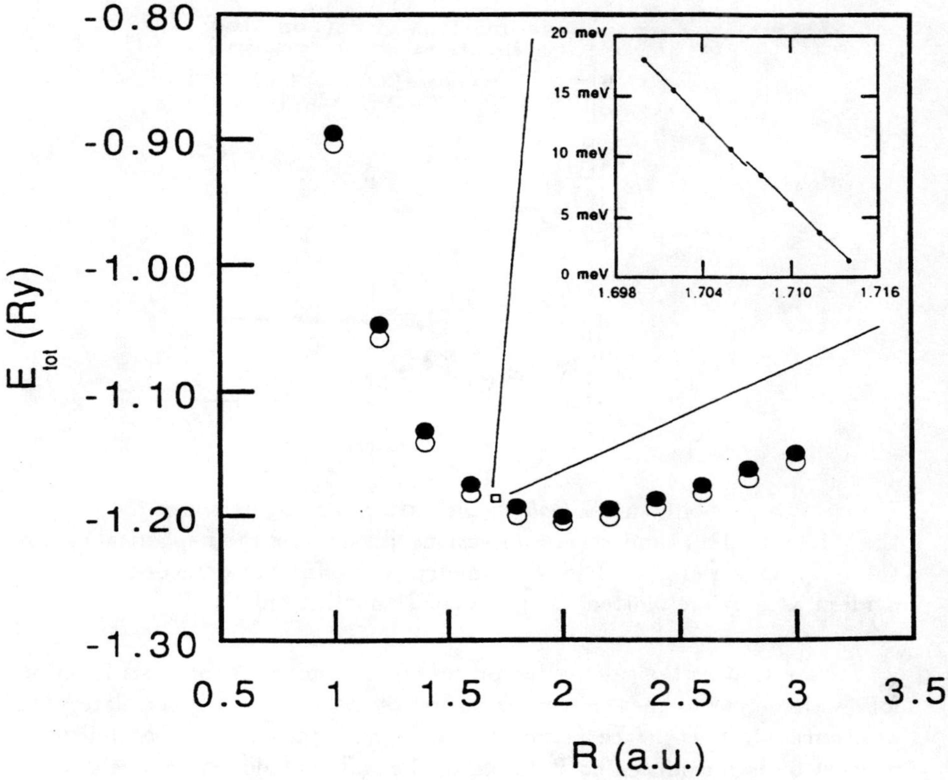

Figure 3: The total energy of a molecular hydrogen ion is shown as a function of the separation between the nuclei. The filled circles are the wavelet values while the open circles are the exact analytic values. The inset shows fine detail of the calculation in the vicinity of a change in basis, illustrating that basis-change effects are at less than the *meV* level.

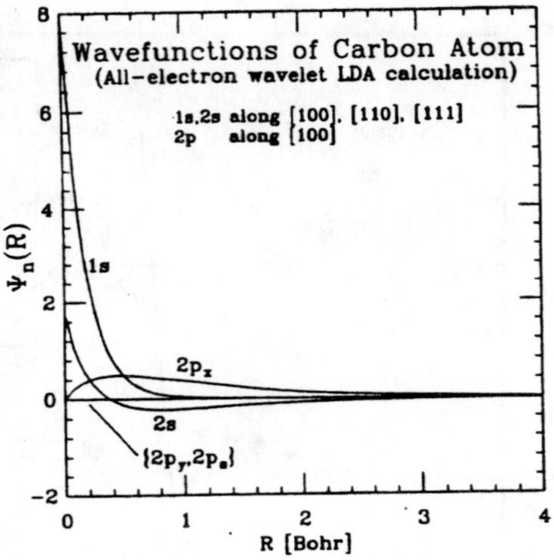

Figure 4: States of C in a 4 *Bohr* cubic lattice. The figure shows the 1s and 2s along the <100>, <110> and <111> directions, illustrating their spherical symmetry and the cusp at the origin. The p symmetry of the further extended $2p_{\{x,y,z\}}$ states is evident as they are plotted along the [100] direction only.

Note that as the calculation proceeds, the centers of the basis functions do not follow the nuclei as they move; the *underlying* basis set is not correlated to the ionic positions. Just as in the plane wave case, this ensures that the finite underlying wavelet basis introduces *no* Pulay terms for a fixed calculational cell. Although, in practice, it *is* possible to use the full underlying basis, it is much more convenient to introduce the support spheres as we have done above. This does introduce a position dependence into the basis by selecting the basis set as illustrated in the right panel of Fig. 1. However, simply increasing the size of the support radii to where the wave function coefficients for the wavelets near the edges of their respective spheres are near zero controls the magnitude of resulting Pulay corrections and eliminates the need for their explicit calculation. The effect on the present calculation from sudden changes in the basis set is extremely small, as the inset in Fig. 3 shows. The discontinuity in the energy is extremely small ($0.3meV$) as is the jump in force/slope ($\approx 1meV/\text{Å}$).

3.4 The future: LDA Carbon Atom

Using a compactly supported basis still under development, we have carried out a full, self-consistent, all electron calculation within the local density approximation [8] of a periodic array of Carbon atoms on a 4 *Bohr* ($\approx$ 2Å) cubic lattice. Fig. 4 reports the results of this calculation. The spherical symmetry of the calculated 1s and 2s states is evident from the fact that the curves for these states along the three principle cubic directions all lie perfectly on each other. The symmetry of the 2p

states is evident from the fact that the x- ([100]-) direction is in the nodal plane of the $2p_y$ and $2p_z$ states. The figure also illustrates that this basis reproduces well the cusp conditions on the s states and that the high resolution required to represent the $1s$ peak ($R \approx 0.2$ *Bohr*) is needed only in a tiny fraction ($\approx 3 \cdot 10^{-4}$) of the volume occupied by the $2p$ states ($R \approx 3$ *Bohr*).

4. CONCLUSIONS

We have developed a 3D wavelet formalism that is applicable to continuous physical systems in general and to electronic structure calculations in particular. We have demonstrated its potential power by performing calculations of the deepest core states of all the nuclei on the periodic table and of the interaction energy of the H_2^+ molecule. These results show that a wavelet expansion with a small number of basis functions gives an accurate description of the electronic wave functions both in atomic core regions and in chemical bonds. We have also demonstrated the feasibility of full, all electron LDA calculations within the framework of multiresolution analysis by presenting the results of a calculation of the states of the carbon atom.

Work currently is underway to evaluate the competitiveness of the resulting computational framework with plane wave, augmented plane wave [APW] and traditional LCAO-type approaches. In comparison to the plane wave approach, we expect wavelets to prove most advantageous in situations which require a spatial resolution which varies significantly throughout space, including systems involving first row elements or transition metals. Also, the local nature of the wavelet basis ensures that the wavelet transform maps far more naturally than does the fast Fourier transform onto the latest generation of massively parallel computer architectures.

Finally, one of the primary advantages of the MRA approach is the exponential scale on which it treats different frequencies. This yields the highly efficient $\log_2 Z$ scaling we noted above and distinguishes MRA from moving-window Fourier transform approaches, such as Wilson's generalized Wannier basis[9], which place frequencies on a linear scale. The exponential layout of frequencies also builds concepts from multigrid *algorithms* directly into the wavelet *basis*. MRA couples long and short length scales so that simple steepest-descent minimization applied to the coefficients of a wavelet expansion corresponds to a multigrid relaxation, without the need for coding a complex algorithm and while maintaining all of the advantages of a uniformly complete basis.

ACKNOWLEDGMENTS

This work was supported in part by ONR Grant No. N00014-92-J-1752, U.S. JSEP Contract No. DAAL-03-86-K-0002, the Cornell Laboratory of Atomic and Solid State Physics, the Material Science Center at Cornell, and the Cornell Theory Center. T.A.A. also would like to thank M. Parrinello for his thoughtful questions about this work.

REFERENCES

1. I. Daubechies; *Ten Lectures on Wavelets*; Philadelphia: SIAM; 1992.

2. M. B. Ruskai *et al.*; *Wavelets and their Applications*; Boston: Jones and Bartlett; 1992.

3. C. K. Chui; *An Introduction to Wavelets*; Boston: Academic Press; 1992.

4. C. K. Chui, ed.; *Wavelets: A Tutorial in Theory and Applications*; Boston: Academic Press; 1992.

5. M. C. Payne *et al.*; "Iterative minimization techniques for *ab initio* total-energy calculations: molecular dynamics and conjugate gradients"; *Reviews of Modern Physics* Vol. 68; 1992; p. 1045.

6. P. Pulay; "*Ab initio* calculation of force constants and equilibrium geometries in polyatomic molecules: I. Theory"; *Molecular Physics* Vol. 246; 1969; p. 197.

7. D. R. Bates, K. Ledsham and A. L. Stewart, "Wave functions of the hydrogen molecular ion"; *Phil. Trans. Roy. Soc. London* Vol. 246; 1953; p. 215.

8. W. Kohn and L. J. Sham; "Self-consistent equations including exchange and correlation effects"; *Physical Review* Vol. 140; 1965; p. A1133.

9. Wilson; "Generalized Wannier Functions"; *preprint*; Cornell University; 1987.

Toward Teraflop Computing
and New Grand
Challenge Applications

ISBN-1-56072-247-9

QUANTUM SIMULATION STUDIES OF BIPOLARONS IN CESIUM-AMMONIA SOLUTIONS

Zhihong Deng[†], Michael L. Klein[†], and Glenn J. Martyna[‡]

[†]Department of Chemistry, University of Pennsylvania, Philadelphia, PA 19104
[‡]Department of Chemistry, Indiana University, Bloomington, IN 47405

Dilute cesium-ammonia solutions have been studied by quantum simulation. The ammonia solvent is made fully polarizable and the cations, here cesium, are explicitly included. The solvent and ions are treated classically and the electronic degrees of freedom are handled using the Car-Parrinello method and Density Functional Theory. At *ca*. 0.5 mole percent metal (MPM), the solvated electrons spontaneously spin-pair to form large peanut shaped species called bipolarons. The electrons still exist as bipolarons at *ca*. 1 MPM but well separated from each other. The bipolarons exhibit no strong tendency to be oriented either parallel or perpendicular to each other. We have investigated the effect of the counter ions and the system size on the structure and dynamics of the bipolarons at *ca*. 1 MPM and found it to be small.

1. INTRODUCTION

The evolution of spin-pairing in dilute metal-ammonia solutions has been extensively studied experimentally [1,2,3,4]. For metal concentrations above 10^{-3} MPM, there is a marked drop in the spin susceptibility per electron. The conductivity per electron also falls off and reaches a minimum at *ca*. 0.1 MPM [1]. These observations have been interpreted to indicate that the electrons form associated spin-paired species such that at *ca*. 0.1 MPM, spin-pairing is essentially complete with almost 80% of the electrons spin-paired [1]. However, the optical absorption spectrum of the solution is relatively unchanged from that at low metal concentration and the volume of the spin-paired species is approximately twice the volume of an isolated electron [1]. observations that suggest the association is weak. In order to explain these results, Mott has proposed an electron distribution resembling that of a hydrogen molecule with a binding energy of a few tenths of an eV above that of two isolated solvated electrons [5].

Previous simulation studies employing Path Integral Monte Carlo (PIMC) and Car-Parrinello Local Spin Density Functional (CP-LSDA) methods [6,7] have confirmed Mott's inferences about the electronic states at *ca.* 1 MPM. In the singlet state, the electrons spin pair and form peanut shaped cavities with peaks in the electron density about 6.5 Å apart [6,7]. These spin-paired species are the so called "bipolarons". Despite this success, several issues remain to be explored. For example, to what extent is the stability of the bipolaron affected by the metal counter ions? Is there a finite size effect on the structure and dynamics of the bipolaron? Are the bipolarons associated at 1 MPM and is there any difference in the properties of bipolarons at different metal concentrations? In this paper, these issues are addressed with specific reference to cesium-ammonia solutions.

2. CAR-PARRINELLO CALCULATIONS

The polarizable model proposed in our previous work on lithium-ammonia solutions [8] is employed in the present calculations. The ammonia solvent is made fully polarizable and the cations, here cesium, are explicitly included [8]. The fully polarizable ammonia model is constructed from a rigid point-charge ansatz [9]. The electronic degrees of freedom associated with the valence electrons are taken to interact with the ammonia and the alkali cations via pseudopotentials. Specifically, the pseudopotential used to describe electron-ammonia interactions contains the appropriate electrostatic interactions and both polarization and repulsion contributions from the nitrogen [8,10]. For the $e^- - Cs^+$ interaction, the s-wave pseudopotential compilation of Bachelet is used as a local potential [8,11]. This simplification is justified because, in cesium-ammonia solutions, the cesium cations are solvated by ammonia molecules and isolated from close contact with the electron density [1]. The Cs^+-ammonia and the $Cs^+ - Cs^+$ interactions are described by pair-potentials [8]. Local Spin Density Functional theory is used to treat electronic exchange and correlation [8,12,13,14]. The dipole polarizability of the ammonia nitrogen is included. Both the ammonia-ammonia and ammonia-metal ion contributions to the polarization energy are treated fully self-consistently and the electronic part in the pair approximation. Electron-electron coupling terms in the polarization energy are neglected. The polarizability of the cesium cations themselves is neglected. The effect of this approximation remains to be investigated. The details of the potentials, as well as the treatment of the many-body polarization energy, are described elsewhere [8].

With these potentials, the electronic states in cesium-ammonia solutions at 0.5 MPM and 1 MPM are examined. The simulation cell (~ 29Å on edge) consisted of 512 ammonia molecules plus two or four cesium atoms, respectively. The volume of the simulation cell is taken to be [1]:

$$V_s = V_{NH_3} + n_e \cdot V_e + n_I \cdot V_I \tag{1}$$

where V_{NH_3} is the volume of 512 ammonia molecules at a typical liquid density, $\rho_{NH_3} = 0.023 Å^{-3}$, and the parameter, $V_e = 65 Å^3$, is the excess volume per electron and $V_I = 125 Å^3$ is the excess volume per Cs^+ ion [1]. The structure, energetics and dynamics of the bipolarons obtained from the present studies are compared to those obtained in earlier work [6,7]. at 1 MPM using a smaller cell (~ 22Å on edge) containing 256 ammonia molecules and two excess electrons. Through such comparisons, a possible system size effect on our previous low concentration studies [6,7]. can be assessed.

The electronic states of the system were determined using Local Spin Density Functional Theory [12,13]. In this scheme, the energy of a N-electron system is written as

$$E_{KS}^{LSDA}[n(\mathbf{r})] = -\frac{\hbar^2}{2m}\int d\mathbf{r} \sum_{i,\sigma} \psi_{i\sigma}(\mathbf{r})\nabla^2\psi_{i\sigma}(\mathbf{r}) \tag{2}$$

$$+ \int d\mathbf{r} V_{ext}(\mathbf{r})n(\mathbf{r}) + \frac{1}{2}\int\int d\mathbf{r}d\mathbf{r}' \frac{n(\mathbf{r})n(\mathbf{r}')}{|\mathbf{r}-\mathbf{r}'|} + E_{xc}[n_1(\mathbf{r}), n_{-1}(\mathbf{r})]$$

where $n(\mathbf{r}) = n_1(\mathbf{r}) + n_{-1}(\mathbf{r})$, $n_\sigma(\mathbf{r}) = \sum_{i=1}^{N_\sigma} |\psi_{i\sigma}(\mathbf{r})|^2$ and $N_1 + N_{-1} = N$. The self-consistent equations for the Kohn-Sham (KS) orbitals are then

$$\left[-\frac{\hbar^2}{2m}\nabla^2 + V_{ext}(\mathbf{r}) + \int d\mathbf{r}' \frac{n(\mathbf{r}')}{|\mathbf{r}-\mathbf{r}'|} + \frac{\delta E_{xc}(\mathbf{r})}{\delta n_\sigma(\mathbf{r})}\right]\psi_{i\sigma}(\mathbf{r}) = \epsilon_i \psi_{i\sigma}(\mathbf{r}) \tag{3}$$

where the exchange correlation energy is defined as $E_{xc}(\mathbf{r}) = \int d\mathbf{r} n(\mathbf{r})[\epsilon_x(\mathbf{r}) + \epsilon_c(\mathbf{r})]$. The form of the spin polarized $\epsilon_x(\mathbf{r})$ and $\epsilon_c(\mathbf{r})$ are taken from Perdew and Zunger [14]. The lowest spin state was studied in the present paper.

The single-particle orbitals have been expanded in a plane wave basis set using a cutoff of $k_{max} = 18\pi/L$, where L is the edge of the simulation cell. Only the Γ point is used in the calculations because of the large size of the unit cell (512 ammonia molecules) and the liquid nature of the system. The plane wave cutoff was tested on a few representative configurations and found to give energies to within a few percent of the fully converged results.

The structure and dynamics of the system was determined using the Car-Parrinello method [15,16]. In our model of metal-ammonia solutions, the ammonia molecules and metal cations move on a Born-Oppenheimer (BO) energy surface generated by the electrons and the induced dipoles

$$U_{BO}(\{\mathbf{R_i}\}) = \min_{\mu_{i_s}} \{V_{pol}^s[\{\mathbf{R_i}\}, \mu_{i_s}]\} + \min_{\psi_i} \{E_{KS}[\{\mathbf{R_i}\}, \psi_i]\}. \tag{4}$$

That is, the electrons must be in the instantaneous ground state and the induced dipoles must satisfy the minimization condition at every solvent configuration [8].

The Car-Parrinello approach is applied to this system by treating the plane wave expansion coefficients of the orbitals in the LSDA expression for the ground state energy (cf. Eq. 2) as dynamical variables and assigning them a small fictitious mass, m_e ($m_e = 64$ a.u.) and a very low temperature, T_e ($T_e = 0.02$ K) [15,16]. Similarly, the components of the induced dipoles on the nitrogen atoms are also treated as dynamical variables and assigned another small fictitious mass, m_p ($m_p = 600$ a.u.) and the low temperature, T_p ($T_p = 5$ K) [17,18]. The system is propagated according to a Hamiltanian consisting of the kinetic energy of the ions and ammonia molecules, the kinetic energy of the basis set parameters, the kinetic energy of the induced dipoles, the pair additive portion of the ammonia-ammonia, ion-ion and ammonia-ion interactions, the electronic energy, and the many-body polarization energy of the solvent [8]. The masses, m_e and m_p, have no physical meaning, but control the time scale of the motion of the electrons and the induced dipoles, respectively. In practice, the fictitious mass of the basis set parameters and the induced dipoles are adjusted for each concentration studied until an adiabatic separation of the dynamics of these fast variables and solvent is attained.

Simulations were run for 30 ps for each state point studied using the Velocity Verlet integration algorithm [19] and a time step of 8 a.u. ($\sim 2\times10^{-4}$ ps). The large temperature differences between the slow ammonia molecules and metal ions (at 260K) and fast but cold ($T < 5K$) degrees of freedom associated with the induced dipoles and basis set parameters, are maintained using a modification of the Nosé-Hoover canonical dynamics scheme, the so-called MKT chain method [8,20,21]. Here, independent chains of thermostats are placed on each orbital, the induced dipole moments, the metal cations, and the translational and rotational degrees of solvent molecules [8]. The MKT chains were found to maintain temperature control very well and, as a result, deviations from the Born-Oppenheimer surface were observed to be less than 5 percent during a typical 30 ps trajectory which takes about 150 CPU hours on the C90 CRAY.

4. RESULTS

The cesium-ammonia solutions were examined at concentrations corresponding to *ca.* 0.5 MPM and 1 MPM using the Car-Parrinello LSDA method. At *ca.* 0.5 MPM, the valence electrons of the cesium atoms ionize and then associate to form a peanut shaped bipolaron (see Fig. 1). The distance between the average position of spin-up and spin-down density is about 6.5 Å which is about the same as that of the 1 MPM singlet-state bipolaron previously studied [7,8]. The bipolaron is observed to fluctuate and reorient. At times, the two electrons move closer than 6.5 Å with a concomitant shape change from peanut-like to more spherical. However, when the electrons "rebound" to the peanut shape, the bipolaron is oriented differently. The electrons at *ca.* 0.5 MPM never collapse to a single spherical cavity, but remain at least 3.5Å apart. The cesium cations are solvated in the bulk ammonia solvent and are not in close contact with the electron density. The average distance between the two cesium cations is about 12Å. The self diffusion coefficient of cesium ions is about 0.2 $Å^2/ps$, which is less than half of that of the ammonia solvent, 0.5$Å^2/ps$.

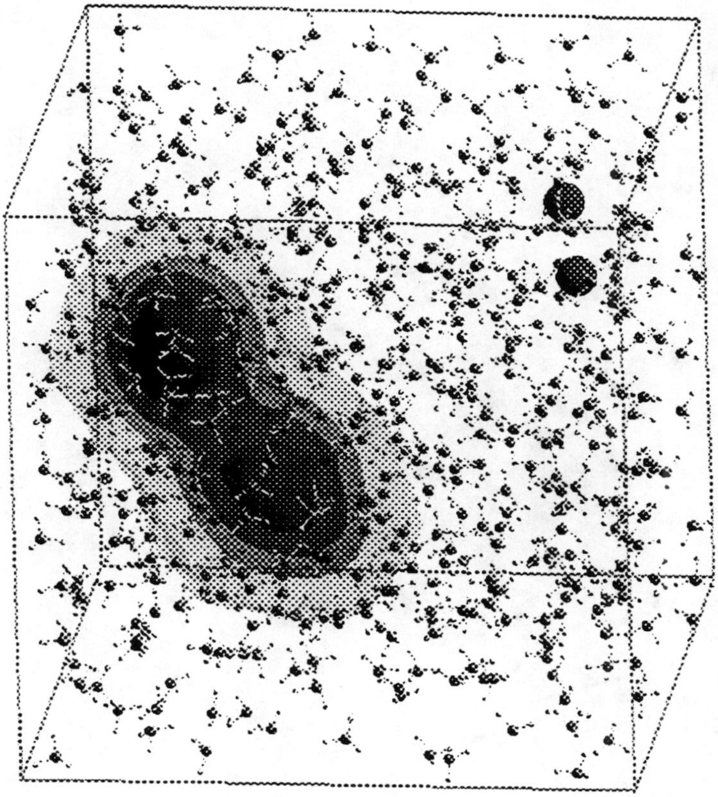

Figure 1 The electron density of a representative configuration of a cesium-ammonia solution at *ca*. 0.5 MPM taken from the present Car-Parrinello LSDA calculations using the polarizable solvent model. The simulation cell ($\sim 29\AA$ on edge) consists of 512 ammonia molecules and two cesium atoms. The Cs^+ ions are shown as spheres and ammonia molecules with ball and stick representation. The outermost contour contains 95% of the electron density.

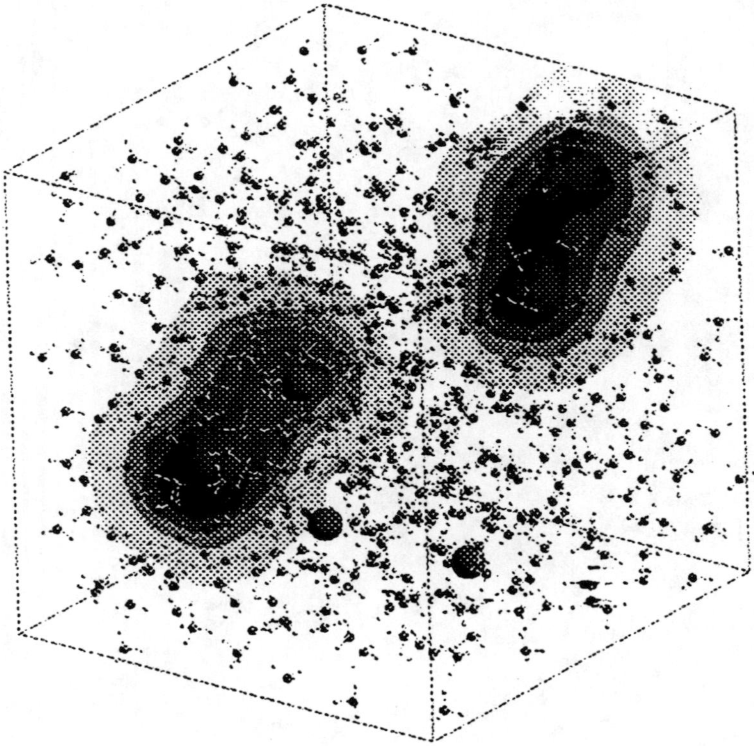

Figure 2 The electron density of a representative configuration of a cesium-ammonia solution at *ca*. 1 MPM taken from the present Car-Parrinello LSDA calculations using the polarizable solvent model. At this instant, the two bipolarons are parallel to each other but do not remain so. The simulation cell ($\sim 29\AA$ on edge) consists of 512 ammonia molecules and four cesium atoms. The Cs^+ ions are shown as spheres and ammonia molecules with ball and stick representation. The outermost contour contains 95% of the electron density.

At *ca.* 1 MPM, the electron density is still localized. The four electrons in the simulation cell exist as two separate bipolarons, see Fig. 2. Each bipolaron is very similar to those found in our earlier studies using a simpler model and a smaller simulation cell [7,8]. The distance between the average position of spin-up and spin-down density in each bipolaron remains about 6.5 Å. The two bipolarons are well separated and constantly change their shape and orientation, moderated by the solvent fluctuation. The bipolarons sample all possible relative orientations, including parallel and perpendicular configurations. The cesium cations are, again, solvated in ammonia and isolated from close contact of the electron density.

In order to further quantify and compare the bipolarons obtained from different systems, the average energy of the bipolaron and its component parts, V_{e-NH_3}, V_{e-e}, V_{xc} and kinetic energy per electron were calculated and compared. The energetics of different bipolarons were found to be almost identical. Hence, no detectable system size effects were revealed in the present study.

4. CONCLUSION

The behavior of bipolarons in cesium-ammonia solutions has been studied using a polarizable solvent model. A possible finite size effect on the structure and dynamics of the bipolaron was also examined by employing a larger simulation cell ($\sim$ 29Å on edge) than in previous studies. The bipolarons at *ca.* 0.5 MPM are very similar to those at *ca.* 1 MPM. Essentially, no difference was found between studies at 1 MPM using a simulation cell with 256 ammonia molecules plus two excess electrons and a larger cell with 512 ammonia molecules and 4 cesium atoms. The present results give added confidence to our work at higher metal concentrations.

ACKNOWLEDGEMENTS

We would like to thank John Shelley for indispensible help in creating the three dimensional graphics software. Also, ZD thanks Cray for a Research Fellowship and GJM thanks NSF for a Posdoctoral Research Associateship in Computational Science and Engineering (ASC 91-08812). The research described herein was supported by the National Science Foundation under CHE 92-24536. Some of the computations benefitted from use of facilities provided by NSF/DMR 91-20668. The bulk of the computing was performed at the Pittsburgh Super Computing Center on the CRAY C90 under grant MCA 93S020.

REFERENCES

1 J. C. Thompson, *Electrons in Liquid Ammonia*, London: Oxford University Press, 1976.

2 G. Lepoutre and M. J. Sienko; (Editors) *Metal-Ammonia Solutions*, New York: W. A. Benjamin, Inc, 1963.

3 J. Jortner and N. R. Kestner; (Editors) *Electrons in Fl- uids*, New York: Springer-Verlag, 1973.

4 Colloque Weyl IV, "Electrons in Fluids-the Nature of Metal-Ammonia Solutions", *J. Phys. Chem.*, 1975, **79**, 2789.

5 N. F. Mott, *Metal-Insulator Transition*, 2nd ed, London: Taylor & Francis, 1990.

6 Z. Deng, G. J. Martyna, and M. L. Klein, *Phys. Rev. Lett.*, 1992, **68**, 2496.

7 G. J. Martyna, Z. Deng, and M. L. Klein, *J. Chem. Phys.*, 1993, **98**, 555.

8 Z. Deng, G. J. Martyna, and M. L. Klein, *J. Chem. Phys.*, 1994, **100**.

9 R. W. Impey and M. L. Klein, *Chem. Phys. Lett.*, 1984, **104**, 579.

10 G. J. Martyna and M. L. Klein, *J. Phys. Chem.*, 1991, **95**, 515.

11 G. Bachelet, D. Hamann, and M. Schluter, *Phys. Rev. B*, 1982, **26**, 4199.

12 S. Lundqvist and N. H. March; (Editors) *Theory of the Inhomogeneous Electron Gas*, New York: Plenum Press, 1983.

13 R. O. Jones and O. Gunnarsson, *Rev. Mod. Phys*, 1989, **61**, 689.

14 J. P. Perdew and A. Zunger, *Phys. Rev. B*, 1981, **23**, 5048.

15 R. Car and M. Parrinello, *Phys. Rev. Lett.*, 1985, **55**, 2471.

16 D. K. Remler and P. A. Madden, *Mol. Phys.*, 1990, **70**, 921.

17 M. Šprik and M. L. Klein, *J. Chem. Phys.*, 1988, **89**, 7556.

18 M. Sprik, *J. Phys. Chem.*, 1991, **95**, 2283.

19 W. C. Swope, H. C. Andersen, P. H. Berens, and K. R. Wilson, *J. Chem. Phys.*, 1982, **76**, 637.

20 G. J. Martyna, M. Tuckerman, and M. L. Klein, *J. Chem. Phys.*, 1992, **97**, 2635.

21 G. J. Martyna and M. L. Klein, "Liouville Operator Analysis of the Car-Parrinello Method", 1994.

Toward Teraflop Computing
and New Grand
Challenge Applications

ISBN-1-56072-247-9

TOWARDS RELIABLE LARGE SCALE SIMULATIONS OF MATERIALS PROPERTIES

Jeremy Broughton

Code 6692,
Naval Research Laboratory,
Washington,
DC 20375.

ABSTRACT

We discuss dominant issues in the simulation of materials properties and possible ways to proceed in mitigating them. Precision, speed and reliability are perhaps principal amongst these issues and we focus on improved tight-binding schemes, true density functionals and neural nets as solutions. Each of these methods relies upon fitting to a data base and here too we suggest improvements beyond the local density functional theory beloved of condensed matter physicists. The overarching goal is to develop energy estimators that are sufficiently simple or user friendly that simulators will be encouraged to use them.

I. INTRODUCTION

In determining or predicting materials properties from an atomistic point of view, there are several, interacting issues with which we must be concerned. I say "interacting" because it is difficult to discuss one alone out of context with the others:

* **SYSTEM SIZES** With the advent of parallel machines with large amounts of memory, we seem to be in a good situation here. Simulations of more than a million atoms are increasingly commonplace[1].

* **PRECISION** This is a touchy issue. For some simple well characterized systems, like inert gases or ionic systems, the accuracy with which it is possible to describe atom-atom interactions is very high using empirical potentials. But for non-trivial systems, such as the mid-block transition elements where covalency and metallicity combine, no useful empirical potentials exist and we are forced to use ab-initio methods. Here, state of the art is approx. 100 atoms and only one or a few atomic configurations can be attempted[2]. Current experience shows that ab-initio methods are good at describing energy <u>differences</u> well (eg phonons) - differences between relatively like systems. Plane wave methods coupled with pseudopotentials allow ab-initio simulations again of 100 atoms but for at most a few thousand configurations - these simulations tend to be confined to p-block semiconductors[3].

* **ELAPSED TIME/ CONFIGURATION SPACE** Of all the issues confronting the simulator, this is the one that needs most inspirational work. Typical total elapsed times are 10^{-9} seconds for an empirical potential simulation and 10^{-11} seconds for an ab-initio semiconductor simulation. Many interesting properties relax on these timescales - as long as we are away from a critical point - but there are many others that do not. Examples of the former include positional correlation functions, pressure and energy. Examples of the latter include crystal growth, defect migration, protein folding, hydrodynamic phenomena.

* **METASTABILITY** This too needs much work. The issue here is one of "correct starting points" for a

simulation and of statistical mechanical accuracy. A good example of the former is a grain boundary in which the naive picture of bringing two crystals together to form the boundary and locally relaxing may not be a useful starting point - but such a system may be indefinitely stable on simulation timescales. A good example of the latter involves generating ergodic ensembles in situations which may be inherently non-ergodic (and maybe we are unaware of the fact!).

It is difficult to talk about each issue above independently because, for example, issues of system size may be fine for empirical potential systems because the memory required per atom for evaluation of the Hamiltonian may be very compact. But as soon as we start needing matrices for the evaluation of Hamiltonians (as in ab-initio methods), system sizes must drop dramatically (by several orders of magnitude) even on large memory machines even when we are only interested in a single configuration. In the rest of this paper we will be primarily concerned with the interacting triangle of issues of (1) precision, (2) system size and (3) elapsed time. We try to improve each of these simultaneously by developing better (ie trustworthy, robust and transferable) simple Hamiltonians. We do this first by generating highly precise data bases against which to parametrize energy schemes later. These schemes will be transferable tight-binding (TB) methods, true (electron) density functionals and neural net (NN) estimators. **The goal we wish to achieve, above all, is for these estimators to be sufficiently simple that users do not have to be quantum physicists to employ them - i.e. simulators interested principally in stat. mech. will be their chief protagonists.**

II. HIGHER PRECISION AB-INITIO

This is work being performed in concert with Warren Pickett and David Singh. The basis of much ab-initio work in condensed matter physics is density functional theory due to Hohenberg and Kohn[4]:

$$E_{Tot} = E_{KE} + E_{NN} + E_{EN} + E_{EE} + E_{XC} \quad (1)$$

Here, KE, NN, EN, EE and XC refer to kinetic energy, nucleus-nucleus, electron-nucleus, electron-electron and exchange-correlation terms. In principle, all these terms are functionals only of the electron density and E_{Tot} is the ground state energy of the multi-electron multi-nucleus system. This equation is the foundation of much of what we will discuss in this paper. Modern implementation of this equation is through the so-called Kohn-Sham[(5)] equations which expand the electron density in terms of occupied one-electron wavefunctions. Such expansion gives rise, via the KE term, to matrices and turns Eqn. (1) into a self-consistent diagonalization problem.

If we can handle the KE term in some other way, then we will have achieved considerable timesavings because the diagonalization step will have been avoided. This is the subject of the section on a true kinetic energy functional. The "mystery" term is the XC. This is the term that accounts for the Fermionic (Pauli principle) nature of electrons as well as the many-body nature of the interacting electron gas. It is often approximated via:

$$E_{XC} = \int \rho(\bar{r})\, \varepsilon_{XC}(\rho)\, d\bar{r} \tag{2}$$

in the so-called local density approximation (LDA). Here, the ϵ_{XC} is the exchange-correlation energy density which has been parametrized for the uniform electron gas and is essentially looked-up from a table. The **exact** expression for E_{XC} is[6]:

$$E_{XC} = \iint \frac{\rho(\bar{r})\,\rho(\bar{r}')}{|\bar{r} - \bar{r}'|} [g^{*}(\rho;\bar{r},\bar{r}') - 1]\, d\bar{r}\, d\bar{r}' \tag{3}$$

where we have assumed as in (2) that we are dealing with a spin-unpolarized system. (The equations get a little more complicated when we deal with unequal up and down spins in a system). The g here is the coupling-constant averaged pair distribution function of the electron gas. This depends upon electron density as well as r and r'. In general it is not spherically symmetric. However, we at NRL (and David Singh in particular) have implemented the following approximation to (3):

$$E_{XC} = \iint \frac{\rho(\bar{r})\,\rho(\bar{r}')}{|\bar{r} - \bar{r}'|} [g^{*}(\rho;|\bar{r} - \bar{r}'|) - 1]\, d\bar{r}\, d\bar{r}' \tag{4}$$

Here, the g^* is assumed to be spherical. For each point r in space a search is performed to find the g^* (which, remember, is density dependent) for which there is exactly one electron excluded by the exchange-correlation hole (this sum rule is an exact requirement). It is found that (4) is a much better approximation than (2) and that bond lengths and cohesive energies are obtained more accurately for a wide range of systems[7]. In actuality, little is known about g^* and David Singh has to make use of informed guesses in the literature as to the form of g^*[8].

With this as background, Warren Pickett and myself are implementing Variational Monte Carlo (VMC) and Diffusion Monte Carlo (DMC) on the uniform <u>and</u> spin polarized electron gas. Even less is known about the spin dependence of g^*. We bother with the latter because of increasing interest being paid to magnetic systems - these are systems where LDA (and its spin analogue) often fails worst. Using VMC and DMC g^* is obtained statistically but for a fully interacting many-body electron gas. We use a "*" to denote that the g's we require are actually coupling-constant averaged; that is we need the average g along the path between the non-interacting mean-field (Hartree-Fock) gas and the fully interacting gas[8]. An example of a VMC-derived g^* for a system comprising 81 up and 33 down electrons at the low density of r_s=8 is given in Fig.1. The dashed-line is the Perdew-Wang model[8].

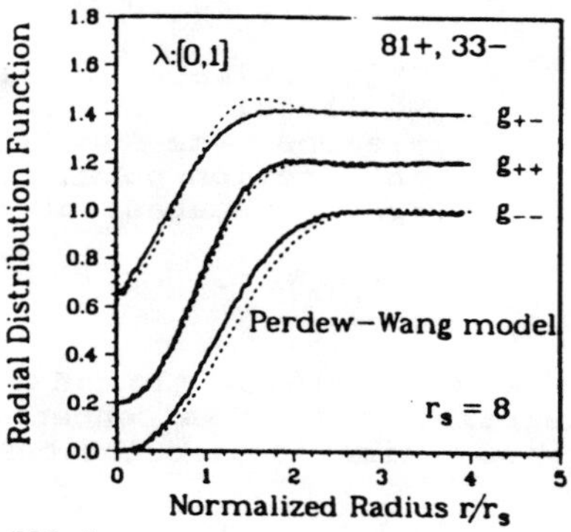

FIG.1.

In due course, we hope to parametrize g^* for all densities and all polarizations for use in non-local (or "weighted") density functional calculations such as those of David Singh's.

III. PARAMETRIZATION SCHEMES

In terms of moving through configuartion space more rapidly, there are two possible approches to be taken. The first involves smarter equation of motion integrators and smarter Monte carlo methods. We will not discuss these here. The second, the subject of this paper, is to make use of simple but accurate energy estimators:

* **SEMI-EMPIRICAL TIGHT-BINDING** Here we are involved with an electronic Hamiltonian in which we concentrate specifically on parametrizing the matrix elements. Such schemes, if transferable, would be the estimator of choice to des-

	cribe phase transitions involving changes in electronic properties (eg. silicon and gallium arsenide melting; H_2 at high pressures).
* **KE DENSITY FUNCTIONAL**	This too involves an electronic Hamiltonian but there are no matrix elements. Instead we seek a functional form for the kinetic energy term in Eqn.1 in terms only of the density and, perhaps, its gradients. We have started to apply these ideas to the graphenes. The degrees of freedom in the problem are now the atomic positions and the electron density (expanded in Gaussians) is constrained to be positive definite.
* **NEURAL NETS**	This estimator involves <u>no</u> electronic Hamiltonian. Instead, the neural net "learns" the functional form of the interaction potential between particles from a database of total energies.

<u>IIIA. TIGHT-BINDING</u>

We concentrate here on matrix elements <u>not</u> basis functions. Indeed we do <u>no</u> integrals. Instead we concentrate on parametrizing matrix elements against ab-initio calculations. The matrix elements have the form:

$$\langle \phi_i | H | \phi_j \rangle \qquad (5)$$

where i and j are combined site and azimuthal quantum number indices (s,p,d), H is the effective one electron Hamiltonian of LDA and ϕ are local basis functions. We are concerned typically with only valence matrix elements. The idea is to find a simple functional form for these matrix elements so that their values may be trivially obtained from look-up tables. Construction of the H-matrix is then very fast. Because the basis functions are local, the matrix size is not large (typically 4N X 4N for a p-block system; where N is the number of atoms and 4 derives from s,p_x,p_y,p_z basis functions) and is sparse (the non-zero range of the matrix element depends upon the range of overlap of ϕ on sites i and j;[9] i.e. approx. 5Å). When coupled with the plethora of new Order (N)[6] methods appearing in the literature for the evaluation of total energies (which rely usually upon finite range of Wannier-type states in a system - one can always transform from canonical orbitals to more localized states without changing the energy), semi-empirical tight-binding techniques become <u>very</u> attractive; that is if their sometime unreliable reputation can be improved.

This reputation is due to two factors: poor transferability

(ie the matrix elements may be fit to those of a given structure but do not transfer accurately to other structures - sometimes because of non-physicality (eg blatant non-monotonicity with distance between atoms i and j) and sometimes because of too restricted a database) and no charge consistency. Often TB schemes are orthogonal; that is no overlap (S) matrix is employed - this too adds to non-transferability. Lastly, little or no schemes exist for making the matix elements environment dependent; in other words existing schemes have the magnitude of the matrix element being a function only of the relative positions of atoms i and j[17]. Below we will describe how to eliminate most of these deficiencies.

Typically total energy schemes based upon TB have assumed an ansatz[17]:

$$E_{Tot} = 2\sum_{n=1}^{\#occ} \epsilon_n + \frac{1}{2}\sum_{i}^{N}\sum_{j}^{N} F(r_{ij}) \tag{6}$$

The total energy is written as a sum over doubly occupied eigenvalues of the TB Hamiltonian plus a sum over atomic pairs of a repulsive term, F, which only depends upon the scalar distance r_{ij}. Actually such an expression has been shown to have some theoretical justification. Harris and Foulkes[18,19] showed that the LDA Hamiltonian when written only in terms of a guessed input electron density would be stationary:

$$E_{Tot} = 2\sum_{n=1}^{\#occ} \epsilon_n + F(\rho_{in}) \tag{7}$$

The eigenvalues are obtained from a single diagonalization of the LDA Hamiltonian based upon the input density and the second term involves only integrals over such density. Foulkes and Haydock[20] went on to show that if the total input density is a superposition of atomic densities and if the second term is cluster expanded to second order, then an equation of the form (6) is reobtained. Eqn. 6 actually works quite well even in charge transfer systems (eg alkali halides) even when the input density involves neutral atoms! The total energy does not match LDA; it is approximately rigidly shifted from it. The cluster expansion is required because the E_{XC} term is non-linear in the density (see Eqn.2).

What do we do to solve the deficiencies of traditional TB? Firstly, we fit to matrix elements not eigenvalues of ab-initio calculations in our database (the former are the more fundamental objects!). Secondly, we employ an overlap matrix. And thirdly both the on-site and off-diagonal elements are environment dependent. At first we will work within the spirit of Harris-Foulkes-Haydock and assume that (1) no charge consistency is required and (2) the total density is the sum of spherical atomic densities. What does the LDA Hamiltonian operator then look like?:

$$H(\bar{r}) = -\frac{1}{2}\nabla^2(\bar{r}) + \sum_{k=1}^{N} V_k^{Coul}(|\bar{r} - \bar{R}_k|) + V_{XC}(\bar{r}) \qquad \textbf{(8)}$$

The Coulomb terms are linearly seperable into atomic components because of the linearity of Poisson's equation. A typical matrix element then has the form:

$$\begin{aligned} H_{ij} &= \langle\phi_i|H|\phi_j\rangle \\ &= \langle\phi_i|-\frac{1}{2}\nabla^2|\phi_j\rangle + \sum_{k=1}^{N} \langle\phi_i|V_k^{Coul}|\phi_j\rangle + \langle\phi_i|V_{XC}|\phi_j\rangle \end{aligned} \qquad \textbf{(9)}$$

$$S_{ij} = \langle\phi_i|\phi_j\rangle$$

The kinetic energy terms (T) and overlap terms (S) are obtainable trivially from dimer calculations. Indeed the two are related by:

$$T_{ij} = -\frac{1}{2}\nabla_{ij}^2 S_{ij} \qquad \textbf{(10)}$$

They may be fit by a polynomial in distance between atoms i and j, and simple trigonometric terms very much in the spirit of Slater and Koster[21]. <u>All</u> matrix elements are made to go smoothly to zero at approx. 5Å.

The Coulomb terms require a database of trimers for their evaluation because the matrix elements are a function of the positions of atoms i,j,k. Niklewski and Sankey[22] have worked out the exact analytic form for such terms, but it is complicated and not very user friendly. What we require is a simple analytic form which we obtain by <u>assuming</u> that both each ϕ and each V_k^{Coul} can be represented by a single effective Gaussian. Then the integrals involve products of Gaussians on different centers which can be reduced (using the properties of Gaussians) to an integral over a Gaussian on a single center. By so-doing, the functional form of the Coulomb matrix elements turns out to be:

$$H_{ij}^{Coul} = F(R_{ij}) \sum_{k=1}^{N} G(R_{pk}) \tag{11}$$

where the point p is located between atoms i an j (mid-point for ss matrix elements and to-be-fit for sp terms). F and G are functions to be fit and can be simple polynomials.

The exchange-correlation matrix elements are the most problematic. We cluster expand V_{XC}^{Tot} to second order and use similar ideas to those employed for the Coulomb terms. The discussion of this term is too lengthy to include here; but the end result is that this matrix element has the form:

$$H_{ij}^{XC} = \frac{1}{2} P(R_{ij}) \sum_{l} \sum_{m} Q(R_{pq}) \tag{12}$$

where now tetramers are required in the ab-initio data base and the point p is as in (11) and the point q is exactly mid-way between atoms l and m. P and Q are, again, functions to be fit. Eqns.11 and 12 become slightly more complicated when the basis functions involve p-orbitals; simple trigonometric functions need to be included.

Lastly, the $F(\rho_{in})$ of Eqn.7 may be handled in a very similar way to the foregoing analysis. The net result is that for an s,s',p basis of dense hydrogen (up to 1.5 Mbar), off-diagonal matrix elements are obtained relative to an ab-initio database at a wide range of densities correct to 0.05eV whereas the on-site are accurate to 0.02eV. Total energies are obtained, relative to LDA, accurate to 50K/atom (ie 0.1 kcal/mole).

Of course, this test whilst tough (hydrogen densifies by a factor of ten upon going from zero pressure to 1.5Mbar) involves little charge transfer. The next step, not yet fulfilled, will involve including charge consistency. Given that the Harris-Foulkes prescription is so powerful and because spherical symmetry is so appealing (as regards simplicity of the matrix elements), our first attempt will involve an assumption such as the following:

$$\rho^{Tot} = \sum_{i=1}^{N} \rho_i^q(|\bar{r} - \bar{R}_i|) \tag{13}$$

where the atomic densities are still spherical but the parametrization we attempt will be a function also of the q's. Self-consistent minimization of the ensuing Hamiltonian will involve variation with respect to these spherical charges.

Before leaving this section we note that Furrukh Khan and coworkers[23] have parallelized a fictitious Langrangian form of a self-consistent TB Hamiltonian and obtained very impressive performance on Intel Paragon machines even <u>without</u> invoking Order (N) methods. (They enforce orthogonality of occupied orbitals by a Gram-Schmidt scheme). They can do 10,000 time steps on a 512 processor Paragon for 1024 silicon atoms in 15 hours - and this uses the $O(N^3)$ orthogonalization scheme which takes over 90% of the time. Use of O(N) methods should produce even more impressive performance.

IIIB. KINETIC ENERGY FUNCTIONALS

This is work that has been performed in conjunction with Karl Johnson, Daniel Brown and Mark Pederson. As we have said, Eqn.1 is, in principle, a functional of the electron density. If we could find a functional form <u>in terms of the density</u> for the KE, then all that would be required is minimization the total energy with respect to the density. If this density is expanded in terms of local functions (eg Gaussians), then the majority of the work will just involve two center integrals which have a finite range cut-off. In other words the problem becomes O(N). <u>No</u> matrices are involved; <u>no</u> orthogonalization is involved; <u>no</u> diagonalization is required.

This idea has been somwhat of a Holy Grail for some time and many significant works by <u>very</u> able practitioners have appeared in the literature[24-29]. Most of this work has been oriented towards finding universal functionals (i.e. they work for <u>any</u> system) of the electron density. The most recent effort has been by Wang and Teter[29] who used a non-local functional and obtained impressive results; they found that their functional reproduced total energies rather well using the exact LDA density and that subsequent minimization of the energy using this KE functional with respect to the density changed the total energy only slightly. Whether such energies are good enough for simulation purposes remains to be seen. But the bottom-line is that the prognosis for such approaches is rather good.

We take a slightly different tack; a less ambitious goal but more likely therefore to produce higher accuracy. Such accuracy of course is required for simulation (remember that kT at room temperature is $1/40^{th}$ eV and these are the energy scales of stat. mech.) The idea is to find KE functionals that are <u>atom specific</u>; that is, within a certain range (distance or density) of each atom, the KE functional depends upon the atom's identity but outside that range where the density is small and slowly varying the KE functional is universal. One is more likely to meet with success using such a separation; it is the conceptual basis of much of computational condensed matter physics (eg. pseudopotentials and APW schemes rely upon similar separations). Where the density is large and rapidly varying, atom specificity enhances our chances of finding a functional and yet the overall utility and ease of use is not compromised.

Historically the two most important terms which occur time and again in KE functionals are the Thomas-Fermi-Dirac (TFD) for the uniform electron gas and the Weizsacker (W) which involves gradient terms and is the first order corection in the gradient expansion for a KE functional for a non-uniform gas:

$$T_{TFD} = C_{TFD}\int (\rho(\bar{r}))^{\frac{5}{3}} d\bar{r}$$

$$T_W = C_W\int \frac{|\nabla\rho(\bar{r})|^2}{\rho(\bar{r})} d\bar{r} \tag{14}$$

Here, T is the total kinetic energy of the electron gas. The W term also, by itself, gets the KE correctly for 1s systems like hydrogen. There are a couple of ways to write the W term because of Green's theorem; one involving the (gradient of ρ)^2 and the other involving the Laplacian of ρ. The "C"s are constants.

However, the gradient expansion explodes at fourth order for atomic systems. There have been several suggestions that a way to proceed might be to assume that:

$$T(\rho) = T_W(\rho) + somethingelse \tag{15}$$

where the "something else" is to be determined/fit. Deb and Ghosh[30] tried the following ansatz for (spherical) <u>atoms:</u>

$$T(\rho) = T_W(\rho) + C\int f(r)(\rho(r))^{\frac{5}{3}} d\bar{r} \tag{16}$$

Here, f(r) was fit to the kinetic energy density arising out of Hartree-Fock calculations for many atoms in the periodic table. Once this f(r) was found, they then relaxed the positive definite electron density of the system and found that (1) the shell-structure of the density was retained and (2) relaxation of the density away from the Hartree-Fock result was small. These observations are cause for optimism; but still the energies, so obtained, are probably not good enough for simulation <u>and</u> this work to-date has only involved atoms.

Because we are interested in molecules and condensed systems, we chose to use the following ansatz:

$$T(\rho) = T_W(\rho) + C\int f(\rho)(\rho(r))^{\frac{5}{3}} d\bar{r} \tag{17}$$

The function to-be-fit is now a function of ρ. This now allows for deviations from spherical symmetry which the f(r) in Eqn.16 did not. Our system for exploration of these ideas was carbon and the graphenes. Our database involves LDA calculations on carbon atoms in three different valence configurations (one non-spherical) and the most graphitic region of a naphthalene molecule. We fit $f(\rho)$ to the KE density of the naphthalene and to the total kinetic energies of the three carbon atoms. The results are given below for total kinetic energies/atom in Hartrees:

Method	"graphite"	$s^1(p^1)^3$	$s^2(p^{2/3})^3$	$s^2(p^1p^1p^0)$
LDA	37.4743	36.8614	37.1619	37.1547
$T(\rho)$	37.4749	38.8623	37.1630	37.1533

The idea of using several systems in the data base, of course, is to increase the probability of transferability of the kinetic energy functional to carbon in any environment. We have not yet tried to minimize the energy with respect to the density using this functional, but the initial signs are promising. In future we might imagine increasing our data base to include diamond and derivatives of the kinetic energy functional (to encourage the total energy to be at a variational minimum) in our fit.

$f(\rho)$ in Eqn.17 actually is a functional of both ρ and the Weizsacker term. Its form is still being optimized, but the idea will be that existing LDA codes will be trivial to modify to make use of the KE functional. Such codes already have all the integration schemes necessary within them. All that will be required is that subroutines that evaluate the KE will be replaced by something very simple and the calls to diagonalization packages will be eliminated.

One can easily imagine that fictitious Lagrangian type methods can be invoked when we want to do molecular dynamics: the electronic degrees of freedom (these will be coefficients of the basis functions by which we represent the <u>density</u>) will have their own timescale and may be thermostated via Nose-type schemes to keep them near the Born-Oppenheimer surface[31,32].

Exactly what sort of performance, compute speed-wise, may be expected from such methods is not yet known. But as we have said, these methods will scale as O(N) and should be orders of magnitude faster than conventional LDA. As a parting comment, regarding accuracy, we have fitted the KE funtional to LDA-derived kinetic-energy densities but <u>there is nothing to stop us from fitting to KEs derived from more accurate schemes such as the generalized gradient approximation or the weighted density functional scheme described in section II above.</u>

IIIC. NEURAL NETS

This is work that has been performed with Andrew Skinner. Neural nets, as applied to condensed matter physics, are a new idea. In principle there are many ways in which such systems might be used: predicting densities of states given only a few moments; predicting properties of alloys given those of the constituents; analytically continuing Green's function data from the imaginary plane onto the real axis, predicting ways in which proteins might fold, and so on. Here we apply NNs to the problem of interatomic potentials.

We start with the observation that empirical potentials have proved very powerful in the simulation of systems for which the asymptotics are well known. For example, simple metals are well described by embedded atom[33] and effective medium theories[34]; ionic systems are well approximated by shell[35] and Gordon-Kim[36] models; physically bonded systems are treated well by multipole methods. But for covalently bonded systems (such as p-block and mid-d-block elements) no such asymptotics are available (unless one is interested only in perturbing around an equilibrium structure) and we are somewhat at a loss as to how to proceed.

Our idea is to train a NN to "find" its own functional form given a data base of total energies of the system of interest. Training, or learning, in a NN is a non-linear optimization problem. Once training is complete on a <u>representative</u> sample of systems, the question will be "how well does this trained net do on systems not in the original data base". Given experience in many areas of pattern recognition, the answer is often "very well". If successful, neural nets may then be used as energy estimators in a Monte Carlo program.

We have started with a "proof-in-principle" since so little is known about the training of such nets for applications such as the one we envision. We have tried training NNs on the Lennard-Jones and Stillinger-Weber[37] (SW) (useful for silicon under certain conditions) potentials. If we can describe these well, and learn pitfalls as we go, then there is hope to describe real databases (eg those from LDA).

There is a vast array of NN architectures and concepts from which one might choose. We selected to use the most common, the feed forward adaptive net. Data flows unidirectionally through the net. It consists of input, "hidden" and output nodes (perceptrons). In principle, only one hidden layer (perhaps containing an infinite number of nodes!) is needed to fit any function. Fig.2 shows the environment of a typical perceptron; we use in our example one in which there are just three inputs although there may be more or less than this. Data values {x} flow from the left along the input connections. Associated with each connection is a weight {w}.

FIG.2.

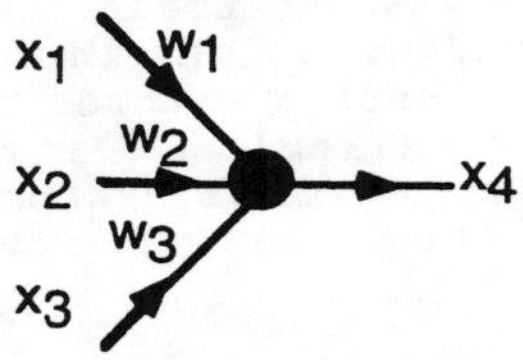

The output, x_4, is obtained as some function of the input weights multiplied by their respective data values:

$$x_4 = h(\sum_{i=1}^{3} w_i x_i) \quad (18)$$

By analogy with the behavior of neurons, the function (h) is assumed to be a hyperbolic tangent although, generalizing, it may be anything.

Connecting nodes together into a net implies that we are going to have a set of weights (the unknown variables in our problem) to determine. Futhermore, the topology of a net (i.e. its connectivity) is something which also is open to choice. In principle, this connectivity may be made part of the optimization process but we will not address this issue here. It turns out that describing a pair potential like the Lennard-Jones is very simple and training of the weights is easy. So we will concentrate here on the Stillinger-Weber potential which proved difficult to train and yet, in so doing, we learnt many lessons as to how we might handle real (LDA) databases.

Consider the network below (Fig.3):

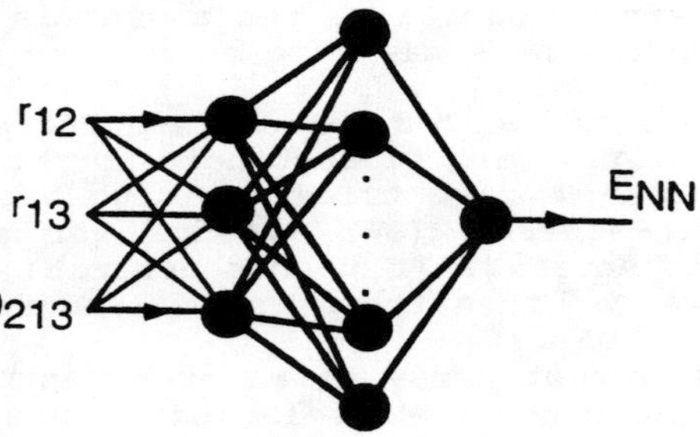

FIG.3.

We chose this to describe the three-body part of the SW potential. Note that we have two hidden layers. The database consists of a wide range of bond lengths and angles for trimers for which the SW energy is computed. We wish to train the NN (find the weights) such that for all trimer configurations in our database, the NN produces the correct SW energy. There are three input nodes corresponding to two bond lengths and the included angle in a given triplet. For each triplet, these three values are presented to the input nodes. The output node (on the right) produces the energy (E_{NN}) to be compared with the SW energy. Training then consists of minimizing an objective function so that for all elements of the database, the ouput energy is closest in a least-squares sense to the true SW energy. This is a highly non-linear problem. Our data base consists of 130 sets of triplets. Our node count is such that we need to find approx. 100 independent weights. (Note that two inputs involve bond lengths; the output energy should be independent of the order in which these are presented to the net - thus a certain symmetry is imposed upon the weights as a constraint).

We chose to try five different optimization techniques: back propagation (much beloved of the NN community but it is merely steepest descent), simulated annealing (SA) as implemented by Monte Carlo, genetic algorithms (which at about the time we were considering using them for our application were being tried also by others in the NN community), conjugate gradient and the swarm search. The latter was of our own invention; we noticed that several of the most fruitful optimization techniques invented since the 1960s involved analogy with the natural world. This method, described elsewhere, is based upon how insects find food.

Genetic algorithms (GA), like the swarm search, are based upon a population of points moving through phase space. GA rely upon survival-of-the-fittest ideas. We deal with a population of networks each with its own set of weights. We rank these nets according to their degree of fitness (i.e. objective function). We then act upon these nets via genetic operators of which the following are most common: mutation, reproduction and crossover - each borrowed from its analogue in natural genetics. In a given generation, mutation is applied approx. 10% of the time - a random node in a random net is selected and its incoming weights are modified by a random amount. Reproduction involves selecting one of the "fitter" nets and duplicating it. Crossover involves taking two of the "fitter" nets and switching incoming weights to equivalent nodes in those two nets. The population is then reranked according to the objective function and the worst are killed off to mainatin constant population. The cycle is then repeated. The population will evolve to become more fit.

To synposize our findings, we note that back propagation is the slowest way to train our three-body net. And that GA and SA are the fastest. Conjugate gradient is <u>not</u> good to apply from a random starting point - it gets stuck too easily in local minima. But even GA and SA reach a plateau region after an initial training period - they find the region of the global (or at least a very good) minimum. So at this point we turn on conjugate gradient and the objective function always plummets to values <u>such that the trained net would be perfectly acceptable for estimating energies in a Monte Carlo simulation instead of the direct SW.</u> We have tried these training ideas on up to 600 weigths and find that they work well.

We have not yet, however, finished our proof-in-principle. A future LDA database will involve not just isolated triplets but unit cells containing many atoms. It may then be necessary to train several nets simultaneously. For example, in the case of the SW system, given an energy versus volume database of several lattice structures we would have to train a two-body and three-body net simultaneously. Using SA or GA followed by conjugate gradient, this presents no problem. The results are shown in Fig.4:

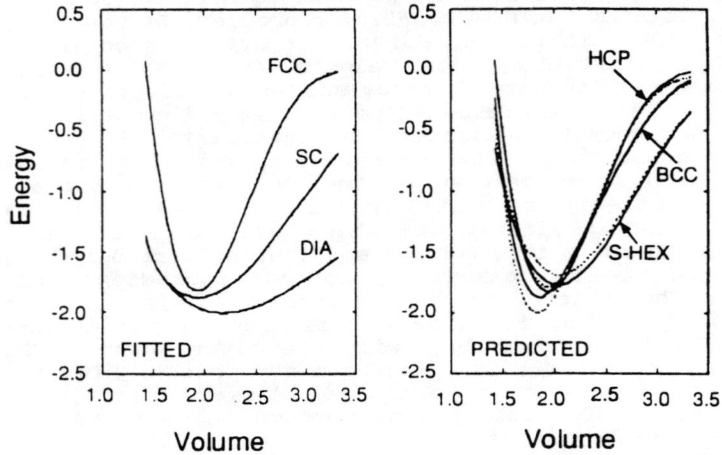

FIG.4.

On the left hand side we see that the actual SW energy for these structures and the trained energy are indistiguishable. On the right, we compare the actual and fitted energies for structures <u>not</u> in the database. They do quite well, but not well enough. Why is this? The answer comprises a second lesson from our proof-in-principle. The training set of structures contain very specific angles between particles and there is not enough information contained within the database to describe the SW system.

The answer to this conundrum lies in choosing a broad distribution of bond lengths and bond angles in our database. We do this by placing particles (eight, say) at random in unit cells of different densities. When we do this, however, the resulting distributions with angle and length are not flat. Fig.5 shows the result (filled circles) for one density:

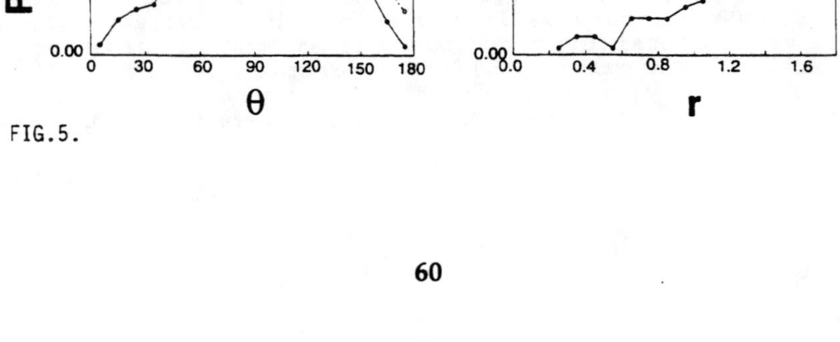

FIG.5.

In order to obtain the best representative data base we then apply reverse Monte Carlo (RMC) techniques to "structure refine" the contents of these unit cells so that the resulting distributions are flat. Fig.5 also shows how well RMC (open circles) does at accomplishing this.

At the time of writing, we have not yet trained our two-body plus three-body nets on this new database, but we feel the prognosis is now good that we will soon complete our proof-in-principle successfully. The final step will be to try an LDA database on a real material. This begs the question as to what NN topology we will try, but we have hope that connectivity may be successfully folded into a training scheme using GAs. Lastly, of course, physical insight can also be used to design a NN for a given system.

As regards computation time and training time, we note that GAs and swarm searches can be very efficiently parallelized. Further, the very simple operations necessary to compute a result from a neural net means that compared with schemes IIIA and IIIB above, it is likely to be very fast. The NN topology is likely to be such that local information around each atom will be all that is required and therefore the compute time will again scale as O(N).

IV. CONCLUSION

We have discussed many issues relating to how to perform useful simulations on real materials such that (1) useful system sizes may be achieved, (2) useful elapsed times (i.e. 10^{-9} secs or more) may be attained and (3) high precision, reliability and transferability are within reach. Also, we have described how to obtain better data bases via (1) going beyond LDA and (2) finding representative data bases. Much work still needs to be done to extend timescales very significantly and to find smarter ways to circumvent metastability problems.

V. ACKNOWLEDGEMENT

I wish to thank ONR for partial support of this work. Also I would like to thank Mark Pederson, Andrew Skinner, Karl Johnson, Daniel Brown, David Singh and Warren Pickett for excellent insights and collegiality during (and beyond!) this work.

REFERENCES

1) A.Nakano, R.Kalia and P.Vashishta, this issue; F.F.Abraham, this issue.

2) D.J.Singh, H.Krakauer, C.Haas and W.E.Pickett, Nature, 365,(1993),39.

3) R.Car and M.Parrinello, Phys.Rev.Lett. 55,(1985),2471.

4) P.Hohenberg and W.Kohn, Phys.Rev. 136,(1964),B864.

5) W.Kohn and L.J.Sham, Phys.Rev. 140,(1965),A1133.

6) D.C.Langreth and J.P.Perdew, Solid State Commun. 17,(1975),1425.

7) D.J.Singh, Phys.Rev. B48,(1993),14099.

8) J.P.Perdew and Y.Wang, Phys.Rev. B46,(1992),12947.

9) W.Yang, Phys.Rev.Lett. 66,(1991),1428.

10) J.Galli and M.Parrinello, Phys.Rev.Lett. 69,(1992),3547.

11) M.S.Daw, Phys.Rev. B47,(1993),10895.

12) X-P.Li, R.W.Nunes and D.Vanderbilt, Phys.Rev. B47,(1993),10891.

13) F.Mauri, G.Galli and R.Car, Phys.Rev. B47,(1993),9947.

14) W.Kohn, Chem.Phys.Lett. 208,(1993),167.

15) P.Ordejon, D.A.Drabold, M.P.Grumbach and R.Martin, Phys.Rev. B48,(1993),14646.

16) D.Drabold and O.F.Sankey, Phys.Rev.Lett. 70,(1993),3631.

17) L.Goodwin, A.J.Skinner and D.G.Pettifor, Europhys.Lett. 9,(1989),701.

18) J.Harris, Phys.Rev. B31,(1985),1770.

19) W.M.C.Foulkes, PhD. Thesis, Cambridge University, (1988).

20) W.M.C.Foulkes and R.Haydock, Phys.Rev. B39,(1989),12520.

21) J.C.Slater and G.F.Koster, Phys.Rev. 94,(1954),1498.

22) O.F.Sankey and D.J.Niklewski, Phys.Rev. B40,(1989),3979.

23) M.L.Yeh and F.S.Khan, Phys.Rev. B, submitted.

24) J.Goodisman, Phys.Rev. A1,(1970),1574.

25) R.Baltin, Z.Naturforsch. A27,(1972),1176.

26) M.Levy, J.P.Perdew and V.Sahni, Phys.Rev. A30,(1984),2745.

27) W.Yang, R.G.Parr and C.Lee, Phys.Rev. A34,(1986),4586.

28) A.E.DePristo and J.D.Kress, Phys.Rev. A35,(1987),438.

29) L-W.Wang and M.P.Teter, Phys.Rev. B45,(1992),13196.

30) B.M.Deb and S.K.Ghosh, Int.J.Quan.Chem. 23,(1983),1.

31) P.E.Blochl and M.Parrinello, Phys.Rev. B45,(1992),9413.

32) M.Sprik, J.Phys.Chem. 95,(1991),2283.

33) M.S.Daw and M.I.Baskes, Phys.Rev.Lett. 50,(1983),1285.

34) K.W.Jacobsen, J.K.Norskov and M.J.Puska, Phys.Rev. B35,(1987),7423.

35) B.G.Dick and A.W.Overhauser, Phys.Rev. 112,(1958),90.

36) R.G.Gordon and Y.S.Kim, J.Chem.Phys. 56,(1972),3122.

37) F.H.Stillinger and T.A.Weber, Phys.Rev. B31,(1985),5162.

Toward Teraflop Computing
and New Grand
Challenge Applications

ISBN-1-56072-247-9

CONJUGATE GRADIENT ELECTRONIC STRUCTURE ALGORITHMS ON SERIAL AND PARALLEL MACHINES

James F. Annett

The Pennsylvaina State University, Department of Physics,
University Park, PA 16802.

INTRODUCTION

The capacity to perform large scale quantum mechanical calculations of electronic states in solids and molecules has increased enormously in recent years, opening up new exciting avenues for research in physics and chemistry. Partly the advances are due to the tremendous increases in available computer power, and partly they are due significant advances the numerical algorithms. Within the framework of the Density Functional Theory (DFT) approach to the electronic structure problem the most modern algorithms use fast iterative methods. For example, the Car Parinello algorithm of 1985[1] was the first such algorithm, while conjugate gradient based techniques have also been developed in recent years[2, 3]. With these new methods and high performance computers it is now possible to perform first principles quantum mechanical calculations for systems with several hundred inequivalent atoms[4]. Further advances will come both from further improvements in the algorithms, and in developing newer methods which are especially well suited for scalable parallel machines.

We have been developing a set of programs based upon efficient conjugate gradient methods for solving the electronic structure problem. Although the basic approach here is similar to those described in recent reviews[5, 6] there are several important technical innovations. Since the standard techniques are quite well known, the following paragraphs will only describe the key improvements. The topics discussed include the construction of more accurate and reliable projection operator pseudopotentials, a fast unconstrained conjugate gradient energy minimization algorithm, and a new method for Brillouin zone integration in metallic systems which preserves the unconstrained minimization algorithm. All of these can be implemented on parallel machines in a way similar to other conjugate gradient and Car Parinello techniques[6]. We are also experimenting with a new local basis for the wavefunctions, which would allow substantially greater parallelism than the conventional plane wave basis and also include the advantages of an adaptive grid method.

RELIABLE AND ACCURATE PROJECTION OPERATOR PSEUDOPOTENTIALS

In a DFT[7] pseudopotential calculation the total electronic energy can be cast into the following form:

$$E[\rho_v] = \sum_i < \psi_i| - \frac{1}{2}\nabla^2 + V_{ps}|\psi_i > + \frac{1}{2}\int d^3r d^3r' \frac{\rho_v(\mathbf{r})\rho_v(\mathbf{r}')}{|\mathbf{r}-\mathbf{r}'|} + E_{xc}[\rho_v], \quad (1)$$

where $|\psi_i>$ are an orthonormal set of wavefunctions, corresponding to the valence electron density $\rho_v(\mathbf{r})$. The external potential due to the ion cores V_{ps} is the sum of ionic pseudopotentials. The functional E_{xc} is the exchange correlation energy, which is usually approximated by the local density approximation (LDA)[7]. Notice that it is not necessary to include any core electron density contributions to E_{xc}[8], provided the pseudopotentials are generated from Hartree Fock core atomic calculations[10, 11].

The form of the pseudopotential V_{ps} is critical to the speed and accuracy of the calculations. The well known Hamann, Shluter and Chiang[9] norm conserving pseudopotentials give accurate physical results, but are inefficient in very large scale calculations. This is because acting on a basis of plane wave states the pseudopotentials have a very large number of non-zero matrix elements. I.e. $V_{GG'}(k) =< k, G|V_{ps}|k, G'>$ is non zero for almost all values of G, G' and k (where $|k, G> \equiv \exp(i(\mathbf{k}+\mathbf{G}).\mathbf{r})/\sqrt{V}$). If there are N_G plane waves and N_k special k-points in the Brillouin zone, then multiplication by the pseudopotential takes $N_G^2 N_k$ operations, which is prohibitive for large systems where N_G might be 10^5 or more.

A simple way to obtain a pseudopotential which can be applied much more efficiently was derived by Kleinman and Bylander[12]. They noted that the following projection operator:

$$V^{KB} = V_{loc} + \frac{V_{nl}|0><0|V_{nl}}{<0|V_{nl}|0>} \quad (2)$$

was identical to the non-local pseudopotential when acting on a state $|0>$ (the atomic pseudo orbital), and that its factorized structure allows its product with the plane wave vectors to be evaluated in order $N_G N_k$ steps. Here V_{nl} is the non-local part of the pseudopotential, defined by $V_{ps} - V_{loc}$, where V_{ps} the conventional norm-conserving pseudopotential and V_{loc} is an arbitrary function chosen as the local part of the pseudopotential. While this form is much more efficient it suffers from poorer transferability and is not always reliable, since in some cases spurious solutions can occur.

In our calculations we are using a simple improved version of the above projection operator pseudopotential. The idea is simply to ensure that the pseudopotential operator gives exact results on a larger space of states. It is straightforward to show that

$$V^{KB2} = V_{loc} + \sum_{ij} V_{nl}|i> [M^{-1}]_{ij} < j|V_{nl} \quad (3)$$

where $M_{ij} =< i|V_{nl}|j >$, is exact when evaluated on any linear combination of the states $|i>$. If the set of $|i>$ approaches completeness then the operator becomes identical to the standard norm-conserving pseudopotential. In practice 2 or 3 operators (compared to 1 for the original KB potential) are sufficient to greatly improve the transferability of the potential without adding too much to the computational burden. For example, for a carbon pseudopotential constructed in the C II ion, the C II ion ionization energy is 24.2423, 24.2402, 24.2407 eV for 1, 2 or 3 projection operators, rapidly approaching the full semi-local potential limit of 24.2404eV[13]. The extra accuracy is also important in eliminating the spurious solutions which come from bad choices of V_{loc} in equation 3[12]. For example in constructing a pseudopotential for carbon or silicon it is best to make V_{loc} the p pseudopotential to keep the number of operators to a minimum. With only one KB projector for the s level the s state becomes unstable and drops into a spurious solution with lower energy than the true s level. With two s projectors the spurious solution is eliminated, and highly accurate results for atomic or solid carbon or silicon can be obtained, which are quite comparable to results with the full HSC potential[13].

UNCONSTRAINED CONJUGATE GRADIENT MINIMIZATION

Stich et.al.[2] and by Teter et.al[3] developed the first conjugate gradient minimization techniques for DFT calculations. They noted that the CG method is one of the fastest numerical techniques available for general purpose minimization, and well suited for minimizing the density functional energy functional. As a numerical scheme it is a much more efficient method than the traditional approach of solving the Schrodinger equation with a trial potential and iterating to self-consistency.

Our conjugate gradient algorithm is a very simple implementation of the CG minimization idea, but it has the advantage of using an unconstrained minimization scheme[14]. The original DFT functional requires a finding a set of orthogonal wavefunctions, $|\psi_i>$ which minimize the energy. The orthogonality constraints must be imposed during the Car Parinello or CG iteration. The simpler alternative which we developed was to minimize the energy using a general set of non-orthogonal (but linearly independent) wavefunctions, $|\phi_i>$, which can then used to evaluate the energy and its derivatives. For example one can easily obtain an equivalent orthogonal set by solving:

$$|\phi_i>= \sum_j |\psi_j> R_{ji} \tag{4}$$

where R is the Cholesky factorization of the overlap matrix:

$$<\phi_i|\phi_j> \equiv S_{ij} = \sum_k R^*_{ik} R_{kj}. \tag{5}$$

Almost identical versions of this algorithm were developed by by us[14], Galli and Parinello [15], and Arias, Payne and Joannopulous[16]. The details of the algorithm and its performance are described in ref. [14].

CONJUGATE GRADIENT METHOD FOR METALS

For metallic systems there is an additional problem in all Car Parinello or conjugate gradient based methods. The problem arises because of the Fermi surface. Most Car Parinello type calculations either make the approximation of only a single special k point in the Brillouin zone integration (which is a reasonable approximation in a large unit cell), or assume uniform band occupation throughout the Brillouin zone (which is correct for semiconductors). One scheme to treat metallic systems with a energy minimization scheme has been proposed by Averill and Painter[17], and another was proposed by Arias et.al.[16]. Both schemes introduce new variational parameters corresponding to variable occupations of states which are varied so as to minimize the energy. We initially tried a similar method but rejected it because of poor numerical convergence.

Our current approach to the Brilliouin zone integration takes a quite different approach. The idea is to always work in the zero temperature limit with integral state occupations. The key idea is that the Fermi surface shape itself is a suitable variational parameter. In other words, for any given Fermi surface shape (defined by the discontinuity in occupation number $n(\mathbf{k})$), an energy can be evaluated. The energy formula is:

$$E[\rho_v] = \sum_{n,k} w_k < \psi_{n,k}| -\frac{1}{2}\nabla^2 + V_{ps}|\psi_{nk} > + \frac{1}{2}\int d^3r d^3r' \frac{\rho_v(\mathbf{r})\rho_v(\mathbf{r}')}{|\mathbf{r}-\mathbf{r}'|} + E_{xc}[\rho_v], \quad (6)$$

where $n(\mathbf{k})$ is the number of occupied energy bands, $|\psi_{nk}>$, at that $\mathbf{k}$ point, and $w_k$is the quadrature weight for the special $\mathbf{k}$ points in the Brilloiun zone. The true Fermi surface is the one which minimizes these energies. A simple iteration scheme which implements these ideas is currently being tested. The key difference with the other methods which have been proposed is that we never use variable state occupations. The occupation number is always an integer at any $\mathbf{k}$ point, and so the full unconstrained conjugate gradient minimization can be easily applied. Details of this method and numerical test results will be described soon[18].

TOWARDS INCREASED PARALLELISM

The techniques outlined above are already well suited for parallel machines. In terms of number of total number of floating point operations the dominant steps are, the time taken to orthogonalize the functions at eack $\mathbf{k}$ point,

$$t_1 = O(N_k N_b^2 N_G) \quad (7)$$

the time to Fourier transform the wavefunctions

$$t_2 = O(N_k N_b N_G \ln N_G) \quad (8)$$

and the time to Cholesky decompose the overlap matrices,

$$t_3 = O(N_k N_b^3). \quad (9)$$

Here N_k is the number of k points, N_b is the maximum number of states per k point, and N_G is the number of terms in the Fourier expansion of the wavefunctions. For typical systems $t_1 >> t_2 >> t_3$ on scalar machines. Each of these dominant operations consists of straightforward linear algebra and can be implemented on parallel machines.

However, in order to increase the basic underlying parallelism in the calculation, we are developing a novel alternative to the traditional plane wave basis set. Although plane waves have a number of advantages, such as the speed of the FFT on serial machines, on parallel machines the FFT may become a bottleneck since it requires a large amount of data transfer among processors. Also, the FFT grid makes it necessary to evaluate the wavefunction and density on a uniform grid of points in real space. A basis set which has the capability to become adaptive could potentially speed up many types of calculations.

The alternative we are exploring is the use of cubic B-splines to provide a smooth local representation of the wavefunction at each point in space. An advantage of B-splines is their smoothness (twice differentiable for cubic B-splines), and so electronic wavefunctions expanded in this basis are automatically smooth. The simplest version of the B-spline basis set divides the unit cell along one axis, into a number of knots, z_i, $i = 1, n$. The knots need not be uniformly spaced thus allowing a denser grid in some regions of space than others. On these knots we can construct a set of piecewise polynomial functions, $f_m(z)$, which are smooth and have the crucial property that they have compact support (vanish outside a finite region); $f_m(z) = 0$ if $z < z_{m-2}$ or $z > z_{m+2}$. These functions are well known, and are the B-splines (basis splines)[19]. To construct three dimensional wavefunctions one can repeat the same process for the x and y axes, hence forming a basis as the tensor product of these functions. A simpler alternative is to retain the plane wave expansion for the x and y functions. The expansion of the wavefunctions is thus:

$$\psi_{ik}(\mathbf{r}) = \sum_{G,m} c^{ik}_{G,m} \exp(i(\mathbf{K}+\mathbf{G}).\mathbf{R}) f_m(z). \tag{10}$$

Here $\mathbf{K} \equiv (k_x, k_y)$, $\mathbf{G} \equiv (G_x, G_y)$, and $\mathbf{R} \equiv (x, y)$. The advantages of this representation of the wavefunction is that (a) it can be made adaptive, since the knot spacing and Fourier transform cut off can be chosen independently in different regions of space. (b) The parallelism is considerably increased, since in Fourier transforming from reciprocal to real space we have n independent 2-D FFTs, instead of one three dimensional FFT. There is essentially no data passing overhead in the transform if we assign different processors different regions of space. Furthermore overlap integrals and the electron kinetic energy can all be computed quickly using simple sparse matrix methods since the B-spline functions are compact. For example the overlap and kinetic energy matrix elements have the simple form:

$$< \psi_{i,k} | \psi_{j,k} > = \sum_{G,n,m} c^{ik*}_{G,n} c^{jk}_{G,m} S_{nm} \tag{11}$$

$$< \psi_{i,k} | -\frac{1}{2}\nabla^2 | \psi_{j,k} > = \sum_{G,n,m} c^{ik*}_{G,n} (\frac{1}{2}(\mathbf{K}+\mathbf{G})^2 S_{nm} + T_{nm}) c^{jk}_{G,m}. \tag{12}$$

These are fast to compute and require almost no data transfer, since S_{nm} and T_{nm} are banded matrices as a consequence of the spatial localization of the B-spline functions. We have found that this basis does indeed work well for numerically solving the Schrodinger equation. Currently we are developing a full conjugate gradient based program based upon these ideas.

References

[1] R. Car and M. Parinello, Phys. Rev. Lett. **55** 2471 (1985).

[2] I. Stich, R. Car, M. Parinello and S. Baroni, Phys. Rev. B **39** 4997 (1989).

[3] M.P. Teter, M.C. Payne and D.C. Allan, Phys. Rev. B **40** 12255 (1989).

[4] I. Stich et.al. Phys. Rev. Lett. **68**, 1351 (1992); K.D. Brommer et.al. ibid. 1355 (1992).

[5] M.C. Payne et.al. Rev Mod Phys **64**, 1045 (1992).

[6] K.D. Brommer et.al. Computers in Physcis **7**, 350 (1993).

[7] P. Hohenberg and W. Kohn, Phys. Rev. **136**, B864 (1964); W. Kohn and L. J. Sham, Phys. Rev. **140**, A1133 (1965).

[8] S.G. Louie, S. Froyen and M.L. Cohen, Phys. Rev. B **26** 1738 (1982).

[9] D.R. Hamann, M. Schluter and C. Chiang, Phys. Rev. Lett. **43**, 1494 (1974).

[10] D.M. Bylander and L. Kleinman, Phys. Rev. B **43**, 12070 (1991).

[11] J.F. Annett, Phys. Rev. Lett. **69**, 2244 (1992).

[12] L. Kleinman and D.M. Bylander, Phys. Rev. Lett. **48** 1425 (1982).

[13] J.F. Annett, to be published.

[14] G.S. Welsh and J.F. Annett, Phys. Rev. B. to be published.

[15] G. Galli and M. Parinello, Phys. Rev. Lett. **69**, 3547 (1992).

[16] T.A. Arias, M.C. Payne and J.D. Joannopulous, Phys. Rev. Lett. **69**, 1077 (1992).

[17] F.W. Averill and G.S. Painter, Phys. Rev. B **46**, 2498 (1992).

[18] J.F. Annett, to be published.

[19] "Splines and Variational Methods", P. M. Prenter (Wiley 1975).

Toward Teraflop Computing
and New Grand
Challenge Applications

ISBN-1-56072-247-9

LARGE SCALE ATOMISTIC FIRST PRINCIPLES STUDY OF ADSORPTION AND SURFACE DIFFUSION

V. MILMAN, S.J. PENNYCOOK, and D.E. JESSON,
Solid State Division, Oak Ridge National Laboratory,
Oak Ridge, TN 37831

M.C. PAYNE, I. STICH, and M.H.LEE
Department of Physics, Cambridge University,
Cambridge CB3 0HE, UK

1. INTRODUCTION

Computer simulation of atomistic processes is an important tool in understanding the properties of condensed matter at a microscopic level. The best way to reproduce the rich variety of experimentally observed effects in the simulation is to use the quantum mechanical description of the ion-electron interactions in a solid. Such calculations although increasingly popular [1] make high demands on the computing power available. The systems of practical interest to surface physics include at least hundreds (or even thousands) of atoms, and their *ab initio* study inevitably requires parallel supercomputers. In this paper we describe the total energy calculations of the adsorption and migration properties of a single Ge adatom on the Si(100) surface. This system is typical in complexity for modern large scale simulations and presents a good test case to show the methodology and its application to surface science problems.

The study of fundamental processes in the Si-Ge epitaxial growth is of considerable scientific and technological interest [2]. One of the most important questions is the identification of the binding sites for Ge adatoms on the Si (100) surface and the determination of the activation energy for surface diffusion.

Recent STM observations suggest that the behavior of a Ge adatom is essentially similar to that of a Si adatom. The Ge islands have the anisotropy of approximately 1000:1 at 500 K, and the diffusion barrier in the fast direction is estimated to be 0.62 eV [3].

Measurements such as these provide an excellent starting point for theoretical investigation. The only reliable approach for this system is to start from first principles. It is known that empirical potentials describe incorrectly the bonding and diffusion of the Si adatom on Si(100) surface (see [4] for a review). None of the empirical potentials available can reproduce even the correct sign of the energy difference between the asymmetric (buckled) and symmetric reconstructions of the Si(100) surface. One expects that the Si-Ge interaction is described by empirical potentials even less accurately.

In the following sections we discuss the parallel implementation of the conjugate gradient technique for *ab initio* pseudopotential studies of large systems and present our results for Ge adsorption and diffusion on the Si(100) surface.

2. COMPUTATIONAL SCHEME

We used the pseudopotential total energy approach for the electronic structure calculation. The electronic minimization was performed using band by band algorithm of the conjugate gradient method. The detailed description of this technique is given elsewhere [1,4]. A supercell with (100) slab geometry and the c(4x4) surface cell contained 12 layers of Si (192 atoms) and two Ge adatoms with inversion symmetry imposed (Figure 1). The two innermost layers were kept fixed at their bulk positions. A single Γ-point was used for the Brillouin zone sampling, with an energy cutoff for the plane wave expansion of 10 Ry (about 30000 plane waves). The size of this system makes the computational project feasible only with the use of massively parallel computers. Our calculations were carried out on the Intel computers iPSC/860 and Paragon at the ORNL Center for Computational Science. The details of the implementation of the CETEP pseudopotential code are given in [5], so we just summarize the main points of the parallelization strategy.

The CETEP utilizes the fact that parts of the Hamiltonian are local in either real or reciprocal space, and so the data related to each electronic wavefunction are spread between the processors using space decomposition. We choose the decomposition regions so as to balance the node load and to utilize the structure imposed by the transpose FFT method. The FFT application to wavefunctions is simplified by the fact that some columns would be empty due to the difference between the cutoff for wavefunctions and for the charge density [1]. The main communication overhead occurs in the 3D FFT procedure that is performed as a sequence of 1D transforms with a number of global data exchanges. The nonlocal potential operations are performed in real space taking advantage of the short range of the corresponding operators.

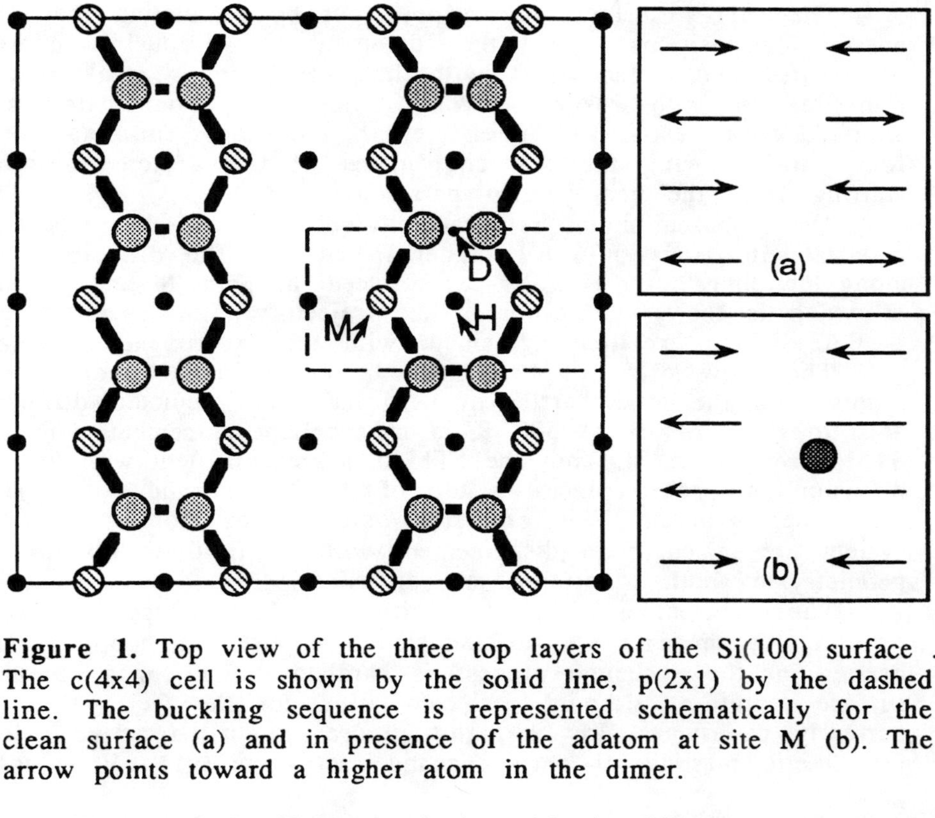

Figure 1. Top view of the three top layers of the Si(100) surface . The c(4x4) cell is shown by the solid line, p(2x1) by the dashed line. The buckling sequence is represented schematically for the clean surface (a) and in presence of the adatom at site M (b). The arrow points toward a higher atom in the dimer.

The parallel efficiency of the code is difficult to assess on the present Paragon computers with their limited memory per node as one cannot study big system using small number of nodes. On the other hand, an artificial increase of the number of nodes for a small system results in large communication overheads since each node carries too few wavefunction components. The execution time decreased by a factor of 1.6 when using 128 nodes of the Paragon XP/S 35 as compared to 64 nodes. We consider this ratio as a good scaling taking into account that the node load is below the optimum level in case of the 128 node configuration.

To summarize our experience of using CETEP on massively parallel computers, the main gain is not in the speed-up due to a higher number of processors, but in the ability to approach complex problems that are not tractable by other means.

3. ENERGY SURFACE FOR THE Ge ADATOM

The energy surface was mapped out by calculating the total energy for positions x,y of the adatom in the irreducible quarter of the p(2x1) surface cell with the simultaneous total energy minimization with respect to all other ionic coordinates and wave-function expansion coefficients. The local minima were found by allowing the x,y coordinates of the adatom to relax starting from the nearby grid point.

The global minimum is located at point M, and the metastable pedestal site H is 0.06 eV higher in energy. The diffusion path along the dimer rows is a zig-zag between the point M and the site D which is the saddle point of the trajectory. The barrier height is 0.62 eV in excellent agreement with the experimental estimate [3]. The slow diffusion trajectory has two inequivalent saddle points with the total barrier of 0.95 eV. The predicted diffusion anisotropy of 2000:1 at 500 K is in excellent agreement with the STM observations [3]. Thus the STM data are consistent with the Ge diffusion that takes place on top of the dimers and not in the interdimer trough. The empirical simulations for the Si-Ge system are in complete disagreement with *ab initio* results for the geometry of both adsorption and diffusion.

There is always a possibility of the surface diffusion occuring by an exchange mechanism as opposed to hopping. The barrier for the exchange process is hard to define for a complex surface structure, although its calculation for the Ge adatom is currently underway. However, this process might be active solely for kinetic reasons, as each exchange act costs 0.11 eV in total energy.

The most controversial issue in the comparison of *ab initio* and empirical results is the bonding geometry. We find that the bond length between the adatom and the surface atoms is close to the Si dimer bond length. In equilibrium the Ge adatom at site M is bonded to two dimers from the same row, and all bond lengths are about 2.39 Å. The distance from the adatom to the second-layer Si atom is only 2.46 Å, but the electron charge density distribution shows that there is no directional bond to this atom. Adsorption at the site H causes formation of four long bonds of 2.48 Å with the dimer bond stretching to 2.52 Å.

The adatom causes maximum strain on dimer bond when it is

located at the saddle point for the hopping across the trough, or in its vicinity. The distance between the dimer atoms becomes 3.3 Å which is already closer to the bulk distance of 3.84 Å than to the dimer bond at the clean surface, 2.30 Å. No such dimer breaking effect caused by the Si adatom has been found [6].

4. EFFECT OF ADATOM ON DIMER BUCKLING

The interplay between the dimer buckling and the energetics of adsorption and surface diffusion has not been addressed before because of the small energy effect involved and of the prohibitively large size of the corresponding supercell.

During atomic relaxation of the originally symmetric dimers we always observed spontaneous buckling. Its character depends strongly on the adatom position. With the adatom at site H the dimer row free of adatoms is only slightly perturbed compared to the clean asymmetric (2x1) reconstructed surface. The influence of the adatom is confined then to one dimer row where buckling is entirely suppressed within our supercell.

The picture is qualitatively different in the vicinity of the Ge adatom at the binding site M when both rows are affected (Figure 1) . The dimers bonded to the adatom are slightly tilted in the same direction by 0.16 Å, and the amplitude grows to 0.43 Å for the next dimers in the same row. A new effect can be seen as a result of the relative proximity of the Ge adatom to the next dimer row. In that row the two dimers nearest to the adatom has a strong in-phase buckling (0.62 Å). There is no direct bonding between these dimers and Ge atom, so this configuration becomes possible due to the second-layer atom displacements. The elastic strain caused by the adatom prevails over the energy gain due to the ferroelectric ordering of buckled dimers and results in the formation of a 1D stacking fault. Since a Si adatom would produce a qualitatively similar structure, we suggest that the buckling defects observed on Si (100) [7] might correspond to single Si adatoms. Their imaging gives the only experimental information available on the binding site of the adatom.

CONCLUSIONS

The first large scale *ab initio* study of the Ge bonding and migration on the Si(100) surface has been performed. The activation barriers for diffusion in fast and slow directions are 0.62 and 0.95 eV, respectively, in excellent agreement with the experimental STM results. We identify the localized buckling defects observed in STM as being due to the adatom bonded at the equilibrium site implying that the study of single adatoms is experimentally accessible.

ACKNOWLEDGMENTS

This research was sponsored by the Division of Materials Sciences, U.S. Department of Energy, under contract DE-AC05-84OR21400 with Martin Marietta Energy Systems, Inc., by an appointment to the Oak Ridge National Laboratory Postdoctoral Research Program administered by the Oak Ridge Institute for Science and Education. This research is part of the Grand Challenge project on first principles simulation of materials properties, funded under the High-Performance Computing and Communications Initiative.

REFERENCES

1. M.C.Payne, M.P.Teter, D.C.Allan, T.A.Arias, and J.D.Joannopoulos, "Iterative minimization techniques for *ab initio* total energy calculations - molecular dynamics and conjugate gradients", *Rev. Mod. Phys.*, Vol. 64, No. 4, 1992, pp. 1045-97.
2. D.E.Jesson, S.J.Pennycook, J.-M.Baribeau, and D.C.Houghton, "Step-driven lateral segregation and long-range ordering during Si_xGe_{1-x} epitaxial growth", *Phys. Rev. Lett.*, Vol. 68, No. 13, 1992, pp. 2062-5.
3. M.G.Lagally, "An atomic level view of kinetic and thermodynamic influences in the growth of thin films", *Jpn. J. Appl. Phys.*, Vol. 32, No. 3B, 1993, pp.1493-501.
4. V.Milman, D.E.Jesson, S.J.Pennycook, M.C.Payne, M.H.Lee, and I.Stich, "*Ab Initio* Study of the Binding and Diffusion of a Ge Adatom on the Si(100) Surface", in: "*Mechanisms of Thin Film Evolution*", eds. S.M.Yalisove, C.V.Thompson, D.J.Eaglesham, MRS 1993 Fall Meeting Proceedings (to be published).
5. L.J.Clarke, I.Stich, and M.C.Payne, "Large scale *ab initio* total energy calculations on parallel computers", *Comp. Phys. Commun.*, Vol. 72, No. 1, 1992, pp. 14-28.
6. G.Brocks, P.J.Kelly, and R.Car, "Binding and diffusion of a Si adatom on the Si(100) surface", *Phys. Rev. Lett., Vol.* 66, No. 13, 1991, pp. 1729-32.
7. R.A.Wolkow, "Direct observation of an increase in buckled dimers on Si(100) at low temperature", *Phys. Rev. Lett.*, Vol. 68, No. 17, 1992, pp. 2636-9.

Toward Teraflop Computing and New Grand Challenge Applications

ISBN-1-56072-247-9

R. M. Fye

MS 1111
Sandia National Laboratories
P.O. Box 5800
Albuquerque, New Mexico 87185

ABSTRACT

Quantum effects lead to some of the most interesting and useful material properties: for example, magnetism and superconductivity. For many materials, the only well-controlled method for understanding such properties is quantum Monte Carlo simulations. We consider here quantum Monte Carlo simulations on the Intel iPSC/860 hypercube. Specifically, we consider simulations of two interacting magnetic impurities in a metal. We first discuss the model, the Monte Carlo method, and different parallelization strategies. We compare run times with those for highly vectorized code on the CRAY YMP, and conclude with numerical results and a summary discussion.

Many materials properties are not reliably modelled by traditional techniques such as Hartree-Fock or LDA calculations, currently used by such companies as Gaussian, Biosym, Schroedinger Inc., etc. These techniques, while very useful, use uncontrolled approximations which can lead to quantitatively or even qualitatively incorrect results. However, recently developed quantum Monte Carlo (QMC) methods can now be used to study certain materials properties without the use of uncontrolled approximations[1]. These QMC methods, however, are more computationally intensive than the traditional methods. For this reason, we explore here the issues in parallelizing a class of quantum Monte Carlo algorithms, and report results obtained using such an algorithm on the iPSC/860 hypercube.

Specifically, we simulate a model describing two interacting magnetic impurities in a metal, the two-impurity spin-$\frac{1}{2}$ Kondo model. This model is given by the Hamiltonian

$$H = H_0 + H_I, \tag{1}$$

where

$$H_0 = \sum_{\vec{k},s} \epsilon_{\vec{k}} c^{\dagger}_{\vec{k},s} c_{\vec{k},s} \tag{2}$$

and

$$H_I = J \sum_{j=1}^{2} \vec{S}_j \bullet \vec{S}_c(\vec{R}_j). \tag{3}$$

H_0 refers to the conduction electron band and H_I to the interactions between the spins and the conduction electrons. More specifically, the $\epsilon_{\vec{k}}$'s are the conduction electron energies; $s = \uparrow, \downarrow$ refers to spin; $j = 1, 2$ refers to the two impurities; the $\vec{S}_j$'s are the impurity spins; and

$$\vec{S}_c(\vec{R}_j) = \sum_{s,s'} c^\dagger_{js} \left(\frac{1}{2} \vec{\sigma}_{ss'} \right) c_{js'} \tag{4}$$

is the normalized conduction electron spin at location $\vec{R}_j$, with $\vec{\sigma}$ the vector of Pauli spin matrices.

Calculations using the so-called "energy-independent coupling constants" (ECC) approximation found unexpected behavior in a certain parameter regime of this model: certain normally finite quantities diverged as the temperature $T \rightarrow 0$, which would lead to striking experimental consequences[2,3]. We simulate here this desired parameter regime in order to determine whether the predicted behavior is an intrinsic property of the model itself or whether it arises simply from the ECC approximation.

The most efficient strategy for parallelizing a QMC algorithm can depend in general upon the algorithm used, the architecture of the machine, and even the parameters simulated. For our simulations, we use the "impurity algorithm" of Hirsch and Fye[4,5]. We consider MIMD rather than SIMD machines, due to the increasing prevalence of the MIMD architecture. We ran our simulations on a 64-node Intel iPSC/860; however, our general arguments apply to MIMD machines with other architectures.

The bulk of the computer time in the impurity algorithm goes into repeatedly "updating" the elements of an $L \times L$ matrix. Here, L typically ranges from 50 to 1000, with the change in a given matrix element independent of the changes in the other elements for a particular update. This updating occurs each time that a proposed Monte Carlo move is accepted. The Monte Carlo process can be considered a "guided random walk". There are thus two obvious approaches to parallelization. The first is to distribute the calculations for a single "walk" over all the nodes of a parallel machine, which we will call here the "distributed calculation" approach. The second, which we will call the "distributed walks" approach, is to allow each node of the machine to conduct its own simulation ("walk"), collecting the results from all of the nodes at the end of the computation. We discuss the "distributed walks" approach first.

There are two relevant Monte Carlo time scales in discussing this approach. The first, $N_{therm.}$, is the average number of Monte Carlo steps to go from a randomly selected initial configuration to the region in phase space of high probability, where one begins sampling. The second, $N_{stat.}$, is the number of steps necessary to obtain the desired statistical precision in measured observables. In our studies of the Kondo two-impurity Hamiltonian using the impurity algorithm, we have found that $N_{therm.} << N_{stat.}$; for example, at low temperatures $N_{therm.} \approx 50$ and $N_{stat.} \approx 200,000$. In general, it appears that the inequality $N_{therm.} << N_{stat.}$ holds for both the impurity algorithm and more commonly used QMC lattice algorithms[6,7,8].

On a machine of P nodes, we then find that the simulation time S_1 is given by

$$S_1 = \alpha_1 \log_2(P) + \alpha_2 L^3 N_{therm.} + \alpha_2 L^3 \left(\frac{N_{stat.}}{P} \right) + \alpha_3 L^2 \left(\frac{N_{stat.}}{P} \right). \tag{5}$$

Here terms of order lower than $\log_2(P)$ or L^2 have been neglected, a hypercube architecture has been assumed, and the "α_i's" are constants. The first term in this expression refers to the "fan-in" and "fan-out" of data to all the nodes at the beginning and end of the simulation. The second term refers to the fact that the walk on each node must be independently "thermalized", starting from node-dependent initial configurations. The third term refers to matrix updating and occasional inversions, the same operations referred to in the second term. The last term refers to the measurement of desired quantities.

The parallelized algorithm is "scalable", with the speed proportional to the number of nodes, if the third and/or fourth terms of this expression dominate. The first term of S_1 is in general comparatively negligible. (This holds for current mesh architecture parallel machines as well.) Thus, assuming L large, the condition for scalability is simply $N_{therm.} << \frac{N_{stat.}}{P}$. This inequality is in general well satisfied for most current simulations; for example, the Kondo two-impurity numbers above give $P << 4,000$, satisfied by most currently-used and planned MIMD machines. Further, a "problem" usually consists of from 10 to several hundred simulations with different temperatures and parameters. Therefore, for treating a given "problem" defined in this way, the above condition on P becomes even easier to satisfy, since different "blocks" of smaller P on a particular machine can be allocated for running the different simulations. Thus, it appears that this "distributed walks" method of parallelization will be scalable at least for this and the next generation of MIMD parallel supercomputers. Further, it appears reasonably efficient in practice. For example, one finds comparable speeds when a highly vectorized version of the above-mentioned Kondo two-impurity code is run on a single node of a Cray YMP and when a parallelized version is run on 64 nodes of an Intel Gamma, as seen in Table 1. This speed comparison between the two machines compares favorably with other parallelization efforts; for example, one finds that Cray and Intel run times for vectorized and parallelized molecular dynamics codes are also roughly the same on the Cray and on the 64-node Intel Gamma[9,10]. In addition, further speed-ups are also possible on the parallel machines by reducing cache memory overflow (if necessary) or using pipelining capabilities (if available).

Table 1. Comparison of algorithm run times on CRAY YMP and Intel iPSC/860 for two different matrix sizes L.

	1 CRAY YMP Processor	64-node Intel iPSC/860
L=52	0.50 sec.	0.27 sec.
L=292	5.38 sec.	7.07 sec.

As mentioned previously, the second method of parallelization is to distribute the calculations for a single Monte Carlo run over all the nodes of the machine, the so-called "distributed calculation" approach. Such an approach leads for a hypercube architecture to a simulation time S_2 given by

$$S_2 = \beta_1 L \log_2(P) N_{total} + \beta_2 \frac{L^3}{P} N_{total} + \beta_3 \frac{L^2}{P} N_{total} + \beta_4 \frac{L^2}{\sqrt{P}} N_{total}, \qquad (6)$$

where $N_{total} = N_{therm.} + N_{stat.}$ and, again, terms of lower order in $N_{therm.}$, $N_{stat.}$, and P have been neglected. Here, the first term refers to the "fan-in" and "fan-out" of data to all the nodes for matrix updating and measurements. The second and third terms refer, respectively, to the matrix updating and part of the inversion and to measurements, all of which are distributed over the P nodes. The fourth term refers to the so-called "torus wrap" method of matrix inversion[11], currently the fastest known such method on large parallel machines. For sufficiently large L ($L^2 >> P \log_2(P)$), we see that this approach is also scalable. If the nodes of the machine operate in scalar mode, α_2 of Eq. 5 is equal to β_2 of Eq. 6. In that case, we see that there is a regime where the two parallelization approaches will be equally fast if $N_{therm.} << \frac{N_{stat.}}{P}$. However, if the nodes have some pipelining capability, then α_2 may be less than β_2, so that the "distributed walks" approach will be faster.

From the above considerations only, it would seem that the "distributed walks" approach is the generally preferable one for efficient parallelization. However, each node must then have sufficient memory to store all the data for its own walk, a memory requirement here proportional to L^2. This is in contrast to the "distributed calculation" method, where the memory requirements themselves can also be distributed. In the Kondo two-impurity simulations, we have found it necessary to use 32-Mbyte iPSC/860 nodes at the lowest temperatures (largest L) studied. In this case, the dollar cost of memory per node can be an order of magnitude or more greater than the cost for the associated iPSC/860 chip. The two-impurity simulations here require significantly more memory than other "impurity algorithm" simulations which have been performed; however, barring breakthroughs in memory storage capability, it is clear that the "distributed calculation" approach to parallelization must eventually become the method of choice for sufficiently large L.

Considerations similar to those above apply to codes which utilize the widely-used lattice "BSS" algorithm[6,7]. Such codes are usually less efficiently vectorizable than "impurity algorithm" codes, suggesting a greater speed-up for parallel computers when compared to vector machines. Memory requirements for these algorithms scale as N^2, where N refers to system size. In general, however, we have found that the BSS memory requirements are less than those of the "impurity algorithm" for problems and parameter regimes considered interesting. Further, the bottleneck for many problems of interest is not system size but rather the so-called "sign problem"[7], which necessitates a large number of independent data points to obtain good statistics. Thus, the "distributed walks" approach to parallelization is even more useful for this class of algorithms.

We show in Fig. 1 the normalized staggered susceptibilty $T_k \chi_s$ versus $log(\frac{T}{T_k})$ for the two Kondo impurities. Here, T is the temperature; T_k is the normalizing "Kondo temperature"[12]; and χ_s is the unnormalized staggered susceptibilty of the two spins. For at least one of the two parameter sets that we simulated, denoted in the figure by x's and filled circles, this susceptibility was predicted show signs of divergence[5] as the temperature $T \to 0$. The fact that there is no sign of a divergence strongly suggests that the unusual behavior predicted by calculations using the ECC approximation is a result of the approximation, and is not an intrinsic property of the Hamiltonian itself.

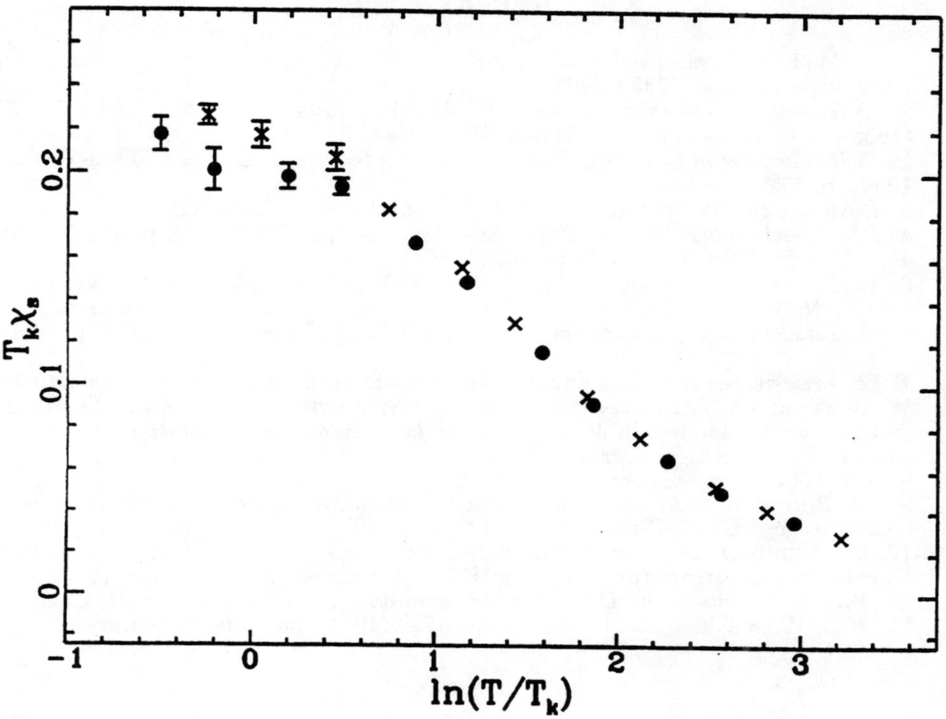

Figure 1. Normalized staggered susceptibility $T_k \chi_s$ versus $ln(\frac{T}{T_k})$.

In summary, we have analyzed the parallelization of a class of quantum Monte Carlo algorithms and have used one of these algorithms to simulate the behavior of two interacting magnetic impurities in a metal. The speeds on a 64-node Intel iPSC/860 were comparable to those using a single CRAY YMP processor. We found no evidence for "anomalous" behavior of the two impurities, predicted by calculations which used the energy-independent coupling constants (ECC) approximation. Our results suggest that any such behavior is a result of using the ECC approximation rather than an intrinsic property of the two-impurity model itself.

ACKNOWLEDGEMENTS

This work was supported by the Applied Mathematical Science Program, U.S. Department of Energy, Office of Energy Research, and was performed at Sandia National Laboratories operated for the U.S. Department of Energy under contract No. DE-AC04-76DP00789. An early portion of the work was also supported by IBM through an IBM postdoctoral fellowship and by the National Science Foundation under grant DMR86-15454.

REFERENCES

1. R. M. Fye, *Phys. Rev.* **B33**, p. 6271 (1986); R. M. Fye and R. T. Scalettar, *Phys. Rev.* **B36**, p. 3833 (1987).
2. B.A. Jones, C.M. Varma, and J.W. Wilkins, *Phys. Rev. Lett.* **61**, p. 125 (1988); B.A. Jones and C.M. Varma, *Phys. Rev.* **B40**, p. 324 (1989); B.A. Jones, in *Field Theories in Condens. Matter Phys.*, Z. Tesanovic (Ed.), (Addison-Wesley, 1990), p. 87.
3. I. Affleck and W.W. Ludwig, *Phys. Rev. Lett.* **68**, p. 1046 (1992).
4. J.E. Hirsch and R.M. Fye, *Phys. Rev. Lett.* **56**, p. 2521 (1986); R. M. Fye and J. E. Hirsch, *Phys. Rev.* **B38**, p. 433 (1988).
5. R.M. Fye and J.E. Hirsch, *Phys. Rev.* **B40**, p. 4780 (1989); R.M. Fye, *Phys. Rev. Lett.* **72**, p. 916 (1994).
6. R. Blankenbecler, D.J. Scalapino, and R.L. Sugar, Phys. Rev. **D24**, p. 2278 (1981).
7. For reviews, see E.Y. Loh and J.E. Gubernatis, in *Electronic Phase Transitions*, W. Hanke and Y.V. Kopaev (Ed.) (Elsevier, Amsterdam, 1990); and H. De Raedt and W. von der Linden, in *Monte Carlo Methods in Condensed Matter Physics*, K. Binder (Ed.) (Springer, Berlin, 1990).
8. S.R. White, private communication.
9. S.J. Plimpton, in *Proceedings of 5th Distributed Memory Computing Conference* (published by IEEE), Charleston, SC (April, 1990).
10. S.J. Plimpton and G. Heffelfinger, in *Proceedings of Scalable High Performance Computing Conference* (published by IEEE), Williamsburg, VA (April, 1992).
11. B.A. Hendrickson and D.E. Womble, submitted to *SIAM J. Sci. Stat. Comput.*
12. K.G. Wilson, *Rev. Mod. Phys.* **47**, p. 773 (1975), and references therein.

Toward Teraflop Computing
and New Grand
Challenge Applications

ISBN-1-56072-247-9

STUDY OF DIFFUSION IN Si BY MONTE CARLO SIMULATION*

Q. S. Zhang, J. A. Van Vechten, and T. K. Monson

Center for Advanced Materials Research
Department of Electrical and Computer Engineering
Oregon State University, Corvallis, OR 97331

A program for Monte Carlo simulation of point defect diffusion and interaction in diamond and zinc-blend crystal structures has been developed, called VIDSIM (Vacancy and Interstitial Diffusion Simulator). VIDSIM allows atom level simulation of diffusion with user-specified parameters (such as bond energies), user-specified mechanisms, and user-specified initial configuration and boundary conditions. Vacancy, interstitial, anti-site and substitutional defect distributions resulting from the simulations may be examined as a function of time. For a 160 million-atom system, VIDSIM runs at a speed of 800 atom hops per second on a personal computer with a 33 Mhz 486 microprocessor.

We report here the latest result of a computer simulation designed to examine the diffusion into Si of Au or transition metals. The simulation demonstrates interesting results re vacancy (V) clusters and Au distribution of both interstitials (Au_i) and substitutionals (Au_{Si}).

1. INTRODUCTION

Diffusion in semiconductor has long been of great interest due to its importance in industry as well as in science. There is a large theoretical and experimental literature on the issue.[1-11] A variety of models for point defect migration, interaction and reaction have been proposed and a great amount of theoretical work has been done to account for, in one way or another, experimental results or observations. Yet, there is much controversy over the validity of the models or mechanisms, such as kick-out (KO)[6,9] and Frank-Turnbull (FT) [2] mechanism, because there have been no rigorous connection

* Supported in part by Komatsu Silicon USA, Inc. and by SEH America, Inc. and previously by the Air Force Office of Scientific Research and by Wacker Siltronic.

between atom level assumption and macroscopic consequences prior to our simulation program. Our program is written in C programming language as defined by the ANSI standard, and has been offered internationally at the cost of the media since 1989. Almost 100 copies have been distributed. For most differential equations which describe the diffusion processes, there exist no analytical solutions. We noticed that, even the simpler models suffer from one major deficiency: the relationship between the atom level assumptions and their macroscopic consequences are extremely complex; and attempts at analytical solutions appear always to involve approximations, passages to limits, neglected processes and imposition of boundary conditions.[5,7,10-12]

VIDSIM[13] was developed to resolve the relation between atom level assumptions and macroscopic consequences. It assumes no differential equation. It uses an atom level Monte Carlo algorithm and involves an enormous amount of computation to obtain statistically significant results. The program models the evolution of a user-defined initial set of defects in space and time for any mechanisms the user chooses to simulate. The complex relationship between assumptions and consequences is thus obtained without any of the approximating passage to limits that have confused the previous literature. We have conducted several research projects[1,13,14,15] using VIDSIM on diamond and zinc-blend structure semiconductor. For example, our simulations of Au diffusion[1] into Si have demonstrated that the commonly-accepted kick-out mechanism cannot produce a U-shaped (symmetrical) concentration profile when diffusion proceeds from an asymmetrical initial condition with Au on only one side of a crystal. We have carried out the several billion event simulations by running two dozen PC's in student computer labs, which would otherwise be idle for most of time. For a 160 million-atom system, for example, VIDSIM runs at a speed of 800 atom hops per second on a personal computer with 33 Mhz 486 microprocessor. Simulation results from teraflop computing provide an insight into the dynamic processes of diffusion in crystals of interest.

Detailed description of VIDSIM program is presented in reference 13.

2. SIMULATION OF Au DIFFUSION IN Si VIA FRANK-TURNBULL MECHANISM

We now report our latest work on a computer simulation designed to examine the diffusion into Si of Au via Frank-Turnbull mechanism. Result is applicable to Cu or Pt or similar transition metals, which, like Au, migrate mainly as interstitials but reside primarily as substitutional impurities. This particular simulation assumes that no Si self interstitials, Si_i's are initially present and none can be produced during the diffusion process, that there are vacancies initially present as clusters in the bulk and that single vacancies can be created and annihilated at the surfaces normal to x direction. It also assumes that a source of Au_i is on the normal surface of the positive x boundary where Au_i will be annihilated if it returns there, and a reflexive boundary condition for

Au_i is imposed on the far side, i.e., the negative x boundary. While vacancies are generated at a rate of $1.84x10^{-9}$ per surface site per attempt period (a.p.), which, in Si, is estimated to be 74 fs, the zone boundary phonon period, the Au_i source injects Au_i on the surface at a rate of $1.84x10^{-9}$ per attempt period per surface site or 184 injections (on average) per diffusion step $r \equiv 5x10^6$ a.p.. The sample simulated is 2000 a thick in x direction and 100 a both in the y and z directions, where a is the lattice constant for the material of interest. Periodic boundary conditions are imposed on the y and z directions. Initially the sample is perfect except for 19 clusters of 5 V's (V_5) each spaced at 100 a intervals in the x direction through the bulk of the sample, which corresponds to a concentration [V] = $3.0x10^{16}$ cm^{-3}, a conservative estimated of [V] at the melting temperature based on the positron lifetime results reported by Dannefaer etc.[18]

We assert that the above conditions are appropriate for the case that Au-Si molten alloy has formed on one side and that an amorphous thermal oxide layer, with no molten alloy, is present on the far side.

We collect an ensemble of 16 of the sample runs of simulation, each of which extends to 240 steps of $5x10^6$ a.p. i.e., $12x10^9$ a.p.. There were a total of about $5x10^{10}$ atomic hops in the simulation. Of the $7.0x10^5$ Au atoms injected, 1030 are retained as Au_{Si} and 180 are retained as Au_i at the end. Of $1.4x10^6$ vacancies injected, 2460 are retained. Note that less than 0.2% of the defects that are introduced survive at the end of this simulation.

3. RESULTS OF COMPUTER SIMULATION AND DISCUSSIONS

We show in Table 1 the rates at which vacancy clusters of various sizes emit V's and diffuse for a particular set of atom level assumptions[13].

We observe that, for the simulation of clusters of type V_5, most of the original clusters break up into single vacancies after 4 r simulation time; they do not migrate a significant fraction of the 100 a initial minimum spacing between them before they totally disperse. Those scattered V's from the original clusters join newly diffusing-in V's from the surfaces and can form new clusters of various sizes. Simulation shows that there are clusters of size of 6, 7, 8 that form spontaneously from single vacancies during the process. We notice that

Table 1. Diffusivity and mean time to emit one or more vacancy from clusters of n vacancies. Time unit $r \equiv 5x10^6$ a.p.. These values result from the parameters assumed (See ref. 1 and ref. 13).

n=	1	2	3	4	5	6	7	8	17
$D_n(a^2/r)$	1177	594	559	419	236	4.0	47	171	1.5
E_n (r)	--	0.66	0.39	0.41	0.35	11.3	3.25	2.25	> 5

there are "magic numbers" for which small clusters are particularly stable, e.g., n = 6. Some of these also diffuse very slowly. We suppose that small clusters of such size account for the 450 ps signal observed in many, but not all positron annihilation spectra[17]. We also study the sample with a 17 V (V_{17}) cluster initially present and find out that the simulation requires a great deal of commuter effort because there is so much atomic diffusion around the surface of the cavity. Having simulated a total time of 20 r, we have observed no emission of any V from such a cluster. Thus, we conclude that the mean time to emit a V exceeds 5 r. These clusters also diffuse very slowly. We suggest that such large clusters correspond to the 1.5 ns signal in all positron annihilation spectra and for the D defects that are so difficult to anneal out[16].

We observe that for the vacancy distribution at step 160, as shown in Fig.1, there is a peak at the location somewhere around 1650 a, i.e., about 350 a from the far surface. Investigation shows that the vacancy clusters, esp. of size 6, (V_6) which is surprisingly stable, are responsible for the sharp rise in the profile. Distribution of V_6 at several steps are shown in Fig. 2.

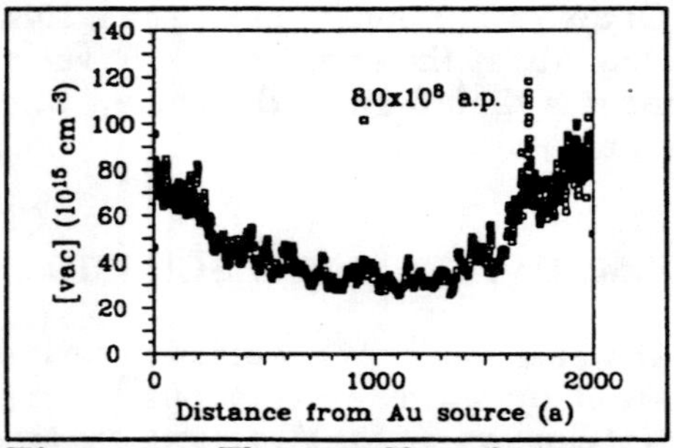

Figure 1. The profile of vacancy concentration in the sample at step 160.

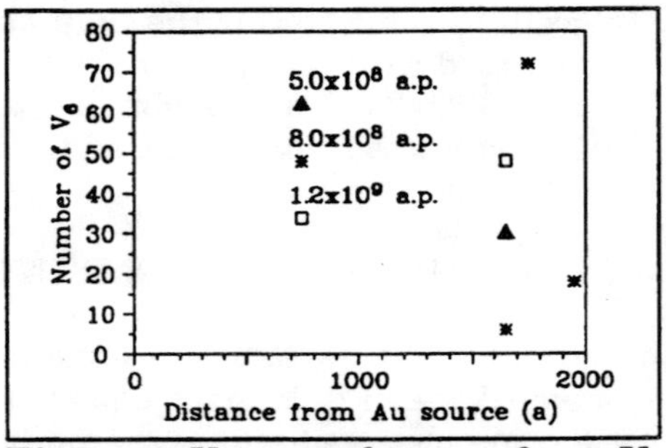

Figure 2. Vacancy clusters of type V_6 observed at step 100, 160 and 240.

In Fig. 3 we show the profile of divacancies, $[V_2]$, which demonstrates a U shape. Since the [V](x) for single vacancies is not uniform, as shown in Fig. 1, some variation in $[V_2]$ as predicted from the Law of Mass Action if "local equilibrium" is assumed. This would imply $[V_2]$ should vary as $([V])^2$. Also, it is obvious that $[V_2]$ profile should dip at the sample surfaces because annihilating boundary conditions for vacancies of kind of both single and cluster are imposed.

Fig. 4 shows a profile of Au_{Si} for t = $1x10^8$, $2x10^8$, $4x10^8$, and $1.2x10^9$ a.p., and Fig. 5 demonstrates the distribution of Au_i concentration through the sample at the same time period as in Fig. 4.

From the Fig. 4 and Fig. 5, we see the distribution of Au_i is similar to that of Au_{Si} and not much more uniform despite the fact that the Au_i have a diffusivity of 22,894 a^2 r^{-1}, 19 times the diffusivity of the V's and dramatically larger than the effective diffusivity of Au_{Si}'s. The ratios of concentrations on both

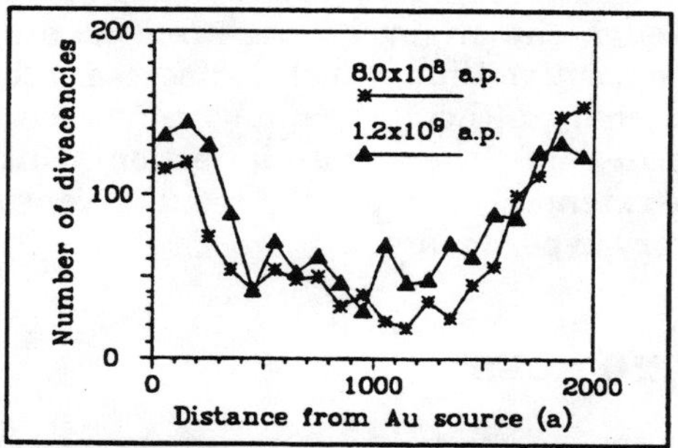

Figure 3. The profile of divacancies, V_2 in the sample, observed at step 100 and 240.

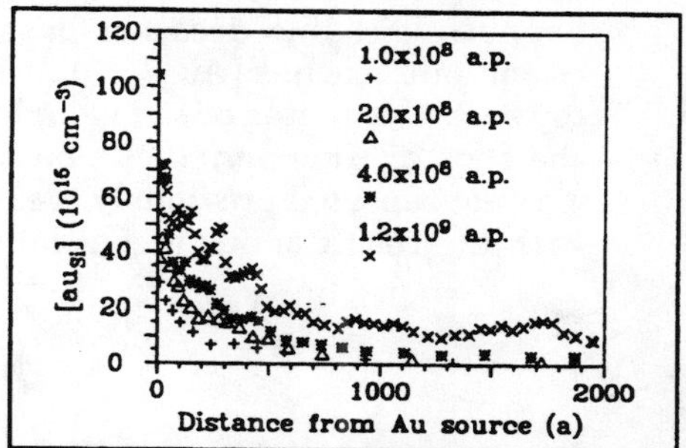

Figure 4. The profile of Au substitutionals in the sample, observed at step 20, 40, 80 and 240.

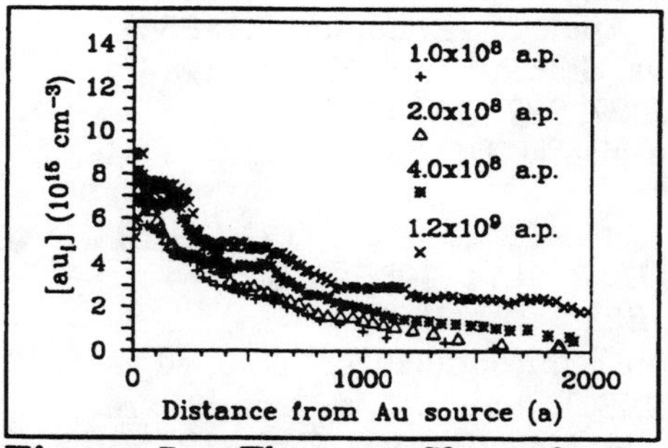

Figure 5. The profile of Au interstitials in the sample, observed at step 20, 40, 80 and 240.

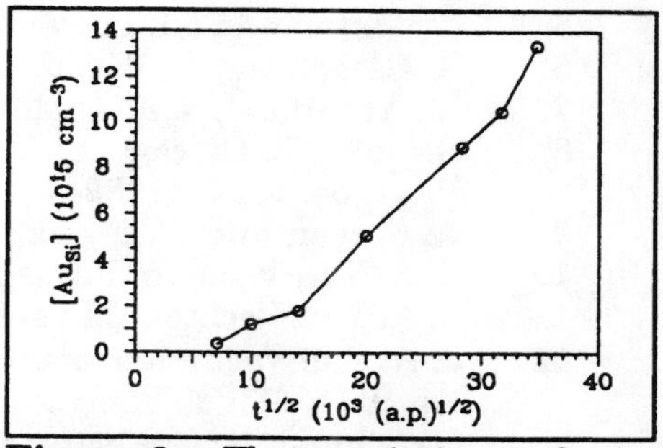

Figure 6. The variation of Au substitutionals in the center of the sample versus the square root of diffusion time.

surfaces for both Au_{Si} and Au_i are observed to be about the same, which is similar to the result[1] we reported when we simulated Au diffusion into Si assuming KO model. In simulating KO model, we allowed no V's and made the Si_i's diffuse less rapidly than the Au_i's. However, there is no rise of $[Au_{Si}]$ near the far surface. The results shown in Fig. 4 are contrary to the assertions or assumptions of many previous investigators, particularly those who advocate the KO mechanism. In contrast to the monotonic distribution of Au_i shown in Fig. 4, they assert that since the Au_i diffuses so rapidly, a uniform distribution of Au_i will be established from the very beginning of the diffusion. We also note that the $[Au_i]$ rises with $[Au_{Si}]$ at the far side and the profile of $[Au_i]$ tends to be flat at the far side as simulation time elapses. The flatness of $[Au_i](x)$ near the far end is a result consistent with the reflexive boundary conditions used in our simulation.

In Fig. 6 we show the variation of [Au_{Si}] in the center versus the square root of time. The trend shown is not exactly that as reported in previous literature[5,8]. Two distinctions are found. First, the best fit of linear regression shows that the best straight line does not pass through the origin, as the previous authors' claim, but reaches [Au_{Si}] = 0 at finite positive time, which is necessary for Au_i to reach the center of the sample. Secondly, although the longer time data and the shorter time period can be fitted to a line, there is an inflection point that was not reported previously. To some extend, the simulation result is consistent with the result of our recent laboratory experiments.

REFERENCES

1. J. A. Van Vechten, U. Schmid, Zhang, Q.-S., J. of Electronic Materials, Vol. 20, 431 (1991).
2. F. C. Frank and D. Turnbull, Phys. Rev. 104, 617 (1956).
3. A. Seeger, Phys. Status, Solidi (a) 61, 521 (1980).
4. U. Gosele, W. Frank and A. Seeger, Appl. Phys., 23, 661 (1980).
5. D. Mathiot and J. C. Pfister, J. Appl. Phys., 55, 3518, (1984).
6. A. Seeger and K. P. Chilk, Phys. Status Solidi 29, 455, (1968).
7. M. Yoshita, Jpn. J. Appl. Phys. 27, 967, (1988).
8. S. Coffa, L. Calcago, S. U. Campisano, G. Calleri and G. Ferla, J. Appl. Phys, 64, 6291 (1988).
9. A. Seeger, and W. Frank, J. Electron. Mater. 14a, 159 (1985)
10. J. A. Van Vechten, Phys. Rev. B 33, 2674 (1986)
11. J. A. Van Vechten, Phys. Rev. B38, 9913 (1989)
12. J. A. Van Vechten, Handbook on Semiconductors, Vol. 3, ed. S. P. Keller, (North Holland, Amsterdam, 1980) Chapter 1, p. 1 and therein.
13. U. Schmid, N. C. Myers, and J. A. Van Vechten, Comp. Phys. Commun. 58, 329(1990).
14. Q. S. Zhang, J. A. Van Vechten and R. K. Graupner, "Fundamental studies of diffusion by computer simulation of atomic process on the giga event scale with microcomputers in parallel", (To be published)
15. T. K. Monson, J. A. Van Vechten, and Q. S. Zhang, Phys. Rev. B 49, Part 2, 2972 (1994)
16. S. Dannefaer, P. Mascher, and D. Kerr, Phys. Rev. Lett. 56, 2195 (1986)
17. P. J. Roksnoer and M. M. B. Van den Boom, J. Cryst. Growth 53, 563 (1981).
18. S. Dannefaer, T. Bretagnon, K. Abdurahman, D. Kerr, and S. Hahn, Defect Engineering in Semiconductor Growth, Processing and Device Technology, Material Research Society Symposium Proceedings, Vol. 262, 1992, ed. S. Ashok, J. Chevallier, K. Sumino, E. Weber.

Toward Teraflop Computing
and New Grand
Challenge Applications

ISBN-1-56072-247-9

LATTICE QCD AT ONE TERAFLOP

Gregory Kilcup
Department of Physics
The Ohio State University
174 West 18th Ave
Columbus, Ohio 43210

OVERVIEW

A group of physicists, computer architects and engineers has teamed together and proposes to build a machine capable of running at a sustained teraflop on a variety of scientific problems. The machine is an accelerated version of Thinking Machine Corporation's (TMC) next generation machine, and is currently being designed at MIT. If constructed, the machine will become a nationally accessible scientific facility sited at MIT, and may become a commercial product. A major driving force behind this collaboration has been the desire to perform the next generation of lattice field theory calculations. In this talk I describe some of the physics motivations for this project, and give an overview of the hardware project.

LATTICE QCD AND THE STANDARD MODEL

The development of the Standard Model of particle physics must rank as one of the great intellectual triumphs of the past two to three decades. Several Nobel prizes have been awarded for putting various pieces in to place, including the theoretical prediction of the fourth quark, the experimental discoveries of the fourth and fifth quarks, the theoretical prediction of W and Z particles, and their experimental discovery. As a result of these developments we have a coherent picture of all the known particles, including a very successful quantum field theory of their strong, weak and electromagnetic interactions. As far it is known, this theory accommodates every experimental result we have to date. As a matter of principle, the Standard Model allows one to express almost any quantity one cares to calculate—e.g., the proton mass, the neutron lifetime, the thermal conductivity of silicon—in terms of the fundamental constants of nature which enter the model as free parameters. Of these there are nineteen: 6 quark masses, 3 lepton masses, the W-boson mass, the Higgs boson mass, 3 coupling constants, 4 mixing angles, and the strong-CP angle. Much if not most of the work currently done in elementary particle physics in some way revolves around these parameters, either trying to extract their values from experiment, or trying to extract predictions from candidate super-theories, such as Grand Unified Theories or superstrings.

The link between the 19 parameters of the Standard Model and any particular experiment is a theoretical calculation. For processes involving only the weak and electromagnetic interactions, there is a reliable calculational technique in the form of weak coupling perturbation theory. Such calculations require perseverance, but on the computational side demand only resources sufficient to run a symbolic manipulator and perform integrals in a few dimensions. By contrast, for nearly anything involving the strong interactions these techniques fail. This situation is unfortunate in that almost every process we care to look at does involve the strong interactions. In particular, of the Standard Model parameters mentioned above, 12 have to do with quarks, and therefore with the strong interaction. There are analytical techniques—e.g. QCD sum rules, or the $1/N$ expansion—which provide some semiquantitative guidance, but the only reliable first-principles technique currently available for the strong interaction is lattice gauge theory. Thus lattice QCD is central to almost any research on the Standard Model.

One may distinguish at least three types of motivations for going to the effort of studying QCD on the lattice. In the first category of calculation, one would like to verify that QCD is indeed the correct theory of the strong interactions, and that lattice QCD can successfully reproduce both qualitative and quantitative features of the real world. Among the achievements lattice QCD can already claim in this area are:

- A convincing demonstration of confinement and chiral symmetry breaking, starting from first principles.
- A determination of the masses of light hadrons in the quenched approximation
- A determination of heavy quarkonia spectra

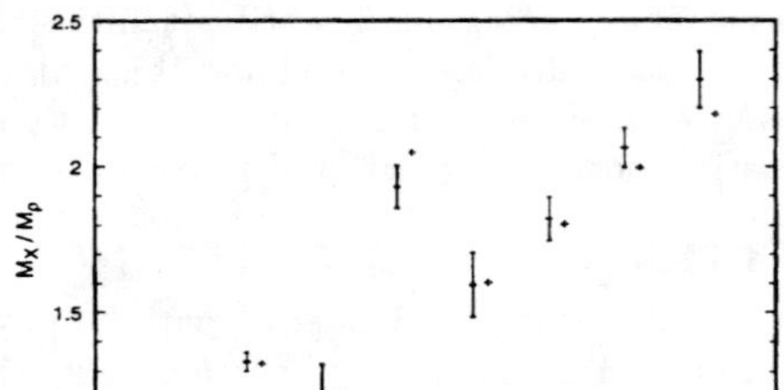

Figure 1: Spectrum of light hadrons as calculated in the quenched approximation on the GF-11. Points *without* error bars indicate the physical values from experiment.

As an example of this class of calculations, in figure 1 we show the recent determination of the masses of the proton and other light hadrons performed by the IBM lattice group on the GF-11. The agreement with experiment is remarkable. Having satisfied oneself that lattice QCD is a reliable tool (and along the way that QCD is in fact the correct theory of the strong interaction), the second class of calculations then seeks to understand a variety of details of hadronic structure, and in some cases to make predictions for phenomena which have not yet been uncovered in the laboratory. These can then be useful guides to experimenters. Among calculations already performed in this category would be

- Determination of the strong coupling constant, α_S
- Determination of quark masses
- The only reliable characterization of the properties of the phase transition to quark matter at high temperature, starting from first principles.
- Computations of hadronic form factors and wavefunctions
- Predictions for the masses of glueballs and exotic mesons in the quenched theory

As an example of these calculations, in figure 2 we compare the results of recent lattice determinations of strong coupling constant with determinations from experiment. We see that the even this first round of calculations, the lattice calculations are among the most precise. In the very near future the error bars on the lattice numbers will decrease dramatically, at which point the lattice calculation will set the standard.

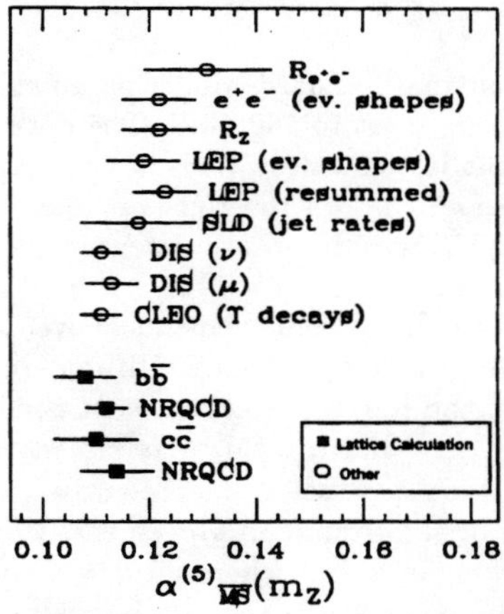

Figure 2: Various lattice and non-lattice determinations of α_S.

The third type of motivation is to learn about physics beyond QCD itself. In the category of calculation one wants to separate out strong interaction "corrections" to processes involving other weaker underlying interactions. This information then combines with experiment to constrain the parameter space of the Standard Model and its possible extensions. Examples of calculations which have impact on the rest of particle physics are these:

- Determination of matrix elements for processes such as $K \to \pi\pi$, $D \to K^* e\nu$, $B \to K^*\gamma$
- The most precise determination of the parameter B_K
- Determination of heavy quark decay constants f_B, f_D, etc.
- Determination of the Isgur-Wise function for heavy quark transitions

As an example of these type calculation, in figure 3 we show the current constraints on two important Standard Model parameters which come from combining experimental data with lattice and other calculations of the relevant matrix elements. We see that the lattice results already significantly sharpen our knowledge of the Standard Model parameters.

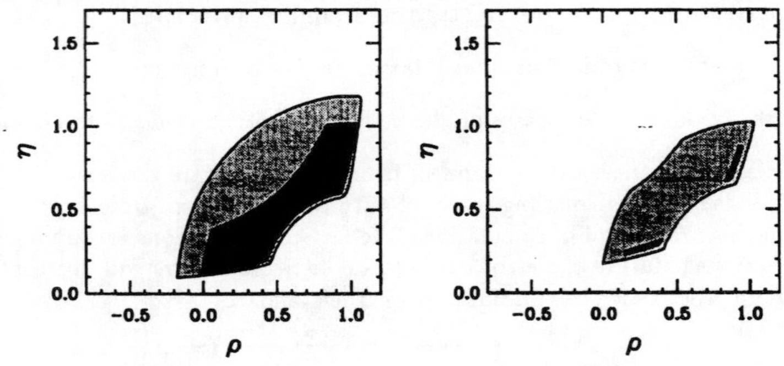

Figure 3: Constraints on the Standard Model parameters ρ and η from the experimental values of ϵ and x_d, with m_{top} set to 160 GeV. The dark and shaded regions show the constraints with and without lattice calculations of the matrix elements. The plot on the left shows the current situation; that on the right assumes a factor of five improvement in the experiment determining V_{cb}, with no improvement in the matrix element calculations.

As demonstrated by the list of achievements above, lattice computations have begun to make significant impact on the rest of physics. Ultimately it is expected that lattice QCD will provide the most precise and reliable calculations of almost all strong interaction quantities. For some quantities, e.g. B_K and α_S, this may already be the case. Improvements on the calculation of most of these quantities are presently limited by computational power and the relatively slow pace of algorithmic improvement. In particular, a truly definitive lattice calculation requires working in regime where the lattice spacing is smaller than any physically relevant scale, and at the point where the quark masses take on their (very small) physical values. The conventional parameterization of these quantities is given by the gauge coupling β, and the pion mass m_π. Figure 4 shows the regions of this parameter space accessible by gigaflop and teraflop resources for both "quenched" and "unquenched" or "dynamical" calculations. Evidently, with a teraflop class machine one could reach the scaling regime for quenched calculations, while definitive dynamical calculations will presumably await another improvement in algorithms. A more detailed discussion of the physics goals which could be reach on a teraflop facility is given, e.g. in ref. [1].

LATTICE QCD ENGINES

Like many other fields of computational physics, lattice gauge theory has a seemingly insatiable appetite for computer cycles. Unlike most other fields, though, lattice QCD also has developed a history of building its own hardware. Figure 5 shows where these lattice QCD engines fit in a plot of theoretical peak speed for a variety of computers. We see that there has been over a decade of development of lattice machines (even longer if one includes the early Caltech hypercube in this category), with steady exponential growth. Almost all of

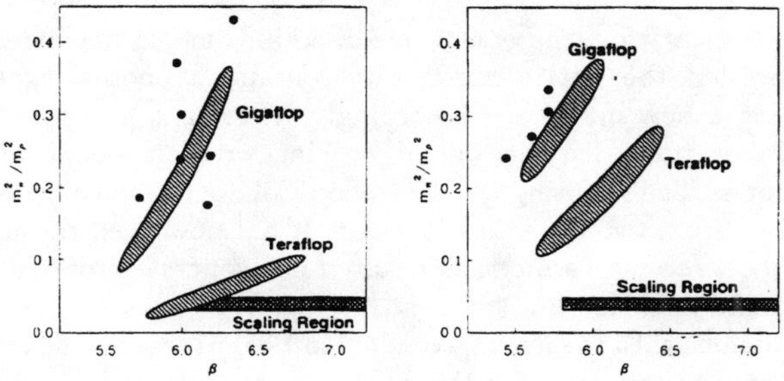

Figure 4: Regions of parameter space accessible at one gigaflop and at one teraflop, for quenched (left) and dynamical (right) calculations. Dots indicate parameter choices in recent calculations.

these machines have been one-of-a-kind lattice QCD engines, built to run in the laboratory for a year or two. In part, the development of these machines has made sense because the computationally intensive kernels—the inversion of large sparse matrices—involve only local, nearest neighbor communication, thus allowing one to live with only simple communications networks. In part, this development has been possible because the programs are small enough that one can write most of the code is assembly language if needed. Most of all, these projects made sense in terms of the cost/performance ratio as compared to commercial machines.

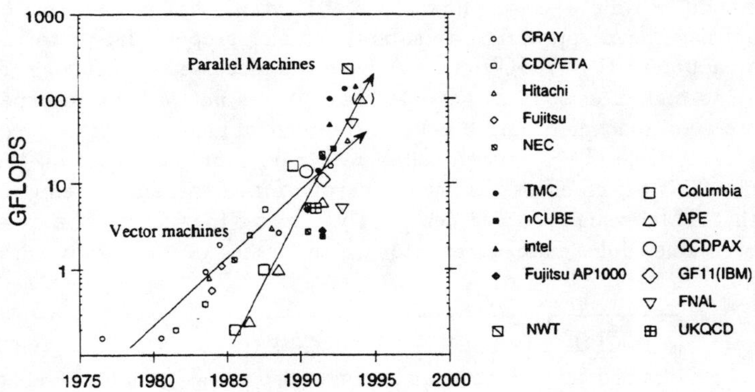

Figure 5: Peak speed of a vector and parallel supercomputers, as compiled in Ref. [3]

Figure 5 also shows that in the last few years we have passed through a cross-over, in which the commercial vendors have jumped from the vector supercomputer growth curve to parallel machines. The presence of commercial vendors in this market has eliminated the orders of magnitude advantage in building one-of-a-kind parallel machines, but if one is willing to work, there is a margin to squeeze out some gain in price/performance. In particular there are currently two or three new lattice QCD engines in the design or construction pipeline.

THE QCD TERAFLOP COLLABORATION

Even if it is clear that the era of one-of-a-kind lattice machines must eventually end, it is also clear that the lattice community contains a pool of expertise which can be of use in designing a new machine. Accordingly, in 1990, a group of lattice QCD physicists formed a collaboration with the aim of working with an industrial partner to produce a teraflop computer. The resulting QCD Teraflop Collaboration comprises about 40 theoretical physicists drawn from two dozen institutions. It has now been through three generations of projects, the most recent of which has resulted in a concrete proposal currently under review at NSF, DOE and ARPA.

After discussions with the leading vendors in 1990, it was decided that Thinking Machines afforded the best opportunity for the collaboration. By the end of 1992 the project was solidly underway. The design effort migrated to MIT, which hosted a fruitful collaboration involving computer architects from the Laboratory for Computer Science, engineers from Lincoln Laboratory, computer designers from TMC, and several lattice physicists. Initial funding for the design phase of project came principally from MIT and from ARPA. By March 1993 the team produced a detailed design for a teraflop machine, based on TMC's CM-5. The central idea was to replace TMC's vector unit with a newly designed part which would run ten times faster. The speed up was achieved by (a) quadrupling the number of vector units, (b) gaining a factor of two for 32-bit operations, and (c) turning up the clock. Had this project been proposed and funded, the timeline called for a prototype machine to be built in the summer of 1994, with a full teraflop machine running in mid-1995. Part of the appeal of this project was the idea that this turbocharged vector unit, or some close relative, could have been offered by TMC as an upgrade to existing CM-5 sites. However, at the point in time when the first phase of hardware design had been completed [2], and it would have been appropriate to submit a major proposal for prototype construction, it became apparent that TMC's energies were best focussed on bringing its next generation product to market as soon as possible, Since it was not realistic to expect that the CM-5 based teraflop machine would become a commercial product, that project was abandoned. At the same time, TMC invited collaboration on a project based on the next generation machine. This design effort has been underwa for a year, and is being refined at the same time that TMC refines its own design. By working together from day one, we believe we have been able to design an accelerator which meshes very naturally with TMC's standard machine.

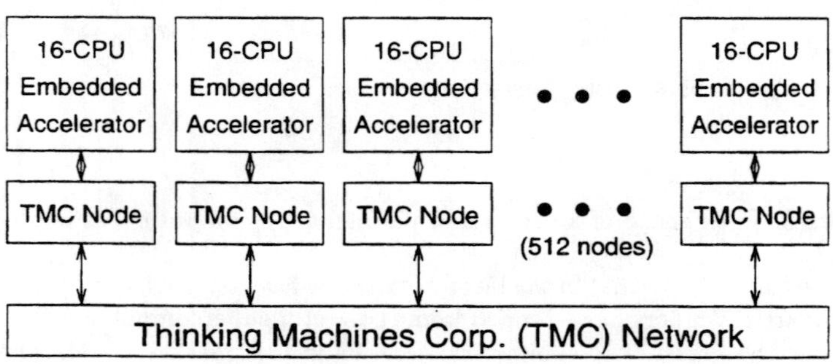

Figure 6: System architecture

THE TERAFLOP MACHINE

The proposed teraflop machine is based on TMC's next generation product. The basic idea is to build a 16-processor accelerator board which will plug into TMC's basic node, as illustrated in figure 6. Off-node communications is handled by TMC's network. Figure 7 shows the accelerator node in slightly more detail. Simple economics has driven us to design for of the commodity CPU chips, and pairs of these are bundled together with a single memory controller and 64MB of DRAM. Eight such pairs are connected to TMC's node a PCI bus to our custom ASIC. Lincoln Laboratory will produce the necessary ASICs. It will require 512 of these accelerated supernodes to reach a sustained teraflop.

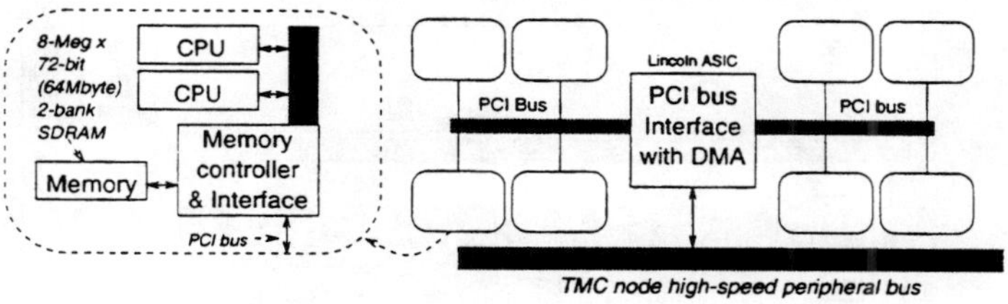

Figure 7: Nodal architecture

The parameters of the machine have been chosen so that even with the smallest problem size one would consider, there is enough bandwidth to feed the processors at near their peak speed. Figure 8 shows the bandwidth utilization for a conjugate gradient solver on a 32^4 grid, assuming the accelerator CPUs run at 80 percent of their peak. In this extreme case some busses are loaded at over half of their theoretical capacity. However, as one increases to realistic problem sizes, the demands on the network drop correspondingly. In figure 9 we show the utilization of the key resources as a function of problem size. The loads are comfortably small.

In the first phase of design, we have only done a crude estimate of the network performance, e.g. assuming aggregate loads which are constant in time, and ignoring collisions as different processors compete for the same resources. As the process has evolved, though, Lincoln Laboratory has written a simulator which models the behavior of individual pieces of the system clock by clock. The simulator allows one to study the performance on actual code fragments and monitor operations such as prefetches, cache reads, contention for memory, etc. Applied to the conjugate gradient solver discussed above, the simulator confirms that the naive estimate of network performance is realistic. Indeed it seems safe to assume that we will be able to get even more than 80% of the theoretical peak performance.

GENERAL USE

If the teraflops project proceeds to completion, we expect a large number of scientific applications will be run on it. We have done detailed analyses of a few sample problems—ocean modeling, *ab initio* electronic structure and molecular dynamics—and verified in each case that one can expect nearly one teraflop sustained performance. Thus this machine should of general interest to the scientific community.

We expect that the first 512 node machine would be sited at MIT and used primarily for lattice QCD when it is initially turned on. However, the MIT facility would quickly evolve

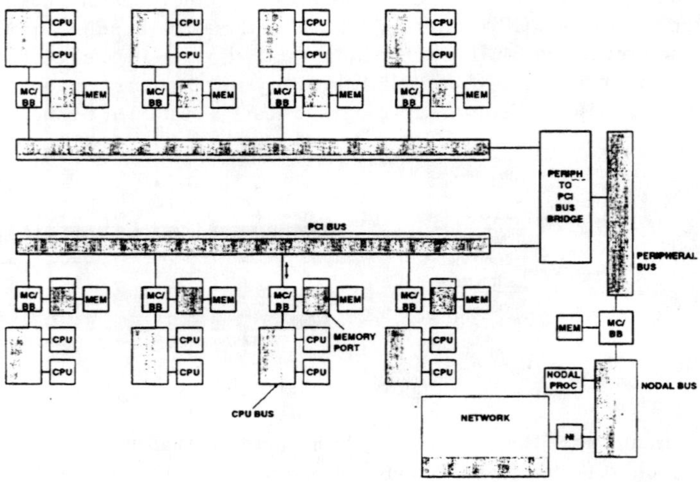

Figure 8: Traffic on the accelerator busses for 32^4 lattice. The shaded regions indicate the fraction of the resource used.

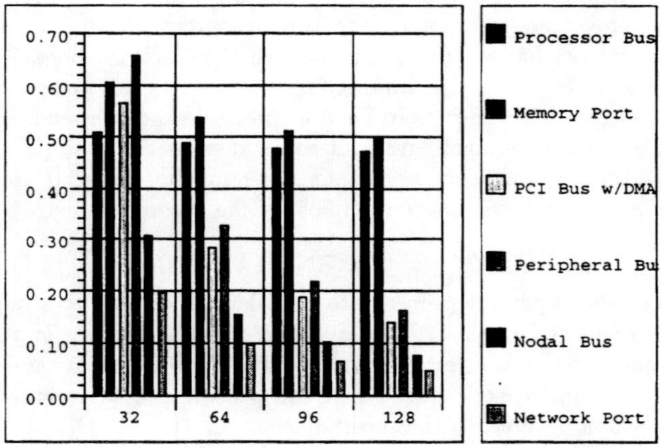

Figure 9: Bandwidth Utilization for QCD at 80% of Peak

into a nationally available resource, with most of the available time allocated by familiar mechanisms, such as the NSF Metacenter committees.

We also expect that if the project is as successful as we envisage, the accelerator architecture will be made available as an add-on or upgrade to TMC's standard product line. Such accelerated machines could find their way into the existing national centers. In addition, it is not impossible that the same accelerator, or a version of it, could be made available for workstations.

WHY THIS PROJECT MAKES SENSE

We believe this Multidisciplinary Teraflops project makes sense at a variety of levels. In broad terms, the desirability of this sort of enterprise, bringing together teams of scientists and engineers from university and industry, has been laid out a number of times, most recently in the NSF's Blue Ribbon Panel report entitled "From Desktops to Teraflops". More specifically we can itemize some key elements in our strategy for exploiting these scientific opportunities and designing and building a cost-effective general purpose teraflops computer.

- Exploitation of locality of problems in physical science in two, three, and four dimensions.

There is a large class of important computationally intensive problems in physical science which are highly local in two, three, or four space-time dimensions and which thus possess generic features which are exploited by the teraflops architecture. Because of their locality, when these problems are partitioned into sub-volumes to be calculated in parallel on nodes of a massively parallel computer, the ratio of computation on a node to communication between nodes increases as the ratio of volume to surface of the partition. For large partitions, the data may be moved in large blocks between nodes, thereby using the communication network efficiently and allowing overlap of computation and communication. For this class of problems, cost/performance is optimized by greatly increasing the processing power of the node to the point at which the communication network is fully utilized, thereby balancing the investment in communication and computation. This project thus explores and develops a new region of design space in which we increase that processing power per node by an order of magnitude by building an embedded accelerator containing 16 superscalar processors to achieve 3.2 GFlop/sec.

- General Purpose Architecture

Previous machines built to obtain higher performance for QCD than available on commercial machines have, by necessity, incorporated special purpose features severely limiting their applicability to general problems in computational science. They have generally utilized single-precision arithmetic, used restrictive communications networks, and employed primitive, labor intensive software environments. To meet the broad objectives of contemporary computational science and to have significant impact on the national effort in high performance computing, we have designed a general purpose teraflops computer utilizing superscalar processors attaining their peak speed in double precision and running high-level software and we employ a general communications network.

- Utilization of Commodity Components.

The key to the cost/performance of the teraflops computer is the use of commodity chips for the components of highest replication in our design. Whereas in the past, it was advantageous to design special-purpose components to optimize the performance for an application like QCD, it is no longer possible for a small design group to compete effectively with the enormous engineering effort which is being devoted to the the design of the next generation superscalar processors by the major vendors. Market forces and economy of scale will clearly drive the unit cost of these processors well below the fabrication cost of special purpose ASICS. These same market forces will motivate the production of associated memory controllers and bus interfaces and will assure the availability of high level software far more sophisticated than could be produced for a one-of-a-kind design.

• Utilization of Thinking Machines' next generation platform.

We take advantage of the full communications and software infrastructure of Thinking Machines' next generation platform. By collaborating early in the design cycle we have both the access to information and the input to design decisions to ensure maximum compatibility between our arithmetic accelerator and Thinking Machines' node. In particular, we will design the accelerator so that standard TMC software will run on the node and be able to access the memory on the accelerator.

• Concentration of design effort on a single element—the embedded accelerator.

Given the finite manpower and resources at our disposal, it is a crucial feature of our project that we are able to concentrate our effort on the design and construction of a single element, where it can have timely and decisive impact. Indeed, it is the limited scope of our effort and the efficient utilization of existing infrastructure which makes our aggressive development schedule and low development costs possible.

• Insulation from details of TMC node design.

Other than connecting to the peripheral bus used in the TMC node, the architectural details of our embedded accelerator are to a very large extent independent of the details of the design of the TMC node. In particular, there is no need to use the same processors, memory controllers, memory, or other components that TMC uses. This independence protects us to the the maximum extent possible from the obvious need any vendor has in developing its next-generation product in a highly competitive and rapidly evolving market to keep a number of design options open and bind crucial elements as late as possible in the design cycle. An additional advantage is the fact that our accelerator can be used directly in a workstation employing the same peripheral bus, providing both an ideal software development environment for the teraflops computer and an extremely powerful addition to the workstation marketplace.

• Performance analysis

Key design decisions in this project are optimized on the basis of detailed performance analysis of a range of computationally intensive problems including QCD, *ab initio* calculations of condensed matter systems, global ocean modeling, and molecular dynamics. The balance of computation and communication and the fractional utilization of datapaths for these applications are described later in this proposal. As the project evolves, successively more detailed simulations of these applications will be performed to optimize every aspect of the design.

To be successful, this project will now need a coordinated collaboration between the relevant government agencies. It is our hope that ARPA will be interested in continuing to fund the computer architecture design, that NSF will be interested in funding the machine insofar as it is a general purpose scientific tool, and that DOE will contribute isofar as the machine will be able to address fundamental issues in elementary particle physics.

References

[1] S.Aoki et al., "Physics Goals of the QCD Teraflop Project", *Int. J. Mod. Phys.* C2 (1991) 829.

[2] A. Anderson *et al.* "An Arithmetic Accelerator for the CM-5 Computer", Lincoln Laboratory project report SCS-1 (1993).

[3] Iwasaki, "Computers for Lattice Field Theories", *Nucl. Phys.* (Proc. Supp.) B34 (1994) 78.

Toward Teraflop Computing and New Grand Challenge Applications

ISBN-1-56072-247-9

MICRODYNAMICS OF BRITTLE FRACTURE: A PARALLEL MOLECULAR DYNAMICS INVESTIGATION

Farid F. Abraham, D. Brodbeck, R. A. Rafey, W. E. Rudge
IBM Research Division
Almaden Research Center
650 Harry Road
San Jose, CA 95120-6099

Abstract

Implementing molecular dynamics on the IBM SP1 and PVS parallel computers, we have studied the fracture of two-dimensional notched solids under tension using million atom systems. Many recent laboratory findings occur in our simulation experiments, one of the most intriguing being the dynamic instability of the crack tip as it approaches a fraction of the sound speed. A detailed comparison between laboratory and computer experiments is presented.

Although much work in the study of fracture in brittle materials and at interfaces has been done over some 70 years, the mechanisms that govern the structure and dynamics of cracks are not well understood (1,2). Linear elasticity theory typically assumes that cracks are smooth and predicts that they accelerate to a limiting velocity equal to the Rayleigh speed of the material. However experiment tells us that, in a typical fracture sequence, an initially smooth and mirrorlike fracture surface begins to appear misty and then evolves into a rough, hackled region with a limiting velocity of about two-thirds the Rayleigh speed. Also, in some brittle materials, the crack pattern can also exhibit a wiggle of a characteristic wavelength. Recent experiments by Swinney and colleagues (3-5) have shown violent crack velocity oscillations beyond a speed of about one-third the Rayleigh speed and exhibited correlation with the roughness of the crack surface. They concluded that a dynamical instability of the crack tip governs the crack velocity behavior and the morphology sequence of 'mirror, mist and hackle (1).'

With the advent of scalable parallel computers, computational molecular dynamics now has the potential to be a very powerful tool to provide immediately insights into the nature of fracture dynamics. We have studied two dimensional triangular solids with up to 1500 atoms on a side, or about one half of a micron in length. Like Swinney (3-5), our interest was to study two-dimensional 'mode one' loading. We were able to follow the crack propagation over sufficient time and distance intervals so that a comparison with experiment became feasible.

We assume that the interatomic forces are a combination of a Lennard-Jones (LJ) 12:6 with a spline cutoff. Quantities are expressed in terms of reduced units: lengths are scaled by the parameter σ, the value of the interatomic separation for which the LJ potential is zero, and energies are scaled by the parameter ϵ, the depth of the minimum of the LJ potential. Reduced temperature is therefore kT/ϵ. Our choice of the simple LJ force law is dictated by our interest to study the microscopic features of brittle fracture common to a large class of real physical systems. The

LJ potential can be used to represent a generic "brittle" material. The parallel molecular dynamics program is implemented on the IBM PVS using 16 nodes, and on the IBM SP1 using 64 nodes. For 2,027,776 atoms, the update time per time step is 0.9 seconds on the SP1.

In this paper, our system is a 2D rectangular slab of atoms with L atoms on a side, where the length $L = 712$. A triangular notch of 10 lattice spacings is cut midway along the lower horizontal slab boundary and a outward strain rate $d\epsilon_y/dt = 0.0001$ is imposed on the outer most columns of atoms defining the opposing vertical faces of the slab. Hence, a linear velocity gradient is established with $-V < v_x < +V$ and creates an ever increasing lateral tension on the solid slab. The solid fails at the notch tip when the solid has been stretched by $\sim$ 3 per cent. At that point, the imposed strain rate remains constant and the simulation is continued until the growing crack has traversed the total length of the slab. We briefly summarize the material properties of the LJ 2D solid (6). The longitudinal sound speed c_l at zero temperature and pressure is ~ 9, and the transverse sound speed $c_t = c_l/(3)^{1/2}$. The Rayleigh speed c_R is somewhat less than the transverse sound speed.

Figures 1 and 2 graphically summarize our nonzero strain rate simulation. Figure 1 shows (a) the crack tip position (in units of reduced length) and (b) the crack tip speed (in units of the Rayleigh sound speed), both as a function of reduced time. Figure 1(c) is an expanded view of the crack tip speed for early time. From Fig. 1a, we find that the crack tip achieves a limiting speed equal to 0.57 of the Rayleigh speed c_R. However, the "instantaneous" tip velocity is very erratic (Fig. 1b) after reaching a speed of $0.3c_R$. Before a time of about 70 and a speed less than $0.3c_R$, the acceleration of the crack tip is quite smooth (Fig. 1c); but with the onset of the erratic fluctuations of the tip speed, there is significant deceleration of the propagating crack. Each of theses features in Figs. 1a, b and c are in agreement with Swinney's et al. experiment (3,4).

Figure 2 shows the time evolution of the propagating crack using a gray-scale rendering of the instantaneous local transverse velocity v_x, or transverse strain rate, which goes from dark grey for the most negative v_x to light grey for the most positive v_x. Initially, the brittle crack propagates in a straight line and leaves "mirror" cleaved surfaces. Periodic stress waves immediately appear with failure. Corresponding to the onset of the erratic oscillations of the tip speed, at a tip speed of $0.3c_R$, the crack begins oscillating back and forth in the transverse direction at approximate angles of plus and minus 30 degrees from the vertical (the original direction of crack motion). Accompanying the oscillating 'zig-zag' excursions of the growing crack is significant compression and plastic flow in the regions immediately next to the newly created surfaces. Each time the crack 'zigs' or 'zags,' a propagating atomic displacement along two adjacent rows of atoms that are $\pm$ 30 degrees to the vertical occurs, which is initiated at the vertex of the change of direction and travels at about the longitudinal sound speed c_l. These 'dislocations' appear as slanted, inverted V being emitted from the moving crack tip, first to the right and then to the left, and may be traced back to their origin by constructing an imaginary line 30 degrees from the vertical which passes through the V. When the dislocation hits the top free boundary, an atomic step is formed. Because the solid is being stretched at a nonzero strain rate, it must "try to keep up" which the lateral boundary expansion; this means mechanical failure, and the obvious one is fracture. This could occur by a single fracture (which is seeded by a notch), multiple internal fracture due to the occurrence of voids, as well as 'necking' by slipping atomic rows of atoms for a finite thick slab. We observe the single fracture plus necking. While dislocation emission is associated with ductile fracture, it would be misleading to identify this experiment as representing ductile fracture. Our system has an exaggerated critical strain for tip failure, which is about 3 percent and a factor of ten larger than experiment (3,4). This is necessary to achieve a fracture dynamics that is sufficiently fast to follow by molecular dynamics. Increasing the strain during tip propagation forces the slab to relieve the additional strain by the sliding of atomic rows, and the resulting dislocations provide an excellent signature for crack oscillation. However, they are not the origin of the oscillation.

This microscopic fracturing has associated with it a larger-scale characteristic wavelength and a growing coarse-grain roughness which is shown in Fig. 3. In Fig 3a, the profile of one of the fractured surfaces is presented as a function of crack distance from the originating failure point, and a wavelength of $\sim 120\sigma$ is apparent. From the profiles, the roughness, or width, as a function of this distance are calculated (7) and presented in Fig. 3b. We find that the width w scales with length L, according to the relation $w = L^{\zeta}$, where $\zeta = 0.81$. This result is in agreement with recent conjectures of a "universal" roughness exponent for the crack surface of real brittle materials (7).

We may look toward teraflop computing by making the following projection. For the 2 million atom system simulated for 200,000 time steps, the wall-clock time is 24 hours using an IBM SP1 with 128 nodes and at a sustained performance of 10 GFlops. A parallel computer with 2000 nodes and with a node speedup of ~ 7 would have a sustained performance of one teraflop for our problem and could be realized in 5 to 6 years. At that time, we could simulate 62 million atoms for 1.3 million time steps for the same 24 hour wall-clock time.

Acknowledgement: A preliminary study of fracture was initiated by FFA at LANL in collaboration with B. L. Holian. With Holian's help, P. Lomdahl at LANL repeated our effort of destroying a 2D slab using "explosive" strain rates. This was reported on the cover of Computers In Physics, 7, 382 (1993). Holian's and Abraham's contributions to Lomdahl's study were later acknowledged by R. LeSar of LANL (private communication and Computers In Physics, to be publish). The collaboration was terminated, and the present work is independent of that effort.

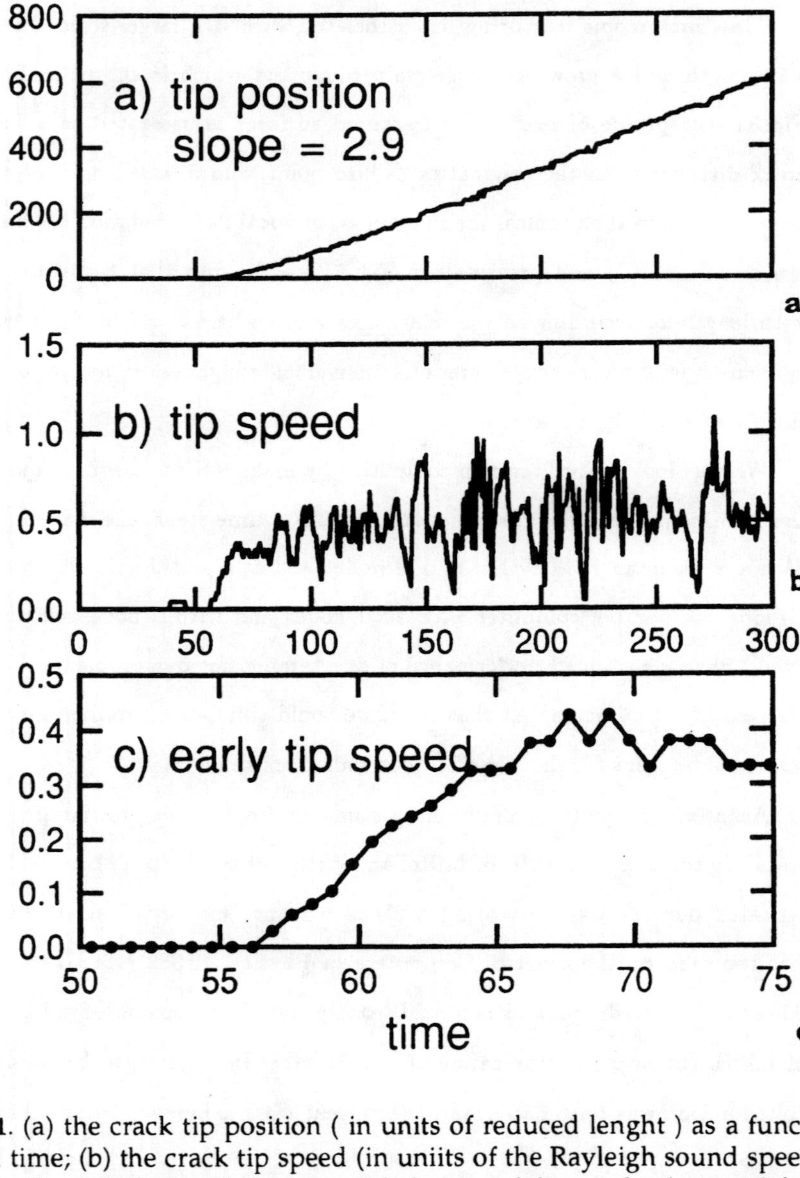

Figure 1. (a) the crack tip position (in units of reduced lenght) as a function of reduced time; (b) the crack tip speed (in uniits of the Rayleigh sound speed) as a function of reduced time; (c) an expanded view of the crack tip speed for early time.

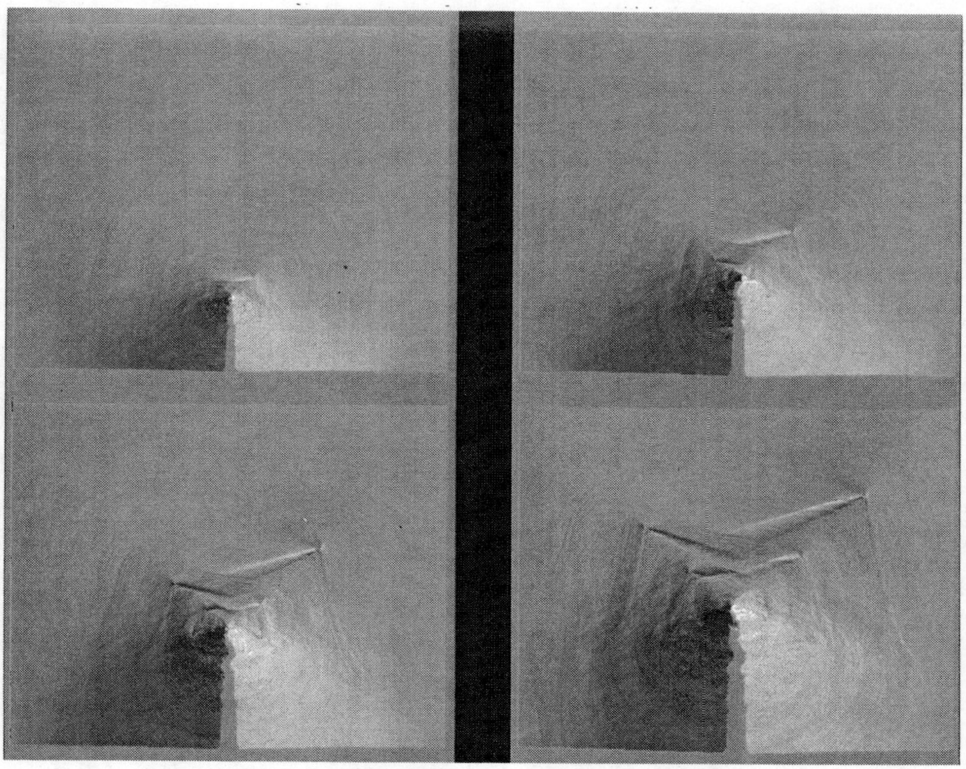

a

Figure 2. The time evolution of the propagting crack is shown using a gray-scale rendering of the instantaneous local transverse velocity υ_x, or transverse strain rate, which goes from dark grey for the most negative $\upsilon_x$to light grey for the most positive υ_x. The time sequence goes from left to right and top to bottom . The frames are reduced times a) 126, 144, 162 180 and b) 198, 234, 270 and 306.

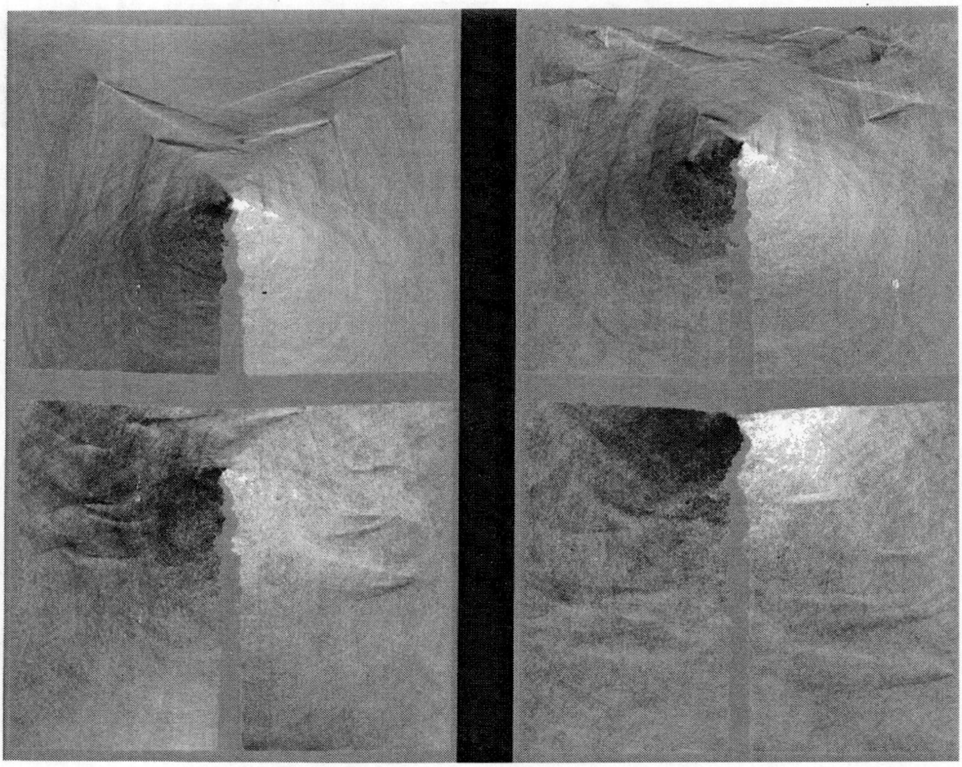

b

Figure 2. *(continued))*

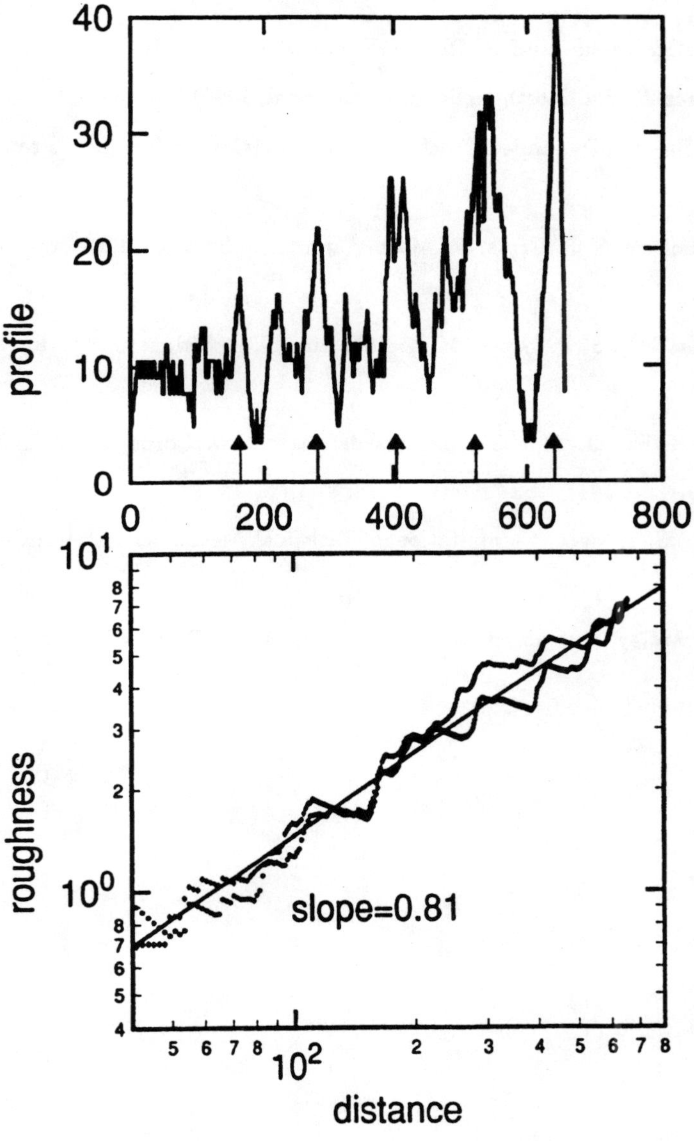

Figure 3. The (a) profile of a fractured surfaced and (b) the roughness of the fractured surface are prresented as a crack distance from the originating failure point.

References

1) H. J. Herrmann and S. Roux, editors, Statistical Models for the Fracture of Disordered Media (North-Holland, Amsterdam, 1990).

2) L. B. Freund, Dynamical Fracture Mechanics (Cambridge Univ. Press, New York, 1990).

3) J. Fineberg, S. P. Gross, M. Marder and H. L. Swinney, Phys.Rev.Lett., 67, 457 (1991).

4) J. Fineberg, S. P. Gross, M. Marder and H. L. Swinney, Phys.Rev., B45, 5146 (1992).

5) S. P. Gross, J. Fineberg, M. Marder, W. D. McCormick and H. L. Swinney, Phys.Rev.Lett., 71, 3162 (1993).

6) Wm. G. Hoover, Computational Statistical Mechanics (Elsevier, Amsterdam, 1991).

7) K. J. Måløy, A. Hansen, E. L. Hinrichsen and S. Roux, Phys.Rev.Lett., 68, 213 (1992).

Toward Teraflop Computing and New Grand Challenge Applications

ISBN-1-56072-247-9

MILLION-PARTICLE SIMULATIONS OF FRACTURE IN SILICA GLASS: MULTIRESOLUTION MOLECULAR DYNAMICS APPROACH ON PARALLEL ARCHITECTURES

AIICHRO NAKANO, RAJIV K. KALIA, AND PRIYA VASHISHTA
Concurrent Computing Laboratory for Materials Simulations
Department of Computer Science and Department of Physics & Astronomy
Louisiana State University, Baton Rouge, LA 70803

ABSTRACT

For realistic modeling of materials, a molecular-dynamics (MD) algorithm is developed based on multiresolutions in both space and time. Materials of interest are characterized by effective interatomic potentials including the long-range Coulomb and three-body covalent potentials. The long-range Coulomb interaction for bulk systems with the periodic boundary conditions is computed with the Reduced Cell Multipole Method. Medium-range non-Coulombic interactions are computed with the Multiple Time-Step approach. Separable tensor decomposition scheme is used to compute three-body potentials. Interactions on different spatial scales are computed using different time scales. For a 4.2 million-particle SiO_2 system, one MD step takes only 4.8 seconds on the 512-node Intel Touchstone Delta machine. The constant-grain parallel efficiency of the program is $\eta' = 0.92$. The program was also benchmarked on a 128-node IBM SP1 machine.

The multiresolution MD simulations are applied to the study of the pore interface growth and the roughness of fracture surfaces in silica glasses. During uniform dilation of silica glasses, the average pore radius, R, and the width, W, scale with the pore size, s, as $R \sim s^{\nu}$ and $W \sim s^{\mu}$ with $\nu = 0.49 \pm 0.02$ and $\mu = 0.50 \pm 0.03$. When the mass density is reduced to 1.40 ± 0.04 g/cm^3, the pores grow catastrophically to cause fracture. The roughness exponent for fracture surfaces, $\alpha = 0.87 \pm 0.02$, supports experimental claims about the universality of α.

1. Introduction

Molecular dynamics (MD) simulation is becoming an integral part of computer-aided materials development. Design of some materials requires large-scale MD simulations. Examples include porous glasses. Porous silica has recently been the focus of many investigations [1]. This environmentally safe material has numerous technological applications [2]: It is used in thermal insulation of commercial and household refrigerators; in passive solar energy collection devices; in particle detectors; and in catalysis and chemical separation. (There is an exciting possibility of utilizing it as an embedding framework in optical switches made of quantum-confined microclusters [3].) Since these applications are due to the remarkable porous structure of the system, it is important to understand the size and spatial distributions of pores and the morphology of pore interfaces.

Since porous glasses are composed of large-scale structural units, each consisting of 10^3 to 10^5 particles, the simulation system must comprise at least 10^6 to 10^7 particles. To prepare a well-thermalized MD configuration and calculate the mechanical and thermal properties, the multimillion-particle simulations need to be run for 10^5 to 10^7 time steps. For simulations to be completed within reasonable time schedule, it is therefore crucial to achieve a speed of a few seconds per step.

For systems interacting via simple binary potentials with short range, this requirement -- to simulate *multimillion particles* at a speed of *a few seconds/step* -- has been satisfied by recent advancement in numerical techniques and parallel computing technology [4]. However, the requirement is yet to be met for realistic modeling of materials. Realistic materials modeling relies on high-quality interatomic potentials. They must include the effects of the long-range Coulomb interaction, charge-dipole interaction, steric hindrance, and bending and stretching of covalent bonds [5]. Each of these potentials requires enormous computing and accordingly a special algorithm.

We have developed a highly efficient MD algorithm based on multiresolutions in both space and time for systems with the long-range Coulomb forces and three-body potentials. Hierarchical spatial resolution is introduced to compute the Coulomb forces, and forces from different spatial regions are calculated using different time scales.

Performance of the multiresolution molecular dynamics (MRMD) algorithm is tested on the 512-node Intel Touchstone Delta machine at Caltech and the 128-node IBM SP1 system at Argonne National Laboratory.

The MRMD simulations are applied to the study of the pore interface growth and the roughness of fracture surfaces in porous silica glasses. We study the pore growth during uniform dilation of silica glasses. When the mass density is reduced to a critical density, the pores grow catastrophically to cause fracture. The roughness of the fracture surfaces is investigated.

2. Multiresolution molecular dynamics algorithm

The most prohibitive computational problem arises from the Coulomb potential. Because of its long range, each atom interacts with all the other atoms in the system. Therefore the evaluation of the Coulomb potential for an N-particle system requires $O(N^2)$ operations, which makes large-scale MD simulations difficult. Recent development of hierarchical algorithms [6-8] has revolutionized the computation of the Coulomb potential. The Fast Multipole Method (FMM) uses truncated multipole expansion and local Taylor expansion for the Coulomb potential field [8]. By computing both expansions recursively on a hierarchy of cells, the Coulomb potential is computed with O(N) operations, see Fig. 1 (b).

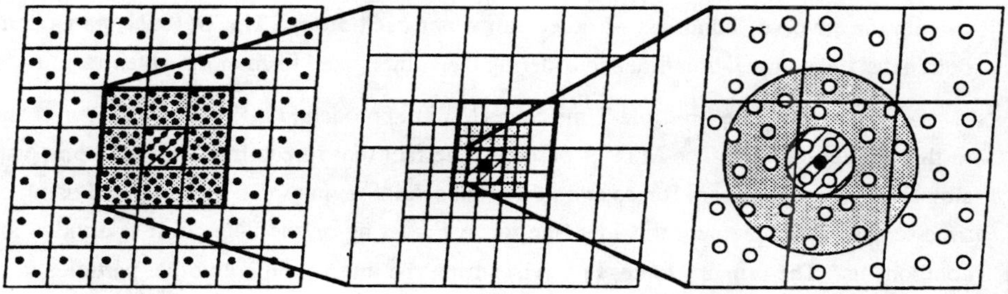

(a) (b) (c)

Fig. 1: Schematic representation of spatial multiresolution for a two-dimensional system. (a) Periodically repeated images of the original MD box (hatched). Replacing each well-separated image by a small number of particles with the same leading multipole expansions reduces the computation enormously while maintaining the necessary accuracy. (b) A hierarchy of cells in the FMM. (c) The near-field forces on a particle (solid circle) are due to the primary (open circles within the hatched area), secondary (open circles within the shaded area), and tertiary (the other open circles) neighbor atoms.

For many simulations in materials science, the periodic boundary condition is used to minimize the surface effects. Summation over infinitely repeated image charges must be carried out to compute the Coulomb potential. The conditionally convergent series is traditionally calculated by the Ewald method [9]. Though the Ewald algorithm scales practically linearly for moderate system size [9], the computation becomes prohibitive for larger systems. Ding, Karasawa, and Goddard have developed the Reduced Cell Multipole Method (RCMM) which makes the computation of the Coulomb potential feasible for periodic systems with multimillion-particle unit cell [10]. They observe that distant images each including multimillion particles can be replaced by a small number of particles which have the same leading multipoles as the original system. The Ewald summation is applied to these reduced images with little computation effort and reasonable accuracy, see Fig. 1 (a).

Another computational difficulty arises from the non-Coulombic part of the interatomic potential. In most materials, the potential in medium range (up to the cut-off length, $r_c = 5$ - 10

Å) is a complicated function of the interatomic distance, r, so that the multipole expansion is not applicable. Therefore the finest cell in the FMM must be larger than r_c. Between atoms residing in well-separated finest cells which do not share any corner, the interatomic forces are Coulombic and the FMM and RCMM are used to compute these far-field forces. On the other hand, within the nearest-neighbor cells the interatomic forces (near-field forces) must be computed directly without using multipoles. With r_c = 5 - 10 Å, the direct near-field force calculation involves hundreds of other atoms per each atom. The $O(10^2N)$ pair computation dominates the computation time, considering the complicated form of the potential at $r < r_c$.

We employ the Multiple Time-Step (MTS) approach [11-13] to reduce the computation in this spatial regime. The MTS is based on the fact that forces from farther atoms vary more slowly in time. Therefore forces from different spatial regimes can be computed using different time scales. To implement this idea, the force, $\mathbf{F}_i$, acting on the ith particle is divided into three components. The primary force, $\mathbf{F}_{i,p}$, arises from the interaction with other particles in a sphere of radius, r_a, around the ith particle. The primary cut-off length, r_a, is chosen so that only the bonding atoms are classified into this category. Also, we choose $r_a > r_0$, so that three-body forces are entirely primary forces [13]. The secondary force, $\mathbf{F}_{i,s}$, consists of pairwise interactions in the range $r_a < r_{ij} < r_c$. The secondary cut-off length, r_c, is chosen such that beyond this length, the interatomic potential can be regarded as purely Coulombic. The tertiary force, $\mathbf{F}_{i,t}$, arises from the particles beyond $r_{ij} > r_c$ and within the nearest-neighbor cells, Fig. 1 (c). In our MD simulations of SiO_2 systems, the primary, secondary and tertiary forces on each atom are typically due to a few, 50, and 300 atoms, respectively. $\mathbf{F}_{i,p}$ is calculated at every MD step. On the other hand, $\mathbf{F}_{i,s}$ and $\mathbf{F}_{i,t}$ are calculated at intervals of $n_1\ \Delta t$ and $n_2\ \Delta t$, respectively. Typical values we choose for n_1 and n_2 are 15 and 120. In between $\mathbf{F}_{i,s}$ and $\mathbf{F}_{i,t}$ are extrapolated according to the Taylor series. The MTS algorithm achieves an order-of-magnitude speedup of the direct force calculations [11]. On parallel computers, the communication overhead is shown to be reduced significantly by the MTS method [12,13].

For describing the bending and stretching of covalent bonds, three-body potentials are widely used [5]. However, triple sums involved in three-body potentials make the computation inefficient. The computation of three-body potentials can be made efficient by decomposing them into separable tensor components [13,14]. The resulting expression for the three-body potentials involves only double sums, which is evaluated much more efficiently. Speedup of factor two is thus achieved [13].

We have developed a highly efficient MD algorithm based on multiresolutions in both space and time. The long-range Coulomb potential in periodic systems are computed with the RCMM and FMM, while the medium-range non-Coulombic potentials are computed with the

MTS method. The three-body potentials are calculated using the separable tensor decomposition. Forces from different spatial regions are computed using different time scales. The far-field forces vary even more slowly than the tertiary forces. Accordingly, the far-field forces are computed at an interval of $n_2 \Delta t$ without the Taylor extrapolation. Fifth-order Gear's algorithm is used to integrate the equations of motion [15]. Figure 2 schematically represents the Multiresolution MD (MRMD) algorithm.

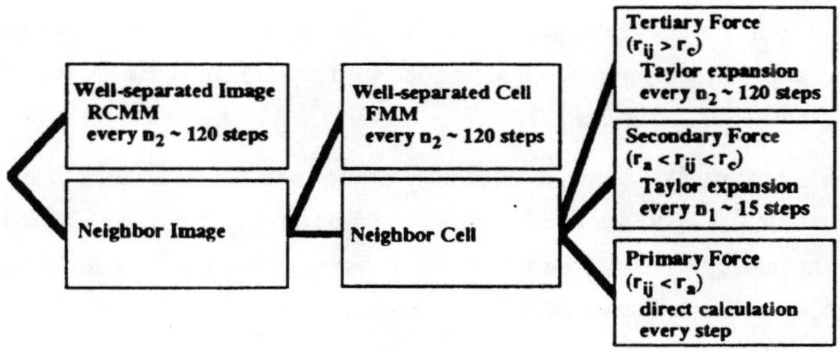

Fig. 2: Schematic of the multiple time steps used in the MRMD algorithm. The Coulomb potential from the well-separated images is computed with the RCMM at every n_2 steps. The far-field potential within the nearest-neighbor images is computed with the FMM at every n_2 steps. The near-field forces are classified into the primary, secondary and tertiary forces according to the interatomic distances. They are updated at every one, n_1, and n_2 steps, respectively.

3. Implementation of the multiresolution molecular dynamics on parallel computers

We use the divide-and-conquer strategy based on domain decomposition to implement the MRMD algorithm on parallel computers [9,12,13]. The total volume of the system is divided into p subsystems of equal volume, and each subsystem is assigned to a node in an array of p processors. The data associated with particles of a subsystem are assigned to the corresponding node.

To calculate the near-field forces on a particle in a subsystem, the coordinates of the boundary particles in the 26 neighbor subsystems must be copied from the corresponding nodes. Here, we distinguish the primary- and secondary-boundary particles. In a subsystem, primary boundary particles to the nth neighbor (n = 1,...,26) subsystem are located within a distance $r_a + \delta$ from the boundary with the nth neighbor, where δ is a small positive number. Similarly, secondary boundary particles are those which are within a distance $r_c + \delta'$ from the boundary but are not the primary particles, where δ' is another small distance.

At every n_1 steps, lists of the primary- and secondary-boundary particles are constructed. The data associated with the listed primary- and secondary-boundary particles are then copied to the neighbor nodes, using message passing routines. The particle data are augmented including these copied particles. At the other steps, only the primary-boundary particles are copied which have been defined at the latest update of the primary-boundary-particle list. Only the coordinates and not their derivatives are copied. In the actual code, the message passing to the 26 neighbor nodes is completed in total of six steps, by sending the boundary-particle information to east, west, north, south, up and down neighbor nodes sequentially. The corner and edge boundary particles are copied to proper neighbor nodes by forwarding some of the received boundary particles to other neighbor nodes [13].

After every n_1 MD steps, a resident particle may have moved out of the subsystem to which the particle has been assigned. Before the next n_1 steps start, we check the coordinates of the N resident particles. Those particles which have moved out of a subsystem are sent to the proper neighbor nodes, and are added to the resident particles there.

In the parallel MTS algorithm, message passings associated with the secondary boundary particles are skipped for n_1 steps, and only message passings performed every time step are those associated with the primary boundary particles, the number of which are very small. Consequently, the MTS method reduces the size of messages dramatically [13].

The implementation of the hierarchical codes on parallel computers have been reported before [16-18]. Suppose the processors are logically organized as a cube of size $p_x \times p_y \times p_z$. For a deeper tree level, $l \geq \log_2[\max(p_x , p_y , p_z)]$, each cell is uniquely assigned to a processor (We consider only those cases where $\max(p_x , p_y , p_z) \leq 2 \min(p_x , p_y , p_z)$). In the FMM, the hierarchical computation of Coulomb forces in a node involves only the multipoles of two skin-layer cells from the nearest-neighbor nodes at each level. In our MRMD algorithm, the multipoles of $8^l / p$ cells per a node are augmented with the copied multipoles to form an array consisting of multipoles of $(2^l/p_x + 2)\ (2^l/p_y + 2)\ (2^l/p_z + 2)$ cells at each layer.

However, for lower levels, the number of cells becomes smaller than the number of processors. Here more than one processors are assigned to one physical cell. Consequently many processors become idle or alternatively they duplicate the same computation. In our parallel implementation of the MRMD algorithm, the multipoles for all the cells in a lower level, $l < \log_2[\max(p_x , p_y , p_z)]$, are set to be global variables.

The problem of idle processors at lower levels of tree is inherent in all the hierarchical algorithms. It reduces the theoretical minimum parallel execution time to be O(logN) for an N particle system using N processors [16,17]. For multimillion-particle simulations on less than

512 processors, however, the number of the finest cells, N_{cell}, is much larger than p. For such large grain sizes, we found that the idle processor problem is negligible and the program is practically scalable as demonstrated by the parallel efficiency analysis in the next section.

4. Performance of multiresolution MD algorithm on parallel computers

We carry out performance tests of the MRMD algorithm on parallel computers. The physical system is SiO_2 modeled with a realistic interatomic potential [5]. The machines we use are the 512-node Intel Touchstone Delta at Caltech and the 128-node IBM SP1 at Argonne. All the calculations are done in 64-bit precision.

Figure 3 shows execution time of the MRMD program on the Delta and SP1 as a function of the number of processors, p. The MTS parameters are chosen as $n_1 = 15$, $n_2 = 120$, and the Taylor expansion is cut off at the first time derivative. Up to quadrupoles are considered for the FMM and RCMM. Here we scale the system size linearly with the number of processors so that the number of particles, N = 8,232 p. For a 4.2-million particle SiO_2 system on the 512 nodes Delta, one MD step takes only 4.84 seconds. The execution time increases only slightly for larger systems.

Figure 3 also shows the time spent for communication expressed as a fraction of the total execution time. For the 512-node Delta, communication spends only 8.1 % of the total execution time. The small communication overhead makes the program efficient even for larger p.

On the SP1, the computation is more than four times faster than on the Delta, but the communication performance is comparable, see Fig. 3. For a 0.53-million particle SiO_2 system on 64 nodes of the SP1, one MD step takes 1.11 seconds and the communication overhead is 15.2 %.

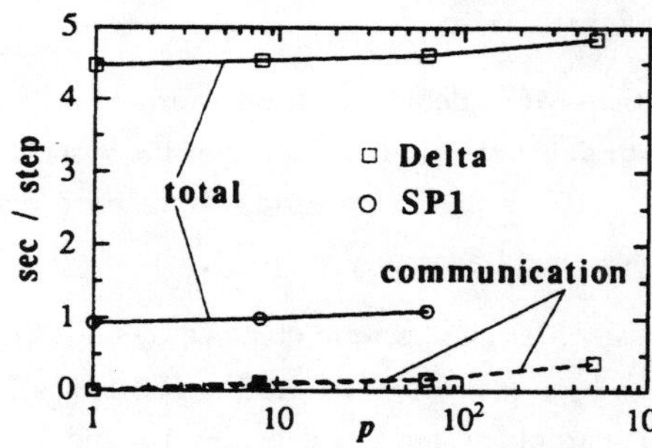

Fig. 3: Execution time of the MRMD program (solid curves) for 8,232p particle SiO_2 systems on p processors. Open squares and open circles are the results on the Delta and SP1, respectively. Communication overhead (dashed curves) of the same program.

Next we examine the parallel efficiency of the MRMD program. We first define the speed of the MRMD program as a product of the total number of particles and time steps executed in a second. The constant-grain speedup is given by the ratio between the speed of p processors and that of one processor. The constant-grain efficiency, η', is the constant-grain speedup divided by p [13]. For a 4.2-million particle SiO_2 system on the 512 nodes Delta, we estimate $\eta' = 0.924$. Since the processing power of each node in the SP1 is greater than that of Delta but the communication speed remains similar (see Fig. 3), the parallel efficiency of the MRMD program on the SP1 is smaller than on the Delta.

5. Million-particle MD simulation of fracture in silica glass

In recent years, a great deal of progress has been made in understanding the morphology of surfaces and interfaces. Scale-invariant surface fluctuations related to different growth processes have been observed in a wide variety of systems [19, 20]: vapor deposition; fluid flow in porous media; sedimentation of granular materials; and thin-film growth. The root mean square surface fluctuations averaged over a distance l obey the scaling relation [19, 20],

$$W \sim l^{\alpha} . \tag{1}$$

Recent experiments on a wide variety of materials reveal that fracture surfaces also exhibit scaling properties embodied in Eq. (1). Bouchaud, Lapasset, and Planès have measured the same value of α (≈ 0.80) for four different aluminum alloys [21]. Måløy et al. have found that the roughness exponent of cracks in a variety of brittle materials is also close to 0.8 [22]. This led them to suggest that the roughness exponent for fracture surfaces has a universal value. However, the universality of the roughness exponent, especially on the nanometer scale, is still an unresolved issue [23].

Million-particle MD calculations are performed on amorphous silica, investigating the growth of pores with a decrease in the density of the system. The systems we have simulated contain up to 1.12×10^6 atoms. Simulations have been performed on IBM's 128-node SP1 system at Argonne National Laboratory.

The low-density MD glasses were obtained by uniformly expanding the well-thermalized normal-density glass by a factor of 1.01-1.03 at 600 K [24,25]. Figure 4 shows snapshots of pores in 1.12×10^6-particle systems at densities 1.8 and 1.4 g/cm^3. The pores begin to form when the density of the system is reduced to 1.8 g/cm^3. Further decrease in the density of the system causes an increase in the number of pores and also the pores coalesce to form larger entities.

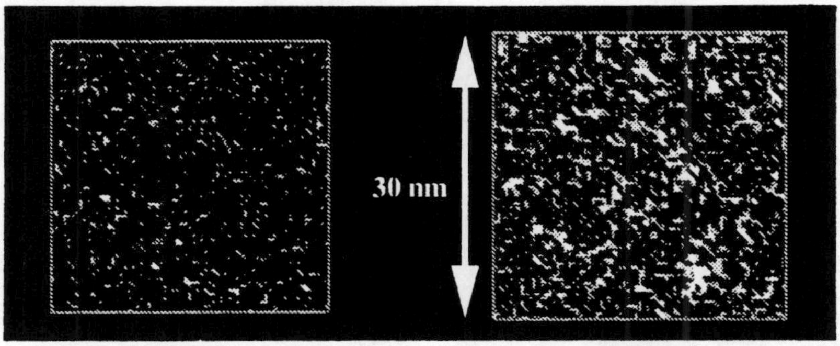

1.8 g/cm3 **1.4 g/cm3**

Fig. 4: Snapshots of two-dimensional slices of MD configurations of silica (1,119,744 particles) at densities 1.8 g/cm^3 and 1.4 g/cm^3. Dark and bright pixels represent silica and pores, respectively.

The roughness of pore interfaces is examined by calculating the width, W [26],

$$W = \left\{ \frac{1}{N_s} \sum_{i=1}^{N_s} \left(\left| \mathbf{r}_i' - \mathbf{r}_o \right| - R \right)^2 \right\}^{1/2} , \tag{2}$$

as a function of the pore volume, s. In Eq. (2), $\{\mathbf{r}_i'\}$ denote points at the interface and $\mathbf{r}_o$ and R are the center and radius of a pore, respectively:

$$R^2 = \frac{1}{N_s} \sum_{i=1}^{N_s} \left| \mathbf{r}_i' - \mathbf{r}_o \right|^2 ; \; \mathbf{r}_o = \frac{1}{N_v} \sum_{i=1}^{N_v} \mathbf{r}_i ; \tag{3}$$

where $\{\mathbf{r}_i\}$ denote points inside a pore.

The pore radius and the interface width scale as $R \sim s^{\nu}$ and $W \sim s^{\mu}$, respectively [26], with exponents $\nu = 0.49 \pm 0.02$ and $\mu = 0.50 \pm 0.03$. The exponent $d = 1 / \nu$, which is the fractal dimension of pores, is 2.05. This agrees with the prediction that d = 2 for unpercolated pores [27]. Within statistical error, we find the same values of ν and μ for porous silica at various densities between 1.7 and 1.4 g/cm^3.

Snapshots of pores in Fig. 4 reveal that there is a dramatic increase in the size of pores when the mass density is reduced to the critical value, ρ_c. Near ρ_c, we find that the density dependence of the average pore size is given by,

$$S_{av} = \frac{\sum_s s^2 n(s)}{\sum_s s\, n(s)} \sim |\rho - \rho_c|^{-\gamma} , \tag{4}$$

where n(s) is the number of s-clusters per site. The best fit for the MD results is obtained with ρ_c = 1.40 ± 0.04 and γ = 1.89 ± 0.15. The latter is close to the universal value (= 1.8) for percolation in three dimensions [27].

In Fig. 5 (a) we show one of the surfaces of the percolating pore. The roughness of this fracture surface is calculated from the height-height correlation function, $g(\sigma)$ [28]:

$$g(\sigma) = \left\langle [h(y+y_0, z+z_0) - h(y_0, z_0)]^2 \right\rangle^{1/2} \; ; \; \sigma = (y^2 + z^2)^{1/2}, \qquad (5)$$

where h(y, z) is the highest vertical coordinate at the point (y, z). The dependence of the height-height correlation function on the in-plane distance σ is characterized by two regimes separated by the correlation length ξ: For $\sigma < \xi$, $g(\sigma) \propto \sigma^\alpha$; and for $\sigma > \xi$ the heights become uncorrelated and $g(\sigma)$ tends to $\sqrt{2}(\langle h^2\rangle - \langle h\rangle^2)^{1/2}$. Figure 5 (a) shows that the MD results for $g(\sigma)$ are well-described by the relation, $g(\sigma) \sim \sigma^\alpha$ with α = 0.87 ± 0.02 for σ < 100 Å. Experimental measurements on bakelite, concrete, steel, and aluminum alloys indicate that the roughness exponent α has a universal value 0.8 [20]. (Simulations of random fuse models [29] and two-dimensional Lennard-Jones system [30] also obtain α = 0.8.) The MD results for the roughness exponent agree with experimental measurements, thus lending further support to claims that the roughness exponent of fracture surfaces is a material-independent quantity. Furthermore, the MD results indicate that the universality of the roughness exponent may prevail even at length scales ≤ 10 nm.

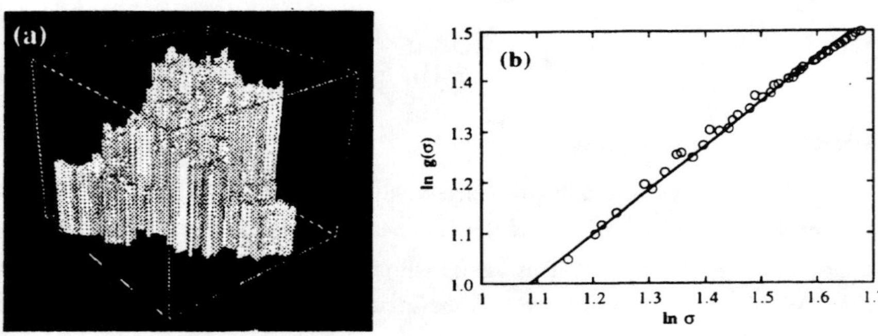

Fig. 5: (a) Snapshot of a fracture surface resulting from a percolating pore in silica glass at a mass density of 1.4 g/cm³. (b) Height-height correlation function (open circles) versus the in-plane distance, σ, for the fracture surface shown in (a). The solid curve is the best fit, $g(\sigma) \sim \sigma^\alpha$, with $\alpha = 0.87 \pm 0.02$ for $\sigma < 100$ Å.

6. Conclusion

The multiresolution MD algorithm is applicable for large-scale simulations with realistic interatomic potential including the long-range Coulomb and three-body potentials. Multimillion particle simulations take only a few second per step on advanced parallel computers such as the Intel Touchstone Delta and the IBM SP1. Large-scale MD simulations reveal that during uniform dilation of silica glasses pores are "all skin and no flesh" ($R \sim \sqrt{s}$ and $W \sim \sqrt{s}$) [31]. When the density of the system is reduced to a critical density, the cātastrophic growth of the largest pore causes fracture in the system. The roughness exponent of resulting fracture surfaces is close to the experimental value (0.8) for many ductile and brittle materials.

7. Acknowledgment

We would like to thank Dr. R. Pandey for stimulating discussions. This work was supported by the U.S. Department of Energy, Grant No. DE-FG05-92ER45477. A part of these simulations were performed on the 128-node IBM SP1 computer at Argonne National Laboratory and the 512-node Intel Touchstone Delta at Caltech. The computations were also performed on the Intel iPSC/860 in the Concurrent Computing Laboratory for Materials Simulations (CCLMS) at Louisiana State University. The facilities in the CCLMS were acquired with the Equipment Enhancement Grants awarded by the Louisiana Board of Regents through Louisiana Education Quality Support Fund (LEQSF).

8. References

1. J. M. Drake and J. Klafter, Physics Today **43**, 46 (1990).
2. J. Fricke, J. Non-Cryst. Solids **121**, 188 (1990); ibid. **147&148**, 356 (1992).
3. G. D. Stucky and J. E. MacDougall, Science **247**, 669 (1990).
4. See for instance, D. C. Rapaport, Comput. Phys. Commun. **62**, 217 (1991).
5. P. Vashishta, R. K. Kalia, J. P. Rino, and I. Ebbsjö, Phys. Rev. B **41**, 12197 (1990).
6. A. W. Appel, SIAM J. Sci. Stat. Comput. **6**, 85 (1985).
7. J. Barnes and P. Hut, Nature **324**, 446 (1986).
8. L. Greengard and V. Rokhlin, J. Comput. Phys. **73**, 325 (1987).
9. R. K. Kalia, S. W. de Leeuw, A. Nakano, and P. Vashishta, Comput. Phys. Commun. **74**, 316 (1993).
10. H.-Q. Ding, N. Karasawa, and W. A. Goddard, Chem. Phys. Lett. **196**, 6 (1992); J. Chem. Phys. **97**, 4309 (1992).

11. W. B. Streett, D. J. Tildesley, and G. Saville, Mol. Phys. **35**, 639 (1978).

12. R. K. Kalia, A. Nakano, D. L. Greenwell, P. Vashishta, and S. W. de Leeuw, Supercomputer **54 (X-2)**, 11 (1993).

13. A. Nakano, P. Vashishta, and R. K. Kalia, Comput. Phys. Commun. **77**, 302 (1993).

14. D. Frenkel, in *Simple Molecular Systems at Very High Density*, eds. A. Polian and P. Loubeyre (Plenum, New York, 1989) p. 411.

15. C. W. Gear, *Numerical Initial Value Problem in Ordinary Differential Equations* (Prentice-Hall, Englewood Cliffs, NJ, 1971).

16. F. Zhao and S. Lennart Johnsson, SIAM J. Sci. Stat. Comput. **12**, 1991 (1420).

17. L. Greengard and W. D. Gropp, in *Parallel Processing for Scientific Computing*, ed. G. Rodrigue (SIAM, Philadelphia, 1989) p. 213.

18. J. A. Board et al., Chem. Phys. Lett. **198**, 89 (1992).

19. M. Kardar, G. Parisi, and Y. C. Zhang, Phys. Rev. Lett. **56**, 889 (1986).

20. *Kinetics of Aggregation and Gelation*, eds. F. Family and D. P. Landau (North Holland, Amsterdam, 1984), and references therein.

21. E. Bouchaud, G. Lapasset, and J. Planès, Europhys. Lett. **13**, 73 (1990).

22. K. J. Måløy, A. Hansen, E. L. Hinrichsen, and S. Roux, Phys. Rev. Lett. **68**, 213 (1992).

23. V. Y. Milman, R. Blumenfeld, N. A. Stelmashenko, and R. C. Ball, Phys. Rev. Lett. **71**, 204 (1993).

24. First MD simulations on porous silica were performed by J. Kieffer and C. A. Angell, J. Non-Cryst. Solids **106**, 336 (1988).

25. A. Nakano, L. Bi, R. K. Kalia, and P. Vashishta, Phys. Rev. Lett. **71**, 85 (1993).

26. M. Plischke and Z. Rácz, Phys. Rev. Lett. **53**, 415 (1984).

27. D. Stauffer, *Introduction to Percolation Theory* (Taylor & Francis, London, 1985); R. Zallen, *The Physics of Amorphous Solids* (John Wiley & Sons, New York, 1983).

28. G. Palasantzas and J. Krim, Phys. Rev. B **48**, 2873 (1993).

29. A. Hansen, E. L. Hinrichsen, and S Roux, Phys. Rev. Lett. **66**, 2476 (1991).

30. F. F. Abraham, in this book.

31. B. B. Mandelbrot, *Fractals: Form, Chance, and Dimension* (Freeman, San Francisco, 1977).

Toward Teraflop Computing and New Grand Challenge Applications
ISBN-1-56072-247-9

THE DESIGN OF BIOMOLECULES USING NEURAL NETWORKS AND THE DOUBLE ITERATED KALMAN FILTER

Ruth Pachter, James A. Lupo, Steven F. Fairchild, Robert L. Crane, and W. Wade Adams
Wright Laboratory, Materials Directorate, Wright-Patterson Air Force Base, Ohio 45433

ABSTRACT

In our continuing efforts towards the design of nonlinear optical chromophore containing polypeptides, an integrated computational approach has been developed. The design of chromophore containing biomolecular materials with defined secondary and tertiary structures by means of novel predictive tools is reported, while the effects of the nonlinear optical chromophores would then be studied with molecular dynamics simulations. A neural network is trained to predict the spatial proximity of C-alpha atoms that are less than a given threshold apart, while the double-iterated Kalman filter (DIKF) technique (coded in PROTEAN2) is then employed with a constraints set that includes these pairwise atomic distances, and the distances and angles that define the structure as it is known from the protein's sequence. The results for test cases demonstrate that this integrated approach is useful for molecular structure prediction at an intermediate resolution. The PROTEAN2 code has been ported to the Thinking Machines Incorporated CM-5 and the multiprocessor Cray C-90, and timing comparisons are discussed, particularly with the same models in the autotasking (multiprocessor) mode on a CRAY C90. While small molecular models were found to run much faster on the C90 than on the CM5, the CM5 surpassed the C90 on larger models.

1. INTRODUCTION

Chromophore containing biomolecules may be well-suited for use as nonlinear optical materials [1,2,3,4], enabling the flexibility of controlling structure at the tertiary or even quaternary level, thus providing temporal stability through packing phenomena. For example, the rod-like coiled-coil structures are of interest for such an application, although other biopolymers may be of importance. In the first stage, an expert system was used to develop the training set consisting of specific protein structures obtained from the Brookhaven Protein Data Base (PDB), with the data files being preprocessed to extract the backbone atomic coordinates and calculate the appropriate torsion angles. Secondary structural motifs are determined by searching for sequential residues whose torsions fall within a user defined tolerance. A neural network then learns to predict secondary structure [5,6], but moreover the spatial proximity of C-alpha atoms. The DIKF [7] algorithm is subsequently employed to elucidate the structure using a data set that includes these pairwise atomic distances, and the distances and angles that define the chemistry and stereochemistry of the molecular structure. It is notable that the neural network constraints set was found to be adequate compared to modeling with an exhaustive set of all C-alpha pair distances derived from the crystal structure of Crambin [8].

2. METHODS

2.1 Neural Networks

Neural networks are trained on the dependence between the amino acid sequence and the distance relation between proximate C-alpha 's in the polypeptide backbone. Tertiary structure information is generated in the form of binary distance constraints between the C-alpha atoms, being 1 if their distance is less than a given threshold, and 0 otherwise. The proteins used in the training set were the first 48 of the set collected by Kabsch and Sander [9], while several of the last sixteen proteins in this set were used for testing (total of 8315 residues). A feed forward neural network with one hidden layer was used, and backpropagation was the learning algorithm. Details of the this neural network application are described elsewhere [10].

2.2 Double-Iterated Kalman Filter

The structural molecular model of a polypeptide consisting of N atoms is described by the mean cartesian coordinates (so-called state vector **x**), and the covariance matrix **C(x)**, that contains the dependence of atomic coordinates on one another based on the known constraints. The elements of **C** for any two atoms i, j are symmetric:

$$C(x_{ij})= \begin{matrix} \sigma_{xixj} \sigma_{xiyj} \sigma_{xizj} \\ \sigma_{yixj} \sigma_{yiyj} \sigma_{yizj} \\ \sigma_{zixj} \sigma_{ziyj} \sigma_{zizj} \end{matrix} \quad (1)$$

The matrices on the diagonal of the covariance matrix $[C(x_{ii})]$ describe the extent of three-dimensional uncertainty in the position of the i-th atom, and the covariance between two variables (the matrices on the off-diagonal of the covariance matrix) estimates their correlation.

Distance and dihedral angle measurements **z** are represented by:

$$\mathbf{z} = \mathbf{h(x)} + \mathbf{v} \quad (2)$$

where $\mathbf{z}$ is the observed value of the data, $\mathbf{h}(\mathbf{x})$ expresses the mathematical relationship between the state vector variables and the observed data value, and $\mathbf{v}$ represents the variance of the data.

Given this information, a sequential linear estimator for the minimum variance estimate of the state is obtained by the extended Kalman filter for non-linear measurement functions [7]:

$$\mathbf{x}(+) = \mathbf{x}(-) + \mathbf{K}\ \{\mathbf{z} - \mathbf{h}(\mathbf{x}(-))\};\ \mathbf{C}(+) = \mathbf{C}(-) - \mathbf{K}\ \mathbf{H}\ \mathbf{C}(-) \tag{3}$$

where (-) signifies a previous structural representation, to be sequentially updated (+).

The criterion for the choice of the Kalman estimator gain matrix $\mathbf{K}$:

$$\mathbf{K} = \mathbf{C}(-)\ \mathbf{H}^{T}\ \{\mathbf{H}\ \mathbf{C}(-)\mathbf{H}^{T} + \mathbf{v}\}^{-1} \tag{4}$$

is to minimize a weighted scalar sum of the diagonal elements of the error covariance matrix $\mathbf{C}$. The term within the inverse in the expression for $\mathbf{K}$ represents the variance of the observed measurement ($\mathbf{C}(\mathbf{z}) = \mathbf{C}(\mathbf{h}(\mathbf{x})) + \mathbf{v}$). The first-order Taylor approximation of $\mathbf{C}(\mathbf{h}(\mathbf{x}))$ is $\mathbf{HCH}^{T}$, where $\mathbf{H}$ is the derivative of the data model, $\mathbf{h}$, and $\mathbf{H}^{T}$ is the transpose of $\mathbf{H}$. The derivatives of the distance model are calculated analytically, while the derivatives of the dihedral angle data model are approximated by using a finite difference calculation. Note that in addition to the optimality of $\mathbf{K}$ contained in its structure, it can also be seen as the 'ratio' between the uncertainty in the estimate and that of the measurement.

The extended Kalman filter approach is used to obtain higher-order non-linear filters by an iterative procedure :

$$\mathbf{x}(+)_{k} = \mathbf{x}(-) + \mathbf{K}_{k}\ \{\mathbf{z} - [\mathbf{h}(\mathbf{x}(+)_{k-1}) + \mathbf{H}(\mathbf{x}(-) - \mathbf{x}(+)_{k-1})]\} \tag{5}$$

with a similar expression for $\mathbf{C}(+)_{k}$ for any iteration k. This iterative procedure is carried out for each one of the distance and dihedral angle constraints. However, since the filter is not optimal in the non-linear case ($\mathbf{h}(\mathbf{x})$ in equation (1)), residual inaccuracies may still result. Therefore, the mean positions obtained after all data are introduced are used for another cycle (l) of updating. The covariance matrix is re-set to its initial large value in order to allow the atoms freedom to move in response to the constraints, and all measurements are re-introduced into the system for each of these doubly-iterated cycles. The successive l cycles are repeated until all of the constraints are satisfied to within a pre-set threshold of standard deviations for the error $\mathbf{e}$:

$$\mathbf{e} = (\mathbf{h}(\mathbf{x}_{final}) - \mathbf{z}) / \sqrt{\mathbf{v}}. \tag{6}$$

The DIKF technique has been extensively tested and analyzed, indicating that a known structure can be reproduced with the DIKF algorithm to within a small RMS error, even when a limited (ca. 20% of all possible interatomic distances) data set is used [11,12,13]. Several applications using NMR NOE data utilizing this novel method proved the approach successful [14,15,16,17,18].

3. COMPUTATIONAL DETAILS

The PROTEAN2 code written in FORTRAN 77 [19] is heavily dependent on basic linear algebra routines. The routines are encapsulated in a few small, well vectorized user written subroutines that made the program a good candidate for porting to the data parallel programming model used by FORTRAN 90 on the CM5. The user routines could be replaced with routines from the Connection Machine Scientific Support Library (CMSSL). Porting the code to the CM5 was undertaken as a three step process. First, the speedup potential was analyzed by benchmarking the PROTEAN2 linear algebra subroutines against the optimized subroutines in the CM Scientific Support Library (CMSSL). A simple test problem using square arrays and vectors dimensioned to 1024 was created. The CMSSL routines ran this test 17 times faster than the equivalent PROTEAN2 routines on a single Cray X-MP cpu (this test was performed prior to gaining access to the C90). The FORTRAN 77 code was than translated with the assistance of the CMAX utility, further modified by hand, and then tested for correctness. The 'brute force' translation ran nearly 238 times slower on the CM5 than it did on the X-MP. Once correct results were obtained, the PROTEAN2 linear algebra routines were replace with CMSSL routines, requiring some adjustment to the code's internal data structures. Note that accessing multiple processors on the C90 is achieved by compiling the program with the autotasking option. An environment variable is then set to specify how many processors to use at run time.

It is important to note that numerical accuracy and stability are of interest in computational studies, in addition to the usual emphasis on good speedup performance. Slight changes in the results can be expected for the same code run on different machines due to differences in precision and floating point operations on the various hardware platforms. Moreover, the division of work among processors may subtly change the order of operations and introduce accuracy problems due to round-off error. To investigate possible numerical effects, the results from runs made with various numbers of nodes were compared.

4. RESULTS AND DISCUSSION

The neural network results for Crambin [10] were used for the application with the DIKF. The model system consisted of 327 atoms and pseudo-atoms, 1122 distance constraints, including bond lengths, distances implied by bond angles, non-bonded distances within well-defined secondary structural motifs, and 37 dihedral angle constraints. The input to the PROTEAN2 program [19] is automated [20]. Good convergence was obtained, and a comparison with the experimental X-ray structure [8] results in total all-atom average RMS of 2.4Å [10]. Similarly, we have tested the genetically engineered Eglin-C [21]. The model consists of 530 atoms, with 1689 distance and 87 dihedral constraints. A comparison with the experimental X-ray structure [23] results in total all-atom average RMS of 3.2Å [10]. These results indicate that such an integrated approach may be useful for an intermediate biomolecular structure prediction, to be further refined by energy minimization and molecular dynamics.

Further, two systems were used for benchmarking, particularly Eglin-C, and the *E. Coli trp* repressor (a 25 kD dimer) whose structure has been determined previously from NMR data using the DIKF [14,15,17]. This molecular system contains 1504 atoms, with 6014 constraints. The *trp* repressor model was tested on two C90 nodes, and on 128, 256, and 512 CM5 nodes, while Eglin-C was tested on two C90 nodes, and on 32, 128, and 256 CM5 nodes.

The timing statistics for the CM5 and those for the C90 are shown in Table 1. The data was gathered from internal timing instrumentation code, but is affected somewhat by system load on both machines. Clearly, the CM5 achieves much higher parallel efficiency than does the C90. For the *trp* repressor model, assuming perfect scaling, the C90 would require 11 nodes to equal the speed of the CM5. The poor scaling performance on the CM5, and the rapid increase in speed as compared to the C90, show the importance of electing the most efficient machine for a given problem.

Programs that are largely dependent on linear algebra routines, such as PROTEAN2, obviously benefit from the data parallel programming model on the CM5. However, until FORTRAN 90 compilers become standard on more machines, the code will remain unportable, and will have to be supported in FORTRAN 90 and FORTRAN 77 versions. The sequential version currently executes under any UNIX f77 compiler, but the FORTRAN 90 version is hardwired to the CM5 [22].

Table 1: Run Statistics for CM5 and C90 Jobs

Molecular System	Computer System	Number of Nodes	Parallel Efficiency	CPU a (sec)	Memory (MByte)
	CM5				
Eglin-C		32	(N/a)	449	132
		128	66%	436	230
		256	(NA)	492	384
Trp Repressor		128	82%	6799	944
		256	(NA)	7098	1065
		512	(NA)	8106	1372
	C90				
Eglin-C			46%	117	118
Trp Repressor			62%	12269	992

[a] Time required for machine to complete one iteration.

ACKNOWLEDGMENT

This research was supported in part by the Army Research Office contract number DAAL03-89-C-0038 with the University of Minnesota Army High Performance Computing Research Center (AHPCRC). The AHPCRC Thinking Machines Inc. CM5 timing results are based upon a beta version of the software and, consequently, is not necessarily representative of the performance of the full version of this software.

REFERENCES

1. B. F. Levine, C. G. Bethea, E. Wasserman, and L. Leenders, *J. Chem. Phys.* **68** (1978) 5042.

2. T. Ishii, T. Wada, A. Garito, H. Sasabe, and A. Yamada, *Mat. Res. Soc. Symp. Proc.* **175** (1990) 129.

3. T. Cooper, L. Natarajan, R. Strasser, R. Pachter, and R. Crane, *ACS Pol. Prep.* **33** (1992) 1018.

4. R. Pachter, T.M. Cooper, L.V. Natarajan, R.L. Crane, and W.W. Adams, Biopolymers **32** (1992) 1129.

5. L. H. Holley and G. Karplus, *Proc. Natl. Acad. Sci. U.S.A.* **86** (1988) 152, and references therein.

6. S.B. Fairchild, R. Pachter, R. Perrin, R.L. Crane, and W.W. Adams, presented at the American Crystallographic Association, Pittsburgh PA, August, 1992.

7. A. Gelb, "Applied Optimal Estimation", MIT Press, 1984.

8. M.M. Teeter, *Proc. Nat. Acad. Sci. USA* **81** (1984) 6014.

9. W. Kabsch and C. Sanders, *FEBS Letters*, May 1983.

10 R. Pachter, S.B. Fairchild, J.A. Lupo, R.L. Crane, and W.W. Adams, *Mat. Res. Soc. Symp. Proc.*, Fall 1993 meeting.

11. R. B. Altman and O. Jardetzky, *Methods in Enzymology* **177** (1989) 218.

12. R. Altman, R. Pachter, and O. Jardetzky, in "Protein Structure and Engineering", (O. Jardetzky, ed.), Plenum Press, New York, pp. 79 (1989).

13. R. Pachter, R. Altman, and O. Jardetzky, *J. Magn. Reson.* **89** (1990) 578.

14. C.H. Arrowsmith, R. Pachter, R. Altman, S.B. Iyer, and O. Jardetzky, *Biochemistry* **29** (1990) 6332.

15. R. Altman, C.H. Arrowsmith, R. Pachter, and O. Jardetzky, "Computational Aspects of the Study of Biological Macromolecules by NMR Spectroscopy" (J. C. Hoch, ed.) pp. 375, Plenum Press, New York (1991).

16. R. Pachter, R. Altman, J. Czaplicki, and O. Jardetzky, *J. Magn. Reson.* **92** (1991) 648.

17. C.H. Arrowsmith, R. Pachter, R. Altman, and O. Jardetzky, *FEBS Eur. J. Biochemistry* **202** (1991) 53.

18. R. Altman, R. Pachter, and O. Jardetzky, *J. Appl. Magn. Reson.* **4** (1993) 441.

19. R. Altman, R. Pachter, C.A. Carrara, and O. Jardetzky, O., PROTEAN2: QCPE **10**, 596 (2) (1990).

20. R. Pachter, programs: PROPARE, PROCON, PROCOPY, unpublished.

21. C.A. McPhalen and M.N.G. James, *Biochemistry* **27** (1988) 6582.

22. J. A. Lupo, unpublished results.

Toward Teraflop Computing
and New Grand
Challenge Applications

ISBN-1-56072-247-9

MOLECULAR DYNAMICS ON PARALLEL COMPUTERS: APPLICATIONS FOR THEORETICAL BIOPHYSICS

Thomas Bishop, Helmut Heller and Klaus Schulten
Beckman Institute and Departments of Chemistry and Physics,
University of Illinois at Urbana-Champaign,
405 North Matthews, Urbana, Illinois 61801 USA

Abstract

Molecular dynamics is a valuable aid for refining the observed structure of biopolymers, for understanding the structure–function relationship of biopolymers, and for the rational design of drugs. In order to accurately characterize biopolymers, it is often necessary to explicitly include solvent or other environments, namely water, ions or cellular membranes resulting in system sizes of tens of thousands of atoms. The resulting large systems can only be simulated on massively parallel computers.

A molecular dynamics program, EGO, has been developed to run on parallel computers in order to simulate large systems. EGO, which was written in OCCAM II and runs on transputers, has been used to conduct simulations of biologically significant systems. Two transputer systems, based on the INMOS T805 processor, have been employed for molecular dynamics: a custom built 60-node system and a Parsytec GCel-64 with 64-nodes. EGO has recently been rewritten in C to run under the machine–independent coordination languages Charm and PVM, so that simulations can be conducted on a workstation cluster.

The program EGO has been applied to simulations of a protein-DNA complex in a water envelope resulting in a system of 13,500 atoms. The simulations have required dedicated computational resources of one month per simulation. Results from the simulations indicate that the so–called DNA binding domain of the glucocorticoid receptor protein induces a bend of approximately 35° in the DNA.

1 INTRODUCTION

X-ray crystallographic techniques have revealed the structure of numerous biological structures. These techniques have been sufficiently developed so that larger and more complex systems, including bonded heterogeneous molecular structures, are becoming available. In fact any recent issue of *NATURE* is likely to contain a newly derived crystallographic structure of biological importance. These static views provide insight into the structural behavior of the molecules revealing common structural motifs that nature has exploited. However, there still exist experimental difficulties in crystallizing or analyzing a particular structure so that the structure analyzed is not necessarily the one of interest, and the crystalline environment may not be the native environment of the system being studied. This is definitely the case for biological systems in which membranes, water, and ions are abundant in the native environment. Molecular dynamics, which relies on an approximate initial conformation, is therefore a complementary tool for refining these systems and for investigating the dynamical degrees of freedom [7,27]. In particular by explicitly including lipids, water, and/or ions the molecular structure of interest may be refined in a natural environment, thus removing the effects of crystal packing. A major drawback of this approach is that the explicit inclusion of the environment significantly increases the number of particles for a given simulation, and, therefore, demands the most powerful computers available, namely parallel computers.

2 MOLECULAR DYNAMICS

2.1 Theory

Molecular dynamics is a classical approach to describe the time evolution of a system of atoms, which remains a valid approximation as long as no covalent chemical bonds are created or destroyed over the course of the simulation. (For a review of molecular dynamics principles see [1]) In this approach, Newton's equations of motion are numerically solved with each atom being represented as a point mass. The Verlet algorithm [39] is most often used for the numerical integration. The position, r_i , of atom i at time $t + \Delta t$ is determined by

$$\left.\begin{array}{rcl} r_i(t+\Delta t) & = & 2r_i(t) - r_i(t-\Delta t) + \mathbf{F}_i(t)\frac{(\Delta t)^2}{m_i} \\ \mathbf{F}_i(t) & = & -\nabla_i \mathbf{E}(r_1(t), \ldots r_N(t)) \end{array}\right\} \quad (1)$$

where $\mathbf{F}_i(t)$ denotes the force acting on the i-th atom, m_i and r_i denote the mass and position of the i-th atom, and N denotes the total number of atoms. ∇_i is the differential operator $(\frac{\partial}{\partial x_i}, \frac{\partial}{\partial y_i}, \frac{\partial}{\partial z_i})^T$. The accuracy of the Verlet algorithm is determined by the time step, Δt, which must be shorter than the fastest motion. The most rapid motion is due to the vibration of hydrogen atoms along covalent bonds which requires a time per integration step of 0.25 fs. This limit is many orders of magnitude below the time scales of relevant processes in biochemistry such that structural molecular dynamics simulations usually require about 10^6 integrations steps, and the resulting time scale accessible to molecular dynamics simulations is still short by a factor of 10^3 – 10^6 for many other important processes.

The total energy function(2) typically employed to describe the interactions between atoms consists of several components:

$$\mathbf{E} = \underbrace{\mathbf{E}_{\text{bond}} + \mathbf{E}_{\text{angle}} + \mathbf{E}_{\text{dihedral}} + \mathbf{E}_{\text{improper}}}_{\mathbf{E}_{\text{bonded}}} + \underbrace{\mathbf{E}_{\text{elec}} + \mathbf{E}_{\text{vdW}} + \mathbf{E}_{\text{hbond}}}_{\mathbf{E}_{\text{nonbonded}}} \quad (2)$$

The components of the total energy are broken down into two categories, the bonded and the nonbonded interactions. The bonded interactions describe interactions between atoms which are linked by covalent bonds and include: $\mathbf{E}_{\mathbf{bond}}$ to describe high frequency vibrations along covalent chemical bonds, $\mathbf{E}_{\mathbf{angle}}$ to describe bending motions between two adjacent bonds, $\mathbf{E}_{\mathbf{dihedral}}$ to describe torsional motion around a bond, and $\mathbf{E}_{\mathbf{improper}}$ to describe the planar orientation of one atom relative to three other atoms. The nonbonded interactions describe interactions between atoms which are not linked by covalent chemical bonds and include: $\mathbf{E}_{\mathbf{elec}}$ the pair-wise Coulomb energy between charged atoms, $\mathbf{E}_{\mathbf{vdW}}$ the pair-wise van der Waals energy, and $\mathbf{E}_{\mathbf{hbond}}$ the hydrogen bond energy. $\mathbf{E}_{\mathbf{elec}}$ is computationally the most expensive calculation since the long range nature involves all possible pairs of atoms in the system which results in the scaling of the computational requirements as $(N)^2$.

2.2 Implementation

The restriction to such short time steps and the large number of atoms typically involved in biological systems limits the total length of a simulation accessible to molecular dynamics. In fact molecular dynamics simulations conducted on high performance workstations are currently limited to a few thousand atoms and overall simulation periods of a few nanoseconds. These problems can be overcome by employing parallel computers and more advanced algorithms.

New algorithms have addressed the problem on two fronts. One front attemps to increase the time per integration step through implicit schemes, Langevin formulations, or constraining rapid degrees of freedom [28, 30, 38, 40]. The other front explicitly addresses the evaluation of the long range Coulomb interactions since it is computationally the most expensive calculation. Standard molecular dynamics practice is to incorporate a distance cut-off beyond which no Coulomb interactions are calculated, thus reducing the number of interactions which must be calculated for any given atom. An appropriate switching function must be incorporated so that the forces do not terminate abrubtly at the cut-off boundry. However, this implementation presents errors which become serious for systems containing significantly charged groups [8, 23], and as they exist in many biological systems, i.e., the phosphate groups of DNA or the charged head groups of membrane lipids. Hierarchical distance class methods [15, 16, 36] and multipole expansions [3, 14] are alternatives to distance cut-off methods. These approaches preserve the long range nature of the Coulomb interactions while not demanding unacceptable computational resources.

Hierarchical distance class methods are based on a spherical subdivision of interatomic distances into several distance classes. The relative motion of neighboring atoms, which will be grouped in the innermost distance class, will have the most influence on the direction and magnitude of the electrostatic forces and accordingly these forces are calculated at every step. Non-neighboring atoms, grouped in outer distance classes, will have a lesser influence on the direction and magnitude of the electrostatic forces so that these forces are updated less frequently. The reduced number of calculations for distant interactions results in a speed-up by a factor of six to ten without a significant loss of accuracy [16]. The *Fast Multipole Method* by Greengard and Rokhlin [14] is based on an approximate analytic solution of the Coulomb interactions that has also proven successful for molecular dynamics calculations conducted on high performance workstations [4], and is currently under development for parallel applications [13].

3 EGO

EGO [2, 18, 19] is a molecular dynamics package that is I/O compatible with the widely used molecular dynamics packages X-PLOR [9] and Charmm [6]. EGO was originally programmed in OCCAM II to utilize a system of transputers. Long range Coulomb interactions are accurately represented in EGO by implementing a distance class method [16] and parallelization is achieved by distributing the atoms among the computational nodes. Each node contains the required parameters for its "own" set of atoms, such as type, mass, charge and coordinates, while the atoms which reside on the other nodes are "external". The calculation of the pair-wise forces proceeds in two phases. In the first phase each node calculates in parallel with all the other nodes the pair-wise force between every atom of its "own" set. This phase requires no communication since all information about a node's "own" atoms is stored locally. In the second phase interactions between a node's "own" atoms and all "external" atoms are calculated. This phase requires communication between the nodes, and EGO has implemented a systolic double ring topology [17, 20, 31, 33] for the communication (see figure 1). The first ring consists of the host node and the network nodes, some of which may be exclusively devoted to hydrogen bonding calculations. The second ring contains only the network nodes which have not been set aside for hydrogen bonding calculations. For a transputer based machine in which every processor has four independent communication links the double ring topology is implemented as follows: the first ring is connected by two antiparallel unidirectional OCCAM II channels, while the second ring is connected using the two remaining links of each transputer. On other parallel platforms the hardware topology may not necessarily be configured as a ring, but the communication pattern remains essentially the same.

The first ring is used to send a copy of a node's "own" atoms to the neighboring node in a clockwise direction. When the "external" coordinates are received each node calculates a subset of the pair interactions between its "own" set and the "external" set of atoms. In the next communication step the "external" set of atoms is passed along the first ring in a clockwise direction to the next node. In this manner the individual sets of coordinates, one for each node, are simultaneously passed around the ring until each node receives back its "own" set. When each node receives back its "own" set of coordinates, every set has made a complete revolution around the ring, and therefore all pair-wise interactions have been computed.

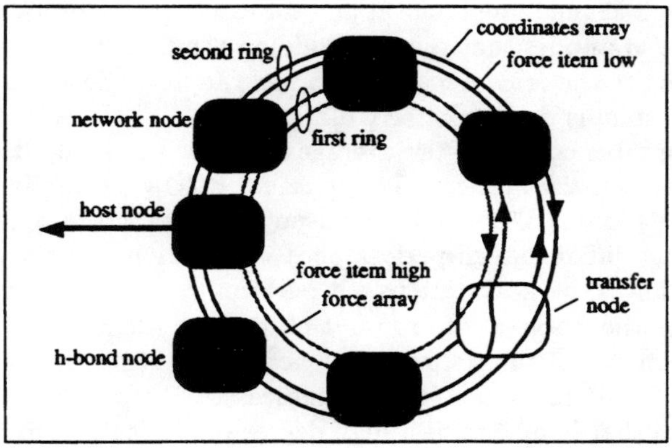

Figure 1:
Double ring topology of EGO. (Picture adapted from [19].)

Newton's third law of motion can be applied to cut the amount of computations in half but forces have to be communicated. Two kinds of force data are communicated, force items and force arrays. The force array is the result of the pair-wise interactions between "external" atoms and a node's "own" atoms. These forces are computed as soon as the "external" coordinates arrive. The force array is communicated entirely on the second ring and lags behind the coordinate array by one transfer step since forces can only be calculated after the coordinates are known. For a transputer implementation separate channels are used for the force array and the coordinate array since the channels can be operated in parallel.

Non-pair interactions involve three atoms(angle interactions) or four atoms(dihedral or improper interactions). The participating atoms may be located on several different nodes. In order to calculate these many-body interactions the necessary coordinates must be selected from the coordinates array as each set of "external" coordinates is passed around the ring and temporarily stored locally. When the complete set of coordinates necessary for a many-body interaction, up to four, has accumulated on the "owner's" node, the force is calculated. These forces are sent out one by one as force items to the nodes which "own" the atoms contributing to the interaction. The force item communication is done on two channels, which form topologically a spiral. One channel, the force item low channel, is on the first ring; the other channel, the force item high channel is on the second ring. New forces are entered on the force item low channel and each node listens on this channel to receive forces that it "owns". In order to avoid a possible deadlock situation in which all nodes are attempting to forward a force item but can not do so because an item is stuck in the channel, the force item high channel is introduced. The only operations on this channel are the forwarding of items and the removal of items belonging to the "owner". One and only one node passes information from the force item low to the force item high channel, so that forces on the the first ring spiral into the second. Since the only operations on the force item high channel are removal and forwarding of information, it can never deadlock. This also implies that the one node on the force item low channel which passes information to the force item high channel can never deadlock and guarantees that the whole system is deadlock free [10].

The following table compares the average run time per integration step of EGO to X-PLOR for various size systems. The times for EGO were obtained on a Parsytec GCel containing 64 Inmos T805 30Mhz transputers. Two sets of times were obtained for X-PLOR using different high-performance workstations. For small systems and short cut-off distances the workstations out perform the transputer system; however, for larger systems the workstations run out of memory (denoted by err) and cannot match the performance of the transputer. The number of nodes exclusively devoted to the hydrogen bond calculation are also indicated. Performance analysis of EGO has demonstrated that it maintains a high degree of efficiency throughout the simulation [35].

number of atoms	HP-735 64Mb			SGI R4400-150Mhz 80Mb			Parsytec GCel 64 nodes 4Mb per node
cut-off	9Å	19Å	29Å	9Å	19Å	29Å	
1,175	0.48	1.29	1.86	1.63	6.01	8.39	4.98(5 h–bond nodes)
7,475	2.8	16.49	err	12.53	68.26	163.81	9.20(3 h–bond nodes)
13,566	8.52	err	err	28.67	179.62	err	25.13(3 h–bond nodes)

4 APPLICATION

EGO has been used to conduct molecular dynamics simulations of a specific domain of the glucocorticoid receptor interacting with DNA. The glucocorticoid receptor is a member of a family of proteins that regulate transcriptional activity within specific cells. The complete regulatory mechanism is not fully understood although it is known that the receptor must recognize and bind a particular sequence of DNA. For a review of this class of hormone receptors see [32]. The proteins in this family of receptors are called steroid hormone receptors and are responsible for the development and differentiation of a wide range of tissues which include: skin, bone, behavioral centers in the brain, and secondary reproductive tissues. The steroid hormones which activate the receptors include: glucocorticoids, estrogens, progestins, androgens, mineralcorticoids, ecdysteroids, vitamin D, RAR and thyroid hormone [12,22,26].

The X-ray crystallographic structure in [24] was used as the starting point for our molecular dynamics investigation. This structure was modified to remove additional base pairs from the DNA which had been added to enhance crystal formation. This modification restored the oligonucleotide to the naturally occurring sequence that the glucocorticoid receptor binds. Test simulations were then conducted on the system in vacuum. Results indicated that the protein–DNA system in vacuum was not stable; therefore, water was added to the system. The instability of DNA in vacuum agrees with other simulations of DNA [5, 11, 37], and with the fact that the conformation of DNA is dependent on the environment [34]. The necessity of including explicit waters resulted in a rather large system size of approximately 13,500 atoms. Using the 64 nodes of a Parsytec GCel-64 required approximately one month of run time to complete a 90 ps simulation. The results indicate that the protein induces a bend in the DNA of approximately 35° which agrees with results obtained from gel-mobility shift assay studies of the estrogen receptor complex [29, 25]. The estrogen receptor is also a member of the steroid hormone receptor family and has a high degree of structure and sequence homology with the glucocorticoid receptor. In addition to the bending, several energetically favorable contacts between protein and DNA have been identified which were not observed in the crystallographic study [24].

5 DISCUSSION

Since parallel computers have proven to be an efficient and effective means of addressing the issues of large scale simulations, EGO has been rewritten in C to run under the machine-independent coordinate languages Charm and PVM. Charm is being developed by researchers at the University of Illinois to run on a variety of parallel platforms [21]. Once tested and verified for accuracy Charm-EGO and PVM-EGO will be available by anonymous ftp as a tool for investigating biological structures. This comes at a significant time since crystallographic structures of exciting biological systems are being determined regularly. The particular application mentioned in this article demonstrates the success and significance of molecular dynamics in bridging the gap between crystallographic data, which reveals a static all atom structure and macroscopic data, such as gel-mobility shift assay which reveals global structure without any atomic detail.

REFERENCES

[1] M. P. Allen and D. J. Tildesley. *Computer Simulation of Liquids.* Oxford University Press, New York, 1987.

[2] Brad Banko and Helmut Heller. User manual for EGO — Release 1.1. Beckman Institute Technical Report TB-92-07, University of Illinois, 1991.

[3] J. E. Barnes and P. Hut. A hierarchical O(N logN) force calculation algorithm. *Nature*, 324:446, 1986.

[4] John A. Board, Jr., J. W. Causey, James F. Leathrum, Jr., Andreas Windemuth, and Klaus Schulten. Accelerated molecular dynamics simulation with the parallel fast multipole algorithm. *Chem. Phys. Lett.*, 198:89–94, 1992.

[5] Klaus Boehncke, Marco Nonella, and Klaus Schulten. Molecular dynamics investigation of the interaction between DNA and dystamycin. *Biochemistry*, 30:5465–5475, April 1991.

[6] Bernard R. Brooks, Robert E. Bruccoleri, Barry D. Olafson, David J. States, S. Swaminathan, and Martin Karplus. CHARMm: a program for macromolecular energy, minimization, and dynamics calculations. *J. Comp. Chem.*, 4(2):187–217, 1983.

[7] Charles L. Brooks III, M. Karplus, and B. M. Pettitt. *Proteins: A Theoretical Perspective of Dynamics, Structure and Thermodynamics.* John Wiley & Sons, New York, 1988.

[8] Charles L. Brooks III, B. Montgomery Pettitt, and Martin Karplus. Structural and energetic effects of truncating long range interactions in ionic and polar fluids. *J. Chem. Phys.*, 83(11):5897–5908, December 1 1985.

[9] Axel T. Brünger. *X-PLOR.* The Howard Hughes Medical Institute and Department of Molecular Biophysics and Biochemistry, Yale University, New Haven, CT, May 1988.

[10] William J. Dally and Charles L. Seitz. The torus routing chip. *Distributed Computing*, 1:187–196, 1986.

[11] Mats A. L. Eriksson and Aattoo Laaksonen. A molecular dynamics study of conformational changes and hydration of left-handed d(CGCGCGCGCGCG) in a nonsalt solution. *Biopolymers*, 32:1035–1059, 1992.

[12] R. M. Evans. The steroid and thyroid hormone receptor superfamily. *Science*, 240:889–895, 1988.

[13] L. Greengard and W. D. Gropp. A parallel version of the fast multipole method. Technical report, Rept. YALEU/DCS/RR-640, 1988.

[14] L. Greengard and V. Rohklin. A fast algorithm for particle simulation. *J. Comp. Phys.*, 73:325–348, 1987.

[15] Helmut Grubmüller. Dynamiksimulation sehr großer makromoleküle auf einem parallelrechner. Master's thesis, Physik-Dept. der Tech. Univ., Munich, Germany, 1989.

[16] Helmut Grubmüller, Helmut Heller, Andreas Windemuth, and Klaus Schulten. Generalized Verlet algorithm for efficient molecular dynamics simulations with long-range interactions. *Molecular Simulation*, 6:121–142, 1991.

[17] Helmut Heller. *Simulation einer Lipidmembran auf einem Parallelrechner*. PhD thesis, Technical University of Munich, Germany, December 1993.

[18] Helmut Heller, Helmut Grubmüller, and Klaus Schulten. Molecular dynamics simulation on a parallel computer. *Molecular Simulation*, 5:133–165, 1990.

[19] Helmut Heller and Klaus Schulten. Parallel distributed computing for molecular dynamics: Simulation of large heterogeneous systems on a systolic ring of transputers. *Chemical Design Automation News (CDA News)*, 7(8):11–22, August 1992.

[20] W. D. Hillis and J. Barnes. Programming a highly parallel computer. *Nature*, 326:27, 1987.

[21] L. V. Kale. The chare kernel parallel programming language and system. In *Proc. of the International Conf. on Parallel Processing*, volume 2, pages 17–25, 1990.

[22] Vincent Laudet, Catherine Hänni, Jean Coll, Francois Catzeflis, and Dominique Stéhelin. Evolution of the nuclear receptor gene superfamily. *EMBO J.*, pages 1003–1013, 1992.

[23] Richard J. Loncharich and Bernhard R. Brooks. The effects of truncating long-range forces on protein dynamics. *Proteins: Structure, Function, and Genetics*, 6:32–45, 1989.

[24] B. F. Luisi, W. X. Xu, L. P. Freedman, K. R. Yamamoto, and P. B. Sigler. Crystallographic analysis of the interaction for the glucocorticoid receptor with DNA. *Nature*, 352:497–505, 1991.

[25] G. Redeuith M. Sabbah, S. Le Ricousse and E. Baulieu. Estrogen receptor-induced bending of the xenopus vitellogenin A2 gene hormone response element. *Biochemical and Biophysical Research Communications*, 185(3):944–952, 1992.

[26] Ernest Martinez, Francoise Givel, and Walter Wahli. A common ancestor DNA motif for invertebrate and vertebrate hormone response elements. *EMBO J.*, 10:263–268, 1991.

[27] J. A. McCammon and S. C. Harvey. *Dynamics of Proteins and Nucleic Acids*. Cambridge University Press, Cambridge, 1987.

[28] S. Miyamoto and P. A. Kollman. SETTLE: An analytical version of the SHAKE and RATTLE algorithm for rigid water models. *J. Comp. Chem.*, 13:952, 1992.

[29] Ann M. Nardulli and David J. Shapiro. Binding of the estrogen receptor DNA-binding domain to the estrogen response element induces DNA bending. *Molecular and Cellular Biology*, 12:2037–2042, 1992.

[30] A. M. Nyberg and T. Schlick. On increasing the time step in molecular dynamics. *Chem. Phys. Lett.*, 198:538, 1992.

[31] N. S. Ostlund and R. A. Whiteside. A machine architecture for molecular dynamics: the systolic loop. In B. Venkataraghavan and R. J. Feldman, editors, *Macromolecular Structure and Specificity: Computer-Assisted Modeling and Applications*, pages 195–208. Annals of the NY Acad. of Sciences 439, New York, 1985.

[32] M. G. Parker, editor. *Nuclear Hormone Receptors*. Academic Press, San Diego, CA, 1991.

[33] A. R. C. Raine, David Fincham, and W. Smith. Systolic loop methods for molecular dynamics simualtion using multiple transputers. *Comput. Phys. Commun.*, 55:13–30, 1989.

[34] Wolfram Saenger, editor. *Principles of Nucleic Acid Structure*. Springer–Verlag, New York, NY, 1984.

[35] Amitabh Sinha, Helmut Heller, and Klaus Schulten. Performance analysis of a parallel molecular dynamics program. *Comput. Phys. Commun.*, 1994. In press. [Beckman Institute Technical Report TB-92-13].

[36] W. B. Streett, D. J. Tildesley, and G. Saville. Multiple time-step methods in molecular dynamics. *Mol. Phys.*, 35(3):639–648, 1978.

[37] S. Swaminathan, G. Ravishanker, and D. L. Beveridge. Molecular dynamics of B–DNA including water and counterions: A 140–ps trajectory for d(CGCGAATTCGCG) based on the GROMOS force field. *J. Am. Chem. Soc.*, 113:5027–5040, 1992.

[38] W. F. van Gunsteren. Constrained dynamics of flexible molecules. *Mol. Phys.*, 40(4):1015–1019, 1980.

[39] Loup Verlet. Computer 'experiments' on classical fluids: I. Thermodynamical properties of Lennard-Jones molecules. *Physical Review*, 159(1):98–103, July 1967.

[40] Guihua Zhang and Tarmar Schlick. LIN: A new algorithm to simulate the dynamics of biomolecules by combining implicit-integration and normal mode techniques. *J. Comp. Chem.*, 1993. In press.

Toward Teraflop Computing
and New Grand
Challenge Applications

ISBN-1-56072-247-9

PHONONS IN SOLID C_{60} AND GRAPHITIC TUBULES

Jin Yu, Lingsong Bi, Rajiv K. Kalia, and Priya Vashishta

Concurrent Computing Laboratory for Materials Simulations
Department of Physics and Astronomy, Department of Computer Science
Louisiana State University, Baton Rouge, LA 70803-4001

ABSTRACT

Using a unified interaction model which consists of a tight-binding potential for the intramolecular interaction and a Lennard-Jones and bond charge model for the intermolecular interaction, phonon dispersion and density of states of solid C_{60} have been calculated in the energy range from 0 to 210 meV. The intermolecular phonon density of states shows peaks around 2.3 and 3.7 meV, and extends to 7.6 meV. Inter- and intramolecular phonons are well separated by a gap of nearly 22 meV. The intermolecular phonon modes show strong dispersion, so do the intramolecular modes with energy below 70 meV. The calculated phonon spectrum agrees very well with recent inelastic neutron scattering experiments. The effects of orientational disorder and pressure on the inter- and intramolecular phonons of solid C_{60} have been investigated. Intermolecular phonon modes are sensitive to orientational disordering which softens libron modes. Most Raman and infrared active modes show strong pressure dependence. Inter- and intramolecular phonon spectra at various pressures (up to 56 kbar) are presented and results are compared with the available experiments.

The phonon dispersion and density of states of graphitic tubules with various helicities and diameters have been studied by tight-binding molecular dynamics method (TBMD). Compared with graphite, phonon modes in tubules are softened by the curvature. Unique features of the graphitic tubule with special emphasis on the low frequency modes are discussed. Sound velocities in graphitic tubules have also been calculated as functions of tubule helicity and diameter. Effects of compressing and stretching on the phonon spectra and sound velocities of the graphitic tubules are also discussed.

1. INTRODUCTION

Over the past few years, tremendous effort has been made to understand the structure, orientational order, rotational dynamics, and inter- and intramolecular interactions in fullerite and their compounds.[1-9] It is now well established that upon crystallization, the centers of C_{60} clusters form a face-centered-cubic (*fcc*) crystal (a_0=14.2 Å) with the fullerene molecules rotating almost freely at room temperature. On cooling below 250 K, solid C_{60} undergoes a first order structural phase transition from an orientationally disordered *fcc* phase to an orientationally ordered simple cubic (*sc*) structure (a_0=14.05 Å) with four molecules per unit cell located on four different cubic sublattices having different orientations.[10]

Using a unified interaction model which consists of a tight-binding potential[11] for the intramolecular interaction and a Lennard-Jones and bond charge model[6] for the intermolecular interaction, we have investigated the vibrational spectra of solid C_{60}. Both the inter- and intramolecular phonon density of states and dispersion have been calculated for crystalline C_{60}.[12] Effects of orientational disorder on the lattice dynamics of solid C_{60} have been studied. The calculated phonon spectrum agrees very well with inelastic neutron-scattering experiments.[13,14]

Recently high-pressure studies of solid C_{60} have attracted considerable interests.[15-19] Since pressure is the only variable which allows the delicate and continuous tuning of the strength of the intermolecular potentials and rotational barriers which control the motions of the C_{60} molecules, detailed investigation of the effects of pressure in solid C_{60} both experimentally and theoretically would provide very useful and important information about the nature of the interaction in solid C_{60}. We report the result of our TBMD study of the pressure effect on the inter- and intramolecular phonon spectra of solid C_{60}, and compare our result with available experiments. The pressure dependence of sound velocities, elastic constants, bulk modulus and specific heat have also been studied.[20]

Most recently a new form of carbon -- graphitic tubule was discovered in carbon rods under arc discharge by high-resolution transmission-electron microscopy.[21] It is the fourth member of the carbon family with dimension of 1 (diamond in 3D, graphite in 2D, and fullerene in 0D). A microtubule has the form of a rolled graphitic sheet with a diameter of a few nanometers. The carbon atom hexagons on the tubule are usually arranged in a helical fashion about the tubule axis.

Due to the crystalline perfection, various possible helical structures, and the dimensionality as well as the high efficiency of production,[22] graphitic tubules may possess unusual mechanical, electronic and optical properties which may find considerable technological applications. Recent theoretical studies[23,24] have shown that the electronic properties of graphitic tubule strongly depend on its helical structure. It can be metallic or semiconducting which implies that the electronic property of graphitic tubule can be tuned by changing its geometric parameters.

Although intensive studies of the structure and the electronic properties of graphitic tubules have been carried out,[23-31] and the relationship between the structure symmetry and lattice dynamics of graphitic tubule have been discussed,[32,33] to the best of our knowledge, so far no detailed theoretical results of the phonon dispersion and density of states of graphitic tubules based on realistic models are available.

In this paper, we also report the results of a tight-binding molecular-dynamics (TBMD)[34-39] study of the phonon dispersion and density of states of graphitic tubules. It has been found that, compared with graphite, phonon modes in tubules are softened by the curvature. While overall the spectra of graphitic tubule resembles that of graphite, especially when the tubule diameter is large, unique features are present in the low-frequency part of the spectra (< 50 meV). These low-frequency modes, which are the signature of the tubule structure, are sensitive to the diameter and the helical arrangement. The nature of the modes are analyzed and detailed comparison with unrolled graphite sheet is carried out.

This paper is organized as the follows. In Sec. II, the tight-binding model for carbon (XWCH model)[11] and the unified interaction model[12] of solid C_{60} are briefly discussed. In Sec. III, the results of the phonon dispersion and density of states of solid C_{60} are presented. The effects of orientational disorder and pressure are discussed. The results of the phonon dispersion and density of states of graphitic tubules with various helicities and diameters are presented in Sec. IV. The effects of compressing and stretching on the phonon spectra of graphitic tubules are discussed. The sound velocities in graphitic tubules are calculated as functions of tubule diameter and helicity. A brief conclusion is given in Sec. V.

2. MODEL

Carbon is unique among all the elements in that it can form strong covalent bonds with various coordination numbers. Due to the quantum nature of the directional chemical bonding, the description of carbon system by a classical potential becomes inadequate. Although first-principles methods (local-density-functional theory) are available, at present time their applications are still limited to small systems (~100 particles) because of enormous computing resource needed for such calculations. For systems in the range of 200 to 500 atoms (800 to 2000 electrons), an alternative approach is the tight-binding approximation.

Recently, by fitting to the results of first-principles calculations of electronic band structure and volume-dependent binding energies of various crystalline carbon phases, Xu, Wang, Chen, and Ho have proposed a transferable tight-binding potential for carbon[11]. In an empirical tight-binding approximation, the carbon-carbon interaction energy can be written as

$$E = E_{bs} + E_{rep}, \qquad E_{bs}=\sum_{n}^{occ} < \psi_n | H_{tb} | \psi_n >.$$

The tight-binding Hamiltonian H_{tb} is constructed with a minimal basis of sp^3 orbitals:

$$H_{tb}=\sum_{i}\sum_{\alpha=s,p} \varepsilon_\alpha a^{+}_{i,\alpha} a_{i,\alpha}+\sum_{i,j}\sum_{\alpha,\beta=s,p} v_{\alpha,\beta}(r_{ij}) a^{+}_{i,\alpha} a_{j,\beta},$$

where the operator $a_{i,\alpha}$ annihilates an electron in orbital α at atom i. ε_s and ε_p are the on-site energies of s and p orbitals, respectively. The hopping integral, $v_{\alpha,\beta}(r_{ij})$ is assumed to scale as a function of the interatomic separation. E_{bs} is the band-structure energy. E_{rep} is a short-ranged repulsive potential energy representing the ion-ion repulsion and the correction to the double counting of the electron-electron interaction in E_{bs}. A detailed description of the XWCH tight-binding potential for carbon has been given by Xu *et al.*.[11]

Such a tight-binding potential model not only reproduces well the binding energies and bond lengths of the crystalline carbon with different coordination numbers, but also describes well the properties of several complex carbon systems far away from the ground state. These include micro-clusters, liquid, and amorphous carbon.[40] Therefore, this model should provide a good approximation for describing C_{60} and graphitic tubules.

Since the minimum separation (~3 Å) between any pair of atoms on different C_{60} clusters is large compared with the C-C covalent bond length (~1.4 Å), solid C_{60} can be regarded as a typical molecular crystal. This assumption is valid at least in the case that when the temperature and pressure are not too high. For a molecular crystal, the total energy is a sum of the intra- and intermolecular interaction energies.

In our unified approach, we use the XWCH model[11] to describe the intramolecular interaction and adapt a modified bond-bond charge model[6] for the intermolecular interaction in solid C_{60}. The interaction between molecules μ and ν is written as follows:

$$V(\mu,\nu)=\sum_{i,j=1}^{60} 4\varepsilon\left\{\left[\frac{\sigma}{|r_{i\mu}-r_{j\nu}|}\right]^{12}-\left[\frac{\sigma}{|r_{i\mu}-r_{j\nu}|}\right]^{6}\right\}+\sum_{m,n=1}^{90}\frac{q_m q_n}{|b_{m\mu}-b_{n\nu}|}\,\mathrm{erfc}\left(\frac{|b_{m\mu}-b_{n\nu}|}{b_0}\right)$$

where $\boldsymbol{r}_{i\mu}$, $\boldsymbol{b}_{m\mu}$ are the coordinates of the i-th C-atom and the m-th bond center of molecule μ, respectively. q_m is the effective charge of the m-th bond and a Coulomb interaction in conjunction with an error function is used to account for the interaction between bond charges. Parameters ε and q_L are determined by fitting to the lattice constant (a=14.05 Å) of the low temperature simple cubic structure and the bulk modulus (B=18 GPa) of solid C_{60}.[41] The parameters of the potential are: σ=3.407 Å, ε=2.8486 meV, b_0 =14.0 Å and q_L=0.30 $|e|$, where e is the electron charge. Because we use a different parametrization procedure, our arameters are slightly different from those used by Lu *et al.*.[6] In Lu *et al.*'s bond-charge model, the bulk modulus is calculated to be about 9.6 GPa,[42] which is much lower than the experimental measurement.[41] T. Yildirim and A. B. Harris[42] have shown that the atom-bond model of Sprik *et al.* [7] results in an even lower bulk modulus of about 8.7 GPa.

In this unified model, all the degrees of freedom of C_{60} molecule in solid are treated explicitly. This approach not only permits the calculation of the intermolecular phonon dispersion and density of states, but also predicts the modifications of the intramolecular vibrational modes when the molecules form a solid and when the solid is under pressure.

3. PHONON DISPERSION AND DENSITY OF STATES OF SOLID C_{60}

The phonon dispersion curves along some high symmetry directions in the first Brillouin zone are shown in Fig. 1. Since there are four C_{60} molecules per unit cell, there are 720 branches of dispersion curves. The lowest 24 branches correspond to the intermolecular phonon modes and the remaining higher-energy branches correspond to the intramolecular vibrational modes. Fig. 1 shows that intermolecular and intramolecular phonon modes are well separated by a large gap of about 22 meV. This validates the rigid-molecule approximation. Surprisingly, the intramolecular phonons also show significant dispersions, especially those with energy below 70 meV. For comparison, in Fig. 1 we have also plotted the vibrational spectrum of an isolated C_{60} molecule together with the symmetry notation and degeneracy calculated with the XWCH model.

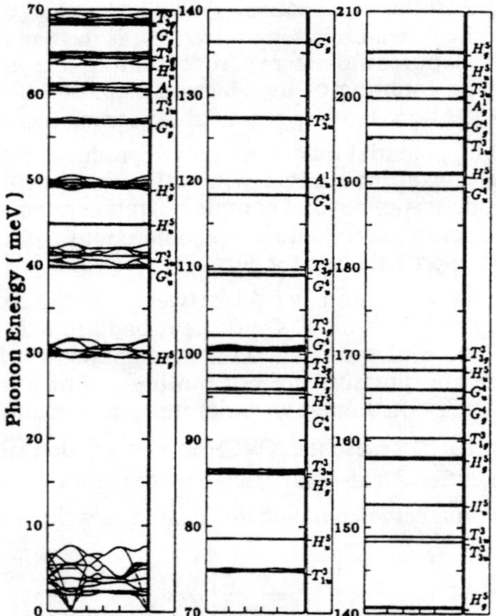

Figure 1. Phonon dispersion curves of solid C_{60} along some high symmetry directions in the first Brillouin zone and the vibrational frequencies of an isolated C_{60} molecule. (The symmetry of the C_{60} molecule is indicated by the icosahedral I_h group label, the number on the label's shoulder indicates the degeneracy of the corresponding group representation.)

In Fig. 2, the calculated intermolecular phonon dispersion and density of states are compared with the neutron scattering experiments.[13] The calculated intermolecular phonon density of states shows strong features around 2.3 and 3.7 meV. The highest intermolecular phonon mode is around 7.6 meV. The calculated phonon spectrum agrees very well with the experimental measurements.

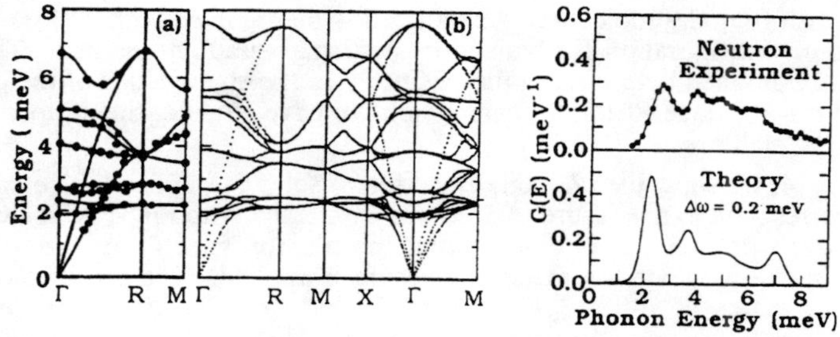

Figure 2. Comparison of the calculated intermolecular phonon dispersion and density of states of solid C_{60} with experiment measurements. (The experimental data are from Pintschovius et al. 1993)

3.1 Effect of Orientational Disorder

In a recent neutron diffraction experiment[43] on powder samples below T_c (250 K), there is evidence for two possible orientations of each C_{60} molecule. These orientations correspond to $\Gamma = \Gamma_1$ and $\Gamma = \Gamma_1 + 60° = \Gamma_2$ respectively, where $\Gamma_1 = 22°$. Here Γ is an orientation parameter. The probability that a molecule has an orientation Γ_1 is found to be 0.853, independent of the temperature as long as it is below 90 K.

To simulate the effect of the orientational disorder, we start with i molecules in the Γ_2 orientation and the remaining 4-i molecules in the unit cell in the Γ_1 orientation (the configuration is denoted by {4-i, i}, i = 0,1,2,3,4). This initial configuration is thermalized and then relaxed with the conjugate-gradient method. The configuration {4,0} is the ground state with $\Gamma = 23.45°$. The system with configuration {1,3} is found to be unstable and relaxes to the orientationally ordered ground state {4,0}. The configuration {0,4} initially with $\Gamma = 82°$ relaxes to a final configuration corresponding to $\Gamma = 70.54°$. In this configuration, hexagons and single (long) bonds of a C_{60} molecule face single bonds and hexagons of the nearest neighbor molecules, thereby maximizing bond-charge interactions.

We have calculated the phonon dispersion relation and density of states for each of the final configurations obtained by starting from the initial configuration {4,0}, {3,1}, {2,2} and {0,4}. In Fig. 3, we display the phonon density of states of the systems with different orientational orders: (a) {4,0}; (b) {3,1}; (c) {2,2}; and (d) {0,4}. Clearly, the intermolecular phonon spectrum is sensitive to the degree of orientational disordering which softens libron modes.

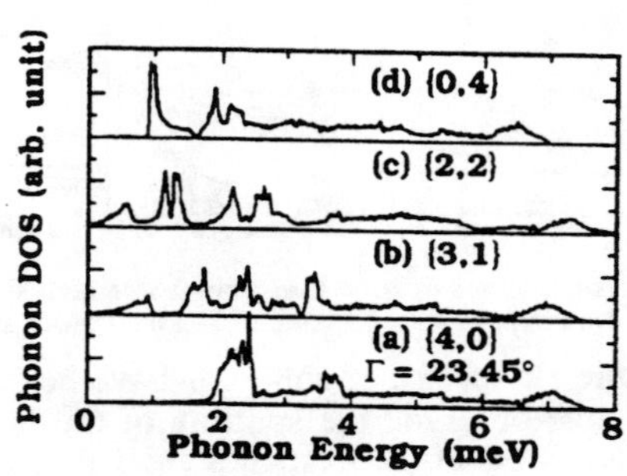

Figure 3. Intermolecular phonon density of states for four orientational configurations: (a) {4,0}; (b) {3,1}; (c) {2,2}; and (d) {0,4}.

3.2 Effect of Pressure

Using the unified model, we have calculated the phonon dispersion and density of states of solid C_{60} at various pressures. For a given pressure or a given lattice constant, the system with four C_{60} molecules per unit cell is thermalized with TBMD and then the final equilibrium configuration is obtained by conjugate gradient method. The stability of the system is examined by checking the positivity of the eigenvalues of the dynamical matrix. In the pressure range (0 to 56 kbar) which we have studied, the simple cubic structure is found to be stable.

In Fig. 4, we show the phonon dispersion of solid C_{60} with a lattice constant of 13.50 Å, which correspond to a pressure of 56 kbar. Compared with Fig. 1 which corresponds to the case of zero pressure, it is evident that the phonon spectra are broadened and shifted upward in energy when the external pressure is applied. The pressure dependent phonon density of states of solid C_{60} is shown in Fig. 5. The libron modes shift to higher frequencies with a rate about 0.05 meV/kbar (0.4 cm^{-1}/kbar). Intramolecular phonon modes also show strong pressure dependence. When pressure is applied, the lower frequency modes are broadened into bands, and the higher frequency modes are split and shifted toward higher energy. Intramolecular phonon modes shift toward higher frequencies with a rate up to 0.11 meV/kbar (0.88 cm^{-1}/kbar). Most Raman and IR active modes show strong pressure dependence. The high energy Raman (H_g) modes and the IR active (T_{1u}) modes are shifted upward and split into doublet or triplet. The splittings increase with increasing pressure.

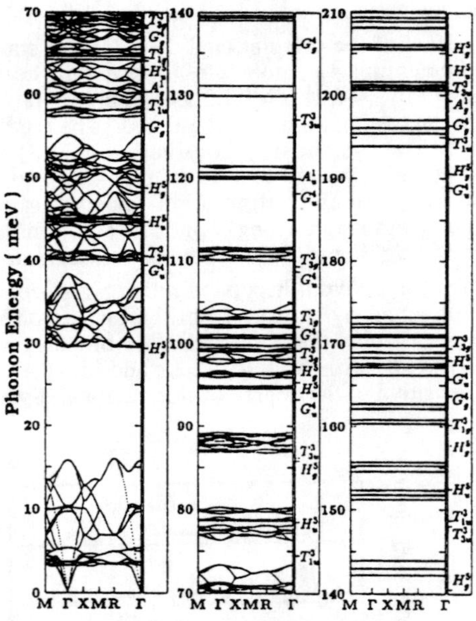

Figure 4. Phonon dispersion curves of solid C_{60} along some high symmetry directions in the first Brillouin zone when the system is under a pressure of 56 kbar (lattice constant a = 13.50 Å).

Recently high-pressure IR spectra of solid C_{60} have been measured up to 32 kbar by Huang *et al* .[15] They have observed the splitting of the IR active T_{1u} modes when the pressure is above 14 kbar. Most of the IR modes show positive pressure dependence with slope ranging from 0.25 to 0.44 cm^{-1}/kbar. Our theoretical calculation agrees reasonably well with the experimental observation.

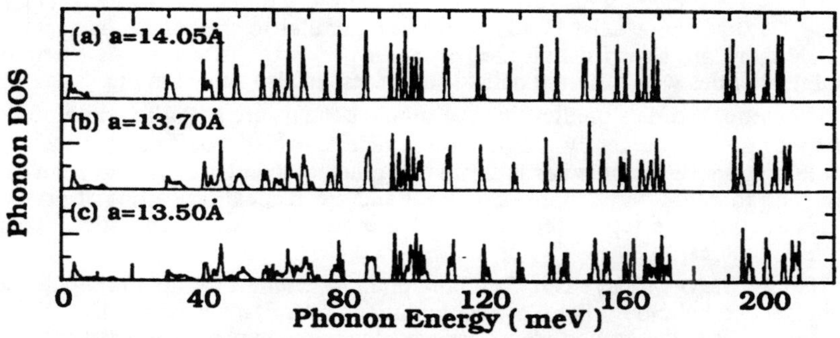

Figure 5. The intermolecular phonon density of states of solid C_{60} at different pressures. (a) p=0 kbar, a=14.05 Å; (b) p=26 kbar, a=13.70 Å; and (c) p=56 kbar, a=13.50 Å.

4. PHONON DISPERSION AND DENSITY OF STATES OF GRAPHITIC TUBULES

The structure of a graphitic tubule can be described by choosing two lattice points on a graphite sheet. Denoting a fixed lattice point by **O**(0,0), a specification of another lattice point, $\mathbf{R}_n(n_1,n_2)$, which will fold onto **O** uniquely defines the tubule structure. (See Fig.6). Alternatively, the lattice vector $\mathbf{R}_n$ or the index (n_1,n_2) can be used to specify the graphitic tubule. Here we denote it by $T(n_1,n_2)$ or $T(l_1,l_2)N$, where $n_1 = l_1 \cdot N$, $n_2 = l_2 \cdot N$, and N is the largest common divisor among n_1 and n_2. (l_1,l_2) determines the helicity of the tubule and N determines the rotational symmetry of the tubule (the tubule axis is a C_N axis). For a given vector $\mathbf{R}_n$ one can always find another vector $\mathbf{R}_m$ (m_1,m_2) such that $\mathbf{R}_n \cdot \mathbf{R}_m = 0$. For one-to-one correspondence, the parameters are confined by $n_1 \geq n_2 \geq 0$, and there is no common divisor among m_1 and m_2. $\mathbf{R}_n$ and $\mathbf{R}_m$ determine the tube diameter and the unit cell length of the tubule, respectively. The diameter (D), the length (L), and the number of carbon atoms (N_c) per unit cell are given by:

$$N_c = 2(n_1m_2 - n_2m_1) = 2N(l_1m_2 - l_2m_1),$$

$$D = \frac{|\mathbf{R}_n|}{\pi} = \frac{a}{\pi}\sqrt{n_1^2 + n_1n_2 + n_2^2}, \qquad L = |\mathbf{R}_m| = a\sqrt{m_1^2 + m_1m_2 + m_2^2},$$

where a is the lattice constant of the graphite, and (m_1,m_2) satisfy:

$$\frac{m_1}{m_2} = -\frac{n_1 + 2n_2}{2n_1 + n_2} = -\frac{l_1 + 2l_2}{2l_1 + l_2}.$$

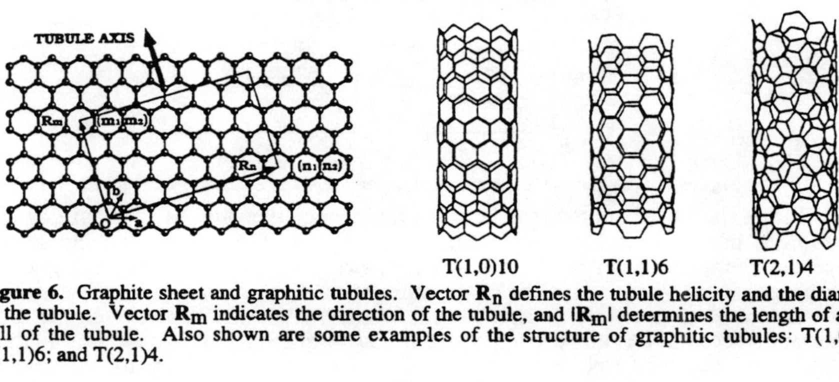

Figure 6. Graphite sheet and graphitic tubules. Vector $\mathbf{R}_n$ defines the tubule helicity and the diameter of the tubule. Vector $\mathbf{R}_m$ indicates the direction of the tubule, and $|\mathbf{R}_m|$ determines the length of a unit cell of the tubule. Also shown are some examples of the structure of graphitic tubules: T(1,0)10; T(1,1)6; and T(2,1)4.

Two special cases with simple helicity are the tubules: T(1,0)N and T(1,1)N. In the tubule T(1,0)N, there exist bonds which are parallel to the tubule axis, while in tubule T(1,1)N there are bonds which are perpendicular to the tubule axis. Some examples of graphitic tubules with different helical structures are also shown in Fig. 6.

Theoretical studies predict that the tubule T(1,1)N are metallic while others are semiconducting.[23,24] Recently magnetoresistance and Hall coefficient measurements on a bundle of graphite nanotubules indicate that graphitic tubules behave as semi-metals.[44] We focus our attention on phonons, structural and mechanical properties of graphitic tubules. In this section, we report the results of the phonon spectra and sound propagation in graphitic tubules.

Using TBMD we have calculated the phonon spectra of graphitic tubules with various diameters and helicities. For a given graphitic tubule, first we thermalize it with TBMD and then quench it to the ground-state configuration with the conjugate-gradient method. Once the ground-state configuration is obtained, the force matrix is directly constructed by numerically differentiating the forces calculated by the Hellmann-Feynman theorem.

The phonon dispersion relation and density of states of some graphitic tubules are shown in Figs. 7 and 8. To understand these helicity dependent phonon spectra, we have also calculated the phonon spectra of the corresponding unrolled graphite sheet with a finite width that is equal to the circumference of the tubule. There is a one-to-one correspondence of the phonon modes between the graphitic tubule and the finite unrolled graphite sheet. In a graphitic tubule, two acoustic modes with amplitudes perpendicular to the tubule axis become degenerate with a finite slop at Γ, while for the unrolled graphite, the acoustic modes are not degenerate and the lowest mode has a zero slop at Γ which corresponds to the translational motion perpendicular to the graphite plane. A finite number of peaks emerge from the low-frequency part of the spectrum of graphitic tubules, which is mainly due to the real periodic boundary condition around the tubule circumference. These lower-frequency modes are mainly radial modes including the breath mode. The higher-frequency modes correspond to the tangent modes. For a graphitic tubule with N_c particle per unit cell, there are $3N_c$ modes. Among them 4 modes have vanishing frequency at Γ, corresponding to 3 translational modes and one rotational mode (about the tubule axis). There are $(3N_c+6)/2$ distinct nonvanishing vibrational frequencies at Γ, among them 10 modes are nondegenerate and others are double degenerate.

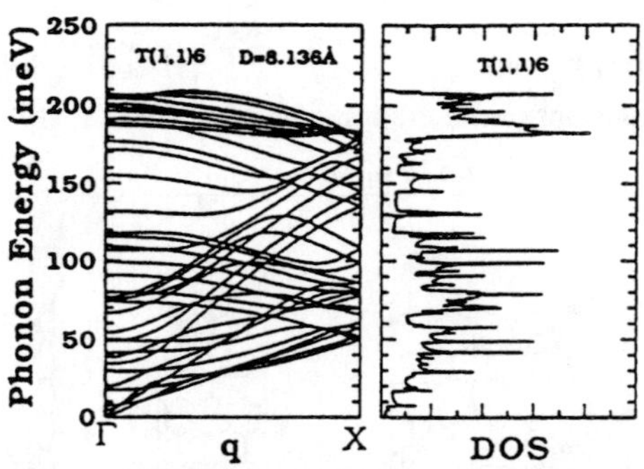

Figure 7. The phonon dispersion and density of states of the graphitic tubule T(1,1)6.

Fig. 9 shows the comparison between the phonon densities of states of graphite and the graphitic tubules with helicities T(1,0)N and T(1,1)N with various diameters. As one can see that the number of peaks in the low-frequency region of the spectra of graphitic tubule is proportional to the diameter of the tubules. As the diameter increases, the tendency toward graphite is clearly demonstrated. When the tubule diameter is larger than 15Å, its phonon spectrum has already approached that of graphite. It is clear that high-frequency modes are softened by the curvature. Compared with graphite, the finite curvature of

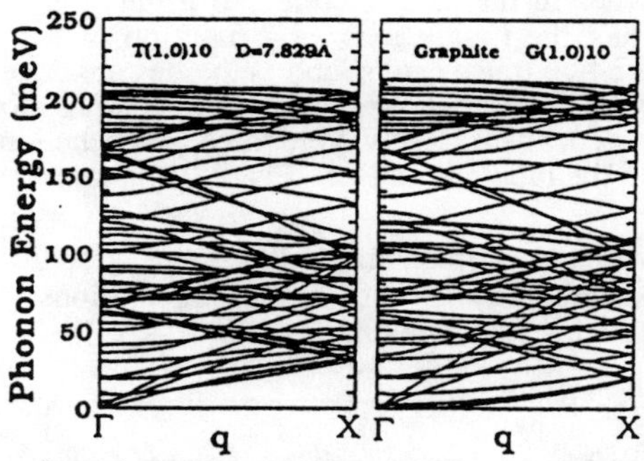

Figure 8. The phonon dispersion of the graphitic tubule T(1,0)10 compared with that of an unrolled graphite G(1,0)10 which has a finite width that is equal to the circumference of the tubule.

graphitic tubule has two major effects: one is the hybridization of the π bonds with the σ bonds, and the other is the repulsion between the π orbitals inside the graphitic tubule. As in the case of a C_{60} molecule, the effect of the first one is surplus that of the second in graphitic tubules.

Another interesting observation is that the spectra of graphitic tubules in the frequency region from 120 to 180 meV deviate strongly from that of graphite. These higher-frequency modes are the tangent modes. In this frequency region, the spectra are sensitive to the helical structure of the tubule, therefore this window provides the information about of the helicity of graphitic tubules.

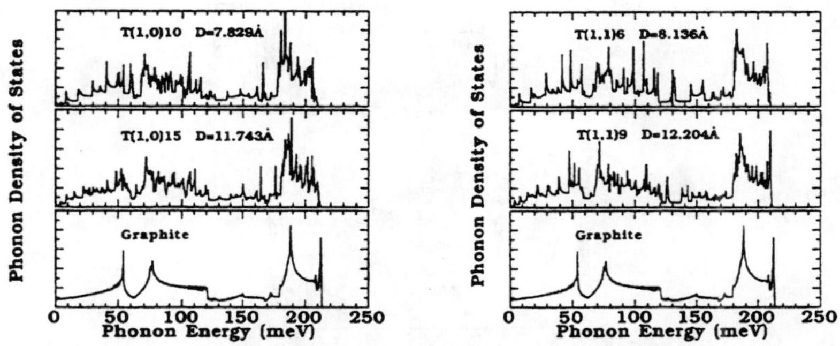

Figure 9. The phonon density of states of graphitic tubules T(1,0)N and T(1,1)N as function of tubule diameters and compared with that of an infinite graphite.

The effect of compressing and stretching on the structure and dynamical properties of the tubules has been studied. Fig. 10 shows the binding energy per particle as a function of tubule unit cell length for T(1,1)N, T(2,1)N, T(3,1)N, and T(1,0)N. Tubules with helicity T(1,0)N and T(1,1)N are the two limiting cases. Tubules with helicity T(1,0)N that have bonds parallel to the tubule axis are easy to compress but hard to stretch, while the tubules with helicity T(1,1)N are hard to compress but easy to stretch. The behavior of tubules with other helicities is just between that of tubules T(1,0)N and T(1,1)N. As the diameter increases, the difference between different helicities becomes smaller.

Fig. 11 shows the phonon density-of-states of the graphitic tubule T(1,1)7 as a function of the tubule unit cell length. Fig. 11 reveals that high-frequency optical phonons are sensitive to external stress. Although the shift of the lower-frequency modes is small, the strengths of these mode are quite sensitive to the external stress. We have also calculated the longitudinal and transverse sound velocities in graphitic tubules from the slopes of the acoustic phonon branches in the long-wavelength limit. Fig. 12(a) shows the speed of sound propagating along the tubule axis as a function of the tubule diameter for two different helicities. The two transverse sound velocities are degenerate. The longitudinal velocity of sound is lower than that in graphite. Both the transverse and longitudinal sound velocities are helicity dependent. However, for a given helicity, the sound velocities depend only weakly on the tubule diameter. Fig. 12(b) shows the effect of external stress on sound velocities.

Recently, Iijima *et al.* have demonstrated that single graphitic tubule about 700Å long can be obtained experimentally.[45] Our model calculations will be useful in guiding experiments in characterizing fullerene tubules.

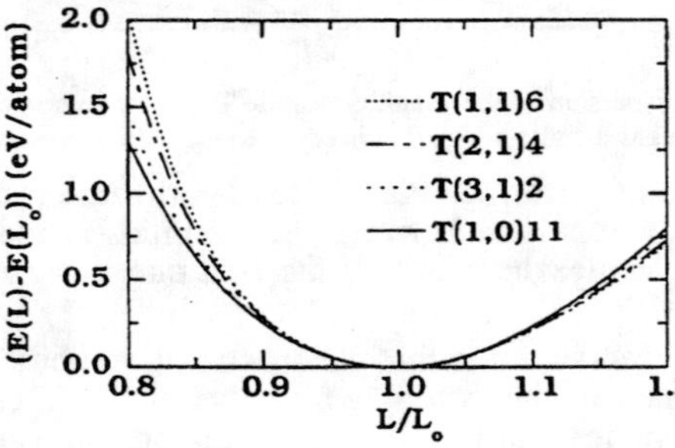

Figure 10. Tubules under compressing and stretching: The binding energy per particle of graphitic tubules T(1,1)6, T(2,1)4, T(3,1)2, and T(1,0)11 as a function of unit cell length.

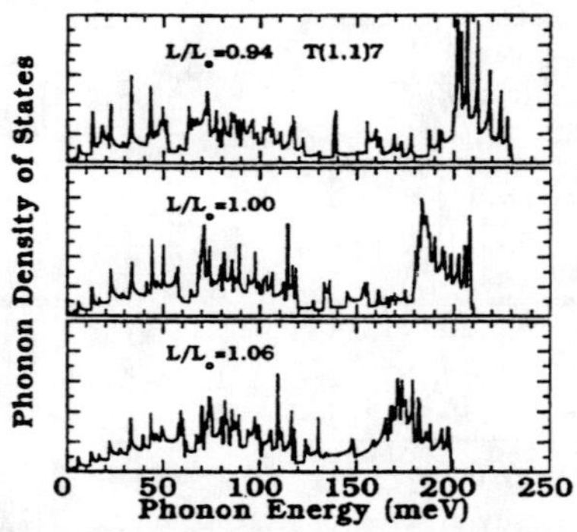

Figure 11. The effect of compressing and stretching on the phonon spectrum of graphitic tubule: T(1,1)7.

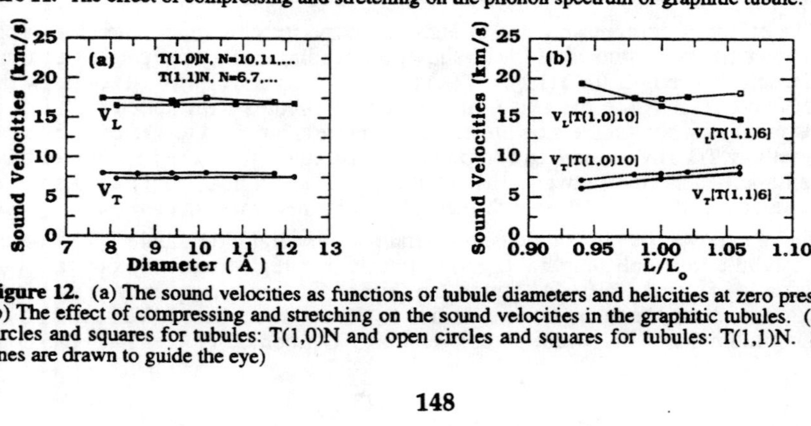

Figure 12. (a) The sound velocities as functions of tubule diameters and helicities at zero pressure; (b) The effect of compressing and stretching on the sound velocities in the graphitic tubules. (Solid circles and squares for tubules: T(1,0)N and open circles and squares for tubules: T(1,1)N. Solid lines are drawn to guide the eye)

5. CONCLUSION

We have calculated the dispersion and density of states of intermolecular and intramolecular phonons of solid C_{60}. The calculations are based on a unified model which includes an intramolecular tight-binding interaction and an intermolecular Lennard-Jones and bond-charge potential. The calculated phonon spectra are in good agreement with inelastic neutron scattering experiments. The effect of orientational disorder on the phonon spectrum of solid C_{60} has been examined. Phonon spectrum of solid C_{60} at various pressures (up to 56 kbar) has been calculated. The work on the effect of pressure on the inter- and intramolecular vibrational spectra to a large extent and the effect of orientationally disorder to a smaller extent demonstrates the usefulness of treating the solid C_{60} within the unified model discussed in this paper.

Using a tight-binding molecular dynamics method, we have calculated the phonon dispersion and density-of-states of graphitic tubules with various helicities and diameters. A detailed comparison with graphite sheet has been carried out. We have found that in the phonon spectra of graphitic tubules, there are two interesting frequency regions: the first one is the low-frequency region (< 50 meV), and the other one is the high-frequency region from 120 to 180 meV. Owing to the real periodic boundary condition around the tubule circumference, the phonon spectra of graphitic tubules in the low-frequency region show strong features with the number of peaks directly proportional to the diameter of the tubules. In the high-frequency region, the phonon spectra show strong helicity dependence. Therefore it provides the window to obtain the information about the helical structure of tubules. The sound propagation in graphitic tubules has also been studied. We find that the sound velocities along the tubule axis are helicity dependent, but for a given helicity the sound velocities depend only weakly on the tubule diameter. The effect of compression and stretch on the phonon spectra and sound velocities in the graphitic tubules have also been investigated, A detailed analysis of the nature and symmetry of the phonon modes in graphitic tubule will be reported elsewhere.

ACKNOWLEDGMENTS

We thank Drs. A. Nakano and W. Jin for useful discussions. We are grateful to Dr. K. M. Ho for sending us their tight-binding potential parameters before publication. This work was supported in part by the NSF, Grant: ASC-9310314. The computations were performed using the facilities of the Concurrent Computing Laboratory for Materials Simulations (CCLMS) at Louisiana State University. The facilities in the CCLMS were acquired with the Equipment Enhancement Grants awarded by the Louisiana Board of Regents through Louisiana Education Quality Support Fund (LEQSF).

REFERENCE

1. H. W. Kroto, J. R. Heath, S. C. O'Brien, R. F. Curl, and R. E. Smalley, *Nature* **318**, 162 (1985).
2. W. Kratschmer, L. D. Lamb, K. Fostiropoulos, and D. R. Huffman, *Nature* **347**, 354 (1990).
3. Y. Guo, N. Karasawa, and W. A. Goddard III, *Nature* **351**, 464 (1991).
4. Q. Zhang, J. Yi, and J. Bernholc, *Phys. Rev. Lett.* **66**, 2633 (1991).
5. O. Gunnarsson, S. Satpathy, O. Jepsen, and O.K. Anderson, *Phys. Rev. Lett.* **67**, 3002 (1991).
6. L. Lu, X. Li, and R. M. Martin, *Phys. Rev. Lett.* **68**, 1551 (1992); X. Li, J. Lu, and R. M. Martin, *Phys. Rev. B* **46**, 4301 (1992).
7. A. Cheng and M. L. Klein, *Phys. Rev. B* **45**, 1889 (1992); M. Sprik, A. Cheng, and M. L. Klein, *J. Phys. Chem.* **96**, 2027 (1992).
8. M. B. Walker, *Phys. Rev. B* **45**, 13849 (1992).

9. E. Burgos, E. Halac, and H. Bonadeo, *Phys. Rev. B* **47**, 7542 (1993).
10. J. E. Fischer, P. A. Heiney, A. R. McGhie, W. J. Romanow, A. M. Denenstein, J. P. McCauley Jr., and A. B. Smith III, Science **252**, 1288 (1991).
11. C. H. Xu, C. Z. Wang, C. T. Chan, and K. M. Ho, *J. Phys: Condens. Matter* **4**, 6047 (1992).
12. J. Yu, R. K. Kalia, and P. Vashishta, *Appl. Phys. Lett.* **63**, 3152 (1993); J. Yu, L. Bi, R. K. Kalia, and P. Vashishta, *Rev. Phys. B* **49**, 5008 (1994).
13. L. Pintschovius, B. Renker, F. Gompf, R. Heid, S. L. Chaplot, M. Haluska, and H. Kuzmany. *Phys. Rev. Lett.* **69**, 2662 (1992); L. Pintschovius, et al.,*Proc. Int. Winterschool on Electronic Properties of Novel Materials* (H. Kuzmany, ed.) Springer Series on Solid State Science (1993).
14. C. Coulombeau, H. Jobic, P. Bernier, C. Fabre, D. Schutz, and A. Rassat, *J. Phys. Chem.* **96**, 22 (1992).
15. Y. Huang, D. F. R. Gilson, and I. S. Butler, *J. Phys. Chem.* **95**, 5723 (1991).
16. F. Moshary, N. H. Chen, and I. F. Silvera, *Phys. Rev. Lett.* **69**, 466 (1992).
17. G. A. Samara, L. V. Hansen, R. A. Assink, B. Morosin, J. E. Schirber, and D. Loy, *Phys. Rev. B* **47**, 4756 (1993).
18. D. W. Snoke, K. Syassen, and A. Mittelbach, *Phys. Rev. B* **47**, 4146 (1993).
19. Y.-N. Xu, M.-Z. Huang, and W. Y. Ching, *Phys. Rev. B* **46**, 4241 (1992).
20. J. Yu, R. K. Kalia, and P. Vashishta, *J. Chem. Phys.* **99**, 1001 (1993).
21. S. Iijima, *Nature* **354**, 56 (1991).
22. T. W. Ebbesen, and P. M. Ajayan, *Nature* **358**, 220 (1992).
23. J. W. Mintmire, B. I. Dunlap, and C. T. White, *Phys. Rev. Lett.* **68**, 631 (1992).
24. N. Hamada, S. Sawada, and A. Oshiyama, *Phys. Rev. Lett.* **68**, 1579 (1992).
25. G. B. Adams, O. F. Sankey, J. B. Page, M. O'Keeffe, and D. A. Drabold, *Science* **256**, 1792 (1992).
26. J.-C. Charlier and J.-P. Michenaud, *Phys. Rev. Lett.* **70**, 1858 (1993).
27. M. S. Dresselhaus, G. Dresselhaus, and R. Saito, *Phys. Rev. B* **45**, 6234 (1992).
28. M. R. Pederson and J. Q. Broughton, *Phys. Rev. Lett.* **69**, 2689 (1992).
29. D. H. Robertson, D. W. Brenner, and J. W. Mintmire, *Phys. Rev. B* **45**, 12592 (1992).
30. C. T. White, D. H. Robertson, and J. W. Mintmire, *Phys. Rev. B* **47**, 5485 (1993).
31. Jae-Yel Yi and J. Bernholc, *Phys. Rev. B* **47**, 1708 (1993).
32. R. A. Jishi and M. S. Dresselhaus, *Phys. Rev. B* **45**, 11305 (1992).
33. R. A. Jishi, M. S. Dresselhaus, and G. Dresselhaus, *Phys. Rev. B* **47**, 16671 (1993).
34. C. Z. Wang, C. T. Chan, and K. M. Ho, *Phys. Rev. B* **39**, 8586 (1989).
35. F. S. Khan and J. Q. Broughton, *Phys. Rev. B* **39**, 3688 (1989).
36. K. Laasonen and R. M. Nieminen, *J. Phys. C* **2**, 1509 (1990).
37. M. Menon and R. E. Allen, *Phys. Rev. B* **33**, 7099 (1986).
38. O. F. Sankey and D. J. Niklewski, *Phys. Rev. B* **40**, 3979 (1989).
39. D. Tomanek and M. A. Schluter, *Phys. Rev. Lett.* **56**, 1055 (1986).
40. C. Z. Wang, K. M. Ho, and C. T. Chan, *Phys. Rev. Lett.* **70**, 611 (1993).
41. S. Duclos, K. Brister, R. C. Haddon, A. R. Kortan, and F. A. Theil, *Nature* **351**, 380 (1991).
42. T. Yildirim and A. B. Harris, *Phys. Rev. B* **46**, 7878 (1992).
43. W. I. F. David, R. M. Ibberson, T. J. Dennis, J. P. Hare, and K. Prassides, *Europhys. Lett.* **18**, 219 (1992).
44. S. N. Song, X. K. Wang, R. P. H. Chang, and J. B. Ketterson, *Phys. Rev. Lett.* **72**, 697 (1994).
45. S. Iijima and T. Ichihashi, *Nature* **363**, 603 (1993).

LARGE-SCALE CALCULATIONS OF THE QUANTUM DYNAMICS OF MOLECULAR COLLISIONS AND REACTIONS

Donald G. Truhlar,[a] David W. Schwenke,[b] Steven L. Mielke,[a] Melissa S. Reeves,[a] Robert W. Numrich,[c] Dean H. Briesemeister,[a] David C. Chatfield,[a] Ronald S. Friedman,[a] Martine Kalke,[a] Gregory J. Tawa,[a] and Michael J. Unekis[a]

[a]Department of Chemistry, Chemical Physics Program, and Supercomputer Institute, University of Minnesota, Minneapolis, MN 55455-0431
[b]NASA Ames Research Center, Moffett Field, CA 94035-1000
[c]Cray Research, Inc. 655F Lone Oak Drive, Eagan, MN 55121

1. INTRODUCTION

Calculation of the accurate quantum dynamics of few-body systems in chemical physics is a challenging class of problems for scientific computation.[1,2] The present paper outlines the use of quantum mechanical scattering theory to describe collisions of diatomic molecules with atoms and with other diatomic molecules. Such systems, containing three or four atoms moving in three dimensions, involve nine or twelve Cartesian coordinates, which reduce to six or nine coordinates after removing the overall motion of the center of mass. The potential function, however, depends on only three or six coordinates, and this allows some dimensions to be treated with less effort. A molecular collision of atom A with diatom BC or of diatom AB with diatom CD is described by the time-independent Schrödinger equation with steady-state scattering boundary conditions.[3] In this paper we consider both nonreactive collisions, in which energy is transferred between collision partners that retain their chemical identity and also reactive collisions, in which both energy and particles are transferred.

The relevant Schrödinger equation is the six-dimensional or nine-dimensional (6-D or 9-D) elliptic partial differential equation (PDE),

$$\left[-\frac{\hbar^2}{2\mu}\left(\nabla_{\mathbf{R}}^2+\nabla_{\mathbf{x}}^2\right)+V_0(\mathbf{x})+V_{\text{int}}(\mathbf{R},x)-E\right]\Psi(\mathbf{R},\mathbf{x})=0. \tag{1}$$

In this equation, $\hbar$ is Dirac's h, i.e., Planck's h divided by 2π; μ is the collisional reduced mass; $\mathbf{R}$ is a vector from A to the center of mass of BC or from the center of mass of AB to that of CD; $\mathbf{x}$ denotes the other three or six coordinates (assumed to be scaled to the same reduced mass μ as that for $\mathbf{R}$); V_0 is the potential energy of noninteracting collision partners,

$$V_0(\mathbf{x}) = \lim_{R\to\infty} V(\mathbf{R},\mathbf{x}) \tag{2}$$

where V is the full potential energy; V_{int} is the interaction potential, given by

$$V_{\text{int}}(\mathbf{R},\mathbf{x}) = V(\mathbf{R},\mathbf{x}) - V_0(\mathbf{x}); \tag{3}$$

E is the total energy; and Ψ is the scattering wave function.

The steady-state boundary conditions are nonhomogeneous, and their specification involves two steps. First we define the eigenstates ϕ_γ and eigenvalues ε_γ of the noninteracting collision partners, and then we write the boundary conditions in terms of these. For nonreactive collisions, the eigenstates required are solutions of

$$\left(-\frac{\hbar^2}{2\mu}\nabla_{\mathbf{x}}^2 + V_0(\mathbf{x}) - \varepsilon_\gamma\right)\phi_\gamma(\mathbf{x}) = 0 \tag{4}$$

with homogeneous boundary conditions. Then for $R > a$, where a is the distance at which $V_{\text{int}}(\mathbf{R},\mathbf{x})$ becomes negligible, the boundary conditions are

$$\Psi(\mathbf{R},\mathbf{x}) \sim e^{i\mathbf{k}_{\gamma_0}\cdot\mathbf{R}}\phi_{\gamma_0}(\mathbf{x}) + \sum_\gamma f_{\gamma\gamma_0}(\hat{\mathbf{R}})\frac{e^{ik_\gamma R}}{R}\phi_\gamma(\mathbf{x}) \tag{5}$$

where

$$k_\gamma^2 = \frac{2\mu}{\hbar^2}(E - \varepsilon_\gamma) , \tag{6}$$

$f_{\gamma\gamma_0}$ is an unknown scattering amplitude, corresponding to initial state γ_0 and final state γ, and $\hat{\mathbf{R}}$ is the direction of $\mathbf{R}$.

For reactive collisions, e.g., A + BC $\rightarrow$ AB + C or AC + B, we must enforce boundary conditions for all three arrangements. Let $\alpha = 1$ denote the region of space where A is far from BC, $\alpha = 2$ denote the region where B is far from AC, and $\alpha = 3$ the region where C is far from AB. Let $\mathbf{R}_2$ denote a mass-scaled vector from B to the center of mass of AC and $\mathbf{x}_2$ a mass-scaled vector from C to A; similarly let $\mathbf{R}_3$ denote a mass-scaled vector from C to the center of mass of AB and $\mathbf{x}_3$ a mass-scaled vector from A to B. Then, in addition to eq. (5) we must enforce

$$\Psi(\mathbf{R},\mathbf{x}) \underset{R_\alpha\to\infty}{\sim} \sum_\gamma f^\alpha_{\gamma\gamma_0}(\hat{\mathbf{R}}_\alpha)\frac{e^{ik^\alpha_\gamma R_\alpha}}{R_\alpha}\phi^\alpha_\gamma(\mathbf{x}_\alpha), \quad \alpha = 2,3, \tag{7}$$

where $f^\alpha_{\gamma\gamma_0}$ is an unknown reactive scattering amplitude, and ϕ^α_γ and k^α_γ are defined analogously to eqs. (4) and (6), but in the second and third arrangements.

Typically the wave function of eqs. (1) and (5) is written as a sum of components, each of which has a given total angular momentum J and each of which can be obtained separately. The problem with $J = 0$ is the simplest.

In this paper we consider several challenging applications involving the solution of these equations. The first is the treatment of energy transfer in four-body collisions, in particular inelastic diatom-diatom collisions, for which we have solved eqs. (1)–(6) by converting them into coupled ordinary differential equations in R, using an approach that is called the close coupling method.[1,3,4] These coupled equations are then solved by a propagation method. We also mention the application of such propagation methods to three-body collisions. The final challenging problems we discuss are reactive atom-diatom collisions and nonreactive atom-diatom collisions involving multiple electronic states. For these problems we solve equations (1)–(6) or (1)–(7) by converting them to coupled algebraic equations using a variational principle.[5]

The computers used for the present studies are primarily the Cray-2 large-memory vector supercomputer (and its Cray M92 and C90 successors) and the massively parallel, distributed-memory Connection Machine CM-5 from Thinking Machines Corporation. Some calculations were carried out on a heterogeneous combination of the Cray-2 and CM-5 linked by a High Performance Parallel Interface (HiPPI).

2. CALCULATIONS EMPLOYING PROPAGATION METHODS

Consider the collision of two HF molecules with total angular momentum zero. We write

$$\Psi = \frac{1}{R}\sum_{n=1}^{N} f_n(R)\ \varphi_n\left(\hat{\mathbf{R}},\mathbf{x}\right) \tag{8}$$

where each value of n labels a set of quantum numbers, which is called a "channel," R is the magnitude of $\mathbf{R}$, φ_n is a known basis function (formulated to carry zero total angular momentum), and f_n is unknown. By substituting (8) into (1), we can convert the 9–D PDE into N coupled ordinary differential equations (ODEs) of the form

$$\frac{d^2 f_n}{dR^2} + \sum_{n'=1}^{N} C_{nn'}(R)\ f_{n'}(R) = 0, \qquad n = 1,2,\ldots,N, \tag{9}$$

where the coefficient matrix, which is dense, contains the 8–D integrals

$$C_{n'n}(R) = \int d\hat{\mathbf{R}}\ d\mathbf{x}\varphi^*_{n'}\left(\hat{\mathbf{R}},\mathbf{x}\right)\left\{-\frac{\ell^2}{\hbar^2 R^2} + \nabla^2_{\mathbf{x}} - \frac{2\mu}{\hbar^2}\left[V_{\text{int}}(\mathbf{R},\mathbf{x}) + V_0(\mathbf{x}) - E\right]\right\}\varphi_n\left(\hat{\mathbf{R}},\mathbf{x}\right) \tag{10}$$

where $\mathbf{l}^2$ is the quantum mechanical operator for the square of the angular momentum associated with $\hat{\mathbf{R}}$ motion. These equations must be solved subject to regularity boundary conditions at $R = 0$ and scattering boundary conditions at large R. The unknown scattering amplitudes occur in the large-R boundary conditions. In challenging current applications, $N > 2000$. In future applications one must consider $J > 0$, which leads to much larger N, e.g., $N = O(10^5)$.

This formalism is also applicable to atom-diatom collisions provided we recognize that **x** is 6-D for the four-body case and 3-D for the three-body case. The expansion (8) is inconvenient for applying reactive scattering boundary conditions, but reactive scattering can be treated by equations similar to (8) by replacing the propagation coordinate R by the hyperspherical radius ρ.[6–11] This allows us to make a connection to the work of Kuppermann[11,12] discussed in an earlier paper at this conference by Messina.[13] One difference of that work[11,12] from the work discussed above and from our own approach[6] to using hyperspherical coordinates for reactive scattering is that Kuppermann's basis functions φ_n depend on ρ, whereas ours do not depend on R or ρ. Faster convergence with respect to basis size can be obtained with basis functions optimized as a function of the propagation coordinate,[14,15] but we will not discuss that aspect further in the present paper.

We consider three sets of calculations using propagation techniques to illustrate the progress that has been made and the challenges that remain. The first example involves a parallel strategy that we employed on global-memory vector computers. The second and third examples involve strategies developed for multi-processor machines with distributed memory.

In all three strategies the two-point boundary value problem for $f_n(R)$ is solved by converting it to an initial value problem which is equivalent to propagating N or $2N$ linearly independent solutions from the small-R region to the large-R region and then taking linear combinations of these solutions to satisfy the boundary conditions. Taking advantage of the regularity boundary condition at $R = 0$ allows one to propagate only N solutions. These solutions are arranged as an $N \times N$ solution matrix. Equivalent information may be propagated in the form of an $N \times N$ global $\mathscr{R}$ matrix as discussed below.

2.1 A Strategy for Vector Machines

Our original strategy for large-scale inelastic scattering problems was designed for vector processors, such as the Control Data Corporation Cyber 205 and various Cray computers, especially the Cray-1, Cray X-MP, and Cray-2. Details of the algorithm and its implementation are presented elsewhere,[14–21] so here we only summarize a few importance aspects.

The strategy for solving eq. (9) is to convert the equations to an initial value problem, as in the invariant imbedding[22] method. In particular, we use the $\mathscr{R}$ matrix propagation algorithm.[14,15] In $\mathscr{R}$ matrix propagation, the R axis is divided into sectors, and each step consists of finding the local $\mathscr{R}$ matrix (a matrix relating the reciprocal of the logarithmic derivative of the wave function components at the right of a sector to those at its left) and using this to update the global $\mathscr{R}$ matrix[23] (which relates the logarithmic derivative components at the right side of a sector to their values at the left of the first sector, assuming propagation proceeds left to right). Step sizes may be determined adaptively with little extra effort.[16,19,20] This method is intrinsically stable,[14] and it allows large steps, especially at large R, but the computational effort per step is high, involving the diagonalization of an $N \times N$ matrix and several other matrix operations.[17,20] Nevertheless the code typically spends 90–98% of its time on these highly vectorizable matrix operations, and the method provides an efficient way to solve large-scale problems on vector supercomputers. Memory management can be flexible, and when memory is scarce, one can operate with storage of only two $N \times N$ matrices in central memory.[24]

Because HF has a permanent dipole moment, the interaction potential for HF collisions with HF has a very long range, decaying only as R^{-3}, and many propagation steps, e.g., 300–600, are required to reach the asymptotic region. (Even more steps would be required if it weren't for the valuable feature of $\mathscr{R}$ matrix propagation that one can take very large steps at large R.) It is essential therefore to evaluate the C matrix efficiently. First of all, each element is an 8-D integral. Second, the matrix is dense; since **C** is symmetric, the number of unique elements is $N(N + 1)/2$, and these must be evaluated. Third, **C** must be evaluated at every step. In one approach,[17] the 8-D integrals are computed by a combination of 3-D analytic integration and 5-D numerical quadrature. The 3-D angular integrals were carried out by expanding the interaction potential in terms of orthogonal angular basis functions and then analytically evaluating the integrals involving these expansion functions and the channel basis functions. The determination of the expansion coefficients requires a 3-D numerical quadrature which is independent of N, and the analytic angular integrals involve vector coupling coefficients which are nontrivial to evaluate but independent of v_n and $v_{n'}$, where v_n and j_n denote the vibrational and rotational quantum numbers of a particular monomer in channel n. The two quadratures over the monomer vibrational coordinates are carried out by N^{QV}-point quadrature, which are programmed as an inner vectorized loop of length $(N^{QV})^2$. The outer loops were arranged to avoid unnecessary repetitions, and we used an optimized quadrature scheme[25] to minimize N^{QV}. In particular, we precalculated and stored separate quadrature weights for each combination of monomer vibrational and rotational quantum numbers (thus the weights depend on four indices: v_n, j_n, $v_{n'}$, and $j_{n'}$). The extra storage required for these weights is negligible compared to the computer time savings they afford.

The second approach[19] to the quadratures also involves a preparatory step. In this approach, we refit the interaction potential to a sum of separable products. This allows the $C_{nn'}(R)$ matrix for any R to be constructed from a relatively small number of R-independent matrix elements. This approach makes the cost of the quadrature step almost negligible, but it may require more storage than the first approach, depending on N and the number of separable products. Using the second approach we have solved eq. (9) with N as large as 2472.

Because dense matrix diagonalizations do not usually parallelize well when distributed across processors on a distributed-memory multiprocessor, we explored other strategies for parallelization on such machines.

2.2 Parallelization in the Physical Domain

Each propagation step involves the same arithmetic operations on different data. Therefore one possible approach to parallelization is to assign the sectors, each spanned by a single propagation step, to individual processors. In this strategy one performs many steps simultaneously, obtaining a local $\mathscr{R}$ matrix for each sector or each set of contiguous sectors on a single processor and then combining these into a global $\mathscr{R}$ matrix, in a process corresponding to the reverse of successive bisections. There are several penalties for using this approach. The first disadvantage results from the nature of the boundary conditions. The initial sector has homogeneous boundary conditions at small R, and this causes certain submatrices to start out as zero. As long as the steps are performed in order, these zeros remain zero, and they may be propagated analytically.[16] However, if steps are performed out of order, replacing the global initial value problem by a sequence of boundary value problems across the individual sectors, one must calculate the general solution rather than this simpler particular solution, and this raises the operation count about 35%.

A second disadvantage of parallelization across the physical domain is the inefficiency in treating problems where the number of sectors is less than the number of processors. A third disadvantage occurs when the local $\mathscr{R}$ matrices are combined; this step leads to a load balancing problem. Fourth, to run efficiently this algorithm would require a large memory on each node, especially if I/O is slow.

The strategy presented next does not have these disadvantages.

2.3 A Strategy Based on Parallel Matrix Multiplications

The essence of the next strategy we employed is to use a very simple propagation algorithm consisting of a limited number of primitive matrix operations that can be parallelized across the processors. The algorithm we chose is the de Vogelaere algorithm,[26] for which the effort consists almost entirely of matrix multiplications and QR factorizations,[27] with the latter needed for stability.[28] In practice we found it was more efficient actually to carry out the QR application on the transpose (T) of the solution matrix. In particular the stabilization transformation we used involved the explicit formation of **Q** and its application to four matrices. We then spread each matrix operation over all the processors. In reducing this idea to practice, the implementation we have used to date is to create the C matrices on the Cray-2, then move them via the HiPPI to the CM-5, where the propagation steps are performed. The prototype problem we considered corresponds to vibrational-rotational excitation of H_2 by He.

We simplified our code as much as possible to keep overhead down, and we were able to solve the prototype problem with $N = 509$ on 512 processors of the CM-5 with only 6% overhead. In addition we obtained good speeds on the matrix multiplications and QR stabilization transformations. Figure 1 illustrates the speedups for matrix multiplication as a function of matrix size for one processor on a Cray-2 or C90, for 16 processors on a C90, and for 32, 128, 256,

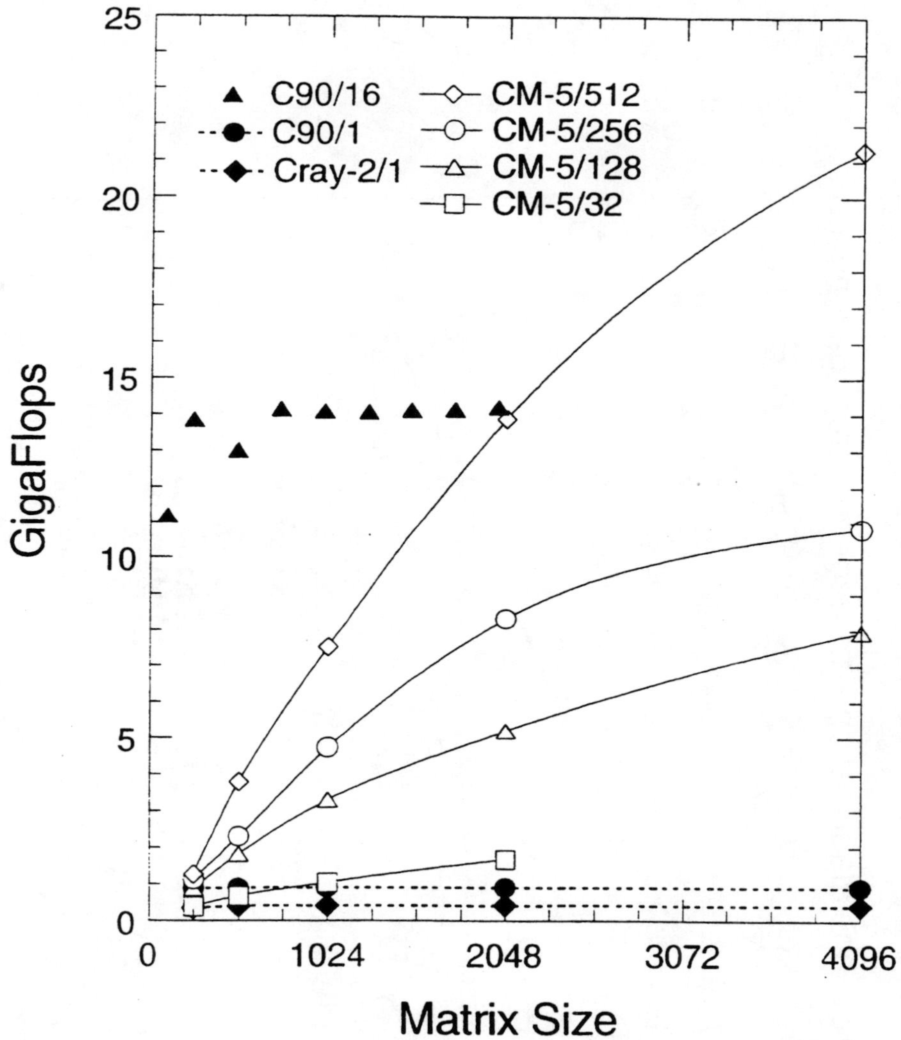

Figure 1. Speeds (billions of floating point operations per second) as functions of matrix size for matrix multiplications required in de Vogelaere algorithm on various computers with various numbers of processors, indicated by the value after /. On the Cray machines, the matrices were stored with leading dimension $2^N + 1$ to avoid bank conflicts. The C90/16 speeds are for a dedicated machine and are taken from Ref. 74, and the other Cray speeds are based on CPU times obtained by the authors in time-share batch mode; in both cases the LAPACK BLAS routine SGEMM is used. The CM-5 speeds are based on elapsed times obtained by the authors using the CMSSL library routine GEN_MATRIX_MULT.

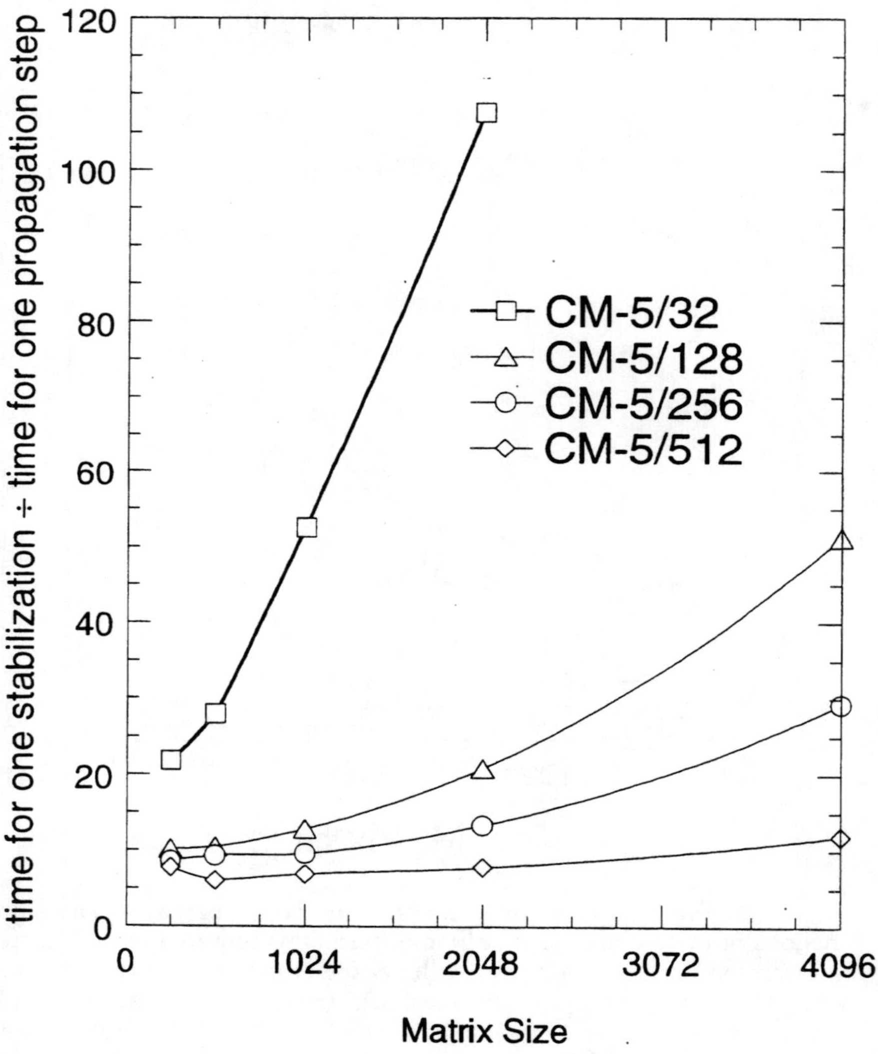

Figure 2. Ratio of time required for a single stabilization transformation to that required for a single propagation step on various partitions of the CM-5 as a function of matrix order.

or 512 nodes of the CM-5. Figure 2 shows the time required on the CM-5 for a stabilization transformation divided by the time for a propagation step, which consists of two matrix multiplies. We found, for the H_2-He problem, that a stabilization needs to be performed on only about 1% of the steps. Thus, when the ratio in Fig. 2 is less than about 100, the efficient matrix multiplications dominate the computer time. Since, as stated above, 94% of the effort in our prototype problem goes into the propagation steps and stabilization transformations, and since the ratio in Fig. 2 is much less than 100 for 512 processors, the excellent speeds on matrix multiplication translate into good performance on the whole algorithm for 512 processors. However, the number of steps required by the de Vogelaere algorithm is large.

Disclaimer. These results are based upon a beta version of the TMC software and, consequently, are not necessarily representative of the performance of the full version of the software.

3. CALCULATIONS EMPLOYING ALGEBRAIC VARIATIONAL METHODS

The description of chemical reactions requires the theory of quantum mechanical rearrangement scattering.[3] For rearrangement collisions we restrict our consideration to three-body systems. For reactive collisions we replace eq. (8) by

$$\Psi = \sum_{\alpha=1}^{3} \sum_{n_\alpha=1}^{N_\alpha} f_{n_\alpha}(R_\alpha)\phi_{n_\alpha}(\hat{\mathbf{R}}_\alpha, \mathbf{x}_\alpha) \tag{11}$$

where $\mathbf{R}_1 = \mathbf{R}$, $\mathbf{x}_1 = \mathbf{x}$, and α is the arrangement quantum number explained below eq. (6). Note that $\mathbf{x}_1$ consists of the BC vibrational coordinate r_1, the BC rotational coordinates $\hat{\mathbf{r}}_1$, and the A-BC angular orbital coordinates $\hat{\mathbf{R}}_1$, with similar definitions for the B-AC and C-AB arrangements. Note also that even if f_{n_α} form an orthogonal set, the basis functions in different arrangements would be nonorthogonal. Furthermore, as explained below eq. (6), we must simultaneously impose collisional boundary conditions in three different coordinate systems. The approach we have found most suitable for attacking such problems is the algebraic variational approach,[5] especially the outgoing wave variational principle[29-38] (OWVP), with basis functions motivated[32,38] by the integral-equation-based generalized[39,40] Newton[41,42] variational principle.

In applying the OWVP, we first partition the interaction potential (3) as

$$V_{\text{int}}(\mathbf{R},\mathbf{x}) = V_1^{\text{D}}(\mathbf{R}_1,\mathbf{x}_1) + V_1^{\text{C}}(\mathbf{R}_1,\mathbf{x}_1) \tag{12a}$$

$$= V_2^{\text{D}}(\mathbf{R}_2,\mathbf{x}_2) + V_2^{\text{C}}(\mathbf{R}_2,\mathbf{x}_2) \tag{12b}$$

$$= V_3^{\text{D}}(\mathbf{R}_3,\mathbf{x}_3) + V_3^{\text{C}}(\mathbf{R}_3,\mathbf{x}_3) \tag{12c}$$

where V_α^{D} is called a distortion potential, and V_α^{C} is a coupling potential. A critical element in this partition is that V_α^{D} does not couple basis functions in different arrangements, but V_α^{C} does. We then write

$$\Psi = \psi_{\text{incoming}}(\mathbf{R}_1,\mathbf{x}_1) + \sum_{\beta} A_\beta \Gamma_\beta\left(\mathbf{R}_{\alpha_\beta},\mathbf{x}_{\alpha_\beta}\right) \tag{13}$$

where ψ_{incoming} is a solution to

$$\left[-\frac{\hbar^2}{2\mu}\left(\nabla_{\mathbf{R}}^2 + \nabla_{\mathbf{x}}^2\right) + V_0(\mathbf{x}) + V_1^{\mathrm{D}}(\mathbf{R},\mathbf{x}) - E\right]\psi_{\text{incoming}}(\mathbf{R},\mathbf{x}) = 0, \tag{14}$$

A_β is a complex coefficient, and each Γ_β is taken as one of three types[36,37] of 6-D basis function in a given arrangement α_β:

- gaussian, centered at $R_\beta^{\mathrm{G}} \neq 0$, in radial translational coordinate R_{α_β}, times an asymptotic vibrational function for r_{α_β} times a 4-D rotational-orbital function $Z_{j\Omega}^{JM_JP}\left(\hat{\mathbf{r}}_{\alpha_\beta},\hat{\mathbf{R}}_{\alpha_\beta}\right)$;
- 2-D gaussian in R_{α_β} and r_{α_β} times $Z_{j\Omega}^{JM_JP}\left(\hat{\mathbf{r}}_{\alpha_\beta},\hat{\mathbf{R}}_{\alpha_\beta}\right)$;
- coupled-channel 6-D Green's function obtained by solving a problem with up to ~50–100 rotationally coupled channels in a single arrangement with a localized inhomogeneity.

The third type of basis function is called a dynamically adapted basis function.[32,38] For reactive scattering one could have all three types of basis function in all three arrangements, leading to a large number of different kinds of integrals.[36] Some economy of coding is achieved by restricting the $\mathbf{x}_\alpha$ dependencies of the forms of the type-1 basis functions and of the inhomogeneities in the type-3 basis functions to be the same.

The computational steps for the OWVP are as follows:

- Compute the radial parts of ψ_{incoming} and the coupled-channel radial Green's functions directly on quadrature grids (for the next step) by high-order finite differences[33,35] (typically a 13-point approximation to d^2/dR_α^2).
- Compute 6-D quadratures over V_{int}, ψ_{incoming}, and basis functions; three dimensions are treated analytically in a body-fixed coordinate frame,[36,43] and three are treated by numerical integration.
- Solve a dense, complex, non-Hermitean linear algebraic system for the coefficients of basis functions and for the complex scattering matrix (which is a matrix of fixed-J scattering amplitudes). Both direct methods involving partitioned matrices[44] and also preconditioned iterative methods[45] have been employed.

For atom-diatom reactive collisions, the state of the art involves treating all J at a given energy with stable convergence of the phases of the scattering matrix elements as required to calculate differential cross sections[46–48] or on a fine energy grid as required to study quantized transition state spectra[49,50] or to calculate thermally averaged rate constants.[51] For atom-diatom collisions involving multiple electronic states,[37,52–54] even low-E, low-J calculations are currently challenging problems. Increasing E or J or the number of electronic states increases the number of channels and hence the number of basis functions required for convergence. The order N of the final dense system of equations is equal to the number of basis functions; the largest calculation we have completed to date has $N = 17413$.[37]

Selected recent applications we have carried out using the algebraic variational method include the following studies:

For the $D + H_2 \rightarrow HD + H$ reaction, we calculated[51] thermally averaged rate constants as a function of temperature and found excellent agreement (< 9%) with a fit[55] to the available experimental values for T = 200–800 K. The comparison is shown in Figure 3. The curve representing experimental results is the three-parameter fit from Ref. 55 to their own and literature[56–58] data. Over the whole region shown, theory agrees with experiment within the 20% reliability of the fit. The theoretical values are based on a potential energy function[59] fit to *ab initio* electronic structure calculations from several sets[59–62] of calculations. This comparison shows that converged quantum dynamics calculations can compete with experimental methods for the accurate determination of chemical kinetics rate coefficients when the potential energy surface is well known. This example suggests two challenges to Teraflop computing: (i) obtaining chemically accurate potential energy surfaces for more complicated systems, and (ii) extending converged quantal kinetics schemes to more complicated systems. At the present time we can calculate converged quantum dynamical rate constants for more complicated atom-diatom systems, but the potential energy surface is not known to chemical accuracy for any system except $H + H_2$ and its isotopomeric analogs.

Converged quantum dynamics calculations have also been compared successfully to experiment for differential cross sections. Recent papers presented such comparisons for the $F + H_2 \rightarrow HF + H$[47] and $H + D_2 \rightarrow HD + D$[48] reactions. The former study is particularly noteworthy in that the experimental results[63] showed strong evidence of participation by quantum mechanical resonance states, but the differential cross sections for the various v' states of HF, where v is the vibrational quantum number and primes denote final-state values, were unreproducible by theory until converged quantum dynamics was combined with a new potential energy function.[47] The latter study was particularly interesting in that it yielded qualitatively different differential cross sections from quasiclassical trajectory calculations[64] for the state-to-state differential cross sections for reaction into various final rotational states. This comparison provides a striking indication of the necessity to solve reactive scattering dynamical problems at the quantum mechanical rather than the classical mechanical level.

A third application area to which we have applied algebraic variational methods is the study of quantized transition states. Transition state theory[65,66] (also called activated complex theory) has provided the dominant quantitative and qualitative framework for understanding chemical kinetics dating back to the 1930s, and quantization of transition states has been considered essential dating back to the seminal work of Wigner[67] and Eyring[66]; consideration of the quantized nature of transition states has been especially indispensable for the

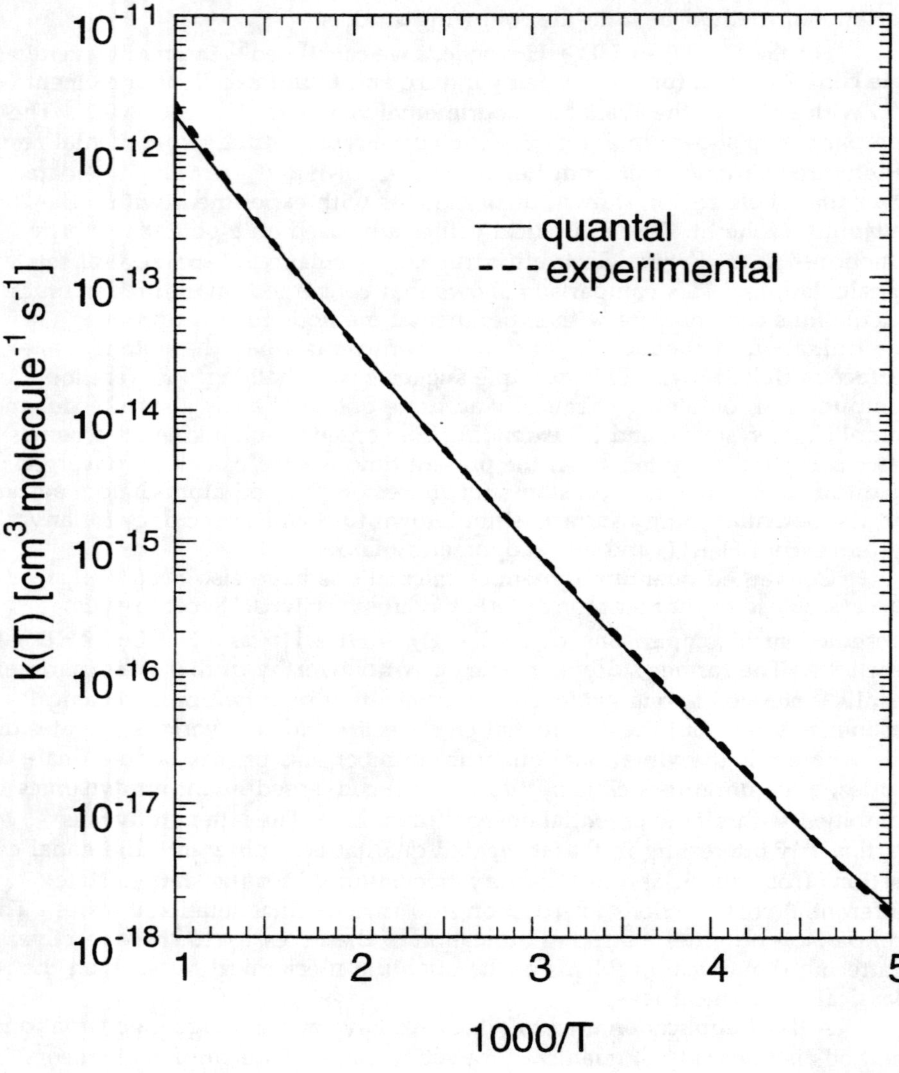

Figure 3. Rate constants vs. 1000/temperature (in degrees Kelvin) for the reaction D + $H_2 \rightarrow$ HD + H. The solid curve represents the values calculated by quantum mechanical theory, and the dashed curve is experiment.

interpretation of kinetic isotope effects.[68] However, the observation of the "spectrum" of the transition state has proved experimentally elusive. Now this spectrum has been observed in accurate quantum dynamics calculations on the $H + H_2$ and $O + H_2$ reactions.[49,50,69]

Figure 4 shows the spectrum of the $O + H_2$ reaction. The top half of this figure shows the cumulative reactive probability $N(E)$ for this reaction, for $J = 0$, with the potential energy function taken from the work of Johnson, Winter, and Schatz.[70,71] This quantity is defined by

$$N(E) = h\rho^R(E)k(E) \tag{15}$$

where h is Planck's constant, $\rho^R(E)$ is the density of states of the reactant (a nondynamical quantity), and $k(E)$ is the converged microcanonical-ensemble quantum mechanical rate coefficient (for the assumed potential energy function). A rate coefficient for a microcanonical ensemble involves an equally weighted sum of all state-to-state reaction probabilities, including all excited states energetically accessible at a given total energy, and that is why it has never been measured experimentally. But, by including the contributions from all states, which is possible in a computational study, one brings out the quantized structure of the dynamical bottleneck to reaction. This is shown in the bottom half of Fig. 4, which is the energy derivative of the top half. Each peak in the lower half of the figure corresponds to a rise in the cumulative reaction probability as the system accesses a new quantized state of the activated complex.

The peaks observed in the transition state spectrum have all been assigned quantum numbers and individual transmission coefficients.[50] In transition state theory, the transmission coefficient of each state of the activated complex is assumed to be unity; and by comparison of thermally averaged rate constants to experiment one can hope at best to determine the average transmission coefficient for all the activated-complex states and hence the average breakdown of the transition state assumption to the extent that this value deviates from unity. The accurate quantum mechanical calculations provide a new level of detail in understanding the validity of the transition state assumption in that we can now see that some quantized dynamical bottleneck states correspond to the unit-transmission-coefficient assumption better than others. For example, the first two peaks in Fig. 4 correspond to activated-complex states that have transmission coefficients of 0.96 and 0.9, respectively, but the third peak, at 0.97 eV, corresponds to a transmission coefficient of only 0.6. The third peak in Fig. 4 is interesting in another way as well. The first two peaks correspond to the ground state and a bend-excited state of the activated complex, but the third state (at 0.97 eV) has the bound stretching motion of the activated complex excited. The energy of this third peak corresponds very closely to the threshold energy for the reaction of H_2 ($v = 1$) with O. This indicates that vibrationally excited reactants principally access the stretch-excited states of the activated complex. We see then that the excited states of the activated complex are *state-specific* doorways between reactants and products, confirming the validity of ideas advanced earlier in approximate theory, in particular in state-specific variational transition state theory.[72] The converged quantum dynamics calculations also identified dynamical bottlenecks

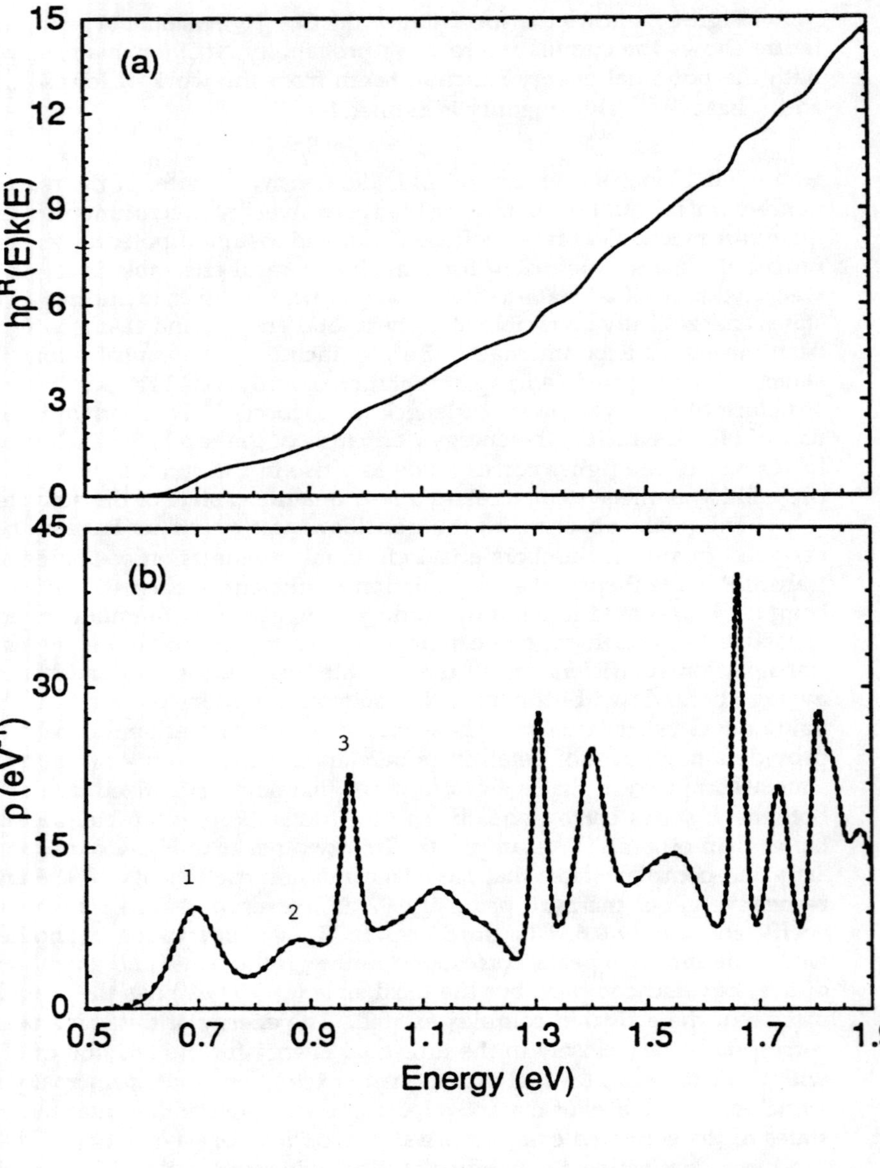

Figure 4. (a) Cumulative reaction probability for the $O + H_2 \rightarrow OH + H$ reaction. (b) Derivative of part (a).

to state-specific reactivity that do not affect the overall rate coefficient; these were called supernumerary transition states of the second kind.[50] This discussion has identified a new role for accurate quantum dynamics calculations—namely, by providing a detailed picture of chemical reactivity at the ultimate level of resolution allowed by quantum mechanics, such calculations can provide insight into the conceptual framework by which we understand phenomena in quantum mechanical systems. The use of large-scale calculations to provide conceptual insight—as well as hard numbers—will be a major challenge for Teraflop computing.

We will close this section with an introduction to a new area which will benefit greatly from Teraflop computing, namely the quantum mechanical treatment of chemical reactions of electronically excited reagents—or "quantum photochemistry."

In 1938, Wigner said,[73] "It seems that one can divide the chemistry of reactions into three groups," the first group being those which exchange translational, rotational, and vibrational energy but do not change electronic state or chemical formula, and the second being those which involve no change in electronic quantum numbers but which may involve a change in constitution. Wigner continued, "The remaining third class deals with reactions which involve a jump in the electronic structure.... It is clearly the most general type and probably the most difficult of all."[73] The accurate quantum mechanical treatment of the dynamics of such systems will be a challenge for Teraflop computers. Meanwhile we have made a start. Our initial efforts in this field have involved the development of a formalism general enough to handle the problem,[36] and a series of calculations[37,52–54] on nonreactive collisions of Na(3*p*) with H_2 at energies above the conical intersection of the ground and first excited electronic state surfaces. These calculations enabled us to discover a new phenomenon, namely the enhancement of molecular energy transfer by the intermediate participation of metastable states associated with the conical intersection region. The metastable states in the vicinity of the conical intersection were assigned quantum numbers, and their lifetimes and decay probabilities into various final states were mapped out.[53,54] We anticipate that additional new phenomena are likely to be uncovered as the calculations are extended to higher energies where chemical reaction becomes possible.

4. SUMMARY

This paper discusses our recent experience with large-scale quantum mechanical calculations for molecular collisions, and it identifies several challenges for Teraflop computation.

ACKNOWLEDGMENTS

The authors are grateful to Bruce C. Garrett, Philippe Halvick, Yi-Ping Liu, and Gillian C. Lynch for invaluable contributions to our overall research effort on some of the systems discussed in this paper. All the work discussed here was supported in part by the National Science Foundation. The work on the CM-5 and on Na(3*p*) + H_2 collisions was also supported in part by the U.S. Army Research Office through the Army High Performance Computing Research Center at the University of Minnesota. The work on Na(3*p*) + H_2 was also supported in part by Cray Research, Inc. and NASA.

REFERENCES

1. R. B. Bernstein (Ed.), *Atom-Molecule Collision Theory,* New York: Plenum, 1979. (779 pp.)
2. A. Laganà (Ed.), *Supercomputer Algorithms for Reactivity, Dynamics, and Kinetics of Small Molecules* (NATO Advanced Science Institute Series C, Vol. 277), Dordrecht: Kluwer, 1989. (441 pp.)
3. N. F. Mott and H. S. W. Massey, *The Theory of Atomic Collisions,* 3rd ed., London: Oxford University Press, 1965. (858 pp.)
4. R. D. Levine, *Quantum Theory of Molecular Rate Processes,* London: Oxford University Press, 1969. (335 pp.)
5. D. G. Truhlar, J. Abdallah, Jr., and R. L. Smith, "Algebraic Variational Methods in Scattering Theory," *Advances in Chemical Physics,* Vol. 25, 1974, pp. 211–293.
6. D. W. Schwenke, D. G. Truhlar, and D. J. Kouri, "Propagation Method for the Solution of the Arrangement-Channel Coupling Equations for Reactive Scattering in Three Dimensions," *Journal of Chemical Physics,* Vol. 86, 1987, pp. 2772–2786.
7. P. G. Hipes and A. Kuppermann, "Lifetime Analysis of High-Energy Resonances in Three-Dimensional Reactive Scattering," *Chemical Physics Letters,* Vol. 133, 1987, pp. 1–7.
8. R. T Pack and G. A. Parker, "Quantum Reactive Scattering in Three Dimensions Using Hyperspherical (APH) Coordinates Theory," *Journal of Chemical Physics,* Vol. 87, 1987, pp. 3888–3921.
9. J. M. Launay and B. Lepetit, "Three-Dimensional Quantum Study of the Reaction H + FH $(vj) \rightarrow HF(v'j')$ + H," *Chemical Physics Letters,* Vol. 144, 1988, pp. 346–352.
10. G. C. Schatz, "Quantum Reactive Scattering Using Hyperspherical Coordinates: Results for H + H_2 and Cl + HCl," *Chemical Physical Letters,* Vol. 150, 1988, pp. 92–98.
11. S. A. Cuccaro, P. G. Hipes, and A. Kuppermann, "Hyperspherical Coordinate Reactive Scattering Using Variational Surface Functions," *Chemical Physics Letters,* Vol. 154, 1989, pp. 155–164.

12. A. Kuppermann and Y.-S. M. Wu, "The Geometric Phase Effect Shows Up in Chemical Reactions," *Chemical Physics Letters*, Vol. 205, 1993, pp. 577–586.
13. P. Messina, "High-performance Distributed Computing Environment," paper at this conference.
14. J. C. Light and R. B. Walker, "An R Matrix Approach to the Solution of Coupled Equations for Atom-Molecule Reaction Scattering," *Journal of Chemical Physics*, Vol. 65, 1976, pp. 4272–4282.
15. N. A. Mullaney and D. G. Truhlar, "The Use of Rotationally and Orbitally Adiabatic Basis Functions to Calculate Rotational Excitation Cross Sections for Atom-Molecule Collisions," *Chemical Physics*, Vol. 39, 1979, pp. 91–104.
16. D. G. Truhlar, N. M. Harvey, K. Onda, and M. A. Brandt, "Applications of Close Coupling Algorithms to Electron-Atom, Electron-Molecule, and Atom-Molecule Scattering," In: *Algorithms and Computer Codes for Atomic and Molecular Quantum Scattering Theory*, Vol. 1, L. Thomas (Ed.), Berkeley: Lawrence Berkeley Laboratory, 1979, pp. 220–289.
17. D. W. Schwenke and D. G. Truhlar, "Large Scale Quantum Mechanical Scattering Calculations on Vector Computers," In: *Supercomputer Applications*, R. W. Numrich (Ed.), New York: Plenum Press, 1985, pp. 215–254.
18. D. W. Schwenke and D. G. Truhlar, "Converged Calculations of Rotational Excitation and V-V Energy Transfer in the Collision of Two Molecules," In: *Supercomputer Simulations in Chemistry* (Lecture Notes in Chemistry Series, Vol. 44), M. Dupuis (Ed.), Berlin: Springer-Verlag, 1986, pp. 165–197.
19. D. W. Schwenke and D. G. Truhlar, "A New Potential Energy Surface for Vibration-Vibration Coupling in HF-HF Collisions. Formulation and Quantal Scattering Calculations," *Journal of Chemical Physics*, Vol. 88, 1988, pp. 4800–4813.
20. M. J. Unekis, D. W. Schwenke, N. M. Harvey, and D. G. Truhlar, "RMPROP: A Computer Program for Quantum Mechanical Close Coupling Calculations for Inelastic Collisions," In: *Modern Techniques in Computational Chemistry: MOTECC–91*, E. Clementi (Ed.), ESCOM: Leiden, 1991, pp. 749–772.
21. M. J. Unekis, D. W. Schwenke, N. M. Harvey, and D. G. Truhlar, "RMPROP–Version 2: A Computer Program for Quantum Mechanical Close-Coupling Calculations for Inelastic Collisions," In: *Modern Techniques in Computational Chemistry: METECC–94*, E. Clementi (Ed.), STEF: Cagliari, 1993, Vol. C, pp. 1–46.
22. R. Bellman and R. Kalaba, "On the Principle of Invariant Imbedding and Propagation through Inhomogenous Media," *Proceedings of the National Academy of Sciences U.S.A.*, Vol. 42, 1965, pp. 629–632.
23. E. P. Wigner and L. Eisenbud, "Higher Angular Momentum and Long Range Interaction in Resonance Reactions," *Physical Review*, Vol. 72, 1948, pp. 29–41.

24. D. W. Schwenke, K. Haug, D. G. Truhlar, R. H. Schweizer, J. Z. H. Zhang, Y. Sun, and D. J. Kouri, "Storage Management Strategies in Large-Scale Quantum Dynamics Calculations," *Theoretica Chimica Acta*, Vol. 72, 1987, pp. 237–251.
25. D. W. Schwenke and D. G. Truhlar, "An Optimized Quadrature Scheme for Matrix Elements over the Eigenfunctions of General Anharmonic Potentials," *Computer Physics Communications*, Vol. 34, 1984, pp. 57–64.
26. R. de Vogelaere, "A Method for the Numerical Integration of Differential Equations of Second Order Without Explicit First Derivatives," *Journal of Research of the National Bureau of Standards*, Vol. 54, 1955, pp. 119–125.
27. G. Strang, *Introduction to Applied Mathematics*, Wellesley: Wellesley-Cambridge Press, 1986. (758 pp.)
28. R. G. Gordon, "New Method for Constructing Wave Functions for Bound States and Scattering," *Journal of Chemical Physics*, Vol. 51, 1969, pp. 14–25.
29. L. Schlessinger, "Use of Analyticity in the Calculation of Nonrelativistic Scattering Amplitudes," *Physical Review*, Vol. 167, 1968, pp. 1411–1423.
30. L. Schlessinger, "Calculation of Some Three-Body Scattering Amplitudes," *Physical Review*, Vol. 171, 1968, pp. 1523–1527.
31. S. C. Pieper, J. Wright, and L. Schlessinger, "Calculations of Three-Particle Scattering Amplitudes Using Local Yukawa Potentials," *Physical Review D*, Vol. 3, 1971, pp. 2419–2424.
32. Y. Sun, D. J. Kouri, D. G. Truhlar, and D. W. Schwenke, "Dynamical Basis Sets for Algebraic Variational Calculations in Quantum Mechanical Scattering Theory," *Physical Review A*, Vol. 41, 1990, pp. 4857–4862.
33. D. W. Schwenke, S. L. Mielke, and D. G. Truhlar, "Variational Reactive Scattering Calculations: Computational Optimization Strategies," *Theoretica Chimica Acta*, Vol. 79, 1991, pp. 241–269.
34. Y. Sun and D. J. Kouri, "Scattered Wave Variational Principle for Atom-Diatom Reactive Scattering: Hybrid Basis Set Calculations," *Chemical Physics Letters*, Vol. 179, 1991, pp. 142–146.
35. S. L. Mielke, D. G. Truhlar, and D. W. Schwenke, "Improved Techniques for Outgoing Wave Variational Principle Calculations of Converged State-to-State Transition Probabilities for Chemical Reactions," *Journal of Chemical Physics*, Vol. 95, 1991, pp. 5930–5939.
36. G. J. Tawa, S. L. Mielke, D. G. Truhlar, and D. W. Schwenke, "Linear Algebraic Formulation of Reactive Scattering with General Basis Functions," In: *Advances in Molecular Vibrations and Collision Dynamics*, Vol. 2B ("Quantum Reactive Scattering"), J. M. Bowman (Ed.), Greenwich: JAI Press, 1994, pp. 45–116.
37. G. J. Tawa, S. L. Mielke, D. G. Truhlar, and D. W. Schwenke, "Algebraic Variational and Propagation Formalisms for Quantal Dynamics Calculations of Electronic-to-Vibrational, Rotational Energy Transfer and Application to the Quenching of the 3p State of Sodium by Hydrogen Molecules," *Journal of Chemical Physics*, Vol. 100, 1994, pp. 5751–5777.
38. Y. Sun, D. J. Kouri, and D. G. Truhlar, "A Comparative Analysis of Variational Methods for Inelastic and Reactive Scattering,," *Nuclear Physics*, Vol. A508, 1990, pp. 41c–61c.

39. D. W. Schwenke, K. Haug, D. G. Truhlar, Y. Sun, J. Z. H. Zhang, and D. J. Kouri, "Variational Basis-Set Calculations of Accurate Quantum Mechanical Reaction Probabilities," *Journal of Physical Chemistry*, Vol. 91, 1987, pp. 6080–6082.
40. D. G. Truhlar, D. W. Schwenke, and D. J. Kouri, "Quantum Dynamics of Chemical Reactions by Converged Algebraic Variational Calculations," *Journal of Physical Chemistry*, Vol. 94, 1990, pp. 7346–7352.
41. R. G. Newton, *Scattering Theory of Waves and Particles*, 2nd ed., New York: Springer-Verlag, 1982. (743 pp.)
42. G. Staszewska and D. G. Truhlar, "Rapid Convergence of Discrete-Basis Representations of the Amplitude Density for Quantal Scattering Calculations," *Chemical Physics Letters*, Vol. 130, 1986, pp. 341–345.
43. D. W. Schwenke, M. Mladenovic, M. Zhao, D. G. Truhlar, Y. Sun, and D. J. Kouri, "Computational Strategies and Improvements in the Linear Algebraic Variational Approach to Rearrangement Scattering," In Ref. 2, pp. 131–168.
44. D. W. Schwenke and D. G. Truhlar, "Localized Basis Functions and Other Computational Improvements in Variational Nonorthogonal Basis Function Methods for Quantum Mechanical Scattering Problems Involving Chemical Reactions," In: *Computing Methods in Applied Sciences and Engineering*, R. Glowinski and A. Lichnewsky (Eds.), Philadelphia: SIAM, 1990, pp. 291–310.
45. M. S. Reeves, D. C. Chatfield, and D. G. Truhlar, "Preconditioned Complex Generalized Minimal Residual Algorithm for Dense Algebraic Variational Equations in Quantum Reactive Scattering," *Journal of Chemical Physics*, Vol. 99, 1993, pp. 2739–2751.
46. S. L. Mielke, R. S. Friedman, D. G. Truhlar, and D. W. Schwenke, "High-Energy State-to-State Quantum Dynamics for $D + H_2(v = j = 1) \rightarrow HD(v' = 1, j') + H$," *Chemical Physics Letters*, Vol. 188, 1992, pp. 359–367.
47. S. L. Mielke, G. C. Lynch, D. G. Truhlar, and D. W. Schwenke, "A More Accurate Potential Energy Surface and Quantum Mechanical Cross Section Calculations for the $F + H_2$ Reaction," *Chemical Physics Letters*, Vol. 213, 1993, pp. 10–16; erratum: in press.
48. S. L. Mielke, D. G. Truhlar, and D. W. Schwenke, "Comparison of Theoretical and Experimental Differential Cross Sections for the $H + D_2$ Reaction," *Journal of Physical Chemistry*, Vol. 98, 1994, pp. 1053–1057.
49. D. C. Chatfield, R. S. Friedman, D. G. Truhlar, B. C. Garrett, and D. W. Schwenke, "Global Control of Suprathreshold Reactivity by Quantized Transition States," *Journal of the American Chemical Society*, Vol. 113, 1991, pp. 486–494.
50. D. C. Chatfield, R. S. Friedman, G. C. Lynch, D. G. Truhlar, and D. W. Schwenke, "The Nature and Role of Quantized Transition States in the Accurate Quantum Dynamics of the Reaction $O + H_2 \rightarrow OH + H$," *Journal of Chemical Physics*, Vol. 98, 1993, pp. 342–362.
51. S. L. Mielke, G. C. Lynch, D. G. Truhlar, and D. W. Schwenke, "*Ab Initio* Chemical Kinetics: Converged Quantal Reaction Rate Constants for the $D + H_2$ System," *Journal of Physical Chemistry*, to be published.

52. D. W. Schwenke, S. L. Mielke, G. J. Tawa, R. S. Friedman, P. Halvick, and D. G. Truhlar, "Converged Quantum Mechanical Calculations of Electronic-to-Vibrational, Rotational Energy Transfer Probabilities in a System with a Conical Intersection," *Chemical Physics Letters*, Vol. 203, 1993, pp. 565-572.
53. S. L. Mielke, G. J. Tawa, D. G. Truhlar, and D. W. Schwenke, "Energy Transfer through Exciplex Funnel States," *Journal of the American Chemical Society*, Vol. 115, 1993, pp. 6436–6437.
54. S. L. Mielke, G. J. Tawa, D. G. Truhlar, and D. W. Schwenke, "Partial Widths of Feshbach Funnel Resonances in the Na(3p)·H_2 Exciplex," *International Journal of Quantum Chemistry Symposia*, Vol. 27, 1993, pp. 621–632.
55. J. V. Michael and J. R. Fischer, "Rate Constants for the Reaction D + H_2 → HD + H over the Temperature Range 655–1979 K, by the Flash Photolysis-Shock Tube Technique," *Journal of Physical Chemistry*, Vol. 94, 1990, pp. 3318–3323.
56. B. A. Ridley, W. R. Schulz, and D. J. Le Roy, "Kinetics of the Reaction D + H_2 = HD + H," *Journal of Chemical Physics*, Vol. 44, 1966, pp. 3344–3347.
57. A. A. Westenberg, N. de Haas, "Atom-Molecule Kinetics Using ESR Detection II. Results for D + H_2 → HD + H and H + D_2 → HD + D," *Journal of Chemical Physics*, Vol. 47, 1967, pp. 1393–1405.
58. D. N. Mitchell and D. J. Le Roy, "Rate Constants for the Reaction D + H_2 = DH and H at Low Temperature using ESR Determination," *Journal of Chemical Physics*, Vol. 58, 1973, pp. 3449–3453.
59. A. J. C. Varandas, F. B. Brown, C. A. Mead, D. G. Truhlar, and N. C. Blais, "A Double Many–Body Expansion of the Two Lowest–Energy Potential Surfaces and Nonadiabatic Coupling for H_3," *Journal of Chemical Physics*, Vol. 86, 1987, pp. 6258–6269.
60. B. Liu, "*Ab Initio* Potential Energy Surface for Linear H_3," *Journal of Chemical Physics*, Vol. 58, 1973, pp. 1925–1937.
61. P. Siegbahn and B. Liu, "An Accurate Three-Dimensional Potential Energy Surface for H_3," *Journal of Chemical Physics*, Vol. 68, 1978, pp. 2457–2465.
62. M. R. A. Blomberg and B. Liu, "The H_3 Potential Surface Revisited," *Journal of Chemical Physics*, Vol. 82, 1985, pp. 1050–1051.
63. D. M. Neumark, A. M. Wodtke, G. N. Robinson, C. C. Hayden, and Y. T. Lee, "Molecular Beam Studies of the F + H_2 Reaction," *Journal of Chemical Physics*, Vol. 82, 1985, pp. 3045–3066.
64. F. J. Aoiz, V. J. Herrero, O. Puentedura, and V. Sáez Rábanos, "State-Resolved Differential Cross Sections for the H + D_2 ($v = 0, j$) → HD (v', j') + D Reaction from Quasiclassical Trajectory Calculations," *Chemical Physics Letters*, Vol. 198, 1992, pp. 321–327.
65. H. Pelzer and E. Wigner, "Über die Geschwindigkeitskonstate von Austauschreaktionen," *Zeitschrift für physikalische Chemie, Abteilung B* (Leipzig), Vol. 15, 1932 , pp. 445–471.
66. H. Eyring, "The Activated Complex in Chemical Reactions," *Journal of Chemical Physics*, Vol. 3, 1935, pp. 107–115.

67. E. Wigner, "Über das Überschreiten von Potentialschwellen bei chemischen Reaktionen," *Zeitschrift für physikalische Chemie, Abteilung B* (Leipzig), Vol. 19, 1932, pp. 203–216.
68. L. Melander and W. H. Saunders, Jr., *Reaction Rates of Isotopic Molecules*, New York: John Wiley & Sons, 1980. (331 pp.)
69. D. C. Chatfield, R. S. Friedman, D. W. Schwenke, and D. G. Truhlar, "The Control of Chemical Reactivity by Quantized Transition States," *Journal of Physical Chemistry*, Vol. 96, 1992, pp. 2414–2421.
70. B. R. Johnson and N. W. Winter, "Classical Trajectory Study of the Effect of Vibrational Energy in the Reaction of Molecular Hydrogen with Atomic Oxygen," *Journal of Chemical Physics*, Vol. 66, 1977, pp. 4116–4125.
71. G. C. Schatz, "A Coupled States Distorted Wave Study of the $O(^3P) + H_2$ (D_2, HD, DH) Reaction," *Journal of Chemical Physics*, Vol. 83, 1985, pp. 5677–5686.
72. B. C. Garrett and D. G. Truhlar, "Thermal and State–Selected Rate Constant Calculations for $O(^3P) + H_2 \rightarrow OH + H$ and Isotopic Analogs," *International Journal of Quantum Chemistry*, Vol. 29, 1986, pp. 1463–1482.
73. E. Wigner, "The Transition State Method," *Transactions of the Faraday Society*, Vol. 34, 1938, pp. 29–41.
74. E. C. Anderson and J. Dongarra, "Performance of LAPACK: A Portable Library of Numerical Linear Algebra Routines," Proceedings of the IEEE, Vol. 81, 1993, pp. 1094–1102.

Toward Teraflop Computing
and New Grand
Challenge Applications

ISBN-1-56072-247-9

EXACT QUANTUM CHEMISTRY FROM HIGH PERFORMANCE COMPUTING AND MONTE CARLO METHODS

James B. Anderson

Department of Chemistry
The Pennsylvania State University
University Park, PA 16802

INTRODUCTION

In one of the first papers to discuss the many-electron problem Dirac [1] noted in 1926 that "The underlying physical laws necessary for the mathematical description of a large part of physics and the whole of chemistry are thus completely known, and the difficulty is only that the exact application of these laws leads to equations much too complicated to be soluble." He went on to say, "It therefore becomes desirable that approximate practical methods of applying quantum mechanics be developed, which can lead to an explanation of the main features of complex atomic systems *without too much computation*."

Today, our definition of 'too much computation' is substantially different and our objective is not simply 'an explanation of the main features' but has become the exact description of these features obtained from exact solution of the Schrödinger equation.

The exact solution of the Schrödinger equation for many electron systems is one of the Grand Challenges to Computational Science [2]. More specifically, the challenge is that of overcoming 'the node problem' or 'the sign problem in quantum Monte Carlo'[3,4].

In fact, it is now possible to obtain exact solutions of the Schrödinger equation for systems of a few electrons [5-11]. These systems include the molecular ion H_3^+, the molecule H_2, the reaction intermediate H-H-H, the unstable pair H-He, the stable dimer He_2, and the trimer He_3. The quantum Monte Carlo method used in solving the time-independent Schrödinger equation for these systems is exact in that it requires no physical or mathematical assumptions beyond those of the Schrödinger equation. As in most Monte Carlo methods there is a statistical or sampling error which is readily estimated.

In this chapter we review the exact quantum Monte Carlo method, its successful applications thus far to systems of a few electrons, and the prospects for successful applications to larger systems. Approximate methods applicable to larger systems are mentioned, but the emphasis is on 'exact' quantum chemistry.

QUANTUM MONTE CARLO

There are many different Monte Carlo methods which might be used for solving the Schrödinger equation, but only three of these are currently popular in calculations of electronic structure. The three are collectively referred to as quantum Monte Carlo methods (QMC). They are the variational quantum Monte Carlo method (VQMC), the diffusion quantum Monte Carlo method (DQMC), and the Green's function quantum Monte Carlo method (GFQMC).

The variational method is the same as conventional analytic variational methods except that the integrals required are evaluated by Monte Carlo procedures. The expectation value of the energy is determined for a trial function ψ_T using Metropolis sampling based on ψ_T^2. The expectation value <E> is given by an average of local energies, $H\psi_T / \psi_T$ or E_{loc}.

As in analytic variational calculations the expectation value $< E >$ is an upper limit to the true value of the energy E. In determining $< E >$ it is not necessary to carry out analytic integrations; and, since only differentiation of the trial wavefunction is required to evaluate the local energy, the trail wavefunction may take any desired functional form. Thus, relatively simple trial functions may incorporate electron correlation effects rather accurately and produce expectation values of the energy well below those of the Hartree-Fock limit. Except in the limit of a large number of terms the VQMC method is not an exact method.

The diffusion and Green's function methods are based on the similarity of the Schrödinger equation and the diffusion equation and the use of a random walk process to simulate diffusion. The relation of the Schrödinger equation to the diffusion equation and to diffusion was noted as early as 1932 by Wigner [12], and a random walk simulation of the Schrödinger equation was discussed by Metropolis and Ulam [13] and by King [14] in 1949.

The time-independent Schrödinger equation, $H\psi = E\psi$, for a single particle is given by

$$\frac{\hbar^2}{2m}\nabla^2\psi(\vec{X}) - V(\vec{X})\psi(\vec{X}) = -E\psi(\vec{X}), \qquad (1)$$

where the potential energy V is a function of position. The equation has as solutions the eigenfunctions $\psi(\vec{X})$ together with their eigenvalues E_i.

In the solution of partial differential equations it is in some cases easier to solve the corresponding transient equation than to solve a steady-state equation directly. If we introduce an imaginary time τ and define the transient function

$$\psi(\vec{X},\tau)=\psi(\vec{X})e^{-E\tau}, \tag{2}$$

$\psi(\vec{X},\tau)$ obeys the relations

$$\frac{\partial\psi(\vec{X},\tau)}{\partial\tau}=-E\psi(\vec{X},\tau) \tag{3}$$

and

$$\frac{\partial\psi}{\partial\tau}=\frac{\hbar^2}{2m}\nabla^2\psi-V\psi. \tag{4}$$

The wavefunction $\psi(\vec{X},\tau)$ consists of a spatial function $\psi(\vec{X})$ changing exponentially with time. There is an infinite number of solutions having energies higher than the lowest-energy or ground-state solution. If an initial function contains components of the ground-state wavefunction and higher-state wavefunctions the more rapid exponential decay of the higher-energy wavefunctions, as indicated by Eq. (2), ensures that the solution at large values of is the lowest-energy solution.

The Schrödinger equation in imaginary time, Eq. (4). is identical in form to Fick's diffusion equation to which a first-order reaction rate term is added,

$$\frac{\partial C(\vec{X},t)}{\partial t}=D\nabla^2C(\vec{X},t)-kC(\vec{X},t). \tag{5}$$

In the language of mathematics the two equations are 'isomorphic'. Diffusion can be simulated by a random walk procedure with particles subject to random motion, moving in a time interval Δt a distance ΔX in one direction or the other in each of the three dimensions.

The diffusion quantum Monte Carlo method for solving the Schrödinger equation in one dimension is a repeated sequence of operations. An initial collection of particles (hereafter, psi particles or psips) is distributed on a line. Time is advanced one step Δt and each psip is moved right or left one step Δx. Then each psip gives birth to a new psip with a probability $P_d = -V\Delta t$ if V is negative or disappears with a probability $P_d = -V\Delta t$ if V is positive. Time is advanced another step and the process is repeated. With increasing time and number of iterations the normalized distribution of psips approaches a 'steady-state' distribution fluctuating about an average stead-state distribution which corresponds to the lowest-energy wavefunction satisfying the time-independent Schrödinger equation.

The Green's function quantum Monte Carlo method is similar to the DQMC method but takes advantage of the properties of Green's functions useful in solving the steady-state diffusion equation. The GFQMC method was proposed first by Kalos [15] for nodeless systems and we describe it here for nodeless systems. The challenge of systems with nodes is discussed in a later section.

The time-independent Schrödinger equation, Eq. (4), may be written in the form

$$-\nabla^2\psi(\vec{X})+k^2\psi(\vec{X})=k^2\frac{V(\vec{X})}{E}\psi(\vec{X}). \tag{6}$$

The Green's function for Eq. (6) which satisfies the boundary conditions for a problem in electronic structure (i.e., $\psi\rightarrow 0$ as $X\rightarrow\infty$) is a known function. Sampling is based on that property of the Green's function which reproduces the wavefunction from itself,

$$\psi(\vec{X})=\int d\vec{X}^{\prime}G_0(\vec{X},\vec{X}^{\prime})\frac{V(\vec{X}^{\prime})}{E}\psi(\vec{X}^{\prime}). \tag{7}$$

Repeated application of Eq. (7) to an initially arbitrary wavefunction produces a wavefunction which is the lowest-energy solution to the Schrödinger equation for the boundary conditions specified. A psip in the first distribution may be transferred to the second distribution by multiplying its weight by sampling the Green's function distribution and moving the psip to its new position. Repetition for an initially arbitrary collection of psips leads to a set of psips which is a sample of points from the lowest-energy wavefunction for the boundary conditions and any other constraints imposed. Further repetition continues the sampling.

The DQMC and GFQMC methods yield samples of the wavefunction from which, in principle, all the properties of a system may be determined. The energy is usually evaluated using an importance sampling scheme proposed by Grimm and Storer [16] to obtain highest accuracies in the energy.

NODE STRUCTURE

For a system of either bosons or fermions the wavefunction must have the correct properties of symmetry and antisymmetry. Except in the simplest cases the wavefunction for a system of n fermions is positive and negative in different regions of the 3n-dimensional space of the fermions. The regions are separated by one or more (3n - 1)-dimensional hypersurfaces which cannot be specified except by solution of the Schrödinger equation.

The procedures described above for DQMC and GFQMC lead to the lowest-energy solutions for boson systems which are nodeless ground-state wavefunctions. They also lead to the ground-state in the case of two electrons (fermions) of opposite spin for which the wavefunction is symmetric to the exchange of the two electrons. For a system of two or more electrons of the same spin the wavefunction must be antisymmetric to the exchange of electrons of the same spin and must contain one or more nodal hypersurfaces. The treatment of systems with nodes requires that the solutions be constrained to the appropriate antisymmetry.

In the first forty years of quantum chemistry the question of the structure and properties of nodal hypersurfaces received very little attention. Only recently, with a knowledge of node structure required for developing Monte Carlo methods, have the structure and properties of nodal hypersurfaces been examined in detail.

For a molecule with m spin-up electrons and n spin-down electrons the node structure is approximately that of the product of two functions, one for spin-up and the other for spin-down electrons. The 3m-dimensional configuration space of spin-up electrons is divided by a (3m - 1)-dimensional nodal hypersurface into two geometrically similar regions nested together face-to-face. The (3n - 1)-dimensional nodal hypersurface for the spin-down electrons has equivalent characteristics.

SOLUTIONS TO THE NODE PROBLEM

Unless the psip distribution in a DQMC or GFQMC calculation is restricted in some way it will proceed to the nodeless ground-state wavefunction of a boson system. The problem of restricting the distribution in order to obtain the desired solutions for fermion systems--the node problem--has been the subject of a number of investigations and these have led to a variety of methods for restricting the solutions. Two of these are especially useful: the fixed-node method and the exact cancellation method.

The fixed-node method, proposed by Anderson [3] in 1975 for use with diffusion Monte Carlo calculations, allows the treatment of ground and excited states with use of approximate nodal surfaces which act as sinks for diffusing psips. The nodal hypersurfaces are boundaries on which the wavefunction is fixed at zero and the Schrödinger equation is, or may be, solved exactly within these boundaries. The fixed-node method has been found to be remarkably successful in many cases, for small molecules and large [4, 17-22]. Nevertheless, unless the nodal surfaces used are exactly correct, the fixed-node method yields only an upper bound to the true energy and is not an exact method.

In another method cancellation of positive and negative psips in close proximity is used to stabilize the positive and negative populations. Arnow, Kalos, Lee, and Schmidt [23] devised an exact cancellation method for GFQMC in which partial cancellations are made on the basis of overlapping distributions of positions for pairs of positive and negative psips. Coker and Watts [24] used cancellation of psips in close proximity in DQMC to obtain stable populations. Anderson, Traynor, and Bobhosian [25] reported an improved exact cancellation method for GFQMC, described in detail below, which has produced excellent results for a number of small systems. Zhang and Kalos [26] have reported a somewhat different type of cancellation scheme.

EXACT CANCELLATION SCHEME

We describe here an exact cancellation scheme which is based on the earlier exact cancellation scheme of Arnow *et al.* [23] and incorporates some of the best features of fixed-node, released-node, and other cancellation methods. The method takes full advantage of the symmetric and antisymmetric properties of wavefunctions and it offers pairwise cancellations of psips as well as self-cancellations and multiple collective cancellations. The method is 'exact' as defined above and it has been applied successfully to a number of few-electron systems.

The basic idea of cancellation is most easily illustrated with the case of the first excited state of a particle in a two-dimensional box. A quantum Monte Carlo calculation for the excited state can be carried out with positive and negative psips, initially separated left right. In the absence of cancellation the two populations spread through-out the available configuration space, penetrate each other, and independently approach the symmetric distribution for the ground state. If positive and negative psips in close proximity are allowed to cancel each other, the two populations tend to cancel each other and produce separated distributions, in which the net population on the left of center is positive and that on the right of center is negative. Without any control a fluctuation in populations will eventually lead to the dominance of either positive or negative psips and one of the ground-state distributions. But, if the two populations are controlled to maintain equal numbers of positive and negative psips and if cancellations are properly executed, the net distribution evolves to that of the exact wavefunction.

There are several ways of cancelling positive and negative particles. Some of these are rigorously correct but not efficient and some are efficient but not rigorously correct. One might cancel positive and negative particles occupying the same position, but the probability of two psips occupying the same position is vanishingly small. One might cancel psips within an arbitrary distance of each other, but that would lead to a bias in the distributions. Fortunately, there is one way which is rigorously correct and reasonably efficient for systems of a few electrons: cancellation on the basis of the overlap of the distributions to which the psips are moved.

In our own work [30] we have used an improved procedure which eliminates the overlap integral, facilitates multiple cancellations, and climinates the computationally expensive conditional acceptance of moves. The improved procedure may be considered a Monte Carlo version of the earlier procedure.

EXACT CANCELLATION: STABILITY

The essential requirement for a successful calculation is a high ratio of positive to negative psips. In the absence of cancellation equal numbers of positive and negative psips in all regions will lead to an indetermiant value for the energy. In the words of the well known song, "You've got to ac-cent-tchu-ate the positive, E-lim-my-nate the negative, Latch on to the affirmative, Don't mess with Mister Inbetween." [27].

Of course, a high ratio of negative to positive would serve just as well. It is the in-between that one must avoid. The way to accentuate the positive is to promote cancellation in every way possible. The number of ways is at present limited to increasing the density of psips and optimizing the step sizes and energy, which are not independent. A variety of other possibilities remains unexplored.

The obvious way of increasing psip density is to increase the number of psips up to the limit of available computer memory. Beyond that one can make full use of symmetry to concentrate psips in a single region of configuration space.

EXACT CANCELLATION: COMPUTATIONAL DETAILS

Computations using the exact cancellation scheme outlined here are relatively easy to carry out. For systems of 2-6 electrons the programs used consist of 200-800 Fortran statements and the bulk of the statements are those for evaluating trial functions and their derivatives. The memory requirements vary with the number of electrons and the number of psips required for stability, but work stations such as the IBM RISC 6000-580 have been found adequate for the few-electron problems we have treated.

Our calculations have been performed on various IBM RISC 6000 machines, the IBM 3090-600S, the Cray C90, and the Thinking Machines CM-2 and CM-5 Connection Machines. Each of these machines, as well as an individual processor on the massively parallel CM-5, is easily capable of running programs with 20,000 psips and with a little care as many as 200,000 psips.

The calculations are by their nature easily carried out on vector and parallel machines. For very high accuracies one needs an accumulation of results and it is unimportant whether one has a few long runs or many short runs. The runs can be carried out entirely independently on separate processors of a massively parallel machine.

In using IBM RISC work stations we found it convenient, especially when using machines not our own, to set up these machines for runs at low priority of about 24 hours duration, which on completion automatically E-mail the results to us, select a new random number seed, and begin another run. In this way we could keep dozens of low cost computers fully and usefully occupied with very little human effort.

A full two-electron, two-proton calculation [5] for H_2 to determine its exact energy without the Born-Oppenheimer approximation, performed on a 32,768-processor Thinking Machines CM-2, was the first quantum calculation to be reported for a massively parallel machine.

THE MOLECULAR ION H_3^+

The ground state of the molecular ion H_3^+ has two electrons of opposite spin and thus no nodes in its wavefunction. Exact Green's function cancellation is not required in QMC calculations for this system; but, the results are, of course, exact for such calculations and the use of cancellation permits large step sizes and leads to very high accuracies. The most recent exact QMC calculation, which is now a few years old, yielded an energy accurate within ±0.000 001 hartrees (i.e., within 0.0016 kcal/mole).

The molecular ion H_3^+ has a long history in quantum chemistry. It is the simplest polyatomic molecule (or molecular ion) and for that reason has served as a test species for developing theoretical methods in quantum mechanics. The first calculations were analytic variational calculations by Hirschfelder [28] in 1938 yielding an energy of -1.2929 hartrees. The most recent Monte Carlo calculations are our own [6] of a few years ago yielding -1.343 835 ±0.000 001 hartrees.

Our own experience with H_3^+ reflects the improvement in methods and computers since 1975. The results are listed in Table 1 and they show an improvement in accuracy from ±0.013 to ±0.000 001 hartrees, a factor of 13,000.

Table 1. Some QMC results for the ground-state energy of H_3^+ in its equilateral-triangle nuclear configuration with R = 1.6500 to 1.6600 bohrs.

Reference	Year	Method	Separation bohrs	Energy hartrees
[3]	1975	DQMC	1.66	-1.344 ± 0.013
[4]	1976	DQMC	1.66	-1.341 4 ± 0.004 3
[29]	1981	DQMC	1.65	-1.343 9 ± 0.000 2
[30]	1987	GFQMC	1.65	-1.343 76 ± 0.000 03
[31]	1988	GFQMC	1.65	-1.343 877 ± 0.000 054
[6]	1992	GFQMC + cancellation	1.65	-1.343 835 ± 0.000 001

THE MOLECULE H_2

The ground state energy of the molecule H_2 has been determined in GFQMC calculations by Traynor, Anderson, and Boghosian [5] without the use of the Born-Oppenheimer or any other adiabatic approximations. The complete four-body problem of two electrons and two protons was treated as inseparable.

The history of accurate calculations for H_2 begins with the work of James and Coolidge [32] in 1933 which represented one of the first successes in solving the Schrödinger equation for molecules. More accurate results have since been obtained by many others, including in the 1960's Kolos and Roothaan [33] and Kolos and Wolniewicz [34] who used a variational approach together with a method by Born [35] for separating the complete Hamiltonian into two parts and neglecting off-diagonal terms in what is called an adiabatic approximation. This is an improvement over the Born-Oppenheimer approximation in which additional terms are neglected.

The calculated energies have been sued to predict the dissociation energy of H_2 and that in turn has been compared with the results of experimental measurements. As the accuracies of experiments and theory both improved the results shifted back and forth a bit, sometimes in agreement, sometimes not.

Our calculations were performed on a 32,768-processor Thinking Machines CM-2 Connection Machine operated with 20-30 psips per processor. The processors were operated independently for blocks of iterations, in which the number of psips in a processor but not their total weight was fixed, interrupted at intervals of 100 iterations for redistributions among the processors to obtain approximately equal weights. The calculation time was about 60 hours. On a full-size 65,536-processor CM-2 the time would be about 30 hours and the average speed would be 1500 megaflops or 1.5×10^9 floating point operations per second.

The energy obtained, which includes the vibrational zero-point energy, was -1.164024 ± 0.000 009 hartrees. This corresponds to a dissociation energy of 36 118.6 ± 2.0 cm^{-1}, without taking into account any relativistic effects. With relativistic and radiative corrections the dissociation energy of H_2 becomes 36 117.9 ± 2.0 cm^{-1}. This value overlaps the best prior theoretical values as well as the best experimental values.

For the more accurate quantum Monte Carlo calculations currently underway we expect the higher accuracy afforded by the exact cancellation algorithm, the better trial function, and a still faster computer will allow us to challenge the accuracies of the best existing calculations and experiments.

POTENTIAL ENERGY SURFACE FOR THE REACTION $H + H_2 \rightarrow H_2 + H$

In 1956 Boys, Cook, Reeves, and Shavitt [36] published their pioneering paper entitled "Automatic Fundamental Calculations of Molecular Structure". In this paper they described the first 'computer' calculations of electronic structure and reported results for several systems including the system of three H atoms. They found the minimum in the classical barrier for the reaction $H + H_2 \rightarrow H_2 + H$ to occur for the collinear configuration H-H-H with separations of 1.757 bohrs having a height of 9.7 kcal/mol relative to reactants $H + H_2$ calculated with the same basis set.

Some 38 years later we find their calculations to be remarkably accurate and their predictions remarkably correct. An exact quantum Monte Carlo calculation [7] shows the barrier height to be 9.61 ± 0.01 kcal/mol relative to $H + H_2$ at the minimum which occurs for a collinear configuration with separations of 1.757 bohrs.

The exact quantum Monte Carlo calculations described here have produced a potential energy surface accurate to within ± 0.01 kcal/mol at the saddle point and within ± 0.01 kcal/mol or better elsewhere on the surface. With this surface, essentially exact full-quantum calculations of reactive scattering, now carried out in a number of laboratories, can predict all the major observables for this reaction more accurately than they can be measured at the present time.

It is likely that, having moved ahead of experiment for the reaction $H + H_2 \rightarrow H_2 + H$ theory will remain ahead forever. Both theory and experiment for this reaction will certainly be improved but theory is likely to maintain its lead.

The accuracy of the Monte Carlo calculation for the H-H-H saddle point configuration is ±0.000 014 hartrees or 3 cm^{-1}. Clementi *et al.* [37] recently speculated that an analytic variational calculation for H-H-H accurate to within 10 cm^{-1} of the exact value "would call for somewhere around 3500 years" on a computer similar to the one used for the Monte Carlo calculation. As Clementi *et al.* pointed out, there are many opportunities for significant reductions in the computational effort for analytic variational calculations and it may be possible to 'reduce the task to 10 to 20 years" or even less [37]. Other workers suggest 10 to 20 hours is a possible. There are also many opportunities for improving the Monte Carlo calculations. In any case three months is a lot less time than three millenia.

THE HELIUM DIMER He_2

The helium dimer presents another one of those problems which has been waiting a long time for an exact solution. The exact cancellation scheme has now provided a solution in the form of exact values of the potential energy for points on the Born Oppenheimer potential energy curve. Those points provide an excellent confirmation of experimental measurements: their error bars straddle the experimental-theoretical compromise potential energy curve of Aziz and Slaman [38] which successfully predicts a variety of experimental measurements.

The term 'basis set superposition error' was introduced to the literature of quantum mechanics by Liu and McLean [39] in their 1973 paper describing their first calculation of the helium-helium interaction. In that work and in two subsequent investigations Liu and McLean [40,41] made repeated improvements in eliminating basis set superposition error in extensive CI calculations. Their sequence of results for the minimum in the potential curve relative to separated atoms is 9.5 K in 1973, -10.76 K in 1975, and -10.94 K in 1989.

The accurate prediction of the helium-helium potential is an extremely difficult problem. The well depth is about 11 K (about 0.000 035 hartrees) and one would like an accuracy of at least one percent of the depth or 0.1 K (0.000 000 3 hartrees). The total electronic energy is about that of two separated helium atoms or -5.807 448 hartrees, so that the desired accuracy is about one part in 2 x 10^7 of the total energy and one part in 3 x 10^5 of the correlation energy.

The recent calculations of Liu and McLean [41] yield total electronic energies 1200K above the exact values for the total energies. Yet, the relative values of the energies, obtained as the differences in total energies of interacting atoms and separated atoms calculated with the same basis set, are in excellent agreement with the exact Monte Carlo results and the potential energy derived from experiments. Nevertheless, one should be cautions about relative errors of less than 0.1 K in calculations with total errors of 1200 K.

The exact quantum Monte Carlo calculations of Anderson, Traynor and Boghosian [10] gave very high accuracies for the helium-helium interaction energies. The calculations were performed on Thinking Machines CM-5 Connection Machine computers with 32 to 250 processors. The speed and memory of each processor were sufficiently high that completely independent calculations with 20,000 psips could be performed on each processor. Thus, the calculations were fully parallel.

Energies were determined for eight internuclear distances in the range of 3.0 to 15.0 bohrs as well as for infinite separation. Results are listed in Table 2. The error bars of the calculated interaction energies straddle the analytic variational results of Liu and McLean [54] and the experimental-theoretical compromise potential of Aziz and Slaman [38]. The exact quantum Monte Carlo interaction energies are not 'better' but they are known to be free of basis set superposition error, any other systematic error, and any inputs beyond the basic constants. In the exact quantum Monte Carlo case one may judge the experimental curve by how well it agrees with the theoretical curves rather than the reverse.

Table 2. Intermolecular potential for the helium-helium system calculated by exact quantum Monte Carlo method [10]. Other values are listed for comparison.

	Potential Energy, K		
Internuclear distance	Theory	Experiment	Theory
bohrs	Exact QMC[a]	Aziz-Slaman[b]	Liu-McLean[c]
3.0	3812. ± 96.	3792.	3767.
4.5	60.0 ± 1.9	58.5	
5.0	-0.41 ± 0.78	-0.39	-0.33
5.6	-10.94 ± 0.17	-10.97	-10.94
6.6	-6.25 ± 0.10	-6.36	
7.5	-3.05 ± 0.10	-3.06	3.057
9.0	0.96 ± 0.10	-0.99	-0.985
15.0	-0.04 ± 0.05	-0.042	
	+0.01 ± 0.02	(0.0)	(0.0)

[a]Ref. [10] [b]Ref. [38] [c]Ref. [41]

DISCUSSION

It is clear that the Green's function cancellation method described in these pages can provide 'exact' results for molecular sytems of a few electrons. In the past half century available computer speeds have increased by a factor of ten about every four years. Speeds have increased from about 10 floating point operations per second in 1945 to about 10^{12} floating point operations per second in 1994 with a significant change in cost. And there is no end in sight. Thus, one can expect calculations for few-electron systems to become relatively cheaper and correspondingly more accurate.

For not-so-few-electron systems and larger systems predictions are much more difficult. Adding an electron increases the dimensionality of a problem by three and increases the degree of difficulty of cancellation by a factor of ten at the very least. Without any improvements in technique, one might then expect to progress to larger problems at a rate no faster than an additional electron every four years. That would seem discouraging except for the fact that improvements in quantum Monte Carlo methods continue to be made at a fairly rapid pace. There is a backlog of good ideas in the quantum Monte Carlo area waiting for its practiitoners to find the time to develop them. Some of these are sure to lead to better 'exact' quantum Monte Carlo calculations. Others are sure to lead to better approximate quantum Monte Carlo calculations--not exact, but very, very accurate--more accurate than those of any other method for larger systems.

ACKNOWLEDGMENT

Support of this work by the National Science Foundation and the Office of Naval Research is gratefully acknowledged.

REFERENCES

1. P. A. M. Dirac, Proc. Roy. Soc. (London) A123, 1929, p. 714.
2. B. J. Alder, *Fut. Gen. Comp. Sys.* Vol. 5, 1989, p. 191.
3. J. B. Anderson, *J. Chem. Phys.* Vol. 63, 1975, p. 1499.
4. J. B. Anderson, *J. Chem. Phys.* Vol. 65, 1976, p. 4121.
5. C. A. Traynor, J. B. Anderson, and B. M. Boghosian, *J. Chem. Phys.* Vol. 94, 1991, p. 3657.
6. J. B. Anderson, *J. Chem. Phys.* Vol. 96, 1992, p. 3702.
7. D. L. Diedrich and J. B. Anderson, *Science*, Vol. 258, 1992, p. 258.
8. D. L. Diedrich and J. B. Anderson, *J. Chem. Phys.* (in press).
9. A. Bhattacharya and J. B. Anderson, *Phys. Rev. A.* (in press).
10. J. B. Anderson, C. A. Traynor, and B. M. Boghosian, *J. Chem. Phys.*, Vol. 99, 1993, p. 345.
11. A. Bhattacharya and J. B. Anderson, *J. Chem. Phys.* (in press).
12. E. P. Wigner, *Phys. Rev.* Vol. 40, 1932, p. 749.
13. N. Metropolis and S. Ulam, *J. Am. Stat. Assoc.* Vol. 44, 1949, p. 335.
14. G. W. King, in Proceedings IBM Computation Seminar, Endicott, New York, 1949 (International Business Machines Corp., New York, 1951), p. 92.
15. M. H. Kalos, *Phys. Rev. A.* Vol. 128, 1962, p. 1791.
16. R. C. Grimm and R. G. Storer, *J. Comput. Phys.* Vol. 7, 1971, p. 134.
17. J. B. Anderson, *Int. J. Quant. Chem.* No. 15, 1979, p. 109.
18. P. J. Reynold, D. M. Ceperley, B. J. Alder, and W. A. Lester, *J. Chem. Phys.* Vol. 77, 1982, p. 5593.
19. F. Mentch and J. B. Anderson, *J. Chem. Phys.* Vol. 80, 1984, p. 2675.

20. D. R. Garmer and J. B. Anderson, *J. Chem. Phys.* Vol. 86, 1987, p. 4025.

21. D. R. Garmer and J. B. Anderson, *J. Chem. Phys.* Vol. 86, 1987, p. 7237.

22. L. Mitas, E. L. Shirley, and D. M. Ceperley, *J. Chem. Phys.* Vol. 95, 1991, p. 3167.

23. D. M. Arnow, M. H. Kalos, M. A. Lee, and K. E. Schmidt, *J. Chem. Phys.* Vol. 77, 1982, p. 5562.

24. D. F. Coker and R. O. Watts, *Mol Phys.* Vol. 58, 1986, p. 1113.

25. J. B. Anderson, C. A. Traynor, and B. M. Boghosian, *J. Chem. Phys.* Vol. 95, 1991, p. 7418.

26. S. Zhang and M. H. Kalos, *Phys. Rev. Lett.* Vol. 67, 1991, p. 3074.

27. J. Mercer and H. Allen, Ac-cent-tchu-ate The Positive, Harwin Music Corp., New York, 1944.

28. J. O. Hirschfelder, *J. Chem. Phys.* Vol. 6, 1938, p. 795.

29. F. Mentch and J. B. Anderson, *J. Chem. Phys.* Vol. 74, 1981, p. 6307.

30. J. B. Anderson, *J. Chem. Phys.* Vol. 86, 1987, p. 2839.

31. C. A. Traynor and J. B. Anderson, *Chem. Phys. Lett.* Vol. 147, 1988, p. 389.

32. H. M. James and A. S. Coolidge, *J. Chem. Phys.* Vol. 1, 1933, p. 825.

33. W. Kolos and C. C. J. Roothaan, *Rev. Mod. Phys.* Vol. 32, 1960, p. 219.

34. W. Kolos and L. Wolniewicz, *Rev. Mod. Phys.* Vol. 35, 1963, p. 473; *J. Chem. Phys.* No. 43, 1965, p. 2429; No. 49, 1968, p. 404.

35. M. Born, *Nachr. Akad. Wiss. Phys.* Vol. 1, 1951, p. 2149.

36. S. F. Boys, G. B. Cook, C. M. Reeves, and J. Shavitt, *Nature* Vol. 178, 1956, p. 1207.

37. E. Clementi, G. Corongiu, D. Bahattacharya, B. Feuston, D. Frye, A. Preiskorn, A. Rizzo, and W. Xue, *Chem. Rev.* Vol. 91, 1991, p. 679.

38. R. A. Aziz and M. J. Slaman, *J. Chem. Phys.* Vol. 94, 1991, 8047.

39. B. Liu and A. D. McLean, *J. Chem. Phys.* Vol. 59, 1973, p. 4557.

40. B. Liu and A. D. McLean, unpublished results (1975); Cited by B. Liu and A. D. McLean, *J. Chem. Phys.* Vol. 72, 1980, p. 3418.

41. B. Liu and A. D. McLean, *J. Chem. Phys.* Vol. 92, 1989, p. 2348.

PARALLEL PROCESSING WITH THE *AB INITIO* PROGRAM GAMESS

Theresa L. Windus, Michael W. Schmidt andMark S. Gordon

Department of Chemistry
Iowa State University
Ames, IA 50011

1. INTRODUCTION

The last decade has seen a large increase in the use of parallel methods in ab initio algorithms [2,3]. Most of the applications have been limited to self-consistent field (SCF) theory [2], however several groups have been delving into the use of parallel processing in post-SCF methods [3]. Examples are the work on integral transformations [3a-3d], MP2 energies [3e-3f], configuration interaction (CI) energies [3g-3i], coupled cluster energies [3j], and our recent work on multi-configurational SCF (MCSCF) energies and gradients [3a].

Our focus in the development of parallel electronic structure methods has been the program suite GAMESS (General Atomic and Molecular Electronic Structure System). The motivation for this endeavor had been twofold: (1) to develop new methods to improve computational efficiency and (2) to apply the new parallel methods to previously unapproachable problems in chemistry.

This paper will concentrate on an overview of the parallelization and selected applications of GAMESS. Section 2 will concentrate on a brief description of the overall model used to parallelize GAMESS, a brief description of the parallel implementation of the SCF code, and chemical applications using that code. Section 3 will concentrate on the parallel implementation of MCSCF energies and gradients.

2. SCF

While there are several different hardware and programming models available, the parallelization of GAMESS is accomplished using the single program, multiple data (SPMD) model assuming a distributed memory machine. This method also works on shared memory machines, but much more memory and communications are required than would be used for a program that is optimized to use shared memory. GAMESS also uses a "peer" model where all of the nodes execute essentially all of the code. This is in contrast to the traditional master-slave model where the slave nodes typically execute only certain portions of the code and the master node assigns tasks for the slaves to execute.

Adoption of the SPMD and peer models allows GAMESS to remain as one code that is relatively easy to maintain. The programmer does not have to continually think about the difference between the master and the slave code and make sure that the code works for both types of nodes. This method also allows as much of the program to perform in parallel as possible (i.e. trying to avoid sequential bottlenecks). The one exception to the peer model is that input and output is handled in a master-slave manner. The "master" node reads the input and broadcasts it to the "slave" nodes. In this manner, each node will have all of the information needed for subsequent calculations. The "master" node is also responsible for producing only one copy of the output.

TCGMSG was chosen to perform the parallel communications for GAMESS. This program is a message passing library developed by Harrison [4]. TCGMSG is portable across many different types of platforms, including groups of UNIX workstations connected by Ethernet, true parallel distributed memory machines such as the Touchstone Delta, and true parallel shared memory machines such as an Alliant. It uses the best type of communication available to the particular hardware it is running on. The portability feature and availability on UNIX workstations is very important for usability by the general chemical community that might not have access to "true" parallel machines.

Another reason for the choice of TCGMSG is that it was developed by a quantum chemist for use in computational chemistry codes. Therefore, it has many of functions needed for communications in a program such as GAMESS. Only a dozen routines are actually used for communication, so that the number of new functions needed to parallelize the code is small.

It is important to emphasize that there is only one universal version of GAMESS. The same version of GAMESS is used for both parallel and sequential applications. When running in sequential mode, GAMESS links to "stub" routines that function properly for one node. In order to run in parallel, GAMESS is relinked to the TCGMSG library instead of these stubs.

GAMESS calculates energies and gradients for all of the Hartree-Fock (HF) wavefunctions (restricted HF (RHF), unrestricted HF (UHF), restricted open-shell HF (ROHF) and generalized valence-bond (GVB)) in parallel. While parallelization of portions of these calculations is not new [2], the scope of the parallelization in GAMESS is. As much of the code as possible was parallelized to achieve reasonable overall scalability. Since the parallelization of the SCF portions of GAMESS has been presented elsewhere [2a], only a brief description will be included here.

The sections of the SCF code modified to run in parallel are: one-electron integrals, one-electron effective core potential (ECP) integrals, two-electron integrals, matrix multiplications, matrix diagonalization, one-electron gradient integrals, one-electron ECP gradient integrals, and two-electron gradient integrals. The matrix diagonalization is actually only semi-parallelized. When molecular symmetry is used, the Fock operator is in a block diagonal form, and each of these blocks is sent to a processor which diagonalizes its block using a sequential diagonalization routine. The final result is then accumulated on all nodes through a global summation routine. The methods for parallelizing the other sections have been discussed in previous work [2a] and will not be discussed here.

Since the gradients are parallelized, several other functions of GAMESS also work in parallel. These important features are molecular geometry optimization, transition state searching, intrinsic reaction coordinate following, and numerical hessians (second derivatives of the wavefunction with respect to nuclear coordinates). These functions are necessary to explore general chemical systems and reactions (which is our end goal).

The composite results of our work on parallel SCF calculations show that the current algorithm is scalable to about 256 nodes for relatively large molecules containing 250 - 400 basis functions on a system such as the Touchstone Delta. Our results also show that it is very useful to have at least two kinds of load balancing available. Currently, GAMESS uses a static load balancing technique (dubbed LOOP balancing) which is used to partition work into many relatively small pieces. This type of load balancing works best when the CPUs used are of approximately the same speed and work load. The other technique used is dynamic load balancing (dubbed NXTVAL balancing) which uses a shared counter (kept by TCGMSG) to distribute tasks to each processor when that processor completes its current task. Since communication is involved with the shared counter, the tasks are relatively larger than those used in the LOOP balancing method. This type of load balancing works best when the CPUs are of different speeds or work loads.

As mentioned in a previous paragraph, numerical hessians can be calculated in parallel once the gradients are parallelized. The hessian establishes the nature of a stationary point on the potential energy surface; that is, whether the molecular structure corresponds to a minimum, a saddle point, or a higher order saddle point. We have also recently developed an algorithm for the parallelization of analytic hessians for a small number of processors [5]. In this algorithm, different parts of the calculation are sent to different processors. For example, one processor performs the atomic to molecular integral transformation calculation, while one or more processors calculate the two-electron hessian integrals. The interested reader is referred to reference 5 for more information about this implementation.

With all of these parallel tools at hand for exploring chemical systems, we now summarize some of the applications that are currently being performed with GAMESS. Perhaps the largest volume of published applications using parallel GAMESS have been reported by Cundari and coworkers [6]. This work has centered on transition metal reactivity. In particular, methane activity has been explored with several transition metal complexes and the comparisons with experiment are very encouraging. Much of this work was performed on the iPSC/i860 and CM-5 at Oak Ridge National Laboratory.

Because of the dramatic increase in computational speed using parallel algorithms, our research group has undertaken a concerted effort to explore several systems involving cage molecules of the form

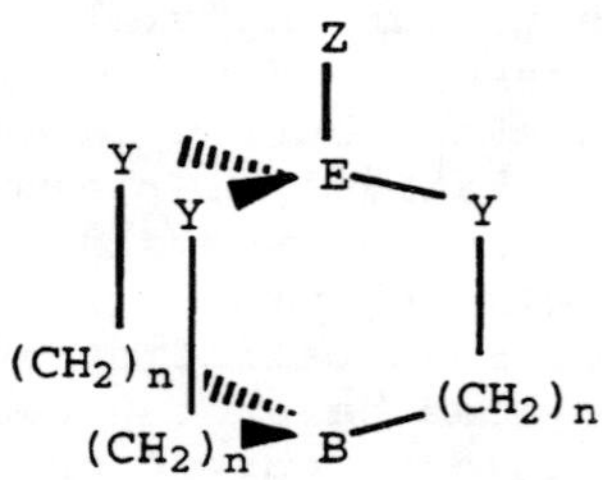

One series of compounds are the cyclophanes, in which B = benzene, E = C or Si, Z = H, Y = O or CH_2, and n = 2 or 3 [7]. Experimentally, this system is interesting because the Z = H substituent may be either inside the cage (endo) or outside the cage (exo), depending on the nature of E. The calculations shed some light on the importance of electrostatic interactions and cage size on the ability of the ligand attached to Si to be endo vs. exo.

Another series of cage compounds are the azaphosphatranes, that have been studied with B = N, Y = NH or $N(CH_3)$, E = P, n = 2, and Z = unsubstituted, H^+, F^+, Cl^+, CH_2, CH_3^+, NH, NH_2^+, O, or OH^+ [8]. Experimentally, the parent azaphosphatrane (Z = unsubstituted) is known to be an extremely strong base (the conjugate acid has a pK_a of 27 in dimethylsulfoxide). Based on our calculations, two new bases are proposed (Z = CH_2 or NH) to be stronger than the parent base and are currently undergoing experimental investigation [9].

Silatranes, azasilatranes and carbosilatranes also fall into this general class of cage molecules. The molecules under consideration have B = N, n = 2, E = Si, Y = CH_2, NH, or O and Z = H, F, OH, NH_2, CH_3, Cl, SH, PH_2, or SiH_3 [10]. The main focus of this research is the Si-N (E-B) transannular bond distance, determining what substituents lengthen or shorten the distance, and the nature of electronic or steric effects of the substituents.

Most of the cage complex calculations were performed on the CalTech Touchstone Delta. However, an Intel Paragon (at the San Diego Supercomputer Center) and two RS/6000s using an Ethernet connection were also used in the latter stages of the calculations.

Among the other types of applications currently using parallel GAMESS are the determination of high energy inorganic benzene isomers using a CM-5 (at the Army High Performance Computation Center at the University of Minnesota) [11], the determination of intramolecular hydrogen bonding in epsilon-aminohexanoic acid using a Paragon (at the University of Graz) [12], and the determination of regioselectivity in organic reactions using electrostatic potential maps on an iPSC/i860 (at Kirtland Air Force Base) [13].

While all of the above applications have involved academic researchers, several researchers from government labs and industry are also using parallel GAMESS. One such example involves calculations at Phillips Laboratory-Edwards Air Force Base on Si_4H_6 (tetrasilabicyclo-butane). This molecule is being explored for its potential as a fuel additive to the usual liquid H_2/liquid O_2 fuel for the space shuttle main engine. These calculations are being performed on the Touchstone Delta and on a cluster involving seven RS/6000s and one Silicon Graphics machine [14].

An example of industrial usage of parallel GAMESS is the Amoco Chemical Company investigation of the reaction kinetics of hydrocarbons and their radicals. The thermochemistry is obtained from GAMESS optimized structures of the reactants, products and transition states. An example suite of reactions might be

$$RH + \cdot CH_3 \rightarrow CH_4 + R\cdot$$

where R ranges from C_1 to C_{12}. To do these calculations, an RS/6000 550, an SG Iris 4D/35, and an SG Indigo R4000 have been used sequentially and in parallel with other workstations on site [15].

The foregoing is just a sampling of the applications that are currently using parallel GAMESS. In general, the goal of all of the above studies has been to provide insight to experiments and to predict new experimental results. These calculations could not have been performed in a timely manner without the use of parallel algorithms and computers.

3. MCSCF

While methods for the parallelization of the SCF portions of quantum chemistry codes have been expolored for quite a while, very little research has been done on post SCF methods. One particular area which has received little attention is the MCSCF method.

One of our recent research areas is the parallelization of the MCSCF energies and gradients. Again, our main goal is to perform chemistry using parallelization as a tool. However, since this research is still in its infancy (the code was only released to the public in early February 1994), no applications have as yet used the parallel MCSCF code. Since our research in this area is described elsewhere [3a], only an outline of the algorithm will be given here.

One of the problems with the parallelization of MCSCF codes is that there are several potential bottlenecks. Therefore, different types of calculations result in different computational bottlenecks. For instance, a calculation with a large number of virtual orbitals (relative to core or active orbitals) and a small active space will have the transformation as a bottleneck. On the other hand, a calculation with a relatively small occupied space but a large number of configuration state functions (CSFs) (large active space) will have the CI diagonalization as a bottleneck. In order to try to accommodate the different types of MCSCF calculations, all portions of the MCSCF energy calculation were parallelized as much as possible, WITHOUT a large amount of rewriting of code.

The MCSCF code in GAMESS is based on the graphical unitary group approach (GUGA). For more in depth information about the GUGA approach the reader is referred to reference 16. The basic steps in a GUGA MCSCF energy calculation are 1) obtaining an initial guess for the molecular orbitals (MOs), 2) calculating the atomic integrals, 3) generating the distinct row table (DRT) containing information about the configuration state functions (CSFs) used in the calculation, 4) transforming the atomic integrals into molecular integrals, 5) sorting the molecular integrals with all indices in the core and active spaces into an order needed by the next step, 6) calculating the contributions to the CI Hamiltonian matrix, H, 7) obtaining the CI eigenvectors, C, by diagonalizing H, 8) calculating the one- and two-electron density matrices, 9) forming the Lagrangian (the orbital gradient) and the orbital hessian, 10) forming the augmented orbital hessian, 11) solving the Newton-Raphson (NR) equations to improve the orbitals, and 12) repeating steps 4 - 11 until convergence is achieved.

The first three of these steps are performed sequentially on all of the nodes. Therefore, after step three, each node has available to it the molecular orbitals, ALL of the atomic integrals, and the DRT. Even though the sequential nature of these three steps will degrade overall performance, they are performed only once in an energy + gradient calculation and therefore, are only a small part of the overall calculation. Also, the algorithm for parallelization of the transformation (step 4) will require each node to have the complete list of atomic integrals.

Step 4 is the first step involved in the MCSCF iterations. From this step to step 11, every effort is made to parallelize as much of the code as possible. Several parallel algorithms for the transformation are available [3b-3f]. However, none of these is particularly practical for the model of programming employed here: SPMD on distributed memory machines. (The exception may be reference 3f which was published after this work was done.)

The current transformation in GAMESS is incorporated from Hondo 8 [17]. A schematic of the parallel transformation is given in Figure 1. Since this transformation performs passes over the atomic integrals (either on disk as assumed in this discussion or calculated directly) forming batches of molecular integrals, it is very natural to parallelize the transformation by allowing each processor to form a batch (or batches) of transformed integrals and put them on its local disk. Therefore, at the

Figure 1: Schematic of the parallel transformation.

```
      SUBROUTINE TRANSFORM
C
C     ME = the processor's ID number
C     NPROC = number of processors
C     initialize parallel
C
      IPCOUNT = ME -1
      NEXT = -1
      MINE = -1
C
C     Begin passes over the atomic integrals to form subsets
C     of the transformed integrals (IJ/KL).
C
      MINKL = 1
   10 MAXKL = MINKL + SIZE_OF_PASS
C
C     Select NXTVAL or LOOP balancing ...
C
         IF (PARALLEL) THEN
            IF (NXTVAL) THEN
               MINE = MINE + 1
               IF (MINE.GT.NEXT) NEXT = NXTVAL()
               IF (NEXT.NE.MINE) GO TO 20
            ELSE
               IPCOUNT = IPCOUNT + 1
               IF (MOD(IPCOUNT,NPROC).NE.0) GO TO 20
            END IF
         END IF
         CALL SUBTRANS()
   20    CONTINUE
         IF (MAXKL.EQ.NUMKL) THEN GO TO 30
C
C     NUMKL = maximum number of KL indices
C
         MINKL = MAXKL + 1
         GO TO 10
   30 CONTINUE
      END
```

end of this step, each processor has a subset of the transformed integrals on its local disk. This type of parallelism equates to parallelization at the loop level (at least globally). Both methods of loop balancing (LOOP and NXTVAL) are implemented in all of the parallel steps unless otherwise noted.

If the number of loops is evenly divisible by the number of processors, the algorithm shows excellent speedups (see reference 3a for examples). However, if the number of loops is not evenly divisible by the number of processors, load imbalance will occur. The number of loops is effectively chosen by the amount of memory used for the transformation. By effective memory management, the number of loops can be made evenly divisible by the number of processors.

The largest advantage to an algorithm such as this for the integral transformation is that it requires no communication between the processors (minimal communication if NXTVAL load balancing is used). This is much different than the algorithms that have partial lists of atomic orbitals on each node and require considerable amounts of communication to perform the transformation.

After the transformation, the integrals with all indices in the core and active space must be sorted (step 5). Since each processor has a partial list of the transformed integrals, each processor sorts the integrals it has into a sort array and then a global summation is performed. After this summation, each node has the complete list of sorted integrals and puts it onto its own local disk space.

Once the integrals have been sorted, contributions (GUGA loops) to the Hamiltonian matrix can be calculated (step 6). Because of dependencies in the code that calculates the GUGA loops, parallelization of the CPU time could not be achieved. However, by parallelization of the output routine, the loop disk space is spread across all of the nodes. By allowing each node to store a subset of the loops, larger calculations can be done than would normally be permitted in a sequential run since the disk space needed by the loops can become quite large for large numbers of CSFs. Also, by spreading out the loop storage across the nodes, the next step parallelizes quite nicely.

The next step (step 7) is the generation of H using the loops and the diagonalization of H. Most of the time involved in this step is formation of H from the loops since an iterative Davidson diagonalization procedure [18] is used for the actual diagonalization. Since each node forms a partial H from its subset of loops and then a global summation is performed, this step actually shows remarkable speedups [3a]. The diagonalization itself is performed sequentially on each node. Each node then ends up with the complete CI eigenvectors and eigenvalues on local disk. This is necessary for the next step.

The generation of the one- and two-electron density matrices (step 8) processes the CI vectors through the same loop generation code used in step 6. Therefore, CPU time is not effectively decreased during this step, but the disk space for the loops is again spread across all of the nodes. The generated loops (which are spread out across all of the nodes) are then read in, labeled, and sorted. Each node performs these three steps on the subset of loops available to it and then a global summation is performed to generate the complete density matrices. The result of the global summation is that each node has the complete density which is then stored onto a local disk.

The next step (step 9) uses the density matrices and the transformed integrals to form the Lagrangian and the orbital hessian. Remember, each node has the complete density but only a subset of the transformed integrals available to it. So, each node forms contributions to the Lagrangian and the orbital hessian and then a global summation is performed to obtain the complete results on each node. This part of the calculation requires as much memory as would be required in the sequential algorithm. This is because each node needs to hold the density, Lagrangian, and orbital hessian in memory during the calculation.

The next two steps (steps 10 and 11) are sequential. Step 10 (formation of the augmented orbital hessian [19]) takes very little time and therefore, does not significantly effect the overall parallel efficiencies. Step 11 (solution of the NR equations), on the other hand, can take significant amounts of time depending on the nature of the MCSCF calculation. This step is essentially finding the lowest eigenvector of the augmented hessian. Since diagonalizations have not been parallelized in GAMESS, this step remains one of the large sequential bottlenecks for the calculation.

Parallelization of steps 4-11 as described above result in very good speedups for several types of MCSCF computations (see reference 3a for specific timing examples). However, it is obvious from the above discussion that the two places needing more work are the calculation of loops which only parallelizes the loop output routine and the solution of the NR equations which is totally sequential and can be a significant bottleneck even in sequential calculations.

The above discussion describes the parallelization of the MCSCF energies. However, in order to study chemical reactions, parallel gradients are needed. Therefore, the rest of this section will describe the parallelization of the MCSCF gradient code.

A schematic of the gradient code is given in Figure 2. The gradient code for MCSCF is the same code used for SCF gradients except that the density is different.

Figure 2: Schematic of gradient code.

```
      SUBROUTINE JKDER
C
C     ME = this processor's ID number
C     NPROC = number of processors
C
C     initialize parallel work
C
      IPCOUNT = ME - 1
      NEXT = -1
      MINE = -1
      CALL TRF2DM
C                          begin the 4 loops over shells
      DO 100 I =
         .
        DO 200 J =
           IF (NXTVAL balancing AND PARALLEL) THEN
             MINE = MINE + 1
             IF (MINE.GT.NEXT) NEXT = NXTVAL()
             IF (NEXT.NE.MINE) GO TO 200
           END IF
           .
           DO 300 K =
              .
             DO 400 L =
                IF (LOOP balancing AND PARALLEL) THEN
                  IPCOUNT = IPCOUNT + 1
                  IF (MOD(IPCOUNT,NPROC).NE.0) GOTO 400
                END IF
                .
C     generate integrals with density on disk
                CALL DABCI()
 400         CONTINUE
 300       CONTINUE
 200    CONTINUE
      CONTINUE
      END
```

Before the loops over shells are entered, the MCSCF density which is in the molecular orbital basis must be transformed into the atomic orbital basis. This transformed density is then used inside the innermost shell loop to calculate the two-electron gradient integrals.

In order to parallelize the two electron gradient integral calculation the density on each node after the

Table I: Time in seconds for SiC_3H_6 MCSCF gradient.

	p=1	p=2
1e- gradient	2.61	1.33
density transformation	16.91	16.69
density sort	57.28	51.35
2e- gradient	212.93	105.47

transformation (after the call to TRF2DM) must be the same density that is needed (at the call to DABCI) by that node to perform its subset of gradient integrals. To accomplish this, only the LOOP (static) load balancing technique is used. If the NXTVAL (dynamic) method was used, there would not be a straightforward way of ensuring that each node would have the density it needs.

During the transformation step, each node performs the transformation sequentially. The transformed integrals are then sorted and put out to disk. At the point of sorting, each node puts only the density it will need for the gradient integral calculation on its local disk.

A preliminary timing example is given in Table I. This example is for SiC_3H_6 using the 6-31G* basis set giving 76 basis functions [20]. This test was run on two dedicated IBM RS/6000 370s.

As can be seen in this example, the transformation and sorting of the density takes a non-trivial amount of time. The small amount of speedup in the density sort step is due to the parallel I/O obtained from having the density written out by two nodes instead of one. Future work will concentrate on parallelization of these two steps (the transformation and sorting of the density).

4. CONCLUSIONS

The overall parallelization of the ab initio electronic structure code GAMESS has been presented. While quite a lot of work is still needed to parallelize the complete package, the SCF and MCSCF energies and gradients have very good efficiencies. With these portions of the code parallelized, optimizations, transition state searches, intrinsic reaction coordinate following, and numerical hessians are also available in parallel.

Many applications of the parallel SCF code have been presented. Most of these applications have facilitated interactions with experimentalists and give predictive results in a timely manner.

Future work will involve improvement of the MCSCF parallelization including improvements in the loop generation code and parallelization of the diagonalization needed in the NR step. Also targeted for future parallel work is the MP2 energy code and the analytic hessian code.

ACKNOWLEDGMENT

This work was supported by a grant from the Air Force Office of Scientific Research (93-1-0105), a Department of Education GAANN fellowship to TLW and through the assistance of the Advanced Research Projects Agency.

REFERENCES

1. Current address: Department of Chemistry, Northwestern University, 2145 Sheridan Road, Evanston, IL 60101

2.a. M.W. Schmidt, K.K. Baldridge, J.A. Boatz, S.T. Elbert, M.S. Gordon, J.H. Jensen, S. Koseki, N. Matsunaga, K.A. Nguyen, S. Su, T.L. Windus, M. Dupuis, and J.A. Montgomery, Jr., *J.Comput.Chem.*, Vol. 14, 1993, 1347

b. M.F. Guest, R.J. Harrison, J.H. van Lenthe, and L.C.H. van Corler, *Theor.Chim.Acta*, Vol. 71, 1987, 117

c. M. Dupuis and J.D. Watts, *Theor.Chim.Acta*, Vol. 71, 1987, 91

d. R. Ernenwein, M.M. Rohmer, and M. Benard, *Comp.Phys. Comm.*, Vol. 58, 1990, 305

e. M.M. Rohmer, J. Demuynck, M. Benard, R. Wiest, C. Bachmann, C. Henriet, and R. ERnenwein, *Comp.Phys.Comm.*, Vol. 60, 1990, 127

f. R.J. Harrison and R.A. Kendall, *Theor.Chim.Acta*, Vol. 79, 1991, 337

g. M.D. Cooper and I.H. Hillier, *J.Comp.-Aided Mol.Design*, Vol. 5, 1991, 171

h. S. Kindermann, E. Michel, and P. Otto, *J.Comp.Chem.*, Vol. 13, 1992, 414

i. H.P. Luthi, J.E. Mertz, M.W. Feyereisen, and J.E. Almlof, *J.Comp.Chem.*, Vol. 13, 1992, 160

j. M. Feyereisen and R.A. Kendall, *Theor.Chim.Acta*, Vol. 84, 1993, 289

k. The whole issue *Theor.Chim.Acta*, Vol. 84, 1993

3.a. T.L. Windus, M.W. Schmidt, and M.S. Gordon, "Parallel Algorithm for Integral Transformations and GUGA MCSCF", accepted *Theor.Chim.Acta*

b. R.A. Whiteside, J.S. Binkley, M.E. Colvin, and H.F. Schaefer III, *J.Chem.Phys.*, Vol. 86, 1987, 2185.
c. L.A. Covick and K.M. Sando, *J.Comp.Chem.*, Vol. 11, 1990, 1151
d. R. Wiest, J. Demuynck, M. Benard, M.M. Rohmer, R. Ernenwein, *Comp.Phys.Comm.*, Vol. 62, 1991, 107
e. J.D. Watts and M. Dupuis, *J.Comp.Chem.*, Vol. 9, 1988, 158
f. A.C. Limaye and S.R. Gadre, *J.Chem.Phys.*, Vol. 100, 1994, 1303
g. R.J. Harrison, *J.Chem.Phys.*, Vol. 94, 1991, 5021
h. R.J. Harrison and E. Stahlberg, *CSCC Update*, Vol. 13, 1992, 5
i. M. Schuller, T. Kovar, H. Lischka, R. Shepard, and R.J. Harrison, *Theor.Chim.Acta*, Vol. 84, 1993, 489
j. A.P. Rendall, T.J. Lee, and R. Lindh, *Chem.Phys.Lett.*, Vol. 194, 1992, 84

4. R.J. Harrison, *Int.J.Quantum Chem.*, Vol. 40, 1991, 847

5. T.L. Windus, M.W. Schmidt, and M.S. Gordon, *Chem.Phys.Lett.*, Vol. 216, 1993, 375

6.a. T.R. Cundari and M.S. Gordon, *J.Am.Chem.Soc.*, Vol. 115, 1993, 4210
b. T.R. Cundari, *Organometallics*, Vol. 12, 1993, 1998
c. T.R. Cundari, S.O. Sommerer, and W.J. Stevens, *Chem. Phys.*, 178, 1993, 235
d. T.R. Cundari, *Organometallics*, Vol. 12, 1993, 4971
e. T.R. Cundari, "Calculation of a Methane C-H Oxidative Addition Trajectory: Comparison to Experiment and Methane Activation by High-Valent Complexes.;", *J.Am.Chem.Soc.* in press.
f. T.R. Cundari; S.C. Critchlow; R.R. Conry; E. Spaltenstein; K.A. Hall; S. Tahmassebi, J.M. Mayer, "Rhenium-Oxo-Bis(acetylene) Anions: Structure, Properties, and Electronic Structure Comparison of Re-O Bonding with That in Other Rhenium-Oxo Complexes;", *Organometallics*, in press
g. T.R. Cundari, "Methane Activation by Group VB Bis(Imido) Complexes;", *J.Am.Chem.Soc.*, submitted
h. T.R. Cundari and M.S. Gordon, "Effective Core Potential Studies of Transition Metal Chemistry;", *Coord. Chem. Rev.*, in preparation
i. M.T. Benson, T.R. Cundari, S.J. Lim, H.D. Nguyen, and K. Pierce-Beaver, "An Effective Core Potential Study of Transition Metal Chalcogenides. Part I. Molecular Structure;", *J.Am.Chem.Soc.*, submitted

7. M.W. Schmidt and M.S. Gordon, "Endo and Exo Hydrogens in Cyclophanes", in prepration

8. T.L. Windus, M.W. Schmidt, and M.S. Gordon, "Theoretical Investigation of Azaphosphatranes", in preparation

9. J.G. Verkade, private communication

10. M.W. Schmidt, T.L. Windus, and M.S. Gordon, "Structural Trends in Silicon Atranes", in preparation

11. N. Matsunaga and M.S. Gordon, "Inorganic Benzene Isomers: Prismanes", in preparation

12. M. Ramek, "Ab-initio SCF Investigation of the Intramolecular Hydrogen Bonding in epsilon-Aminohexanoic Acid", *Int. J. Quant. Chem.: Quant. Biol. Symp.*, submitted

13.a. G.A. Kraus, J. Li, M.S. Gordon, and J.H. Jensen, *J.Am.Chem.Soc.*, Vol. 115, 1993, 5859
b. G.A. Kraus, J. Li, M.S. Gordon, and J.H. Jensen, "Regiocontrol by Remote Substituents. A Direct Total Synthesis of Racemic Hongconin", *J.Org.Chem.*, in press

14. J.A. Boatz and M.S. Gordon,"Bond Stretch Isomerism in Strained Organosilicon Compounds", in preparation

15. J.T. Golab, private communication

16.a. B. Brooks and H.F. Schaefer III, *J.Chem.Phys.*, Vol. 70, 1979, 5092
b. B. Brooks, W. Laidig, P. Saxe, N. Handy, and H.F. Schaefer III, *Physica Scripta*, Vol. 21, 1980, 312
c. B.O. Roos in *Methods in Computational Molcular Physics*, (G.H.F. Diercksen and S. Wilson Eds.) Dordrecht, Holland: D. Reidel Publishing, 1983

17. M. Dupuis, S. Chin, and M. Marquez, "CHEM-Station and HONDO" in *Relativistic and Electron Correlation Effects in Molecules and Clusters* (G.L. Malli Ed.) NATO ASI Series, New York: Plenum Press, 1992

18. E.R. Davidson, *J.Comput.Phys.*, Vol. 17, 1975, 87

19. D.R. Yarkony, *Chem.Phys.Lett.*, Vol. 77, 1981, 634

20. H. Shimizu and M.S. Gordon, unpublished results

Toward Teraflop Computing
and New Grand
Challenge Applications

ISBN-1-56072-247-9

A SINGLE ARRANGEMENT VARIATIONAL METHOD FOR QUANTUM MECHANICAL REACTIVE SCATTERING CALCULATIONS

B. Ramachandran,[(a)] **Xudong Wu**[(b)] **and Robert E. Wyatt**[(b)]

(*a*) *Department of Chemistry, Louisiana Tech University, Ruston, LA 71272*
(*b*) *Department of Chemistry and Biochemistry, University of Texas, Austin, TX 78712*

ABSTRACT

We present a variational method that reduces the formally three arrangement problem of atom-diatomic molecule reactive scattering to a one arrangement problem. The method leads to a large matrix equation **AC** = **B**. By representing the solution on grid points selected in the physically relevant regions of the potential surface, we reduce **A** to a smaller, sparse and structured matrix. The sparsity and the structure of **A** are both exploited in gaining substantial savings in storage, and in obtaining the solutions using either iterative refinement or the Generalized Minimal Residual (GMRes) method. Either approach permits full exploitation of vector or massively parallel computer architectures. The results of applying the method to a few three-dimensional atom-diatomic molecule reactions are presented.

1. INTRODUCTION

The atom-diatomic molecule reactive scattering problem, A+BC→products, is a complicated example of the quantum mechanical three-body problem. Many reactive scattering calculations in the recent past[1] have used three sets of mass-weighted (or mass-scaled) Jacobi coordinates,[2] one for each atom+diatom combination (or "arrangement"): A+BC, B+AC and C+AB. The scaling of the Jacobi vectors causes the coordinates for the different arrangements to be at acute angles to each other, causing nonorthogonal overlaps between functions in the different arrangements.[3] All these calculations ultimately involve the solution of a large matrix equation of the type **AC** = **B** for the unknowns **C**. Although these calculations are impressive, it has proved to be difficult to extend such treatments to heavier atoms and molecules. The main difficulty is the sheer size of the matrix **A**, and the fact that

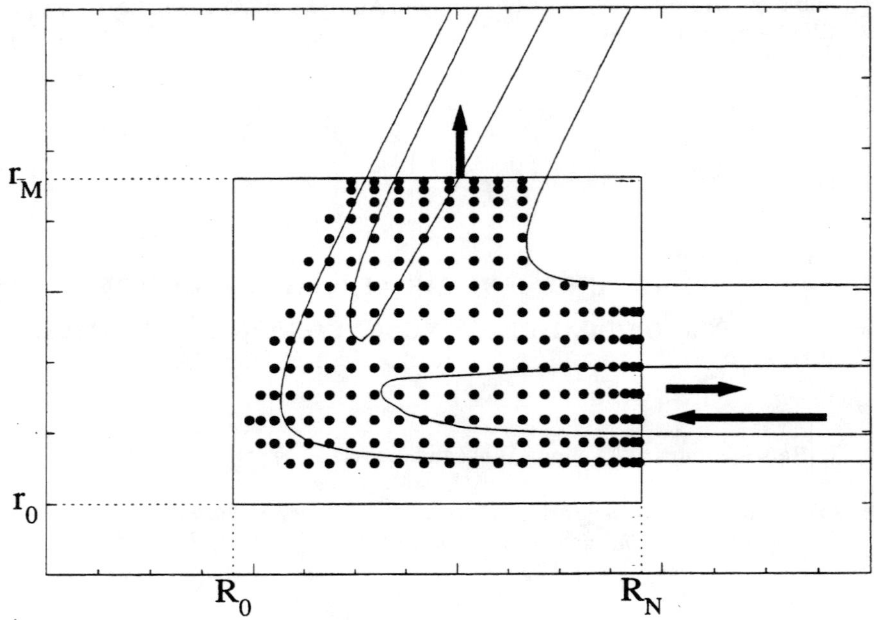

Figure 1. A schematic summary of the essential features of the method. The scattering problem is solved in the rectangular region, and the S-matrix boundary conditions are applied at $R = R_N$ and $r = r_M$, as indicated by arrows. Two contours of the potential as well as the DVR points selected by applying the energy cut-off criteria are shown.

A tends to be dense. In addition, the nonorthogonal "exchange" matrix elements in **A** can also lead to linear dependency for very large matrices.

This paper presents one of the many attempts[4–6] to reduce the size of **A** as well as to eliminate the exchange matrix elements from it. In this method,[6] the scattering problem is solved in a rectangular region defined in terms of mass-weighted Jacobi vectors[2] for the reactant arrangement (***R***, ***r***) as shown in Figure 1. The Kohn variational method for the log-derivative matrix[7–9] is used to compute the log-derivative matrix at the boundaries (R_0, R_N; $r = r_M$) and (r_0, r_M; $R = R_N$), with the gradients computed *perpendicular to the boundaries*, i.e., with respect to R at $R = R_N$ and with respect to r at $r = r_M$. The reactant vib-rotational states are found at $R = R_N$, as functions of r, while those for the products are evaluated as functions of R, at $r = r_M$. The log derivative matrix is converted to the **S** matrix by applying the complex incoming and outgoing wave boundary conditions[8] at $R = R_N$ and $r = r_M$ for the reactants and products respectively, perpendicular to the boundaries. The total reaction probabilities are then found by summing the appropriate column of the reactive block of $|\mathbf{S}|^2$. The method is admittedly approximate in nature, since the product channel boundary conditions are applied in the "wrong direction." However, in spite of this, the method yields very accurate results for a wide variety of reactions, as shown below.

2. THE MATRIX EQUATION AND ITS SOLUTION

A detailed discussion of the Kohn variational principle for the log-derivative matrix is presented in Ref. 8. For the purpose of this discussion, it is sufficient to note that the variational functional for the log-derivative Y can be written as

$$Y = Y_0 + \langle \Psi | H - E | \Psi \rangle, \tag{1}$$

where Y_0 is a "guess" for Y (see Ref. 8). The functions $\Psi^m(R, r, \gamma) = (Rr)^{-1}\psi^m(R, r, \gamma)$, where m denotes the initial state of the reactant diatomic, are solutions of

$$-\frac{\hbar^2}{2\mu}\left(\frac{\partial^2}{\partial R^2} + \frac{\partial^2}{\partial r^2} - \frac{\hat{L}^2}{R^2} - \frac{\hat{j}^2}{r^2}\right)\psi^m + V(R, r, \gamma)\psi^m = E\psi\ , \tag{2}$$

where (R, r, γ) are the mass-weighted Jacobi coordinates for the reactant arrangement, $\hat{L}^2$ and $\hat{j}^2$ are respectively, the operators for orbital and rotational angular momenta, $V(R, r, \gamma)$ is the Born-Oppenhemier potential for nuclear motion,[10] and E is the scattering energy. The functions $\psi^m(R, r, \gamma)$ are expanded in the rectangular region of Fig .1 (with $0 \le \gamma \le \pi$) as

$$\psi^m(R, r, \gamma) = \sum_{i=1}^{N}\sum_{k=1}^{M}\sum_{j,l}^{j_{\max}} u_i(R)v_k(r)Y_{j,l}^{JM}(\gamma)C_{ikjl}^{JM}. \tag{3}$$

The rules of angular momentum coupling[2] dictate that the values of J and j above determine the allowed values of l. For the applications discussed here, we set J=0, and j=0,1,... j_{max}. We now define a grid in the rectangular region of Fig. 1 by picking a set of points $\{R_n\}$ along R and $\{r_m\}$ along r. The functions u_i and v_k are chosen[6] to generate a "discrete variable representation" (or DVR)[11] of the solution on this grid. These functions satisfy the Kroenecker delta conditions $u_i(R_n) = \delta_{in}$, $v_k(r_m) = \delta_{km}$ etc., on the grid. Substitution of this DVR into the variational functional, followed by extremization of the functional with respect to the expansion coefficients C_{ikjl}^{JM}, results in a system of linear algebraic equations

$$\mathbf{AC} = \mathbf{B} \tag{4}$$

to be solved for the coefficients **C**. The order of **A** is given by NMj_{max} which tends to be a very large number. We reduce the size of this matrix by rejecting all points (R_n, r_m) that lie in regions where $V(R, r, \gamma_0)$ is higher than a certain cut-off value. The points (R_n, r_m) thus selected are also shown in Fig. 1, along with the contours of the potential.

The resulting matrix **A**, thanks to the Kroenecker delta properties of the DVR, is a very sparse, structured matrix. The largest matrix elements are concentrated along the diagonal, the great majority of the nonzero elements are concentrated in blocks along the diagonal, and the remaining nonzero elements, which become successively smaller as one moves away from the diagonal, occur in "stripes" parallel to the diagonal. This suggests substantial savings in memory for storing **A**, and also that the problem of Eq. (4) is ideally suited for solution by the several iterative methods available today,[12–14] which do not require the full matrix to be stored in memory. In our applications of the method, we have used two iterative methods to solve Eq.(4), both designed to take full advantage of the structured sparsity of **A**, as described below.

2.1 Iterative Refinement

We write matrix **A** as **A** = **P**+**Q**, where **P** contains the diagonal blocks of A, and **Q** contains the off-diagonal "stripes." This can be solved iteratively as

$$\mathbf{PC}_n = \mathbf{B} - \mathbf{QC}_{n-1}, \tag{5}$$

where $\mathbf{C}_0$, the first "guess" is obtained by setting **Q** = 0. The advantages of this approach are the following. Firstly, the blocks that make up **P** can be stored as separate, smaller matrices, and the stripes in **Q** can be stored as vectors, resulting in tremendous savings in memory. Secondly, the iterative scheme of Eq.(5) involves only one LU decomposition, followed by a series of matrix-vector multiplications. Both steps, especially the latter, are highly suitable for achieving high speeds on vector and parallel computers.

2.2 The Generalized Minimal Residual (GMRes) Method

This is an implementation of the Generalized Minimal Residual (GMRes) method of Saad and Schultz.[13] When applied to a linear algebraic problem **Ac** = **b**, the GMRes algorithm begins with an initial solution vector $\mathbf{c}_0$, and generates the corresponding residual vector $\mathbf{r}_0 = \mathbf{b} - \mathbf{A}\mathbf{c}_0$. At each iteration *n*, a correction $\mathbf{z}_n$ is determined in the Krylov subspace spanned by the vectors $\{\mathbf{r}_0, \mathbf{A}\mathbf{r}_0, \ldots, \mathbf{A}^{n-1}\mathbf{r}_0\}$ so as to minimize the Euclidean norm of the residual $\mathbf{r}_n = \mathbf{b} - \mathbf{A}\mathbf{c}_n$, where $\mathbf{c}_n = \mathbf{c}_0 + \mathbf{z}_n$. The residual $\mathbf{r}_n$ is a non-increasing function of *n*, and in fact, the solution is guaranteed to converge within *N* iterations, where *N* is the order of **A**.

One way to accelerate the convergence is to "precondition" the system of equations so that the initial vector $\mathbf{c}_0$ contains a substantial amount of information regarding the physical nature of the problem.[14] For the systems considered here, we choose the preconditioned system of equations to be

$$(\mathbf{P}^{-1}\mathbf{A})\mathbf{C} = \mathbf{P}^{-1}\mathbf{B}, \tag{6}$$

where, as noted above, **P** is relatively easy to invert because of its block-diagonal structure. The faster convergence in this case is expected from the fact that as **P** tends to **A**, Eq.(6) converges in a single iteration. In actual applications, rather than explicitly use $\mathbf{P}^{-1}\mathbf{A}$, one generates the preconditioned Krylov subspace by a sequence of operations of the type $\mathbf{s} = \mathbf{A}\mathbf{r}$, $\mathbf{t} = \mathbf{P}^{-1}\mathbf{s}$. Once again, the vector or parallel architectures of the computing platforms can be fully exploited for the matrix-vector multiplications involved at each step.[15]

3. APPLICATIONS

We present the results of applying the method described above to three simple reactions with $J = 0$, *viz.*, the D+H_2, H+D_2 and the F+H_2 reactions. The total reaction probabilities can be seen to be accurate over a wide range of scattering energies, even in the case of the F+H_2 reaction, which has a sharp (mass-weighted) angle between the reactant and product arrangements. An extension of the present method to calculate state-to-state reaction probabilities has already been implemented.[16] As expected from the preceding discussion, the convergence of the GMRes method is considerably aided and accelerated by preconditioning the linear system of equations.

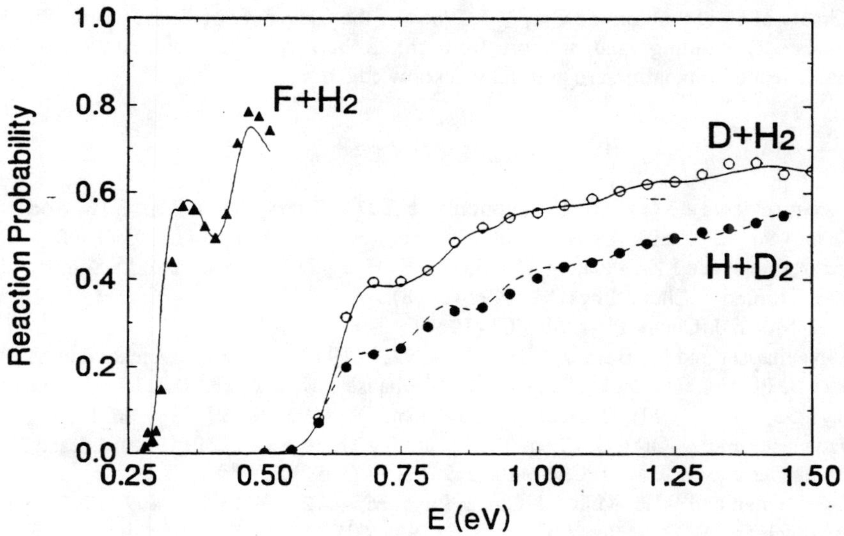

Figure 2. The total reaction probability from the ground state of the reactant molecule for three reactions with $J = 0$. The lines represent the results of the present method, and the symbols the exact results from literature.

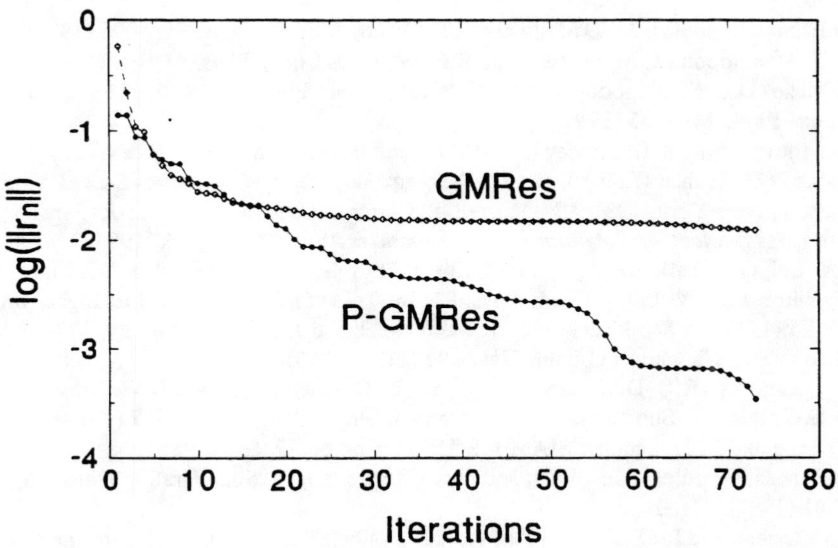

Figure 3. The norm of the residual vector for the F+H_2 reaction at $E = 0.37$ eV plotted against the number of iterations for GMRes without preconditioning, and with preconditioning (P-GMRes).

ACKNOWLEDGEMENT

Grants of CPU time on the Cray Y-MP/864 of the University of Texas Center for High Performance Computing, and support from the Robert A. Welch Foundation and the National Science Foundation are gratefully acknowledged.

REFERENCES

1. Recent reviews are (a) D.E. Manolopoulos and D.C. Clary, Annu. Rep. C (R. Soc. Chem.) **86**, 95 (1989); (b) W.H. Miller, Annu. Rev. Phys. Chem. **41**, 245 (1990).
2. For example, see J.Z.H. Zhang, D.J. Kouri, K. Haug, D.W. Schwenke, Y. Shima and D.G. Truhlar, J. Chem. Phys. **88**, 2492 (1988).
3. W.H. Miller, J. Chem. Phys. **50**, 407 (1969).
4. D. Neuhauser and M. Baer, J. Chem. Phys. **92**, 3419 (1990); D. Neuhauser and M. Baer, J. Phys. Chem. **94**, 185 (1990); D. Neuhauser, M. Baer and D.J. Kouri, J. Chem. Phys. **93**, 2499 (1990); D. Neuhauser, J .Chem. Phys. **93**, 7836 (1990); M. Baer, D. Neuhauser and Y. Oreg, J. Chem. Phys. Faraday Trans. **86**, 1721 (1990); I. Last, D. Neuhauser and M. Baer J. Chem. Phys. **96**, 2017 (1992).
5. T. Seideman and W.H. Miller, J. Chem. Phys. **96**, 4412 (1992); **97**, 2499 (1992); S.M. Auerbach and W.H. Miller, J. Chem. Phys. **98**, 6917 (1993); P. Saalfrank and W.H. Miller, J. Chem. Phys. **98**, 9040 (1993); W.H. Miller, Acc. Chem. Res. **26**, 174 (1993); W.H. Thompson and W.H. Miller, Chem. Phys. Lett. **206**, 123 (1993).
6. X. Wu, B. Ramachandran and R.E. Wyatt, Chem. Phys. Lett. **214**, 118 (1993).
7. D.E. Manolopoulos and R.E. Wyatt, Chem. Phys. Lett. **152**, 23 (1988); **159**, 123 (1989).
8. D.E. Manolopoulos, M. D'Mello and R.E. Wyatt, J. Chem. Phys. **91**, 6096 (1990).
9. D.E. Manolopoulos, M. D'Mello and R.E. Wyatt, J. Chem. Phys. **93**, 403 (1990); M. D'Mello, D.E. Manolopoulos and R.E. Wyatt, Chem. Phys. Lett. **168**, 113 (1990); J. Chem. Phys. **94**, 5985 (1991).
10. See for example, K.D. Lawley (Editor), *Potential Energy Surfaces*, Wiley, New York, 1980; D.G. Truhlar (Editor), *Potential Energy Surfaces and Dynamics Calculations*, Plenum, New York, 1981; J.N. Murrell, S. Carter, S.C. Farantos, P. Huxley, and A. Varandas, *Molecular Potential Energy Functions*, Wiley, New York, 1984.
11. J.V. Lill, G.A. Parker and J.C. Light, Chem. Phys. Lett. **89**, 483 (1983); J.C. Light, I.P. Hamilton and J.V. Lill, J. Chem. Phys. **82**, 1400 (1985); Z. Bacic and J.C. Light, *ibid.*, **85**, 4594 (1986); **86**, 3065 (1987); R.M. Whitnell and J.C. Light, *ibid.*, **90**, 1774 (1989); S.E. Choi and J.C. Light, *ibid.*, **92**, 2129 (1990).
12. For example, see C. Duneczky, R.E. Wyatt, D. Chatfield, K. Haug, D.W. Schwenke, D.G. Truhlar, Y. Sun and D.J. Kouri, Comput. Phys. Commun. **53**, 357 (1989).
13. Y. Saad and M.H. Schultz, SIAM J. Sci. Stat. Comput. **7**, 856 (1986).
14. D.E. Manolopoulos, R.E. Wyatt and D.C. Clary, J. Chem. Soc. Faraday Trans. **86**, 1641 (1990).
15. J.M. Ortega and R.G. Voigt, SIAM Rev. **27**, 149 (1985); J.M. Ortega, *Introduction to Parallel and Vector Solution of Linear Systems*, Plenum, New York, 1988.
16. B. Ramachandran, X. Wu and R.E. Wyatt, manuscript in preparation.

Toward Teraflop Computing
and New Grand
Challenge Applications

ISBN-1-56072-247-9

IMPLEMENTATION OF A PROPAGATION ALGORITHM FOR ELECTRON-HYDROGEN SCATTERING

Y. D. Wang and J. Callaway

Department of Physics & Astronomy
Louisiana State University
Baton Rouge, LA 70803-4001
E-mail: ydwang@rouge.phys.lsu.edu, callaway@rouge.phys.lsu.edu

ABSTRACT

A propagation algorithm was developed to solve systems of two-dimensional coupled partial differential equations in quantum scattering of electrons from hydrogen atoms. The algorithm can treat the full Coulomb interaction of the two electrons. Since solutions are propagated outward to the asymptotic region, our algorithm is extremely effective and suitable for extracting scattering quantities such as S-matrix and K-matrix. The present algorithm is also attractive for its handling of large data arrays, which is a key limit to direct numerical solution of partial differential equations in general. The effectiveness and accuracy of this method were demonstrated through study of elastic, inelastic scattering cross sections and resonance structures below the $n = 3$ threshold.

1. INTRODUCTION

Ever since the birth of modern quantum mechanics, the scattering of electrons from atomic hydrogen has been a subject of extensive study. Understanding effects of long-range electron-electron interaction has been a major challenge for this simple Coulombic three-body system. Since the structure of atomic hydrogen is exactly known, the study of electron-hydrogen collisions can provide a testing ground for sophisticated scattering models and theories. During the last twenty years, the study of electron-hydrogen scattering has evolved as high performance computers and advanced computational techniques have been introduced. Despite significant progress, this field remains active and challenging largely due to the complexity of the three-body character of the system.

Theoretical study of electron-hydrogen scattering process ultimately requires the solution of a two-electron Schrödinger equation. Various formalisms have been proposed using perturbative, close-coupling, and variational methods. However, efforts devoted to obtaining direct numerical solution of the Schrödinger equation are relatively scarce. [1-6] We have recently developed a propagation algorithm[1] which avoids the use of a basis set expansion. In this short paper, we discuss our propagation algorithm and its application to electron-hydrogen scattering. Throughout this paper, atomic units with energy in rydbergs are used unless otherwise stated.

2. BASIC EQUATIONS

Let us consider an electron incident on a target hydrogen atom. We denote the two-electron scattering wave function for a total angular momentum L, total spin S and parity π as $\Psi^{L,S,\pi}(\vec{r}_1, \vec{r}_2)$. It must satisfy the Schrödinger equation

$$H\Psi^{L,S,\pi}(\vec{r}_1, \vec{r}_2) = E\Psi^{L,S,\pi}(\vec{r}_1, \vec{r}_2). \tag{1}$$

where the two-electron Hamiltonian

$$H = -\nabla_1^2 - \nabla_2^2 - \frac{2Z}{r_1} - \frac{2Z}{r_2} + \frac{2}{|\vec{r}_1 - \vec{r}_2|}, \tag{2}$$

with $\vec{r}_i$ $(i = 1, 2)$ specifying the coordinates of the two electrons. The solutions must obey the Pauli principle,

$$\Psi^{L,S,\pi}(\vec{r}_2, \vec{r}_1) = (-1)^S \Psi^{L,S,\pi}(\vec{r}_1, \vec{r}_2), \tag{3}$$

and proper boundary conditions.

To solve Eq.(1), we expand $\Psi^{L,S,\pi}(\vec{r}_1, \vec{r}_2)$ as a complete set of functions in the two-particle coupled spherical harmonics,

$$\Psi^{L,S,\pi}(\vec{r}_1, \vec{r}_2) = \sum_{l_1, l_2} R^{L,S,\pi}_{l_1,l_2}(r_1, r_2) \mathcal{Y}^{L,\pi}_{l_1,l_2}(\hat{r}_1, \hat{r}_2); \tag{4}$$

and obtain a set of coupled partial differential equations

$$\sum_{i=1}^{2} [\frac{\partial^2}{\partial r_i^2} - \frac{l_i(l_i+1)}{r_i^2} + \frac{E}{2} + \frac{2Z}{r_i}] P_{l_1 l_2}(r_1, r_2) + \sum_{l_1' l_2'} V_{l_1 l_2, l_1' l_2'}(r_1, r_2) P_{l_1' l_2'}(r_1, r_2) = 0, \tag{5}$$

where we have put

$$P_{l_1 l_2}(r_1, r_2) \equiv r_1 r_2 R^{L,S,\pi}_{l_1,l_2}(r_1, r_2), \tag{6}$$

and $V_{l_1 l_2, l_1' l_2'}$ is the potential matrix arising from the two-electron Coulomb interaction. This is a set of coupled two-dimensional partial differential equations in the two-electron configuration space (r_1, r_2) (see Fig.1). These equations are coupled through the interaction potential matrix, V.

The boundary conditions are

$$P_{l_1 l_2}(r, r) = 0, \qquad for \;\; S = 1; \tag{7}$$

and

$$[\frac{\partial P_{l_1 l_2}(r_1, r_2)}{\partial r_1}]_{r_1 = r_2} = [\frac{\partial P_{l_1 l_2}(r_1, r_2)}{\partial r_2}]_{r_1 = r_2} \qquad for \;\; S = 0. \tag{8}$$

In addition,

$$P_{l_1 l_2}(r_1, r_2) \longrightarrow r_1^{l_1+1} \quad when \;\; r_1 \;\; \rightarrow 0; \tag{9}$$

$$P_{l_1 l_2}(r_1, r_2) \longrightarrow r_2^{l_2+1} \quad when \;\; r_2 \;\; \rightarrow 0. \tag{10}$$

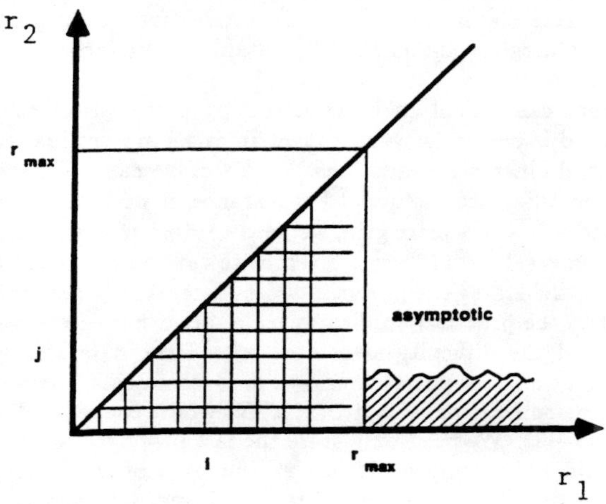

Figure 1: The triangle region for finite difference integration. (from Ref. 1)

The problem now is to solve the set of partial differential equations in the triangle domain shown in Fig.1.

3. NUMERICAL METHODS

The standard close-coupling approach and its derivatives approximate the set of partial differential equations (5) by expanding $P_{l_1 l_2}(r_1, r_2)$ in a complete set of functions of one of the radial variables, say r_2,

$$P_\gamma(r_1, r_2) = \sum_{\gamma'} [1 + (-1)^S P_{12}] f_{\gamma\gamma'}(r_1) u_{\gamma'}(r_2), \tag{11}$$

where P_{12} is the electron-exchange operator, and $u_{\gamma'}(r)$ is a complete set of basis functions. We have introduced a channel index (γ) for ($l_1 l_2$). The original set of two-dimensional partial differential equations (5) is then transformed into a set of one-dimensional integro-differential equations. The integral nature is again due to electron-exchange. This conventional approach to electron-exchange has several drawbacks. The choice of a proper basis set is not clear. Indeed the search for better basis sets to accurately describe continuum states have consumed much efforts during the past twenty years.

Let us explore the possibility of solving the coupled partial differential equations by direct numerical methods. In solving partial differential equations, both finite difference[1,2] and finite element methods are frequently used.[5,6] We choose to work with the finite difference method.[1,2] In Fig.1 we have shown an arrangement of two-dimensional integration grids. Briefly speaking, we may divide the integration area into two regions. The inner region is where both electrons are close to the nucleus and electron-electron interactions are strong. It is essential to retain potential matrix to full order. In the outer region, a general solution can be extremely difficult especially for two free electrons. For excitation processes as we consider in this paper, the situation is much simpler since bound atomic state wave functions decay exponentially. This part of the general asymptotic region is highlighted in Fig.1. An effective and accurate algorithm must be (i) suitable for handling singularities when $r_i \to 0$; (ii) reasonable in storage requirement; (iii) suitable for extracting scattering quantities in the asymptotic region.

The first point can be solved by constructing power series solutions near the singular points. The second is particularly important since we are dealing with a set of coupled two-dimensional partial differential equations. Data storage can be a severe problem for applying higher-order finite difference methods. For instance, if we have m channels (or m number of P_γ functions) and a $N \times N$ square grid, we need to store matrix of dimension (m^2N^2, m^2N^2). For $N = 100$, this is $(10^4m^2, 10^4m^2)$. Even if we take into account the tridiagonal property of some matrices, the storage requirements are large. The requirement of large data storage is a major limit to the practical application of a direct numerical method.

We have solved the difficulty associated with large data storage. Our idea is to seek a propagation solution. In this scheme, we need to calculate two-dimensional propagation matrices of dimension (mi, mi) $(i = 1, 2, 3, ..., N)$ which connect solutions at two neighboring grid lines (say, $i, i+1$). We need only store the last propagation matrix connecting solutions between inner and outer regions. It has a dimension of (mN, mN), which is a significant improvement over the ordinary finite difference scheme. Our approach is similar to an earlier investigation of Poet[3,4] who studied a restricted model case in which only $L = 0$ and only the monopole term of potential matrix (i.e. $1/r_>$) are included. In Poet's case, only one two-dimensional partial differential equation needs to be solved. In the present formulation, we consider a full interaction matrix and m partial differential equations.

We now consider this procedure in more detail. Let N be the total number of equally distributed grid points along the r_1 axis $(1 \leq i \leq N,\ i = 1 \to r_1 = 0)$. Similarly, let N grid points be equally distributed along the r_2 axis $(1 \leq j \leq N,\ j = 1 \to r_2 = 0)$. At each grid point (i, j), there are m number of equations for each channel γ. It is convenient to introduce composite indices, I and J,

$$1 \leq J \leq I \leq mN, \tag{12}$$

incorporating both coordinates and channel indices so that associated with point (i, j), $I = m(i-1) + \gamma$ and $J = m(j-1) + \gamma$. At each point (i, j), an m component vector $P^{(i)}(J) = P_\gamma(r_{1i}, r_{2j})$ and an $m \times m$ matrix $V_{\gamma\gamma'}$ are defined. Now we fix r_{1i} and integrate along r_2. By applying three point finite difference at r_{1i} we have

$$\sum_{J'=1}^{L_1} A_i(J, J')P^{(i-1)}(J') + \sum_{J'=1}^{L_2} B_i(J, J')P^{(i)}(J') + \sum_{J'=1}^{L_3} C_i(J, J')P^{(i+1)}(J') = 0, \tag{13}$$

with $L_1 = m(i-1)$, $L_2 = mi$ and $L_3 = m(i+1)$. The three matrices A, B and C are determined by three-point finite difference formulae. We have shown[1,2] that it is possible to further reduce this three-point equation into an equation relating two successive grid points, say i and $i+1$,

$$P^{(i)}(J) = \sum_{J'=1}^{L_3} D_i(J, J') P^{(i+1)}(J'), \tag{14}$$

where the propagation matrix D can be obtained through recurrence relations

$$D_i(J, J') = - \sum_{J''=1}^{L_2} \tilde{B}_i^{-1}(J, J'') C_i(J'', J'), \tag{15}$$

and

$$\tilde{B}_i(J, J') = B_i(J, J') + \sum_{J''=1}^{L_1} A_i(J, J'') D_{i-1}(J'', J'). \tag{16}$$

All D matrices can be determined by propagation outwards starting from the first one at $i = 1$. Since at $i = 1$, $A_1 = 0$ and $L_2 = m$, $L_3 = 2m$, it can be shown that

$$D_1(J, J') = - \sum_{J''=1}^{n} B_1^{-1}(J, J'') C_1(J'', J'). \tag{17}$$

The finite difference formulae we used are of Numerov type. The Numerov scheme approximates the second-order differential equation

$$\frac{d^2}{dx^2} f(x) + g(x) = 0, \tag{18}$$

by the three-point finite difference formula

$$f(x_{n-1}) - 2f(x_n) + f(x_{n+1}) + \frac{h^2}{12}[g(x_{n-1}) + 10g(x_n) + g(x_{n+1})] = 0. \tag{19}$$

Now consider the following second-order equation containing singularities in x,

$$[\frac{d^2}{dx^2} - \frac{l(l+1)}{x^2} + \frac{2Z}{x}] f(x) + g(x) = 0, \tag{20}$$

where g is regular in x. The function $f \to x^{l+1}$ as $x \to 0$. For $x > 0$, there is no singularity, and the conventional Numerov formula applies. For $x \to 0$, we can derive Numerov-type finite difference formulae by constructing power series near the singular points. There are two cases depending on the value of l. For $l = 0$, the formula near $x = 0$ was given by Poet[3],

$$\begin{aligned} &[-144 + 216hZ - 64(hZ)^2] f(h) + [72 - 36hZ - 4(hZ)^2] f(2h) \\ &+ h^2(60 - 32hZ) g(h) + h^2(6 - 4hZ) g(2h) = 0; \end{aligned} \tag{21}$$

for $l > 0$, we obtained[1]

$$\begin{aligned} &2^{l+1}[hZ(l+3) - (l+1)(2l+3)] f(h) + [lhZ + (l+1)(2l+3)] f(2h) \\ &+ 2^l(l+3) h^2 g(h) + l h^2 g(2h) = 0. \end{aligned} \tag{22}$$

These one-dimensional Numerov finite difference formulae can be applied to two directions to approximate a two-dimensional second-order partial differential equation. We can achieve this by fixing one variable (say r_{1i}) and integrate the other (r_{2j}) at each r_{1i}. Hence, we approximate a two-dimensional second-order partial differential equation at (i,j) by constructing finite differences on a 3×3 square grid with (i,j) being its central grid point. For the set of coupled partial differential equaitons in (5), these formulae give a set of coupled linear equations which can be put into the matrix form of Eq.(13).

The recursive generation of the D matrices is the central element of our numerical procedure. They provide a propagation solution to the set of partial differential equations satisfying the proper boundary conditions. Starting from D_1 near the origin, we can generate D_i for $i > 1$ by successively applying matrix inversions. Though we do not construct wave functions explicitly, the propagation D matrix in the asymptotic region will be sufficient to determine the quantities characterizing scattering.

The propagation scheme is extremely suitable for extracting asymptotic solutions. Scattering matrices such as S and K matrices can be obtained in a straightforward manner from Eq.(14) once the asymptotic functions are determined. Since propagation depends on history, we need not to consider the asymptotic boundary conditions when we calculate D matrices. This is in contrast to many finite difference and finite element methods[5,6] where boundary conditions are included as part of a global matrix and any change in boundary conditions will require a different calculation.

Finally, electron-exchange is included in a direct manner in the present propagation scheme. The exchange of two electrons across the diagonal line ($r_1 = r_2$) can be accomplished by exchanging channel functions. Thus grid points lying on the upper triangle region are related to those in the lower triangle region. This treatment of electron-exchange is quite unique.

4. RESULTS AND DISCUSSIONS

We have applied the propagation method to calculate electron-hydrogen atom scattering below the $n = 3$ threshold. To appreciate the accuracy and effectiveness of the present method, we present in Table I and Table II a small sample of results for elastic scattering phase shifts. These results using close-coupling, variational, finite element and higher-order finite difference methods represent continuous effort towards achieving accurate calculation of phase shift. There is an excellent agreement between present results and other calculations. This comparison shows that the present finite difference scheme is in competitive with the more sophisticated finite element calculations. In the inelastic region below $n = 3$ we have studied $1s - 2s$ and $1s - 2p$ scattering cross sections and resonances. Again our results are in good agreement with other calculations.

In summary, we have successfully established a general propagation algorithm which solves the two-electron Schrödinger equations directly. The algorithm allowing propagation of wave functions is both accurate and effective.

Table 1: Elastic singlet and triplet phase shifts for $e-H$: present results are compared with R-matrix, finite element (FEM), and variational method (from Ref.1.).

k	R-matrix	FEM	Variational	present
		$^1S^e$		
0.1	2.550	2.553	2.5561	2.5545
0.2	2.062	2.066	2.0666	2.0666
0.3	1.691	1.695	1.6963	1.6956
0.4	1.410	1.414	1.4152	1.4147
0.5	1.196	1.200	1.2010	1.2007
0.6	1.035	1.040	1.0408	1.0412
0.7	0.925	0.930	0.9303	0.9302
0.8	–	0.887	0.887	0.8867
		$^3S^e$		
0.1	2.939	2.938	2.9385	2.9392
0.2	2.717	2.717	2.7174	2.7171
0.3	2.500	2.500	2.4997	2.4999
0.4	2.294	2.294	2.2941	2.2939
0.5	2.105	2.104	2.1046	2.1044
0.6	1.933	1.933	1.9328	1.9329
0.7	1.780	1.780	1.7794	1.7796
0.8	–	1.645	1.6438	1.6436

Table 2: Same as in Table I, except for $^1P^o$ and $^3P^o$ (from Ref.2).

k	R-matrix	FEM	Variational	present
		$^1P^o$		
0.1	0.006	0.006	0.007	0.006
0.2	0.015	0.015	0.015	0.016
0.3	0.016	0.016	0.017	0.017
0.4	0.009	0.009	0.010	0.010
0.5	−0.002	−0.002	−0.001	−0.002
0.6	−0.012	−0.012	−0.009	−0.012
0.7	−0.016	−0.015	−0.013	−0.015
0.8	–	−0.007	−0.004	−0.007
		$^3P^o$		
0.1	0.010	0.010	0.011	0.010
0.2	0.045	0.045	0.045	0.046
0.3	0.107	0.107	0.106	0.107
0.4	0.187	0.187	0.187	0.188
0.5	0.270	0.271	0.271	0.271
0.6	0.341	0.342	0.341	0.342
0.7	0.392	0.393	0.393	0.394
0.8	–	0.428	0.427	0.429

ACKNOWLEDGMENTS

This research was supported in part by the US National Science Foundation under Grant No. PHY91-22117.

REFERENCES

1. Y.D. Wang and J. Callaway, "Direct numerical approach to electron-hydrogen scattering," *Physical Review A*, Vol. 48, No. 3, 1993, pp. 2058-2069.
2. Y.D. Wang and J. Callaway, "Direct numerical approach to electron-hydrogen scattering II: $L > 0$," to be published in *Physical Review A*.
3. R. Poet, "Symmetrically coupled partial differential equations in scattering I. Model electron-hydrogen collisions," *Journal of Physics B*, Vol. 13, 1980, pp. 2995-3008.
4. R. Poet, "The exact solution for a simplified model of electron scattering by hydrogen atoms," *Journal of Physics B*, Vol. 11, 1978, pp. 3081-3094.
5. J. Botero and J. Shertzer, "Direct numerical solution of the Schrödinger equation for quantum scattering problems," *Physical Review A*, Vol. 46, No. 3, 1992, pp. R1155-R1158;
6. J. Shertzer and J. Botero, "Finite element analysis of electron-hydrogen scattering," to be published in *Physical Review A*.

Toward Teraflop Computing and New Grand Challenge Applications

ISBN-1-56072-247-9

SIMULATION OF THE COULOMB GAP ON A PARALLEL COMPUTER

Fedor G. Pikus

Department of Physics, University of Utah, Salt Lake City, 84103

I. INTRODUCTION

The idea of the Coulomb gap has been put forward by A. L. Efros and B. I. Shklovskii[1] in 1975. Initially the Coulomb gap was studied in doped bulk semiconductors; later this concept was applied to many three- and two-dimensional systems, where the carriers (usually electrons) are strongly localized and can be considered as classical point charges. The Coulomb gap was shown to have profound implication on the hopping transport (for review see Ref. [2]). Recently the idea of the Coulomb gap was extended for systems of free electrons in a strong magnetic field[3,4], granular metals[5], and high-T_c superconductors[3,6].

Very few theoretical results, related to the Coulomb gap, have been obtained analytically. The numerical simulation has been the main tool of research in this field. This makes the problem of efficient simulation algorithms very important. However, development of the algorithms for Coulomb gap simulation on supercomputers meets significant difficulties. The main source of the problem is the long-range nature of the Coulomb interaction. This means that every electron "feels" the movement of every other electron. Therefore, it is impossible to separate a system of particles with Coulomb interaction into few regions, which would interact only along their borders. Furthermore, after a single electron moves all Coulomb energies in the entire system must be recomputed.

In this paper we describe a new implementation of the Coulomb gap simulation algorithm on a parallel computer. In the next section the basic physics of the Coulomb gap is described. The algorithms, used in the study of the Coulomb gap, are briefly summarised in sections III and IV, and the new algorithm is described in section V. Section VI shows the efficiency of the parallelization of the new algorithm.

II. PHYSICS OF THE COULOMB GAP

The basic idea behind the phenomenon of the Coulomb gap is easy to illustrate. Let us consider a ground state of a system of classical electrons, considered as point charges. The electrons can occupy only discrete points of the space - sites. Any site can be either occupied by one electron or empty. The Hamiltonian of such system has the following form:

$$H = \tfrac{1}{2}\sum_{i,j}\frac{n_i n_j}{r_{ij}} + \sum_i n_i \varphi_i , \tag{1}$$

where n_i is the occupation number of site i, r_{ij} is the distance between the two sites, and φ_i is a random external potential[1]. The occupation number is 1 if the site is occupied by an electron and it is 0 if the site is empty. In this paper we use the units in which the electron charge e=1.

If we take any occupied site i and empty site j, then the work which is needed to move the electron from site i to site j is

$$\Delta W_{ij} = \varepsilon_j - \varepsilon_i - r_{ij}^{-1}. \tag{2}$$

This is also the change in the total energy of the system. Here ε_i and ε_j are the energies of electron on sites i and j, respectively, *taken before the electron has moved*. The term V_{ij} in equation (2) subtracts from the energy of the target site the potential, created by the hopping electron itself.

In the ground state the total energy is minimal by definition. Therefore, all one-electron hops should increase the total energy, which means that ΔW_{ij} must be positive for all sites i and j: $\Delta W_{ij} > 0$, or $r_{ij} > (\varepsilon_j - \varepsilon_i)^{-1}$. Note that in the ground state all empty sites have their energies above the Fermi level μ, while all occupied sites are below μ. If we now consider the sites in an energy strip of the width ε around the Fermi level, we see that the distance r between two sites in this strip cannot be smaller than ε^{-1}. Therefore, the density of states near the Fermi level cannot be larger that the following estimate:

$$g(\varepsilon) \sim \frac{1}{r^d |\varepsilon - \mu|} \sim |\varepsilon - \mu|^{d-1}, \tag{3}$$

where d is the dimensionality of the problem. One can see that the density of states is strongly suppressed in the vicinity of the Fermi level. This is a very general result for the systems with Coulomb interaction: even if this interaction is week compared to other interactions or external disorder, *it cannot be considered as a perturbation* for the states close to the Fermi level.

III. MODELING OF COULOMB GAP

The first studies of the Coulomb gap were done using the algorithms, which find a minimum of the total energy of the system[2,7,8]. Usually such algorithms minimise the energy with respect to all one-electron hops, and sometimes simultaneous hops of small number of electrons are also considered[9]. Such algorithms provide the information about

---

[1] The problem is equivalent to an Ising problem in a random magnetic field with long-range interaction.

the Coulomb gap at zero temperature, when the system relaxes to the ground state and remains there. However, the more realistic situation of the finite temperature cannot be studied by such methods. There is also an inherent problem in these algorithms: they never give the real ground state, but the so-called pseudo-ground state, which has the minimal energy with respect to all electron rearrangements considered. Therefore, it becomes important to model the Coulomb gap at finite temperature.

The finite-temperature modeling of the Coulomb gap is usually done using the Metropolis algorithm, which in this case has a straightforward physical background. Let us start with some configuration of electrons on the sites. The probability of a hop from site i to site j is given by the Boltzmann exponent:

$$p_{ij} = \tau^{-1}, \text{ if } \Delta W_{ij} < 0, \text{ and } p_{ij} = \tau^{-1} \exp\left(-\Delta W_{ij}/T \right), \text{ if } \Delta W_{ij} > 0. \tag{3}$$

Here τ is the predexponential time, determined by the electron-phonon interaction. The algorithm just models the thermal life of the real electron system: at each step, a pair of occupied and empty sites is selected randomly. Then, the program computes the energy difference ΔW and generates hop with the probability, given by Eq. (3). The *simulation time* is measured in attempts to perform a hop (so, the time τ is used as a unit). So, as applied to the Coulomb gap, this algorithm models the evolution of the system in the *real time*.

Any quantity one wants to calculate, such as density of states, has to be averaged over all configurations (i.e. all arrangements of the electrons on the sites) to get an average over the Gibbs ensemble:

$$\langle X \rangle = \sum_i X_i \exp\left(-\frac{W_i}{T} \right) \left[\sum_i \exp\left(-\frac{W_i}{T} \right) \right]^{-1} \tag{5}$$

Here X is the quantity to be averaged, i denotes the number of configuration, and the sum is taken over all configurations. In practice the sum over all configurations is replaced by the sum over a subset of *representative configurations*. In the Metropolis algorithm, the summation is carried out over all encountered configurations. Physically, this means that we start from some initial configuration and let the motion of electrons, caused by the interaction with thermal phonons, take place for as long as it needed for the system to equilibrate.

IV. SCALAR, VECTOR, OR PARALLEL?

It was already noted that the implementation of the Metropolis algorithm, or any other algorithm for Coulomb gap modeling, on advanced computer architectures is a difficult problem, far from its final solution. Most of the computations are done on scalar computers, such as workstations. The reason for this is that the energies of *all* sites have to be recalculated after a single electron hop. To speed up the recalculation of Coulomb energies, the lattice model has been widely used[2,4]. In this model the sites are located not randomly, but form a regular lattice, usually a square one. Then the interaction energy depends only on the difference between the site numbers and can be stored as tables. Then the energy recalculation becomes a completely matrix operation. Therefore, the lattice model allows to vectorize a significant part of the calculations. However, this model also leads to a severe problem in computations: crystallisation. At zero temperature the ground state of the Hamiltonian (1) with sites in a lattice is ordered. This problem of crystallisation makes it impossible to do the calculations for the numbers of electrons commensurate with the number of sites, and in the vicinity of such numbers[3,4]. The calculations with random sites are free from such problem, but they are much more expensive, and this usually forces one to use small systems [10].

At low temperatures the most time-consuming part becomes the random search for the electron to hop. At low temperatures the hop probability becomes exponentially small, and many sites must be tried before a hop occurs. Each try involves generation of few random numbers and calculation of the transfer work [Eq. (2)]. Because the result of each try is impossible to predict, these calculations are inherently scalar.

On the other hand, the traditional approaches to the parallelization, such as separation of the system into few weakly interacting parts, so that each node handles only one part, does not seem feasible, because in a Coulomb system there are no weakly interacting parts. Also, it may be not sufficient to consider only nearest-neighbour hops. In our simulations at low temperatures hops as long as 10 average electron-electron distances had to be considered. This means that not only the interaction potential, but also the charge transfer is long-range. In the next section we show an alternative approach to the parallel implementation of the Metropolis algorithm, which is especially suitable for low temperatures and makes use of the biggest computational problem in this regime - the low hopping rate.

V. NEW PARALLEL ALGORITHM

The basic idea behind the proposed algorithm is that because at low temperatures successive electron hops have very low probability, we can *try many hops simultaneously*, on different nodes of a parallel computer. The probability of conflict, when two nodes generate a successive hop at the same time, is very small.

I will now describe the details of the implementation of the Metropolis algorithm on a parallel computer. The algorithm has two levels of parallelization. The lower level, which I call a group, implements the above scheme in the following way: each group consists of a Group Coordinator program and a number N_p of Player programs. At the beginning, the Group Coordinator generates the coordinates of sites and the initial configuration of the electrons on the sites[2]. This configuration is then sent to all Players. Each Player starts its own Monte-Carlo game on the *entire system*, but with different random number sequence. This way each Player tries different site pair for an electron hop. As soon as a Player finds a successful hop, it sends a message to the Group Coordinator and suspends further calculations. The Group Coordinator informs all Players that a hop must be performed. The Players then update the electron occupation numbers and recompute energies, and continue the Monte-Carlo game. Note that the Player which finds the hop does not consider it accepted until the Group Coordinator confirms it. This way the later can solve a conflict,

[2] This implementation uses random sites coordinates, since it allows to avoid the above mentioned crystallisation problem. Also, the benefits of the lattice model are less significant on a scalar computer.

when two Players report a hop simultaneously. Only one hop will be accepted, and the configuration on all Players changes synchronously. So, the group selects site pairs and tries hops about N_p times faster than a single processor. Since at now temperatures this is the main part of the calculations, we can expect a nearly linear increase in performance with N_p until the number of conflicts becomes significant. The results of the test shown below demonstrate that it is indeed so.

The upper layer of parallelization consists of few groups and a main Coordinator program. The Coordinator performs all input-output functions:-it reads the simulation parameters and sends them to Group Coordinators, then it receives the hops, done by all groups, and stores the initial and final sites for each hop in a disk file. This allows to concentrate all input-output functions on one node.

Different groups are completely independent. They either run on different realisations of random site coordinates to achieve an averaging both over time and over disorder, or they start from the same initial configuration with different random number sequences and in generally move into different regions of the configuration space. Note that the later approach can not substitute the groups, because it is important not only to generate many configurations, but to generate *representative*, or typical, configurations. The initial and few subsequent configurations are usually far from equilibrium, and, therefore, must have very small weight. So, it is necessary to do many hops just to reach the thermal equilibrium.

VI. PERFORMANCE OF THE NEW ALGORITHM

In this section I show the performance of the parallel implementation of the Metropolis algorithm on a Parallel Virtual Machine (PVM), organised on a cluster of IBM RS6000 workstations, using PVM version 3.0. All test runs were performed on the system of 900 sites, randomly placed in a square 30 by 30, with 450 electrons. All computations were done with one group, so the parallel machine consisted of one "Coordinator", one "Group Coordinator", and N_p "Players". The computations were done for different temperatures T and different number of Players N_p. For each T and N_p the program was run for 3000 CPU seconds on all nodes. The measure of performance of the program is the number of hops done.

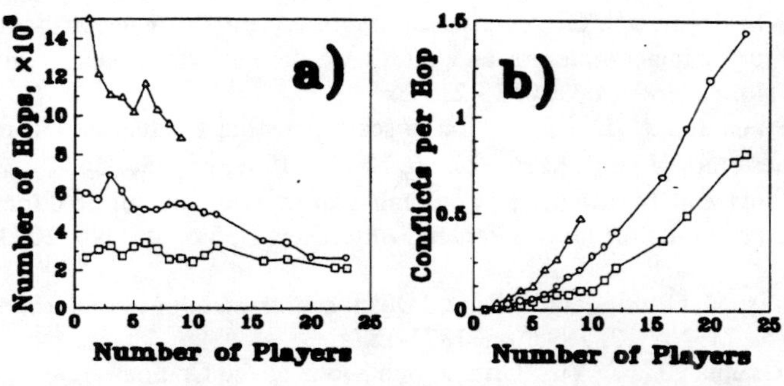

Fig. 1. The number of hops (a) and number of conflicts per hop *vs.* number of Players for different temperatures: T=0.01 (squares), T=0.02 (circles), and T=0.04 (triangles), the temperature unit is the

electron-electron interaction energy at the average distance . Other parameters of the calculations are given in the text. The fluctuations of the performance are due to different load of the workstations by other users.

The Figure 1 shows how the number of hops performed in 3000 CPU seconds depends on the number of Players, and also the number of conflicts per hop (a conflict is a situation when two Players report hops simultaneously). From Fig. 1 one can see that for temperatures below 1/100 of the electron-electron interaction energy at the average distance the performance grows with the size of the group almost linearly up to the largest size of the group, 23. For T=1/50, the optimal size of the group is 10-12. For higher temperatures, the performance per node drops when the second Player is added, but then it stays pretty constant for groups of 2-7 Players. One can also see that for each temperature, i.e. for each hopping rate, there is an optimal size of the group. This size is determined by the individual node performance and the speed of internode connections.

ACKNOWLEDGEMENT

I am grateful to my scientific adviser Prof. A. L. Efros, who guided my research in the physics of Coulomb gap. This work was supported by NSF Grant No. DMR-9116748.

REFERENCES

[1] A. L. Efros and B. I. Shklovskii, "Coulomb Gap and Low-Temperature Conductivity of Disordered Systems", *J. Phys. C*, Vol. *8*, No. 1, 1975, pp. 49-59.

[2] A. L. Efros and B. I. Shklovskii, "Coulomb interaction in disordered systems with localized electron states", In: *Electron-electron interaction in disordered systems* (Ed. A. L. Efros and M. Pollak), Amsterdam:North Holland, 1985, pp. 410-481.

[3] A. L. Efros, "Coulomb gap and transport in classical electron liquid", *Phys. Rev. Lett.*, Vol. 68, No. 14, 1992, pp. 2208-2211.

[4] A. L. Efros and F. G. Pikus, "Classical approach to the gap in the tunneling density of states of two-dimensional electron liquid in a strong magnetic field", *Phys. Rev. B*, Vol. 48, No. 19, 1993, pp. 14694-14697.

[5] R. Chicon, M. Ortuno, and M. Pollak, "Hardening of the Coulomb gap by electron polarons", *Phys. Rev. B*, Vol. 37, No. 18, 1988, pp. 10520-10525.

[6] A. E. Kar'kin *et. al*, "Disordering of single crystals by neutron bombardment: high-temperature superconductors and quasi-two-dimensional metals", Superconductivity, Vol. 5, No. 12, 1992, pp. 2091 - 2107.

[7] F. G. Pikus and A. L. Efros, "Large scale potential fluctuations in plane layers with impurities", *Sov. Phys. JETP*, Vol. 96, No. 10, 1989, pp. 558–563.

[8] A. Mobius and M. Richter, "Coulomb gap in two- and three-dimensional systems: Simulation results for large samples", *Phys. Rev. B*, Vol. 45, No. 20, 1992, pp. 11568-11579.

[9] E. Cuevas, M. Ortuno, and J. Ruiz, "Quantuzation state of granular metals", *Phys. Rev. Lett.*, Vol. 71, No. 12, 1993, pp. 1871-1874.

[10] E. R. Grannan, C. C. Yu, "Critical behaviour of the Coulomb glass", *Phys. Rev. Lett.*, Vol. 71, No. 20, 1993, pp. 3335-3338.

Toward Teraflop Computing
and New Grand
Challenge Applications

ISBN-1-56072-247-9

THE PHASE PROBLEM IN PROTEIN CRYSTALLOGRAPHY: POTENTIAL APPROACHES UTILIZING MASSIVELY PARALLEL COMPUTERS

Edward J. Meehan* and J. Michael Meehan#

*Chemistry Department, University of Alabama in Huntsville and # Department of Computer Science, Louisiana Tech University

ABSTRACT

The phase problem in protein crystallography should be identified as a new grand challenge application. It is a problem of great importance not only for advancing basic science in the field of structural molecular biology but also of great commercial importance due the increasing role of protein crystallography in guiding the rational design of new drugs in the pharmaceutical industry. To reconstruct the structure of a molecule from diffraction data both the intensity and phase of each reflection are required. The intensities are experimentally observable; the phases are not. At present, for protein structures, it is not possible to directly compute the phase of each reflection from information contained in the pattern of diffracted intensities. The high degree of parallelism inherent in some of the new approaches to this problem make the addition of massively parallel computing a natural and very attractive extension.

1. INTRODUCTION

The three dimensional structure determination of protein molecules and other biological macromolecules by the technique of x-ray crystallography has played a central role in molecular biology [1]. It has been the principle technique for establishing the connection between biological function and three dimensional molecular structure. Our detailed knowledge of the structures of DNA, enzymes, hormones, antibodies, DNA-binding proteins, transport proteins, and many other classes of proteins are the result of the successful application of this method [2]. Today this technique is increasingly used in the structural biology programs of the pharmaceutical and biotechnology industries to guide the rational design of new drugs. The number of known protein structures now exceeds six hundred and the rate at which new structures are being reported is accelerating. This remarkable success has been due to recent advances in several areas. Thanks to breakthroughs in the overproduction of proteins by genetic engineering, large quantities of previously rare proteins are now available. The development of high power rotating anode x-ray generators, the availability of extremely intense x-ray beam lines at synchrotron facilities, and the development of electronic and phosphor imaging plate area detector systems have drastically reduced the time and effort required for the careful measurement of the diffracted intensities. Personal workstations with excellent graphic capabilities have made building molecular models into computed electron densities maps much easier. Some progress has even been made on the difficult task of growing diffraction quality crystals. Nevertheless, the structure determination of a protein molecule still remains a formidable undertaking and the usual rate limiting step in this process goes by the name "the phase problem." Indeed the phase problem has always been the fundamental obstacle in the use of diffraction data to establish molecular structure.

In the crystallographic experiment, a crystal is irradiated by an x-ray beam and the intensities of the diffracted x-ray maxima are carefully measured. From each of these intensities a number F(hkl) can be derived. The structure of a molecule can be described by its electron density function ρ(xyz) in three dimensional space. As can be seen from equation (1) the numbers F(hkl) are the coefficients in a Fourier synthesis used to

$$\rho(x,y,z) = \frac{2}{V_c}\sum_{h=0}^{\infty}\sum_{k=-\infty}^{\infty}\sum_{l=-\infty}^{\infty}\left|F(hkl)\right|\cos\left[2\pi(hx+ky+lz)-\alpha(hkl)\right] \tag{1}$$

construct the unknown electron density of the molecule from the experimentally measured diffraction data. V_C is the volume of the unit cell of the crystal. However, equation (1) also shows that an additional piece of information, the phase α(hkl) of each diffraction maxima is required. But this information is unobtainable from the diffraction experiment and this dilemma constitutes the phase problem.

2. ISOMORPHOUS REPLACEMENT METHODS

Since in the general case the phase of each reflection can range in value from 0 to 2π and since the number of reflections for most proteins is at least of the order 10^4, it is easy to see that any attempt to examine all possible phase sets by brute force is doomed for the number of permutations is intractable. How then have crystallographers overcome the phase problem to determine macromolecular structures? The most important approach has been isomorphous replacement. This method was first applied to proteins by Perutz and his coworkers [3] and has been used in the great majority of cases where new unique protein structures were determined. In this method the crystallographer attempts to prepare a series of heavy atom derivatives of the protein crystal that are isomorphous to the native crystal. One hopes that the addition of a very electron dense atom bound to the protein will affect observable changes in the intensities of the diffraction maxima but will not perturb the structure of the native protein. The data collection process is repeated and the intensity of each reflection from the derivative crystal is measured. The next step is to determine the location of the added heavy atom in the unit cell. The common approach is to calculate a Patterson function using the intensity differences between the derivative and native reflections as coefficients. In favorable cases the location of the heavy atoms can be determined. Once the position of the heavy atom is known, both the magnitude and phase of the heavy atom's contribution to each structure factor can be calculated. These are used in conjunction with the measured values of the magnitude of $\mathbf{F_P}$ of the native and the magnitude of $\mathbf{F_{PH}}$ of the derivative to determine the phase of $\mathbf{F_P}$ for each reflection. The basic idea of the method can be understood by examining figure 1 which is known as a Harker construction. The magnitude of $\mathbf{F_P}$ is known from the measured intensity of the native reflection. Likewise the magnitudes of $\mathbf{F_{PH1}}$ and $\mathbf{F_{PH2}}$ are known from the measured intensities of two independent derivatives. The locations of H1 from one

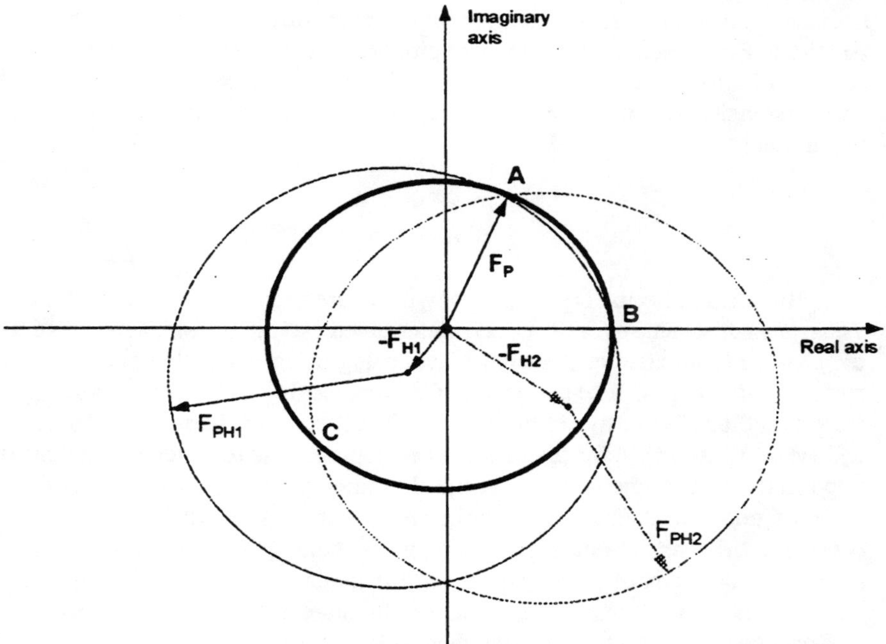

Figure 1. Harker construction for phase determination

derivative and the heavy atom H2 from a second independent derivative have been determined, thus permitting the calculation of the vectors $-\mathbf{F_{H1}}$ and $-\mathbf{F_{H2}}$. We seek the solution to the vector equation $\mathbf{F_P} = \mathbf{F_{PH}} - \mathbf{F_H}$. The first derivative narrows the possible choice of phase of $\mathbf{F_P}$ to the points A or B. This leaves a two fold ambiguity in the phase of each reflection. In the ideal case this ambiguity is resolved by the second derivative which confirms choice A as the unique solution In practice the crystallographer attempts to prepare multiple isomorphous derivatives in order to obtain good indications of the phase of $\mathbf{F_P}$.

The multiple isomorphous replacement method has been augmented by a number of phasing procedures. These include the use of anomalous scattering data, use of the multiple wavelength method with suitable anomalous scatters, and in certain cases molecular replacement techniques [4,5] or the use of noncrystallographic symmetry [6].

Since these methods have obviously been good enough to allow the determination of hundreds of structures, why is there still a problem? The preparation of heavy atom derivatives is often a trial and error process. In many instances the determinations of important structures were delayed for years before suitable derivatives were found. It is a very labor intensive process, tying up the valuable time of the crystallographer as well as consuming the majority of machine time on the expensive diffraction instrumentation. The process requires a continual supply of difficult to prepare diffraction quality crystals. The phases obtained by the method are inherently flawed because the derivative structures are almost never truly isomorphous with the native structure. For these reasons the whole process of protein structure determination would be revolutionized if it were somehow possible to directly calculate the phases from the native intensity data alone. For small molecule crystal structures, methods are available that accomplish just this task.

3. DIRECT METHODS

In small molecule crystallography the phase problem has essentially been solved. Thousands of structures are routinely determined each year. In 80 - 90 % of the cases the phases of the reflections are calculated using information obtained only from the pattern of intensities. The collection of techniques that make this possible is called "direct methods." The award of the 1985 Nobel prize in chemistry to Drs. Jerome Karle and Herbert Hauptman for their role in developing these techniques emphasized the importance of these methods in structural chemistry. The theory of direct methods is based on relatively sophisticated mathematical formalism and any detailed explanation is beyond the scope of this paper. Here, we will only point out that the methods rely on the known atomicity of crystal structures, the random placement of atoms within the unit cell, and the fact that the electron density function is everywhere non-negative. The theory develops restrictions on the phase relationships among linearly dependent reflections. The most useful and famous are known as the Σ_2 relations. Let **h** represent a vector in reciprocal space denoted by the indices hkl (i.e. a reflection), and **k** a second vector h'k'l'. **h-k** is a third vector (reflection) which forms a triplet with **h** and **k**. Reflection triplets like this form a Σ_2 relation. If the phases of two reflections involved in the Σ_2 relation are known they can be used to calculate the phase of the third. If a reflection is a member of multiple triplets the phase is assigned using the tangent formula of Karle and Hauptman [7] (equation 2) or a closely related method.

$$\tan \alpha_{h} \approx \frac{\sum_{k} w_{h}|E_{k}||E_{h-k}|\sin(\alpha_{k}+\alpha_{h-k})}{\sum_{k} w_{h}|E_{k}||E_{h-k}|\cos(\alpha_{k}+\alpha_{h-k})} \tag{2}$$

The E's are normalized structure factors that are calculated from the measured intensities, the w's are weights. In the most widely used direct method program, random phases are assigned to the strong reflections and the tangent formula is used recursively to refine the phases to the most consistent set. The set of phases obtained from one randomly assigned set of starting phases is not guaranteed to refine to the correct solution. So, the procedure is repeated from multiple starting phase sets. For small molecules the tangent formula is robust enough to find the correct phase set in a relative low number of trials, almost always less than 100 and generally about 20.

4. DIRECT METHODS AND PROTEINS

The remarkable success of direct methods in phasing small molecule crystal structures has encouraged researchers to apply these methods to protein structures. To date, these attempts have only achieved limited success. Woolfson and Yao [8] have tested the program SAYTAN [9], which is based on the Sayre-equation tangent formula, on the small protein avian pancreatic polypeptide (APP). A starting basis set of 129 known phases within 3 Angstrom resolution were combined with randomly assigned phases for 1371 strong reflections to 1 Angstrom resolution and subjected to phase refinement. The best phase set produced had a mean phase error of 31.9° and an interpretable electron density map. In subsequent work Mukherjee and Woolfson [10,11] have shown that when high resolution data were used, an essentially correct phase set could be found even starting from only random phases. While these results are encouraging there are many special features of APP which make it a very favorable test case and not representative of proteins in general. These include the presence of a native Zinc atom and extremely high resolution diffraction data.

George Sheldrick has attempted direct method phasing of two other small proteins crambin and rubredoxin, by the phase-annealing approach [12]. For crambin, despite trying 500,000 different random starting phase sets the method failed to net the correct solution. However, when the correct phases were input as the starting set they were stable to phase refinement. In the case of rubredoxin the presence of an iron atom aided the phasing attempts and 1% of the starting phase sets refined to mean phase errors of about 56°. These phases were further improved by Fourier recycling methods. Again both these proteins are unusual in that they diffract to extremely high resolution.

The obvious parallel nature of these calculations suggests ways of improving the chances of success by using massively parallel computing. However, there are good theoretical reason to doubt that a simple extension of conventional direct methods will be able to overcome the phase problem for proteins [12,13]. The probability that the phase relations used by method are correct is inversely proportional to the number of atoms in the structure. As the size of the proteins under study increases the power of direct methods diminish. The derivations of the methods also use atomicity, but it is rare to find protein crystals that diffract to atomic resolution. These objections have prompted researchers to develop new approaches to the problem.

Many of these new ideas were described at a recent conference devoted to this topic [14]. Two of the most promising approaches are the Low-Resolution Real-Space envelope method of S. Subbiah [15,16] and the Entropy Maximization and Likelihood Ranking approach of G. Bricogne [17]. Again, there is a very high degree of parallelism inherent in the calculations performed by each of these methods. Bricogne, Gilmore and their coworkers [18] have recognized this parallelism and divided the computations among five networked SUN workstations, but their ideas have yet to be implemented on a truly massively parallel machine.

REFERENCES

1. T.L. Blundell and L.N. Johnson, *Protein Crystallography*, San Diego, Academic Press Inc, 1976, (556 pp.).
2. C. Branden and J. Tooze, *Introduction to Protein Structure*, New York, Garland Publishing, Inc., 1991, (302pp).
3. D.W. Green, V.M. Ingram, and M.F. Perutz, *Proc. Roy. Soc.*, **A225**, 1954, p. 287.
4. J. Karle, Int. J. Quantum Chem. Symp., 7,1980, 357.
5. W.A. Hendrickson et al., *Proc. Natl. Acad. Sci. U.S.A.*, **86**, 1989, 2190.
6. E. Arnold and M.G. Rossman, *Proc. Natiol. Acad. Sci. U.S.A.*, **83**, 1986, 5489.
7. J. Karle and H. Hauptman, *Acta Cryst.*, **3,** 1950, **181**.
8. M.M. Woolfson and Yao Jia-Xing, *Acta Cryst.*, **A44**, 1988, pp.410-413.
9. T. Debaerdemaeker, C. Tate, and M.M. Woolfson, *Acta Cryst.*, **A44**, 1988, pp. 353-357.
10. M. Mukherjee and M.M. Woolfson, *Acta Cryst.*, **D49**, 1993, pp. 9-12.
11. M.M. Woolfson, *Acta Cryst.*, **D49**, 1993 pp.13-17.
12. G. M. Sheldrick, Z. Dauter, K. S. Wilson, H. Hope, and L.C. Sieker, *Acta Cryst.*, **D49**, pp. 18-23.
13. D. Baker, A. E. Krukowski, and D. A. Agad, Acta Cryst., D49, pp. 186-192.
14. J.P. Gluske, ed, *Direct Methods in Macromolecular Crystallography*, *Acta Cryst.*, **D49**, 1993, 222pp.
15. S. Subbiah, *Science,* **252**, 1991, pp. 128-132.
16. S. Subbiah, *Acta Cryst.*, **D49**, 1993, pp. 108-119.
17. G. Bricogne, *Acta Cryst.*, **D49**, 1993, pp.37-60.
18. G. Bricogne and C. J. Gilmore, *Acta Cryst.*, **A46**, 1990, pp. 284-297.
19. C. J. Gilmore, G. Bricogne, and C. Bannister, *Acta Cryst.*, **A46**, pp. 297-308.
20. C. J. Gilmore, A.N. Henderson. and G. Bricogne, *Acta Cryst.*, **A47**, 1991, pp. 842-846.
21. K. Shankland, C.J. Gilmore, G. Bricogne, and H. Hashizume, *Acta Cryst.*, **A49**, 1993, pp. 493-501.

Toward Teraflop Computing
and New Grand
Challenge Applications

ISBN-1-56072-247-9

ASYMPTOTIC BEHAVIORS OF PAIR INTERACTION POTENTIAL IN A LAYERED 2D SYSTEM

J. D. Fan, Y. M. Malozovsky and J. Cheng*

**Department of Physics Southern University and A & M College,
Baton Rouge, Louisiana 70813**

A pair interaction potential in a layered system with two-dimensional (2D) electron sheets, taking into account electron correlations, is obtained. The potential is derived for arbitrary locations of interacting charges in such a lattice. The local-field factor for a layered electron liquid is evaluated. It is shown that the electron correlations lead to both an attraction between two like charges within a certain range of inter-charge distances in a plane of layers at the intermediate carrier density and a strong oscillating character of the pair interaction at the low carrier density. The pair interaction potential in the direction normal to the plane shows oscillating behavior which is caused by electron correlations. The behaviors of the in-plane and normal-to-plane potential and its asymptotic expressions for different values of the carrier density are also presented. The unusual behaviors of the potential are very edifying and illuminating. This may cast a light on the mystery of high temperature superconductivity.

I. Introduction

There is a number of compounds which have a layered structure and an essentially two-dimensional (2D) electron spectrum such as all the high-T_c cuprate compounds[1], graphite intercalation compounds, semiconductor's superlattices etc. The pair interaction potential for such layered compounds is very important in microscopic description of lattice dynamics, electron-phonon interaction, electron-impurity scattering, and electron-electron interaction, etc. Usually, modeling of lattice dynamics of such layered systems is carried out in terms of long-range Coulomb forces and short-range repulsion potentials[2,3] with a quite large number of adjustable parameters. The use of empirical pair potentials with a number of adjustable parameters, unfortunately, leads to serious uncertainties in the microscopic properties of phonon spectrum, electron-phonon interaction, electron-impurity scattering etc. Furthermore, an isotropic screened Coulomb potential is not suitable for describing microscopic properties of layered systems due to the obvious spatial anisotropy. Anisotropy of the electron spectrum must lead to the strong anisotropy of the pair interaction potential. Moreover, the random phase approximation (RPA) that correctly describes the screening effect at a high electron density is not a very good approximation for the metallic electron density because at the metallic density electron correlations begin to play leading role in screening, and thus essentially affect the pair interaction potential[4].

The description of electron-correlation effects in the isotropic three-dimension (3D) and 2D has been well developed[5,6]. It is also known[6] that the electron-correlation effects in a 2D electron liquid are stronger than in a 3D case. In a layered system with 2D electron sheets the Coulomb interaction is still three-dimensional. It implies that the electron correlations in a layered 2D system (L2DS) should be stronger than in a pure 2D case.

In this paper we consider the asymptotic behavior of the pair interaction potential in an L2DS taking into account correlation effects with local field factor in the Hubbard approximation.

II. Model and Electron Correlations

In order to determine the pair interaction potential we consider two charged particles surrounded by electrons. In the static case the effective interparticle potential between the i-th charge and the j-th charge in a quite general form is defined by the equation

$$\widetilde{V}(\mathbf{R}_i-\mathbf{R}_j) = V_{cc}(\mathbf{R}_i-\mathbf{R}_j) + \int d^3r \int d^3r' V_{ec}(\mathbf{r}-\mathbf{R}_i)\,\chi(\mathbf{r},\mathbf{r}')V_{ec}(\mathbf{r}'-\mathbf{R}_j), \tag{1}$$

where $V_{cc}(\mathbf{R}_i - \mathbf{R}_j)$ is the potential of the direct (bare) inter-charge interaction between the two charges which is assumed to be purely Coulombic, $V_{ec}(r)$ is the electron-charge interaction and $\chi(r, r')$ is the nonlocal susceptibility of the electron sub-system. The dynamical nonlocal susceptibility satisfies the following equation

$$\chi(\mathbf{r},\mathbf{r}',\omega) = \widetilde{\chi}(\mathbf{r},\mathbf{r}',\omega) + \int d\mathbf{r}_1\, d\mathbf{r}_2\, \widetilde{\chi}(\mathbf{r},\mathbf{r}_1,\omega)\, V(\mathbf{r}_1-\mathbf{r}_2)\, \chi(\mathbf{r}_2,\mathbf{r}',\omega), \tag{2}$$

where $V(r)$ is the unscreened Coulomb interaction and $\widetilde{\chi}(\mathbf{r},\mathbf{r}',\omega)$ is the irreducible susceptibility that includes the vertex correction. Here we should note that Eqs.(1)and (2) are quite general.

Now we apply Eqs.(1) and (2) to a model system consisting of electron sheets separated by an interlayer spacing c, and assume that electrons are distributed on the layered planes and the electron spectrum is isotropic in any of the planes. We first consider Eq.(2) for susceptibility, which can be represented for a layered system by

$$\chi_{l,l'}(\mathbf{k}_{\|},\omega) = \widetilde{\chi}_{l,l'}(\mathbf{k}_{\|},\omega) + \sum_{l_1,l_2} \widetilde{\chi}_{l,l_1}(\mathbf{k}_{\|},\omega)\, V_{l_1,l_2}(\mathbf{k}_{\|})\chi_{l_2,l'}(\mathbf{k}_{\|},\omega), \tag{3}$$

where l is the index of the l - th layer and $V_{l,l'}(k_{\|}) = V_0(k_{\|})\exp(-k_{\|}c|l-l'|)$ is the Coulomb matrix element in a layered crystal with $V_0(k_{\|}) = 2\pi e^2/\kappa k_{\|}$ being the Coulomb interaction in a pure 2D case and κ is the dielectric constant of the background lattice. The solution of the Eq. (3) using the relation $\exp(-k_{\|}|z|) = N^{-1}\sum_{k_z} f(\mathbf{k})\exp(-ik_z z)$, where N is the number of layers, can be written as

$$\chi(\mathbf{k},\omega) = \widetilde{\chi}(\mathbf{k},\omega) \;/\; (1 - V(\mathbf{k})\,\widetilde{\chi}(\mathbf{k},\omega)), \tag{4}$$

where $\mathbf{k} = (k_{\|}, k_z)$ and

$$V(\mathbf{k}) = V_0(k_{\|}) \sinh c\, k_{\|} / (\cosh c\, k_{\|} - \cos ck_z) = V_0(k_{\|})\, f(\mathbf{k}), \tag{5}$$

is the Coulomb interaction for a layered crystal with $f(\mathbf{k})$ being the form factor stemming from layering. Assuming that $V_{cc}(r)$ and $V_{ec}(r)$ are purely Coulombic, Eq. (1) can be represented in the Fourier representation by

$$\widetilde{V}(\mathbf{k}) = V_{cc}(\mathbf{k}) + V_{ec}(\mathbf{k})V_{ec}(-\mathbf{k})\,\chi(\mathbf{k},0), \tag{6}$$

where $\chi(\mathbf{k},\omega)$ is defined by the Eq. (4). in the case of the charge interaction, $V_{cc}(\mathbf{k}) = Z_i Z_j V(\mathbf{k})$ and $V_{ec}(\mathbf{k}) = Z_i V(\mathbf{k})$ with the charge number Z_i and the same $V(\mathbf{k})$ as in Eq.(5). For simplicity, we assume that both the bare inter-charge and electron-charge interactions are purely Coulombic. Because of the periodicity of the system in the z-direction, in Eq. (6), the summation over reciprocal lattice vectors is omitted and it suffices to consider k_z in the first Brillioun zone ($-\pi/c \le k_z \le \pi/c$). It can be shown using the equation for the vertex function in a local approximation that the irreducible susceptibility can be expressed as

$$\widetilde{\chi}(\mathbf{k}_{\|},\omega) = \chi_0(\mathbf{k}_{\|},\omega) \;/\; (1+ K(\mathbf{k}_{\|})\,\chi_0(\mathbf{k}_{\|},\omega))\,, \tag{7}$$

where $K(\mathbf{k}_{||})$ is the short range interaction due to the exchange-correlation effects and related to the local field factor by the relation $K(\mathbf{k}_{||}) = V(\mathbf{k})G(\mathbf{k})$ with $G(\mathbf{k})$ being the local field factor, and $\chi_0(\mathbf{k}_{||}, \omega)$ is the usual free-electron response function for a pure 2D electron spectrum. Substituting Eq. (9) into Eq. (6), the frequency-dependent electron susceptibility with the local field correction can be represented by[5]

$$\chi(\mathbf{k},\omega) = \chi_0(\mathbf{k}_{||},\omega) \,/\, \{1 - V(\mathbf{k})[1 - G(\mathbf{k})]\, \chi_0(\mathbf{k}_{||},\omega)\} \tag{8}$$

Now we discuss the local field factor $G(\mathbf{k})$ in an L2DS. The electron-correlation effects in a strongly coupled electron liquid can be considered in terms of two approaches. The first approach[7] uses the time-dependent multiparticle correlation and response functions. In a self-consistent manner, it considers the dynamic correlations in a strongly coupled and degenerate electron liquid. The second, well-known as the STLS [5] (Singwi-Tos-Land-Sjolander) approach, also in a self-consistent manner, accounts for correlations at short distances between two electrons by means of a pair-correlation function. Both approaches are similar in the static case. It is well-known that the STLS approach produces a good quantitative result in the 3D case. The comparison of the numerical simulation[8] for the ground state of a 2D electron liquid with the calculation of Jonson[6], who applies the STLS scheme to the 2D case, shows that the STLS scheme produces a very good accuracy for correlation energy. We thus adopt the STLS approach for the evaluation of the local field factor $G(\mathbf{k})$ in a layered electron liquid.

Let's now consider the STLS scheme in applying to a layered 2D electron liquid. The Hamiltonian that describes the Coulomb interaction of such a many-particle system is given by

$$H = \sum_{m,l} \frac{\mathbf{p}_m^2(l)}{2m^*} + \frac{1}{2} \sum_{\substack{\mathbf{q}\neq 0 \\ l_1,l_2}} \frac{2\pi e^2}{\kappa q}\, e^{-q|l_1 - l_2|c} \left[n_{l_1}^{\dagger}(\mathbf{q})\, n_{l_2}(\mathbf{q}) - n_s \right], \tag{9}$$

where m^* is the electron effective mass, $\mathbf{p}_m(l)$ is the 2D momentum operator of the m-th electron in the l-th layer, $n_l(\mathbf{q}) = \sum_m e^{-i\mathbf{q}\rho_m(l)}$ is the density fluctuation in the l-th layer with the coordinate $\rho_m(l)$ of the m-th electron in the l-th layer, and $\mathbf{q} = \mathbf{q}_{||}$ is the 2D wave vector. Using the equation of motion $\dot{n}_l(\mathbf{q}) = -i\,[\, n_l(\mathbf{q}), H\,]$ we have

$$\ddot{n}_l(\mathbf{q}) = -\sum_m \left[\frac{\mathbf{q}\mathbf{p}_m(l)}{m^*} + \frac{q^2}{2m^*}\right]^2 e^{-i\mathbf{q}\rho_m(l)} - \frac{q^2}{m^*}\, n_s \sum_{l'} \frac{2\pi e^2}{\kappa q}\, e^{-q|l-l'|c}\, n_{l'}(\mathbf{q})$$
$$- \sum_{\substack{\mathbf{q}'(\neq \mathbf{q}) \\ l'}} \frac{\mathbf{q}\,\mathbf{q}'}{m^*} \frac{2\pi e^2}{\kappa q'}\, e^{-q'|l-l'|c}\, n_l(\mathbf{q}-\mathbf{q}')\, n_{l'}(\mathbf{q}') \tag{10}$$

In Eq. (10), if we make summation over l on both sides, then change $l \to l'$ and $l' \to l$ in the last term on the right hand side, there will be no change to the result. But the product of the two density fluctuations becomes $n_{l'}(\mathbf{q}-\mathbf{q}')\, n_l(\mathbf{q}')$ and can be written as

$$\begin{aligned} n_{l'}(\mathbf{q}-\mathbf{q}')\, n_l(\mathbf{q}') &\approx \sum_m e^{-i\mathbf{q}\rho_m(l)} \frac{1}{n_s} \left\langle \sum_{mn} e^{-i(\mathbf{q}-\mathbf{q}')[\rho_n(l') - \rho_m(l)]} \right\rangle, \\ &= n_l(\mathbf{q})\, S_{l,l'}(\mathbf{q}-\mathbf{q}') \end{aligned} \tag{11}$$

where $S_{l,l'}(\mathbf{q}-\mathbf{q}')$ is the structure factor of a layered system and <..> is the static average. Substituting Eq. (11) into Eq. (10) and making the Fourier transformation, Eq. (10) can be written as

$$\tilde{n}(q,q_z) = -\sum_m \left[\frac{qp_m}{m^*} + \frac{q^2}{2m^*}\right]^2 e^{-iqp_m} - \frac{q^2}{m^*} n_s\, n(q,q_z)\Psi(q,q_z)\,, \tag{12}$$

where

$$\Psi(q,q_z) = V(q,q_z) + \frac{1}{n_s}\sum_{\substack{q'(\neq q)\\ q'_z}} \frac{q\,q'}{q^2} V(q',q'_z)\,[S(q-q',q'_z) - 1]\,, \tag{13}$$

is the effective field in a layered system which includes both the Coulomb interaction V(q) (the first term in the right hand side of Eq. (13)) and local field (the second term). Finally, using the fluctuation-dissipation theorem and Eq. (13), the local field factor in the charge density channel can be written as

$$G(\mathbf{k}) = \frac{1}{n_s^2 f(\mathbf{k})} \sum_{\mathbf{k}'} \int_0^\infty \frac{d\omega}{\pi} \frac{\mathbf{k}_{\parallel}\mathbf{k}'_{\parallel}}{|\mathbf{k}_{\parallel}|\,|\mathbf{k}'_{\parallel}|} f(\mathbf{k}')\ \mathrm{Im}\ \chi(\mathbf{k}_{\parallel}-\mathbf{k}'_{\parallel},\mathbf{k}'_z,\omega) \tag{14}$$

where the change $\mathbf{q} = \mathbf{k}_{||}$ was made and $\chi(\mathbf{k}, \omega)$ is the electron susceptibility defined by Eq. (8), and n_s is the 2D electron density, $\mathbf{k}_{||}$ is the in-plane wave vector, f(k) is given by Eq. (5). Note that G(k) is k_z-dependent only due to f(k).

Eqs. (8) and (14) provide a set of equations which have to be solved self-consistently in order to find the local field factor G(k). The simplest assumption in order to estimate Eq. (14) is to take the Hartree-Fock approximation assuming $\chi(\mathbf{k}, \omega) = \chi_0(\mathbf{k}_{||}, \omega)$ which is equivalent to the well-known Hubbard approximation. This is actually the k_z-independent zero-order approximation of Eq. (8). Of course, the higher order approximation of $\chi(\mathbf{k}, \omega)$ is k_z-dependent, but it does not affect the k_z-dependence of G(k) because of the integration in Eq. (14) over k_z. Note the integration of f(k) over k_z in Eq. (14) gives 1, we can therefore have the local field factor in the Hartree-Fock approximation in the form

$$G_H(\mathbf{k}) = \frac{1}{2\,f(\mathbf{k})} \frac{k}{\sqrt{k^2 + k_F^2}}\,, \tag{15}$$

where $k_F = (2\pi n_s)^{1/2}$ is the 2D Fermi momentum. As it follows from Eq.(15), the local field factor for an L2DS even in the Hartree-Fock approximation does quite differ from the pure 2D case because in Eq. (17) there exists a form factor f(k) stemming from layering. Furthermore, as it is seen from Eq. (17), the local field factor is strongly dependent of k_z. Indeed, for $k_z = \pi/c$, the coupling of the nearest pair of planes, $G(k)|_{k\to 0} \approx 1/ck_F$ is a constant, and if $ck_F < 1$, we have $G(k) > 1$. This fact means that in the case of a low electron density, $ck_F < 1$, the electron-correlation effects may lead to 'overscreening' of the original Coulomb interaction. For, k_z=0 , $G(k)|_{k\to 0} \approx ck^2/4k_F$, that is similar to the 3D case. Thus, the local field factor in an L2DS is essentially anisotropic and k_z- dependent. This obviously stems from the spatial anisotropy in such a lattice structure.

III. Major Results and Discussions

Now we can find the effective pair potential using Eqs. (6), (8) and (14). In real space it is defined by the inverse Fourier transformation of Eq. (6)

$$\widetilde{V}(\mathbf{r}-\mathbf{r}') = \frac{c}{(2\pi)^3} \int_{-\pi/c}^{\pi/c} dk_z \int d^2k\ \widetilde{V}(\mathbf{k}) \exp\,[\,i\mathbf{k}(\mathbf{r}-\mathbf{r}')]. \tag{16}$$

According to the self-consistent Eq. (14) for the local field factor, the analytical form of the effective pair interaction potential can not be obtained. However, we can obtain its analytical expression if we use its simple expression Eq. (15). Substituting Eq. (6) into Eq. (16) in terms of Eqs. (5), (8) and (15), the expression of the effective pair interaction potential in an L2DS with the local field factor in the Hubbard approximation reads as

$$\widetilde{V}(\mathbf{r}-\mathbf{r}') = \frac{e^2}{\kappa} Z_i Z_j \Phi(z-z') \int_0^\infty dk\, J_0(k\,|\rho-\rho'|)\, \frac{\sinh ck}{\sqrt{A^2(k)-1}} \left[A(k) + \sqrt{A^2(k)-1}\right]^{-|z-z'|/c} , \tag{17}$$

where $J_0(x)$ is the zero-order Bessel function, Z_i and Z_j are the charge numbers, and z and z' are positions in the z-direction, of two interacting charges under consideration. Others are given as follows

$$A(k) = \left|\cosh ck + \frac{\eta(k)}{k a_B^*} \sinh ck\right|, \qquad \eta(k) = \frac{2\Pi(k)}{1-\alpha P(k)}$$

and

$$P(k) = \Pi(k) \,/\, \sqrt{1+k^2/k_F^2}, \qquad \Pi(k) = 1 - \mathrm{Re}\sqrt{1-4k_F^2/k^2}$$

and $\Phi(x) = -\cos \pi x/c$, if $\alpha P(k) > 1$, otherwise $\Phi(x) = 1$. Where $a^*_B = \kappa/e^2 m^*$ is the effective Bohr radius and $\alpha = e^2/\kappa v_F$ is the interelectronic interaction constant that is related to dimensionless density parameter r_s by the relation $r_s = \sqrt{2}\alpha$. As an illustration, Fig. 2(a) and (b) show behaviors of this potential in a plane and in the direction normal to the plane at the selected doping densities.

It should be mentioned that for a layered 2D system Visscher and Falicov[9](VF) have discussed and obtained the screened Coulomb potential in terms of the standard RPA approximation without consideration of any electron-correlation effects. However, Eq. (17) is obtained with consideration of electron-correlations and can be used for an arbitrary position of an interacting pair of charges: ions or electrons in a layered 2D system. This result has been briefly reported in our previous paper[10]. We present here more details with asymptotic behavior of the pair interaction potential and the recent numerical results which show the amazingly interesting behaviors of the pair interaction potential, especially in the z-direction, which have never been reported elsewhere.

As it is seen from Eq. (17), at the small electron coupling ($\alpha \ll 1$) Eq. (17) turns into the form of the VF screened Coulomb potential, i.e., with the increase of inter-charge distance the potential monotonically decreases without Friedel oscillations in the z direction and with the small Friedel oscillations in a plane of layers. The curve 1 and 2 in Fig. 1a and 1b represent this case.

Let's consider the asymptotic behaviors of the potential. In the case of the high density limit ($\alpha \ll 1$), i.e., in theVF case and a large interlayer spacing $c \gg a^*_B$ we are able to complete the integral of the potential in Eq. (17). It consists of two parts: the screened part and the Friedel oscillatory part. The screened part of the in-plane pair potential is (we assume below that Z =Z '= 1)

$$\widetilde{V}_{scr}(\rho) = \frac{e^2}{\kappa\rho} - \frac{\pi e^2}{\kappa a^*_B}\left[H_0\left(\frac{2\rho}{a^*_B}\right) - N_0\left(\frac{2\rho}{a^*_B}\right)\right], \tag{18}$$

where $H_0(x)$ and $N_0(x)$ are the Struve and Neumann functions of the zero-th order, respectively. If $\rho \gg a^*_B$, it has the asymptotic behavior given by

$$\widetilde{V}_{scr}(\rho) \approx \frac{e^2}{4\kappa\rho}\left(\frac{a^*_B}{\rho}\right)^2 [\, 1 - O\,((\frac{a^*_B}{\rho})^2)\,]\,. \qquad (19)$$

However, the screened part of the pair potential in the direction normal to the plane in this case is

$$\widetilde{V}_{scr}(z) = \frac{e^2}{\kappa z} + \frac{2e^2}{\kappa a^*_B}\, e^{-2z/a^*_B}\, Ei\,(-\frac{2z}{a^*_B}), \qquad (20)$$

where Ei(x) is the integral exponent function, with the asymptotic behavior at the limit of $z >> a^*_B$

$$\widetilde{V}_{scr}(z) \approx \frac{e^2 a^*_B}{2\kappa z^2}[\, 1 - O\,((\frac{a^*_B}{z}))\,] \qquad (21)$$

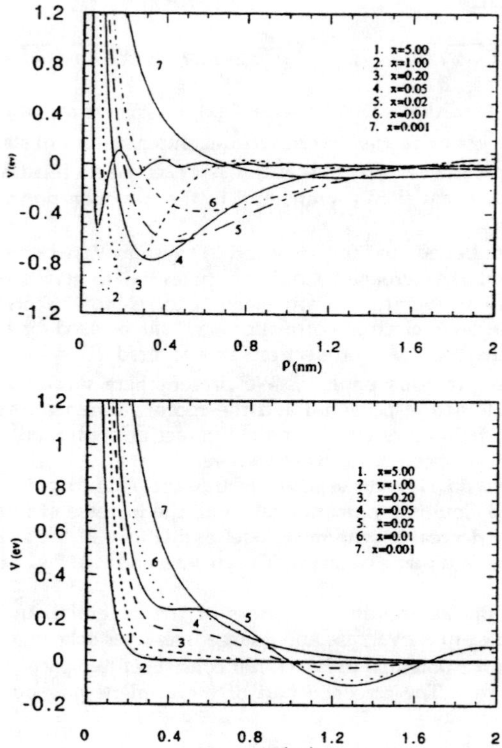

Fig. 1. Pair interaction potential in a layered 2D system for illustrative values of the electron (hole) doping density $x = a^2 n_S$, c= 6.6 Å and a^*_B = 1.0 Å, where n_S is the two-dimensional carriers density, a = 3.8 Å is the lattice constant of the Cu-O plane, c is the interplanar spacing and a^*_B is the effective Bohr radius of electron.
a) in-plane potential; b) potential in the direction normal to a plane.

Moreover, the screened part of a pair interaction potential in the case of a small interlayer spacing ($c \leq a^*_B$) can be represented approximately by the form of a usual isotropic 3D pair potential such as

$$\widetilde{V}_{scr}(r) \approx \frac{e^2}{\kappa\,|r|} \exp\{ - \frac{2\,|r|}{a^*_B} \sqrt{1 + a^*_B / c}\ \} \tag{22}$$

The Freidel part of the in-plane pair potential in the case of a large interlayer spacing ($c >> a^*_B$)

$$\widetilde{V}_{Friedel}(\rho) \approx - \frac{e^2 a^*_B}{2\kappa\,(1 + a^*_B\, k_F)^2} \frac{\sin 2k_F\,\rho}{\rho^2} \tag{23}$$

For a small interlayer spacing ($c < a^*_B$) it is given by

$$\widetilde{V}_{Friedel}(\rho) \sim - \frac{e^2 a^*_B}{2\,\kappa} \sqrt{\frac{c}{a^*_B}} \frac{\sin 2k_F\,\rho}{\rho^2}. \tag{24}$$

As seen from these expressions the screened part of the potential does not depend on k_F at all, only the Friedel part depends on k_F. The potential in the direction normal to the plane does not have the Friedel part in the case of $\alpha < 1$.

The situation, however, crucially changes if the interelectron coupling is quite strong, i.e. $\alpha > 1$. In this case the potential at a certain range of inter-charges distances may be negative (Fig. 1a,b). This is due to the 'overscreening' of the Coulomb interaction caused by the electron correlations in such a particular structure. The minimum of the potential in this case ($\alpha >> 1$) corresponds to the interparticle distance

$$\rho^{-1}_{min} \sim k_F\,(2\alpha)^{2/3}[\ (2\alpha)^{2/3} - 1]^{-1/2} \tag{25}$$

Furthermore, in the case of the intermediate density of carriers when $ck_F > 1$ the screened part of the in-plane potential has the form ($\rho >> k_F^{-1}$)

$$\widetilde{V}_{scr}(\rho) \sim - \frac{e^2}{\kappa\,\rho}\ e^{-\rho\, k_F} \tag{26}$$

with the screening length $\sim k_F^{-1}$, whereas the Friedel part has the same form as Eqs. (23) and (24).

In the case of a quite low density of carriers ($ck_F < 1$) the pair potential for large interparticle distances $\rho > k_{cr}^{-1}$ becomes strongly oscillating

$$\widetilde{V}(\rho) \sim - \frac{e^2}{\kappa} \frac{\cos k_{cr}\rho}{\rho}, \tag{27}$$

where $k_{cr} \approx \sqrt{(a^*_B + c)^{-2} - k_F^2}$ is the critical in-plane wave vector which corresponds to the wave vector of the charge density wave instability. Moreover, this form of the pair interaction potential coincides with the form of the Friedel part of the pair potential in the one-dimensional case. Further, such a form of the pair potential leads to the insulating state in a layered Fermi liquid. It is also interesting to notice that the pair interaction potential in the z direction also becomes strongly oscillating in the case of a strong coupling ($\alpha > 1$)

$$\widetilde{V}(z) \approx \frac{k_F e^2}{2\kappa} \cos \frac{\pi z}{c} \{ 1 - \frac{\pi}{2} [\, H_1(k_F z) - N_1(k_F z)\,]\} \tag{28}$$

where $H_1(x)$ and $N_1(x)$ are the Struve and Neumann functions of the first order, respectively. Its asymptotic behavior at the limit of $z >> k_F^{-1}$ takes the form

$$\widetilde{V}(z) \sim -\frac{e^2}{\kappa k_F} \frac{\cos \pi z/c}{z^2} [1 - O(1/k_F^2 z^2)] \tag{29}$$

It should be pointed out that the oscillating behaviors of the pair interaction in the direction normal to the plane completely differ from the in-plane Friedel oscillations and are caused by the electron correlations in such a particular structure. Thus, it follows from the asymptotic behaviors of the pair interaction potential above that the consideration of the correlations in a layered 2D Fermi liquid strongly affects the form of the pair interaction and leads to the following main peculiarities: (i) in the intermediate density the in-plane pair interaction has a strong short-range attractive character with a small Friedel oscillating part at the large interparticle distance; (ii) at the low density the in-plane pair interactions becomes strongly oscillating in character and is similar to the behavior of the pair interaction in the one-dimensional case; (iii) the pair interaction in the direction normal to the plane has oscillating part caused by correlations in a layered Fermi liquid.

Fig. 1a and Fig.1b present the behaviors of the pair interaction in a plane and in the direction normal to the plane, respectively, for the illustrative values of the 2D carriers density n_s (actually, for Cu-O oxides the corresponding doping density $x = a^2 n_s$, where a = 3.8 Å is the lattice constant of a Cu-O plane, is adopted in the plots for the convenience in comparison with the phase transition diagram of oxides[11]). One can see from these two figures how the shape of pair potential changes with the change of x.

From the two figures, it is obvious that

(a) In the intermediate range of the doping density, especially for the doping density corresponding to the superconducting phase, for instance, $0.05 \leq x \leq 0.3$ ($3.46 \times 10^{13} cm^{-2} \leq n_s \leq 2.08 \times 10^{14} cm^{-2}$)for LaSrCuO compounds[12], the area of the negative parts of potential is definitely larger than that of the positive parts.

Meanwhile, the potential in the z-direction is strongly screened at short distances and then presents a plateau that indicates its enforcement and then converges to a common point, 3c/2, to be zero. The nodes where the potential in the z-direction vanishes are given by (n+1/2)c, where n is an integer;

(b) As the density increases, the in-plane potential tends to the Visscher-Falicov type, i.e., it presents clear Friedel oscillations with gradually weakening amplitudes and the negative part also becomes narrower and shallower while the interaction along the normal direction is strongly screened.;

(c) As the density decreases, the in-plane potential shows a wider and shallower negative part in oscillations with longer wavelengths than that at high densities, in the meantime, the potential in the z-direction is getting stronger, and the plateau looks more apparent and even form a bump (for x=0.03 or $n_s = 2.08 \times 10^{13} cm^{-2}$, not shown in Fig. 1b);

(d) Finally, at the extremely low density the potential behaves as weakly screened coulombic repulsion without appreciable Friedel oscillations being seen while the plateau in the z-direction potential disappears at all. What one can see is a weakly screened Coulumb potential.

Here we should point out that the oscillatory nature of the potential in the z-direction completely differs from the Friedel oscillations and in fact represents a new effect caused by electron correlations in a layered system.

IV. Summary of Conclusions

It is therefore concluded from our calculations and presentations that

(i) The electron correlations in an L2DS are much stronger than in a pure 2D or 3D case and essentially affect the behaviors of pair interaction potential;

(ii) The local field factor is anisotropic and has a strong dependence on the direction of the wave vector. It means that in an L2DS the pair-correlation function will essentially be anisotropic as well;

(iii) The consideration of the correlation effects in a layered 2D electron liquid leads both to an apparent short range attractive interaction (the 'negative' part of pair interaction) in any of layered planes, and to oscillations of potential in the direction normal to the plane. It seems that this behavior of the pair interaction potential in an L2DS is crucial in understanding high temperature superconductivity[11,13] and important in dynamics and stability of such layered lattices.

(iv) The feature of the plateau and nodes in the potential in the z-direction is very luring. It may be used to explain antiferromagnetism in the insulating phase and the co-existence of superconductivity and antiferromagnetism in the superconducting phase;

(v) Finally, the indirect part of pair interaction described in terms of the electron sub-system can be used for the evaluation of electron-phonon interaction in an L2DS. In addition, a static pair interaction potential can also be applied to the evaluation of electron-impurity scattering and electron-electron interaction in an L2DS.

IV. Acknowledgements

This research is sponsored by the Air Force Office of Scientific Research, Air Force System Command, USAF, under Grant No. AFOSR 91-0337. The numerical calculations were performed on the CRAY supercomputer provided by the National Center for Supercomputing Applications, University of Illinois at Urbana Champaign.

V. References

* Present address: Center for Advanced Microstructures Device, Louisiana State University, Baton Rouge, LA 70803

1. W. E. Pickett, Rev. of Modern Phys. 61,433(1989).
2. M. Evain, M. A. Beno, J. M. William, J. Am. Chem. Soc. 110, 614 (1988); S. L. Chaplot, Phys. Rev. B, 42, 2149 (1990).
3. P. A. Deimier, Phys. Rev. B 38, 6596 (1988); R. C. Baetzold, Phys. Rev. B 42, 56 (1990).
4. K. S. Singwi, M. P. Tosi, Correlations in Electron Liquids in *Solid State Physics* (Academic Press, 1981), Vol. 36, 224.
5. K. S. Singwi, M. P. Tosi, R.H. Land, A. Sjolander, Phys. Rev. 176, 589 (1968).
6. M. Johnson, J. Phys. C: Sol. St. Phys. 9, 3055, (1976).
7. A. Nakano, S. Ichimaru, Phys. Rev. B 39, 4930 (1989).
8. B. Tanatar, D. M. Ceperley, Phys. Rev. B 39, 5005 (1989).
9. P. B. Visscher, L.M. Falicov, Phys. Rev. B3, 2541(1971).
10. Y. M. Malozovsky and J. D. Fan, Phys. Rev. B 49,4334(1994).
11. Y. M. Malozovsky and J. D. Fan, Phys. Rev. B (submitted)
12. H. Takagi, Y. Tokura, S. Ushida, Physica C162-164,1101(1989). Also, S.Ushida, H. Takagi, Y. Tokura, Physica C162-164,1677(1989).
13. M. Randeria, J.M. Duan, L. Y. Shieh, Phys. Rev. Lett. 62, 981(1989).

II. PARALLEL ALGORITHMS, TOOLS AND LANGUAGES

Toward Teraflop Computing
and New Grand
Challenge Applications

ISBN-1-56072-247-9

LIBRARIES FOR PARALLEL PARADIGM INTEGRATION

Ian Foster and Ming Xu

Mathematics and Computer Science Division
Argonne National Laboratory
Argonne, Illinois 60439, U.S.A.

ABSTRACT

A programming paradigm is a method for structuring programs in order to reduce the complexity of the programming task. In parallel programming, task and data parallelism are the most common paradigms, although object, functional, logic, and database parallelism are also used. Most existing programming languages and tools are designed to support either task parallelism or data parallelism. Yet there are many applications that can benefit from a combination of both paradigms. For example, image processing problems can exploit the regularity of data-parallel computation within each stage of a pipeline. This process requires tools that support both task and data parallelism and that allow task- and data-parallel components to interact. In particular, it should be possible to reuse libraries developed in either paradigm in a variety of situations. To meet these requirements, we have designed a small set of extensions to Fortran, called Fortran M, that provides a framework on which portable, reusable libraries can be built to implement programming paradigms. In this paper, we illustrate the approach by showing how it is used to implement libraries for file I/O, message-passing, and data-parallel computation.

1. INTRODUCTION

Most existing parallel programming tools are designed to support a single-program multiple-data (SPMD) or *data-parallel* programming model, in which each processor executes the same program but operates on different data. This model is fundamental to data-parallel languages such as C* and High Performance Fortran and accounts for the bulk of programs written in message passing libraries such as MPI, p4, and PVM. The advantages of the data-parallel approach include regular communication patterns and ease of programming and debugging.

Nevertheless, an increasing number of parallel applications have a richer structure in which threads of control may execute different programs and may be created and deleted dynamically. This is the case, for example, in multidisciplinary simulation, in which a complex system (such as an aircraft) is constructed by coupling models of system components (such as fluid dynamics, structural mechanics, surface heating, and controls). Similarly, image-processing algorithms often have a heterogeneous pipeline structure that is not naturally represented in an SPMD context. These applications require what is often called *task* parallelism.

Data and task parallelism are often seen as opposing approaches to programming. Yet in practice we find that applications frequently include both task- and data-parallel components. For example, although the interactions between the components of a multidisciplinary simulation involves task parallelism, individual components may well admit to a data-parallel solution. In these and other applications, the ability to integrate multiple paradigms in a single program has the potential for improving both programmer productivity and performance. A lack of tools, however, makes the development of such *multiparadigm* applications difficult in practice.

In this paper, we introduce an approach to multiparadigm programming based on language extensions. The idea is to define a small set of extensions to an existing sequential language that can be used to specify concurrency, communication, synchronization, and mapping. They also provide what we call *compositionality*, meaning that program components encapsulating concurrency, communication, and mapping decisions can be reused in different situations without concern for internal implementation details. The extended sequential language is then used to write *paradigm libraries* that support various paradigms. Thanks to compositionality, paradigm libraries can be integrated in flexible ways to implement multiparadigm programs. In this paper, we use an extended Fortran called Fortran M (FM) [6] to illustrate the approach; however, the basic ideas are language independent. In a related effort, colleagues at Caltech are using an extended C++ for the same purpose [3].

To explore the utility of the FM extensions for multiparadigm programming, we have been working with colleagues to develop libraries for the integration of message passing, for data parallel programming [5, 2], for redirection of file I/O, for scientific programming "templates," and for exploitation of parallelism in automatic differentiation [1]. In this paper, we describe the mechanisms used to support the first three of these applications.

2. FORTRAN M

Fortran M (FM) is a language designed by researchers at Argonne and Caltech for expressing task-parallel computation [6]. It comprises a small set of extensions to Fortran and provides a message-passing parallel programming model, in which programs create processes that interact by sending and receiving messages on typed channels. Two key features of the extensions are their support for determinism and modularity.

FM is currently defined as extensions to Fortran 77; however, equivalent extensions can easily be defined for Fortran 90. For clarity, we use some Fortran 90 syntax in subsequent sections when discussing integration of FM and HPF.

```
program aerodynamics
inport (integer, real x(10,20), real y(10,20)) pi
outport (integer, real x(10,20), real y(10,20)) po
...
channel(in=pi,out=po)
channel(in=qi,out=qo)
...
processes
   processcall controls(pi,qo)
   processcall structures(qi,po)
endprocesses
end


process controls(inp,outp)
inport (integer, real x(10,20), real y(10,20)) inp
outport (integer, integer, real x(10,10,3)) outp
...
send(outp) i, j, a
receive(inp) nstep, u, v
...
end
```

Figure 1: Sketch of a Multidisciplinary Program, Using FM

2.1 Concurrency and Communication

FM provides constructs for defining program modules called ***processes***; for specifying that processes are to execute concurrently; for establishing typed, one-to-one communication ***channels*** between processes; and for sending and receiving messages on channels. Send and receive operations are modeled on Fortran file I/O statements but operate on ***port variables*** rather than unit numbers.

The FM programming model is dynamic: processes and channels can be created and deleted dynamically, and references to channels can be included in messages. Nevertheless, computation can be guaranteed to be deterministic; this feature avoids the race conditions that plague many parallel programming systems. Determinism is guaranteed by defining operations on port variables to prevent multiple processes from sending concurrently, by requiring receivers to block until data is available, and by enforcing a copy-in/copy-out semantics on variables passed as arguments to processes. Nondeterministic constructs are also provided for programs that operate in nondeterministic environments.

Figure 1 illustrates the use of several FM constructs. The first code fragment uses the **channel** statement to create two channels and a process block (delineated by **processes** and **endprocesses** statements) to create two processes called **controls** and **structures**. These execute concurrently, on the same or different processors. The second code fragment implements the **controls** process; it uses the **send** and

receive statements to send and receive data on the ports passed as arguments. Message formats are defined by the port declarations, allowing a FM compiler to generate efficient communication code and to convert to a machine-independent format in a heterogeneous environment.

2.2 Resource Management

FM resource management constructs allow the programmer to specify how processes and data are to be mapped to processors and hence how computational resources are to be allocated to different parts of a program. These constructs influence performance but not correctness. Hence, we can develop a program on a uniprocessor and then tune performance on a parallel computer by changing mapping constructs.

FM process placement constructs are based on the concept of a virtual computer: a collection of virtual processors, which may or may not have the same shape as the physical computer on which a program executes. A virtual computer is an N-dimensional array, and mapping constructs are modeled on array manipulation constructs. The **processors** declaration specifies the shape and dimension of a processor array, the `location` annotation maps processes to specified elements of this array, and the **submachine** annotation specifies that a process should execute in a subset of the array. For example, the following code places the **controls** and **structures** processes on different virtual processors.

```
processors(2)
...
processes
  processcall controls(...) location(1)
  processcall structures(...) location(2)
endprocesses
```

In contrast, the following code places each process in a submachine comprising 10 virtual processors. This would be useful, for example, if the processes were themselves parallel programs, written in FM or using a SPMD library.

```
processors(20)
...
processes
  processcall controls(...) submachine(1:10)
  processcall structures(...) submachine(11:20)
endprocesses
```

3. FILE INPUT/OUPUT LIBRARIES

Our first example of a paradigm library is almost trivial but nevertheless useful. This is a file I/O compatibility library (FIOCL). With FIOCL, programs that were designed originally to interact with their environment by reading and writing files can be integrated into a task-parallel framework by reinterpreting file read and write operations as receive and send operations on channels. The library uses FM processes to encapsulate different programs and channels to represent the "virtual files" on which these programs perform read and write operations.

A program that is to be integrated into an FM framework must be modified to incorporate calls to FIOCL subroutines `assoc_inport` and `assoc_outport`. These associate a Fortran file with an FM inport or outport, respectively, and cause subsequent read or write operations on the file to be implemented as receive and send operations. The program must also be converted into a process. It can then be plugged together with other programs by FM code that creates the required channels and passes the associated inports and outports to these programs.

We illustrate the approach with an example similar to that used in the preceding section. Figure 2 sketches versions of programs `controls` and `structure` that have been adapted to operate by using the FM file I/O library. The two programs are assumed to read and write file data, respectively. To allow the two programs to operate concurrently, we add to both programs a `process` declaration and add three statements (indicated by comments) that declare a port, include some definitions, and specify that the file operated on by the program is to be associated with a port. Subsequent open, read, and write operations then operate on the specified files. The code that sets up the necessary channel and invokes the two components is also shown.

We have not yet discussed the mechanism by which I/O statements are made to operate on ports rather than files. In a language such as C, I/O operations are implemented as library calls; hence, it would suffice to link application programs with a modified I/O library that checked each I/O operation to see whether it concerned a file or a channel. As this approach is not possible in Fortran, we introduce a simple preprocessor that replaces I/O calls with calls to library routines. For example, a `write` statement is replaced with "`call fiocl_write`".

4. MESSAGE-PASSING LIBRARIES

We now describe a message-passing compatibility library (MPCL) that allows programs developed using message-passing (MP) libraries (e.g., p4, PVM, Express) to be integrated into a more general task-parallel framework. This allows MP programs to be invoked from FM and permits MP programs to call FM routines. The invoking program can use FM virtual computer constructs to specify the resources (virtual processors) that will be available to the MP program; the MP program executes as if these virtual processors were physical processors, and performs ordinary MP calls. Various FM data structures can be passed as arguments to the MP program. These data structures can be either replicated or partitioned over virtual processors. Ports passed as arguments allow an MP program to communicate with other program components. Figure 3 illustrates some of these ideas. The enclosing oval represents a FM process, with local data structures `X` and `Y`. The enclosed execution graph represents initiation of an MP program on four virtual processors, with argument `X` scattered and `Y` replicated.

MPCL consists of two components: an interface routine that sets up the N^2 channels required to allow N processes to communicate with each other, and then invokes an MP program in N processes; and a set of FM implementations of a particular

```
        program aerodynamics
        inport (integer n, character buff(n)) pi
       -outport (integer n, character buff(n)) po
        channel(in=pi,out=po)                    ! Create channel
        processes                                ! Create processes
          processcall controls(pi)
          processcall structures(po)
        endprocesses
        end

        process controls(pi)
        inbdrpoft. for) copmmunication
        inkFibel/'@ibbiary' definitions
        callAssosiateifiporwith inpdata',pi)
        ...
        open(unit=11, file='indata')
        ...
        read(11,99) a, b, c
99      format(3F10.2)
        ...
        end

        process structures(po)
        outpOutpo(rt.fo) cqmmunication
        inkFibel/'@ibbiary' definitions
        callAssosiateofitpwith( inpotdata', po)
        ...
        open(unit=9, file='outdata')
        ...
        write(9,99) a, b, c
99      format(3F10.2)
        ...
        end
```

Figure 2: Using the File I/O Library

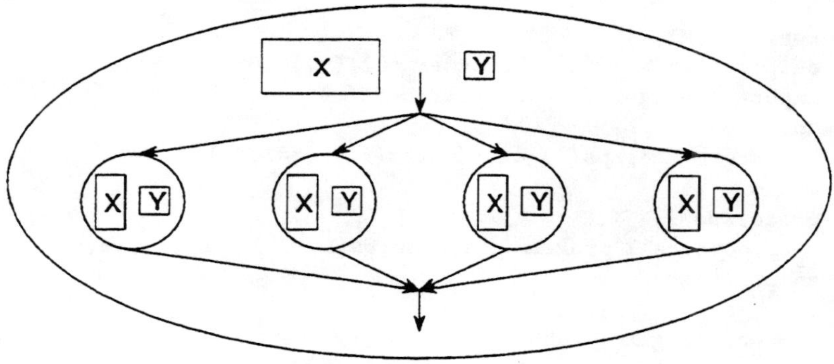

Figure 3: Invoking a Message-Passing Program from FM

MP library's routines (e.g., **p4send**, **p4recv**, etc., in p4). MPCL currently supports subsets of the p4, PICL, and Express libraries.

The interface code has a structure similar to that shown in Figure 4. This example program is intended to initiate execution of the MP program **prog**, passing FM variables **X** and **Y** as arguments (partitioned and replicated, respectively). It creates **N** instances of a process **prog_wrap**, passing each an array of **N** outports, which can be used to send messages to the other processes, and a single inport, on which messages from other processes are received. The **N** outports destined for a single process are associated with that process's inport by the nondeterministic **MERGER** construct. The subroutine **prog_wrap** stores the ports and other information passed as arguments in a common block (defined in the include file **mp.inc**) and then invokes **prog**.

The FM implementations of the MP library routines use the channel structure created by the initialization routine to implement send, receive, and other operations. For example, the following is an implementation of a generic **mp_send** operation that allows the caller to specify a tag, message size, message contents, and destination. The array **outps** contains the outports passed as arguments to the **prog_wrap** call and stored in a common block by **stash_ports**.

```
subroutine mp_send(tag,size,msg,dest)
integer tag, size, dest                ! Message tag, size, dest.
character msg(size)                    ! The data to be communicated
include 'mp.inc'                       ! Include file with channels
send (outps(dest)) tag, size, msg      ! Send message to dest
return
end
```

Although the interface code in Figure 4 is not especially complicated, it would nevertheless be useful if we could encapsulate it in a channel setup and message-passing setup library. This library would have to be parameterized with the name of the message-passing process (in our case, **prog**) and the number and distribution of

```
real x(N,M), y
outport (integer n, character buff(n)) outps(N,N)
inport (integer n, character buff(n)) incps(N)
do i=1,N
   merger(in=inps(i),out=(outps(i,j),j=1,N))
enddo
processdo i = 1,N
   processcall prog_wrap(i,N,outps(i,1:N), inp(i), x(i,1:M), y)
endprocessdo

process prog_wrap(num,outps,inp,arg1, arg2)
outport (integer n, character buff(n)) outps(N,N)
inport (integer n, character buff(n)) inps(N)
real arg1(M), arg2
include 'mp.inc'
call stash_ports(num,inp,outps)
call prog(arg1,arg2)
enddo
```

Figure 4: FM Wrapper Code for Message-Passing Program

the user arguments passed (e.g., X and Y). Unfortunately, since Fortran 77 supports neither higher-order functions nor variable-length argument lists, a parameterized library of this sort is not possible.

We circumvent this problem by providing a preprocessor that generates the required interface code. This preprocessor allows the user to use an `mpcall` statement to invoke an MP program and a `scatter` statement to specify that an array variable should be partitioned when passed as an argument to an MP program. (BLOCK distributions in one or two dimensions are currently supported.) Together, these features allow us to replace Figure 4 with the following statements.

```
real x(N,M), y
scatter x(BLOCK,*)
mpcall prog(x,y)
```

The use of these features is further illustrated in the following code fragment, which invokes two MP programs, `controls` and `structures`, one after the other, passing the variable X as an argument to both.

```
program main
processors pr(64)
real x(512, 512)
scatter x(*,BLOCK)
...
mpcall controls(x)
...
```

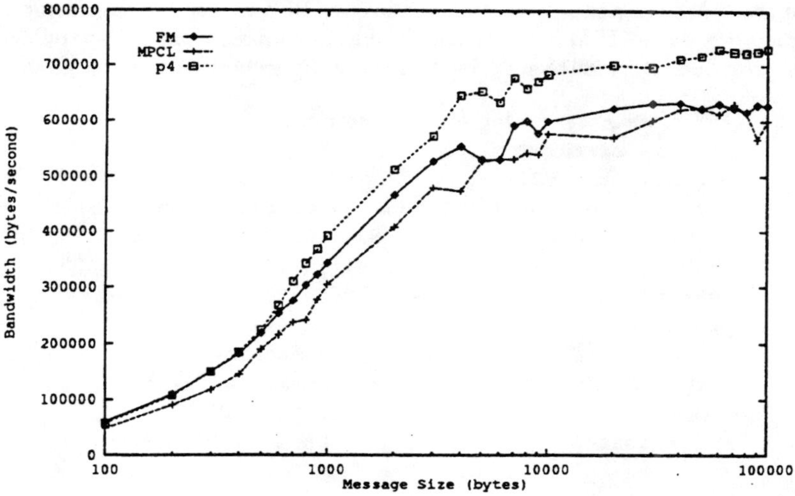

Figure 5: Bandwidth of FM, MPCL, and p4 on Ethernet

```
mpcall structures(x)
```

We are conducting detailed performance studies to determine whether this library-based approach to the integration of message-passing programs leads to significant overhead. Some preliminary results are presented in Figure 5. This shows achieved bandwidth, as measured by timing a simple program that bounces messages of varying size between two processors, on two Ethernet-connected Sparc-2 workstations. Results are given for versions of the program written in FM, in p4 using the compatibility library (MPCL), and in raw p4. We see that FM and p4 provide comparable performance for smaller messages, but that p4 is slightly faster for larger messages. MPCL is consistently about ten per cent slower than FM or p4. We expect that this overhead (which is quite acceptable for many applications) can be reduced significantly.

5. HIGH PERFORMANCE FORTRAN

The mechanisms described in the preceding section can also be used to integrate programs written in High Performance Fortran (HPF). HPF compilers typically compile HPF programs to Fortran plus calls to message-passing libraries. Hence, a simple integration strategy is first to compile the HPF program using an HPF compiler and then to link the resulting code with the FM message-passing library. We have pursued this approach successfully in collaboration with Bhaven Avalani and Alok Choudhary of Syracuse University [5]. This allows us to write code similar to the following. This code fragment implements an image-processing convolution pipeline, in which two input image streams flow through two forward fast Fourier transform (FFT) stages, and then through a multiplication and inverse FFT stage. We have demonstrated this application on the IBM SP1 and shown that this mixed task/data-parallel formulation can provide performance superior to that of a purely data-parallel program.

```
c       FM Main Program for Mixed Algorithm
        program mixed_parallel
        processors pr(24)
        outport (complex x(512,512/8)) outs1(8), outs2(8)
        inport (complex x(512,512/8)) ins1(8), ins2(8)
        channel(in=ins1(:), out=outs1(:))
        channel(in=ins2(:), out=outs2(:))
        processes
          mpcall fft(nimages, outs1) submachine(1:8)
          mpcall fft(nimages, outs2) submachine(9:16)
          mpcall ifft(ins1, ins2) submachine(17:24)
        endprocesses
```

This approach allows the integration of HPF procedures into FM task-parallel programs. FM data structures can be passed as arguments to HPF procedures. This requires either that the FM library has knowledge of the data structures used in the HPF compiler or that the HPF compiler is aware of the format of the FM data structures. We have adopted the former approach.

FM port variables can also be passed as arguments to HPF procedures, providing in principle a mechanism by which HPF programs can communicate with other, concurrently executing, HPF or FM procedures. This can be achieved without extensions to the HPF compiler by (a) representing these variables within HPF in terms of the representation used by the FM compiler (which happens to be integers), and (b) using the HPF extrinsic procedure mechanism to invoke FM procedures that operate on these variables. This approach is simple but inelegant. An alternative approach is to extend HPF with port data types and data-parallel send and receive operations that send and receive arrays and scalars on arrays of outports and inports, respectively. We are currently pursuing this approach in collaboration with Syracuse.

6. RELATED WORK

Two alternative approaches to multiparadigm programming are new languages and libraries. New languages can provide direct support for both the SPMD and task-parallel programming models; however, they can require considerable investment compiler development, code conversion, and user training. In the library approach, paradigm libraries make direct calls to low-level primitives for task creation, communication, and synchronization, rather than using language extensions. This avoids the need for compiler development but lacks desirable properties such as compositionality and compile-time checking.

More limited in scope are approaches based on the use of a task-parallel coordination language able to invoke data-parallel computations. For example, Cheng et al. propose the use of the AVS dataflow visualization system to implement multidisciplinary applications, in which some components may be data-parallel programs [4]. This provides an elegant graphical programming model but is less expressive than the approach described here. For example, cyclic communication structures are not easily expressed. Similarly, Quinn et al. describe work on iWARP in which a configuration language is used to connect Dataparallel C computations [8]. The Dataparallel C programs use specialized versions of C I/O libraries for communication. Process and communication structures are static, and all communication passes via a central communication server.

Subhlok et al. describe a compile-time approach for exploiting task and data parallelism on the iWarp mesh-connected multicomputer [10]. The input program incorporates HPF-like data parallel constructs and directives indicating data dependencies and parallel sections. An appropriate mix of task and data parallelism is then generated automatically by the compiler. The use of FM and data-parallel paradigm libraries permits more general and dynamic forms of task parallelism but also requires more programmer intervention.

7. CONCLUSIONS

We have used three simple examples to show how the FM extensions to Fortran can be used to develop libraries that support the integration of programs developed using diverse paradigms into a single task-parallel framework. These libraries use FM processes to encapsulate message-passing computation, channels to implement communication, and virtual computer constructs to control resource allocation. The resulting programs can be reused in any environment.

In general, we prefer to support the integration of a new paradigm by means of a library rather than additional language extensions. The limitations of Fortran syntax, however, often encourage us to use simple source transformations to facilitate the use of a particular paradigm. In some cases, these transformations are essential (FIOCL); in others, they are cosmetic (MPCL, HPF). These extensions are incorporated in a preprocessor; if they prove to be genuinely useful, we might eventually incorporate them into our FM compiler.

Our future plans include the development of Fortran 90 language extensions to support multiparadigm programs; the more modern constructs provided by Fortran 90, including structured data types and dynamic memory allocation, can support a more powerful set of primitives. We are also investigating compiler and runtime system optimization techniques and the integration of paradigm libraries written in different languages. In the latter area, a particular focus is integration with the CC++ language under development at Caltech [3]. This task is simplified by the fact that CC++ and FM use the same runtime system.

More information on this work is available via Mosaic at the following address:

`http://www.mcs.anl.gov/fortran-m/FM.html.`

In addition, a FM compiler is available from anonymous ftp server `info.mcs.anl.gov`, in directory `pub/fortran-m`.

ACKNOWLEDGMENTS

This research was supported by the NSF Center for Research in Parallel Computation (CRPC) Contract CCR-8809615 and by the Office of Scientific Computing, U.S. Department of Energy, under Contract W-31-109-Eng-38. We are grateful to other members of the CRPC's Paradigm Integration group, particularly Mani Chandy, Carl Kesselman, Robert Olson, and Steven Tuecke, for their many contributions to this work. Dennis Gannon's SAGE project at Indiana University provided transformation tools used in this work.

References

[1] C. Bischof, L. Green, K.Haigler, and T. Knauff, Parallel Calculation of Sensitivity Derivatives for Aircraft Design Using Automatic Differentiation, Preprint MCS-P419-0294, Argonne National Laboratory, Argonne, Ill., 1994.

[2] Chandy, K. M., I. Foster, K. Kennedy, C. Koelbel, and C.-W. Tseng, Integrated Support for Task and Data Parallelism, *Intl. J. Supercomputer Applications*, 8(2), 1994 (in press).

[3] Chandy, K. M., and C. Kesselman, CC++: A Declarative Concurrent Object-Oriented Programming Notation, *Research Directions in Concurrent Object-Oriented Programming*, Gul Agha, Peter Wegner, and Akinori Yonezawa (Eds.), MIT Press, 1993

[4] G. Cheng, G. Fox, and K. Mills, Integrating Multiple Programming Paradigms on Connection Machine CM5 in a Dataflow-based Software Environment, Technical Report, NPAC, Syracuse University, Syracuse, N.Y., 1993.

[5] Foster, I., B. Avalani, A. Choudhary, and M. Xu, A Compilation System That Integrates High Performance Fortran and Fortran M, *Proc. 1994 Scalable High Performance Computing Conf.*, IEEE (to appear), 1994.

[6] Foster, I., and K. M. Chandy, Fortran M: A Language for Modular Parallel Programming, Preprint MCS-P327-0992, Argonne National Laboratory, Argonne, Ill., 1992.

[7] Fox, G., S. Hiranandani, K. Kennedy, C. Koelbel, U. Kremer, C. Tseng, and M. Wu, Fortran D Language Specification, Technical Report TR90-141, Computer Science, Rice Univ., Houston, Texas, 1990.

[8] P. Hatcher and M. Quinn. *Data-Parallel Programming on MIMD Computers*. The MIT Press, Cambridge, Mass., 1991.

[9] High Performance Fortran Forum 1993. High Performance Fortran Language Specification, Version 1.0. Technical Report CRPC-TR92225. Center for Research on Parallel Computation, Rice University, Houston, Texas, 1993.

[10] J. Subhlok, J. Stichnoth, D. O'Hallaron, and T. Gross. Exploiting Task and Data Parallelism on a Multicomputer. In *Proc. 4th ACM SIGPLAN Symposium on Principles and Practice of Parallel Programming*, San Diego, Calif., May 1993.

Toward Teraflop Computing
and New Grand
Challenge Applications

ISBN-1-56072-247-9

OBJECT-ORIENTED METHODS FOR PARALLEL EXECUTION OF ASTROPHYSICS SIMULATIONS

Dennis Gannon, Shelby X Yang, Paul Bode, Vladimir Menkou, and Suresh Srinivas

Department of Computer Science, Indiana University
Bloomington, Indiana 47405, U.S.A.

1 INTRODUCTION

Object-oriented technology now forms the basis for a very large part of the software development industry. This is especially true in the areas of computer graphics, data base, graphical interface design and modern operating systems. We are also beginning to see the emergence of object-oriented methodology in scientific programming.[1] For parallel programming of scientific applications, there exist a number of new tools to help build portable, object-oriented software. Most of them are extensions to C++, the dominant object-oriented programming language. They include COOL [3], CC++ [5, 4], Mentat [13], Charm++, and C** [15]. In addition, there are C++ libraries, such as P++ [17], which provide support for advanced data structure handling in parallel systems. Such libraries are an essential part of applications requiring adaptive structured grids.

In this paper we describe another C++ extension for parallel programming called pC++ [16, 11, 2, 10, 12] and its use in Grand Challenge Cosmology Consortium (GC^3) simulations. Section 2 of this paper contains a brief overview of pC++. In section 3 and 4 we describe the implementation of two GC^3 N-body codes in pC++. Finally, we discuss ideas of how pC++ can be used in adaptive mesh refinement applications.

2 OVERVIEW OF pC++

The goal of the pC++ project is to design a simple extension to C++ for parallel programming that provides:

*This research is supported in part by ARPA under contract AF 30602-92-C-0135, the National Science Foundation Office of Advanced Scientific Computing under grant ASC-9111616, and the National Science Foundation and ARPA Grand Challenge Award, "The Formation of Galaxies and Large-scale Structure."

[1]For example, see the proceedings of the 1993 and 1994 Object-Oriented Numerics Conference.

- parallel object-oriented software that runs without modification on all commercial scalable parallel Multiple Instruction Multiple Data (MIMD) systems,
- an interface to Single Program Multiple Data (SPMD) libraries such as ScaLapack++ [8] and P++,
- an interface to High Performance Fortran (HPF),
- and an interface to "multithreaded" C++ languages like CC++.

We emphasize that pC++, or other object-oriented parallel programming languages, should not be viewed as a replacement for Fortran90 or HPF. Rather, object-oriented parallelism should be a tool to express the types of parallelism that cannot be easily expressed in Fortran. To accomplish this task pC++ exploits the two major characteristics of object-oriented design: encapsulation and inheritance.

Encapsulation reflects the principle of object-oriented language: closely related variables and functions are grouped together into a user-defined data type called *class*. An instance of the data type is called an object and the associated functions are called member functions or methods of the class. Invoking a member function of an object is often viewed as sending the object a message to carry out a specific task. In this way an object-oriented program can be visualized as a network of objects each of which manages its own data structure and operates collectively by sending messages to other objects. This metaphor of communication lends itself perfectly to parallel execution, and most parallel programming extensions to C++ rely on this model.

Inheritance allows a class to inherit selected data members and member functions of other classes, rather than reimplementing them. The inheritance mechanism used to build distributed data structures in pC++ is the same as in C++, *i.e.*, through class derivation.

pC++ has two basic extensions to the C++ language: a mechanism to describe how operations can be invoked over a set of objects in parallel, and a mechanism to refer to an individual object.

A data structure called *collection* is used to describe a set of objects distributed over the processors of a parallel machine. To build a collection of some class type `T`, which is called an *element* class in pC++, one needs a distribution and an alignment object. The distribution object defines a grid and a mapping from the grid to the physical processors on a parallel machine. The alignment object specifies the shape, size, and the mapping of the element objects to the grid points. In addition, a processor object, `Processors`, is needed to represent the set of processors available to use.

```
Processors P;
Distribution D(100,&P,BLOCK);
Align A(20,"[ALIGN(X[i],D[i+10])]");
```

creates a one dimensional grid of a size of 100 which is mapped to the processors of the machine by blocks. If there are 20 processors, grid positions 0 through 4 are mapped to processor 0, positions 5 through 9 are mapped to processor 1, ..., etc. The alignment aligns the logical vector `X[0:19]` with the grid positions `D[10:29]`. Given a distribution, an alignment and the class type of the element objects, it is easy to build a collection. One of the base collections that pC++ collection library provides is the SuperKernel collection. It is designed to be used as the base collection for all other collections. It builds arrays of element objects and provides global name space for the element objects. The declaration

```
SuperKernel<T> MyCollection(&D, &A);
```

creates a collection called MyCollection which is a set of objects of type T.

The most important feature of a collection is the ability to apply a function in parallel across all the element objects. For example, if T is defined as

```
class T{
   ...
 public:
  void foo();
   ...
};
```

where function foo() is a member function of the class, a parallel application of foo() to all the elements would take the following form:

```
MyCollection.foo();
```

To access an individual member of a collection, one can use the overloaded operator () which returns a *global* pointer to an element. For example,

```
MyCollection(i)
```

returns a global pointer to the ith element in the collection. A global pointer is a pointer that spans the entire address space of a distributed memory machine. In this way, any object can have a global address. The following function call

```
MyCollection(i)->foo();
```

is a remote invocation, it sends a message to the processor that contains the ith element and a thread on that processor executes the function. The remote invocation feature is an essential part of pC++ 2.0 and is not part of the current pC++ 1.0 distribution.

Usually, a user would want to create a specialized collection that has properties appropriate for the application at hand. The task of building a new derived collection is almost the same as building a derived class in C++. A collection definition takes the form shown below.

```
Collection MyCollectionType: SuperKernel {
 public:
  // data members here are duplicated on each processor of a
  // parallel system.  members functions here are executed in
  // parallel on all processors of the system.
 MethodOfElement:
  // data members and member functions here are
  // added to the element class.
```

There are two types of data and member functions in a collection definition. Data members and functions labeled as *MethodOfElement* represent new functions and data that are added to each element class. The member functions are invoked just as if they are member functions of the element class. Other data member not labeled as MethodOfElement are duplicated on each processor and the functions are invoked in the SPMD mode.

In the next two sections we will illustrate the use of collection to define parallel data structures for the N-body simulation codes which are a part of the GC^3 project. We will also show how our prototype Fortran interface is used in one of the codes, the Self-Consistent Field code.

3 THE SELF-CONSISTENT FIELD CODE

One of the N-body codes developed by GC^3 researchers is the Self-Consistent Field (SCF) code, which is used to simulate the evolution of galaxies. It solves the coupled Vlasov and Poisson equation for collisionless stellar systems using the N-body approximation approach. To solve Poisson's equation for gravitational potential,

$$\nabla^2 \Phi(\vec{r}) = 4\pi\rho(\vec{r}),$$

density ρ and potential Φ are expanded in a set of basis functions. The basis set is constructed so that the lowest order members well-approximate a galaxy obeying the de Vaucouleurs $R^{1/4}$ projected density profile law. The algorithm used in the SCF code is described in detail in Hernquist and Ostriker 1992 [14].

The original SCF code was written in Fortran77 by Lars Hernquist in 1991. In 1993, the code was converted to Thinking Machines CM Fortran by Greg Bryan. Expirements conducted on the 512-node CM-5 at the National Center for Supercomputing Applications (NCSA) by Greg Bryan indicate that with 10 million particles the CMF code can achieve 14.4 Gflops on 512 nodes of the CM-5 (private communication).

The expansions of the density and potential take the following forms:

$$\rho(\vec{r}) = \sum_{nlm} A_{nlm}\rho_{nlm}(\vec{r}),$$

$$\Phi(\vec{r}) = \sum_{nlm} A_{nlm}\Phi_{nlm}(\vec{r}),$$

where n is the radial "quantum" number and l and m are quantum numbers for the angular variables. Generally, the two sums will involve different expansion coefficients. But the assumption of bi-orthogonality ensures a one-to-one relationship between terms in the expansions for the density and potential. The basis sets ρ_{nlm} and Φ_{nlm} also satisfy Poisson's equation:

$$\nabla^2 \Phi_{nlm}(\vec{r}) = 4\pi\rho_{nlm}(\vec{r}).$$

The basis sets ρ_{nlm} and Φ_{nlm} are given by

$$\rho_{nlm}(\vec{r}) = \frac{K_{nl}}{2\pi}\frac{r^l}{r(1+r)^{2l+3}}C_n^{2l+3/2}(\xi)\sqrt{4\pi}Y_{lm}(\theta,\phi),$$

$$\Phi_{nlm}(\vec{r}) = -\frac{r^l}{(1+r)^{2l+1}} C_n^{2l+3/2}(\xi)\sqrt{4\pi} Y_{lm}(\theta,\phi),$$

where K_{nl} is a number related only to n and l, and $C_n^{2l+3/2}(\xi)$ and $Y_{lm}(\theta,\phi)$ are ultrasperical polynomials and spherical harmonics, respectively. After some algebra, the expansion coefficients become

$$A_{nlm} = \frac{1}{I_{nl}} \sum_k m_k [\Phi_{nlm}(r_k, \theta_k, \phi_k)]^*,$$

where I_{nl} is a number and m_k is the mass of the kth particle. Once the gravitational potential is found, the gravitational force per unit mass can be obtained by taking the gradient of the potential and the particles can be accelerated accordingly.

3.1 The pC++/Fortran Version of the SCF Code

We design a C++ class called `Segment` to represent a subgroup of the N particles used in the simulation. As we have discussed earlier, the major procedure in the SCF code is to compute the sums for the expansion coefficients A_{nlm}. Our approach is to first compute local sums within each `Segment` object. After this, global sums are formed by a global reduction. The global sums are then broadcast back to each `Segment` object where the particles are accelerated by the gravitational force. Fortran subroutines in the original Fortran code now become member functions of the `Segment` class, although subroutines involving inter-element communication and I/O need to be modified. The `Segment` class is declared as follows with many less important variables and member functions omitted:

```
class Segment {
 public:
  FArrayDouble x,y,z,vx,vy,vz,ax,ay,az,mass,
               plm,clm,dlm,elm,flm,dplm;
  double sinsum[lmax+1][lmax+1][nmax+1],
         cossum[lmax+1][lmax+1][nmax+1];
  Segment();
  void compute_polynomial();
  void compute_acceleration();
  void update_position();
  void update_velocity();
};
```

The new data type `FArrayDouble` is a predefined class to contain Fortran double precision arrays. On the CM-5, `FArrayDouble` represents parallel arrays — arrays allocated in the vector processor accelerators' memories. In the above declaration, `x`, `y`, `z`, `vx`, `vy`, `vz`, `ax`, `ay`, `az`, `mass` are one-dimensional arrays that contain the positions, the velocities, the accelerations, and the masses of particles belonging to a `Segment` object, and `plm`, `clm`, `dlm`, `elm`, `flm`, `dplm` contain the expansion coefficients and the values of the polynomial. The `sinsum` and `cossum` contain the local sums and eventually the global sums of expansion coefficients. They are serial arrays on the CM-5 and are allocated in the Sparc chip's memory. Among the class member functions (Fortran subroutines), compute_polynomial computes the polynomials and local sums, compute_acceleration computes the acceleration for each particle, update_position and update_velocity update the positions and velocities of particles.

The collection that distributes the elements, allocates memory, and manages inter-element communication is declared as below. Again, many less important member functions are omitted for brevity:

```
Collection SelfConsistField:public Fortran {
 public:
  SelfConsistField(Distribution *D,Align *A);
  void InParticles();
  void InParameters();
  void OutParticles(int nsnap);
 MethodOfElement:
  virtual void compute_polynomial();
  virtual void compute_acceleration();
  virtual void update_position();
  virtual void update_velocity();
  void read_segment();
  void write_segment();
};
```

Functions declared here are pC++ functions. Their main functionality is to handle the I/O. InParticles, InParameters, and OutParticles read the input files and write to the output files, and read_segment and write_segment are called by InParticles and OutParticles to perform parallel I/O on both the CM-5 and Paragon. Functions that are already defined in element class Segment are declared as virtual functions in this collection declaration. The inherited Fortran collection is a parent collection which handles inter-element communication. Fortran itself is derived from the SuperKernel collection.

The main program is listed below:

```
void Processor_Main() {
 Processors P;
 Distribution D(elem_count,&P,BLOCK);
 Align A(elem_count,"[ALIGN(X[i],D[i])]");
 SelfConsistField&lt;Segment&gt; X(&D,&A);
 // read initial model
 X.InParameters();
 X.InParticles();
 X.compute_polynomial();
 X.ReduceDoubleAdd(offset,variable_count);
 X.compute_acceleration();
 // main loop
 for(n = 1; n <= nsteps; n++) {
  X.update_position();
```

CPU time in seconds spent in main loop without I/O.			
No. of Particles	pC++/CMF on CM5	CMF on CM5	pC++/F77 on Paragon
512	5.4 (76.6)	6.6 (40.9)	5.8
5120	8.6 (75.1)	9.9 (40.9)	25.0
51200	45.8 (89.1)	50.3 (57.4)	332.5
Total CPU time in seconds with parallel I/O			
51200	49.1 (89.1)	58.2 (57.4)	396.3

Table 1: *Execution time in seconds for 100 time steps on 32-node partitions with the expansions truncated at nmax* = 6 *and lmax* = 4. *Numbers in parentheses are amount of memory used in MBytes. The total time includes reading the input model (2.87 MBytes), initializing the system, evolving the system for 100 evolution steps, and writing two output files (2.87 MBytes and 2.46 MBytes).*

```
    X.compute_polynomial();
    X.ReduceDoubleAdd(offset,variable_count);
    X.compute_acceleration();
    X.update_velocity();
    X.OutParticles(n);
  }
}
```

where ReduceDoubleAdd is a reduction function inherited from SuperKernel. offset is measured from the beginning of the class Segment to the beginning of the field sinsum, and variable_count is the total number of array elements is sinsum and cossum. A leapfrog integration scheme is used to advance particles.

3.2 Timing Results

Our experiments with the pC++/CMF SCF code was conducted on the 32-node CM-5 at the University of Maryland and the 88-node Paragon at Indiana University. For comparison, we also ran the CMF SCF code on the CM-5. The results of these experiments are listed in Table 1.

As it can be seen in Table 1, the pC++/CMF code is, in fact, slightly faster than the CMF SCF code in all cases. This can be explained by that the pC++/CMF code is able to use a faster global vector reduction function. The timing results show that our Fortran interface implementation is very efficient. Given the results shown in Table 1 and experiments conducted on NCSA's CM-5 using larger partition sizes, we conclude that the pC++/CMF code can achieve at least the 14.4 Gflop speed of the CMF code.

4 THE PARTICLE MESH CODE

Another N-body code in the dossier of the GC^3 group is the Particle Mesh (PM) code (see Ferrel and Bertschinger 1993 [9]). The particle-mesh method used in the PM code computes long-range gravitational forces in a galaxy or galaxy cluster system by solving the gravitational potential on a mesh. The three-dimensional space is discretized by a three-dimensional grid. An average density for each grid point is then computed using the Nearest Grid Point scheme in which the density value at a grid point is the sum of all masses of the particles nearest to that grid point. Once the density values at the grid points are known, Fourier transforms are performed to compute the potential values at the grid points. And finally, the potential values at the grid points are interpolated back to the particles and the particle positions and velocities are updated. Two data structures that are natural to the particle-mesh method are: a one-dimensional particle list and a three dimensional mesh.

4.1 The Particle List Collection

The particles in the simulation are first sorted according to their affinity to mesh points; particles closest to the same mesh point are neighbors in the sorted list. The sorted list is then divided into segments and each segment forms an element of a particle list collection.

There are two approaches that we can follow when dividing the sorted list. Pertaining to the two approaches are issues of data locality and load balancing. In the first approach, the sorted list is evenly divided so that the segments have the same length. In the second, particles belonging to the same mesh points are grouped into the same segment and segments will have different lengths.

In the first approach, load balancing is ensured because each processor has the same number of particles. However, this approach may cause particles belonging to the same mesh point to be distributed among different elements, thus requiring more inter-element communication and remote update. The second approach allows a greater exploitation of data locality, but there is a potential load balancing problem. As the system evolves, particles (stars or galaxies) tend to group together into clumps. Consequently, some mesh points may have 1000 times more particles than other mesh points, and segments that have these mesh points will have much longer lengths. Since we usually distribute the collection elements, in this case segments, evenly across the processors in a parallel machine, the processors that have those long segments will do more work. We follow the first approach as an initial test.

The `Segment` class is defined as

```
class Segment {
 public:
  int particle_count; // Number of particles in the segment
  double x[particle_count],y[particle_count],z[particle_count],
         vx[particle_count],vy[particle_count],vz[particle_count],
         mass[particle_count];
  ...
};
```

where `x`, `y`, `z`, `vx`, `vy`, `vz`, and `mass` represent the position, the velocity, and the mass of a particle, respectively.

The ParticleList collection is defined as

```
Collection ParticleList : SuperKernel {
 public:
  ParticleList(Distribution *D, Align *A);
  void sortParticles();
 MethodOfElement:
  void pushParticle(Mesh<MeshElement> &G);
  void updateGridMass(Mesh<MeshElement> &G);
  ...
};
```

The function `sortParticles()` is a routine that sorts the particles in lexicographic order according to their positions. The function `pushParticle()` uses the gravitational force to update the positions and velocities of the particles. The argument passed to `pushParticle()` is a collection designed for the mesh data structure. The function `updateGridMass()` is used to add the mass of a particle to the total mass of the mesh point to which it is closest. The importance of this function is that it first loops through the particles local to a segment and accumulates a local total mass for each mesh point. It then adds the local total mass to the mesh point's total mass by a remote update operation on the appropriate mesh point. Because remote updates are expensive, this operation should be infrequent. This is why the particles are sorted to form a list in the beginning.

During the sorting, the particles within each segment are sorted first using the quick sort library sorting function. Then a global sorting is performed using the bitonic sort algorithm [6].

4.2 The Mesh Collection

The mesh is logically a three dimensional array of mesh points each containing the value of density and position. Because FFT is used to solve the gravitational potential equation, the data structure is designed as a two-dimensional collection with each element contains an array of mesh points that have the same x and y coordinates but different z coordinates:

```
class MeshElement {
 public:
  double mass[nz], position[nz];
};
```

The collection `Mesh` is defined as follows:

```
Collection Mesh : SuperKernel {
 public:
  Mesh(double lx, double ly, double lz, Distribution *T, Align *A);
  void computePotential();
  ...
};
```

where function computePotential() computes the gravitational potential using the total mass at each mesh point and lx, ly, lz are the numbers of mesh points in the three x, y, and z dimensions, respectively.

To calculate the gravitational potential (or forces), discrete Fourier transform is used twice: first the density is transformed into the wavenumber domain and then the potential (or force component) is transformed back into spatial domain.

FFT transform in the x-, y-, and z-directions is performed by the Mesh collection. The FFT in the z-direction poses no problems, as for each MeshElement with indices (i,j) the whole array of mesh points with indices (i,j,*) is located in that single MeshElement. Each MeshElement performs the z-FFT on its data without inter-element data communication, and load balancing is also ensured.

To perform FFT in the x-direction, the values of density at mesh points with indices (*,j,k) are collected by the collection element, Mesh(i,j). It then performs sequential FFT and sends back the resulting potential values to the mesh points from which it collected the density values.

To ensure good load balancing, we want all collection elements to participate the x-FFT. If it is known that the number of mesh points in the x-direction is equal to the number of mesh points in the z-direction, we can let all Mesh(*,j) send their kth density value to Mesh(k,j). If the number of mesh points in the x-direction is not equal to the number of mesh points in the z-direction, we can let Mesh(*,j) send their kth density value to Mesh(l,j) where l = (j + k) % lx. The y-direction FFT can be performed in a similar fashion.

4.3 The Main Simulation Loop

In its simplest form the simulation is given by the code below:

```
main(){
 Processors P;
 Distribution DP(segment_count, &P, BLOCK);
 Align AP(segment_count, "[ALIGN(particlelist[i], DP[i])]");
 ParticleList&lt;Segment&gt; particlelist(&DP, AP);
 Distribution DM(x_count, y_count, &P, BLOCK, WHOLE);
 Align AM(x_count, y_count, "[ALIGN(mesh[i], DM[i])]");
 Mesh<MeshElement> mesh(&DP, AP);

 // initialize particle list
 ...
 // main loop
 for(int i = 0; i < number_of_steps; i++){
   mesh.computePotential();
   particlelist.pushParticle(mesh);
   if(needed) particlelist.sortParticles();
   particlelist.updateGridMass(mesh);
 }
 ...
}
```

The main loop involves parallel computation on both Mesh and ParticleList. First the potential is computed in parallel on the grid. Second, the particle velocities and positions are updated. If particles have moved to new grid points, the appropriate data structure updates must then be made. If the particles have moved a lot since the last time they were sorted, the particles are sorted again. Third, the particle masses are accumulated in their corresponding points for the next iteration step.

5 ADAPTIVE GRID AND MULTI-THREADED EXECUTION

pC++ is designed to support parallel programming styles that are not well supported by Fortran90 and HPF. Problems with complex, adaptive data structures are naturally suited for an object-oriented language like C++. Though it is true that Fortran90 supports many advanced data-structure features, they are not as flexible as those in C++ and have not been integrated into HPF.

In this section, we describe the basic design of pC++ collection that will be used in adaptive grid computations. The idea is to allow a mesh to be refined in regions where more resolution is needed, for example, near a congestion of galaxies or stars. We modify the Mesh collection element class so that a grid cell can represent a new finer grid if the cell is in a region where extra resolution is required. The modified MeshElement now called MeshCell is give below:

```
class MeshCell{
 double gravPotential;
 double massDensity;
 int isRefined;  // 1 if the cell is refined
 Mesh<MeshCell> *refinedRegion;
};
```

The resulting data structure, as illustrated for a two dimensional problem in Figure 1 below, is a dynamical structure. Multi-threaded execution plays an important role in this type of parallel programming. Because new collections are created within elements of a collection, we must be able to invoke parallel operations within parallel sections. This type of nested parallelism requires a multi-threaded model of execution.

While it is still too early to evaluate this approach to parallel adaptive structures, we feel that the potential for success is high. The reader should note that there are several other approaches to adaptive parallel grid computation [17, 1, 7].

6 CONCLUSION

In this paper we have show how pC++ is used to design and implement object-oriented software for N-body and adaptive mesh refinement simulations. As a part of the NSF GC^3 effort, pC++ research will focus on problems related to adaptive computations on parallel machines. pC++ 1.0 is now available by anonymous ftp from Indiana University (ftp.cica.indiana.edu in pub/sage). Currently, pC++ runs on the Thinking

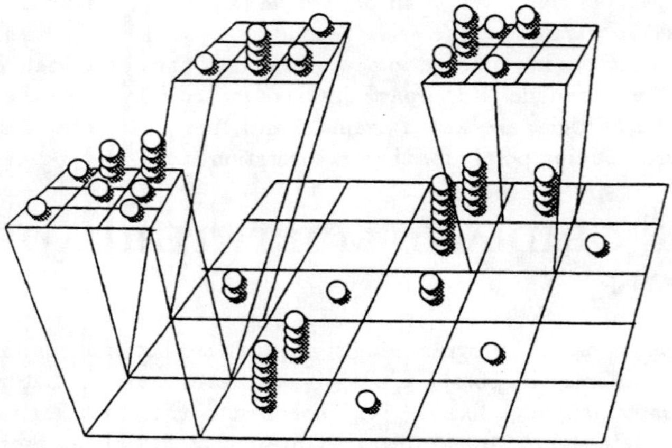

Figure 1: *Adaptive Mesh Refinement. If more resolution is required, the grid cell is refined to form a new mesh structure.*

Machines CM-5, the Intel Paragon, the BBN TC2000, the Kendall Square Research KSR-1, the IBM SP-1, Parallel Virtual Machines (PVM) for workstation clusters, and the Sequent Symmetry. A version for Cray T3D will also soon be available.

pC++2.0 is currently under construction. The key new features in pC++2.0 are multi-threads and global pointers. Multi-threaded execution is important for parallel adaptive structures. Global pointers are an essential requirement for the N-body simulations describe in this paper.

References

[1] S. Bhatt, M. Chen, C-Y Lin, and P. Liu. Object-oriented support for adaptive methods on parallel machines. In *Object Oriented Numerics (OON-SKI)*, pages 266–267, 1993.

[2] F. Bodin, P. Beckman, D. Gannon, S. Yang, S. Kesavan, A. Malony, and B. Mohr. Implementing a parallel C++ runtime system for scalable parallel systems. In *Supercomputing 93*. IEEE Computer Society, 1993.

[3] R. Chandra, A. Gupta, and J. Hennessy. *COOL: a Language for Parallel Programming*, pages 126–148. The MIT Press, 1990.

[4] K. M. Chandy and C. F. Kesselman. Compositional C++: Compositional parallel programming. In *Fourth Workshop on Parallel Computing and Compilers.* Springer-Verlag, 1992.

[5] K. M. Chandy and C. F. Kesselman. CC++: A declarative concurrent object oriented programming notation. In *Research Directions in Object Oriented Programming.* MIT Press, 1993.

[6] T. H. Cormen, C. E. Leiserson, and R.L.Rivest. *Introduction to Algorithms.* MIT Press, 1989.

[7] W. Crutchfield and M. Welcome. Object oriented implementation of adaptive mesh refinement algorithms. In *Object Oriented Numerics (OON-SKI)*, pages 108–122, 1993.

[8] J. Dongarra, R. Pozzo, and D. Walker. An object oriented design for high performance linear algebra on distributed memory architectures. In *Object Oriented Numerics (OON-SKI)*, pages 257–264, 1993.

[9] R. Ferrell and E. Bertschinger. Particle-mesh methods on the connection machine. *International Journal of Modern Physics C*, 1993.

[10] D. Gannon, F. Bodin, P. Beckman, S. Yang, and S. Narayana. Distributed pC++: Basic ideas for an object parallel language. In *Object Oriented Numerics (OON-SKI)*, pages 1–24, 1993.

[11] D. Gannon and J. K. Lee. On using object oriented parallel programming to build distributed algebraic abstractions. In *Conpar-Vap*, pages 769–774. Springer Verlag, 1992.

[12] D. Gannon, S. X. Yang, and P. Beckman. *User Guide for a Portable Parallel C++ Programming System, pC++.* Computer Science Department, Indiana University, available from moose.cs.indiana.edu:/pub/sage by ftp, 1994.

[13] A. S. Grimshaw. An introduction to parallel object-oriented programming with Mentat. Technical Report 91 07, University of Virginia, 1991.

[14] L. Hernquist and J. P. Ostriker. A self-consistent field method for galactic dynamics. *The Astrophysical Journal*, 386:375–397, 1992.

[15] J. Larus, B. Richards, and G. Viswanathan. C**: A large-grain object oriented data-parallel programming language. Technical Report 1126, Computer Science Department, University of Wisconsin, 1992.

[16] J. K. Lee and D. Gannon. Object oriented parallel programming: Experiments and results. In *Supercomputing 91 (Albuquerque, Nov.)*, pages 273–282. IEEE Computer Society and ACM, 1991.

[17] M. Lemke and D. Quinlan. P++, a parallel C++ array class library for architecture-independent development of numerical software. In *Object Oriented Numerics (OON-SKI)*, pages 268–269, 1993.

Toward Teraflop Computing
and New Grand
Challenge Applications

ISBN-1-56072-247-9

Automatic Distribution in HPF *

Siddhartha Chatterjee † John R. Gilbert ‡ Robert Schreiber * Thomas J. Sheffler *

Abstract

Our recent work in compiler and runtime mapping of the array data in a distributed-memory, data-parallel program has concentrated on choosing the parameters of the distribution. We show how a compiler may choose between cyclic, block, and block-cyclic distributions and also decide how to allocate the available processors to array axes.

1 Introduction

One of the major decisions in compiling data-parallel programs for distributed-memory parallel computers is the mapping of data and computation to the multiple processors of the machine. A good mapping minimizes program completion time by balancing the opposing needs of parallelism and communication: spreading the data and work over many processors increases available parallelism, but also increases communication time.

Most compilation systems (*e.g.*, Fortran D [7] and High Performance Fortran [10]) divide the data mapping problem into two phases: *alignment*, in which the relative positions of arrays are determined, and *distribution*, in which arrays are partitioned and mapped to a processor grid. We have dealt with the alignment problem previously [2, 5, 6, 15]. This paper focuses on the distribution problem.

1.1 Distribution

The distribution of an array specifies for each of its dimensions the number of processors p it is spread across and the block size k used in the distribution: element i is located at processor $(i \text{ div } k) \bmod p$. The distribution of a multidimensional array is the tensor product of the distributions of each of its dimensions. The HPF declarations

```
      REAL T(100,200)
CHPF$ PROCESSORS P(4,8)
CHPF$ DISTRIBUTE T(CYCLIC(1),CYCLIC(10)) ONTO P
```

specify the distribution of an array to a 4×8 processor grid with block sizes 1 and 10 in the two dimensions. The mapping of other data arrays is determined by the composition of an alignment to an explicitly distributed array (or an HPF TEMPLATE) and the distribution of the array to the processor grid. (Note that distributing a dimension to one processor is equivalent to forcing that dimension to reside in memory.)

The distribution problem is to determine distribution parameters that minimize the completion time of the program.

*Reprinted with permission from *Proceedings of the Workshop on Environments and Tools for Parallel and Scientific Computing*, edited by Jack J. Dongarra and B. Tourancheau. Copyright 1994 by the Society for Industrial and Applied Mathematics. All rights reserved.

†Research Institute for Advanced Computer Science, Mail Stop T27A-1, NASA Ames Research Center, Moffett Field, CA 94035-1000 (sc@riacs.edu, schreibr@riacs.edu, sheffler@riacs.edu). The work of these authors was supported by the NAS Systems Division via Contract NAS 2-13721 between NASA and the Universities Space Research Association (USRA).

‡Xerox Palo Alto Research Center, 3333 Coyote Hill Road, Palo Alto, CA 94304-1314 (gilbert@parc.xerox.com).

1.2 Problem formulation

In our system, data flow is represented as a directed, edge-weighted graph called the Alignment-Distribution Graph (ADG) [3]. For purposes of distribution, we can view the ADG as consisting of nodes and edges. Nodes represent program operations, and edges connect definitions of array objects to their uses. Alignment and distribution are attributes of array objects. A solution to the distribution problem is a labeling of ADG nodes with distribution parameters.

The ADG makes communication explicit. ADG edges connect the definition of an object to its uses. Communication occurs when the alignment or distribution is different at the end points of an edge. *Realignment* occurs along an edge when the alignment of the object at the tail of the edge is different from its alignment at the head. *Redistribution* occurs along an edge when the distribution of the array at the tail is different from the distribution at the head. Alignments are chosen in a previous compilation phase, and are considered fixed here.

Let δ a mapping from ADG nodes to distributions. The computation time T_{comp} of an ADG node u is a function of its computation, the size of the array object it computes, the alignments of this object, and the distribution $\delta(u)$ at the node.

For example, consider the program fragment

```
REAL A(16), B(24, 32)
A = SUM( B(:,17:32), DIM = 1 )
```

The ADG has a node that takes B into B(:, 17:32) (a "section" node), whose output is connected to a sum-reduction node that produces SUM(, DIM = 1) of its input. In the alignment phase, the alignment of the output of the first node is constrained to be 16 units to the right of the alignment of its input, the alignment of the input to the sum node is chosen to be identical (so there is no realignment on the edge between them) and its output (the array A) is chosen to be aligned to B(K, 17:32) for some K. Now we must choose a distribution for the object to which all these are aligned, namely the array B. We may choose a different distribution at each of the two nodes, although that would not be profitable in this example.

The cost of the first node (the array section) is essentially zero no matter what the chosen distribution. But the second, the sum-reduction, is influenced by this choice. Let us posit, for now, four candidate distributions for B:

```
CHPF$   PROCESSORS P22(2,2)
CHPF$   PROCESSORS P14(1,4)
CHPF$   DISTRIBUTE B(CYCLIC, CYCLIC) ONTO P22
CHPF$   DISTRIBUTE B( BLOCK,  BLOCK) ONTO P22
CHPF$   DISTRIBUTE B(      *, CYCLIC) ONTO P14
CHPF$   DISTRIBUTE B(      *,  BLOCK) ONTO P14
```

If we take the cost of a single-precision floating point add to be unity, and the cost of a message of length n between processors to be $\alpha + n\beta$, then we have the following costs:

CHPF$ DISTRIBUTE B(CYCLIC, CYCLIC) ONTO P22 :: COST $= 96 + \alpha + 8\beta$
CHPF$ DISTRIBUTE B(BLOCK, BLOCK) ONTO P22 :: COST $= 192 + \alpha + 16\beta$
CHPF$ DISTRIBUTE B(*, CYCLIC) ONTO P14 :: COST $= 96$
CHPF$ DISTRIBUTE B(*, BLOCK) ONTO P14 :: COST $= 192$

(The interaction of alignments and distributions is quite important in determining good distributions. The cost of any realignment that occurs on out-edges of an ADG node can also be accounted for at the node [4].) Thus, we include a term T_{node}, called a *node cost*, that accounts for computation and realignment, in our model of completion time. All our techniques assume that the dependence of node cost T_{node} on distribution can be made explicit.

The redistribution cost of an edge (u, v) depends on the weight w_{uv} of the edge, and the distributions $\delta(u)$ and $\delta(v)$ of nodes u and v. Specifically, we assume that the cost of redistribution along edge (u, v) is the product of three terms: a machine parameter ρ that gives the cost per data item of all-to-all personalized communication; the edge data weight w_{uv} (the total data volume carried by the ADG edge); and the ***discrete distance*** $\text{dist}(\delta(u), \delta(v))$, defined to be 0 if $\delta(u)$ equals $\delta(v)$ and 1 if they differ. (We are engaged now in the process of verifying this assumption by experimentation with the CM Fortran compiler running on a CM-5.)

Our model of completion time of the ADG $G = (V, E)$ is

$$T(G, \delta) = \sum_{v \in V} T_{node}(v, \delta(v)) + \rho \left(\sum_{(u,v) \in E} w_{uv} \cdot \text{dist}(\delta(u), \delta(v)) \right). \tag{1}$$

In the sequel whenever we refer to a "cost" we mean either the node cost T_{node} of an ADG node, or the redistribution cost of an edge.

Given the ADG G, the goal is to determine an optimal distribution mapping δ, one that minimizes the completion time $T(G, \delta)$.

We collect here some definitions and facts from graph theory and linear algebra that we will use in the paper. Let $S \subseteq V$ be a subset of the nodes of the ADG. We denote by $G(S)$ the ADG subgraph induced by S. We assume that the set of candidate distributions D has been determined. A distribution mapping of S is a function $\delta : S \mapsto D$. It is ***static*** if $\delta(s)$ is the same for all elements s of S, otherwise it is ***dynamic***. If δ is defined on S, we call the set S static or dynamic depending on whether the restriction of δ to S is static or dynamic.

Let $S \subseteq V$ be given. Define $T_{node}(S, d) = \sum_{v \in S} T_{node}(v, d)$. We denote by $T_{opt}(S)$ the minimum over all $d \in D$ of $T_{node}(S, d)$, and call this the ***static cost*** of $G(S)$. It is the minimum completion time of $G(S)$, given that all nodes in S are constrained to have the same distribution, since there is no redistribution when S is static. Define a ***best static distribution*** of the subgraph $G(S)$ as some distribution d that achieves the static cost of $G(S)$.

A partition of S is a set of disjoint subsets of S whose union equals S. We shall primarily deal with partitions of the nodes of an ADG subgraph $G(S)$ consisting of two subsets, S_1 and S_2. For such a two-way partition, define $\text{cut-cost}(S_1, S_2)$ to be ρ multiplied by the sum of the weights of the edges with one endpoint in S_1 and the other in S_2.

Let X be any undirected, edge-weighted, n vertex graph with vertices V and edges E. The Laplacian matrix of X is the symmetric $n \times n$ matrix defined by

$$L(X)_{ij} = \begin{cases} -w_{ij}, & i \neq j \text{ and } (i,j) \in E \\ \sum_{k \neq i} w_{ik}, & i = j \\ 0, & \text{otherwise.} \end{cases}$$

1.3 Previous work

Most of the previous work in this area has concentrated on the static version or on simplified dynamic versions of the problem. Wholey [16] uses a hill-climbing procedure to determine the distributions for named variables. (A named variable corresponds, in our formulation, to a subset of the nodes of the ADG. Thus, Wholey considers a restricted version of the dynamic problem.) Gupta [9] uses heuristic methods to determine the distribution parameters. He analyzes communication patterns to determine whether block or cyclic distributions are preferable. He then uses an affinity graph framework to determine block sizes. Finally, he allows at most two array dimensions to be distributed across the processors, and determines the proper aspect ratio by exhaustive enumeration.

Kremer [12] shows that dynamic distribution is NP-complete. Bixby *et al.* [1] and Kremer *et al.* [13] present a partial, heuristic solution method. They assume a decomposition of the program into phases, which are program fragments that are executed without changing distribution. Dynamic redistribution therefore only occurs between phases. Their system chooses the distribution of each phase. They solve this restricted problem by reducing it to 0-1 integer programming and employing an efficient branch-and-bound algorithm for such problems. Phases are created by user directives, although they have also proposed using loop nests as phases.

The techniques we present here, in contrast, do not require the user to provide any decomposition of the program. We do not exploit a reduction to another NP-complete problem; rather, we propose a heuristic that directly applies to the distribution problem. In particular, we give a fast algorithm that first determines node subsets to be given the same distribution, and then determines their distributions.

1.4 Organization of the paper

The remainder of the paper is organized as follows. Sections 2 through 4 discuss our algorithm for determining distributions. Section 5 discusses an experimental test of an implementation of the algorithm.

2 The distribution algorithm

The dynamic distribution problem is to choose a distribution mapping δ that minimizes completion time $T(G, \delta)$. Kremer [12] proved that dynamic distribution NP-complete. The distribution problem has some similarities with graph partitioning. Unlike graph partitioning, however, there is no intrinsic balance criterion in our problem formulation; moreover, the tension between node cost and the redistribution cost makes this problem interesting. We therefore seek good heuristics rather than exact algorithms for the problem. This section gives an overview of our algorithm; the following sections discuss details.

Algorithm DCD approximately solves the dynamic distribution problem for an arbitrary ADG subgraph $G(S)$, using the divide-and-conquer paradigm. By applying it to the entire ADG, we produce a distribution mapping. Here, we assume that the set D of allowed distributions is given.

Algorithm DCD (divide-and-conquer distribution):
INPUT: A subset $S \subseteq V$ of ADG nodes.
OUTPUT: A distribution mapping from S to D, and the completion time $T(S)$ that this mapping achieves.
Step 1. [Finished?] Using the criteria described in Section 4, determine if S should have a static distribution. If so, choose a best static distribution of S, with $T(S)$ equal to the static cost of S, and exit. Otherwise go to Step 2.
Step 2. [Divide.] Partition S into two subsets S_1 and S_2, and call Algorithm DCD recursively to determine dynamic distributions $\delta(S_1)$ and $\delta(S_2)$ with costs $T(S_1)$ and $T(S_2)$.
Step 3. [Conquer.] Find the edges of $G(S)$ that connect an endpoint in S_1 with an endpoint in S_2 and for which the endpoint distributions determined in Step 2 are different. Define T_D to be $T(S_1) + T(S_2) + \rho \cdot w(S_1, S_2)$. If T_D is smaller than the static cost of S then return the distribution mapping given by $\delta(S_1) \cup \delta(S_2)$, with cost $T(S) = T_D$, otherwise return a best static distribution of S, with $T(S)$ equal to the static cost of S.

□

In fact, there is also a Step 0, which precedes the first call to Algorithm DCD . Step 0 identifies subsets of ADG nodes that can be made to share a common distribution without worsening the resulting distribution mapping. We then contract each such subset to a single node whose cost table is the sum of the tables of its constituents. This *contraction* step is important for reducing the cost of Algorithm DCD . The contraction criteria are identical to the termination criteria of Step 1.

Rather than requiring user intervention, Algorithm DCD automatically finds sets of nodes that it constrains to share a common distribution. It then determines distributions for these sets. The key to the algorithm is the partitioner, which must choose a partition that groups strongly related nodes in the same subset. Section 3 discusses partitioning strategies, and Section 4 discusses the termination condition.

3 Partitioning

A core routine of Algorithm DCD is the partitioner, which takes a subset of ADG nodes S and partitions it into two subsets S_1 and S_2. Algorithm DCD then independently computes candidate distribution mappings for the induced subgraphs. Our key partitioning heuristic is the following: choose a partition that minimizes $\kappa_S(S_1, S_2)$, which we define to be the sum of the static costs of S_1 and S_2 and cut-cost(S_1, S_2). (The subscript S stands for "static".)

In this section we present an algorithm of polynomial complexity for approximately solving this problem. It encodes the problem as the minimization of a real-valued function of the vertices of the unit n-dimensional cube, and embeds this minimization in an easier continuous problem.

The approximately optimal partitions that this provides could be improved further by a subsequent improvement procedure of Kernighan-Lin type, in which nodes are moved from one subset to the other singly, in order to further reduce κ_S. We do not yet know its complexity, or whether such postprocessing is worthwhile.

3.1 Partitioning via nonlinear optimization

In recasting the partitioning problem in matrix terms, we use techniques seen in spectral graph partitioning methods [14].

Let S be an n-vertex subset of ADG nodes. Assume we are given a partition of S into two disjoint subsets S_1 and S_2. Let x be an n-vector with elements $+1$ and -1 encoding this partition; nodes corresponding to the $+1$ elements of x belong to S_1, while those corresponding to the -1 elements belong to S_2. We use the fact, well known in graph partitioning, that the cost of the edges crossing the cut, cut-cost(S_1, S_2), is given by $\frac{1}{4}\rho x^T Lx$ where L is the Laplacian of $G(S)$.

As above, $D = \{\delta_1, \ldots, \delta_d\}$ is a given set of candidate distributions. Construct the $d \times n$ node-cost matrix C, such that $C_{ij} = T_{node}(j, \delta_i)$ is the node cost of node j with distribution δ_i.

To get the static costs of S_1 and S_2, we need to extract the nodes belonging to each set. Let e be the n-vector of all 1's. Given that the elements of x are $+1$ and -1, we see that the corresponding elements of the vector $\frac{1}{2}(e+x)$ are 1 and 0, while those of the vector $\frac{1}{2}(e-x)$ are 0 and 1. Element i of the matrix-vector product $\frac{1}{2}C(e+x)$ gives the cost of the $+1$ partition if each node in that partition has distribution δ_i. The static cost of S_1 is therefore $\frac{1}{2}\min_i(C(e+x))_i$, while that of S_2 is $\frac{1}{2}\min_i(C(e-x))_i$. We therefore seek to minimize

$$\frac{1}{4}\rho x^T Lx + \frac{1}{2}\min_i(C(e+x))_i + \frac{1}{2}\min_i(C(e-x))_i \tag{2}$$

over the set of vectors with elements ± 1, not all elements the same. This is the set of vertices of the n-dimensional unit hypercube, without the two elements e and $-e$ whose elements are all of the same sign. We denote this set by H_n.

Rewrite the matrix $C = B - M$, where B is a matrix whose entries are a constant b, larger than $\max_{ij} C_{ij}$; M is the "savings" matrix. The following constrained minimization problem is equivalent to (2):

$$\min_{x \in H_n} \frac{1}{4}\rho x^T Lx - \frac{1}{2}\|M(e+x)\|_\infty - \frac{1}{2}\|M(e-x)\|_\infty. \tag{3}$$

(For a vector z, $\|z\|_\infty$ is the absolute value of the element of z whose absolute value is largest).

Note the two kinds of terms in the cost function. The redistribution term $\frac{1}{4}x^T Lx$ is sensitive only to the edges of the ADG. The other two node-cost terms consider only the node characteristics. The minimization problem (3) is combinatorial, and may be as hard as the original distribution problem! We next present a heuristic, inspired by spectral methods in graph partitioning, for approximately solving (3).

3.2 Heuristic CC

In this section we describe an approximate solution technique. The idea in this algorithm (called CC for convex combinations) is to solve approximately the communication-only problem and the node-only problem in the continuous domain and to then search for the minimizer of (3) among the convex combinations of the two extremal vectors.

The vector that minimizes the communication term $x^T Lx$ among vectors of unit 2-norm is e (since $e^T Le = 0$); among vectors of unit 2-norm orthogonal to e, its minimizer is the eigenvector of L corresponding to the smallest nonzero eigenvalue (called the Fiedler vector). We rescale the Fiedler vector to have unit infinity norm, and call it x_L.

As for the node term, we require a vector x such that $M(x+e)$ and $M(x-e)$ are both large. We choose the second right singular vector of M, scaled to have unit infinity norm; call this vector x_M. We argue in [4] that Mx_M will be nicely linearly independent of Me and that both will be large, making both of $M(e+x)$ and $M(e-x)$ large.

We now search along the line between x_L and x_M for the minimizer, *i.e.*, we seek λ in $[0,1]$ such that the vector $x = \lambda x_L + (1-\lambda)x_M$ minimizes the objective function in (3). Since both x_L and x_M are only determined up to sign, we replace x_M by $-x_M$ if necessary to make the two vectors agree in sign in as many places as possible before beginning this line search. (Consider, otherwise, the effect of $x_M = -x_L$.) we revert to the discrete domain by taking the sign of the continuous minimizer.

We are also looking into quantizing both x_L and x_M, and then looking at the vertices of the subhypercube determined by these two partitions. In this case, ***any*** graph partitioner may be used to produce the vector x_L.

4 Termination

The second unspecified element of Algorithm DCD is the termination criterion that determines when to stop dividing. We could recurse all the way down to single nodes, but this is often unnecessary. In this section, we develop certain results regarding structural properties of ADG subgraphs that tell us when we can safely stop the recursion.

First, some definitions. A subgraph $G(S)$ of the ADG G is ***optimally static*** if some optimal distribution mapping for G assigns the same distribution to all nodes in S.

For $v \in V$, let $\delta_{opt}(v)$ be some distribution d that minimizes $T_{node}(v,d)$. We call $\delta_{opt}(v)$ local minimum cost distribution at v. For any $S \subseteq V$, let $\delta_{opt}(S)$ be a best static distribution of $G(S)$, *i.e.*, some value of d that minimizes $\sum_{v\in S} T_{node}(v,d)$.

S is ***unanimous*** if there is a best static distribution $\delta_{opt}(S)$ that is also a local minimum cost distribution for each node $v \in S$; that is, there is some distribution d such that, for all nodes $v \in S$, $d = \delta_{opt}(v) = \delta_{opt}(S)$.

Define $\Delta(S)$ as $\min_d \sum_{v\in S} T_{node}(v,d) - \sum_{v\in S} \min_d T_{node}(v,d)$. $\Delta(S)$ gives the difference in node-cost between placing the entire node set at its best static distribution and placing each node at its local minimum cost distribution. Clearly, $\Delta(S) = 0$ if and only if S is unanimous; it is a measure of "dissension" in S. Define $\theta(S)$ as $\min_{v\in S}(\min_{d\neq\delta_{opt}(v)} T_{node}(v,d) - T_{node}(v,\delta_{opt}(v)))$. $\theta(S)$ gives the least possible cost of changing the distribution of a node in S from its local minimum to the distribution of next lowest cost. Let $w(S)$ be the total weight of edges with exactly one endpoint in S, multiplied by the communication parameter ρ. Finally, define mincut(S) to be the smallest possible redistribution cost incurred when S is dynamic, *i.e.*, mincut$(S) = \min \text{cut-cost}(S_1, S_2)$ where the minimum is taken over all partitions of S into two nonempty subsets.

Now we give some results regarding the static properties of subgraphs. The proofs, all straightforward, appear in an earlier paper [4].

If $\Delta(S)$ is large, then it is hard to satisfy all nodes with a single, static distribution. Also, if $w(S)$ is also large, then the nodes that border S may "pull" its elements toward different distributions. On the other hand, when $G(S)$ has no low-weight edge cutset, it will be expensive to allow it to be dynamic. These competing factors are directly comparable, as we now demonstrate.

Lemma 1 (Min-cut) *If* mincut$(S) \geq w(S) + \Delta(S)$ *for a set* S, *then* S *is optimally static.*

The next result establishes sufficient conditions for a subgraph $G(S)$ to be optimally static in the special case where it is unanimous. This strengthens Lemma 1 for this case.

Lemma 2 (Unanimous) *If set S is unanimous and* $\text{mincut}(S) + \theta(S) \geq w(S)$, *then S is optimally static.*

The final result shows how an optimally static subgraph may be enlarged while remaining optimally static. One may include nodes that are tied strongly (by heavily weighted edges) in the subgraph.

Lemma 3 (Accretion) *Let S be optimally static and assume $v \notin S$. Define $w(v, S)$ to be ρ multiplied by the sum of the weights of edges connecting v to S, and similarly $w(v, \bar{S})$ is ρ times the sum of the weights of all other v-incident edges. Finally, let range$(v) \equiv (\max_d T_{node}(v, d) - \min_d T_{node}(v, d))$. If $w(v, S) \geq w(v, \bar{S}) + range(v)$, then $S \cup \{v\}$ is optimally static.*

Note that the computation involved in verifying some of the hypotheses above is dominated by the time taken to find the global minimum cut mincut(S). A naive algorithm for this would run n single-source single-sink minimum cut computations (n being the number of nodes in S) for a total cost of $O(n^3)$ or more. Recently, Karger and Stein [11] have recently developed a probabilistic algorithm for this problem with $\tilde{O}(n^2)$ running time.

5 Experiments

We reported previously [4] on some experiments on small graphs designed by hand to capture the essential difficulties of some nontrivial distribution problems, such as in ADI and multizone PDE solvers. Here, we give some results obtained with actual test code. We used the test fragment "Erlebacher", an 800-line ADI kernel from a fluid flow code whose origin is ICASE. The code solves multiple tridiagonal systems by Gaussian elimination. The data of the systems form a three dimensional grid. The code sweeps over this grid in each of the three directions.

The ADG representation of the Erlebacher kernel has 666 nodes. After contraction, in which for this example Lemma 3 is the most useful, 226 nodes remain. The static cost is 1.51×10^9 (where a flop costs one unit). We compute a better dynamic distribution, which has cost 1.29×10^9.

We note that Bixby *et al.* were quite successful in obtaining distribution solutions for Erlebacher using their 0-1 integer programming formulation. Direct comparison of their approach with ours should be quite interesting. At the present time, our implementation involves interpreted Matlab code, and is not efficient. We concur with their suggestion that the integer programming technique and these heuristic techniques can complement one another, with the heuristic techniques used when the IP fails to quickly find an optimal solution. In other words, we may use Algorithm DCD , but switch to an exact IP method once subgraphs become small enough and the resulting IP becomes tractable. Also, initial application of the optimally static lemmas to detect phases appears to be important, no matter what the subsequent solution method.

References

[1] Robert Bixby, Ken Kennedy, and Ulrich Kremer. Automatic data layout using 0-1 integer programming. To appear, *Proceedings of the International Conference on Parallel Architectures and Compilation Techniques (PACT94)*, Montréal, August, 1994. Technical Report CRPC-TR93349-S, Center for Research on Parallel Computation, Rice University, Houston, TX, November 1993.

[2] Siddhartha Chatterjee, John R. Gilbert, and Robert Schreiber. Mobile and replicated alignment of arrays in data-parallel programs. In *Proceedings of Supercomputing'93*, pages 420–429, Portland, OR, November 1993.

[3] Siddhartha Chatterjee, John R. Gilbert, Robert Schreiber, and Thomas J. Sheffler. Modeling data-parallel programs with the alignment-distribution graph. *Journal of Programming Languages*, 1994.

[4] Siddhartha Chatterjee, John R. Gilbert, Robert Schreiber, and Thomas J. Sheffler. Array distribution in data-parallel programs. Submitted to the Seventh Annual Workshop on Languages and Compilers for Parallel Computers, 1994.

[5] Siddhartha Chatterjee, John R. Gilbert, Robert Schreiber, and Shang-Hua Teng. Optimal evaluation of array expressions on massively parallel machines. In *Proceedings of the Second Workshop on Languages, Compilers, and Runtime Environments for Distributed Memory Multiprocessors*, Boulder, CO, October 1992. Published in SIGPLAN Notices, 28(1), January 1993, pages 68–71. An expanded version is available as RIACS Technical Report TR 92.17 and Xerox PARC Technical Report CSL-92-11.

[6] Siddhartha Chatterjee, John R. Gilbert, Robert Schreiber, and Shang-Hua Teng. Automatic array alignment in data-parallel programs. In *Proceedings of the Twentieth Annual ACM SIGACT/SIGPLAN Symposium on Principles of Programming Languages*, pages 16–28, Charleston, SC, January 1993.

[7] S. Hiranandani and K. Kennedy and C. Tseng. Compiling Fortran D for MIMD distributed-memory machines. *Communications of the ACM* 35 (1992) pp. 66–80.

[8] Philip E. Gill, Walter Murray, and Margaret H. Wright. *Practical Optimization.* Academic Press, Orlando, FL, 1981.

[9] Manish Gupta. *Automatic Data Partitioning on Distributed Memory Multicomputers.* PhD thesis, University of Illinois at Urbana-Champaign, Urbana, IL, September 1992. Available as technical reports UILU-ENG-92-2237 and CRHC-92-19.

[10] High Performance Fortran Forum. High Performance Fortran language specification. *Scientific Programming,* 2 (1993) pp. 1–170.

[11] David Karger and Clifford Stein. On $\tilde{O}(n^2)$ algorithm for minimum cuts. In *Proceedings of the 25th Annual ACM Symposium on Theory of Computing*, pages 757–765, 1993.

[12] Ulrich Kremer. NP-completeness of dynamic remapping. Technical Report CRPC-TR93-330-S, Center for Research on Parallel Computation, Rice University, Houston, TX, August 1993. Appears in the *Proceedings of the Fourth Workshop on Compilers for Parallel Computers*, Delft, The Netherlands, December 1993.

[13] Ulrich Kremer, John Mellor-Crummey, Ken Kennedy, and Alan Carle. Automatic data layout for distributed-memory machines in the D programming environment. Technical Report CRPC-TR93-298-S, Center for Research on Parallel Computation, Rice University, Houston, TX, February 1993. Appears in *Proceedings of the First International Workshop on Automatic Distributed Memory Parallelization, Automatic Data Distribution and Automatic Parallel Performance Prediction (AP'93)*, Vieweg Verlag, Wiesbaden, Germany.

[14] Alex Pothen, Horst D. Simon, and Kang-Pu Liou. Partitioning sparse matrices with eigenvectors of graphs. *SIAM Journal of Matrix Analysis and Applications*, 11(3):430–452, July 1990.

[15] Thomas J. Sheffler, Robert Schreiber, John R. Gilbert, and Siddhartha Chatterjee. Aligning parallel arrays to reduce communication. Submitted to Supercomputing'94, Washington DC, November 1994.

[16] Skef Wholey. *Automatic Data Mapping for Distributed-Memory Parallel Computers.* PhD thesis, School of Computer Science, Carnegie Mellon University, Pittsburgh, PA, May 1991. Available as Technical Report CMU-CS-91-121.

Toward Teraflop Computing
and New Grand
Challenge Applications

ISBN-1-56072-247-9

A PARADIGM FOR GRAND CHALLENGE PERFORMANCE EVALUATION[1]

John L. GUSTAFSON

Ames Laboratory, U.S. DOE
Iowa State University, Ames, Iowa

ABSTRACT

The computing community has long faced the problem of scientifically comparing different computers and different algorithms. This difficulty is especially pronounced for "Grand Challenge" computing, and the lack of a performance evaluation paradigm has had a negative effect on the entire HPCC program. Our failure to articulate the goals of some of our Grand Challenges has raised doubts about the program at the federal level. In this paper, a model is proposed that shows a practical way to define and communicate *ends-based* performance of an application, without the *means-based* measures such as "teraflops" or "double precision." Unlike most performance analysis, we incorporate human issues such as monetary cost and program development time into the model. Examples are given to illustrate the paradigm.

1. INTRODUCTION

The term "Grand Challenge" was coined by Nobel Laureate Kenneth G. Wilson, who also articulated the current concept of "computational science" as a third way of doing science. Posing a scientific effort as a specific challenge like "climate prediction" or "protein folding" implies an engineering rather than a research approach, and that there is a point at which one can define success. The Grand Challenge problems have the following in common:

- They are questions to which many scientists and engineers would like to know answers, not just esoterica.
- They are difficult; we don't know how to do them right now.
- We think they can be done by computer, but we think current computers are not "powerful" enough.

[1] This work is supported by the Applied Mathematical Sciences Program of the Ames Laboratory-U.S. DOE under contract No. W-7405-ENG-82.

So how does one know when a Grand Challenge has been solved? In asking researchers this question, I find the question met with resistance, even resentment. Perhaps having a firm test of success means either the effort can be proved unsuccessful (which might mean cessation of funding) or it might be proved successful (which, ironically, also might mean cessation of funding). As long as the frontier of a challenge is ill-defined and movable, a Grand Challenge effort can keep success just out of reach. Can a computational chemist, for instance, define a level of physical accuracy and a molecule complexity at which chemists will have nothing more to study? It seems unlikely that this will happen.

The HPCC program is now under attack because of failure to specify goals. In "HPCC Research Questioned" [6], Fred Weingarten points out that Congress cast 65 dissenting votes against extending HPCC, raising such questions as:

- What are the real goals of the HPCC program?
- How can we measure progress toward those goals or lack thereof?

Somehow we need concrete measures of HPCC progress without making HPCC goals as narrowly-defined as those of a moon shot or a superconducting supercollider.

The solution to this, and to future large-scale computational efforts, lies in effective performance evaluation paradigms. Paradigms such as "A teraflop/s on a real application" are not effective, for reasons explained below. Neither is "the smaller the execution time, the better" by itself, since below some amount of time, other things become more important.

2. ENDS VERSUS MEANS: THE FAILURE OF "FLOP/S"

Suppose a track coach, training runners for mile races, decides that faster running implies more Footsteps Per Second (FSPS). He then makes the even shakier deduction that more FSPS implies faster running, and that his athletes can shift their goals from winning races to practicing to maximize FSPS.

The result, obviously, would be absurd. All the coach would achieve would be a collection of runners taking rapid steps that don't get them very far. Would higher FSPS ratings on a runner imply higher speed on actual races? Probably not. In fact, it might correlate inversely. Yet, this absurdity is exactly what we do when we confuse "flop/s" ratings with scientific goals.

Consider the following example from the NAS Parallel Benchmarks [1]: Four computers can be ranked from "fastest" to "slowest" by peak gigaflop/s ratings as follows:

System	Nominal Gigaflop/s	Nominal Rank
TMC CM-2	15.0	1
Intel iPSC/860	7.7	2
CRAY Y-MP	2.6	3
nCUBE 2	2.4	4

Using the first of the NAS Parallel Benchmarks (one so forgiving of slow interprocessor communications that it goes by the name "EP" for "Embarrassingly Parallel"), the ranking goes as follows for "sustained" gigaflop/s [2]:

Actual Rank	System	Actual Gigaflop/s	Nominal Rank
1	nCUBE 2	2.6	4
2	CRAY Y-MP	1.1	3
3	TMC CM-2	0.44	1
4	Intel iPSC/860	0.36	2

The ranking is almost exactly reversed! The computers with the higher peak flop/s ratings tend to have *lower memory bandwidths*, indicating a tendency of some hardware designers to follow the ARPA design goal of maximum flop/s while ignoring everything else. For a given hardware budget, higher peak flop/s ratings might imply *lower* sustained speed.

Note that the nCUBE 2 exceeds its "peak" gigaflop/s rating. This is because the EP benchmark counts logarithms, square roots, and multiplications modulo 2^{46} as 25, 12, and 19 operations based on the Cray Hardware Performance Monitor, but the nCUBE 2 has instructions that permit it to do these things in fewer operations. This brings up another problem with the use of flop/s as a metric: There is no such thing as a "standard" or "unit" floating-point operation. This fact has been well articulated by Snelling [4].

Consider the following Fortran program segment, where variables beginning with `A-H` and `O-Z` are 64-bit real numbers, and those beginning with `I-N` are integers:

```
Y = X ** ABS(Z)
J = Y + 1
IF (Z .LT. 0.) W = J
Z = SIN(W)
```

In the first line, does an absolute value count as a flop? It means merely zeroing a single bit, so it seems it shouldn't get credit for such work. But many architectures use the floating-point adder functional unit to perform absolute values, which would show it as work on a hardware performance monitor. What should the power function "**" count, when both the base and the exponent are real numbers? Should comparisons with zero as in the third line count as flops, even though they are trivial from the hardware point of view? Of course, the `IF` test introduces an operation count that can only be determined at run time, assuming one counts the integer-to-float conversion `W = J` as a floating-point operation. Estimates for the effort to compute a `SIN` range from about 4 flops for computers with very large interpolation tables to 25 flops as measured by NASA/Ames using a Cray Hardware Performance Monitor. Clearly, flop counts are *not* architecture-independent, yet most of the texts on numerical methods assume that they are.

The main reason flop/s metrics are useless is algorithmic: **Improving an algorithm often often leads to a lower flop/s rate**. Consider a problem that arises in computational chemistry: multiplying two 1000 by 1000 matrices that are each about 10% sparse. If one ignores sparsity, the operation has as its BLAS kernel either an `AXPY` or a `DOT`, depending on outer loop nesting:

Method 1:

```
      DO 1 K = 1,1000
        DO 1 J = 1,1000
          DO 1 I = 1,1000
1           C(I,J) = C(I,J) + A(I,K) * B(K,J)
```

This operation is "Cray food." Traditional vector processors effortlessly get over 80% of peak flop/s ratings on this loop, perhaps with minor restructuring but usually just using the standard Fortran compilers. Unfortunately, only about 1% of the operations contribute to the answer if the A and B matrices are 10% sparse. A sparse code to do the same computation, *even without a sparse storage scheme*, might save operations via something like this:

Method 2:

```
      DO 2 K = 1,1000
        DO 2 J = 1,1000
          IF (B(K,J) .NE. 0.) THEN
            DO 1 I = 1,1000
1             IF (A(I,K) .NE. 0.) C(I,J) = C(I,J) + A(I,K) * B(K,J)
          END IF
2     CONTINUE
```

As anyone who has used vector computers can attest, the IF statements in Method 2 might degrade the flop/s rate by an order of magnitude. A typical performance measure might show Method 1 to run in 1.0 seconds at 2.0 gigaflop/s on a vector computer, but Method 2 to run in 0.1 seconds at 0.2 gigaflop/s on the same computer. From the hardware viewpoint, Method 1 is ten times faster, but from the user viewpoint, Method 2 is ten times faster. By the prevalent HPCC esthetic, Method 2 is less "efficient," farther from its Grand Challenge goal, and thus should not be used. Yet, *it arrives at the answer in an order of magnitude less time*. There are many such examples:

Higher Flop/s Rate	**Quicker Answers**
Conventional Matrix Multiply	Strassen Multiplication
Cholesky Decomposition	Conjugate Gradient
Time-Domain Filtering	FFTs
All-to-All *N*-Body Methods	Greengard Multipole Method
Successive Over relaxation	Multigrid
Explicit timestepping	Implicit timestepping
Recompute Gaussian integrals	Compute Gaussian integrals once, store
Material property computation	Table look-up

The methods on the left persist in the repertoire of scientific computing largely because they keep the front panel lights on, not because they are better methods. There is something seriously wrong with the notion of "efficiency" that awards a higher score to the slower algorithms in the left column.

A related false goal is that of "speedup." As commonly defined, speedup is a metric that rewards slower processors and inefficient compilation [5]. It is especially misleading when measured on fixed-size problems, since the emphasis on time reduction as the only goal implies that parallelism in computing has very limited payoff. The main use of parallel computing hardware is increase in capacity in some performance dimension, not time reduction for problems we can already solve on a single processor.

Increasing *memory* does not always increase the merits of a simulation. A poorly-chosen basis set for quantum chemistry will require more terms and more storage to get the same accuracy in an answer than would a better choice of basis functions. We think using increased memory always means better answers, but this is not the case. We conclude this section with a table comparing means-based measures with ends-based measures:

Means-Based	**Ends-Based**
Flop/s ratings	Time to compute an answer
Bytes of RAM	Detail, completeness in answer
Number of Processors	Problems that can be attempted
Use of commodity parts	Cost and availability of system to end user
Double precision	Match to actual physics
ECC memory	System reliability
Speedup	Product line range

3. A SOLVED GRAND CHALLENGE

In the 1950s and 1960s, the space program was compute-bound. A successful mission had to be very conservative on fuel, and that meant having fast, accurate course corrections to control the rockets. For the computers of that era, ordinary differential equations in real time represented a Grand Challenge.

The USSR, being behind the U.S. in computer technology, initially relied on ground-based computers for mission control because their equipment was too heavy and too bulky to put on board. They incurred the difficulty of transmission delays and having to coordinate multiple transceivers around the globe. The U.S. was able to put most of the computing on board, greatly increasing the safety margin and fuel economy.

Where is this "Grand Challenge" now? It's *solved*, that's where. Computing is no longer regarded as an obstacle to space travel. The challenge did not simply move ever further out of reach. The 1990s Space Shuttle uses the improvements to computing power to manage the multivariate response to aerodynamic effects in the atmosphere, a more difficult task, but the response needed is well within the computing power available.

This example shows that Grand Challenges can be specified precisely, and actually can be "solved." The goal was to supply enough computer guidance to send hardware into space and bring it back safely. Can we be so precise about the current Grand Challenges?

4. "UTILITY" AND "ACCEPTABILITY"

William Pardee [3] has suggested something similar to the following method of thinking about a particular parameter of success: The *utility* of the answer to a Grand Challenge is a function of each aspect of its answer, where positive utility means the answer was worth having and negative utility means the answer is worse than no answer at all (for example, when the answer is misleading). For example, the utility as a function of "decimals of accuracy in the answer" might look like the following:

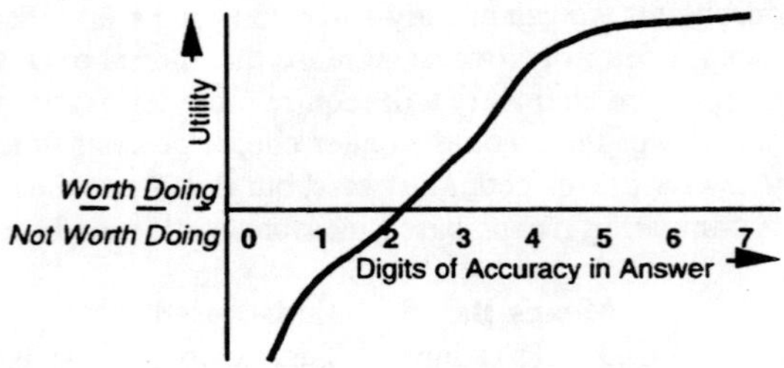

Figure 1. "Utility Curve"

[Note that this is quite different from the amount of precision that might be required in the computation for typical algorithms. We have grown so accustomed to the use of 64-bit arithmetic with 14 to 16 decimals of accuracy in the *computation* that we tend to forget to consider what we need in the accuracy of the *result*.]

A somewhat different model is to define "acceptability," a function bounded by 0 (unacceptable) and 1 (completely acceptable) that is monotone increasing in some parameter, assuming all other parameters are completely acceptable. Such curves might be approximated as "logistic curves," which are functions of the form

$$A(x) = 1 / (1 + e^{a + bx}) \tag{1}$$

where b is less than zero.

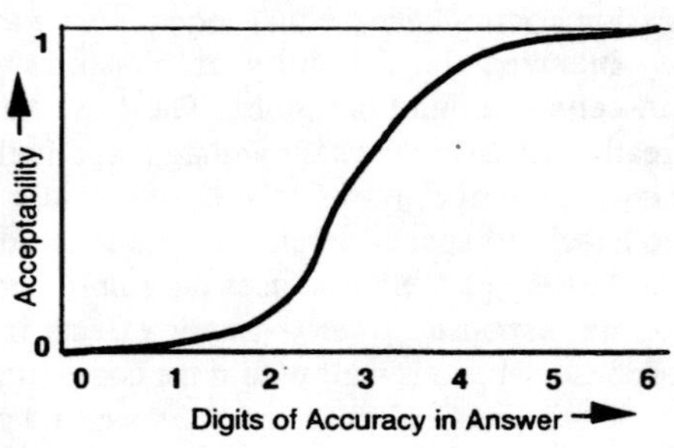

Figure 2. Typical "Acceptability Curve"

Both the Utility model and the Acceptability model ignore cross terms; for example, a chemistry application with 100 atoms and only one decimal of accuracy might be acceptable, but when applied to systems of 3 atoms, only answers accurate to four decimals will be competitive with research done elsewhere. Where cross terms are easy to recognize, it may be more useful to plot utility versus some combination of more than one variable (like, accuracy in decimals times the square root of the number of atoms).

To see why each Grand Challenge community needs to come up with its own set of Acceptability graphs, consider the differences between various groups of scientists regarding *run times*.

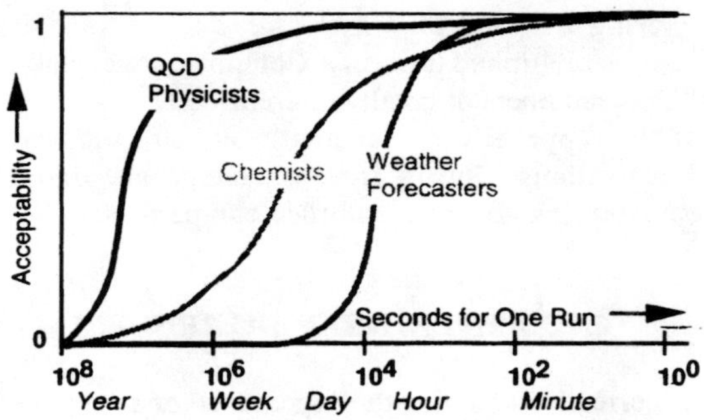

Figure 3. Run time Acceptability Variation by Scientific Culture

From personal observation, QCD physicists have an extraordinary tolerance for execution times that take a significant fraction of a human lifetime; they expect to wait months for a single result. The upper limit of their patience is simply that for runs of more than a year, computer hardware improvements permit those problems to be started later and finished sooner. Chemists and most scientists operate more in the range of several-hour to several-day runs. Weather prediction (not climate prediction) is clearly limited by the time scale of geophysical events. Outside the Grand Challenge community, there are computer applications such as text editing where interactions requiring more than a few seconds are considered intolerable.

If we are to quantify Grand Challenge goals, we have to include not just the measures of closeness to physical reality, but the practical demands of the entire project. There is a tendency to sweep such issues as programming effort and system up time "under the rug" when measuring computing performance. Although they are harder to quantify than operation counts or word sizes, they can be included in the model.

5. THE VARIABLES MOST MODELS LEAVE OUT

Performance studies commonly assume that the only figure of merit one need consider is the reciprocal of the execution time. Putting questions of fixed time versus fixed size scaling for a moment, there are certainly many other things that matter to the computer user, such as:

- Time to create or convert an effective simulation program on a particular architecture
- Initial cost of the system
- Cost per run, or better, the cost for a complete solution to the Grand Challenge
- Probability that any given run on the computer will fail from reliability problems (hardware or operating system software)
- Validity of the answer (non-obvious failure modes)
- Time for each edit-compile-run-debug cycle

Compared to these issues, the question of how close we get to 1 teraflop/s seems moot. All of these variables can be made into specific goals by estimating the Acceptability function and declaring a value at which we declare the subgoal as "met." The acceptabilities A_i can be multiplied to form a Composite Acceptability $A = \Pi_i A_i$, a bit like taking the "AND" Boolean operator on all requirements.

The beauty of this approach is that it allows fair comparison of widely varying architectures and algorithms. One is free to change an algorithm to fit a different architecture without worrying about uncontrolled comparisons.

6. EXAMPLE: GRAPHIC RENDERING

The problem of correctly rendering the appearance of a room defined by the locations, colors, and reflective properties of its surfaces and lights is a Grand Challenge in the computer graphics community. What are the requirements of this challenge?

1) It should be able to handle any geometry or reflection property one might find in a typical building interior.
2) It should take less than one minute to compute.
3) It should cost less than one dollar for each multi-view rendering.
4) The time to make a small alteration to the geometry should be no greater than the time to re-render the image.
5) A video display of the scene should be indistinguishable from a photograph of a real room with the same geometry. More precisely, it should be within 5% of true luminosity at a display resolution of 1024 by 1024 pixels, and should have less than 1% chance of catastrophic failure from any reason.
6) We want to meet these goals by the year 2000, with the equivalent of two full-time people working on it.

This list of goals is *not* the way the graphics community has approached the challenge. You will not find such a specification in the *SIGGRAPH Proceedings* or similar literature. Some researchers keep vague goals similar to these in their head, but the prevailing mode of comparing rendering methods is to display a picture and show that it "looks realistic." There is seldom any mention of the mathematical accuracy, the cost of the system that created the picture, the amount of time spent computing, or the effort to create the program.

By expressing these goals, our program at Ames Lab changed its approach to the rendering problem. Taking each of these goals in turn:

1) We explicitly restrict ourselves to surfaces expressible by convex planar quadrilaterals with diffuse surface reflectivity.
2) We allow some runs to last several hours for the sake of prototyping, but otherwise retain this goal.
3) We retain this goal if one does not figure in the program development cost or the facilities start-up costs.
4) We retain this goal.
5) We relax this goal by tolerating about a 10% deviation from correct luminosity.
6) We are ahead of schedule.

These compromises can be made more precise using the Acceptability functions of each goal. One could fit logistic curves to each goal, and then define the product as the net acceptability. The Acceptability might be a step function for qualitative requirements like point 1.

Point 5 requires a new formulation of the problem. Normally, diffuse surfaces are treated using the "radiosity equation":

$$b(r) = e(r) + \rho(r) \int_S F(r,r')\, b(r')\, dr' \tag{2}$$

where b is the radiosity (or luminosity) in watts or lumens per meter, r and r' are points on surfaces in the scene, e is the emissivity, or light emitted as a source from each point, S is the set of all surfaces, and F is the "coupling factor" that measures the geometric coupling between points in the scene. For diffuse surfaces, the equation is exact.

This is discretized to form a system of linear equations, *but here is where the more explicit goal changed our approach*: We discretize so as to form a rigorous upper bound and lower bound on the solution. The coupling factor F attains a maximum and a minimum for any pair of patches i and j, which are the elements $F_{ij\,max}$ and $F_{ij\,min}$ of the discretized system The upper-bound solution can be initially bounded by the maximum light emissivity e_{max} times the sum of the geometric series for the maximum reflectivity ρ_{max}:

$$e_{max}\,(1 + \rho_{max} + \rho_{max}^{\;2} + \rho_{max}^{\;3} + \ldots) = e_{max} \,/\, (1 - \rho_{max}) \tag{3}$$

The lower bound solution can be bounded by zero. Both bounds are independent of location in the scene. Now we subdivide the geometry, keeping careful track of maxima and minima in the new discretization. The answer is then improved by Gauss-Seidel iteration *without* over relaxation, guaranteeing monotone approach to the correct solution. We alternate the refining of the subdivision with the iteration of the Gauss-Seidel solver to tighten the bounds on the answer, producing steady improvement in the quality of the answer with increased computation. To illustrate this, consider the simple two-dimensional radiosity problem shown in Figure 4.

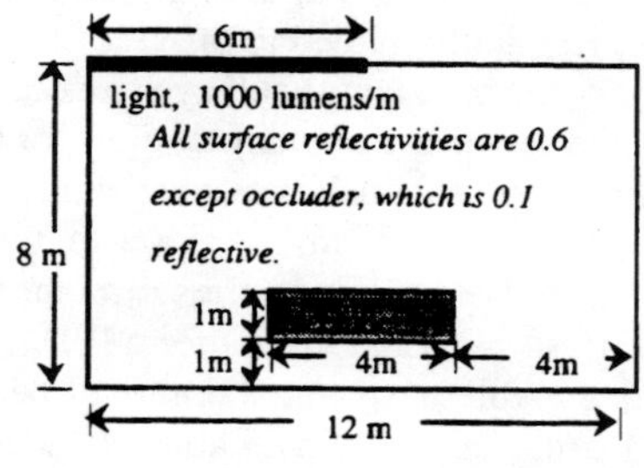

Figure 4. Simple Radiosity Geometry

Figure 5 shows how the true, continuous solution to the equation is bounded by the discrete form, for a coarse discretization. The answer "quality" can now be defined as the reciprocal of the total area between lower and upper bounds.

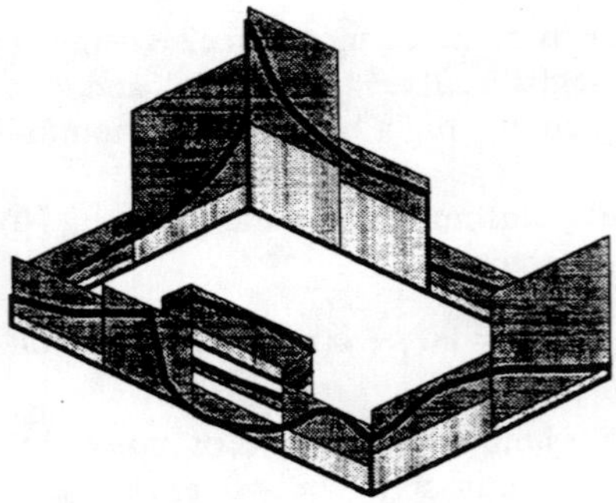

Figure 5. Rigorously Bounded Solution

The use of rigorous bounds for the answer to a continuum problem seems to be rare. Computational scientists tend to use double precision and trust that it represents the true answer except for the last few decimals of a 15-digit answer. This is seldom a valid approach, since discretization error dominates most problems. Once we realized there was no point to requiring 10^{-15} error in the solution with 1% error in the discretization, we were able to make tremendous improvements to our run times. We are currently running graphics rendering problems that would take over a thousand times as long using our old paradigm. Stating our goals clearly caused us to realize that much of our effort was misplaced. A similar approach could well be used for the federal Grand Challenges.

7. TRANSLATING GC GOALS TO HARDWARE DESIGN GOALS

Hardware designers are faced with an ill-defined problem: How does one allocate hardware costs to maximize performance on a Grand Challenge? The naïve approach of "Make every component as high performance (which usually means 'fast' or 'large') as possible" does not work because cost cannot be ignored. Unfortunately, the "Teraflops" goal has sent the message to designers that nothing matters but floating point arithmetic speed. Thus, designers are implicitly guided to provide I/O, memory speed, memory size, ease of use, and MTBF only to the extent that they effect the nominal flop/s rate. This has had a disastrous effect on the suitability of many designs for Grand Challenge applications. Every engineering goal must have subgoals; however, some of our subgoals seem to be the wrong ones in that they lead us farther from, not closer to, the ultimate goal.

Some specifics: A sustained teraflop/s implies a memory size of roughly 1 tera*word* (not tera*byte*), which at 1994 personal computer SIMM prices costs from $250M to $1000M. The processors capable of a net theoretical performance of 1 teraflop/s, in contrast, cost under $5M using currently-available RISC chips. Why, then, is the flop/s performance still regarded as the design challenge? It is the least of our worries.

Balancing memory bandwidth seems to lead to several pitfalls: belief in caches as a complete solution, and reliance on benchmarks that involve unrealistic levels of reuse of data elements (such as matrix multiply). The Level 3 BLAS are characterized by order n^3 operations on order n^2 quantities. Such operations are beloved of marketing departments because they produce high flop/s numbers for advertising claims, but represent a vanishingly small part of Grand Challenge workloads. A better design rule would be to test all computer operations on order n algorithm constructs. To do n multiplies as a memory-to-memory operations in 64-bit precision requires moving $24n$ bytes to or from main memory. Hence, a teraflop/s computer should have a nominal total memory bandwidth of 24 terabytes/s, a daunting figure in 1994. Uncached memory bandwidth has a strong correlation with computer hardware cost. There is no free lunch. In 1994, I estimate the cost of memory bandwidth in a balanced system to be $40 per megabyte/s. The bandwidth for a "sustained teraflop/s" therefore costs about $100M if scaling is linear (optimistic scaling, but realistic for distributed memory systems that rely on explicit message passing).

SUMMARY

We have used the term "Grand Challenge" to organize our HPCC efforts and justify support for large-scale computational research. The goal of "a sustained teraflop per second" is the hardware challenge often mentioned in the same breath as "Grand Challenge." These goals may not lie in the same direction. To the extent that we let the measure of operations per second be an end in itself, we are distracted from the real goal of solving physical problems by computer. For some specific examples, the goals may even be in opposite directions; we can achieve higher nominal flop/s rates only by using less sophisticated algorithms that delay the solution.

If we define all our performance measures in terms of answer goals, these problems disappear. We can compare parallel computers with vector computers with serial computers running all different algorithms without questions of "fairness." With the improved definition, hardware designers can produce computers better suited to our needs, and we can use the systems in a way far better suited to solving the Challenges.

REFERENCES

1. D. Bailey et al., "The NAS Parallel Benchmarks," *Report RNR-91-002*, NASA/Ames Research Center, January 1991.

2. J. Gustafson, "The Consequences of Fixed Time Performance Measurement," *Proceedings of the 25th HICSS Conference*, Vol. III, IEEE Press, 1992.

3. W. Pardee, "Representation of User Needs in Grand Challenge Computation," *Special Report by Pardee Quality Methods* (805) 493-2610 for Ames Laboratory, 1993.

4. D. Snelling, "A Philosophical Perspective on Performance Measurement," *Computer Benchmarks*, J. Dongarra and W. Gentzsch, editors, North Holland, Amsterdam, 1993, pp. 97–103.

5. X.-H. Sun and J. Gustafson, "Toward a Better Parallel Performance Metric," *Proceedings of DMCC6*, ACM, 1991.

6. F. Weingarten, "HPCC Research Questioned," *Communications of the ACM*, Vol. 36, No. 11, November 1993, pp. 27–29.

Toward Teraflop Computing
and New Grand
Challenge Applications

ISBN-1-56072-247-9

PARALLEL EXECUTION OF FINE-GRAINED, IRREGULAR DAGs

Frederic T. Chong * Shamik D. Sharma † Eric A. Brewer ‡
Joel Saltz §

Massachusetts Institute of Technology
University of Maryland

1 INTRODUCTION

Our goal is to execute fine-grained, irregular directed acyclic graphs (DAGs) efficiently on general-purpose, distributed-memory multiprocessors. We explore a range of runtime methods, some of which involve *runtime preprocessing*, an approach shown to be effective with iterative computations [SMC91]. We test our methods on an important real-world application, sparse-matrix triangular solves. In order to maintain generality, we do not use matrix-specific optimizations, yet we achieve unprecedented performance.

Our methods depend heavily upon active messages [E+92] and are closely related to the dataflow paradigm [ACM88]. Active messages greatly reduce overhead by providing user-level communications. We also take full advantage of active message handlers to decrease synchronization and data-copying costs. These mechanisms allow us to take a data-driven approach with fine-grained synchronization. This approach, coupled with reasonable hardware support, facilitates much of our speedups.

*Fred Chong (ftchong@ai.mit.edu) is supported in part by an Office of Naval Research Graduate Fellowship and ARPA contract N00014-91-J-1698

†Shamik Sharma (shamik@cs.umd.edu) is supported in part by EPRI (RP3103-06), ARPA (NAG-1-1485), ONR (SC292-1-22913), and NSF (ASC 9213821).

‡Eric Brewer (brewer@lcs.mit.edu) is supported in part by the National Science Foundation, grant CCR-8716884; by ARPA, contract N00014-91-J-1698; by an equipment grant from Digital Equipment Corporation; and by grants from AT&T and IBM.

§Joel Saltz (saltz@cs.umd.edu) is supported in part by EPRI (RP3103-06), ARPA (NAG-1-1485), ONR (SC292-1-22913), and NSF (ASC 9213821).

```
do i = 1, n
  x(i) = b(i)
  do j = low(i), high(i)
    x(i) = x(i) - t(j)*x(column(j))
  end do
end do
```

Figure 1: An example of a sparse triangular solve

Surprisingly, there have been few studies of irregular, fine-grained DAGs in the dataflow community. Rubin [Rub92] has studied regular, fine-grained DAGs arising from a conjugate gradient problem. While Rubin performed his study on the Monsoon dataflow machine, Yeung and Agarwal [YA93] have studied the same problem on Alewife, a shared-memory, SPARC-based multiprocessor.

Chakrabarti and Yelick [CY93] have studied the Gröebner-basis problem, which results in an irregular DAG. However, this computation is not as fine-grained as the applications we examine. The Gröebner study used consumer-driven techniques, using multithreading to hide the latency of fetching data. Since our application performance can be critical-path bound, we take a data-driven approach instead.

The remainder of the paper is organized as follows: In Section 2, we will describe sparse triangular solves and why they are important. In Section 3, we will describe our experimental platform. Section 4 contains the bulk of our experimental results, as well as describing the runtime methods used in the experiments. Section 5 discusses the costs and benefits of run-time preprocessing. Section 6 describes why the network should be frequently polled. Section 7 presents a detailed breakdown of our application overheads. Given these overheads, we extrapolate the benefits of architectural support for lower-overhead communication in Section 8. We then present our concluding remarks.

2 SPARSE TRIANGULAR SOLVES

For this study, we selected sparse-matrix triangular solve as the source of our fine-grained, irregular DAGs. While parallel computation has generally focused on the easy problems of dense matrix computation, sparse matrices represent a much larger class of scientific computation. Sparse systems arise from simulations of integrated circuits, electric fields, physical structures, power grids, and just about any other real-world system.

Sparse triangular solves involve finding a vector $\vec{x}$ in an equation of the form ($\mathbf{T}\vec{x} = \vec{b}$), where $\mathbf{T}$ is either an upper or lower triangular matrix and $\vec{b}$ is a vector of values. The code for such a computation is given in Figure 1. Figure 2 illustrates the DAG formed by a sparse, lower-triangular matrix. Note that the dependencies

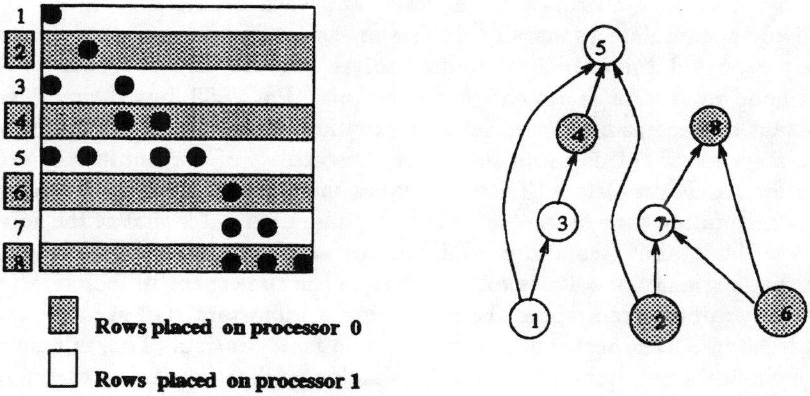

Figure 2: A lower triangular matrix (left) and the resulting forward subsitution DAG (right). The filled circles on the left represent nonzeros in the matrix. The nodes of the DAG correspond to rows of the matrix.

can be quite irregular. Additionally, each arc in the DAG represents only one multiply-accumulate operation. This extremely fine-grain computation, coupled irregular dependencies, makes sparse triangular solves a challenging benchmark for the runtime strategies we will support.

Sparse triangular solves are important in solving linear systems of equations of the form $\mathbf{A}\vec{x} = \vec{b}$, where $\vec{x}$ is a vector of unknowns and $\vec{b}$ is a vector of values. There are various techniques for solving such systems of equations. In direct methods, this system is *completely* factored into $\mathbf{LU}\vec{x} = \vec{b}$ where $\mathbf{L}$ is a lower-triangular matrix and $\mathbf{U}$ is an upper-triangular matrix. The system can then be solved through a straightfoward forward substitution ($\mathbf{L}\vec{y} = \vec{b}$) and a backward substitution ($\mathbf{U}\vec{x} = \vec{y}$). In preconditioned iterative methods, the matrix $\mathbf{A}$ is *incompletely* factored into lower and upper triangular matrices $\mathbf{L}$ and $\mathbf{U}$, which are then used in iterative triangular solves to obtain a solution for $\vec{x}$.

Sparsity patterns of the factored triangular matrices used in direct methods are very different from the incompletely factored matrices. The completely factored matrices have substantially greater fill-in than the incomplete factors.

Our experimental results are based on incompletely factored matrices. We perform parallelization at row-granularity (i.e all computation pertaining to a row is assigned to a single processor). This is a very fine granularity level, with only a few floating point operations per row. With completely factored matrices, we find that even at this level of granularity, parallelism is limited. This is because fill-in during factorization causes the sparsity patterns of completely factored matrices to be very different from those of incompletely factored matrices.

Efficient parallel implementation of triangular solves has been a difficult problem. This problem is due to the extremely small grain of the computation. Each row depends only on a few other rows, and each dependency involves a single multiply-accumulate (generally double-precision floating point). Speedups are rarely reported for sparse triangular solves. Heath and Raghavan [HR93] report good results for factorization on the Intel iPSC/860, but their solves exhibit constant or decreasing performance as the number of processors increases. They obtain speedups of no more than 3 or 4 regardless of the number of processors, even for banded matrices. They downplay the importance of the solve by noting that the running time of the factorization phase dominates that of the solve phase. Lucas, Blank, and Tiemann [LBT87] report similar results. While the time spent in a single triangular solve is much less than the time spent in factorization, there are many applications where the solve time is important. Often there are tens to hundreds of solves performed using a single factorization. This is true not only for preconditioned iterative methods, also for applications using direct methods, where the same factorization of **A** may be used to solve for different right hand side vectors $\vec{b}$. For example, the time spent performing solves is equal to or double that of the time spent factoring in the sequential execution of the ETMSP power grid code [ETM93].

We would like to note that in applications where the solve is repeated several times, it may be more efficient to invert the triangular matrix, converting the solve into an easily parallelizable matrix vector multiplication [AS92]. It is possible to eliminate fill-in during the inversion [PA92]. We have not investigated this technique in this paper.

3 EXPERIMENTAL PLATFORM

In this section, we describe the multiprocessor hardware and communications software that we use in our experiments.

3.1 CM-5

We perform our experiments on the CM-5 [Thi93a]. Each node of the CM-5 has a 33 MHz SPARC processor as well as four vector units. The CM-5 has a fat-tree-based network [L^+92] which provides fairly uniform communications delays and sustainable bandwidth. It also has a control network for global operations. To keep our study architecturally general, we do not use the vector units, nor do we use the control network.

3.2 Strata

For efficient communication and accurate timing, we made extensive use of the Strata communications library [BB94]. Strata is a CMMD-compatible [Thi93b]

[0]We estimated speedups assuming a sequential solve speed similar to that of uncached DAXPY on a single iPSC/860 node [Moy91].

package with high-performance communication and extensive support for timing and debugging. Section 6 discusses the impact of using Strata's communication primitives.

The standard CMMD timers on the CM-5 require kernel calls for each timing event, which cost hundreds of cycles. Strata, however, provides user-level access to the cycle counter on the network interface of every CM-5 node. The overhead for timing with the cycle counter is about 18 cycles: Strata subtracts out the overhead to achieve interval timing with single-cycle resolution. Although we can accurately time a single interval, timing many intervals inflates the execution time and may affect the ordering of interprocessor events. Given the fine-grain nature of the application, adding 18 cycles per timing can be substantial. In cases where this inflation was significant, we instead used the mean difference between code with and without the property of interest. Section 7 covers this technique in more detail.

In general, we timed events that lasted at most one-tenth of the 16.6 milliseconds between timer interrupts. This ensures that the cycle counts are rarely affected by the interrupts, time-slicing, or other processes. [BK94] covers CM-5 timing methodology in more detail.

4 RUNTIME METHODS

We adopt a data-driven approach to DAG computation. Active messages provide an efficient mechanism to communicate the data and synchronize the computation. At any given time, several tasks in the DAG may be ready to execute. The next task may be selected dynamically at compute-time. However, we may also adopt preprocessed schemes, commonly known as *inspector-executor* strategies [SMC91].

A preprocessing step (called an inspector) is used to optimize the execution of the actual computation step (called the executor). The runtime cost of the one-time preprocessing step is amortized over all executions of the executor. Depending on how many times the executor step is carried out, preprocessing of varying complexity and quality can be carried out. We have examined various preprocessing schemes and demonstrate the performance impact of each on sparse triangular solves.

As with any computation, parallelizing a DAG involves determining a "good" distribution of data and computation across processors - a good distribution being one that minimizes communication and maximizes parallelism. Unlike computations without dependencies, parallelizing a DAG also involves determining a computational ordering of the tasks allocated to each processor. Furthermore, each computation must be scheduled to execute only when all incoming dependencies have been satisfied. This requires the specification of suitable synchronization points in the computation. We call the computational structure resulting from distribution, ordering, and synchronization of tasks a *computational schedule*. Determining a computational schedule requires runtime preprocessing, wherein the dependencies are examined before the actual execution of the DAG. We have examined different preprocessing schemes and show the performance impacts of each on our application.

4.1 Task Distribution

For task distribution, we have considered three schemes - block distribution, cyclic distribution and Dominant Sequence Clustering (DSC) [GY92]. We considered block and cyclic distributions of nodes across processors because of their simplicity. While these distributions do not optimize either communication or load balance, their computational preprocessing costs are neglibile. The performance of these regular distributions provides us with a lower bound against which we can compare the performance of other distributions. At the opposite end of the spectrum there are computation-intensive task clustering schemes which look at the entire DAG in order to minimize the critical path length of the DAG [Sar89] [Yan93]. For example, Dominant Sequence Clustering, obtains an allocation by incrementally reducing the critical path length through successive clustering steps. Comparisons show that DSC outperforms most other static-task allocation scheme in both processing time and quality of computation schedules. DSC was intended for statically clustering and scheduling static task graphs at runtime, and is computationally very expensive. We used DSC in our as a runtime preprocessing step in order to determine the performance gains of using a sophisticated, albeit costly, clustering scheme.

4.2 Ordering

Once nodes of the DAG have been distributed across processors, we then need to determine an order in which local elements will be computed. Not all orderings are valid: node B cannot be scheduled before node A if there is a dependence from node A to node B. Determining an optimal ordering is an NP-complete problem. Nonetheless, various heuristics can be applied to obtain schedules of varying quality.

One way to achieve a good ordering without any preprocessing cost is to employ a dynamic data-driven scheme in which each incoming message triggers the appropriate computation. On the CM-5, this can be done via active message handlers. For example, in triangular solves, the computation at each node represents an accumulation. The final incoming data element triggers another active message which sends the computed data element to all other nodes that need the result. The data driven scheme automatically ensures that all dependencies are respected.

Instead of adopting a data-driven method, we can obtain an ordering via preprocessing. For example, global level scheduling, as in [Sal90], partitions the nodes of the DAG into *levels* $L_1 \dots L_n$, such that the nodes in level L_i depend only on nodes in $L_1 \dots L_{i-1}$. Each processor orders its local nodes based on their levels. The resulting schedule is called a *level schedule*. Partitioning the nodes into levels involves a topological sort over the global DAG.

The topological sort, needed to obtain a global level scheduling, has the same fine-grained irregular computational characteristics as a triangular solve. Consequently, the runtime methods we describe for the triangular solve can also be applied to parallelize the topological sort. Currently, however, we perform level scheduling sequentially.

While level scheduling is a reasonable heuristic, it does not try to schedule rows in an order that can overlap computation with communication. For example, the PYRROS package [Yan93], which generates the DSC clusters, also provides a task ordering based on the Ready Critical Path heuristic. This heuristic tries to schedule those tasks on the critical path first so that dependent nodes can be executed earlier. This schedule is much more costly to compute than level scheduling, but given a DSC partition, it can be expected to provide a good ordering.

We have also tried combining dynamic data-driven with prescheduled task distributions. In this hybrid scheme, we use a precomputed DSC mapping and schedule of tasks to processors, but incoming data elements can activate any ready task if the next DSC-scheduled row is not ready.

Note that DSC runtime approaches imply both a task distribution and a schedule.

4.3 Presence Counters

Each node of a DAG must wait until all of the data along its incoming dependencies have arrived before performing its computation and forwarding the result along its outgoing dependencies. In order to ensure such synchronization, we use *presence counters* [ACM88]. A presence counter is used to count the number of items that have arrived. If the computation to be performed on incoming data elements is non-commutative, the presence counter must be placed at the beginning of each task to check for the arrival of all data before computation. On the other hand, if the computation is commutative (as in the accumulates of a triangular solve), the presence counter can be placed at the end of the task to detect completion and indicate forwardability. Checking the presence counter at the end of the computation enhances parallelism since useful computation can be carried out instead of idling while waiting for data. Presence counters are necessary even when tasks are prescheduled since data arriving from off-processor may suffer unbounded delays. This phenomenon is because most modern multiprocessor networks, including the CM-5, do not guarantee delivery within a well-defined amount of time.

Consequently, all of our implementations use presence counters. Most use one counter per matrix row, but the coarse-grain, level-scheduled version attempts to reduce overhead by keeping one counter for many rows. This savings, however, is at the cost of reduced parallelism, since every row sharing the same counter must wait for the presence counter, even if some of them are ready early. We have examined implementations, with both early and late presence checking. We will also precisely measure the cost of maintaining presence counters in Section 7.

4.4 Methods Tested

In this section, we describe several versions of sparse triangular solve implementations. Each of these versions is intended to demonstrate the effectiveness of particular aspects of the runtime support.

Dynamic blocked: This version uses a block distribution of rows based on original node numbers. This is a dynamic implementation without any prescheduled ordering of rows. The computation is ordered by a ready queue, resulting in an order similar to breadth-first traversal of the DAG.

Dynamic cyclic: This version is identical to the one above, except that it uses a cyclic distribution of tasks.

Fine-grained Level-scheduled cyclic: This version distributes rows by cyclicly and uses level-scheduling to order the tasks on each processor. It uses a presence-counter for each row. The check is done at the start to detect when all required data has arrived.

Coarse-grained Level-scheduled cyclic : Rows are distributed in a cyclic fashion. Rows are ordered using level-scheduling and all rows on a processor that belong to the same level are placed in a *group*. Each group of rows shares a presence counter. The presence counter is used to detect readiness. Incoming data is buffered until all data required for execution of the next group has arrived. This scheme is aimed at reducing the overhead of presence-counter checking, but suffers from reduced parallelism.

Prescheduled DSC strict: This is a dynamic implemantaion which uses a precomputed DSC distributon and ordering. The schedule is followed strictly. If a prescheduled row is not ready to be computed, we poll the network until the required data arrives.

Prescheduled DSC hybrid: The rows in this scheme are distibuted according to a DSC distribution. Howeever, this scheme does not follow the DSC ordering strictly. When the next row in the schedule is not ready, we allow other rows to computed if they are ready for execution.

4.5 Benchmarks

We chose four power grid matrices from the Harwell-Boeing [DGL92] benchmark set for our experiments. These sparse matrices come from the BCSPWR set, and represent parts of the Western US Power Network and the Eastern US Power Network. Our matrices were incompletely factored, with the sparsity pattern being identical to that of the original matrix.

In Table 1, we have tabulated the relevant characteristics of these matrices. As can be seen from the table, the matrices are symmetric, very sparse and relatively small. *Max Speedup* is an upper bound calculated by the number of rows divided by the critical path. *DSC Speedup* is the speedup (up to 128 processors) predicted

Table 1: The benchmark BCSPWR matrix set

	Rows	NonZeros	Max Speedup	DSC Speedup	Seq MFLOPS
bcspwr05	274	1033	49.2	10.5	1.9
bcspwr06	1454	3377	103.9	20.6	1.9
bcspwr07	1612	3718	115.1	21.9	1.8
bcspwr10	5300	13571	481.8	77.3	1.6

by the DSC scheduler, which uses an ideal graph model incorporating simple communication and computation costs on the CM5. Seq MFlops is the number of millions of double-precision floating point operations per second our optimized sequential implementation achieves on a single CM5 node.

4.6 Results

Figure 3 summarizes the performance of all of our approaches on each of our benchmarks. The times for one processor come from an optimized sequential code running on a single CM-5 SPARC node. For some of the slower schemes, this explains the rise in execution time from one processor to four processors.

The performance of the dynamic block and cyclic approaches are similar except for bcspwr10. The block distribution is worse in this case because the sparse triangular solve tends to proceed in a wavefront from the first row towards the last row. Our block distribution assigns rows in linear blocks. This distribution can sequentialize this wavefront. The level scheduling schemes provide similar or worse performance. The coarse-grained-level scheme provided little gain over the fine-grained version. As we shall see in Section 7, presence counter overhead is a relatively small fraction of total overhead.

In general, the prescheduled DSC-strict approach performs the best. Since our matrices are relatively small and possess limited parallelism, performance differences are most pronounced in the smaller numbers of processors where DSC can do a better job of optimizing the critical path. As the number of processors increases, DSC has a harder time distributing load without adding communication cost to critical paths. The exception is bcspwr10, our largest matrix, which does possess enough parallelism for all schemes to do fairly well. The fact that the DSC-hybrid approach does not perform as well as the strict approach suggests that very little time is spent waiting for the next scheduled row when another row could be worked on. The added overhead of the hybrid approach clearly negates any gain from decreased wait time.

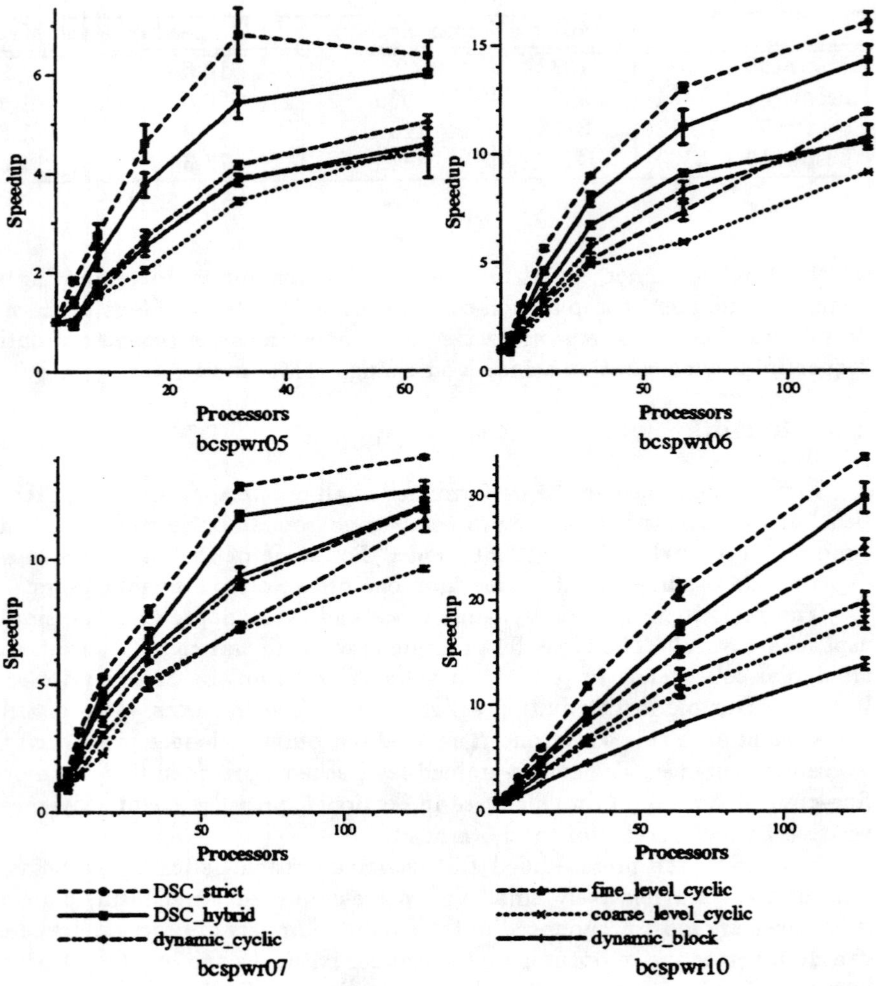

Figure 3: Performance curves for forward substitution using a range of runtime methods on four benchmark matrices. Note that the scales differ between graphs in order to provide maximal resolution between curves within each graph.

Overall, the speedups for both dynamic and preprocessed schemes are quite good for such small. fine-grained problems. Best absolute performance, given 128 processors, for matrices 05, 06, 07, and 10, is 13.1, 29.5, 25.2, and 54 MFLOPS, respectively.

5 PREPROCESSING COSTS

In this section, we compare the cost of preprocessing a DAG to the speedups gained by the resulting schedule and partition. We discover that it is very difficult to make the cost of prescheduling worthwhile at our small computational grain and small problem sizes.

In examining the costs, we must consider both the time to compute the DAG distribution and execution schedule and the time to move the data from its initial distribution to the new distribution. In general, the redistribution of data can be considered a global permutation. Global permutations on the CM-5 can be performed at roughly 2.5 Mbytes per second per processing node [BK94]. The upper triangular bcspwr10 matrix, for example, has 5300 rows, each represented by approximately 24 bytes. There is also a symmetric lower triangular matrix which we must store separately. In the 8 processor case, this gives each node approximately 32 Kbytes to contribute to the permutation. This means that we can complete our permutation in about 13 ms.

Using DSC, bcspwr10 on 8 processors runs about 2.1 ms faster than the dynamic runtime using a cyclic distribution. Iterative methods can take from tens to thousands of iterations to converge. Assuming that we repeat our solve 100 to 1000 times, and multiplying by 2 for both forward and backward solve, we get a total savings of 420 to 4200 ms. Given the low cost of the global permutation, we can apply most of this time against our preprocessing algorithm.

DSC was intended for compile-time use and we only have a sequential implementation to measure. The running time of DSC on a SPARC 1+ (similar in power to a CM-5 SPARC node) on bcspwr10 is on the order of 20 seconds. Even assuming a parallel implementation with perfect speedup on 8 processors, the number of iterations required to make DSC worthwhile is likely to be on the high end.

Fortunately, some applications have a static non-zero structure through different factorizations. Although the values of the matrix we are solving may change, the structure stays the same and we can use the same schedule and data mapping. This may allow us to assume benefits for many thousands of iterations for the cost of one preprocessing computation.

Nonetheless, we conclude that we need even simpler prescheduling algorithms and may need to apply them to larger problems with larger grain size.

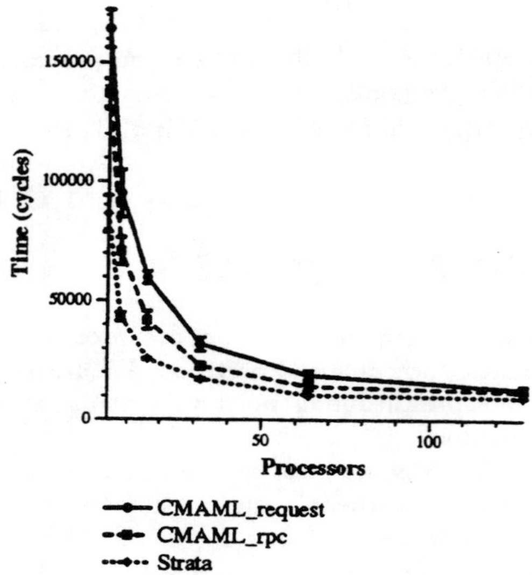

Figure 4: Performance curves for bcspwr07 with static DSC runtime using various send-with-polling routines. Cycle time is 30 ns.

6 NETWORK POLLING

Given the fine-grained nature of the application, we expected active-message overhead to be a substantial fraction of total overhead. Somewhat unexpected was the importance of network-polling policy.

Figure 4 plots the performance of bcspwr07 with the DSC-prescheduled-strict runtime using three different versions of active messages. The **CMAML_rpc** version uses **CMAML_rpc** for sending packets, which only polls if the outgoing packet is blocked. As a result, a processor can go for a long time without polling. This in turn causes other processors to stall until a poll occurs. The key problem is the relative independence of the ability to inject and the need to poll (to allow others to make progress).

We attempt to remedy this problem with our second version, which uses **CMAML_request** to inject packets. **CMAML_request** polls on every injection. Unfortunately, this routine was designed for request-reply protocols, not efficient use of the network. It only injects messages on one side of the network, halving network capacity for our applications. Additionally, both sides of the network are polled, but one side will always be empty. The resulting performance is worse than that of **CMAML_rpc**.

The Strata send routine, however, was designed for efficient use of the network. This version polls on every injection and also uses both the left and right networks, which increases both throughput and network capacity. Strata also has slightly lower overheads than the CMAML versions. Strata reduces communications overhead in our application up to a factor of three relative to the CMAML_rpc version.

The change from CMAML to Strata increases *application* performance by 25 to 30 percent. The importance of polling and the resulting improvements are consistent with the results in [BK94]. Given the limited capacity of the network, it is critical to use both sides of the network, which provides twice as much buffering. Secondarily, it is critical to poll on every injection to avoid stalling other processors. Low-cost interrupts avoid the latter problem, but do not exist on the CM-5 and also would require additional overhead to ensure atomicity.

7 OVERHEADS

In this section, we isolate the overheads in the DSC-strict runtime implementation. With only two multiply-accumulates per dependency, our application is extremely fine grained. Not only does this make both computation and communication overheads highly significant, it also makes the code extremely difficult to measure. Even with lightweight cycle accesses to the cycle counter through Strata, we had to keep timing to a minimum in order to avoid altering the behavior of our codes. As a result, we used a series of incrementally varying codes to isolate relevant overheads.

7.1 Local Overheads

We first focused upon local overheads by comparing the performance of two versions of our parallel code on a single CM-5 SPARC node with that of our optimized sequential solver on the same node. One version of the parallel code contained presence counters and checks, and the other had them removed.

Figure 5 contains the results of these experiments for each of our benchmark matrices. The difference between the parallel code without presence counters and the sequential code constitutes the overhead of using row-based datastructures with local and non-local outgoing dependency information. The difference ranges from 5 to 20 percent of the sequential time, but we expect the actual impact to be on the low end of the range. This is because the higher percentages arise from the cache behavior of the larger matrices. However, when the actual application is run in parallel, the matrices will be distributed across multiple processors, greatly reducing their local working sets.

The difference between the parallel code without presence counters and the code with counters represents the cost of maintaining presence information. This cost is about 30 percent of the sequential time.

With these figures, we expect our total local overhead to be about 40 percent of our sequential time. Given that our application efficiencies range from 15 to 40 percent, we are left with substantial non-local overheads to examine.

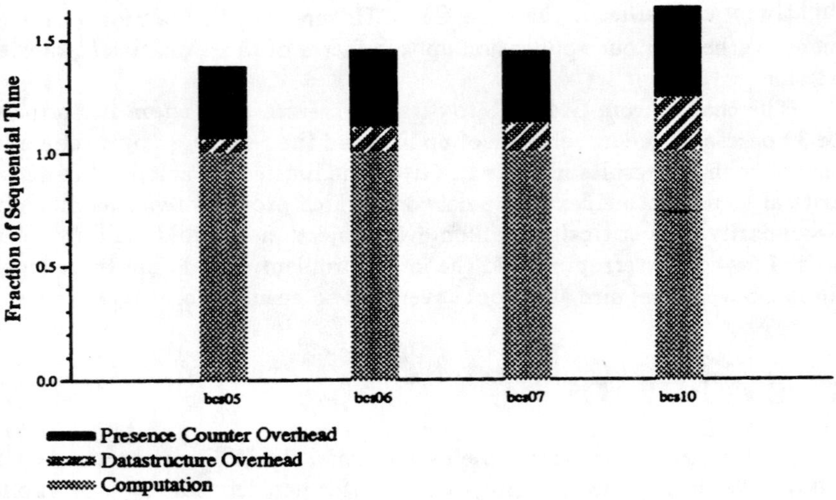

Figure 5: CM-5 single node performance of our parallel code is broken down for each of our benchmarks. Performance is given as a ratio to the single node performance of an optimized sequential implementation. "Computation" equals 1.0 by definition.

7.2 Non-Local Overheads

As we might expect, a portion of our efficiency is lost to idle time caused by critical paths in our schedule. However, we found that a major portion of our overheads comes from send and receive overhead.

Messages received by our application invoke a receive handler which adds the incoming data to the appropriate matrix row and increments two presence counters. Note that the data is multiplied with the appropriate coefficient on the sender's side before communication.

We measured the time for a message to be received and the resulting execution of its handler. We then subtracted the time to execute the handler to obtain the send overhead, which is 81 cycles. The Strata send routine that we use in our applications takes 66 cycles with an uncongested network. Adding our overheads together, this gives us a total *best-case* send and receive overhead of 147 cycles per message.

Now we can calculate the *minimum* overhead in our applications due to send and receive by counting the number of messages sent and received. Figure 6 gives our results for each of our applications. Note that the overhead is substantial and that the data is very consistent, with overheads increasing as matrix size increases. With overheads as nearly as high as 40 percent, it is clear that substantial performance improvements could result from architectures with decreased send and receive overhead.

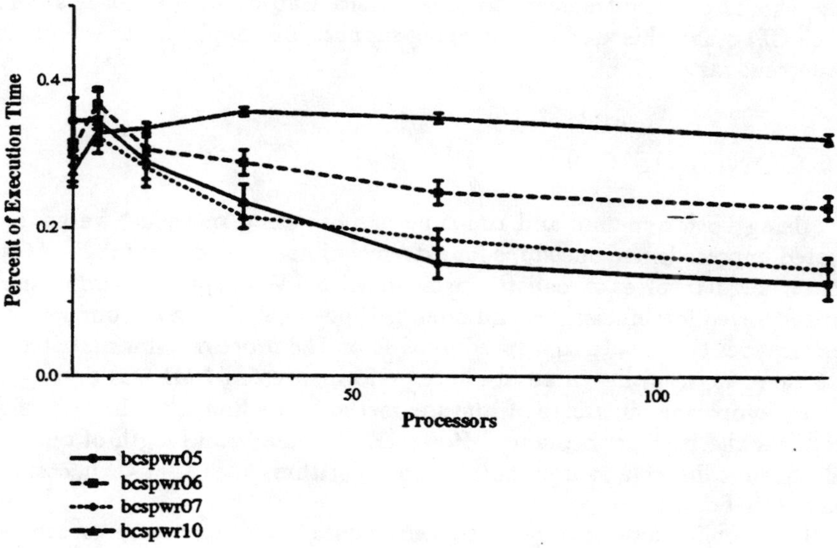

Figure 6: Communication overhead of the DSC-prescheduled-strict runtime.

8 LOWER-OVERHEAD ARCHITECTURES

Although the CM-5 and active messages deliver much lower overheads than earlier systems such as the iPSC/860, send and receive overhead still limits performance on fine-grained applications. Newer systems promise to deliver much lower overheads which directly translates to much higher performance on our applications. The T3D [T3D93], for example, can send a message in 4 cycles and receive a message with similar overhead. The Alewife [ACJ+91] shared-memory multiprocessor has a memory controller which reduces processor overhead to similar levels.

The StarT [Bec93] architecture has an on-processor message interface and can send 256 bits in one clock cycle and can receive 128 bits in one cycle. The J-Machine [D+92] first demonstrated such processor-interface integration, but was not implemented to support the floating point operations necessary scientific applications such as our benchmarks.

With low-overhead architectures, we can expect send and receive overhead of only 3 cycles per 24-byte message in our application. With careful polling policies or inexpensive message interrupts, our applications should not be limited by the capacity of most modern networks. Therefore, a reduction in communication overhead should directly translate to performance improvements in our applications. If the CM-5 had this kind of messaging support, our applications would run 15 to 40 percent faster.

9 CONCLUSION

Using both dynamic and run-time preprocessing methods, we have demonstrated unprecedented speedups for extremely fine-grained, irregular DAGs arising from triangular solves of realistic sparse matrices. While previous implementations have reported low efficiencies and bounded speedups of about 4, our solves exhibit performance that scales to a speedup of 34 on 128 processors for matrices as small as 5300 rows, resulting in an absolute performance of 54 MFLOPS.

In comparing our range of runtime methods, we find that the DSC algorithm produces the best performance. However, the small run length of our problems will make it difficult to implement such algorithms such that their costs are less than their benefits.

Our applications require a frequent message-polling policy to achieve good performance. This policy is not available from the standard CMMD library, but is provided by the Strata communications library.

Finally, our detailed study of overheads revealed that send and receive overheads are still a significant factor on the CM-5, constituting from 15 to 40 percent of our application times. We conclude that our applications would significantly benefit from architectural support for lower-overhead communications.

10 ACKNOWLEDGMENTS

We would like to thank Joel Phillips and Jacob White for discussions on iterative methods; Mustafa Uysal for providing factored matrices; Tao Yang, Apostolos Gerasoulis, and Jia Jiao for providing and supporting the PYRROS code which performs DSC; and Stuart Fiske and Debby Wallach for their comments on drafts of this paper. We are also grateful to AHPCRC Minnesota, for providing access to their CM-5.

References

[ACJ+91] Anant Agarwal, David Chaiken, Kirk Johnson, David Kranz, John Kubiatowicz, Kiyoshi Kurihara, Beng-Hong Lim, Gino Maa, and Dan Nussbaum. The MIT Alewife machine: a large-scale distributed-memory multiprocessor. MIT/LCS/TM 454, MIT, 545 Technology Sq., Cambridge, MA 02139, June 1991.

[ACM88] Arvind, David E. Culler, and Gino K. Maa. Assessing the benefits of fine-grained parallelism in dataflow programs. In *Supercomputing '88*. IEEE, 1988.

[AS92] Fernando Alvarado and Robert Schreiber. Optimal parallel solution of sparse triangular systems. *SIAM Journal of Scientific and Statistical Computation*, 1992. to appear.

[BB94] Eric A. Brewer and Robert D. Blumofe. Strata: A high-performance communications library. Technical Report (to appear). MIT Laboratory for Computer Science, January 1994.

[Bec93] Michael J. Beckerle. Overview of the START(*T) multithreaded computer. In *Proceedings of IEEE COMPCON*, February 1993.

[BK94] Eric A. Brewer and Bradley C. Kuszmaul. How to get good performance from the CM-5 data network. In *International Parallel Processing Symposium*, Cancun, Mexico, April 1994. To Appear.

[CY93] Soumen Chakrabarti and Katherine Yelick. Implementing an irregular application on a distributed memory architecture. In *Proceedings of the Fourth ACM SIGPLAN Symposium on Principles and Practices of Parallel Programming*, pages 169–178, San Diego, California, May 1993.

[D+92] William J. Dally et al. The message-driven processor: A multicomputer processing node with efficient mechanisms. *IEEE Micro*, pages 23–39, April 1992.

[DGL92] Ian S. Duff, Roger G. Grimes, and John G. Lewis. User's guide for the Harwell-Boeing sparse matrix collection. Technical Report TR/PA/92/86, CERFACS, 42 Ave G. Coriolis, 31057 Toulouse Cedex, France, October 1992.

[E+92] Thorsten von Eicken et al. Active messages: a mechanism for integrated communication and computation. In *Proceedings of the 19th Annual Symposium on Computer Architecture*, Queensland, Australia, May 1992.

[ETM93] Analysis of performance accelerator running ETMSP. Technical Report TR-102856, Performance Processors, Inc., Palo Alto, California 94301, October 1993. Research Project 8010-31.

[GY92] Apostolos Gerasoulis and Tao Yang. A comparison of clustering heuristics for scheduling directed acyclic graphs on multiprocessors. *Journal of Parallel and Distributed Computing*, 16:276–291, 1992.

[HR93] Michael T. Heath and Padma Raghavan. Distributed solution of sparse linear systems. Technical Report UIUCDCS-R-93-1793, Department of Computer Science, University of Illinois, Urbana, IL 61801, February 1993.

[L+92] Charles E. Leiserson et al. The network architecture of the connection machine CM-5. In *Symposium on Parallel Architectures and Algorithms*, pages 272–285, San Diego, California, June 1992. ACM.

[LBT87] Robert F. Lucas, Tom Blank, and Jerome J. Tiemann. A parallel solution method for large sparse systems of equations. *IEEE Transactions on Computer-Aided Design*, CAD-6(6):981–991, November 1987.

[Moy91] Steven A. Moyer. Performance of the iPSC/860 node architecture. Technical Report IPC-TR-91-007, Institute for Parallel Computation, School of Engineering and Applied Science, University of Virginia, Charlottesville, VA 22903, May 1991.

[PA92] Alex Pothen and Fernando Alvarado. A fast rerdering algorithm for parallel sparse triangular solution. *SIAM Journal of Scientific and Statistical Computation*, 13:645–653, 1992.

[Rub92] Norman Rubin. Data flow computing and the conjugate gradient method. Technical Report MCRC-TR-25, Motorola Cambridge Research Center, 1992.

[Sal90] Joel H. Saltz. Aggregation methods for solving sparse triangular systems on multiprocessors. *SIAM Journal of Scientific and Statistical Computing*, 11(1):123–144, Jan 1990.

[Sar89] Vivek Sarkar. *Partitioning and Scheduling Parallel Programs for Execution on Multiprocessors.* MIT Press, 1989.

[SMC91] Joel H. Saltz, Ravi Mirchandaney, and Kay Crowley. Run-time parallelization and scheduling of loops. *IEEE Transactions on Computers*, pages 603–611, 1991.

[T3D93] CRAY T3D system architecture overview. Technical report, Cray Research, Inc., 900 Lowater Road, Chippewa Falls, WI 54729, September 1993.

[Thi93a] Thinking Machines Corporation, Cambridge, MA. *CM-5 Technical Summary*, November 1993.

[Thi93b] Thinking Machines Corporation, Cambridge, MA. *CMMD Reference Manual (Version 3.0)*, May 1993.

[YA93] Donald Yeung and Anant Agarwal. Experience with fine-grain synchronization in MIMD machines for preconditioned conjugate gradient. In *Proceedings of the Fourth ACM SIGPLAN Symposium on Principles and Practices of Parallel Programming*, pages 187–197, San Diego, California, May 1993.

[Yan93] Tao Yang. Scheduling and code generation for parallel architectures. Technical Report DCS-TR-299, Rutgers, May 1993.

EXPERIMENTAL RESULTS FOR DATA SHARING ON HIGH PERFORMANCE MULTIPROCESSORS

Craig C. Douglas, Timothy G. Mattson, and Martin H. Schultz

Yale University, Department of Computer Science, New Haven, CT 06520-2158.

**Intel Corp., Supercomputer Systems Division, Beaverton, OR 97006.*

Abstract

In this paper, we compare communication times for a number of portable programming environments running on: ethernet connected workstation clusters, high speed switches for workstation clusters (IBM ALLNODE and the DEC GIGAswtich), the IBM SP-1 MMD computer, and the Paragon XP/S MIMD computer. These benchmarks include a simple, two node ping/pong test and a ring test in which 4 nodes simultaneously shift data around a ring.

From our results, it is clear that as communication patterns become more complex, the performance differences between portable parallel programming environments decreases substantially. Several conclusions were found for the high speed communication networks (i.e. meshes in the Paragon XP/S or crossbar switches in the SP-1, ALLNODE or GIGAswitch). First, the overhead associated with a portable programming environment (TCGMSG) on the Paragon XP/S is negligible compared to the native communication layer. Second, the communication performance of the Paragon XP/S is improving dramatically as new operating systems become available (SUNMOS) and as the message coprocessor is turned on (with OSF/1 R1.2). Finally, the crossbar switches used in the SP-1 and for clustering workstations significantly outperform LAN's and deliver performance that scales with the number of nodes.

1 INTRODUCTION

The effectiveness of a parallel computer is dependent on the rate at which data can be shared among processors. The higher the communication rate,

[1] Author to whom correspondence should be sent: tgm@ssd.intel.com

the more flexibility programmers have in designing their algorithms. This rate isn't the only consideration when programming parallel computers. It is also important to write code that is portable among all major parallel computer systems.

The portability problem has been solved with dozens of programming environments [1, 2] that support portable programming. With so many to choose from, however, selecting which portable programming to use can be a confusing task requiring the user to consider diverse issues such as ease of use, expressiveness, and efficiency. Since many of these criteria are subjective, the tendency is to consider the single objective issue of efficiency.

In an earlier paper [3] we compared the performance of P4 [4], PVM [5], Linda [6], TCGMSG [7] and POSYBL [8] on ethernet connected workstations. We considered two different benchmarks. The first benchmark measured conflict free communication between two nodes (a simple *ping/pong* program). The second benchmark considered a more complicated communication pattern in which data was simultaneously shifted about a ring of four nodes.

This paper describes the extension of these benchmarks to more sophisticated communication environments. In particular, we consider:

- Ethernet networks of higher performance workstations (RS/6000 560's rather than the SPARCstation 1 workstations used in the first project).
- Clusters of RS/6000 560 workstations connected by the ALLNODE switch under development by IBM.
- Clusters of DEC Alpha workstations connected by DEC's crossbar switch, the DEC GIGAswitch.
- The Paragon XP/S MIMD supercomputer.
- The IBM SP-1 MIMD supercomputer.

We also studied a portable communication library from IBM called EUIH. This message passing system runs on the SP-1 as well as local area networks (LAN's) of RS/6000 workstations.

For the Paragon XP/S, we studied three different operating systems to see how the performance is improving as these operating systems evolve. In addition we developed a version of the benchmarks coded in the native communication layer for the Paragon: NX/2. The NX/2 versions of the benchmarks were generated by direct translation of the TCGMSG program into an NX/2 program. This is important to note as well known optimizations were *not* carried out since that would violate the spirit of a portable benchmark.

The benchmarks for the SP-1 used the SP-1's native communication library, EUIH. The EUIH benchmark programs were also run without modification (not even relinking) on an ethernet connected cluster of IBM RS/6000 workstations. Unfortunately, the EUIH benchmark programs were different from our portable benchmark codes. We include the results from these benchmarks, however, since both the EUIH and our portable benchmarks generate identical message patterns. In the future, we will port our portable benchmarks to EUIH so we can maintain strict uniformity in our comparisons.

For our portable benchmarks, no optimization switches were set as the programs were constructed. In addition, we used every programming environment as provided. We used the default compiler flag settings when building the various public domain systems and made no attempt tune the systems for the actual networks used here. This last point extended to the benchmark program themselves as we made no attempt to optimize them for the communication networks under study. To do so would violate our goal of studying portability.

As with the previous study [3], we restricted ourselves to quantitative comparisons of these programming environments even though run time efficiency is not always the most important issue for the application programmer. In the course of a program's existence, issues such as ease of use, debugging, and software maintenance can be far more important than run time efficiency.

This paper begins by describing the computer systems used for the benchmarks. We then describe the results from the two node, ping pong benchmarks for each of the different communication networks. We then see what happens to the performance as contention is added to the benchmark by looking at the four node, ring test benchmarks.

2 COMMUNICATION NETWORKS

A number of different parallel and distributed computer systems were used to generate the results in this paper. The first set of results were taken from [3]. These calculations were carried out on four identical SUN SPARCstation 1 workstations on their own, isolated ethernet network. These workstations had identical, complete file systems and were not running a network file system. Each machine had 8 Mb of random access memory.

The next system consisted of a network of RS/6000 560 workstations with 128 Mb of random access memory on each workstation. These were connected by two different networks: ethernet and a crossbar switch under development by IBM called the ALLNODE switch. Crossbar switches are a major improvement over a LAN based technology such as ethernet. With a crossbar switch, the cluster's aggregate bandwidth increases as more nodes are added. Neither of the RS/6000 networks were isolated, though they were dedicated to our benchmarks during data collection.

The final cluster consisted of a network of DEC Alpha workstations connected by a DEC GIGAswitch. The GIGAswitch is a crossbar switch that supports up to 22 workstations with 100 megabits/second between any two workstations.

Workstation clusters are important sources of supercomputing cycles. The ultimate performance, however, requires a system that can scale up to large numbers of nodes. We therefore were interested in the performance of our benchmarks on a MIMD parallel supercomputer.

At this time, we have results for the Intel Paragon XP/S and the IBM SP-1 MIMD supercomputers. For the Intel Paragon XP/S, we have the following key traits:

- Systems are scalable with delivered systems ranging from 8 to over 1800 nodes.
- Each node contains two Intel i860 processors: one for computation and the other for communication.
- The nodes are connected by a 2D mesh with a peak communication rate between any two nodes of 200 megabytes/second.
- All facets of the system scale: I/O, computation, and the communication network.

Three different Paragon XP/S operating systems were considered in these tests. OSF/1 release 1.1 is the operating system currently shipped with the Paragon XP/S. On this version of the operating system, the message co-processor is not active. This means that communication interrupts the lone i860 processor and the latencies and bandwidths suffer.

The second Paragon XP/S operating system is OSF/1 release 1.2. This operating system utilizes the communication processor and the performance is much improved. This operating system will be shipped to Paragon customers later in 1994. Finally, we considered an operating system developed at the University of New Mexico and Sandia National Laboratory called SUNMOS [9]. It is less flexible than the OSF based operating systems and requires more effort to use, but it is very fast.

The key traits of the IBM SP-1 are:

- Systems are scalable with delivered systems ranging from 8 to 128 nodes.
- Each node contains a RISC System/6000 processor model 370.
- Each rack of the machine contains 16 nodes which are connected to all of the nodes in the rack.
- Each rack is connected to each of the other racks, up to 8 racks.
- Each node can page to disk, which can be local.
- Each node runs a standard version of AIX (IBM's version of UNIX).

Using the EUIH library for message passing, an executable can be made for a cluster of RISC System/6000's that uses either an ethernet or token ring. The same executable can be run on the SP-1 (i.e., no recompiling or relinking) and it will use the fast switch.

3 TWO NODE STUDIES

The experiments described in this section measured the communication time between two nodes. The timings were obtained by measuring the round trip communication time in a so-called *ping/pong* program: a message was sent from one node to the other and then back again.

In each case, every attempt was made to remove network interference effects. For the SPARCstation 1 benchmarks [3], this was easy since the network was isolated and under our control. For the other systems, it was more difficult to minimize network interference, but with patience we were able to collect reproducible results on quiet networks. In every case, we were interested in elapsed time, not CPU time, so the programs accessed the system clock by calling the standard UNIX function *gettimeofday()* for timings.

The average overhead associated with the calls to the timing function was computed and used as a correction factor to the recorded times. This overhead was computed within each test program and was always insignificant compared to the measured round-trip communication times.

Each programming environment was tested by considering 100 iterations for the round trip communication. Each iteration was separately timed and corrected for the overhead associated with calling the clock routine. Once these individual timings were collected, each program called the same statistics analysis routine. Detailed results are available for the SPARCstation 1 network [3]. For each of the other systems, all that is reported is the average bandwidth in megabytes per second. More detailed results will follow in a later technical report.

The key results from the SPARCstation 1 ping/pong benchmark are reproduced in Table 1. From these results, we see clear and consistent performance differences for messages ranging in size from 100 bytes to one megabyte. TCGMSG was significantly faster for all message sizes. P4, PVM and C–Linda (in that order) represent a middle range in performance. Finally, POSYBL was the slowest system and even failed for the largest message size.

There are many advantages to working on an isolated workstation network. However, unless one is able to physically reside at the location of the network, it is awkward to use an isolated network. Therefore, the rest of the two node tests were conducted on shared networks.

In Table 2 we show the two node average bandwidths for a number of different workstation clustering systems. Benchmark performance on the ethernet clusters are in line with our earlier results with the bandwidths found for EUIH essentially matching those from TCGMSG.

The ALLNODE system from IBM delivers in the ball park of a single megabyte/second. This level of performance is surprising in light of the fact that this system should deliver a peak bandwidth of more than 3 megabytes/second. The Linda system used in this study, however, ran on top of a version of TCP/IP

Table 1: Average data transfer rates for the two node studies: ethernet.

Bytes in	Message passing				Virtual shared memory	
message	P4	PVM[1]	PVM[2]	TCGMSG	C–Linda	POSYBL
100	.041	.035	.014	.055	.025	.013
400	.15	.12	.049	.16	.088	.045
1,000	.32	.22	.11	.34	.18	.10
4,000	.52	.45	.19	.63	.38	.26
10,000	.61	.47	.28	.85	.37	.31
40,000	.65	.54	.32	1.0	.47	.29
100,000	.65	.56	.34	.99	.51	.16
400,000	.66	.58	.36	1.0	.54	.094
1,000,000	.66	.57	.35	1.0	.54	—

All rates are in megabytes per second.
[1] Using vsnd/vrcv.
[2] Using snd/rcv.

Table 2: Average data transfer rates for the two node studies: clusters.

Bytes in	Ethernet[1]			ALLNODE[1]	Gigaswitch[2]
message	TCGMSG	Linda	EUIH	Linda	TCGMSG
800	.35	0.23	0.36	0.28	1.1
8,000	.87	0.48	0.80	0.60	4.6
80,000	1.1	0.70	1.1	0.91	9.9
800,000	1.1	0.73	1.1	0.97	11.4

All rates in megabytes per second.
[1] Using a dedicated network of RS/6000 560 workstations.
[2] Using a non-dedicated network of DEC alpha workstations.

developed at Yale University. TCP/IP on the IBM ALLNODE switch is nonoptimal and is undergoing additional tuning at Yale University. Furthermore, Scientific Computing Associates Inc. is optimizing Linda for the switch by using a low level communication layer below TCP/IP. This should provide much better performance and will be included in our future work.

Also in Table 2 we present results for TCGMSG on the DEC GIGAswitch. Given that the peak performance for this benchmark is 12.5 megabytes/second, the 11.4 megabyte/second result is impressive. The DEC GIGAswitch results only include TCGMSG, since at the time of this writing, none of the other programming environments were available on the GIGAswitch (though Linda should be available soon).

In Table 3, we present the ping/pong results for the two MIMD computers studied in this project. The SP-1 achieves performance within 75% of the 12

Table 3: Data transfer rates for two node studies: MIMD supercomputers.

Bytes in message	Paragon XP/S OSF R1.1 NX/2	Paragon XP/S OSF R1.2 NX/2	Paragon XP/S OSF R1.2 TCGMSG	Paragon XP/S SUNMOS NX/2	SP-1 AIX EUIH
800	6.4	4.5	4.2	8.8	5.2
8,000	12.3	18.1	17.9	51.0	7.3
80,000	14.3	25.8	25.6	128.5	8.6
800,000	12.3	27.4	27.2	153.3	8.7

All rates are in megabytes per second.

Megabyte/second peak bandwidth. Comparing to other crossbar switches, the SP-1 switch lags behind the DEC GIGAswitch for large messages but leads the GIGAswitch for small messages. For all message sizes, the SP-1 exceeds the bandwidths observed on the ALLNODE switch.

The performance seen for the the Paragon XP/S leads all other systems studied in this project. The OSF/1 results fell well short of the 200 megabyte/second peak performance. The SUNMOS figure of 153.3 megabytes/second is impressive, however, and is reasonably close to peak performance of 200 megabytes/second. The SUNMOS performance is even more impressive in light of the fact that the release of SUNMOS used in these tests did not utilize the communication co-processor. The next generation of SUNMOS will use the communication co-processor and should provide even better performance.

Another conclusion based on these results is that for TCGMSG, the costs of using a portable communication layer are negligible. This is apparent from the essentially identical performance for TCGMSG and NX/2 systems. This is not surprising since TCGMSG is a very light weight message passing layer on top of NX/2. Tests with PVM and p4 on the Paragon are in progress.

Two node, point-to-point communication tests are an overly simple way to compare programming environments. More complicated communication patterns found in actual applications are essential to make a fair and complete comparison.

4 FOUR NODE STUDIES

We expect communication contention to equalize the performance of the various systems. To test this hypothesis, we developed a benchmark that intentionally created a great deal of contention. This benchmark, called the *ring_test* program, used a four node logical ring and carried out the following steps:

- Start a program on each of the four nodes.

- Construct an array on each node.
- Pass the array from each node to its neighbor, i.e., the nodes shift the data around the ring.
- Repeat this for some number of shifts.

We varied the size of the messages and considered 100 shifts. We timed these shifts and report the net bandwidth for the process. We used the same timing routine as in the two node tests. Since multiple shifts were considered, the timing corrections were insignificant and were omitted.

The key results on the isolated SPARCstation 1 network from [3] are reproduced in Table 4. In this table, we give the average bandwidth (in megabytes per second) as a function of message size for each of the programming environments.

From Table 4 we see that TCGMSG is still the fastest of the systems tested. The ring tests do not maintain the performance differences observed in the two node tests. While the two node tests showed TCGMSG as being approximately 50% faster for the largest message sizes, the four node tests have TCGMSG only 20% faster. We suspect this effect follows from the fact that TCGMSG communication on a network is synchronous. The other programming environments support some low level overlap of the sends and receives, but TCGMSG must synchronize at each send/receive pair. This effect was not present in the two node tests since the ping/pong benchmark is inherently synchronous.

Since TCGMSG communication on a network is synchronous, TCGMSG required that the communication be split into two parts: half the nodes did a send/receive while the other half did a receive/send. This algorithm is referred to in the tables as *SPLIT*. The other programming environments include asynchronous communication, so we had the option of structuring the benchmarks to post all the sends and then all the receives. This is referred to in the tables as *NO-SPLIT*. Both of these options were considered for P4 and PVM. C–Linda and POSYBL hide low level message passing details from the user so we decided to only investigate the NO-SPLIT algorithm for those environments.

PVM's performance dropped once the message sizes became large. This result does not appear when the tests are run on workstations with larger memories, so we suspect the effect is due to paging on the small memory (8 Mbyte) SPARCstation 1 workstations used in these tests.

The p4 results were surprisingly poor for small message sizes. It was suggested to us [10] that this was due to the overhead of establishing the TCP sockets when communication first takes place between any two nodes. Our assumption was that 100 shifts around the ring would offset any startup effects which is why our original tests did not consider this effect. To test this setup-time hypothesis, we modified the p4 NO-SPLIT program so the `ring()` function was called once prior to the timed call to `ring()`. This established the TCP sockets between nodes prior to the collection of timing data. The results of the *two-ring* vs. the original *one-ring* benchmarks are given in Table 5. Notice that

Table 4: Data transfer rates for the four node studies

Bytes in message	Message passing			Virtual shared memory	
	P4[1]	PVM[2]	TCGMSG[2]	C-Linda[1]	POSYBL[1]
800	0.034	0.52	0.50	0.38	0.10
8,000	0.25	0.75	1.12	0.69	0.32
80,000	0.85	0.78	1.06	0.92	0.37
800,000	0.83	0.25	1.05	0.88	—

All rates are in megabytes per second.
[1] NO-SPLIT (i.e. all sends followed by all receives).
[2] SPLIT (PVM used vsnd/vrcv).

Table 5: Average four node bandwidth: p4 overhead estimate.

Bytes in message	p4[1] one-ring	p4[1] two-ring
800	0.02	0.65
8,000	0.15	1.02
80,000	0.66	1.00
800,000	1.02	1.00

All rates in megabytes per second.
[1] Using a dedicated network of RS/6000 560 workstations.

the *two-ring* results are on par with the TCGMSG ring test benchmarks which confirms the startup cost explanation for p4's low performance for small messages. Future versions of the ring test benchmarks will use the *two-ring* version of the program for all of the programming environments.

In Table 6 we show results for TCGMSG, Linda and EUIH on three different networks; RS/6000 560 workstations connected by ethernet, the same workstations connected by the IBM ALLNODE switch, and the DEC Alpha workstations connected by the GIGAswitch. Beginning with the ethernet results, we note that Linda's performance on this network is on par with that of TCGMSG and EUIH. In [3] we argued that buffer management within each programming environment was responsible for performance differences. Therefore, we believe that the higher performance of the RS/6000 workstation relative to the SPARCstation 1 has decreased buffer-management overhead to the point where the various systems deliver similar performance.

With the crossbar switches, the communication performance did indeed scale as the number of nodes increased. The ALLNODE results scaled by a factor of almost 4 which is exactly what we expected since Linda supports fully asynchronous communication in the ring test. TCGMSG on the GIGAswitch can at

Table 6: Average data transfer rates for the four node studies: Clusters.

Bytes in	Ethernet[1]			ALLNODE[1]	Gigaswitch[2]
message	TCGMSG	Linda	EUIH	Linda	TCGMSG
800	0.65	0.62	0.24	0.24	2.00
8,000	1.01	0.82	0.68	2.13	5.78
80,000	0.60	1.00	0.60	3.62	17.2
800,000	1.04	1.02	1.00	3.62	21.4

All rates in megabytes per second.

[1] Using a dedicated network of RS/6000 560 workstations.

[2] Using a non-dedicated network of DEC alpha workstations.

Table 7: Data transfer rates for 4 node studies: MIMD supercomputers.

Bytes in message	Paragon XP/S				SP-1
	OSF R1.1 NX/2	OSF R1.2 NX/2	OSF R1.2 TCGMSG	SUNMOS NX/2	AIX EUIH
800	8.0	8.4	7.9	15.6	11.4
8,000	11.8	14.4	14.3	42.2	14.7
80,000	14.4	42.6	42.2	50.8	13.6
800,000	12.5	42.8	42.7	55.0	14.5

All rates are in megabytes per second for a 4 node square mesh.

most yield a factor of two performance gain since the TCGMSG version of the ring test occurs in two paired transfers. Comparing the two node, GIGAswitch results to the four node benchmark shows the expected factor of two.

In Table 7, we consider the ring_test benchmarks on the two MIMD supercomputers: the Intel Paragon XP/S and the IBM SP-1. First, compare the NX/2 and TCGMSG benchmarks for the Paragon. The NX/2 program was generated from the TCGMSG program by a direct one to one mapping of the TCGMSG communication routines onto the analogous NX/2 routines. Hence, while strictly not portable, the NX/2 benchmark does use a portable algorithm. Notice that TCGMSG and the NX/2 results are essentially the same. Once again, we see that the cost of using a portable communication layer is minimal.

Also in Table 7, the bandwidths for the OSF R1.2 operating system are roughly two times the two node bandwidths from Table 3. This is the expected scaling since the ring communication takes place in terms of two pairs of communications. The OSF R1.1 and SUNMOS results do not scale as well for reasons that are not entirely clear at this point. We suspect that these systems are suffering from additional communication contention as the messages wrap around the ring. By using the fact that the Paragon uses x-y routing for its messages, we could eliminate contention by using a diagonal arrangement of nodes on the Paragon. We did not do this, however, since this would have violated our goal of portable benchmarks. Finally, notice that the R1.2 version of OSF/1 with the active message coprocessor is a substantial improvement over the R1.1 version of OSF/1 and actually approaches the performance of SUNMOS for this test.

The SP-1 bandwidths are consistent across all message sizes. They provide considerably better performance than the DEC GIGAswitch for small message sizes, but somewhat slower performance for large messages. The performance scales well in moving from the two node to the four node benchmarks, however, a full scaling analysis will have to wait for the portable benchmarks. This will be reported in a future paper.

5 CONCLUSIONS

In this paper, we have discussed two simple benchmarks that measure the communication performance of a number of programming environments running on a number of higher performance communication networks:

- Ethernet networks of IBM RS/6000 560 workstations.
- Clusters of RS/6000 560 workstations connected by the prototype cross bar switch from IBM, the ALLNODE switch.
- Clusters of DEC Alpha workstations connected by DEC's crossbar switch, the DEC GIGAswitch.
- The Paragon XP/S MIMD supercomputer.
- The IBM SP-1 MIMD supercomputer.

This work is an extension of our earlier research [3] where we considered these same benchmarks on an isolated ethernet network of SPARCstation 1 workstations.

Several conclusions can be drawn from this paper.

- Buffer management plays an important role in overall communication performance. The impact of buffer management, however, decreases on higher performance workstations.
- As communication patterns become more complex, the performance differences between these programming environments decrease substantially.
- The cost of using a portable communication layer (TCGMSG) on the Intel Paragon XP/S is negligible for these benchmarks.
- The performance of crossbar switches used for clustering workstations and within the SP-1 is impressive and scales as expected with the number of nodes.

- The Paragon XP/S performance is rapidly improving as operating systems such as OSF/1 R1.2 and SUNMOS become available.

This project is a continuing effort. The next step will be to consider the other portable programming environments on the crossbar switches, the SP-1, and the Paragon XP/S. These comparisons carried out on the MIMD computers (the SP-1 and the Paragon XP/S) should prove particularly interesting. With the low latency and high bandwidth of these MIMD supercomputers, if differences do exist in the performance of portable parallel programming environments, the Paragon XP/S and SP-1 should expose them.

The authors gratefully acknowledge the generosity of San Diego Supercomputer Center for providing access to their DEC Alpha farm and DEC GIGAswitch. This work was supported in part by International Business Machines, Intel Corporation, and the Office of Naval Research, grant N00014-91-J-1576.

A number of registered trademarks appear in this paper. ALLNODE and RS/6000 are trademarks of International Business Machines. DEC, Alphas, and GIGAswitch are trademarks of Digital Electronics Corporation. SPARCstation 1 is a trademark of Sun Microsystems. Linda is a trademark of Scientific Computing Associates, Inc. Paragon XP/S and i860 are trademarks of Intel Corporation.

References

[1] L. Turcotte, "A Survey of Software Environments for Exploiting Networked Computing Resources," Tech Report MSM-EIRS-ERC-93-2, Mississippi State University,(1993).

[2] D. Y. Cheng, "A Survey of Parallel Programming Languages and Tools," NASA Ames Research Center Technical Report RND-93-005,(1993).

[3] C. C. Douglas, T.G. Mattson, and M.H. Schultz, "Parallel programming Systems for Workstations Clusters," Yale University Computer Science Department, Technical Report YALEU/DCS/TR-975, (1993).

[4] R. Butler and E. Lusk, "User's Guide to the p4 Programming System," Argonne National Laboratory technical report ANL-92/17, (1992).

[5] V. S. Sunderam, "PVM: A Framework for Parallel Distributed Computing", *Concurrency: Practice and Experience, Vol 2*, pages 315-339, (1990).

[6] N. Carriero and D. Gelernter, *How to Write Parallel Programs: A First Course.* (Cambridge: MIT Press, 1990).

[7] R. J. Harrison,"Portable Tools and Applications for Parallel Computers," *International Journal of Quantum Chemistry, Vol 40*, 847-863, (1991).

[8] G. Schoinas, "Issues on the implementation of Programming SYstem for distributed applications," University of Crete draft technical report, (1992).

[9] K. S. McCurley, "Intel NX compatibility under SUNMOS," Sandia National Laboratories Technical Report, SAND 93-2618, (1993).

[10] R. Butler and E. Lusk, Personal communication, (1993).

Toward Teraflop Computing
and New Grand
Challenge Applications

ISBN-1-56072-247-9

Solving Multiple Objective Linear Programs on the Intel Paragon

Hong Zhang * Malgorzata M. Wiecek †

Abstract

This paper presents a parallel algorithm for solving multiple objective linear programs. The algorithm is implemented on an Intel Paragon multiprocessor. Numerical results for large and extremely large problems are presented.

1 Introduction

Multiple objective linear programming is becoming more prevalent as we enter the information age. Nowadays, almost every important real world decision problem involves more than one objective. However, a multiple objective linear program (MOLP) often has a large number of solutions in the form of extreme efficient points (EEPs) and unbounded efficient edges [1], [4]. The process of finding all of them or even a subset of them is very space and time consuming. This growing importance and enormous computational expense of MOLPs, as well as the structure of the solution set and the availability of high performance computers, motivate to design an algorithm that is capable of solving very large size problems in a short time.

Based on ADBASE [4], [5], a well known sequential computer package, Matthews and Soltys initiated the work on the design of a parallel algorithm for solving MOLPs [2] [3]. Subsequent extensive research resulted in a parallel algorithm whose preliminary testings were carried out on an Intel iPSC/2 multiprocessor [7]. In this paper, we report further improvement of this algorithm, its implementation on an Intel Paragon machine and numerical results obtained for large MOLPs.

*Institute for Computer Applications in Science and Engineering, NASA Langley Research Center, Hampton, VA 23665. On leave from Department of Mathematical Sciences, Clemson University, Clemson, SC 29634, (`hongsu@math.clemson.edu`). Research was supported by the National Aeronautics and Space Administration under NASA Contract No. NAS1-19480.

†Department of Mathematical Sciences, Clemson University, Clemson, SC 29634, U.S.A. (`wmalgor@clemson.clemson.edu`). Research supported in part by the National Science Foundation under contract DMS-9308605.

2 Parallel algorithm

A parallel algorithm is designed based on the well established sequential package ADBASE that solves MOLPs formulated as follows:

$$max\{z = Cx \mid x \in S\}$$

where

$$S = \{x \geq 0 \mid A_{m_1}x \leq b_{m_1}, A_{m_2}x = b_{m_2}, A_{m_3}x \geq b_{m_3}\},$$

C is an $k \times n$ matrix, A_{m_i} are $m_i \times n$ matrices and b_{m_i} are $m_i \times 1$ vectors with nonnegative components, $i = 1, 2, 3$.

In general, generating all EEPs of an MOLP can be viewed as finding a subset of all extreme points associated with the feasible set S. Therefore, solving an MOLP is somehow similar to solving a linear program with multiple solutions. ADBASE consists of three main phases. In Phase 1, a single objective linear program (SOLP) related to the original MOLP is solved for an initial feasible extreme point of the MOLP. Phase 2 searches for an initial efficient extreme point (IEEP) of the problem, and Phase 3 includes generating all efficient extreme points and unbounded efficient edges. In Phase 3, all nonbasic variables of an IEEP are checked for feasibility and efficiency, which identifies all efficient extreme solutions adjacent to the initial one. The feasibility and efficiency test is continued at efficient extreme points subsequently found by performing simplex pivot operations between a current and adjacent efficient extreme point (this operation will be referred to as the *efficient pivot operation*). The bookkeeping includes storing EEPs that have been already found and their bases (referred to as *efficient bases*). The process goes on until all solutions are generated. Assigning the efficient solutions to nodes and efficient edges to arcs, one can construct a graph (referred to as the *EEP-graph*) along which the search can be performed.

A straightforward parallelization of ADBASE, proposed in [2], suffers from dependency upon an IEEP and severe job imbalance. The main idea of parallelization presented in [7] is based on performing Phase I and Phase II in parallel and keeping all processors busy as long as EEPs are being generated. The former is achieved by generating multiple EEPs so each of processors starts its search at a different point of the EEP-graph, and the latter by activating idle processors by the technique of recrashing [3]. As soon as a processor cannot perform any efficient pivot operation from its current EEP, it starts to examine the next EEP on its list by recrashing to this point in a minimum number of pivots. These strategies, incorporated into the basic parallelization, lead to the following parallel algorithm for solving MOLPs.

Parallel Algorithm for MOLPs:

- In parallel, do on each of processors:

  1. Formulate an SOLP from the given MOLP. Find an IEEP by solving this SOLP.

2. Search the subgraph along the nodes and edges that are generated by itself until no more unexamined basis is posted on its list. Whenever a new efficient basis is found, immediately send it to all other processors and check its own buffer for possible new bases sent by other processors.
3. Keep receiving messages from other processors. When a new basis is received, crash to and do efficient pivot operation on it. If the basis leads to a new efficient solution, start a new subgraph search from this newly found point, as described in Step 2.
4. Stop when all processors have finished subgraph search.

This algorithm was tested on an Intel iPSC/2 for some problems, as reported in [7]. The achieved speedups of the algorithm were collected and discussed. The two strategies greatly increased the parallel efficiency of the algorithm, and therefore the process of obtaining all efficient solutions for an MOLP was significantly accelerated on the parallel computer. However, the testing conducted was preliminary and had two major limitations. In Step 1 of the algorithm, all processors started their subgraph search at only two IEEPs, which generated redundant computations in the beginning of the search. Those two IEEPs were found using a combination of two subroutines provided by ADBASE. The other limitation was that the testing problems were too small for good performance evaluation, since in general, parallel algorithms are developed for solving computationally extensive problems.

The research presented in this paper is focused on eliminating the two restrictions mentioned above. Step 1 of the parallel algorithm has been modified in order to simultaneously generate multiple IEEPs using the lexicographic principle. ADBASE is capable of performing the lexicographic maximization process that is carried out in accordance with the recursively defined reduced feasible regions:

$$\begin{aligned} S_0 &= S \\ S_1 &= \{y : c^1 y = max[c^1 x \mid x \in S_0]\} \\ &\vdots \\ S_i &= \{y : c^i y = max[c^i x \mid x \in S_{i-1}]\} \\ &\vdots \\ S_k &= \{y : c^k y = max[c^k x \mid x \in S_{k-1}]\}, \end{aligned}$$

with

$$C = \begin{bmatrix} c^1 \\ \vdots \\ c^k \end{bmatrix}.$$

In particular, the process maximizes the objective functions in the order in which they are stored by rows in criterion matrix C. Obviously, a different maximization process can be obtained from a reordering of the objective functions, or equivalently, a reordering of rows in matrix C. There are $k!$ orderings in all, a number usually much larger than the number of processors available.

A short subroutine that permutes the rows of C has been added into ADBASE. Experiments on all orderings for MOLPs with k objective functions show that the orderings:

$$\begin{aligned} S_0 &= S \\ S_1 &= \{y : c^i y = max[c^i x \mid x \in S_0]\} \\ S_2 &= \{ \qquad \cdots \qquad \} \\ &\vdots \\ &, \end{aligned}$$

$i = 1, \cdots, k$, are guaranteed to generate k different IEEPs. That is, different sets S_1 in this process are guaranteed to produce different IEEPs. When the solution in S_1 is unique, changing the orderings of objective functions in subsequent sets S_i, $i = 2, \cdots, k$, makes no difference in IEEPs produced, which has occurred in the test.

3 Numerical results

The parallel algorithm described in Section 2 was implemented on the Intel Paragon multiprocessor at NASA Langley Research Center. Using ADBASE, testing problems were randomly generated by specifying the number of objective functions (k), number of structural variables (n), and number of constraints (m_1).

An interesting phenomenon observed is that the number of EEPs grows rapidly as $k + n + m_1$, sum of the parameters, increases. For example, the solution sets could grow by several thousand when the number of objective functions is incremented by one. Similar observations were reported in [6], where random problem generation was discussed for creating MOLP test problems. In general, an MOLP may have a huge number of solutions, which is beyond our capability of data processing or exceeds the machine memory capacity. In this situation, finding all efficient solutions is no longer practical and the goal of generating all EEPs could be questioned. However, in the presence of a large number of EEPs, the solution process of MOLPs goes further and involves maximizing a decision maker's overall utility function over the efficient set in order to obtain a (possibly unique) most preferred solution [1], [4]. Obviously, that solution will depend on the choice of the utility function and as such it will not be determined uniquely. Selection of the utility function is a difficult task usually performed by a decision maker (DM), who can make a better choice if more information about the efficient set is available. Therefore, ability to find a subset of the efficient set within a given time period is of great importance, as it may contribute to the DM's learning process about the multiple objective problem under consideration. Using that partial information, the DM can modify the utility function that will better represent his/her preferences.

In this paper, MOLPs that involve more than 5 thousand EEPs are classified as extremely large problems. Accordingly, for small and large MOLPs, the goal is to generate all EEPs as fast as possible; otherwise, to find as many solutions as possible within a given time period.

Table 1 shows the parallel execution times for p processors as well as for sequential ADBASE ($p = 1$) on 7 testing problems. The second column of this table specifies the number of efficient bases and EEPs. For example, problem #3 has 251 efficient bases and 234 EEPs, while problem #1 has 58 efficient bases and 58 EEPs. Parallel execution time is determined by slowest processor.

Table 1: Execution Time (Seconds)

Problem	No. of Solutions	$p = 1$	$p = 2$	$p = 4$	$p = 8$
#1	58	0.7724	0.4951	0.3573	0.3852
#2	129	1.9827	1.0944	0.6551	0.6988
#3	251bas 234ex	5.0659	2.7440	1.8469	1.0997
#4	424bas 402ex	13.4987	7.3755	5.1234	2.7138
#5	818	32.6500	17.0657	9.4557	6.1187
#6	1512bas 1473ex	89.7754	46.9689	25.3096	17.9618
#7	3119	146.1361	76.0051	43.0819	23.7395

For the same testing problems, Table 2 lists the speedup defined as

$$\frac{\text{execution time using 1 processor}}{\text{execution time using } p \text{ processors}},$$

and Figure 1 depicts the parallel efficiency:

$$\frac{\text{speedup on } p \text{ processors}}{p}.$$

In general, when an MOLP includes more solutions to be found, the chances of splitting the work between processors will increase, because there is less chance for more than one processor to be terminated at the same time and thus, to recrash to the same solution. This efficiency increase clearly can be seen from both Table 2 and Figure 1. In addition, as the number of solutions of MOLPs increases, the efficiency of the parallel algorithm goes up quickly to its optimum, as illustrated in Figure 1.

Table 2: Speedup

Problem	No. of Solutions	$p = 2$	$p = 4$	$p = 8$
#1	58	1.56	2.16	2.01
#2	129	1.81	3.03	2.84
#3	251bas 234ex	1.85	2.74	4.61
#4	424bas 402ex	1.83	2.63	4.97
#5	818	1.91	3.45	5.34
#6	1512bas 1473ex	1.91	3.55	5.00
#7	3119	1.92	3.39	6.16

Figure 1

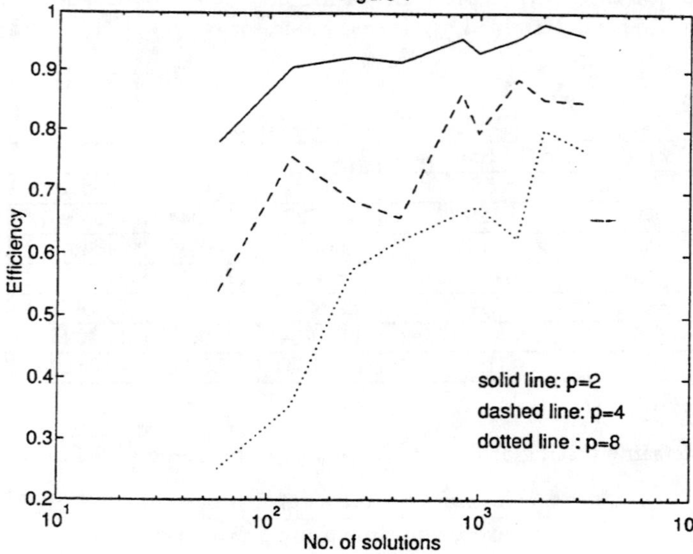

Table 3: Results for Extremely Large Problems

Problem (k, n, m_1)	No. of solutions found in 30 seconds $p=1$	$p=2$	$p=4$	$p=8$	$p=16$	$p=32$	Ratio
(16,100,48)	128	161	213	294	487	492	3.84
(16,102,48)	100	108	127	205	302	332	3.32
(20,110,40)	62	82	110	209	410	527	8.50
(32,110,30)	54	75	106	171	301	587	10.87
(29, 80,70)	30	80	110	178	316	583	19.43
(32,100,30)	24	40	83	195	333	631	26.29
(24,130,20)	20	31	32	71	72	83	4.15
(32,130,20)	12	23	36	46	48	91	7.58
(32,150,50)	5	14	24	27	27	42	8.40
(32,130,67)	3	15	28	32	32	63	21.00

The implementation results on extremely large MOLPs are presented in Table 3. These problems involve huge number of solutions, so they are identified by the input parameters used in the random problem generator of ADBASE and listed in the descending order according to the number of solutions found by one processor in the given time interval. Solutions are found in 30 seconds using p processors. All rows of this table show that more solutions are generated simultaneously when more processors are used. The last column lists the ratios between the number of solutions found using 32 processors and the number of solutions found using 1 processor. The general increasing tendency in this column implies that the algorithm performs better on larger problems.

4 Conclusions

This paper reports the numerical results of applying a parallel algorithm to solving large and extremely large MOLPs on an Intel Paragon multiprocessor. Two performance criteria, the speed-up and parallel efficiency, have been observed. All experiments confirm the general tendency that the both criteria improve as the size of MOLPs solved increases. Further research on refining the parallel algorithm is in progress and new experiments will be reported in the nearest future.

References

[1] V. Chankong and Y. Y. Haimes, *Multiobjective Decision Making - Theory and Methodology*, North-Holland, New York, 1983.

[2] J. L. Matthews, *Solving multiple objective linear programs on a hypercube computer*, M.S. project, Department of Mathematical Sciences, Clemson University, Clemson, SC, (1992).

[3] J. R. Soltys, *A parallel algorithm for multiple objective linear programs*, M.S. project, Department of Mathematical Sciences, Clemson University, Clemson, SC, (1993).

[4] R. E. Steuer, *Multiple Criteria Optimization - Theory, Computation and Application*, John Wiley, New York, 1986.

[5] ——, *Manual for the ADBASE multiple objective linear programming package*, Department of Management Science and Information Technology, University of Georgia, Athens, GA, (1991).

[6] ——, *Random problem generation and the computation of efficient extreme points in multiple objective linear programming*, private communication, (1993).

[7] M. M. Wiecek, H. Zhang, J. L. Matthews, and J. R. Soltys, *A parallel algorithm for multiple objective linear programs*, to appear in Proceedings of the XI International Conference on MCDM, Coimbra, Portugal, (1994).

Toward Teraflop Computing
and New Grand
Challenge Applications

ISBN-1-56072-247-9

Modeling Processor Wait Time for 2-D Parallel Finite Element Applications

Michelle Hribar
Valerie E. Taylor

Department of Electrical Engineering and Computer Science
Northwestern University
Evanston, IL 60208-3118

1 Introduction

The use of parallel processors has made feasible the execution of large scale applications such as finite element analysis. Generally, the speedup is limited by the interprocessor communication used by message-passing parallel machines. To understand the effect of communication on the speedup it is necessary to develop analytical models of the application. In this paper we present a model of the communication of parallel, 2-D finite element problems implemented on the Intel Delta. Our communication model consists of start-up time, transmission latency, and processor wait time due to synchronization. We find that the wait time can account for up to 25% of the total communication time.

2 Parallel Finite Element Method

Parallel finite element analysis divides the work of finite element computations among multiple processors. Parallel FEM requires 3 steps: 1) dividing the domain into subdomains, 2) assigning each subdomain to a processor and 3) executing the method on each processor. We focus on the class of nonlinear, dynamic problems for which the explicit integration step is the most computationally-intensive step. The specific procedure that we use to perform this step is the direct vector procedure that was first described by Belytschko and Chiapetta [2] and Belytschko et al [3]. This approach uses only vectors as storage; the mass matrix is lumped and stored as a vector. The advantages to this approach are the minimal storage requirements and the simplicity of solving for the displacements. We analyzed the WHAMS finite element code [4], which uses the direct vector procedure.

To solve for the displacements over time, strains, stresses and forces must be locally evaluated each time step. Then, the forces must be exchanged between neighboring processors in order to complete the computation of displacements. Due to

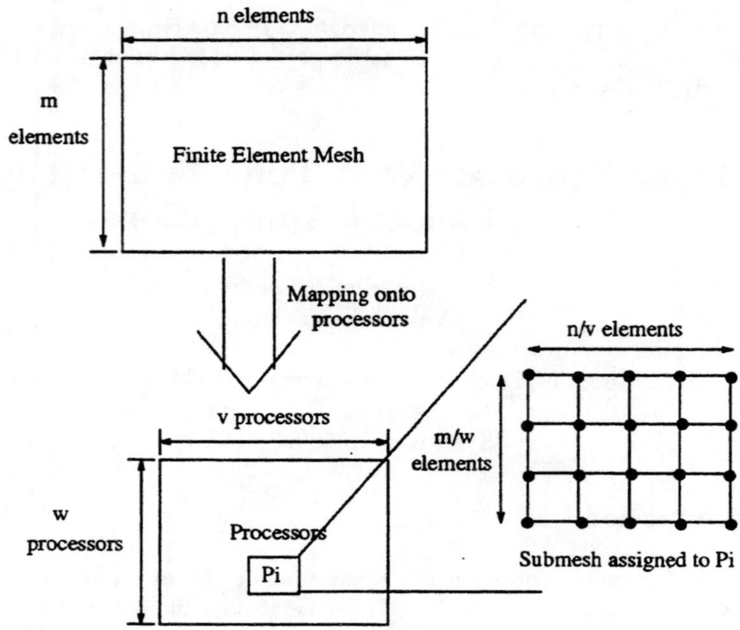

Figure 1: Mapping of multiple elements to a processor.

the dependencies of the computations, however, none of the communication can be overlapped with computation. Hence, we do not consider asynchronous communication; we consider synchronous, forced, and hybrid schemes.

3 Communication

The amount of communication required depends on the number of neighboring processors. Our implementation uses only 4-node quadrilateral elements. When multiple elements are assigned to each processor, the number of nodes it shares with its neighboring processors depends on the position of its neighbors. Figure 1 shows the mapping of multiple elements to processor P_i. The dimensions of the global mesh of elements are m x n and the size of the mesh of processors is w x v. Thus the dimensions of each individual processor P_i's submesh are (m/w) x (n/v) assuming m is a multiple of w and n is a multiple of v. P_i shares $(n/v) + 1$ nodes with each of its north and south neighbors, $(m/w) + 1$ nodes with each of its east and west neighbors, and only 1 node with each of its northeast, northwest, southwest and southeast neighbors.

This communication is often modeled as $\alpha + \beta$*L where α is the startup time of the message, β is the transfer time per byte, and L is the number of bytes in the message. While this model represents the transmission time of a single message, it does not include any wait time that the processors may experience during the communication. We use this model as an initial estimate of communication time.

The α and β parameters used by these models differ for each of the communication protocols available on the Delta. To determine the different parameters for each of the protocols, we measured the time it took to perform a message swap between two neighboring processors. Table 1 gives the α and β parameters that we determined experimentally for the synchronous and forced communication. Forced messages are a special type of synchronous and asynchronous communication that include additional overhead to synchronize and set up a buffer at the destination processor. The normal protocol mechanisms are bypassed resulting in a transmission rates that are two times faster than unforced communication [5].

Message Times		
Type	α	β
Synchronous	100 μsecs	0.2 μsecs
Forced	350 μsecs	0.1 μsecs

Table 1: Times for Different Message Types.

We devised another communication scheme, the hybrid method, to decrease the communication time by using both forced and synchronous messages. Since a processor only shares one node with its northeast, northwest, southwest and southeast neighbors, we use synchronous communication for these messages. The neighbors in the north, south, west and east directions can share larger number of nodes so we use forced messages for this communication.

4 Processor Wait Time

We tested our general communication model described in the previous section by executing the WHAMS code for two problems–128x128 and 64x64 element meshes. We found that the communication model, $\alpha + \beta$*L, is a good predictor of relative performance, but not true performance. When we included a parameter for processor wait time, as described below, we found the new model to be a better predictor of true performance.

4.1 Measuring Wait Time

It is necessary for processors to synchronize with each neighbor to get the desired data. That is, a processor cannot proceed until it completes its message swap with each of its neighbors. Since the processors are not guaranteed to reach the same message swap code at the same time, processors must wait for each other. Table 2 shows the major steps that must be performed in the WHAMS code. This wait time may be caused by three parts of the code: initialization, computation in the main

WHAMS Pseudocode	
Initialize Data Structures with Subdomain Information:	
	1. Read Data File
	2. Construct Data Structures for Communication
	3. Exchange Mass Information
For i = 1 to Maxstep do	
	4. Compute Forces
	5. Exchange Forces
	6. Update Forces
	7. Update Displacements and Velocities

Table 2: WHAMS Pseudocode

loop, and the communication of the forces. The initialization step may be completed in different amounts of time because processors often do not perform I/O in the same amount of time. In addition, constructing the data structures for communication will take less time for the processors on the boundary of the mesh because they do not have as many neighbors. Computation may take different amounts of time because of cache misses that some processors experience but others do not. Finally, wait time may occur because of the communication itself. For example, corner processors need to communicate with only 3 neighbors. Consequently, because of the communication order, it will wait for a neighboring processor to finish communicating with its other neighbors before it can send a message to the corner processor.

To determine how each of these factors affect our measured communication time, we forced the processors to synchronize after different places in the code. From the resulting communication time of the altered code we can determine how each part of the code affects the wait time. The original code is executed as shown in Table 2, without any added forced synchronization. To determine the effect of the initialization step, we put a `GSYNC` after step 3 of the code. `GSYNC` is an Intel primitive that prevents further execution until all processors have reached the statement. Next, to determine the effect of computation and communication, we put a `GSYNC` after step 4 so that the processors were synchronized before they performed the force exchanges in each iteration of the loop. Figure 2 displays the difference in communication times between the original code and the altered code for the 128x128 element mesh problem for the synchronous scheme. Similar plots resulted for the forced and hybrid schemes. The average difference between these communication times are given in Table 3. The graphs and the table show that the greatest factor that affects the wait time is the initialization for all the communication methods. They also show that there is less of a difference between the measured communication times and the theoretical model for the forced communication. This may be because the large overhead of the forced messages hides the synchronization time. Finally, the table shows that even synchronizing the code before the communication of each iteration still results in communication times that are larger than the theo-

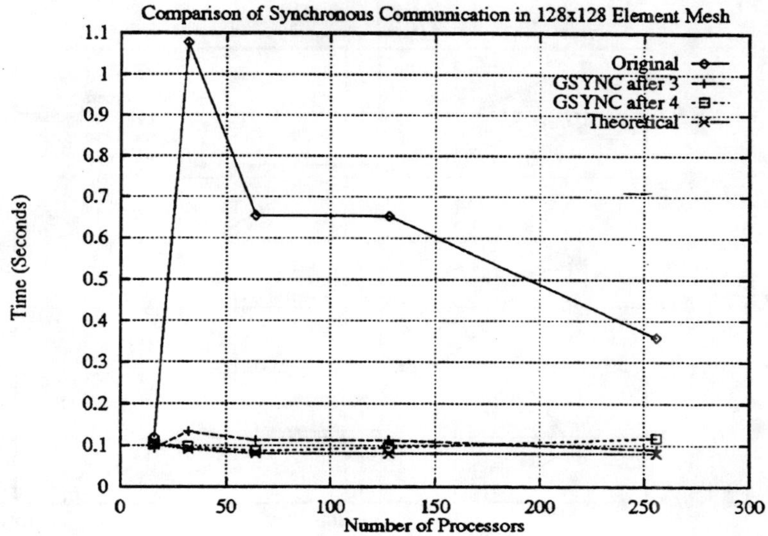

Figure 2: Communication Time of Different Versions (Synchronous) (128x128 element mesh)

retical model. This difference accounts for the amount of waiting that the series of 8 exchanges generates.

Difference in Communication Times						
Difference Type	Sync	% Diff	Forced	% Diff	Hybrid	% Diff
Theor & Original Code	0.4835	555.10	0.4668	285.41	0.4844	391.32
Theor & GSYNC after 3	0.0211	24.25	0.0235	14.42	0.0235	19.02
Theor & GSYNC after 4	0.0128	14.65	0.0160	9.80	0.0214	17.30

Table 3: Synchronization times

4.2 Modified Model

Because our previously described model was based on exchanges between two processors, it did not include time to synchronize. In this section, we present a modified communication model that includes this synchronization time. We add a ω term to represent the time to synchronize to the $\alpha + \beta * L$ model we described in Section 3.

From our results in Section 4.1, we can determine an ω term for each type of communication. While we found that initialization step that included I/O contributed the largest synchronization effect, we do not wish to include this in our model since

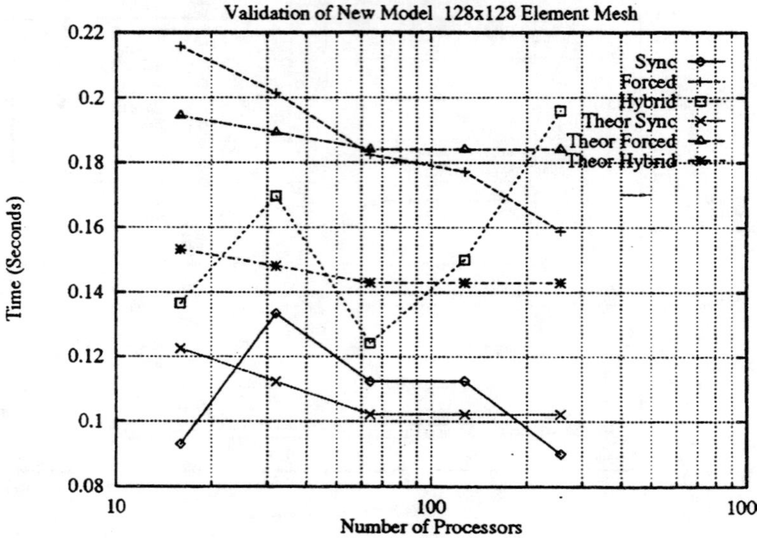

Figure 3: Validation of New Model (128x128 element mesh)

it is not in the main loop of computation. Instead, we assume that the processors are synchronized after the initialization. This assumption is reasonable since it would require just one GSYNC call during the execution of the code. Thus, we focus on the synchronization that results due to the computation and communication within the main loop.

Initially we assume that ω does not depend on message size or processor mesh size. We can then use the values in Table 3 of the average difference between the theoretical model and the code with the GSYNC after the initialization step to determine our ω term for each message. For synchronous messages ω_s is equal to 52.8 μseconds. For forced messages ω_f is 59.0 μseconds. As the table shows, the cumulative wait time accounts for 24.25% of synchronous communication, 14.42% of forced communication, and 19.02% of hybrid communication.

To verify this model, we compare the measured communication time where the processors are synchronized after initialization to our predicted times. Figure 3 shows that our model predicts the times we measured much more closely for the 128x128 element problem with the GSYNC after initialization. As mentioned previously, this problem size uses at most 2 packets per message and at least one processor communicates with all of its neighbors. So, the ω is reasonable for these size messages and processor mesh sizes.

Figure 4 shows that larger message sizes are not correctly predicted by this new model. The first processor mesh size, 18, uses 3 packets for communicating with east and west neighbors and 2 packets for the north and south neighbors. The next processor size, 21, uses 3 packets for communicating with east and west neighbors and 1 packet for the north and south neighbors. The remaining processor mesh

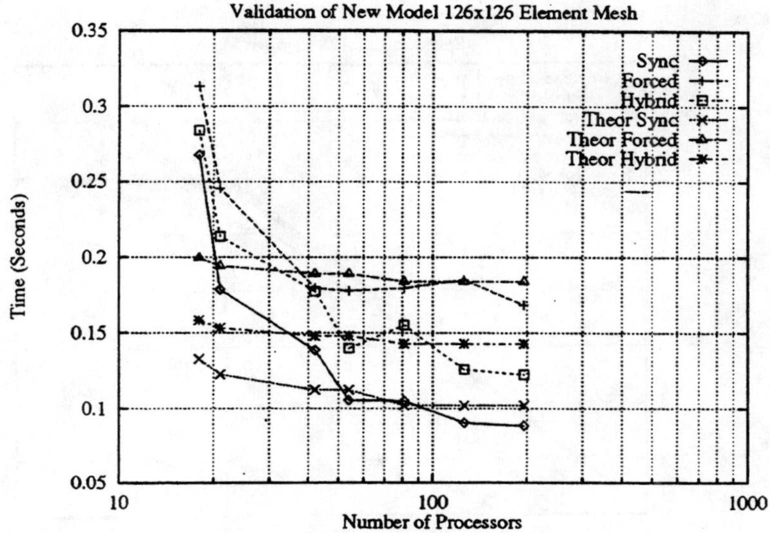

Figure 4: Validation of New Model (126x126 element mesh)

sizes use 1 or 2 packets for communication. As the graph shows, the model does not predict the communication time for these larger messages, but it does for the smaller ones.

Therefore, the ω term must depend on message size and must also depend on the maximum number of neighbors a processor has in a given mesh. Further work is needed to determine the exact relationship between the wait time, message size and processor mesh size. But since the majority of our problems use only small message sizes, we choose to keep ω as a constant.

5 Summary

Using parallel processors is very advantageous for large-scale, computationally intensive applications such as finite element analysis. We know that the speedup of these applications is limited by interprocessor communication. For this reason, we study the communication of of the 2-D parallel finite element WHAMS code on the Intel Delta.

When modeling the speedup of this application, we found that using the common communication model of $\alpha + \beta * L$ greatly underestimates the time the processors spend communicating and processing messages. The processors also spend time waiting to communicate with the other processors. The wait time caused by the main loop of computation and communication represented in our model as ω is up to 25% of the total communication time.

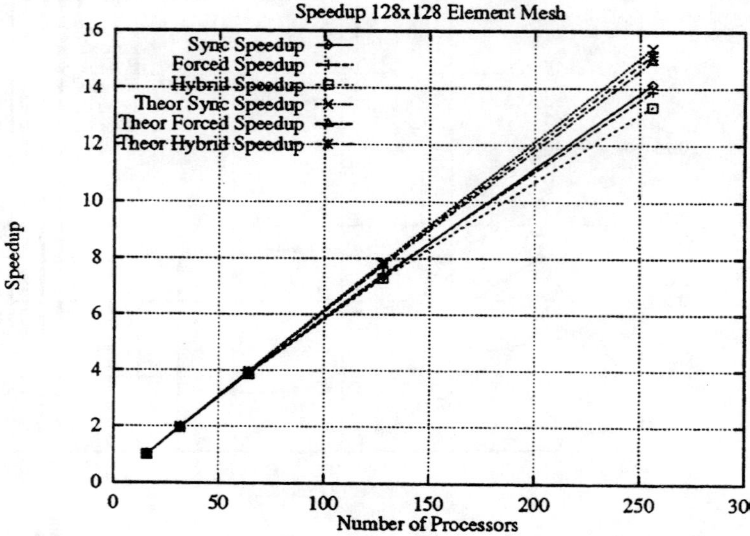

Figure 5: Speedup (128x128 element mesh)

Including this ω term in our model allows us to predict the speedup of our application. Figure 5 shows the measured speedup and the speedup predicted by our model for the 128x128 element problem.

References

[1] A touchstone DELTA system description. Intel Supercomputer Systems Division, February 1991.

[2] T. Belytschko and R. L. Chiapetta. A computer code for dynamic stress analysis of media-structure problems with nonlinearities (SAMSON). Technical Report AFWL-TR-72-104, Air Force Weapons Laboratory, KAFB, 1973.

[3] T. Belytschko, R. L. Chiapetta, and H. Bartet. Efficient large nonlinear transient analysis by finite elements. *Internat. J. Numer. Methods Engrg.*, 10:579–596, 1976.

[4] Hsin-Chu Chen, Hui Gao, and Sanjay Sarma. WHAMS3D project progress report PR-2. Technical Report 1112, University of Illinois CSRD, 1991.

[5] Richard J. Littlefield. Characterizing and tuning communications performance on the Touchstone DELTA and iPSC/860. In *Proceedings of the 1992 Intel User's Group Meeting*, October 1992.

Toward Teraflop Computing and New Grand Challenge Applications

ISBN-1-56072-247-9

A Scalable Parallel Algorithm for Periodic Symmetric Toeplitz Tridiagonal Systems

Xian-He Sun

Department of Computer Science
Louisiana State University
Baton Rouge, LA 70803-4020

Abstract

Symmetric Toeplitz tridiagonal systems arise in many scientific applications. An efficient algorithm, the Simple Parallel Prefix (SPP) algorithm, was previously proposed for solving symmetric Toeplitz tridiagonal systems on SIMD and vector computers. Based on the SPP algorithm, a scalable parallel algorithm is proposed for solving periodic symmetric Toeplitz tridiagonal systems in this study. The newly proposed algorithm has the same parallel computation count as that of the SPP algorithm for non-periodic systems, and it requires only shift communications.

1 Introduction

A matrix is Toeplitz if its entries along each diagonal are the same. Symmetric Toeplitz tridiagonal systems arise in many scientific applications. They appear in multigrid methods, Alternating Direction Implicit (ADI) method, wavelet collocation method, and in line-SOR preconditioners for conjugate gradient methods [3]. In addition to solving PDE's, Toeplitz tridiagonal systems also arise in digital signal processing, image processing, stationary time series analysis, as well as in spline curve fitting [7].

Because of its importance, intensive research has been done on the development of efficient parallel tridiagonal solvers. Many algorithms have been proposed [6], including the well known recursive doubling reduction method (RCD) developed by Stone [2], and the cyclic reduction or odd-even reduction method (OER) developed by Hockney [1]. In general, parallel Toeplitz tridiagonal solvers require global communications which makes them inefficient on distributed-memory architectures. Recently, we have taken a new approach [3, 4]: increasing parallel performance by introducing bounded numerical error. Two new algorithms, namely the Parallel Diagonal Dominant (PDD) algorithm [3] and the Simple Parallel Prefix (SPP) algorithm [4], have been proposed based on this approach for MIMD and SIMD machines respectively. These two algorithms take the advantage of that most of the tridiagonal systems arising in scientific applications are diagonal dominant. Backed by rigorous accuracy analysis, the algorithms truncate communication and computation without degrading the accuracy. Theoretical and experimental results have shown that these two algorithms are efficient, practical and applicable to many scientific applications.

In this paper, a new algorithm is introduced for solving periodic systems. The newly proposed algorithm has the same parallel computation count as that of the SPP algorithm. It requires only shift communications. Since the new algorithm is an extension of the SPP algorithm, it is well believed that the accuracy results regarding the SPP algorithm can be applied to the new algorithm as well. The discussion of the SPP algorithm is given in Section 2. The new algorithm for periodic symmetric Toeplitz tridiagonal systems is introduced in Section 3. The final section gives the conclusion.

2 The Simple Parallel Prefix Algorithm

The Simple Parallel Prefix (SPP) algorithm [4] is a "tearing" algorithm. It first solves a modified system, and, then, it corrects the intermedian result to get the final solution. The SPP algorithm is designed for fine-grain computing. With n processors, it solves an n-dimensional tridiagonal system with $2\lceil \lg(n) \rceil + 1$ AXPY operations. Two prefix communications are required in the computing (tearing) phase and one broadcast communication is needed in the correction phase. When the tridiagonal system is diagonally dominant, both the computing and correction phases can be truncated without influencing the accuracy. The truncation makes the SPP algorithm superior to other existing methods, even on vector machines.

2.1 The SPP Algorithm

We are interested in solving a linear system

$$Ax = d, \tag{1}$$

where A is a symmetric Toeplitz tridiagonal matrix of order n:

$$A = \begin{bmatrix} c & 1 & & & \\ 1 & c & 1 & & \\ & \cdot & \cdot & \cdot & \\ & & \cdot & \cdot & 1 \\ & & & 1 & c \end{bmatrix} = [1, c, 1] \tag{2}$$

and $x = (x_1, \cdots, x_n)^T$ and $d = (d_1 \cdots, d_n)^T$ are n-dimensional vectors. We assume that matrix A is diagonally dominant (i.e., $|c| > 2$).

Computing Phase

The SPP consists of two phases, the computing phase and the correction phase. In the computing phase, the system

$$\tilde{A}\tilde{x} = d \tag{3}$$

is solved, where

$$\tilde{A} = \begin{pmatrix} a & 1 & & \\ 1 & c & \ddots & \\ & \ddots & \ddots & 1 \\ & & 1 & c \end{pmatrix} = a \begin{pmatrix} 1 & & & \\ b & 1 & & \\ & \ddots & \ddots & \\ & & b & 1 \end{pmatrix} \begin{pmatrix} 1 & b & & \\ & \ddots & \ddots & \\ & & \ddots & b \\ & & & 1 \end{pmatrix} = a \cdot [b, 1, 0] \cdot [0, 1, b],$$

a and b are the real solutions of:

$$\begin{cases} a + b = c \\ a \cdot b = 1 \end{cases} \tag{4}$$

Because $a \cdot b = 1$ and $|c| > 2$, we may further assume that $|a| > 1$ and $|b| < 1$. From Eq. (3), $\tilde{x} = a^{-1} \cdot [0, 1, b]^{-1}[b, 1, 0]^{-1}d = b \cdot [0, 1, b]^{-1}[b, 1, 0]^{-1}d$. Let $L = [-b, 0, 0]$. Then

$$[b, 1, 0] = [0, 1, 0] - [-b, 0, 0] = I - L$$

and

$$[b, 1, 0]^{-1} = (I + L^{2^{\lceil \lg n \rceil - 1}})(I + L^{2^{\lceil \lg n \rceil - 2}}) \cdots (I + L^2)(I + L). \tag{5}$$

The superscripts of matrix L represent matrix multiplication. Similarly, let $U = [0, 0, -b]$. Then,

$$[0, 1, b] = [0, 1, 0] - [0, 0, -b] = I - U$$

and

$$[0, 1, b]^{-1} = (I + U^{2^{\lceil \lg n \rceil - 1}}) \cdots\cdots (I + U^2)(I + U).$$

Thus, the solution of Eq. (3) is

$$\tilde{x} = b \cdot (I + U^{2^{\lceil \lg n \rceil - 1}}) \cdots (I + U) \cdot (I + L^{2^{\lceil \lg n \rceil - 1}}) \cdots\cdots (I + L)d. \tag{6}$$

Let $v = (v_1, v_2, \cdots, v_n)^T$ be an n-dimensional vector. Given the special structure of L^i, we find $(I + L^i)v = v + (-b)^i v_{(i)}$, where $v_{(i)} = (0, \cdots 0, v_1, \cdots v_{n-i})^T$ and v_1 is the $i+1$ element of $v_{(i)}$. Similarly, for U^i, we find $(I + U^i)v = v + (-b)^i v^{(i)}$, where $v^{(i)} = (v_{i+1}, \cdots, v_n, 0 \cdots 0)^T$. The operation that a vector plus a multiple of another vector is called the AXPY operation. It can be implemented efficiently on SIMD and vector machines. Equation (6) indicates that Eq. (3) can be solved in $2 \cdot \lceil \lg n \rceil$ AXPY operations. Because $|b| < 1$, and both $||L^i|| \to 0$, $||U^i|| \to 0$ when $n \to \infty$, the AXPY operations can be truncated without influencing the accuracy.

Correction Phase

Our goal is to find the solution of Eq. (1). Modification is needed to convert the solution of Eq. (3) to the final solution. The relation between Eq. (1) and Eq. (3) is given by

$$x = \tilde{x} - \tilde{A}^{-1}V(I + E^T\tilde{A}^{-1}V)^{-1}\tilde{x}_1,$$

where $\tilde{x}_1$ is the first element of vector $\tilde{x}$, and

$$\tilde{A}^{-1}V(I + E^T\tilde{A}^{-1}V)^{-1} = b^2\left(\frac{1-b^{2n}}{1-b^{2(n+1)}}, \cdots, (-b)^i\frac{1-b^{2(n-i)}}{1-b^{2(n+1)}}, \cdots, (-b)^{n-1}\frac{(1-b^2)}{1-b^{2(n+1)}}\right)^T. \quad (7)$$

The final solution is

$$x = \tilde{x} - \tilde{x}_1 z, \quad (8)$$

where vector z is the right side of Eq. (7). Because $|b| < 1$, z can be truncated at some integer k_1 without affecting the accuracy. Furthermore, when n is large, $b^{2(n-i+1)}$, $i = 0, 1, \cdots, k_1$ will be less than machine accuracy, and z is reduced to $\tilde{z} = ((-b)^2, (-b)^3, \cdots, (-b)^{k_1+2}, 0, \cdots, 0)^T$. Totally, without truncation, $2 \lceil \lg(n) \rceil + 1$ AXPY operations are needed to get the final solution.

2.2 Accuracy Analysis

If the Toeplitz matrix under consideration is diagonal dominant, the $2 \lceil \lg(n) \rceil$ AXPY operations in the computing phase can be truncated to $2k$ AXPY operations without influencing the accuracy, where k is an integer less than $\lceil \lg(n) \rceil$. Let x be the solution of the SPP algorithm without truncation and x^* be the corresponding solution with truncation, the accuracy analysis in [4] shows that the relative error under l_1 norm is bounded by

$$\frac{||x - x^*||}{||x||} \le \frac{|b|^k(1+|b|^{n-k})}{1-|b|}\left(1 + \frac{(1-|b|^k)(1+|b|)}{1-|b|}\right)\left(1 + \frac{b^2(1+|b|^{n+1})(1-|b|^n)}{(1-b^2)(1-|b|)}\right). \quad (9)$$

When the order of the tridiagonal system n is large, $|b|^n$ may be smaller than machine accuracy. In this case, the inequality (9) becomes

$$\frac{||x - x^*||}{||x||} \le \frac{|b|^k(1+|b|^{n-k})}{1-|b|}\left(1 + \frac{(1-|b|^k)(1+|b|)}{1-|b|}\right)\left(1 + \frac{b^2}{(1-b^2)(1-|b|)}\right). \quad (10)$$

In general the integer k is quite small. For instance, if the diagonal dominancy, $|c|$, is larger than or equal to 3, k equals 4 and 6 for single precision (10^{-7}) and double precision (10^{-14}) respectively.

3 The New Algorithm

When the boundary conditions are periodic, the discretization matrices of PDE's and other scientific applications are periodic systems. For periodic systems, the matrix A in the equation

$$Ax = d, \tag{11}$$

has the form

$$A = \begin{pmatrix} c & 1 & & 1 \\ 1 & c & 1 & \\ & \ddots & \ddots & 1 \\ 1 & & 1 & c \end{pmatrix} = a \begin{pmatrix} 1 & & & b \\ b & 1 & & \\ & \ddots & \ddots & \\ & & b & 1 \end{pmatrix} \begin{pmatrix} 1 & b & & \\ & 1 & \ddots & \\ & & \ddots & b \\ b & & & 1 \end{pmatrix}, \tag{12}$$

with a and b satisfying the linear system (4). Define

$$L_P = \begin{pmatrix} 0 & & & -b \\ -b & \ddots & & \\ & \ddots & \ddots & \\ & & -b & 0 \end{pmatrix}.$$

Then,

$$I - L_P = \begin{pmatrix} 1 & & & b \\ b & 1 & & \\ & \ddots & \ddots & \\ & & b & 1 \end{pmatrix}.$$

It is easy to verify that the inverse of $I - L_P$ is

$$(I - L_P)^{-1} = \frac{1}{1-(-b)^n}(I + L_P + L_P^2 + \cdots + L_P^{n-1}). \tag{13}$$

The i-th power of L_P has the form

$$L_P^i = \begin{pmatrix} & & (-b)^i & & \\ (-b)^i & & & \ddots & \\ & (-b)^i & & & (-b)^i \\ & & \ddots & & \\ & & & (-b)^i & \end{pmatrix},$$

where the first possible non-zero element in the first column is the $(i+1,1)$-the entry, and the first possible non-zero element in the first row is the $(1, n-i+1)$-th entry. The inverse of matrix $I - L_P$

can be computed through $2^{\lceil \lg(n) \rceil} - 1$ matrix mulplications using the following equality:

$$(I + L + L^2 + \cdots + L^{n-1}) = (I + L^{2^{\lceil \lg n \rceil - 1}})(I + L^{2^{\lceil \lg n \rceil - 2}}) \cdots (I + L) \tag{14}$$

Similarly, let

$$U_P = \begin{pmatrix} 0 & -b & & \\ & \ddots & \ddots & \\ & & \ddots & -b \\ -b & & & 0 \end{pmatrix}.$$

Then

$$(I - U_P)^{-1} = \frac{1}{1-(-b)^n}(I + U_P + U_P^2 + \cdots + U_P^{n-1}) \tag{15}$$

$$= \frac{1}{1-(-b)^n}(I + U_P^{2^{\lceil \lg n \rceil - 1}})(I + U_P^{2^{\lceil \lg n \rceil - 2}}) \cdots (I + U_P). \tag{16}$$

Based on Eq. (12), (14) and Eq. (16), the solution of (11) can be obtained by

$$\begin{aligned} x &= A^{-1}d = a^{-1}(I - U_P)^{-1}(I - L_P)^{-1}d \\ &= \frac{b}{(1-(-b)^n)^2}(I + U_P^{2^{\lceil \lg n \rceil - 1}}) \cdots (I + U_P)(I + L_P^{2^{\lceil \lg n \rceil - 1}}) \cdots (I + L_P)d \end{aligned}$$

It requires $2\lceil \lg(n) \rceil + 1$ matrix-vector mulplications. In general, matrix-vector mulplication needs n^2 operations. Since the matrices L_P^i and U_P^i are special Toeplitz matrices, the required matrix-vector multiplications can be done with AXPY operations. For an n-dimensional vector, $v = (v_1, v_2, \cdots, v_n)^T$,

$$(I + L^i)v = v + (-b)^i v_{(i)}, \tag{17}$$

with $v_{(i)} = (v_{n-i+1}, v_{n-i+2}, \cdots, v_n, v_1, \cdots v_{n-i})^T$, and

$$(I + U_P^i)v = v + (-b)^i v^{(i)},$$

with $v^{(i)} = (v_{i+1}, \cdots, v_n, v_1, v_2, \cdots v_i)^T$. Notice that for matrices U_P^i and L_P^i, the second vector in the AXPY operation is a shift of the first vector along opposite directions. The shift of vector requires "shift" communications on distributed-memory machines. Figure 1 gives the proposed algorithm for solving periodic symmetric Toeplitz tridiagonal systems. With n processors the algorithm finds the solution in $2\lceil \lg(n) \rceil + 1$ AXPY operations for a matrix of order n. Since $|b| < 1$, we may assume that $|b|^n$ is less than machine accuracy and assume that the AXPY operation can be truncated from $2\lceil \lg(n) \rceil + 1$ to $2k + 1$ without degrading the accuracy. The integer k is independent of the order of matrix. Interested readers may refer [4] for detailed accuracy study. Using n processors, each of the three j loops in Fig. 1 can be executed in one AXPY operation.

```
for  i ← 0  to  k − 1  do
  for  j ← 1  to  n  do
    d_j = d_j + (−b)^{2^i} d_{(|j−2^i|) mod(n)}
    j ← j + 1
  i ← i + 1

for  i ← 0  to  k − 1  do
  for  j ← 1  to  n  do
    d_j = d_j + (−b)^{2^i} d_{(j+2^i) mod(n)}
    j ← j + 1
  i ← i + 1

for  j ← 1  to  n  do
  x_j = b · d_j
  j ← j + 1
```

Figure 1. The Proposed Algorithm for Periodic Systems.

4 Conclusion

A scalable parallel algorithm has been proposed for solving periodic symmetric Toeplitz Tridiagonal systems for fine-grain computing. With n processors, the proposed algorithm needs $2\lceil \lg(n) \rceil + 1$ AXPY operations for a system of n equations. Most tridiagonal systems arising in scientific computing are diagonal dominant. The proposed algorithm takes the advantage of diagonal dominancy and truncate the AXPY operations from $2\lceil \lg(n) \rceil + 1$ to $2k + 1$ without influencing the accuracy. The proposed algorithm is an extension of the SPP algorithm [4]. Based on the accuracy analysis and experimental results given in [4], k is quite small. In general, k is equal to 4 and 6 for single and double precision respectively. The truncation of computation and communication makes the proposed algorithm efficient on vector machines, where AXPY operations can be implemented efficiently, as well as on SIMD machines. Since the integer k is independent of the order of matrix, the truncation also makes the algorithm scalable. It is perfectly scalable in terms of *isospeed* scalability [5], that is when problem size increases linearly with the number of processors, the achieved average speed of the algorithm will maintain the same.

References

[1] HOCKNEY, R. A fast direct solution of Poisson's equation using Fourier analysis. *J. ACM 12* (1965), 95–113.

[2] STONE, H. An efficient parallel algorithm for the solution of a tridiagonal linear system of equations. *J. of ACM 20*, 1 (Jan. 1973), 27–38.

[3] SUN, X.-H. Application and accuracy of the parallel diagonal dominant algorithm. ICASE Technical Report, 93-6, ICASE, NASA Langley Research Center, 1993. A short version appears in Proc. of ICPP '93.

[4] SUN, X.-H., AND JOSLIN, R. A simple parallel prefix algorithm for compact finite-difference scheme. ICASE Technical Report, 93-16, ICASE, NASA Langley Research Center, 1993.

[5] SUN, X.-H., AND ROVER, D. Scalability of parallel algorithm-machine combinations. *IEEE Transactions on Parallel and Distributed Systems* (June 1994), 599–613.

[6] SUN, X.-H., ZHANG, H., AND NI, L. Efficient tridiagonal solvers on multicomputers. *IEEE Transactions on Computers 41*, 3 (1992), 286–296.

[7] TAHA, T. R., AND JIANG, P. A parallel algorithm for solving periodic tridiagonal toeplitz linear systems. In *Proc. of the Sixth SIAM Conf. on Parallel Processing for Scientific Computing* (March 1993), pp. 491–496.

Toward Teraflop Computing
and New Grand
Challenge Applications

ISBN-1-56072-247-9

A COMPUTATIONAL STRATEGY FOR EXPLOITATION OF MASSIVE TEMPORAL PARALLELISM IN SOLUTION OF TIME-DEPENDENT PDES

Amir Fijany, Jacob Barhen, and Nikzad Toomarian
Center for Space Microelectronics Technology
Jet Propulsion Laboratory, California Institute of Technology
Pasadena, CA 91109

ABSTRACT

In this paper massively parallel algorithms for solution of time-dependent PDEs are developed. It is shown that, for a wide class of such PDEs, the seemingly strictly sequential time-stepping procedures can be fully parallelized resulting in time-parallel algorithms which offer a massive degree of coarse grain parallelism. The time-parallel algorithms have a simple structure with a minimum of communication and synchronization requirement and hence are particularly efficient for implementation on massively parallel MIMD architectures.

1. INTRODUCTION

The solution of time-dependent PDEs is at the heart of many scientific and *Grand Challenge* applications. The corresponding development of fast and accurate algorithms has been extensively studied in the literature. The advent of massively parallel architectures offers an appealing new opportunity for faster solution of evermore complex problems. However, in order to fully exploit the computing power of these new architectures, existing algorithms must be reexamined, with emphasis on their efficiency for parallel implementation. Eventually, new algorithms may have to be developed that, from the onset, take a greater advantage of the available massive parallelism.

In this paper, we present a novel technique for solution of time-dependent PDEs which is particularly efficient for implementation on emerging massively parallel MIMD architectures. By departing from conventional approaches, our proposed technique allows the solution of such PDEs to be fully parallelized in time resulting in time-parallel algorithms which offer a massive degree of coarse grain temporal parallelism with a minimum of communication and synchronization requirement. We have already applied this technique to the solution of a model problem, i.e., the heat equation [1]. The practical implementation of our time-parallel algorithm for this problem on a massively parallel MIMD architecture, the Intel's Touchstone Delta, has shown that a significant speedup can be achieved even by using a very large number of processors on the order of hundreds [2]. In this paper, we present the general concept underlying our time-parallel computation approach and discuss its domain of efficient applicability. We also analyze key issues in extending our technique to more complex problems which represents a framework underlying our current research effort.

This paper is organized as follows. The time-stepping procedure for solution of time-dependent PDEs and current parallel computation approaches are reviewed in §2. The time-parallel algorithms are presented in §3 along with a discussion on their efficiency and applicability. In §4, time-parallel algorithms for two model problems are presented and their performance is analyzed. Finally, some concluding remarks are made in §5.

2. BACKGROUND

2.1. Time-Stepping Procedures

The algorithms discussed in this paper can be applied to the solution of a wide class of time-dependent PDEs. However, in order to provide a simple illustration for our discussion, let us consider a parabolic equation on a 2D regular domain Ω, with boundary Ω', i.e.,

$$\frac{\partial U}{\partial t} = \mathcal{L}U + f(x,y,t) \qquad \text{in } \Omega, \quad \text{and } T \geq t > 0 \tag{1}$$

with initial and Dirichlet boundary conditions given by

$U_0 = h(x,y)$, in Ω and $t = 0$, and $U = g(x,y)$, on Ω' and $T \geq t > 0$

where $\mathcal{L}$ is a linear elliptic operator and $f(x,y,t)$ is a source vector.

The discretization of Eq. (1) in both time and space, by superimposing a uniform grid of size $\gamma = \Delta x = \Delta y$ on Ω and using a standard finite-difference scheme, leads to a family of time-stepping (or, marching-in-time) methods given by

$$(I + 2\alpha\beta\mathcal{M}_{\mathcal{L}})U^{(m)} = (I - 2\alpha(1-\beta)\mathcal{M}_{\mathcal{L}})U^{(m-1)} + F^{(m)} \quad m = 1 \text{ to } M \tag{2}$$

where I and $\mathcal{M}_{\mathcal{L}}\epsilon\Re^{N^2 \times N^2}$ denote the identity matrix and the matrix arising from the discretization of $\mathcal{L}$, respectively. Here, $\alpha = \tau/2\gamma^2$, $\tau = \Delta t$ is the time step size, $M = T/\tau$, and N is the grid size. Furthermore, $U^{(m)}$ and $F^{(m)}\epsilon\Re^{N^2}$ denote the approximate solution vector at time step m and the vector resulting from the discretization of $f(x,y,t)$ and $g(x,y)$, respectively.

Three methods are usually invoked for solution of Eq. (1). They are characterized in terms of the parameter β as: Explicit method ($\beta = 0$); Implicit method ($\beta = 1$); and Crank-Nicolson (C-N) method ($\beta = 1/2$). The explicit method is conditionally stable, while both the implicit and C-N methods are unconditionally stable. Furthermore, the C-N method is second-order accurate in time, while the implicit method is only first-order accurate.

From a computational point of view, the solution of Eq. (2) is both time (number of time steps, M) and space (size of grid, N) dependent. In the sequel, the term *space-parallel* is used for algorithms that only exploit parallelism in solving Eq. (2) at each time step, while the term *time-parallel* refers to those algorithms that exploit parallelism in the computation of all vectors $U^{(m)}$, $m = 1$ to M.

2.2. Current Trends in Developing Parallel Algorithms

Recent directions in developing fast parallel algorithms for solution of time-dependent PDEs seem to have emerged from two widely acknowledged observations (see, for example, [3,4]) regarding the efficiency of time-stepping methods for parallel computation:

1. The explicit methods, while limited in their range of stability, are highly efficient for parallel/vector processing, since the computation at each time step mainly involves a matrix-vector multiplication (MVM);
2. The implicit and C-N methods, despite their superior numerical properties, are not efficient for parallel/vector processing, since the solution of a linear system is required at each time step.

The first observation has motivated the development of new explicit methods which, while preserve the efficiency for parallel/vector computation, offer better numerical properties [5,6]. Note, however, that the parallelism in these methods is rather fine grain and, even with improved stability, a very large number of time steps is still required. The second observation has led to approaches emphasizing an increase in the efficiency of implicit methods for parallel computation[4,7]. All these approaches result in space-parallel algorithms, since they attempt to parallelize the computation of each step, while the overall computation in time remains strictly sequential.

In fact, it seems that the computation of time-stepping procedures in Eq. (2) is assumed to be strictly sequential in time. This has motivated the development of new approaches, mostly in the form of iterative techniques, to achieve some level of parallelism in time [8]-[13]. However, all these approaches seem to have achieved a rather limited parallelism in time. Indeed, Womble [10] supports the assessment of [14], wherein a simultaneous solution for all the time steps is not considered practical.

In the sequel, we present a technique which, for a wide class of problems, allows the computation in the time-stepping procedures to be fully parallelized in time. Interestingly, for this class of problems, our approach establishes a rather surprising result. *In fact, while our technique can be applied to the solution of the above-mentioned three methods with a similar computational structure, the C-N method is significantly more efficient than the explicit and implicit methods for time-parallel computation.*

3. TIME PARALLEL ALGORITHMS

To motivate the idea of time-parallelism, notice that Eq. (2) simply represents a First-Order Inhomogeneous Linear Recurrences (FOILR). The solution of such recurrences can be computed in $O(\text{Log } M)$ by using, for example, the algorithms in [15]. This indicates that the computation is fully parallelizable in time, wherein the time lower bound of $O(\text{Log } M)$ can be achieved.

From an efficiency stand point, however, such an approach is not practical, since it involves the computation of explicit inverse and powers of matrices in Eq. (2). Starting with highly sparse matrices, this would lead to the generation of increasingly dense and ultimately full matrices. For 2D and 3D problems, the complexity of each step of such a time-parallel algorithm would then be of $O(N^6)$ and $O(N^9)$, respectively, with the overall complexity of the algorithm being of $O(N^6 \text{Log } M)$ and $O(N^9 \text{Log } M)$. Thus, although the complexity of the computation could be reduced in time, it would be significantly increased in the spatial domain. As a result, the computational cost of such time-parallel algorithms would be orders of magnitude greater than that of the best serial algorithm for most practical cases. *Nevertheless, this observation clearly suggests that, insofar as the data dependency in the computation is concerned, the time-stepping procedures can, in principle, be fully parallelized in time.*

3.1. Introduction of Temporal Parallelism in Computation

Motivated by the above observation, we propose a technique which, for a wide class of time-dependent PDEs, allows the time-stepping procedures to be *efficiently* parallelized in time, leading to highly practical algorithms for massively parallel computation. The fundamental idea of our time-parallel computation is to introduce a diagonalization process in the time-stepping schemes. To describe our approach, let us consider the C-N method given by Eq. (2). Note that the matrices on the left- and right-hand sides of the equation are simultaneously diagonalizable, i.e., they have the same set of eigenvectors. Let the Eigenvalue-Eigenvector Decomposition (EED) of the nonsingular matrix $\mathcal{M}_{\mathcal{L}}$ be given by:

$$\mathcal{M}_{\mathcal{L}} = \Theta\Lambda\Theta^{-1}$$

Substituting the above decomposition into Eq. (2) results in

$$(I + \alpha\Theta\Lambda\Theta^{-1})U^{(m)} = (I - \alpha\Theta\Lambda\Theta^{-1})U^{(m-1)} + F^{(m)} \qquad m = 1 \text{ to } M$$

$$\Theta(I + \alpha\Lambda)\Theta^{-1}U^{(m)} = \Theta(I - \alpha\Lambda)\Theta^{-1}U^{(m-1)} + F^{(m)} \qquad m = 1 \text{ to } M$$

Multiplying both sides by the nonsingular matrix Θ^{-1}, we obtain

$$(I + \alpha\Lambda)\Theta^{-1}U^{(m)} = (I - \alpha\Lambda)\Theta^{-1}U^{(m-1)} + \Theta^{-1}F^{(m)} \qquad m = 1 \text{ to } M$$

Let $\tilde{U}^{(m)} = \Theta^{-1}U^{(m)}$, $m = 0$ to M, and $\tilde{F}^{(m)} = \Theta^{-1}F^{(m)}$, $m = 1$ to M. It follows that

$$(I + \alpha\Lambda)\tilde{U}^{(m)} = (I - \alpha\Lambda)\tilde{U}^{(m-1)} + \tilde{F}^{(m)} \qquad m = 1 \text{ to } M$$

Defining the diagonal matrices

$$D_1 = (I + \alpha\Lambda)^{-1}(I - \alpha\Lambda) \text{ and } D_2 = (I + \alpha\Lambda)^{-1} \tag{3}$$

we get

$$\tilde{U}^{(m)} = D_1\tilde{U}^{(m-1)} + D_2\tilde{F}^{(m)} \qquad m = 1 \text{ to } M \tag{4}$$

which is a transformation of Eq. (2) into a diagonal form. In contrast to Eq. (2), however, Eq. (4) is highly efficient for parallel computation. For 2D and 3D problems, the complexity of sequential implementation of Eq. (4) is of $O(MN^2)$ and $O(MN^3)$, respectively. With $O(M)$ processors, the computation can be performed in $O(N^2 \text{Log } M)$ and $O(N^3 \text{Log } M)$ by adapting the algorithms of [15].

3.2. Structure of Time-Parallel Algorithms

Following our discussion regarding the diagonalization process, a high level description of the time-parallel algorithms can be given in terms of the following steps:

1. Compute the eigenpairs of $\mathcal{M}_\mathcal{L}$
2. Compute the diagonal matrices D_1 and D_2 from Eq. (3)
3. Compute $\tilde{U}^{(0)}$ and $\tilde{F}^{(m)}$

$$\tilde{U}^{(0)} = \Theta^{-1}U^{(0)} \tag{5}$$

$$\tilde{F}^{(m)} = \Theta^{-1}F^{(m)} \qquad m = 1 \text{ to } M \tag{6}$$

4. Compute $\tilde{U}^{(m)}$ by solving in parallel the FOILR in Eq. (4).
5. Compute $U^{(m)}$

$$U^{(m)} = \Theta\tilde{U}^{(m)} \qquad m = 1 \text{ to } M \tag{7}$$

If $\mathcal{M}_\mathcal{L}$ is symmetric, then $\Theta^{-1} = \Theta^T$, where T denotes transpose. Thus, in Eqs. (5)-(6), MVM rather than linear system solution is required. For nonsymmetric $\mathcal{M}_\mathcal{L}$, the linear system solutions can be also avoided by noting that Θ^{-1} is the matrix of the eigenvectors of matrix $\mathcal{M}_\mathcal{L}^T$. Thus, if in Step 1 the eigenvectors of $\mathcal{M}_\mathcal{L}^T$ are also computed, then the operations in Eqs. (5)-(6) can be reduced to MVM. In a parallel environment with a sufficient number of processors, this does not degrade the computational efficiency, since the computations for $\mathcal{M}_\mathcal{L}$ and $\mathcal{M}_\mathcal{L}^T$ can be performed in parallel (see also §4.2).

The computations in Steps 1 and 2 are space dependent, and need to be performed once (see below). Steps 3 and 5 highlight the full temporal decoupling. With $O(M)$ processors, the corresponding computation can be performed with a complexity of $O(1)$ in time and of $O(k)$ in space, with no communication among processors, where k stands for the cost of MVM. The only communication occurs in the parallel solution of the FOILR in Eq. (4). As can be seen, our proposed time-parallel algorithms have a highly decoupled structure. For many applications of interest, M is very large (of the order of hundreds or thousands). Thus, such a time-parallel computing approach will lead to a massive degree of coarse grain temporal parallelism with simple communication and synchronization requirements.

Besides Step 1, the most computation-intensive part of the time-parallel algorithms is the MVM in Steps 3 and 5. In general, for 2D and 3D problems, the corresponding cost is of $O(N^4)$ and $O(N^6)$. This represents a major improvement over the direct parallel computation of Eq. (2). However, as will be shown below, for a wide class of problems one can exploit the structure of matrix $\mathcal{M}_{\mathcal{L}}$, so that both the computation of Step 1 and the MVMs in Steps 3 and 5 can be performed with a greater efficiency.

Our time-parallel computing approach can also be directly applied to the explicit and implicit methods, given by Eq. (2), by using the same diagonalization technique. The resulting time-parallel algorithms will have the similar computational structure, the only difference being in the definition of the diagonal matrices D_1 and D_2. For the explicit method, we would obtain $D_1 = I - 2\alpha\Lambda$ and $D_2 = I$ while for the implicit method, we would have $D_1 = D_2 = (I + 2\alpha\Lambda)^{-1}$.

However, in order to satisfy the stability constraints, and achieve the same level of accuracy as the C-N method, both the implicit and explicit methods require a much larger number of time-steps. This implies that, for a given accuracy and overall computation time, the time-parallel computation of the implicit and explicit methods would require a significantly larger number of processors. Thus, for a given number of processors, a time-parallel computation of the C-N method will result in a significantly more efficient overall implementation, with a much better accuracy, than either the implicit or explicit methods.

3.3. Efficiency and Applicability

The basic idea of time-parallel computation is rather simple. It is also general, in the sense that it can directly be applied to other types of time-dependent PDEs, such as first order and second order hyperbolic equations [16]. However, what makes it a highly practical and efficient approach for massively parallel environments is the fact that, for a wide class of practical applications, the computation of eigenpairs of the matrix $\mathcal{M}_{\mathcal{L}}$ can be performed very efficiently. Furthermore, the multiplication of the matrix of eigenvectors by a vector can also be carried out with a great efficiency.

Motivated by the simple structure and massive coarse grain parallelism underlying our approach, we have attempted to identify those problems for which our approach can be applied most efficiently. The two main factors under consideration are:

a. Fast and accurate computation of the eigenpairs of $\mathcal{M}_{\mathcal{L}}$;
b. Fast multiplication of matrix of eigenvectors by a vector.

Although our results are preliminary, rather surprisingly they indicate that a wide class of problems are *readily* well suited for such an approach. Such problems can be characterized as those for which the structure of matrix $\mathcal{M}_{\mathcal{L}}$ can be exploited to achieve a high computational efficiency for the above two factors. In the following, brief discussions of these factors are presented.

3.3.1. Fast Computation of Eigenpairs of $\mathcal{M}_{\mathcal{L}}$

Depending on the structure of $\mathcal{M}_{\mathcal{L}}$, which results from the type of elliptic operator, the boundary conditions, and the considered domain, we can identify three main techniques for fast computation of its eigenpairs. The first and second techniques are more special, in the sense that they take a greater advantage of the specific structure of $\mathcal{M}_{\mathcal{L}}$, while the third technique is more general, wherein only the sparsity of $\mathcal{M}_{\mathcal{L}}$ is exploited.

a. Analytical Expression of Eigenpairs of $\mathcal{M}_{\mathcal{L}}$

For a few simple elliptic operators on a regular domain, the analytical expression of the eigenpairs of $\mathcal{M}_{\mathcal{L}}$ is known *a priori*. Typical example is the Laplace operator on 2D and 3D regular domains. However, our analysis indicates that it is possible to develop analytical formulae for some cases where no such expressions were previously known. The first example is the matrix arising from the application of the C-N method to the solution of a first-order hyperbolic equation. The second example is the matrix arising from the discretization of convection-diffusion type of operators with constant coefficients. The corresponding derivations are discussed in [16].

Even though the class of problems for which the analytical expression of eigenpairs can be derived is rather limited, it needs to be further explored since they are well suited for time-parallel computation. Interestingly, however, as we shall see in the second example of §4, the availability of analytical expressions does not necessarily imply optimal efficiency for our time-parallel computation approach.

b. Divide and Conquer Method

The second method can be considered as a divide and conquer approach, which exploits the specific structure of $\mathcal{M}_{\mathcal{L}}$. It reduces the computation of the eigenpairs of $\mathcal{M}_{\mathcal{L}}$ to the computation of eigenpairs of a set of simpler matrices, e.g., symmetric and nonsymmetric tridiagonal matrices. This method can be applied to a wide class of linear operators on regular domains. Our preliminary analysis [16] indicates that classes of such operators include the Laplace operator in polar and spherical coordinates, separable elliptic operators, some cases of nonseparable elliptic operators, etc..

The advantage of this method is its high efficiency, yielding an optimal computational cost for most cases. It also offers a high degree of coarse grain parallelism, since the computation of eigenpairs of the set of tridiagonal matrices can be performed in parallel. Furthermore, the matrix of the eigenvectors can be obtained as a factor of sparse matrices, which allows its fast multiplication by any vector. This method is further illustrated in the second example treated in §4.

c. General Sparse Matrix Techniques

The third method is more general, and can be used for problems for which the first and the second methods cannot be applied. Regardless of the type of operator and boundary condition, $\mathcal{M}_{\mathcal{L}}$ has a highly sparse structure. Thus, a general approach for efficient computation of its eigenpairs would be based on the use of well known techniques for sparse eigenproblems [17]. *The key point, however, is the fact that we are not interested in explicit computation of the matrix of eigenvectors, but rather in its multiplication with some vector.* Specifically, it is more efficient to obtain the matrix of eigenvectors in a factored form, since its multiplication by a vector can then be performed with a greater efficiency (see below). This is a clear departure from most conventional sparse eigenproblem techniques, wherein the explicit computation of the matrix of eigenvectors is sought.

3.3.2. Fast Multiplication of Matrix of Eigenvectors by a Vector

In general, the matrix of eigenvectors, Θ, is dense. For a 2D problem, the cost of multiplication of Θ by a vector is of $O(N^4)$. Our emphasis on efficient techniques for this MVM is based on the following facts. Computing the matrix Θ in a factored form allows, in most cases, a much faster MVM, e.g., in $O(N^3)$ or even in $O(N^2\text{Log } N)$. For a typical 2D problem with N of the order of hundreds, this would result in *more than two orders of magnitude speedup*, regardless of the degree to which the computation is parallelized in time. Such a significant improvement provides a strong rationale for techniques that compute the matrix of eigenvectors in a factored form and thus, by avoiding its explicit evaluation, also achieve a greater efficiency in computing the eigenpairs of matrix $\mathcal{M}_{\mathcal{L}}$.

4. TWO EXAMPLES OF TIME-PARALLEL ALGORITHMS

In order to better illustrate the concept of time-parallel computation, we briefly discuss its application to two model problems.

4.1. The 2D Heat Equation

As a first example, we consider the solution of a 2D heat equation on a square domain. Note that this model problem has also been considered in [4,5,9,10,12]. For the heat equation, the elliptic operator in Eq. (1) is the Laplace operator. Thus, for the C-N method, Eq. (2) represents a sequence of Poisson equations. By using the *Fast Poisson Solvers* [18] each solution of Eq. (2) can be obtained in $O(N^2\text{Log } N)$, leading to an overall complexity of $O(MN^2\text{Log } N)$ in the framework of the C-N formalism.

On a square domain, the analytical expressions of eigenpairs of the Laplace operator for different boundary conditions are known. For the Dirichlet boundary condition, the matrix Θ is the operator of the 2D Discrete Sine Transform (DST), and is given as $\Theta = \mathcal{Q}P\mathcal{Q}$ where $\mathcal{Q} = \text{Diag}\{Q, Q, \ldots, Q\} \epsilon \Re^{N^2 \times N^2}$ and $Q \epsilon \Re^{N \times N}$ is the operator of 1D DST. Furthermore, $P \epsilon \Re^{N^2 \times N^2}$ is a permutation matrix which arises in application of 2D discrete transforms. Note that, $P^T = P^{-1}$, since P is a permutation matrix and hence is orthogonal.

The multiplication of matrix Θ by any vector is tantamount to performing a 2D DST which can be computed in $O(N^2\text{Log } N)$. Thus, in a parallel implementation using $O(M)$ processors, the computational complexity of the time-parallel algorithm, C_{TP}, is given by

$$C_{TP} = a_1 N^2 \text{Log } N + a_2 N^2 \text{Log } M$$

where a_1 and a_2 are some constants and lower degree terms are neglected. The speedup, S_{TP}, is then obtained as

$$S_{TP} = O((M\,Log\ N)/(Log\ N + Log\ M)) \tag{8}$$

A comparison of our theoretical result, given by Eq. (8), and the practical results of implementation of the time-parallel algorithm on Delta, presented in [2], with those reported in [4,5,9,10,12] for this same model problem clearly indicates the efficiency of our time-parallel computing approach. The results in [2] also support the assessment regarding the efficiency of the time-parallel algorithms for implementation on massively parallel MIMD architectures.

4.2. Laplace Operator in Polar Coordinates

As a second example, we consider the solution of class of problems involving the Laplace operator in polar coordinates. Note that, for this example the analytical expression of eigenpairs of $\mathcal{M}_{\mathcal{L}}$ is not known. However, as shown below, these eigenpairs can be efficiently computed by using the Divide-and-Conquer method of § 3.3.1.

The Laplace operator in polar coordinates is given by

$$\nabla^2 U = \frac{\partial^2 U}{\partial \rho^2} + \frac{1}{\rho}\frac{\partial U}{\partial \rho} + \frac{1}{\rho^2}\frac{\partial^2 U}{\partial \phi^2}$$

The domain Ω is considered to be an annulus between two circles with radii ρ_0 and ρ_1. The mesh points in the ρ-ϕ plane are defined by the points of intersection of the circles $\rho = i\Delta\rho$, $i = q-1$ to $p+1$, and the straight lines $\phi = j\Delta\phi$, $j = 1$ to N, where $\Delta\phi = 2\pi/N$. For simplicity, it is assumed that $\rho_0 = (q-1)\Delta\rho$, $\rho_1 = (p+1)\Delta\rho$ and $K = p - q + 1$. With Dirichlet boundary conditions and using the five-point finite-difference scheme, $\mathcal{M}_{\mathcal{L}}$ is a block tridiagonal matrix given by

$$\mathcal{M}_{\mathcal{L}} = \text{Tridiag}[(1-1/2i)I,\ \ B_i,\ \ (1+1/2i)I] \epsilon \Re^{KN\times KN},\ i = q \text{ to } p$$

where I is the $N \times N$ identity matrix, $B_i = \beta_i B - 2I$ with $\beta_i = (1/i\Delta\phi)^2$, and B is an $N \times N$ symmetric tridiagonal matrix with a periodic structure given by $B =$ Tridiag$[1, -2, 1]$ with $B_{1N} = B_{N1} = 1$. Note that, this periodic structure of B results from the periodicity in ϕ. The following theorem is used in deriving the EED of $\mathcal{M}_{\mathcal{L}}$.

Theorem 1. The EED of the matrix B is given by

$$B = FDF^{-1}$$

where F is the matrix of eigenvectors and $D = \text{Diag}\{d_j\}$, $j = 1$ to N, is the diagonal matrix of eigenvalues, with $d_j = -4\sin^2[(j-1)\pi/N]$.

Proof. See for example [19].

The matrices F and F^{-1} are the direct and inverse 1D Discrete Fourier Transform (DFT) operators. Thus, their multiplication by any vector can be performed in $O(N \, Log \, N)$. From the definition of B_i, it follows that B_i and B share the same set of eigenvectors. The EED of B_i is then given by $B_i = F\lambda_i F^{-1}$ where $\lambda_i = \text{Diag}\{\lambda_{ij}\} = \beta_i D - 2I$, $j = 1$ to N, and $\lambda_{ij} = \beta_i d_j - 2$.

Theorem 2. The EED of $\mathcal{M}_{\mathcal{L}}$ is given by

$$\mathcal{M}_{\mathcal{L}} = \mathcal{F}\mathcal{P}\mathcal{Q}\Lambda\mathcal{Q}^{-1}\mathcal{P}^T\mathcal{F}^{-1} \tag{9}$$

where $\mathcal{F} = \text{Diag}\{F, F, \ldots, F\}$ and Λ is the diagonal matrix of eigenvalues which, along with the matrix $\mathcal{Q}$, is defined below.

Proof. The matrix $\mathcal{M}_{\mathcal{L}}$ can be written as

$$\mathcal{M}_{\mathcal{L}} = \text{Tridiag}[(1 - 1/2i)I, \quad F\lambda_i F^{-1}, \quad (1 + 1/2i)I] = \mathcal{F}\mathcal{R}\mathcal{F}^{-1} \tag{10}$$

where $\mathcal{R} = \text{Tridiag}[(1 - 1/2i)I, \quad \lambda_i, \quad (1 + 1/2i)I]$. The block elements of $\mathcal{R}$ are diagonal. Thus, it can be reduced to a block diagonal matrix $\mathcal{T}$ using

$$\mathcal{R} = \mathcal{P}\mathcal{P}^T\mathcal{R}\mathcal{P}\mathcal{P}^T = \mathcal{P}(\mathcal{P}^T\mathcal{R}\mathcal{P})\mathcal{P}^T = \mathcal{P}\mathcal{T}\mathcal{P}^T \tag{11}$$

where $\mathcal{T} = \text{Diag}\{T_j\}$ and $T_j = \text{Tridiag}\ [(1 - 1/2i), \quad \lambda_{ij}, \quad (1 + 1/2i)]$, $j = 1$ to N and $i = q$ to p. Now, let the EED of T_j be given by $T_j = Q_j\Lambda_j Q_j^{-1}$. Defining $\mathcal{Q} = \text{Diag}\{Q_j\}$ and $\Lambda = \text{Diag}\{\Lambda_j\}$, $j = 1$ to N, it follows that

$$\mathcal{T} = \mathcal{Q}\Lambda\mathcal{Q}^{-1} \tag{12}$$

The EED of $\mathcal{M}_{\mathcal{L}}$, given by Eq. (9), is obtained by substituting Eqs. (11)-(12) into Eq. (10).

The matrix T_j is *sign symmetric*, since the products of pairs of the corresponding off-diagonal elements are all nonzero and positive, and hence has real eigenvalues. Due to this property, all eigenpairs of T_j can be efficiently computed by using, for example, the subroutine RT provided by EISPACK [20]. Multiplication of a vector by Q_j^{-1} corresponds to the solution of a linear system involving a computational cost of $O(K^3)$. However, following our discussion in §3.2., this operation can be reduced to a MVM with a cost of $O(K^2)$ by noting that Q_j^{-1} is the matrix of eigenvectors of matrix T_j^T. Therefore, if the EED of T_j^T is also computed then the matrix Q_j^{-1} is explicitly obtained and its multiplication by a vector represents a simple MVM. For typical values of K of the order of hundreds, this scheme results in a two order of magnitude improvement in the computational efficiency.

Now, let us consider a parallel implementation by using M processors. Assuming $M \geq 2N$, the EED of $2N$ sign symmetric tridiagonal matrices T_j and T_j^T can be performed in parallel, leading to a cost of $O(K^2)$ for Step 1. The diagonal matrices D_1 and D_2 can be computed in $O(KN)$ and the cost of parallel solution of the FOILR in Eq. (4) is of $O(KN\,Log\ M)$. Note that, the matrix of eigenvectors, Θ, is obtained in a factored form as $\Theta = \mathcal{F}\mathcal{P}\mathcal{Q}$. Thus, the multiplication of Θ and Θ^{-1} by a vector in Steps 3 and 5 can be performed with a cost of $a_1K^2N + a_2KN\,Log\ N$, where a_1 and a_2 are constants and lower degree terms are neglected. It then follows that the cost of such implementation of time-parallel algorithm, C_{TP}, is given by $C_{TP} = a_1K^2N + a_2KN\,Log\ N + a_3KN\,Log\ M$, where a_3 is a constant and lower degree terms have been neglected.

The fast Poisson solvers of [18] can be also extended to solution of the problem in polar coordinates. This implies that, for the C-N method, the cost of best serial algorithm for each solution of Eq. (2) is of $O(KN\,Log\ N)$, leading to an overall complexity of $O(MKN\,Log\ N)$. The speedup of the time-parallel algorithm, S_{TP}, is then given by

$$S_{TP} = \frac{MKN\,Log\ N}{a_1K^2N + a_2KN\,Log\ N + a_3KN\,Log\ M} = O((M\,Log\ N)/K)$$

At first glance, it might have seemed that time-parallel algorithms could be more efficiently applied to those problems for which the analytical expression of eigenpairs of $\mathcal{M}_L$ are known, and hence no computation is needed. However, our analysis of the performance of the time-parallel algorithm for this example, for which additional computations are required for derivation of such eigenpairs, appears to clearly indicate the contrary. This result seems to be rather general and shows that, for most cases, *the performance of the time-parallel algorithms will not be degraded due to the need of computing the eigenpairs, if the latter is performed efficiently.*

5. CONCLUSION

We have presented a novel technique for massively parallel solution of time-dependent PDEs. Our discussion on the efficient applicability of this technique clearly indicates that it can be extended to the solution of a wide class of such PDEs. It was shown that, for this class of problems, the C-N method is significantly more efficient than the explicit and implicit methods for time-parallel computation.

We have shown that, by using the first and particularly the second technique of § 3.3.1. for efficient computation of eigenpairs of matrix $\mathcal{M}_{\mathcal{L}}$, our approach can be *readily* applied to a rather large class of problems of practical interest [16]. However, the ultimate generalization of our approach, particularly for solution of problems on irregular domains, requires further research work on analyzing and designing appropriate sparse eigenproblems techniques in the framework of the discussion in §3.3.1.

ACKNOWLEDGEMENT

This research was performed at the Center for Space Microelectronics Technology, Jet Propulsion Laboratory, California Institute of Technology. It was jointly sponsored by Innovative Science and Technology Office of the Ballistic Missile Defense Organization, and by the National Aeronautics and Space Administration, Office of Advanced Concepts and Technology. The support and encouragement of Dr. Paul Messina, Director of the Concurrent Supercomputing Consortium, is greatly acknowledged.

REFERENCES

1. A. Fijany,"Time-Parallel Algorithms for Solution of Linear Parabolic PDEs", Proc. Int. Conf. Parallel Processing (ICPP), Vol. III, pp. 51-55, Aug. 1993.
2. N. Toomarian, A. Fijany, and J. Barhen,"Time Parallel Solution of Linear Partial Differential Equations on the Intel Touchstone Delta Supercomputer", to appear in *J. of Concurrency*, 1994.
3. J.M. Ortega and R.G. Voigt, *Solution of Partial Differential Equations on Vector and Parallel Computers*, SIAM Pub., 1984.
4. E. Gallopoulos and Y. Saad,"On the Parallel Solution of Parabolic Equations," Proc. ACM Int. Conf. on Supercomputing, pp. 17-28, June 1989.
5. G. Rodriguez and D. Wolitzer,"Preconditioned Time-Differencing for the Parallel Solution of the Heat Equation," Proc. 4th SIAM Conf. on Parallel Processing, pp. 268-272, 1990.

6. D. J. Evans,"Alternating Group Explicit Methods for the Diffusion Equation," Appl. Math. Modelling, Vol. 9, pp. 201-206, 1985.
7. S. M. Serbin,"A Scheme for Parallelizing Certain Algorithms for the Linear Inhomogeneous Heat equation," SIAM J. Sci. Stat. Comput., Vol. 13(2), pp. 449-458, March 1992.
8. E. Lelarasmee et al,"The Waveform Relaxation Method for the Time Domain Analysis of Large Scale Integrated Circuits," IEEE Trans. Computer-Aided Design, Vol. 1, pp. 131-145, 1982.
9. J. H. Saltz and V. K. Nail,"Towards Developing Robust Algorithms for Solving Partial Differential Equations on MIMD Machines," Parallel Computing, Vol. 6, pp. 19-44, 1988.
10. D. E. Womble,"A Time-Stepping Algorithm for Parallel Computers," SIAM J. Sci. Stat. Comput., Vol. 11(5), pp. 824-837, 1990.
11. W. Hackbusch,"Fast Numerical Solution of Time Periodic Parabolic Problems by a Multigrid Method, SIAM J. Sci. Stat. Comput., Vol. 2, pp. 198-206, 1981.
12. G. Horton and R. Knirsch,"A Time-Parallel Multigrid-Extrapolation Method for Parabolic Partial Differential Equations," Parallel Computing, Vol. 18, pp. 21-29, 1992.
13. S. Vandewalle and R. Piessens,"Efficient Parallel Algorithms for Solving Initial-Boundary Value and Time-Periodic Parabolic Differential Equations," SIAM J. Sci. Stat. Comput., Vol. 13(6), pp. 1330-1346, Nov. 1992.
14. G. Strang and G. J. Fix, *An Analysis of the Finite Element Method.* Prentice-Hall, Englewood Cliffs, NJ, 1973.
15. R. Hockney and C. Jesshope, *Parallel Computers.* Adam Hilger Ltd., 1981.
16. A. Fijany, J. Barhen, N. Toomarian "On the Structure of Time-Parallel Algorithms for Solution of Time-dependent PDEs," In preparation.
17. S. Pissanetzky, *Sparse Matrix technology.* Academic Press, 1984.
18. B. Buzbee, G. Golub, and C. Nielson,"On Direct Methods for Solving Poisson Equations," SIAM J. Numer. Anal., Vol. 7, pp. 627-656, 1970.
19. C. Van Loan, *Computational Frameworks for Fast Fourier Transform.* SIAM Pub., Philadelphia, 1992.
20. B.T. Smith *et al, Matrix Eigensystem Routines- Eispack Guide.* 2nd Ed., Springer Verlag, 1976.

Toward Teraflop Computing
and New Grand
Challenge Applications

ISBN-1-56072-247-9

THE STUDY OF ANISOTROPIC SUPERCONDUCTORS WITH A PARALLEL, SPARSE TRUST REGION NEWTON METHOD

Lois Curfman McInnes * and Mario Palumbo †

Mathematics and Computer Science Division
Argonne National Laboratory
Argonne, IL 60439

ABSTRACT

In this paper we study the magnetic properties of anisotropic type-II superconductors by minimizing the free energy functional within the three-dimensional anisotropic Ginzburg-Landau model. A finite-dimensional approximation of this functional produces a very large, sparse optimization problem with $O(10^6)$ degrees of freedom. Newton-like methods have proven to be robust and efficient for solving such problems. In particular, we employ a sparse, parallel version of a trust region Newton method that uses the preconditioned conjugate gradient technique to approximate a minimizer of the resulting quadratic function. Our computations are done within the framework of the Simplified Unconstrained Minimization Solvers (SUMS), a portable and extensible software library that provides robust solution strategies for both uniprocessor and multiprocessor architectures.

We present computational results on the IBM SP1 for determining the minimum energy of a single tilted vortex in an anisotropic superconductor. Such a calculation is fundamental to the understanding of the angular dependence of the lower critical field as well as the detailed nature of the vortex "chain" state.

1. INTRODUCTION

The magnetic properties of anisotropic type-II superconductors have recently received a great deal of scientific attention, mainly because of the discovery of the so-called high-temperature superconducting compounds. Type-II superconductors are characterized by a vortex or mixed state in which superconductivity

*This work was supported by an appointment to the Distinguished Postdoctoral Research Program sponsored by the U.S. Department of Energy, Office of University and Science Education, and administered by the Oak Ridge Institute for Science and Education.

†This work was supported by the Office of Scientific Computing, U.S. Department of Energy, under Contract W-31-109-Eng-38.

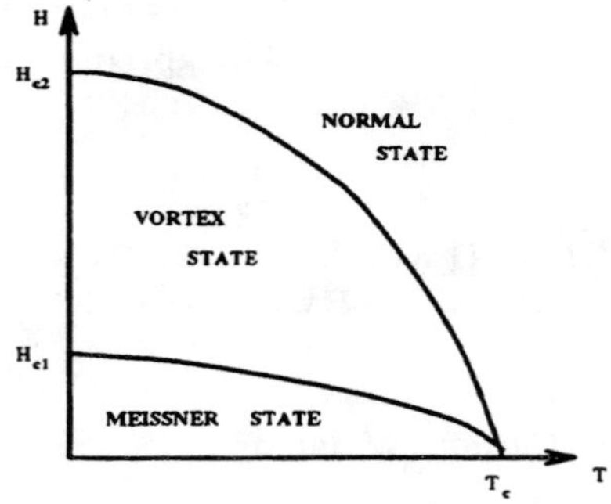

Figure 1: Phase Diagram of a Conventional Type-II Superconductor. The axes represent the temperature, T, and the applied magnetic field strength, H.

coexists with a local magnetic induction. Figure 1 presents the phase diagram of a typical type-II superconductor. In the Meissner phase the material is completely superconducting, with a finite local magnetic induction existing in only a thin layer near the surface. In the normal state superconductivity is destroyed, while the local magnetic induction is uniform throughout the sample. In the vortex state, however, regions of superconductivity and finite magnetic induction coexist through the formation of magnetic vortices, which are essentially quantized tubes of magnetic flux separated from the superconducting regions of the sample by circulating supercurrents. At a given temperature, T, the vortex state is separated from the normal state by the upper critical field, $H_{c2}(T)$, while the vortex and Meissner states are separated by the lower critical field, $H_{c1}(T)$. The behavior of the lower critical field as a function of the direction of the applied field is the focus of our considerations in this paper.

In this paper we study the effect of anisotropy on the lower critical field of a *uniaxial* superconductor, which has only one anisotropic direction. Nearly all of the known anisotropic superconducting systems are uniaxial. We will see that the presence of anisotropy leads to significant qualitative differences in the behavior of the lower critical field with respect to isotropic materials.

We perform all calculations within the framework of the anisotropic Ginzburg-Landau model, which provides an accurate description of the macroscopic behavior of anisotropic superconducting materials. The presence of anisotropy makes the model inherently three-dimensional, so that for most applications analytic study is intractable. Thus, to analyze many of the effects of anisotropy on basic superconducting properties requires numerical simulations. For realistic systems, minimization of the Ginzburg-Landau free energy functional produces a challenging optimization problem with $O(10^6)$ degrees of freedom and no unique solution.

Problems such as this demand a robust and efficient solution strategy as well as the computational resources of high-performance computers. We employ a sparse, parallel version of a trust region Newton method that is especially effective for this class of problem. Our computations are done within the framework of the Simplified Unconstrained Minimization Solvers (SUMS), a portable and extensible software library for both uniprocessor and multiprocessor architectures.

The remainder of this paper is organized as follows. In Section 2 we present the problem formulation, while in Section 3 we describe the sparse, parallel minimization strategy. Finally, in Section 4 we present computational results that provide insight into the magnetic properties of type-II syperconductors.

2. PROBLEM FORMULATION

To study the magnetic properties of anisotropic materials, we seek the global minimizer of the anisotropic Ginzburg-Landau free energy functional. For the case of uniaxial superconductors, the total free energy over some volume Ω is given by

$$\mathcal{F}[\psi, \boldsymbol{A}] = \int_{\Omega} \left(\mathcal{F}_{cond}[\psi] + \mathcal{F}_{grad}[\psi, \boldsymbol{A}] + \mathcal{F}_{field}[\boldsymbol{A}]\right) d\Omega, \tag{1}$$

where ψ is a complexed-valued order parameter, and $\boldsymbol{A}$ is the magnetic vector potential. The three terms in the free energy are typically referred to as the condensation, gradient, and field energy terms, respectively, and can be written in dimensionless form within the Cartesian coordinate system as follows:

$$\mathcal{F}_{cond}[\psi] = -|\psi|^2 + \frac{1}{2}|\psi|^4 \tag{2}$$

$$\mathcal{F}_{grad}[\psi, \boldsymbol{A}] = |(\nabla_{xy} + i\boldsymbol{A}_{xy})\psi|^2 + \gamma\,|(\nabla_z + iA_z)\psi|^2 \tag{3}$$

$$\mathcal{F}_{field}[\boldsymbol{A}] = \kappa^2\,|\nabla \times \boldsymbol{A}|^2, \tag{4}$$

where γ is the mass anisotropy factor, and κ is the Ginzburg-Landau parameter, both of which are material-dependent. The physical quantities of interest in this model include the local density of superconducting electrons, given by $|\psi|^2$, and the local magnetic induction, $\boldsymbol{B} = \nabla \times \boldsymbol{A}$.

A noteworthy feature of the free energy functional is its invariance under a gauge transformation. That is, given any pair $\{\psi, \boldsymbol{A}\}$ and any scalar function ϕ, there exists another pair $\{\psi', \boldsymbol{A}'\}$ defined by

$$\psi' = \psi e^{-i\phi}, \qquad \boldsymbol{A}' = \boldsymbol{A} + \nabla\phi, \tag{5}$$

that leaves the free energy and, in fact, all physical observables, unchanged. This symmetry property implies that there is no unique solution to the anisotropic Ginzburg-Landau model, since any solution is only known up to a gauge transformation. Numerically this indicates the presence of a large null space, which presents a nontrivial obstacle in the minimization process.

By definition, the lower critical field of a type-II superconductor is the lowest field at which vortices first enter the sample. If we take $\varepsilon_v(\theta_B)$ to be the energy of an isolated vortex, then in our dimensionless units the lower critical field is given by

$$H_{c1} = \frac{1}{(2\pi\kappa)^2}\sqrt{\left(\frac{\partial\varepsilon_v}{\partial\theta_B}\right)^2 + \varepsilon_v^2}, \tag{6}$$

where θ_B refers to the angle between the uniaxial direction and the average magnetic induction. This expression is valid only if vortices always repel each other in all directions, which is not true in the case we are analyzing. However, the attraction between vortices is quite small in the parameter ranges we consider. We return to this point in Section 4 to estimate a bound on the error introduced by this approximation.

To simplify our work, we introduce an approximation to the free energy which makes the resulting system quasi-two-dimensional (Preosti, 1993). We assume that the average magnetic induction, $\langle \boldsymbol{B} \rangle$, makes an angle θ_B with repect to the uniaxial direction. We then rotate the coordinate system such that the $\hat{z}$ axis lies along the direction of $\langle \boldsymbol{B} \rangle$, and we assume there is no variation along the vortex. In this way all gradients with respect to z are zero, so that the free energy term is simplified accordingly.

3. PARALLEL, SPARSE MINIMIZATION STRATEGY

Discretization of the domain Ω with n_g grid points produces the unconstrained optimization problem

$$\min\{\mathcal{F}(\boldsymbol{x}) : \boldsymbol{x} \in \Re^n\}, \tag{7}$$

where $\mathcal{F}$ is the free energy functional, $\boldsymbol{x}$ consists of the magnetic vector potential and order parameter evaluated at the grid points, and $n = 5n_g$ for the three-dimensional case. Recently, Newton-like methods have proven to be robust and efficient for solving such minimization problems arising within the context of superconductivity. Garner et al. (1992) and Jones and Plassmann (1993a) considered a damped, inexact Newton method with a line search. Instead, we employ a trust region Newton scheme that uses the preconditioned conjugate gradient method to determine an approximate minimizer of the resulting quadratic function. This approach was first described by Steihaug (1983), and a uniprocessor version is included within MINAPCK-2 (Moré, 1993). We use a new parallel, sparse implementation that is part of the Simplified Unconstrained Minimization Solvers (SUMS) library (Gropp and McInnes, 1994) for numerical solution of unconstrained minimization problems in both uniprocessor and multiprocessor environments.

3.1 Trust Region Newton Method

The trust region approach is based on the fact that Newton-like methods employ a quadratic model of the objective function around the current iterate, $\boldsymbol{x}_k$. Thus, the reduction $\mathcal{F}(\boldsymbol{x}_k + \boldsymbol{s}) - \mathcal{F}(\boldsymbol{x}_k)$ is modeled by

$$q_k(\boldsymbol{s}) = \boldsymbol{g}(\boldsymbol{x}_k)^T \boldsymbol{s} + \frac{1}{2}\boldsymbol{s}^T H_k \boldsymbol{s}, \tag{8}$$

where $\boldsymbol{g}(\boldsymbol{x}_k) = \nabla \mathcal{F}(\boldsymbol{x}_k)^T$, and $H_k = \nabla^2 \mathcal{F}(\boldsymbol{x}_k)$ is the symmetric Hessian matrix. Since the model is accurate only in a neighborhood of the current iterate (called the trust region), we determine the succeeding trial step, s_k, to be the approximate minimizer of the quadratic constrained within the trust region. Thus, the resulting subproblem is to solve

$$\min\{q_k(s) : \|s\| \leq \Delta_k\}, \tag{9}$$

where Δ_k is a positive parameter, and $\|\cdot\|$ is the Euclidean norm in $\Re^n$. If $\mathcal{F}(x_k + s)$ is sufficiently reduced, then the step is accepted and Δ_k can be increased; otherwise, the step is rejected and Δ_k should be reduced.

We solve the minimization problem (9) inexactly using the preconditioned conjugate gradient method. In particular, we employ incomplete Cholesky factorization of the augmented Hessian matrix, as given by

$$H_k + \gamma_k I \approx LL^T, \tag{10}$$

where I denotes the identity matrix, and γ_k is a positive scalar that is computed at each iteration. This modification overcomes difficulties inherent in the superconductivity problem, since the Hessian, $\nabla^2\mathcal{F}(x^*)$, is positive semidefinite at the solution.

3.2 Parallel, Sparse Solution within SUMS

We describe the minimization of the free energy functional using the SUMS package, with emphasis on the library's unique features that facilitate the customized solution of a wide variety of application problems. SUMS is a portable, parallel minimization package that is designed to be flexible and extensible, so that it easily adapts to the continually changing multiprocessor environments and the steadily advancing state-of-the-art in computational linear algebra. We note that SUMS is part of the multi-level PETSc (Portable, Extensible Tools for Scientific computation) library (Gropp and Smith, 1993), which provides support for flexible data structures, vector and matrix-vector operations, direct and iterative linear solution techniques, preconditioning strategies, domain decomposition tools, communication routines, and performance monitors.

The problem considered in this work has a regular domain with a uniform discretization. The parallel implementation employs a two-dimensional grid decomposition and a distributed sparse row scheme for matrix data. Thus, each processor stores the unknowns as well as the corresponding rows of the Hessian matrix that are associated with its grid points. The SUMS library is particularly useful for this case since it is designed to be data-structure-neutral, so that the natural storage formats for vectors and matrices can be dictated by the user's application.

A modular design is used for the minimization routines within SUMS, thereby enabling experimentation with newly developed solution strategies and customization according to the user's needs. For example, this modularity facilitates the incorporation of the parallel incomplete Cholesky factorization approach and triangular solution strategy of Jones and Plassmann (1992), which are used for the preconditioning phase of the conjugate gradient method in solving the trust region subproblem.

4. COMPUTATIONAL RESULTS

We present computational results for determining the lower critical field of a single tilted vortex in an anisotropic superconductor. We also estimate a bound on the error introduced by our assumption of an isolated vortex. All of the following computational experiments were performed on the IBM SP1, where we employed from one through thirty-two nodes, depending on the particular problem size.

Figure 2 shows a cross section of the magnetic induction, B_z, in the xy-plane in the rotated coordinate system. This result was generated with $\kappa = 2$, $\gamma = 5$, and $\theta_B = 75$ degrees. The dark regions on either side of the field's center indicate areas of negative magnetic induction, which should act to attract neighboring vortices. We expect this interaction to be weak, since the magnitude of the minimum value of B_z is less than one percent of the maximum value. Because the negative region is deepest for $\theta_B \approx 75$ degrees, this is a reasonable bound on the error of our "isolated vortex" approximation.

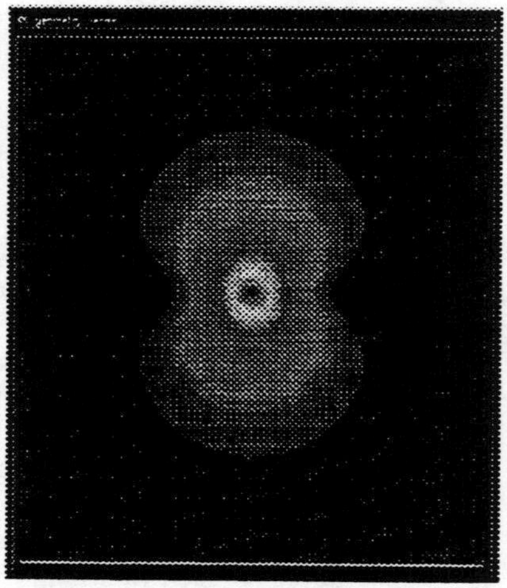

Figure 2: Cross-Section of Magnetic Induction

Figure 3 illustrates the results of our calculations of the lower critical field, H_{c1}, as a function of the angle of the *applied* field H. In our dimensionless units, the average magnetic induction is given by

$$\langle \boldsymbol{B} \rangle = \frac{2\pi}{N_x a_x N_y a_y}, \tag{11}$$

where we assume that the number of grid points in each direction is $N_x = N_y$. Also, the separation between grid points taken to be $a_x = a_y = .25\xi$, where

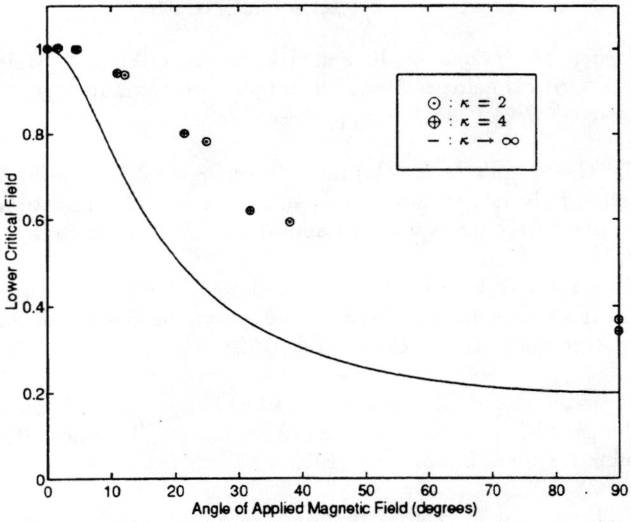

Figure 3: Lower Critical Field Versus Angle of Applied Magnetic Field, θ_H

ξ denotes the correlation length. For each point on the graph a series of runs was performed with the system sizes gradually being increased (or, equivalently, the average magnetic induction gradually being decreased), until the calculated value of H_{c1} was established to three significant figures. Using $\gamma = 5$ for all experiments, we considered the cases $\kappa = 2$ and $\kappa = 4$. To assure isolation of the vortex being studied, these cases required $N_x = 400$ and $N_x = 800$, respectively, and produced minimization problems with $O(10^6)$ degrees of freedom.

The lower critical field for the London limit, $\kappa \to \infty$, which is computed analytically using (6), is represented by the solid line of the graph. We clearly see that the qualitative features of the plots are quite similar for the low κ cases and the London limit. Although quantitative differences between the low κ cases and the London limit are evident, we anticipate that further studies with higher κ parameters will indicate a continuation the trend exhibited in Figure 3.

ACKNOWLEDGEMENT

We acknowledge our scientific collaborators: William Gropp and Jorge Moré (Mathematics and Computer Science Division, Argonne National Laboratory), and Gianfranco Preosti (Physics Department, Purdue University).

REFERENCES

J. Garner, M. Spanbauer, R. Benedek, K. Strandburg, S. Wright, and P. Plassmann; "Critical fields of Josephon-coupled superconducting multilayers"; *Physical Review B*; Vol. 45 1992; pp. 7973–7983.

W. D. Gropp and L. C. McInnes; Users manual for the Simplified Nonlinear Equation Solvers and Simplified Unconstrained Minimization Solvers; Technical Report; Argonne National Laboratory; (*In preparation*).

W. D. Gropp and B. F. Smith; The design of data-structure-neutral libraries for the iterative solution of sparse linear systems; Technical Report MCS-P000-0393; Argonne National Laboratory; 1993.

M. T. Jones and P. E. Plassmann; BlockSolve v1.1: Scalable library software for the parallel solution of sparse linear systems; Technical Report ANL-92/46; Argonne National Laboratory; 1992.

M. T. Jones and P. E. Plassmann; "Computation of equilibrium vortex structures for type-II superconductors"; *Int. J. Supercomputing Applications*; Vol. 7 1993; pp. 129–143.

J. Moré. Unpublished information; Mathematics and Computer Science Division; Argonne National Laboratory; 1993.

G. Preosti. Unpublished information; Physics Department; Purdue University; 1993.

T. Steihaug. "The conjugate gradient method and trust regions in large scale optimization"; *SIAM J. Numer. Anal.*; Vol. 20 1983; pp 626–637.

Toward Teraflop Computing
and New Grand
Challenge Applications

ISBN-1-56072-247-9

DISTRIBUTED INTERPRETIVE COMPUTING ENVIRONMENT (DICE): A TOOL FOR PROTOTYPING DISTRIBUTED OPERATING SYSTEMS

J. Michael Meehan
Computer Science Department
Louisiana Tech University

The **D**istributed **I**nterpretive **C**omputing **E**nvironment (**DICE**) has been designed and implemented in order to provide a flexible testbed with which to perform investigations into distributed computing. In particular we wish to investigate alternative designs for various issues in distributed operating systems design. The system is structured as a relatively small kernel running on top of an extended m-code (***Xm-code***) interpreter. The extended m-code interpreter can be thought of as the CPU the runs the kernel as well as the user level processes. Separate copies of the interpreter and kernel execute on each participating node in the network. The kernels cooperate, using the underlying network communication procedures built into the interpreter, to provide distributed system capabilities. The kernel supports transparent process migration and remote process management. Support for extensive profiling capabilities has been built into the interpreter creating an environment from which the performance of distributed algorithms can be easily investigated under actual experimental load conditions. This paper explains the capabilities provided by DICE, a brief overview of how it is implemented, and discusses how it is being utilized to investigate several issues related to distributed operating system design.

1. INTRODUCTION

Experimental distributed operating systems have been developed either from the ground up (**Amoeba, V**) [7,8][2] or have been constructed by modifying **UNIX** [1] source code (**Mach**, **LOCUS**). [6] Due to the size and complexity of these systems and the fact that they must ultimately control the bare hardware, they are difficult to use for rapidly prototyping new design approaches and producing experimental results. The fundamental idea behind the DICE system is to provide a system which can be used on any available collection of networked computers to perform experimental investigations in distributed computing. In order to achieve this, the system is constructed on top of an interpreter. The instruction set executed by this interpreter is derived from m-code developed for the Lilith project at ETH Zürich. [4,9] We have extended the m-code instruction set for our purposes and refer to it as Xm-code. The DICE kernel is written in Modula-2 and is compiled to Xm-code to be executed by the interpreter. The DICE kernel is fully multitasking and schedules processes to be executed by the Xm-code interpreter in the same fashion as any traditional operating system. The kernel implements a collection of SVCs

(Supervisory Calls) to support I/O, file operations, interprocess communication and synchronization, and other traditional operating system support facilities.

The system is self-contained in that all development tools required for creating user level processes or new versions of the kernel can be executed from within the DICE environment. Only the Xm-code interpreter, which must execute on the native system, must be developed outside the DICE environment. DICE provides a Modula-2 compiler for generating Xm-code capable of compiling itself. A user shell program is provided with features modeled after the UNIX C-Shell. DICE provides a loader, a dynamic linker, and a stand-alone linker. In addition, a standard set of utility programs is provided for developing within the DICE environment. The entire system is ported to a new collection of hardware by simply providing an Xm-code interpreter for the new platform. The Xm-code interpreter provides four basic abstractions on which everything else resides. These are:

- artificial instruction set for architecture independence
- network communication abstraction
- native operating system independence
- native window system independence

In addition to providing a uniform abstraction for the instruction set on which everything else is built, the interpreter also provides a network communication abstraction. The kernel and all Xm-code processes utilize a uniform communications abstraction ultimately provided by the Xm-code interpreter. This communication abstraction can be implemented using any underlying network transport capability provided by the native machine. In this fashion, the system is not only platform independent in terms of the instruction set of the native hardware but is also independent of the actual underlying network support. All algorithms in the kernel used to implement process migration, remote process management, load balancing, etc., rely on the abstract network communications capability provided by the Xm-code interpreter.

SVCs to the DICE kernel, to perform operations such as file I/O, are ultimately carried out by having the kernel invoke special privileged Xm-code instructions, which in turn cause the interpreter to utilize the appropriate facilities of the native operating system. The implementation of the windowing system capabilities presented to a DICE process are implemented in a similar fashion.

2. DISTRIBUTED COMPUTING CAPABILITIES

The kernel provides in a completely transparent manner for Xm-code process migration and load balancing on the participating nodes. The user may over-ride the normal load balancing algorithm by requesting that the system fork a process on a specified node. Additionally, the user may request that a process not be a candidate for migration under the control of the load balancing algorithm. In this manner, the user may set up a distributed computing experiment specifically tailored for some purpose. All connections for interprocess communication and synchronization are handled automatically by the kernels for the user irrespective of where the processes actually execute. When an SVC request is received by a kernel from a locally executing process which must be serviced by another kernel the SVC request is converted to a request sent as a message to the appropriate kernel. That kernel receives the request, performs the work, and sends the results back to the originating kernel. The interaction between kernels is of a request response type. The kernel to kernel protocol exploits this behavior by using the response message as an implicit acknowledgment for the request message. The local kernel assigns a transaction number to the process which made the SVC request and blocks it. The process is thus blocked waiting on the completion of a specific transaction number. The request message consists of a transaction number, a function indicator, and parameters appropriate for that function. The response sent by the remote kernel consists of a transaction number, a function indicator, and the results. The transaction number in the response message matches that of the request message. These transaction numbers are uniquely assigned by the requesting kernel. If the requesting kernel does not receive a response within a time interval less than or equal to a time-out value set as a parameter in the kernel, the requesting kernel will re-transmit the request and increment a retry count. If the response does not arrive after a specified number of retries, set as a kernel configuration parameter, the requesting kernel assumes that the request cannot be handled and returns an error code to the process making the SVC request. The process can then take whatever action it deems appropriate. The three types of messages used by the kernels to communicate are *request, response, and advertisement.* Most request message types are used by the kernel to request another kernel to perform some work on behalf of a process. Every system call defined in the system has a corresponding request message type. The additional request message types *transfer, datatransfer, changeofaddress,* and *removefwdrec* are used to support process migration. The request message types *terminate, unsuspend* and *kill* are used for remote process management. The advertisement message type *Hello* is used by a kernel at boot time to inform the other kernels of its presence. The advertisement message *Bye* is broadcast by a kernel at shutdown time to notify other kernels it will no longer participate in the distributed system. The advertisement message type *Utilization* is broadcast by a kernel to inform other kernels of its load statistics at that particular time. This message is used to support the load balancing algorithm.

3. RESEARCH AREAS CURRENTLY UNDER INVESTIGATION USING DICE

The system is currently being utilized as an experimental tool in three primary areas of investigation. These are: kernel to ***kernel protocol design***, ***load balancing algorithms***, and ***fault tolerance***. Kernel to kernel protocol design deals with questions concerning how to best provide support for transparent process migration. The DICE system as currently implemented provides kernel support for process migration, from any node, to any other node, at any time regardless of the current state of the process. This differs from the process migration capabilities implemented in other systems. Some systems do not allow a process to be migrated at all after it is initially placed. This limits the system to only being able to support a static load balancing algorithm. In order for the system to be able to dynamically respond to varying loads the kernel must support a capability to migrate a process from one node to another after it has initially been placed. Systems which support this, such as **Sprite**, [3,5] currently do so in a limited fashion. In order for these systems to migrate a process from the node at which is was initially placed to another node, they first send the process back to the home (originating) node and then send it to the new destination. Other systems restrict the set of processes which can be considered for migration to only those processes which are not currently in a blocked state. These restrictions are used to avoid the problem which arises when the event occurs for which the blocked process was waiting.

The DICE system has been used to implement a number of load balancing algorithms from the literature and to conduct experiments into their performance under various loads. The data obtained from these experiments has been utilized to design a novel load balancing strategy which, it is hoped, will be capable of scaling to large numbers of nodes without incurring excessive message overhead. If a periodic transmission of load statistics is used for each kernel to inform each other kernel the message overhead quickly becomes excessive for large numbers of kernels. Even if a piggybacking scheme is employed to reduce the number of messages required to propagate the state information the number of messages required and the processing of those messages during peak load times remains a significant overhead. We have been investigating schemes in which the absence of a message during a time interval itself has information content related to the relative load of the system.

The DICE system is being utilized to implement a prototype kernel providing process-level fault tolerant capabilities. This experimental kernel is designed to provide fault tolerance through replication as a service to user processes in a transparent manner. The prototype design supports automatic failure detection and re-replication. Shadow files are transparently provided for replicated processes which interact with the file system. The shadow files are *coalesced* upon termination of the fault-tolerant process work group. In addition, the design provides for a capability to verify the correct operation of replicated processes through voting by utilizing what we refer to as marker posting . Markers are posted by an application and tagged with an identifying label. Like markers from the replicated tasks are collected by the system and compared. When a discrepancy is detected in the markers the system kills the malfunctioning process based on a majority vote and arranges to replicate a new copy from one of the survivors. Fault tolerance is to be implemented as a facility of the shell. The user issues a command of the form *ft n command,* where *n* is the level of replication desired and command is any valid command. The capability may be utilized directly by a process by making a system call to a special version of fork. There remain a number of outstanding design issues related to how to provide fault tolerance through process replication as a transparent facility of the operating system.

SUMMARY

The DICE system provides a very capable environment with which to conduct experimentation in distributed operating system design and distributed computing in general. The implementation provides a system which can be readily ported by the researcher to any available collection of networked computers. The system has been operational at Louisiana Tech University since Fall 1993. DICE is currently being utilized to perform experiments concerning **kernel to kernel protocol design, load balancing algorithms** capable of scaling to large numbers of nodes, and process level **fault tolerant capabilities** provided as a feature of the kernel. Plans for future investigations utilizing the system include performance measurement of distributed algorithms and the design of high level language concurrency features for distributed computing.

References

1. [Bach86] Bach, J. Maurice, The Design of the UNIX Operating System, Prentice-Hall, Inc.Englewood Cliffs, N.J. ,1986.

2. [Cheriton88] Cheriton, D. R., "The V Distributed System," Communications of the ACM, Vol. 31, No. 3, March 1988, pp 314-333.

3. [Douglis91] Douglis, Fred and Ousterhout J., "Transparent Process Migration: Design Alternatives and the Sprite Implementation," Software Practice and Experience, Vol. 21(8), August 1991.

4. [Jacobi82] Jacobi, Christian, "Code Generation and the Lilith Architecture," Diss. 7195, ETH Zürich, 1982.

5. [Ousterhout88] Ousterhout, John, "The Sprite Network Operating System," IEEE Computer, February 1988, pp 23-36.

6. [Popek85] Popek, G. J., and Walker, B. J., *The LOCUS Distributed System Architecture*, Cambridge, Mass: The MIT Press, 1985.

7. [Tanenbaum85] Tanenbaum, A.S. and Renesse R.Van, "Distributed Operating Systems," ACM Computing Surveys, Vol. 17, #4, December 1985, pp 433-438.

8. [Tanenbaum90] Tanenbaum, A. S., van Renesse, R., van Staveren, H., Sharp, G. J., Mullender, S. J., Jansen, J., van Rossum, G., "Experience with the AMOEBA Distributed Operating System," *Communications of the ACM*, Vol, 33, No. 12, December 1990, pp. 46-63.

9. [Wirth81] Wirth Niklaus, "The Personal Computer Lilith," A.I.Wasserman Ed., Software Development Environments, IEEE Computer Society Press, 1981.

Toward Teraflop Computing and New Grand Challenge Applications
ISBN-1-56072-247-9

SINGLE COSET ENUMERATION IN PARALLEL

Armando L. Caro *caro@cs.widener.edu*

Widener University, Computer Science Department

INTRODUCTION

Computational group theory, the algorithmic content of group theory, has gained a lot of attention in the past few decades. Among some important applications we can mention crystallography, and the sporadic simple group construction. A group may be specified in different ways. One of the most common ways to specify a group is that of presentations. A presentation for a group G is a pair (X, R) where X is the set of generators of the group, and R is a set of words over X called the set of relators of G. A presentation is finite if both X and R are finite sets. A finite group has a finite presentation. However, given a finite presentation of a group, the problem of determining whether the group is finite or not is a well known undecidable problem.

One of the central problems in computational group theory is the following: Given a finite presentation for a group, construct its multiplication table. Several algorithms have been designed to solve this problem. The standard algorithm was proposed in 1936 by Todd-Coxeter [1]. The other existing algorithms are variations of this. No standard parallel algorithm has been developed to solve this problem. Only one parallel algorithm has been proposed by Akl [3], but it is mostly sequential. The parallelism is kept to a minimum in his work. The standard approach to do coset enumeration of a group is by constructing a multiplication table. Perhaps a better structure to use is that of a Cayley graph: Given a group G, let γ be the set of generators ${g_i}_{i=1}^{i=k}$ of the group. A Cayley graph for G is a graph C(V,E) such that:

1. $v \in V \Leftrightarrow v \in G$.

2. $\forall v \in V, \forall g \in \gamma \exists$ two edges $(v, x_g), (y_g, v) \in E$.

3. $x \in \gamma \Rightarrow \exists e_x = [w, v] \Leftrightarrow x * w = v$, where * is the group binary operation.

A right coset of a subgroup H of a group G is a set of the form: Hg= { x ∈ G , x = hg for some h ∈ H}. A left coset can be similarly defined.
By constructing a graph for the cosets of a non-trivial subgroup of G, we save space, since we get [G]/[H] cosets, instead of [G] elements! [G] is the cardinality of G. Single coset enumeration is the most standard approach to construct the multiplication table for the group presented as G(X,R). Double coset enumeration was introduced by Conway[2] in 1984. This approach saves even more space by dividing the number of elements by one more subgroup. To the present, no parallel algorithm has been proposed for double coset enumeration of finite groups, and of course, none has been implemented.

2. PROBLEMS

The main problem to be solved is:
Construct a multiplication table for a given finite group G starting from a finite presentation of it. Instead of working directly with the *elements* of the group, one works with *cosets* of a non-trivial subgroup in order to minimize the table obtained, and consequently save storage space in the actual implementation of the algorithms.

2.1 Example

The following example is worked out in detail by Leech[4]. Consider the presentation ({A,B,C}, { ABC', BCA',CAB' }), where A', B' and C' stand for their inverses. This is called a fibonacci group: each generator is the product of the two preceeding generators in cyclic order. A multiplication table is given by Leech[4] using a sequential *algorithm* to construct the multiplication table and the relator tables. He used single coset enumeration techniques with I, the identity element of the group, as the subgroup to generate the cosets. He also presented this example using the subgroup generated by A to generate cosets.

3. SEQUENTIAL GROUP ALGORITHMS

The fundamental algorithm for *single coset enumeration* of groups is due to Todd and Coxeter [1]. An algorithm for *double coset enumeration* was later given by Conway [2].

3.1 Single Coset Enumeration

1. Introduction. Consider a finitely presented group G(X,R), where X is an inverse generating set and the relator xx' has been added to R for all x in X. The subgroup H used for enumerating cosets is generated by words W over R.

2. Table. In the standard Todd-Coxeter algorithm a set S of single cosets is maintained. A function f: SxX $\Rightarrow S \bigcup \{0\}$ is constructed. f(s,x) = x" means that sx = x" is the action of G on the set of cosets S. A consistency condition f(s,x) = s" $\neq$ 0 iff f(s,x')= s. This means that inverses have the expected behavior. Initially, the table is empty, and hence, f(s,x) = 0 for all x in X. The table is progressively updated, retaining the consistency conditions. Cosets that are distinct in G must be distinct in S. If a coset is generated more than once, later references to the same coset are made equivalent to the previously generated coset.

3. Pushing Relators. To *push* (r,s), a relator-coset pair, where r = x1x2...xn: calculate s(0) = s,$s^{(i)} = s^{(i-1)}x_i$, until either:

   (a) $s^{(n)} is found, and s^{(n)} = s$. Then there is a coincidence of type A; or

   (b) $s^{(j-1)}x_j = 0$ for some j smaller than or equal to n. Then calculate $s''^{(i-1)} = s''^{(I)}x'_i$, until either

      i. $s''^{(j-1)}$is found when a coincidence of type A is recorded $s^{(j-1)} = s''^{(j-1)}$; or

      ii. $s''^{(l)}x_l = 0$. If l = j we have shown that $s^{(j-1)}x_j = s''^{(l)}$. Otherwise, we define new cosets to be $s^{(j)}...s^{(l-1)}$ and record type B conincidences $s^{(j-1)}x_j = s^{(j)}, ..., s^{(l-1)}x_l = s''^{(l)}$.

4. Processing Coincidences.

   - Type A Coincidence. When s= s"

     (a) If s or s" has been deleted replace then by their undeleted images.

     (b) If now s= s" stop, otherwise without losing generality, s < s"

     (c) Empty s", by generating, for each non-zero entry f(s",x) = s"', the type B conincidence s"x = s"' and then setting f(s",x) = f(x"', x') = 0.

     (d) Delete the coset s" and record that its undeleted image is s.

   - Type B coincidence. When sx = s":

     (a) Replace s and s" by their undeleted images.

     (b) If f(s,x) = 0 set f(s,x) = s" and f(s", x') = s and stop.

     (c) If f(s,x) = s" then stop.

     (d) Let s"' = f(s,x) generate the type A coincidence s" = s"'.

The type B coincidence was what Leech [4] called deduction. Conway[2] proposed an inprovement to this by using double coset enumeration. However, a discussion of two coset enumeration of groups (both sequential and parallel) is beyond the scope of this paper.

PROPOSED PARALLEL ALGORITHM

In the above mentioned algorithms a group multiplication table was used to store their data. I decided to follow the development by Akl [3], which uses a directed graph to store their data. In a sequential manner, we can think of the construction done in the following fashion:
Start by placing the identity elemnent I at the root of the tree. **repeat**

1. Add nodes to the tree by *pushing* all the relators to all existing nodes
2. if a vertex X(W) is considered and is not present, insert it and label it arc(X,W).
3. if a vertex is reached at the end of a cycle, other than the one that should have been there, it is made equivalent to the previous cycle. The first word is kept, the second is deleted.

until all words in the tree are *rightly connected.* A word W in the tree is rightly connected when it is connected such that R_iW = W , for all R_i in R (the set of relators).

If we observe this algorithm carefully, we can conclude that the construction of such a graph, whose nodes represent the elements of the group, and whose edges are used to represent the relations among these elements, could profit significantly from a parallel approach. Before we start the construction in parallel, we add all inverses to the set of generators X, and all pairs xx' to the set of relators R.
The construction, as the sequential version, starts with one vertex representing the identity element (or the subgroup H). Two parallel processes : *verify, push* can be used in the construction thus:
The parallel process *push* would try to push every relator onto every node in the graph which is not *rightly connected* yet. The process *verify* would try to verify the newly generated word is not in *tuple space* as a node. If a conflict occurs, the two words which have to be set equivalent, are tagged with the younger one. By considering the vertices in the graph at each step through the construction we avoid the sequential *collapse* routine which is common to all sequential versions of this algorithm.

algorithm SINCOSET

{ L is the list of word vertices which are not yet reducible
W is reducible to W' iff W[] = X'

W is irreducible iff W[] = nil }
Set L = I /* I is "outed" to tuple–space as a new node in the graph to be explored

```
while (1) {
 do in parallel ∀ nodes W_0 in L
do in parallel  ∀ R_n R_(n-1)...R_1
    W ← W_0
    push (R,W)
     L ← L∪ {W}
    verify L
 end do in parallel
 end do in parallel
end while
end algorithm SINCOS
```

Termination of the algorithm is guaranteed for presentations of finite groups. When there are no more nodes in tuple space to be verified, the procdure stops. As the nodes are generated in parallel, they are verified in parallel, hence, doing away with the standard sequential procedure to collapse the graph after its creation.

5. FUTURE WORK

Future work involves the empirical investigation of this approach via a proper implementation on a MIMD machine with shared memory. The author has written an initial version in Linda using our twenty-node network at Delaware. Conclusive results heve not been generated yet due mainly to lack of time to perform proper testing. As a future recommendation it is suggested to modify the parallel algorithm above to do double coset enumeration of finite groups as presented by Conway [2].

6. CONCLUSION

Even though further testing has to be done in order to obtain some conclusive results, it is clear that the proposed approach is significantly better than the previous ones, few of which have been implemented!. By letting the processors work independently on different nodes of the graph, and sharing their finding via the tuple-space, we significantly reduce the time involved in constructing the Cayley's graph for the group presented. It has been previously suggested by Akl [3] that each processor generate a graph independently of the rest of the processors, and at random times checks with other processors to exchange information. This approach seemed rather week, since the graph could be generated by many processors simultaneously, which is a waste of resources, and defeats the purpose of parallelism!

REFERENCES

[1] J.A. Todd, and H.S.M. Coxeter, "A Practical Method for Enumeration Cosets of a Finite Abstract Group". *Proc. Edinburg Math. Soc.* Vol. 2, No 5 1936, pp. 26-34.

[2] J.H. Conway. "An algorithm for Double Coset Enumeration?" In: *Computational Group Theory.* Proceedings of London Mathematical Society Symposium on Computational Group Theory. Ed: M.D. Atkinson. Montreal:Academic Press. 1984.

[3] S. AKL, G. Labonte, M. Leeder, and K. Qiu. " On Doing Todd-Coxeter Coset Enumeration in Parallel". *Discrete Applied Math.* Vol. 34, 1991. pp. 27-35.

[4] J. Leech, " Coset Enumeration" In: *Computational Group Theory.* Proceedings of London Mathematical Society Symposium on Computational Group Theory. Ed. M.D. Atkinson. Montreal: Academic Press. 1984.

[5] R.H. Gilman. "Enumeration of Double Cosets". *J. Pure and Appl. Alg.* Vol:26. 1982. pp. 183-188.

[6] S.A. Linton. " Double Coset Enumeration". *J. Symbolic Computation.* Vol:12. 1991. pp. 427-438.

[7] G. Havas, and J. Cannon. " Algorithms for Groups". *The Australian Computer Journal.* Vol: 24. 1992. pp. 51-60.

Toward Teraflop Computing and New Grand Challenge Applications

ISBN-1-56072-247-9

SOLVING LINEAR RECURRENCE SYSTEMS ON PARALLEL COMPUTERS

Marcin Paprzycki[1] Przemysław Stpiczyński[2]

[1] Department of Mathematics and Computer Science, University of Texas of the Permian Basin, Odessa, TX 79762, e-mail: paprzycki_m@gusher.pb.utexas.edu
[2] Numerical Analysis Department, Marie Curie-Skłodowska University, Pl. Marii Curie-Skłodowskiej 1, 20-031 Lublin, POLAND, e-mail: przem@golem.umcs.lublin.pl

Abstract. Two divide and conquer algorithms for the solution of a linear recurrence system of order m of n equations are introduced. The arithmetical complexity of the proposed algorithms is discussed. It is shown that for large n the optimal number of processors is $O(\sqrt{n})$ and that for the optimal number of processors the time complexity of the proposed algorithms is $O(\sqrt{n})$. It is also shown that for fixed n and fixed number of processors p the theoretical speed-up decreases as the order of the system m increases. The results of experiments on a 20-processor Sequent are presented.

Keywords. Linear recurrence systems, parallel algorithms, divide-and-conquer, shared-memory multiprocessors, speedup.

1. INTRODUCTION

The final phase of several numerical algorithms reduces to the solution of a linear recurrence system of order m for n equations. Many parallel algorithms for solving this problem have been proposed [1–4, 6–9, 11, 12]. In [12] two medium grain efficient divide and conquer parallel algorithms were presented and their theoretical implementation on a linear array of processors with message passing facilities was discussed. It has been recently shown that both algorithms have very good numerical properties [13].

The major purpose of this paper is to show that these algorithms can be efficiently implemented on shared memory MIMD multiprocessors. Section 2 contains a short description of the proposed algorithms. Their arithmetical complexity functions are presented and discussed in Section 3. In Section 4 the results of the experiments on a 20-processor Sequent Symmetry are presented and analyzed.

2. PARALLEL ALGORITHMS

Let us define a linear recurrence system of order m for n equations, where $m \le n$:

$$x_k = \begin{cases} 0 & \text{if } k \le 0, \\ f_k + \sum_{j=k-m}^{k-1} a_{kj} x_j & \text{if } 1 \le k \le n. \end{cases} \tag{1}$$

Computation of values x_k reduces to the system of linear equations

$$(I - A)\mathbf{x} = \mathbf{f} \qquad \text{where } I, A \in R^{n\times n} \text{ and } \mathbf{x}, \mathbf{f} \in R^n, \tag{2}$$

where $\mathbf{x} = (x_1, \ldots, x_n)^T$, $\mathbf{f} = (f_1, \ldots, f_n)^T$ and $A = (a_{ik})$ with $a_{ik} = 0$ for $i \le k$ or $i - k > m$.

Without loss of generality we can assume that n is divisible by p (where 'p' is the number of processors) and $q = n/p > m$. The system (2) can be written in the following block form

$$\begin{pmatrix} L_1 & & & & \\ U_2 & L_2 & & & \\ & U_3 & L_3 & & \\ & & \ddots & \ddots & \\ & & & U_p & L_p \end{pmatrix} \begin{pmatrix} \mathbf{x}_1 \\ \mathbf{x}_2 \\ \vdots \\ \mathbf{x}_{p-1} \\ \mathbf{x}_p \end{pmatrix} = \begin{pmatrix} \mathbf{f}_1 \\ \mathbf{f}_2 \\ \vdots \\ \mathbf{f}_{p-1} \\ \mathbf{f}_p \end{pmatrix}, \tag{3}$$

where $L_j \in R^{q\times q}$, $\mathbf{x}_j$, $\mathbf{f}_j \in R^q$ for $j = 1, \ldots, p$ and $U_j \in R^{q\times q}$ for $j = 2, \ldots, p$. Vectors $\mathbf{x}_j$ satisfy the following recurrence relation

$$\begin{cases} \mathbf{x}_1 = L_1^{-1}\mathbf{f}_1, \\ \mathbf{x}_j = L_j^{-1}\mathbf{f}_j - L_j^{-1}U_j\mathbf{x}_{j-1} & \text{for } j = 2, \ldots, p. \end{cases} \tag{4}$$

Let U_j^k denote the kth column of the matrix U_j. Since $U_j^k = 0$ for $j = 2, \ldots, p$ and $k = 1, \ldots, q - m$ we obtain the following formula for Algorithm 1:

$$\begin{cases} \mathbf{x}_1 = L_1^{-1}\mathbf{f}_1, \\ \mathbf{x}_j = \mathbf{z}_j - \sum_{k=0}^{m-1} x_{(j-1)q-k}\mathbf{y}_j^k & \text{for } j = 2, \ldots, p, \end{cases} \tag{5}$$

where $L_j\mathbf{z}_j = \mathbf{f}_j$ and $L_j\mathbf{y}_j^k = U_j^{q-k}$ for $k = 0, \ldots, m - 1$.

To develop the second algorithm let us observe that each matrix U_j can be written as

$$U_j = -\sum_{k=1}^{m}\sum_{l=k}^{m} \beta_j^{kl}\mathbf{e}_k\mathbf{e}_{q-m+l}^T, \tag{6}$$

where $\beta_j^{kl} = a_{(j-1)q+k,(j-1)q-m+l}$ and $\mathbf{e}_k$ denotes the kth unit vector of R^q. Substituting into (5) we obtain the following formula for Algorithm 2 (for more detailed description of both algorithms see [12])

$$\begin{cases} \mathbf{x}_1 = L_1^{-1}\mathbf{f}_1, \\ \mathbf{x}_j = \mathbf{z}_j + \sum_{k=1}^{m} \alpha_j^k\mathbf{y}_j^k & \text{for } j = 2, \ldots, p, \end{cases} \tag{7}$$

where $\alpha_j^k = \sum_{l=k}^{m} \beta_j^{kl} \mathbf{e}_{q-m+l}^T \mathbf{x}_{j-1}$, $L_j \mathbf{y}_j^k = \mathbf{e}_k$ for $k = 1, \ldots, m$, and $L_j \mathbf{z}_j = \mathbf{f}_j$.

Methods (5), (7) are examples of *divide-and-conquer* algorithms. First, several linear recurrence systems of order m for q equations are to be solved separately (in parallel). Second, a set of values needs to be calculated in each block and communicated to the next block effectively decoupling the original system. This is the sequential part of all three algorithms. Finally, the solution to the original problem is calculated independently in each block (in parallel).

3. COMPLEXITY OF THE ALGORITHMS

Let us first modify for the shared memory computer the arithmetical complexity formulas for (1) formally developed in [12]. Let τ_a denote the time of the execution of the basic arithmetic operation *multiply and add*. The complexity of a sequential algorithm for solving (1) can be expressed by the following formula

$$T_1(n) = m\left(n - \tfrac{m+1}{2}\right) \tau_a. \tag{8}$$

The complexity of Algorithm 1 is represented by:

$$T_{p,1}(n) = m\left[mp + (m+2)\tfrac{n}{p} - \tfrac{1}{2}(m^2 + 6m + 1)\right] \tau_a, \tag{9}$$

whereas the complexity of Algorithm 2 is defined by:

$$T_{p,2}(n) = m\left[(\tfrac{3}{2}m + \tfrac{1}{2})p + (m+2)\tfrac{n}{p} - (m^2 + \tfrac{9}{2}m + \tfrac{1}{2})\right] \tau_a, \tag{10}$$

A number of observations can be made about the above complexity functions.

1. The arithmetical complexity functions for the parallel algorithms have the same overall structure as the functions for other divide and conquer algorithms (see for instance [5, 10]).
2. Algorithm 2 gives better time complexity results for a small number of processors.
3. For small m and large n the optimal number of processors for both parallel algorithms is of order $O(\sqrt{n})$.
4. For small m, large n and an optimal number of processors $p_{opt} = O(\sqrt{n})$ both parallel algorithms perform in time $O(\sqrt{n})$.
5. For fixed p and m the increase in n does not increase the speedup.
6. For fixed n and p the increase of m decreases the speedup.

The last two properties are illustrated on Figure 1 which represents the predicted speedup for various values of m, optimal and fixed p and for $n = 1000, \ldots, 10,000$. It should be noted that for $n = 10,000$ the optimal number of processors $p_{opt} \approx 100$.

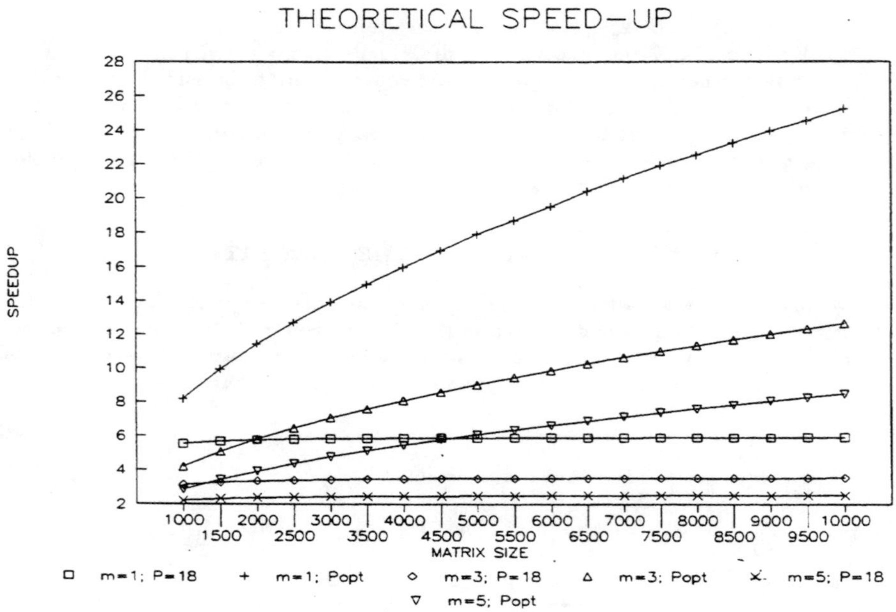

Figure 1: Effects of changes in p, m and n on the theoretical speedup.

4. RESULTS

The experiments were performed on a 20 processor Sequent Symmetry. The code was implemented using Fortran 77 and Sequent provided parallelization primitives (DOACROSS). Each result presented here is an average of multiple runs on an empty machine. For programming simplicity it was assumed that n is divisible by p. Since one of the processors is running the operating system and since 19 is not an optimal divisor, the largest number of processors used was 18.

Figure 2 presents the comparison between speedups of the two proposed algorithms for $n = 6930$ (which was the biggest size we were able to fit into the memory for $m = 8$), $m = 1$, 4 and 8, and $p = 2, \ldots, 18$. Speedup of both algorithms was calculated against the same sequential algorithm.

It should be pointed out that the wavy shape of the curves is partially caused by the fact that the experiments were not carried out when the number of processors p was not a divisor of the system size n. As predicted, for increasing m the practical speedup decreases. There is no performance improvement for $p = 2$ as the overhead of the parallel solution is bigger than the gains from parallelization. As m increases it takes more and more processors to obtain any speedup. It can be also observed that, in all cases, Algorithm 2 gives better performance than Algorithm 1. This is a general result that we have observed in all experiments with large n and for which we do not have a complete explanation. From now on we will report the performance of Algorithm 2 only.

Figure 3 compares the performance of Algorithm 2 for $m = 1$ for various matrix sizes. A couple of observations can be made. First, the system overhead can be observed for $p > 12$ for matrix sizes up to $n = 5040$. Only for the largest system size

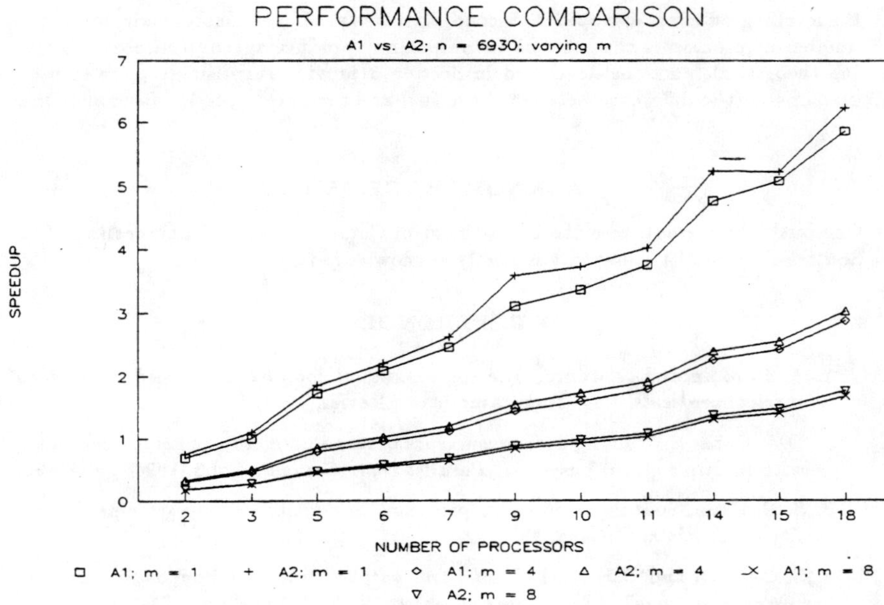

Figure 2: Comparison between the two algorithms for various m.

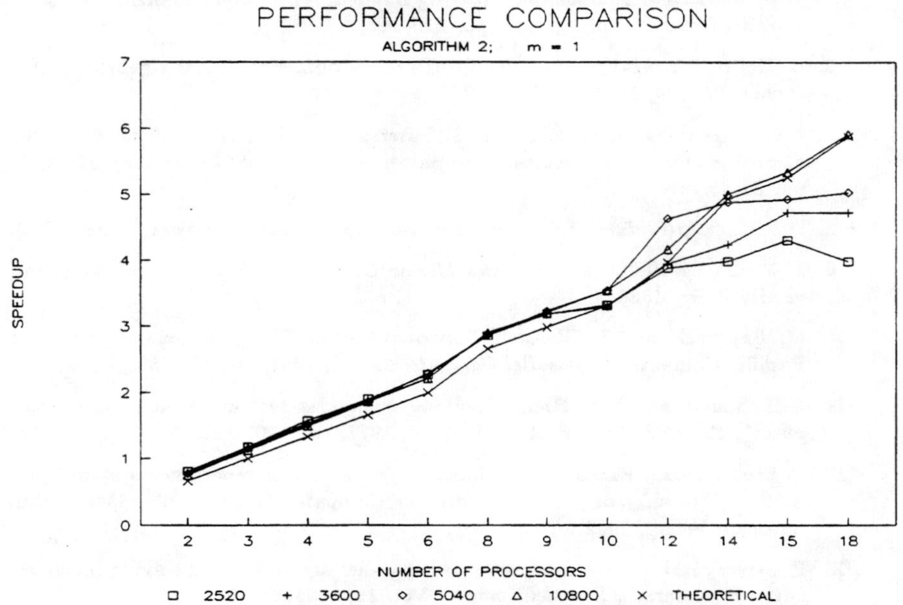

Figure 3: Performance of Algorithm 2 for various n.

the levelling-off effect disappears. Second, as it was predicted theoretically, for a given number of processors the increase in n does not produce speedup increase. Third, the theoretical functions developed in Section 3 provide surprisingly good speedup predictions (the difference between the actual and predicted speedup is smaller than 5%).

ACKNOWLEDGEMENT

Computer time grant from the Department of Computer Science Engineering of the Southern Methodist University is kindly acknowledged.

REFERENCES

1. A. Borodin and I. Munro, *The computational complexity of algebraic and numerical problems*, New York: American Elsevier, 1975.
2. D.A. Carlson, "Solving linear recurrence systems on mesh–connected computers with multiple global buses", *J. Parallel Dist. Comput.* Vol.8, 1990, pp. 89-95.
3. S.-C. Chen, Speedup of iterative programs in multiprocessing systems, University of Illinois at Urbana, 1975.
4. S.-C. Chen and D.J. Kuck, "Time and parallel processor bounds for linear recurrence systems", *IEEE Trans. Comput.* Vol. 24, 1975, pp. 701-717.
5. J. Dongarra and L. Johnsson, "Solving Banded Systems on Parallel Processor", *Parallel Comput.* Vol. 5, 1987, pp. 219-246.
6. D. Heller, "A survey of parallel algorithms in numerical linear algebra", *SIAM Review* Vol. 20, 1978, pp. 740-777.
7. A.C. Greenberg, R.E.Lander, M.S. Paterson and Z. Galil, "Efficient parallel algorithms for linear recurrence computation", *Inf. Proc. Letters* Vol. 15, 1982, pp. 31-35.
8. D.J. Kuck, *Structure of Computers and Computations*, New York: Wiley, 1978.
9. J. Modi, *Parallel Algorithms and Matrix Computations*, Oxford: Oxford University Press, 1988.
10. M. Paprzycki and I. Gladwell, "Solving Almost Block Diagonal Systems on Parallel Computers", *Parallel Comput.* Vol. 17, 1991, pp. 133-153.
11. A.H. Sameh and R.P. Brent, "Solving triangular systems on a parallel computer", *SIAM J. Numer. Anal.* Vol. 14, 1977, pp. 1101-1113.
12. P. Stpiczyński, "Parallel algorithms for solving linear recurrence systems", in: L. Bougé et al. eds., *Lecture Notes in Computer Science* Vol. 634, Berlin: Springer–Verlag, 1992, pp. 343-348.
13. P. Stpiczyński, "Error analysis of two parallel algorithms for solving linear recurrence systems", *Parallel Comput.* Vol. 19, 1993, pp. 917-923.

Toward Teraflop Computing
and New Grand
Challenge Applications

ISBN-1-56072-247-9

An OtOt Strategy for Race Detection in Parallel Programs

Suresh K. Damodaran-Kamal and Joan M. Francioni
Computer Science Department
University of Southwestern Louisiana
Lafayette, LA 70504-1771
email: {skd, jf}@cacs.usl.edu

Abstract

Multiple threads of execution and nondeterminism make testing and debugging of parallel programs difficult. In this paper, a strategy for combating the effects of these problems is presented. The use of this strategy is demonstrated with an example.

1 Introduction

Parallel programs have more than one thread of execution, whereas sequential programs have only one. In addition, parallel programs can exhibit different behaviors in different executions for the same set of input data. A consequence of this nondeterministic behavior is the occurrence of races that causes difficult-to-detect bugs.

Current approaches to parallel program testing and debugging do not advocate any specific strategy. In this paper, we propose and specify the ingredients of a $One-Thread-at-One-Time$ (OtOt) strategy for race detection and debugging of message passing parallel programs. This strategy advocates that a programmer needs to concentrate on only one thread of execution at one time while debugging an entire program. The advantage of using the OtOt strategy over not using such a strategy is the reduced intellectual burden.

The rest of the paper is organized as follows. In Section 2, we give a justification for the deployment of a strategy in testing and debugging parallel programs. The description of the OtOt strategy is in Section 3. A brief description of the user interface of a debugger we have implemented based on the OtOt strategy is given in Section 4, and Section 5 concludes the paper.

2 Why Do We Need a Strategy?

A debugging strategy is required due to the problems related to the probe effect and the maze effect. We briefly describe the probe effect and maze effect below.

2.1 Probe Effect

Dynamic race detection mechanisms in software invariably introduce a *probe effect* [4]: the attempt to gain information about a nondeterministic program results in modifying the behavior of the program. In a program with races, the process of monitoring or modifying the run-time characteristics of a program in some way (say, by inserting a print statement) can mask the appearance of a race.

This is called the probe effect. Trace-based race detection tools are also susceptible to the probe effect because of the need to instrument the source to obtain the trace. Moreover, if the program has a race, the trace will record only one possible execution sequence of the program for a given input. Any strategy to test or debug a parallel program must be able to counter the probe effect to be effective.

2.2 Maze Effect

Parallel programs have multiple threads of control in contrast to the single thread of control of a sequential program. Typically a programmer debugs many threads of control simultaneously. While debugging one thread of control, one has to keep in mind where the controls of execution in the other threads are as well. Besides the fact that the multiple threads are progressing on their own, at varying rates, the execution behavior in some threads is also affecting the execution behavior in other threads at varying times. In many cases, it is difficult for the programmer to keep track of all the threads at the same time. The result of this is to get lost in the maze of threads of execution. This is the *maze effect.* To counter the maze effect requires a technique of debugging parallel programs that can alleviate the burden of thinking about many threads of execution at the same time.

3 An OtOt Strategy

An OtOt (One-Thread-at-One-Time) strategy consists of concentrating on a particular thread of execution, called the *controlled thread*, in a race detection or a debugging session. Other threads, or processes, are debugged relative to the controlled thread.

An instance of an OtOt strategy for message passing parallel programs is called *controlled execution* [2]. In controlled execution, the execution of one of the processes in a parallel program is controlled by blocking message delivery to that process alone. When a process is thus blocked at a *suspend point*, all the messages that could possibly become available to the controlled process at that time are made available to it. Given all these messages in the queue at the same time, the user can then compare the messages for races. This method can be continued in each process, one process at a time. Controlled execution is implemented by embedding a simple algorithm in the mail delivery system. It has been shown in [2] that controlled execution based methods do not suffer from the probe effect.

In a message passing parallel program, execution control can be comprehended by following the thread of execution in each process and the message flow among processes. In the next section, we describe how message flows can be followed, while keeping a frame of reference on a single process.

Following Execution Flow

The OtOt strategy permits us to define a sensible mapping of the sequential debugger actions, such as break point, single step, etc., to parallel debugging. This capability is considered very useful in parallel debugging [6]. Such a mapping can also reduce the semantic gap between the sequential and parallel debuggers. We show below how execution flow can be followed using the mapping provided by the OtOt strategy. This technique has been implemented in a debugger (called *mdb*) [3] for Parallel Virtual Machine (PVM) [5], a popular message passing parallel environment.

A suspend point, which occurs just prior to a blocking receive, is where *mdb* stops execution of the controlled process. Thus, a suspend point can be considered as a "parallel breakpoint." At a suspend point, *mdb* automatically invokes a console so that the users have access to a variety of commands. A **step** command takes the execution of the controlled process ahead by one "parallel step," that is the duration up to the next suspend point. Other commands to go forward in a thread of execution can be found in Section 4 and in [1]. It is possible to do sequential debugging by invoking sequential debuggers at any suspend point. Controlled execution permits sequential debuggers to be used in conjunction with a parallel debugger without causing the probe effect. We describe source level debugging below.

Source Level Debugging

Since *mdb* is based on controlled execution, which overcomes the probe effect, it is possible to set up any commonly available sequential debugger to work with *mdb*, and thereby facilitate source level debugging. When a controlled process is at a suspend point, it is possible to attach this process to a sequential debugger. This is because the controlled process is waiting for the receive system call to PVM to return before doing further processing. Executing the controlled process under a sequential debugger facilitates viewing the receive code. This also provides a symbolic source level debugging capability. A **catch** command provided by *mdb* gives instant access to the sequential debugger on any specified instance of a process presently executing in the parallel program.

By combining source level debugging and controlled execution, the flow of an execution can be followed by users without the maze effect. The suspend points in the controlled process ensure that a frame of reference is available during execution.

4 User Interface of mdb

Basically, *mdb* allows users to see and experiment with all the messages that could possibly be available in the receive queue (RQ) of a specific receive event. The commands available to the user are listed below. There are two modes of execution in *mdb*: manual and automatic. The switching from one mode to another is transparent to the user.

Commands common to both modes:

- **eval** [<expression>] : evaluate a semantic expression over the messages in RQ. By default this command will use the previously defined semantic expressions. In the absence of a semantic expression, equality of msgtypes of two messages will constitute a race.
- **print** [<expression>] : Display the messages in RQ that satisfy the given expression. By default all the messages are displayed.
- **stop at** [<expression>] : Stop at the next suspend point where this expression is true.
- **stop at** <msgtype> : Stop at the next suspend point after this type of message arrives.

Automatic (Testing) Mode Commands:

- **run** : Execute up to the first race or until termination.
- **run to** $< nn >$: Execute up to the $< nn >$ suspend point.
- **continue** : Continue execution from where execution has stopped. In cases where more than one message may be delivered to the receive, the selection of a message for delivery will be arbitrary.

- **replay** : Replay the last execution traced. While being replayed, the execution mode switches to manual.

Manual (Debugging) Mode:

- **step** : Execute until the next suspend point. While replay, the saved trace will be delivered.
- **next** [<integer>] : By default, deliver all messages in the RQ, and stop at the first subsequent suspend point. With a parameter, this is repeated at each of the subsequent suspend points.
- **deliver** [<msg>] : Deliver the specified message.
- **continue** : Switch mode to automatic.
- **catch** [< *process* >] : Catch the process and run it under a sequential debugger. Without parameters, the controlled process will be caught.
- **ps** : Show the status of processes running under *mdb*.
- **where** : Display the current position in the program in terms of suspend points.

4.1 A Bug Detection Exercise

Based on the Jacobi Relaxation Method, consider a program to solve a set of three variable linear equations. The equations are

$$x_1^{(k+1)} = \frac{1}{a_{11}}(b_1 - x_2^{(k)} - x_3^{(k)}),$$

$$x_2^{(k+1)} = \frac{1}{a_{22}}(b_2 - x_3^{(k)} - x_1^{(k)}),$$

$$x_3^{(k+1)} = \frac{1}{a_{33}}(b_3 - x_1^{(k)} - x_2^{(k)}).$$

Each process calculates one variable and broadcasts the value of the variable to the other processes. Each process receives a message from each of the other processes. This message has the structure: < *x_index*, *x_iterno*, *x_value* >. In a message, *x_value* is the *x_iterno*th iteration value of *x_index*. The *x_value* is calculated and sent by each of these process. These messages have a msgtype of 3. At the receipt of this message, the receive code distinguishes the messages based on the *x_index* value in each message. Each process assumes the initial values of all variables to be zero.

During execution, this program hangs after executing some iterations. The hanging occurs after an arbitrary number of iterations, making it clear that the program has an erroneous race condition. The following are the steps in debugging this problem using *mdb*.

Step 1. We run the program in with one of the value calculating processes as the controlled process.

Step 2. At the very first suspend point, there is a race. With the *catch* command we investigate the receive code of the controlled process. On examining the messages at the suspend point and the receive code, we find that we need to be more specific about the race conditions. Therefore, we add `@3:x_index == x_index';` as a semantic expression. This expression means that it is acceptable to have messages with the msgtype 3, but if their *x_index* values match, then it is a race. This also reflects the way the receive of the message interprets the message.

Step 3. We run the program again.

Step 4. To our surprise, we find a race again at a suspend point!

Step 5. Again, we find that there are two messages with the same *x_index*, but with different iteration numbers at that receive. This situation occurs because each process calculates the *x_value* by itself, assuming zero as the initial values of all *x_index* variables. Also when the controlled process sends the first iteration value, the other processes also calculate the second iteration *x_values*. Therefore, the receive has a race!

Step 6. We use a more specific semantic expression this time.

```
@3:x_index==x_index' && x_iterno==x_iterno';
```

This expression does not give a race over the messages in the receive queue. We change the receive code to reflect this semantic expression, and thus rectify the error.

5 Conclusion

The probe effect and the maze effect are two problems that make race detection as well as general purpose debugging difficult in message passing parallel programs. We advocate the use of a One-Thread-at-One-Time (OtOt) strategy to test or debug parallel programs. Controlled execution, an on-the-fly technique to implement the OtOt strategy, can counter both the maze effect and the probe effect. We have implemented *mdb*, a debugger that incorporates the OtOt strategy for the Parallel Virtual Machine (PVM) message passing parallel programming environment.

References

[1] DAMODARAN-KAMAL, S. K., AND FRANCIONI, J. M. *mdb*: A semantic race detection tool for PVM. Tech. Rep. TR-93-5-5, Center for Advanced Computer Studies, University of Southwestern Louisiana, November 1993.

[2] DAMODARAN-KAMAL, S. K., AND FRANCIONI, J. M. Nondeterminacy: Testing and debugging in message passing parallel programs. In *Proceedings of the 3rd ACM/ONR Workshop on Parallel and Distributed Debugging* (May 1993). Also in ACM SIGPLAN Notices, 28,12 (Dec 1993).

[3] DAMODARAN-KAMAL, S. K., AND FRANCIONI, J. M. *mdb*: A semantic race detection tool for PVM. In *Proceedings of the 1994 Scalable High Performance Computing Conference* (Knoxwille, TN, May 1994). To appear.

[4] GAIT, J. A probe effect in concurrent programs. *Software - Practice and Experience 16*, 3 (March 1986), 225–233.

[5] GEIST, A., BEGUELIN, A., DONGARRA, J., JIANG, W., MANCHECK, R., AND SUNDERAM, V. PVM 3.0 user's guide and reference manual. Tech. Rep. ORNL/TM-12187, Oak Ridge National Laboratory, Oak Ridge, TN 37831-6367, May 1993.

[6] WORKSHOP ON DEBUGGERS FOR HIGH PERFORMANCE COMPUTERS. Industry panel. In *Proceedings of the Supercomputer Debugging Workshop '93* (Portland, Oregon, November 1993).

Subject Index